ICONOGRAPHIC INDEX TO OLD TESTAMENT SUBJECTS
REPRESENTED IN PHOTOGRAPHS AND SLIDES OF PAINTINGS
IN THE VISUAL COLLECTIONS, FINE ARTS LIBRARY,
HARVARD UNIVERSITY

GARLAND REFERENCE LIBRARY
OF THE HUMANITIES
(VOL. 729)

ICONOGRAPHIC INDEX TO OLD TESTAMENT SUBJECTS REPRESENTED IN PHOTOGRAPHS AND SLIDES OF PAINTINGS IN THE VISUAL COLLECTIONS, FINE ARTS LIBRARY, HARVARD UNIVERSITY

Helene E. Roberts

GARLAND PUBLISHING, INC. • NEW YORK & LONDON
1987

Library of Congress Cataloging-in-Publication Data

Roberts, Helene, E.
   Iconographic index to Old Testament subjects
represented in photographs and slides of paintings in
the visual collections, Fine Arts Library, Harvard
University.

   (Garland reference library of the humanities ;
vol. 729)
   1. Bible. O.T.—Illustrations—Slides—Catalogs.
2. Bible. O.T.—Illustrations—Photographs—Catalogs.
3. Paintings—Slides—Catalogs. 4. Painting—
Photographs—Catalogs. 5. Harvard University. Fine
Arts Library—Catalogs. I. Harvard University.
Fine Arts Library. II. Title. III. Series: Garland
reference library of the humanities ; v. 729.
ND1430.R63 1987   755′.4   86-25830
ISBN 0-8240-8345-8 (alk. paper)

Printed on acid-free, 250-year-life paper
Manufactured in the United States of America

CONTENTS

Preface   vii

Introduction   ix

Index of Concepts, Terms, and Proper Names   3

Iconclass Classification of Old Testament Themes
Listing of Themes and Paintings Representing
Them   77

PREFACE

This _Iconographic_ _Index_ _to_ _Old_ _Testament_ _Subjects_ came into being in response to the many questions from users seeking to find works of art depicting particular subjects. The photographs and slides in the Visual Collections of the Fine Arts Library at Harvard University are organized according to the media and culture of art objects, but lack a subject access. This is the first of a projected series of guides to various iconograhic subjects that will help to fill this need. We hope eventually to extend our subject indexing to include the New Testament, mythology, historical scenes, allegory, literary subjects, landscapes and genre subjects and to extend our indexing into other media than painting, including architecture, sculpture, drawings, manuscripts and the minor or decorative arts.

Most collections of record photographs of art works, such as Harvard's, share this method of organization by media and culture. For the traditional art historian, concerned primarily with schools and styles of art, this system of organization works quite well. More and more art historians, however, are approaching art from different perspectives, often more concerned with content and subject, than with form and style. Furthermore, scholars from other disciplines are increasingly studying visual materials, and for them, subject access is of vital importance.

The Visual Collections contains more than one million images in various formats: photographs, 35mm. slides, lantern slides, negatives and postcards. Without subject access one can only find specific works by particular artists or cultures, or by using the catalogue, find all the works of art located in a particular museum or collection. One can find Bactrian coins or Turner's _The_ _Evening_ _of_ _the_ _Deluge_, if that is what one is looking for, but, it would take an exhaustive search, one so huge it would be impractical, to compare Turner's _Deluge_ with other artist's depiction of the subject, or with other scenes of sea disasters. With the _Iconographic_ _Index_ _to_ _Old_ _Testament_ _Subjects_, it will at least be possible to perform the first part of this search with much greater ease. In time it will be possible to do both, and perhaps, with modern technology, to see the relevant images presented before one on a video screen.

In conceiving this project we envisioned using a complex computer system which would allow for sophisticated searches. However, as it became clear that such a system would not be funded, we decided to go ahead with a simpler concept which would assemble the most important information, above all listing the paintings which depict each specific scene in the Old Testament. We had also hoped to adopt a system which would have made addition of new material easier and more flexible. The present system does allow for updating, but only in large batches at stated intervals. Once we had typed the entries, we could not add new acquisitions in this volume. We thus already have a sizeable collection of new entries accumulated which will have to wait for a new edition.

Initially we had planned to list these paintings under the Biblical chapter and verse containing each scene. But finding the Iconclass classification system superior, we adopted it. Iconclass preserves the sequence of Biblical chapter and verse while adding non-Biblical material associated with Biblical characters. It has a place, for example, for the story of the baby Moses, trampling on Pharaoh's crown and being tested for his intentions by having to choose between a bowl of hot coals and one of cherries. The story does not occur in the Bible, but since it was depicted several times by artists it seems best to include it with the other stories of Moses' childhood. Iconclass also expands certain scenes into their pictorial variations. A brief Biblical verse may provide only a narrative outline which artists have elaborated and depicted in a variety of ways. Iconclass provides a breakdown of those variations.

In looking ahead to the indexing of other topics, we decided that Iconclass would have even greater advantages than it does with the indexing of Old Testament themes. Whereas the Old Testament themes follow the Biblical text fairly closely, the same is not true of other subjects. Particularly in the case of genre scenes, a large category in any collection concerned with paintings, no text exists. Iconclass presents an existing, carefully worked out system geared to works of art. Furthermore, it is an international system and one used by other collections engaged in subject indexing. By virtue of its alphanumerical categories, it is tied to no particular language. If one looks ahead to a possible sharing of cataloguing information such considerations are important.

Iconclass also has the advantage of providing a large Index of proper names, objects and concepts that are associated with the scenes which it classifies. If one looks under camels, for example, in the Index, one is referred to the scene of Rebekah at the Well, a scene which is often depicted with camels. The Biblical text and the scene title, however, do not mention camels. Thus Iconclass allows for a whole complex of ideas associated with a scene to be listed and found by users. The usefulness, therefore, of the listing of paintings goes far beyond finding depictions of the Biblical scene itself; it also allows one to make a search for ideas, objects and concepts that are connected to the scene. A smaller Index has been constructed for this volume which contains only those names and terms which refer to the Old Testament scenes represented in the Visual Collections. If one looks in the Index portion in the front of the volume, one finds a listing of proper names, objects and concepts, each of which refers to Iconclass numbers. In the second part of the volume one finds these Iconclass numbers organized numerically. A list of paintings depicting the relevant scene will be found under each number.

I would like to thank the people who have worked on this project: Christian E. Fritze, who in the Work-Study program helped with the initial stages of this project; David Wallack, who assigned most of the Iconclass numbers to the retrospective material; Anne C. Strugnell, who assembled and typed the Index of terms from the larger Iconclass Index, and who assigned many of the Iconclass numbers to new materials and typed cards for them; Elizabeth Drumwright, who typed the listing of themes with paintings depicting them; and to Wolfgang Freitag, the Fine Arts Librarian, who supported the project in many ways including the finding of the necessary special funds which supported this project. We wish to give special thanks to Leendert Couprie and the many people who improved the original Iconclass system and readied it for publication, and to the Royal Netherlands Academy of Arts and Science who gave us permission to use it.

INTRODUCTION

Although subject access is a commonplace and
accepted practice in book libraries, it is much
rarer in visual libraries. Anyone who has used one
of the few visual libraries with subject indexing
such as the Photographic archives in the Warburg
Institute in London, the Decimal Index to the Art
of the Low Countries in the Hague, or the Princeton
Index to Christian Art at Princeton University,
knows the great advantage they afford in giving one
access to visual materials. The same advantage can
also be gained by using such subject indexes to
visual materials as Thomas H. Ohlgren's Illuminated
Manuscripts: an Index to Selected Bodleian Library
Color Reproductions and its Supplement also
published by Garland Publishing, Inc.

At the most elementary level, subject indexing
provides an additional way to find a work of art.
In most visual libraries one must know the name of
the artist of the work in order to locate it.
Occasionally the name of the artist may slip one's
mind; then it is difficult or sometimes impossible
to find the work for which one is looking. If one
is in a collection with subject indexing, however,
one can locate that particular work if one
remembers only the title or theme of the work.

One can also find attributions and influences
through comparisons of works of the same subject.
By noting similarities in composition and handling
of a theme, one can find material to support
attributions and provide evidence for the influence
of one artist upon another. Thus even those art
historians who use a traditional approach to their
subject can profit from using a collection that
provides subject indexing to its collections.

There is, of course, one traditional approach
to art history, that of the iconographic or
iconological, which has long centered on the
interpretation of the subject of paintings and the
matching of the subject with the text related to
it. This is still a viable approach to works of
art, and one which, in the contemporary world, is
often given a new twist, one which brings it under
the umbrella of semiotics.

It is in these newer approaches to art history
where one can find great use for subject indexing.
If one is concerned with placing a work of art in
its historic context, reading its semiotic message
or analyzing its narrative devices, then the subject
of the work becomes more important than its style or
its composition. Both the titles of studies in art
history in Dissertation Abstracts and the papers
given at present day art conferences, reveal the
great changes that have occurred in art history, and
have increased the desirability of subject indexing
for visual collections.

One of the most obvious fields for which a
subject index is of great value is that of the
relationship of art and religion. The great battles
between the Iconoclasts and those who defended the
use of religious imagery in churches can be traced
in the type and frequency of religious imagery in
paintings. Many religious controversies, whether
bitter conflicts between Catholicism and
Protestantism, or esoteric theological polemics on
sacred texts, are reflected in religious paintings,
just as are the multitudinous arguments between
diverse sects and factions. Although an index such
as ours cannot deal with all the possible
interpretations or arcane readings of each Old
Testament theme, it does list the paintings which
depict such themes and arrange them by their
national schools, so that they can be located and
compared by scholars who have the necessary
knowledge and background to make the subtle
interpretations.

Some of the variations in the depiction of
Biblical themes do not relate to theological
arguments, but to differences in translation.
Moses, for example, when he comes down from talking
with God on Mount Sinai, has reacted to the
experience with an alteration in his appearance.
Although some Biblical translations describe this
change as a shining of the skin of his face, others

render it as a growth of horns on his head.
Depictions of Moses reflect these different
translations, some of them showing him with horns,
other with rays of light shooting from his
forehead. Bringing together scenes depicting
Moses may help to suggest the sources used by the
various artists depicting Moses.

William Blake called the Bible, "the Great
Code of Art," reflecting the central place that
this religious text has had in thinking and
conceptualizing throughout the medieval period,
the Renaissance, the seventeenth, eighteenth and
nineteenth centuries, and even in the present
day. (Included in the index are twentieth century
paintings as well as those from earlier periods.)
Biblical stories were depicted on walls to teach
the unlettered, on altarpieces to inspire the
devotion of the worshipper, and in books to
illuminate and supplement the text. The meaning
of Biblical texts and the images that expressed
them thus became not only relevant in a religious
setting, but permeated and colored thinking at
all times and in every situation. It is,
therefore, necessary to understand the meanings
expressed by a religious painting if one is to
understand the historical context surrounding the
painting. Leaders of state, for example,
associated themselves with religious figures in
works of art in order to gain authority and
approval for their actions. They commissioned
painters to give a religious interpretation to
secular actions or, as patrons, to provide gifts
to the Church, gifts which they hoped might bring
forgiveness for their sins. Old Testament themes,
in particular, lent themselves to a flexibility of
use in commenting on secular matters, since they
were not tied so closely to the more sacred and
devotional function of New Testament themes.

Paintings of Old Testament themes not only
helped to bring Biblical stories to life, and to
lend meaning to contemporary events, but they were
often entertaining as stories in their own right.
Many Biblical stories dealt with the same

emotional crises that touched the lives of the
people who saw them. Eve's disobedience, Adam's
giving in to temptation, Sarah's childlessness,
Hagar's expulsion, Jacob's marriage to the wrong
woman, all must have been recognizable as human
situations with a universal appeal and message. How
various ages and countries depicted these emotional
stories, how frequently the domestic aspect of these
stories were emphasized is not without interest.

Feminist art historians have found significant
changes in the depiction of Old Testament women
throughout the ages. Judith, for example, described
in the Bible as a heroine who saved her people, is
often, in later years, transformed into an evil
castrating woman, a killer of men. The depiction of
other women, Eve, Delilah, Ruth, Bathsheba among
them, reflect attitudes, not only toward religion,
but toward social and sexual relations between men
and women.

The narrative techniques, how a story is told
visually, can be studied with profit in Old
Testament themes. The artist faces a special
problem in trying to show the passage of time in
dramatic action. Although using the static medium
of a flat canvas, and restricted realistically to
capturing one point in time, the artist must
nevertheless follow a verbal text that describes
serial actions through time. The artist must evoke
the action that has gone before and suggest what
will happen following the action. The devices used
by the artist are many, varying with the artistic
conventions of his time and factors related to the
story chosen for depiction.

The listings include several narratives that
are no longer accepted as authentic books of the Old
Testament: the books of Tobit, Susannah (a part of
Daniel), and the Maccabees. As these books were
formerly a part of the Vulgate and other versions of
the Bible, and as many paintings depict scenes from
them, these Apocryphal books have been retained here
as part of the iconographical listings. They
include one of the painters' favorite themes in the
story of Susannah, and one of the most charming, in

the story of Tobias and the Angel.

One of the more important interpretive
devices used with Old Testament materials is that
of typology, where an Old Testament figure or
scene is seen as a precursor to a matching New
Testament figure or scene, or to some
non-Biblical figure or scene. Many altarpieces
merge scenes from the Old and New Testaments in a
complex commentary relating meanings from both
parts of the Bible. The Iconclass classification
system allows for a special category showing
these relationships. Unfortunately, most of them
will not be noted in this volume, but will have
to wait until the volumes indexing New Testament
and mythological subjects are completed.

Although it is neither comprehensive nor
complete, we have chosen to publish this index of
Old Testament themes depicted in photographs and
slides in the Visual Collections because such
an index is urgently needed. We hope that it
will help visual librarians who are faced with
questions about Old Testament subjects and about
the broader concepts, objects and ideas which are
associated with them.

Figure 1. 71 A 3 GENESIS 1:26 - 2 CREATION OF ADAM AND EVE.

Sir Edward Burne-Jones, Days of Creation. Sixth Day:
Creation of Adam and Eve. Harvard University, Fogg
Art Museum, 1943.459. (Courtesy of the Harvard University
Art Museums, The Fogg Art Museum, Grencille L. Winthrop
Bequest)

Figure 2. 71 A 61 GENESIS 3:24 GOD EXPELS ADAM AND EVE
FROM PARADISE AND HAS THE TREE OF LIFE GUARDED BY AN ANGEL
WITH A FLAMING SWORD.

James Jacques Joseph Tissot, Illustrations of the Hebrew
Bible, No. 4: Adam and Eve Driven from Paradise. 1896-1902.
New York, Jewish Museum, 52.71. (Courtesy of the Jewish
Museum, New York)

Figure 3. 71 A 62 GENESIS 3:24 ADAM AND EVE OUTSIDE EDEN, WHOSE ENTRANCE IS GUARDED BY SHINING CHERUBIN.

Thomas Cole, Expulsion from Eden. Boston, Museum of Fine Arts, 47.1188 (Karolik Collection) (Courtesy of the Museum of Fine Arts, Boston)

Figure 4.   71 C 13 13 11 GENESIS 22:11-12   WHEN ABRAHAM HAS
HIS HAND RAISED TO KILL ISAAC, AN ANGEL RESTRAINS ABRAHAM'S
HAND.

Caravaggio, Sacrifice of Abraham. Florence, Palazzo Uffizi.
Alinari, 49849 (Courtesy of Alinari/Art Resources, NY)

Figure 5. 71 D 13 31 GENESIS 39:12-13 POTIPHAR'S WIFE CATCHES
JOSEPH BY HIS ROBE, USUALLY WHILE LYING IN BED: JOSEPH
ESCAPES LEAVING HIS CLOAK BEHIND IN HER HAND.

Raphael (and assistants), Old Testament subjects: Joseph
and Potiphar's wife. Rome, Vatican, Loggie. Anderson,
4316 (Courtesy of Alinari/Art Resources, NY)

Figure 6. 71 T 56 APOCRYPHA TOBIT 6:3 TOBIAS CAPTURES THE
FISH AND PULLS IT ON LAND.

Alessandro Varotari (Il Padovanino), Tobias and the Angel.
Princeton, University, Museum of Art, 78-14. (Courtesy
of the Art Museum, Princeton University. Gift of Mrs.
Douglas Delanov)

INDEX OF CONCEPTS, TERMS, AND PROPER NAMES

AARON
11 I 62(AARON)   Aaron (not in biblical context)
71 E 1-71 E 4   Story of Moses and Aaron

ABEL
71 A 7   The labors of Adam and Eve; infancy
of Cain and Abel
71 A 8   The story of Cain and Abel

ABIGAIL
71 H 24   David and Abigail

ABINADAB
71 H 32 12   Death of Jonathan and his brothers
Abinadab and Melchi-shua

ABINADAB'S SONS
71 H 62 2   The ark is placed on a cart driven
by the sons of Abinadab; David and the
people dance and make music before the ark

ABIRAM (SON OF ELIAB)
71 E 31 7   Rebellion of Korah (Core), Dathan
and Abiram, and their punishment

ABISHAI
71 H 25 2   David and Abishai invade Saul's
encampment at night, while Saul and his
soldiers are sleeping

ABRAHAM
71 C 1   Story of Abraham

ABSALOM
71 H 84 9   Absalom, put to flight on a mule,
remains hanging by his hair in an oak tree

ABUSE
71 W 52   Job on the dunghill with Satan (or
devils) abusing and tormenting him; Job's
wife may be present

ACCEPTING
see RECEIVING

ACCLAMATION
see PROCLAMATION

ACCOMPANYING
see COMPANION(S)
see LEADING

ACCOUNTING
see CALLING TO ACCOUNT

ACCUSING
see also BEFORE
see also BETRAYING
see also ORDEAL
see also REBUKING
71 D 13 4   Potiphar's wife before her husband:
she accuses Joseph of trying to violate
her, using the cloak as evidence
71 D 17 31   Joseph accuses his brothers of
being spies and throws them in prison
71 P 41 3   The elders accusing Susanna before
the people, laying their hands on her head
or unveiling her
71 Q 74 1   Esther accuses Haman

ACHAN
71 E 52 5   Achan's sin (aftermath of the fall
of Jericho)

ACHIA
see AHIJAH

ADAM
71 A 3   Creation of man; the Garden of Eden
71 A 4-71 A 5   Temptation and Fall

ADAM (cont.)
71 A 6   Expulsion of Adam and Eve from Paradise
71 A 7   The labors of Adam and Eve; infancy
of Cain and Abel
71 A 82 3   Adam and Eve discover the dead
body of Abel and grieve over it

ADDRESSING
see WARNING

ADMISSION (REFUSED)
see REFUSING (ADMISSION)

ADMITTING
see RECEIVING A PERSON

ADMONISHING
see ADVISING
see REBUKING
see WARNING

ADOLESCENCE
see YOUTH

ADOPTION
see also FOUNDLING
see also UPBRINGING
71 E 11 26   When Moses is old enough, his
mother brings him to Pharaoh's daughter,
who adopts him

ADORATION
see WORSHIPPING
71 E 13 53   Adoration of the golden calf (which
may be standing on a pillar, and is
sometimes depicted as a dragon)

ADORNING
see TOILET (MAKING)

ADVANCEMENT (PROMOTION)
see PROMOTION

ADVANCES
see COURTING

ADVERSITY
see MISFORTUNE

ADVISING
see also ADMONISHING
see also INSTRUCTING
71 F 65   Naomi advises Ruth to seek Boaz'
protection

AFFLICTION
see SUFFERING

AFRAID
see FEAR

AGAG (KING)
71 G 36   Samuel summons Agag to be brought
before him

AGREEMENT
see MARRIAGE CONTRACT

AGRICULTURE
see FARMER
see FIELDS

AHAB (KING)
71 M 11   Elijah announces to King Ahab that
God will bring a long drought in the land
to avenge the apostasy of Israel

AHAB'S DESCENDANTS
71 K 31 14   Ahab's descendants are slain and
their heads are piled up in two heaps at
the city gate

AHASUERUS (KING)
71 Q   Story of Esther

AHIJAH
71 I 72   Meeting of Jeroboam and the prophet
Ahijah; Ahijah rends his garment in twelve
pieces, ten of which he gives to Jeroboam

AI
71 E 52 6   The city of Ai is taken by stratagem

AIJALON
71 E 52 94 2   Joshua orders the sun and moon
to stand still over Gibeon and Aijalon until
the Amorites who had besieged the city
of Gibeon are routed

AIR (IN THE)
see also ASCENSION
see also FALLING
see also HEAVEN
see also JUMPING
see also SKY
see also THROWING (BEING THROWN)
71 P 43 33   The prophet Habakkuk, carried by
his hair by an angel, brings food to Daniel
who sits unharmed between the lions

ALARM
71 E 31 53   The spies, except for Caleb and
Joshua, bring startling reports which upset
the people - reconnaissance of Canaan

ALLEGORY
N.B. personifications, symbols, allegories,
emblems, etc. of particular subjects must be
looked for in the ICONCLASS volumes (System
and Bibliography) under the notations denoting
the subject concerned. Attributes of
personifications from Ripa are to be found in
the Bibliography only.
11 I 62(...)3   Specific aspects, e.g.
allegorical and symbolical aspects of male
persons from the Old Testament (not in
biblical context)
11 I 63(...)3   Specific aspects, e.g.
allegorical and symbolical aspects - female
persons from the Old Testament

ALLIANCE
see also COVENANT
71 C 31 95   Jacob and Laban make an alliance:
a pile of stone is erected and an animal
is sacrificed

ALPHABET
see LETTER(S)

ALTAR
see also SACRIFICING
71 C 25 42   Isaac builds an altar
71 E 13 52   Aaron makes a golden calf and
has it placed on a pedestal or altar
71 E 13 53 1   Aaron builds an altar and offers
a sacrifice to the golden calf
71 I 43 23 4   Prayer of Solomon: Solomon kneels
before the altar
71 M 43 21   As Elijah prays, God sends fire
which burns up not only his sacrifice but
also the altar itself; the people fall
prostrate
71 O 32 2   Purification of Isaiah: an angel
touches Isaiah's lips with a burning coal,
taken from the altar with tongs - Isaiah's
visions

AMINADAB
see ABINADAB

AMORITES
71 E 52 94   Joshua and his army make a surprise
attack on the Amorites who are besieging
the city of Gibeon

ANANIAS (OF BABYLON)
11 I 62(THREE HEBREWS)21   The three Babylonian
youths Ananias (Shedrach), Azarias (Abed-
nego), Misael (Mesach) invoked in distress,
and for resurrections
71 P 13   The story of the three Hebrews in
the fiery furnace

ANGELS
71 A 61   God expels Adam and Eve from paradise
and has the tree of life guarded by an angel
with a flaming sword
71 A 72 3   An angel instructs Adam in
agricultural activities
71 C 11 93 2   An angel meets Hagar at the
fountain on the way to Shur and persuades
her to return
71 C 12 2   The visit of the three angels (three
men) - story of Abraham
71 C 12 4   The destruction of Sodom and
Gomorrah: Lot and his family flee to Zoar,
carrying their belongings; an angel may
be showing the way
71 C 12 84 11   An angel appears and reveals
a well of water to Hagar
71 C 13 13 11   When Abraham has his hand raised
to kill Isaac, an angel restrains Abraham's
hand
71 C 31 21   The dream of Jacob: while sleeping
on the ground with a stone for a pillow
Jacob sees a ladder reaching from earth
to heaven with angels going up and down;
usually with God at the top of the ladder
71 C 32 2   Jacob and the angel
71 E 11 45   At an inn, God (or the angel of
God) tries to kill Moses
71 E 11 73 2   The plague of the first-born:
the destroying angel passes through the
land and kills every Egyptian first-born
of man and animal
71 E 12 22 1   The people pass over on dry land
(Egyptians not or barely visible); the angel
of God and the pillar of cloud may be shown
at the rear
71 E 33 14   An angel holding a sword bars the
way and causes Balaam's ass to turn aside;
the angel is invisible to Balaam
71 F 31 1   Annunciation of Samson's birth to
the wife of Manoah by an angel
71 F 31 2   Annunciation of the birth of a son
to Manoah and his wife
71 L 24 38   At night, an angel of the Lord
decimates the Assyrian camp: 185,000
soldiers are killed
71 M 53   An angel wakes Elijah; a loaf of
bread and a jar of water are usually at
Elijah's head
71 O 32 2   Purification of Isaiah: an angel
touches Isaiah's lips with a burning coal,
taken from the altar with tongs - Isaiah's
visions
71 P 13 4   To his astonishment King
Nebuchadnezzar sees four men (one of them
usually represented as an angel) in the
furnace; the king commands them to come
forth
71 P 43 33   The prophet Habakkuk, carried by
his hair by an angel, brings food to Daniel
who sits unharmed between the lions
71 T 4-71 T 7   The angel Raphael - the book
of Tobit
71 W 2   The 'sons of God' (angels) with Satan
gather before God - story of Job
71 Z 31   Heliodorus in the temple, attacked
by a man (or angel) on horseback and two
other men (or angels)

ANGER
see also REVENGE
71 E 13 54 1   On seeing the idolaters Moses
breaks the tables of the law

71 Q 74 11   King Ahasuerus gets up in a fury and goes into the palace garden

ANIMAL(S)
see also KILLING - ANIMAL
see also MONSTER(S)
see also SACRIFICING
71 A 25   Creation of the animals - Genesis
71 A 33 3   Adam naming the animals
71 A 35 3   Adam is given dominion over all created things
71 B 32 21   The gathering of the animals in pairs - story of Noah
71 B 34 21   The animals leave the ark

ANIMATING
71 A 31 1   The man (Adam) comes to life: usually God reaches out his hand or breathes life into his nostrils

ANNA (WIFE OF TOBIT)
71 T   - The book of Tobit

ANNOUNCING
see also ANNUNCIATION
see also REPORTING
71 B 31 21   God announces a flood and commands Noah to build an ark
71 M 11   Elijah announces to King Ahab that God will bring a long drought to avenge the apostasy of Israel

ANNUNCIATION
71 F 31 1   Annunciation of Samson's birth to the wife of Manoah by an angel
71 F 31 2   Annunciation of the birth of a son to Manoah and his wife

ANOINTING
71 H 11 5   Samuel anointing David in the presence of his father Jesse and his brothers
71 H 41 2   David anointed king by the tribe of Judah
71 H 48 2   David anointed king by the elders of Israel
71 H 88 32   Solomon anointed king by Zadok; all the people rejoice and blow their trumpets

APOSTASY
see IDOLATRY

APPARITION
see GHOST(S)

APPEALING
see PLEADING

APPEARANCE
see also ANGEL(S)
see also ANNUNCIATION
see also DREAM
see also VISION
71 C 12 84 11   An angel appears and reveals a well of water to Hagar
71 F 21 21   The angel of the Lord appears to Gideon, who is usually shown threshing wheat
71 H 31 52   The ghost of Samuel appears to the witch of Endor; Saul falls prostrate to the ground

APPEARANCE OF GOD
see GOD

APPLE(S)
71 A 4-71 A 5   Temptation and Fall

APPOINTING
see CHOOSING
see LOT

ARARAT (MOUNT)
71 B 33 2   The ark of Noah comes to rest on Mount Ararat

ARAUNAH
71 H 54 63   By the command of God the angel stops destroying the Israelites at the threshing-floor of Araunah (Ornan) the Jebusite

ARBITRATION
see INTERVENING

ARGUING
see OBJECTING

ARK
71 B 3   Story of Noah
71 E 52 22   The Israelites leave their camp to cross the Jordan; the priests, carrying the ark, lead the march
71 E 52 42   The Israelites march around Jericho: in the procession the main body of the soldiers comes first, next are seven priests who blow on trumpets, followed by the priests carrying the ark and a rear guard
71 H 62   The Ark of the Covenant is brought to Jerusalem
71 I 43 23 2   The Ark of the Covenant is brought into the temple; a cloud fills the house of the Lord

ARM(S)
see ARM(S) RAISED
see ARM(S) STRETCHED
see CROSSED ARMS

ARM(S) RAISED
see also ARM(S) STRETCHED
see also WORSHIPPING
71 C 13 13 1   When Abraham has his hand raised to kill Isaac, God or the hand of God restrains Abraham's hand
71 C 13 13 11   When Abraham has his hand raised to kill Isaac, an angel restrains Abraham's hand
71 E 12 23   With his people safe on the shore, Moses raises his hands and causes the water to return; Pharaoh's army perishes in the water (Red Sea)
71 E 12 72 1   Moses sitting on a rock, arms held up by Aaron and Hur; the Amalekites are defeated

ARM(S) STRETCHED
see also ORDERING
see also REACHING
71 E 11 72 2   The plague of frogs: Aaron stretches out his hand over the water of Egypt; frogs come out and cover the land

ARMOUR
71 H 14 32   David receives Saul's armour - story of David and Goliath

ARMS (WEAPONS)
see WEAPON(S)

ARMY
see also SOLDIER(S)
71 E 12 23   With his people safe on the shore, Moses raises his hands and causes the water to return; Pharaoh's army perishes in the water (Red Sea)
71 E 12 23 1   Pharaoh and his army engulfed in the Red Sea (Israelites not or barely visible)

ARMY-CAMP
see CAMP

ARRESTING
  71 D 13 5   Joseph is arrested and sent to
  prison

ARRIVAL
  see also **DISEMBARKATION**
  see also **RECEIVING A PERSON**
  see also **RETURNING**
  71 C 21 5   The return journey and arrival in
  Canaan (Eliezer and Rebekah)
  71 I 33 1   The queen of Sheba comes to Solomon
  with a train of camels loaded with gifts
  71 T 59   The arrival at Ecbatana

ARROW(S)
  see also **BOW AND ARROW**
  see also **KILLING**
  71 B 15 1   Lamech kills Cain: Cain is
  accidentally shot dead by an arrow of the
  blind Lamech, who is assisted in the hunt
  by his son Tubalcain
  71 H 32 13   Saul wounded by an arrow
  71 K 29 45   When Jehoram realizes Jehu's
  treason, he turns his chariot round to flee,
  but Jehu shoots an arrow that strikes
  Jehoram in the back; the king falls dead
  in his chariot
  71 N 61 1   Elisha tells Joash to shoot an
  arrow through the window towards Syria and
  predicts that Joash will be victorious

ARTAXERXES
  see **AHASUERUS (KING)**

ASCENDING
  see also **ASCENSION**
  see also **CLIMBING**
  71 C 31 21   The dream of Jacob: while sleeping
  on the ground with a stone for a pillow
  Jacob sees a ladder reaching from earth
  to heaven with angels going up and down;
  usually with God at the top of the ladder

ASCENSION
  71 F 31 4   Manoah's sacrifice; the angel
  ascends in the flames
  71 T 79 2   The angel Raphael disappears into
  the sky

ASENATH
  71 D 24 21   Jacob blesses Manasseh and Ephraim
  with arms crossed; Joseph may be shown
  trying to uncross them or expressing (with
  Asenath) his disapproval

ASH
  see **ASHES**

ASHES
  71 H 81 23   Amnon sends Tamar away; Tamar puts
  ashes on her head, rends her garment, lays
  her hand on her head and leaves crying
  71 W 51   Job covered with sores (or boils)
  takes his abode on a dunghill (pile of
  ashes) and scrapes his body with a potsherd

ASHORE
  see **SHORE**

ASKING
  see also **BEFORE**
  see also **INTERROGATION**
  see also **INVITING**
  see also **INVOKING**
  see also **PERMISSION**
  see also **PRAYING**
  see also **PROPOSAL**
  see also **RIDDLE**
  71 C 27 6   Esau seeks his father's blessing;
  Isaac realizes he has mistakenly blessed
  Jacob instead of Esau

  71 E 11 81   During the night Pharaoh sends
  for Moses and Aaron and begs them to depart
  71 F 15 1   Deborah (sitting under a palmtree)
  beseeches Barak to attack Sisera and his
  army
  71 F 21 43   Twice Gideon asks the Lord to show
  him a sign with a sheep's fleece before
  his raid against the Midianites
  71 M 21 1   Elijah asks the widow of Zarephath
  to fetch him some food
  71 Q 5   Mordecai asks Esther's help
  71 Q 74 2   Haman begs Esther for his life
  71 Q 82   Esther entreating Ahasuerus: she falls
  at the king's feet and asks him to revoke
  the decree against the Jews; the king holds
  out his sceptre to her (Esther may be
  holding the decree)

ASLEEP
  see **SLEEPING**

ASMODEUS
  71 T 64 2   Tobias lies the fish's heart and
  liver on glowing coals; the evil spirit
  Asmodeus disappears
  71 T 64 21   The angel binding Asmodeus

ASS
  see also **ASS' JAW-BONE**
  see also **DONKEY**
  see also **MULE**
  71 C 13 11   Abraham with Isaac, an ass and
  the servants on their way to Moriah
  71 E 11 44   Moses departs for Egypt: he carries
  his rod and is accompanied by his wife and
  sons upon an ass
  71 E 33 14   An angel holding a sword bars the
  way and causes Balaam's ass to turn aside;
  the angel is invisible to Balaam
  71 E 33 14 1   Balaam strikes his ass, whereupon
  the ass lies down and starts to speak
  71 W 31 11   The theft of Job's oxen and asses
  by the Sabeans

ASS' JAW-BONE
  71 A 82   The killing of Abel: Cain slays him
  with a stone, a club or a jaw-bone,
  alternatively with a spade or another tool
  as weapon
  71 F 35   Samson and the jaw-bone of an ass

ASSASSINATING
  see **MURDERING**

ASSAULTING
  see **ATTACKING**

ASSEMBLING
  71 B 32 21   The gathering of the animals in
  pairs - story of Noah
  71 H 22 21   David's family and men join him
  in the cave Adullam
  71 W 2   The 'sons of God' (angels) with Satan
  gather before God - story of Job

ASSEMBLY
  see **ASSEMBLING**
  see **BANQUET**
  see **FEAST**

ASSISTANT
  see **HELP**

ASTIN (QUEEN)
  71 Q 21   The feast of Ahasuerus (Xerxes,
  alternatively Artaxerxes); the downfall
  of Queen Vashti (Astin)

ASTONISHMENT
  see **WONDER**

ATTACKING
see also **VIOLATING**
71 Z 31   Heliodorus in the temple, attacked by a man (or angel) on horseback and two other men (or angels)

ATTENDANT
see **SERVANT**

AUDIENCE
see **BEFORE**
see **LISTENING**

AUREOLE
see **RAY OF LIGHT**

AUTHORITY
see **POWER**

AVENGING
see also **REVENGE**
71 M 11   Elijah announces to King Ahab that God will bring a long drought in the land to avenge the apostasy of Israel

AWAITING
see **WAITING**

AWAKING
71 B 35 22   Noah awakes from his slumber and curses Canaan, son of Ham
71 F 37 7   Samson wakes up and finds his hair and strength gone; he is taken prisoner
71 M 53   An angel wakes Elijah; a loaf of bread and a jar of water are usually at Elijah's head

AZARIAS
11 I 62(THREE HEBREWS) 21   The three Babylonian youths Ananias (Shedrach), Azarias (Abednego), Misael (Mesach) invoked in distress, and for resurrections
71 P 13   The story of the three Hebrews in the fiery furnace

BAAL
71 M 4   Elijah defies the priests of Baal; the end of the drought

BABEL
see also **BABYLON**
71 B 4   Story of the Tower of Babel

BABY
see also **BIRTH**
see also **EXPOSING**
see also **FOUNDLING**
see also **MOTHER AND CHILD**
see also **SUCKLING**
71 E 11 23 1   Moses (alone) in the bulrushes
71 E 11 25   Moses is either presented to Pharaoh's daughter or surrounded by women fondling him

BABYLON
see also **BABYLONIAN CAPTIVITY**
71 B 4   Story of the Tower of Babel
71 O 78 34   Jeremiah prophesies the destruction of Babylon

BABYLONIAN CAPITIVITY
71 L 4   The Babylonian Captivity of the Jews
71 X 1(Ps.137:1) 1:71 L 4   'By the rivers of Bablyon...' - the Hebrews in captivity lamenting by the riverside

BACKWARD MOVEMENT
71 B 35 21 11   Shem and Japheth walking backwards towards Noah

BAD LUCK
see **MISFORTUNE**

BAG
see **SACK**

BAGOAS
71 U 44 2   The murder of Holofernes is discovered (by Bagoas)

BAKER
71 D 14   - Story of Joseph in prison

BALCONY
71 H 71   David, from the roof (or balcony) of his palace, sees Bathsheba bathing

BALD
71 V 22   After a three-day sojourn in the belly of the monster Jonah is cast on dry land; Jonah may be shown nude and bald-headed

BANISHING
see also **EXPELLING**
71 C 12 8   The banishment of Hagar and Ishmael

BANQUET
see also **FEAST**
71 H 24 5   The banquet in Nabal's house
71 H 81 5   Amnon is murdered at Absalom's banquet
71 P 22   During Belshazzar's banquet a hand appears and writes on the wall (MENE, MENE, TEKEL, and PARSIN (UPHARSIN)); King Belshazzar is frightened

BARAK
71 F 15   The time of Deborah and Barak - the book of Judges

BARLEY
71 F 65 1   Ruth brings the barley home to Naomi and tells her what has occurred in the fields of Boaz

BARN
    71 D 16 42 11   Joseph opens the storehouse
    and sells corn

BARRENNESS
    71 C 12 24 3   The promise of a son is renewed;
    Sarah, overhearing it, laughs incredulously

BASKET
    71 E 11 24 1   Moses is pulled out of the water
    by the servants
    71 E 12 54 1   The gathering of manna (in
    baskets and pots)

BATHING
    see also TOILET (MAKING)
    71 E 11 24   The finding of Moses: Pharaoh's
    daughter comes to bathe with her maidens
    in the river and discovers the child
    floating on the water
    71 H 71   David, from the roof (or balcony)
    of his palace, sees Bathsheba bathing
    71 N 16 2   Naaman comes to the Jordan, dips
    himself seven times and is cured
    71 P 41 2   Susanna bathing, usually in or near
    a fountain and sometimes accompanied by
    two female servants

BATHSHEBA
    11 I 63(BATHSHEBA)   Bathsheba (not in biblical
    context)
    71 H 7   David and Bathsheba

BATTLE
    see also ARMY
    see also ATTACKING
    see also DEFEAT
    see also FIGHTING
    see also VICTORY
    71 F 83 3   Second battle between the
    Philistines and the Israelites at Eben-ezer;
    the Israelites defeated again
    71 H 32   Battle between the Israelites and
    the Philistines
    71 H 74 2   Uriah is killed in the battle
    71 Z 39   A heavenly rider, in white garment
    and with weapons of gold, helps the
    Maccabees in their battle against Lysias

BATTLE-FIELD
    see BATTLE

BEACH
    see SHORE

BEAM (LIGHT)
    see RAY OF LIGHT

BEAR
    71 H 14 31   David kills a lion and a bear (or
    tells Saul about it)

BEARING (CARRYING)
    see CARRYING

BEATING
    see also SCOURGING
    see also STRIKING
    71 A 82   The killing of Abel: Cain slays him
    with a stone, a club or a jaw-bone,
    alternatively with a spade or another tool
    as weapon

BEAUTY

    see LOVE AT FIRST SIGHT
    see TOILET (MAKING)

BECKONING
    71 F 37 5   Samson asleep in Delilah's lap;
    she is usually shown beckoning to a
    Philistine or putting a finger to her lips

BED
    see also BIRTH
    see also COUCH
    see also LOVER(S)
    see also SICK PERSON
    see also SLEEPING
    71 C 11 91 1   Sarah brings Hagar to Abraham,
    who is usually shown lying in bed
    71 C 27 4   Isaac lying in bed blesses Jacob
    who, disguised in Esau's clothes, brings
    food to his father; Jacob's hands and neck
    are covered with goatskins
    71 D 13 31   Potiphar's wife catches Joseph
    by his robe, usually while lying in bed;
    Joseph escapes leaving his cloak behind
    in her hands (possibly with a naked child
    lying in a crib)
    71 H 84 6   David receives beds, vessels, food
    and other presents from Shobi, Machir, and
    Barzillai

BEDROOM
    see BED

BEFORE
    see also ACCUSING
    see also ANNOUNCING
    see also APPEARANCE
    see also ASKING
    see also BOWING
    see also COMPLAINING
    see also GIVING
    see also KNEELING
    see also MEETING
    see also MESSENGER
    see also OFFERING
    see also ORDERING
    see also PRESENTING A PERSON
    see also REBUKING
    see also RECEIVING A PERSON
    see also VISITING
    see also WARNING
    71 E 11 64   Moses and Aaron before Pharaoh;
    Aaron performs the miracle of the rod
    changing into a snake
    71 H 14 51   David brings Goliath's head to
    Saul
    71 I 13   Bathsheba comes before Solomon
    71 I 32 4   Both mothers come before Solomon
    - the judgement of Solomon
    71 I 33 2   The queen of Sheba before Solomon,
    testing him with questions
    71 P 25   Daniel, when brought before King
    Belshazzar, interprets the writing on the
    wall
    71 Q 6   Esther before Ahasuerus
    71 W 2   The 'sons of God' (angels) with Satan
    gather before God - story of Job

BEGGING
    see ASKING

BEGINNING
    see also ORIGIN
    71 A 1   'In the beginning...' the ordering
    of chaos

BEHEADING
    71 H 14 43   David beheads Goliath with a sword
    71 U 42 73   Holofernes beheaded by Judith with
    his own sword; the maidservant may be
    keeping watch

BEHOLDING
    see LOOKING

BEING
    see HUMAN BEING
    see MONSTER(S)

BELIEVER
    see FAITH

BELOVED
     71 X 21   Shulammite, the beloved woman - Song
               of Solomon

BELSHAZZAR (KING)
     71 P 2   Daniel and King Belshazzar

BENAIAH
     71 H 52 64   Benaiah kills two men, and then
               a lion, in a pit on a snowy day

BENDING
     see BOWING

BENEDICTION
     see BLESSING

BENJAMIN
     71 C 32 62   Birth of Benjamin: Rachel dies
               in childbirth
     71 D 18 1   Judah persuades the afflicted Jacob
               to consent to the departure of Benjamin
     71 D 18 11   Jacob's farewell to Benjamin
     71 D 18 5   The feast at Joseph's house: the
               amazement of the brothers at being seated
               according to their age; Benjamin is honored
               with extra food
     71 D 19 1   Joseph has his silver cup placed
               in Benjamin's sack
     71 D 19 3   The brothers before Joseph: Judah
               pleads for Benjamin and offers to be
               retained as a slave in his stead

BERIT MILAH
     see CIRCUMCISION

BETHEL
     71 C 32 5   Jacob at Bethel

BETHLEHEM
     71 F 62   Naomi's return to Bethlehem

BETHULIAH
     71 U 43   Judith and her maidservant on their
               way back to Bethuliah

BETRAYING
     71 K 29 45   When Jehoram realizes Jehu's
               treason, he turns his chariot round to
               flee, but Jehu shoots an arrow that strikes
               Jehoram in the back; the king falls dead
               in his chariot

BEWAILING
     see LAMENTING

BILDAD
     71 W 54 1   Eliphaz, Bildad and Zophar go to
               Job to console him over his misfortunes
               (the three friends may be depicted as kings)

BINDING
     see also CHAINING
     71 C 13 12   Preparations for the sacrifice,
               e.g. Abraham binding Isaac
     71 D 17 52   Joseph comes back, picks out Simeon
               and has him bound
     71 F 37 32   Samson is bound by Delilah with
               new ropes
     71 P 13 3   After the furnace has been heated
               seven times more, the three Hebrews are
               bound and thrown into the fire; their
               executioners are burnt by the flames
     71 T 64 21   The angel binding Asmodeus

BIRDS
     71 A 25 1   Creation of birds and fishes

BIRTH
     see also EMERGING

71 C 24 3   Birth of the twins: Jacob clutches
               Esau's heel
     71 C 32 62   Birth of Benjamin: Rachel dies
               in childbirth

BIRTHRIGHT
     71 C 24 41   Esau, returning hungry from the
               hunt, sells his first birthright for a
               potage of lentils

BITING
     71 E 32 41   When the people complain again
               about the food, God sends poisonous snakes;
               many die of snake-bites - book of Numbers

BLACK
     see also BLACK AND WHITE
     71 C 31 61   Laban agrees to give Jacob all
               the black and spotted sheep and goats as
               wages

BLACK AND WHITE
     71 C 31 61   Laban agrees to give Jacob all
               the black and spotted sheep and goats as
               wages
     71 C 31 63   Jacob puts peeled rods in the
               animal's drinking troughs to make the beasts
               bear spotted young

BLAMING
     see ACCUSING

BLESSED FOOD
     71 H 21 21   David receives the hallowed bread

BLESSING
     71 A 35 2   God blesses Adam and Eve;
               institution of marriage
     71 A 81 1   God (or the hand of God) appears
               and blesses Abel - sacrifice
     71 B 34 31   God blesses Noah and gives him
               his commandments
     71 C 11 71   Melchizedek blesses Abraham
     71 C 32 22 1   Jacob receives a new name,
               Israel, and is blessed by the angel
     71 D 24 21   Jacob blesses Manasseh and Ephraim
               with arms crossed; Joseph may be shown
               trying to uncross them or expressing (with
               Asenath) his disapproval

BLINDNESS
     71 B 15 1   Lamech kills Cain: Cain is
               accidentally shot dead by an arrow of the
               blind Lamech, who is assisted in the hunt
               by his son Tubalcain
     71 F 37 8   The blinding of Samson
     71 F 37 81   The blind Samson in Gaza, bound
               with brass chains
     71 K 21 43   Jeroboam's wife in disguise visits
               the old and blind Ahijah, but he, having
               been warned by God, recognizes her; he
               predicts the death of her son and Israel's
               punishment for Jeroboam's sin
     71 T 3   Tobit's blindness

BLOOD
     71 A 83 11   Abel's blood cries out for revenge
     71 D 12 71 1   Joseph's brothers stain Joseph's
               coat with the kid's blood
     71 D 12 8   Joseph's blood-stained coat is
               brought and shown to Jacob
     71 E 11 72 1   The plague of water turned to
               blood; as Pharaoh goes down to the Nile,
               Aaron strikes the surface of the river
               with his rod; the water turns into blood
               and all the fish die

BLOSSOMING
     see ROD (FLOWERING)

BLOW(S)
     see BEATING

BLOWING
see TRUMPET

BOARDING
see EMBARKATION

BOAZ
71 F 6   - The story of Ruth

BODY
see CORPSE

BOIL(S)
see also LEPROSY
71 F 83 51 2   God punishes the inhabitants
of Ashdod with emerods or boils
71 W 51   Job covered with sores (or boils)
takes his abode on a dunghill (pile of
ashes) and scrapes his body with a potsherd
71 W 52 1   Job is smitten from head to foot
with sores by Satan, or dragon-like monsters
that blow poisonous smoke on Job

BOILING
see CAULDRON

BONE(S)
71 E 12 11   Moses takes the bones of Joseph
with him
71 N 7   Elisha's bones
71 O 93 3   Ezekiel's vision of the valley
of the dry bones

BOOTH
see also TABERNACLE
see also TENT
71 V 42   The prophet Jonah withdraws from
Nineveh; he builds a booth and while
enjoying the shade of a plant (gourd or
vine) which God made grow for him, he awaits
the destiny of the city

BORDER
see BOUNDARY

BOTTLE
see FLASK

BOULDER(S)
see STONE(S)

BOUND PERSON
see BINDING

BOUNDARY
71 E 13 22   The people get ready for the coming
legislation: they wash their clothes and
set bounds round the mountain

BOW
see BOW AND ARROW

BOW AND ARROW
see also SHOOTING
71 C 12 83   Hagar and Ishmael (often with
bow and arrow) depart

BOW AND QUIVER
see BOW AND ARROW

BOWING
71 D 17 3   Admitted in Joseph's presence, the
brothers bow down before him
71 D 18 4   When Joseph gets home, he receives
his brothers; they bow down before him and
give him the presents
71 F 64 3   Boaz speaks to Ruth; Ruth usually
bowing down, or kneeling before him
71 N 13 24   The Shunammite woman rides out
with her donkey to Elisha, bows down before
him and taking hold of his feet, entreats
him to come with her

BOX
71 F 83 62   The Ark of the Covenant and the
box with the guilt offering, drawn by two
cows, sent back to Israel

BOY
see CHILD
see FATHER AND SON

BRACELET
71 C 21 33   Rebekah receives ear-rings and
golden bracelets from Eliezer
71 C 33 27 1   Judah's love-affair with Tamar;
he gives her his signet(-ring), bracelets
and staff

BRAND
71 F 34 3   Samson ties three hundred foxes
two by two by their tails with a fire-brand
in between; with the torches on fire he
lets them go into the cornfields of the
Philistines which are set aflame

BRAZEN
71 E 32 4   The brazen serpent - book of Numbers

BREAD
see also FEEDING
see also LOAF
71 C 11 7   The meeting of Abraham and
Melchizedek, the high priest and king of
Salem, who brings bread and wine
71 C 12 82   Abraham provides Hagar and Ishmael
with bread and a jug of water
71 H 21 21   David receives the hallowed bread
71 H 62 8   David places the ark in a tent,
burns offerings before the Lord and
distributes bread, meat and wine to everyone

BREAKING
see also COLLAPSING
see also DESTRUCTION OF IDOLS
71 E 11 27 1   Moses and Pharaoh's crown:
Pharaoh playfully places his crown on the
head of the infant Moses, who throws it
to the ground and tramples on it; or Moses
breaks the crown while playing
71 E 13 54 1   On seeing the idolaters Moses
breaks the tables of the law
71 F 21 64   The attack on the Midianites:
Gideon and his men blow their trumpets,
break their pitchers, and hold their lamps
71 F 38 3   Samson breaks the pillars; the
temple of Dagon collapses, killing all that
are in it

BREAST(S)
see SUCKLING

BREATHING
see ANIMATING

BREEDING
71 C 31 63   Jacob puts peeled rods in the
animal's drinking troughs to make the beasts
bear spotted young

BRIDAL CHAMBER
see WEDDING-NIGHT

BRINGING
see BEFORE
see GIVING
see LEADING

BROKEN
see BREAKING
see POTSHERDS

BROTH
see SOUP

BROTHER(S)
see also TWIN(S)
71 D 11 Joseph incurs the hatred of his brothers

BROW
see FOREHEAD

BUCKET
71 W 53 12 Job's wife pouring a bucket of water over him

BUILDING
see also ALTAR
see also BUILDING A CITY
71 B 42 1 The building of the Tower of Babel; Nimrod may be present, supervising or assisting the construction
71 H 51 4 The building of David's palace

BUILDING A CITY
71 A 84 2 Cain building the city of Enoch

BULL
see OX

BULRUSHES
see REED(S)

BUNCH OF GRAPES
see GRAPE(S)

BURIAL
see also FUNERAL
71 C 22 41 Abraham is buried by Isaac and Ishmael in the cave of Machpelah
71 E 11 31 21 Moses buries the body of the Egyptian taskmaster in the sand
71 T 24 Tobit buries the dead in secret

BURNING
see also BURNING (CITY)
see also BURNING ALIVE
see also COAL(S)
see also FIRE
see also SACRIFICING
see also SETTING ON FIRE
71 E 11 41 1 A burning bush attracts Moses' attention
71 E 11 42 The burning bush - calling of Moses
71 K 31 22 2 The images of Baal are destroyed and burned

BURNING (CITY)
71 C 12 42 Sodom and Gomorrah burning

BURNING ALIVE
see also FIRE
71 P 13 3 After the furnace has been heated seven times more, the three Hebrews are bound and thrown into the fire; their executioners are burnt by the flames

BURNING BUSH
see BUSH

BURNT OFFERING
see SACRIFICING

BURYING
see BURIAL

BUSH
71 C 12 84 1 Hagar sits weeping after having put Ishmael under a bush to die
71 C 13 14 A ram caught in a thicket is sacrificed instead of Isaac
71 E 11 41 1 A burning bush attracts Moses' attention
71 E 11 42 The burning bush - calling of Moses

BUTLER
71 D 14 - Story of Joseph in prison

CAIN
71 A 7 The labors of Adam and Eve; infancy of Cain and Abel
71 A 8 The story of Cain and Abel
71 B 15 1 Lamech kills Cain: Cain is accidentally shot dead by an arrow of the blind Lamech who is assisted in the hunt by his son Tubalcain

CALAMITY
see MISFORTUNE

CALF
see also GOLDEN CALF
71 C 12 24 2 Abraham orders the preparation of a calf and other food

CALLING
see SHOUTING

CALLING TO ACCOUNT
see also INTERROGATION
71 A 52 1 God calls Adam and Eve to account for their deed
71 A 83 1 The Lord calls on Cain to account for his deed

CALLING TO ARMS
see PREPARATIONS - BATTLE, WAR

CAMEL
71 C 31 84 Jacob on the way to Canaan with his family, his flocks, camels and all his possessions
71 I 33 1 The queen of Sheba comes to Solomon with a train of camels loaded with gifts

CAMEL'S SADDLE
71 C 31 94 1 Rachel hides the teraphim in a camel's saddle and sits on it

CAMP
see also TENT
71 C 11 65 Abraham calls all the men in his camp together and sets out in pursuit of the four kings
71 D 17 71 At their camp one of Joseph's brothers finds money in his sack
71 E 12 8 Jethro's visit to Moses: with Zipporah and her two sons he comes to the desert where Moses is encamped

CANAAN
71 C 21 5 The return journey and arrival in Canaan (Eliezer and Rebekah)
71 C 31 84 Jacob on the way to Canaan with his family, his flocks, camels and all his possessions
71 E 31 5 Reconnaissance of Canaan - book of Numbers
71 E 46 1 Moses from Mount Nebo views the promised land
71 E 52-71 E 53 The conquest of Canaan by the Israelites under Joshua's leadership
71 E 54 The division of Canaan

CANAAN (SON OF HAM)
71 B 35 22 Noah awakes from his slumber and curses Canaan, son of Ham

CANDELABRUM
see CANDLESTICK

CANDLESTICK
71 I 43 22 4 The seven-branched candlestick - temple of Solomon

CANNIBALISM
see DEVOURING

CANTICLE
see SINGING

CAPE (CLOAK)
see CLOAK

CAPTAIN
see OFFICER

CAPTIVE(S)
see also DEFEAT
see also LIBERATING
see also PRISONER
see also RELEASING
71 D 17 52   Joseph comes back, picks out Simeon
and has him bound

CARAVAN
see also CAMEL(S)
see also TRAVELLING
71 C 32 21   Jacob sends his family and caravan
across the river Jabbok, and stays behind

CARESSING
see also LOVER(S)
71 E 11 25   Moses is either presented to
Pharaoh's daughter or surrounded by women
fondling him

CARGO
see LOAD

CARMEL (MOUNT)
71 N 13   Elisha and the Shunammite woman

CAROUSAL
see FEAST

CARRIAGE
see CART
see CHARIOT

CARRYING
see also CARRYING ON THE SHOULDERS
71 C 13 11 1   The servants are left behind
while Abraham and Isaac (usually carrying
wood) climb the mountain
71 E 52 22   The Israelites leave their camp
to cross the Jordan; the priests, carrying
the ark, lead the march
71 H 32 45   The inhabitants of Jabesh-Gilead
take away the bodies of Saul and his sons
71 P 43 33   The prophet Habakkuk, carried by
his hair by an angel, brings food to Daniel
who sits unharmed between the lions
71 T 32   Old Tobit leaves the banquet and
carries the dead man into a house
71 T 58   Tobias and the angel Raphael continue
their journey; usually Tobias carrying the
fish

CARRYING ON THE SHOULDERS
71 E 31 52   The spies take away some of the
fruits of Canaan and return, usually
carrying a large bunch of grapes on a pole

CARRYING-POLE
71 E 31 52   The spies take away some of the
fruits of Canaan and return, usually
carrying a large bunch of grapes on a pole

CART
71 H 62 2   The ark is placed on a cart driven
by the sons of Abinadab; David and the
people dance and make music before the ark

CASKET
see BOX

CASTING (MOULDING)
see MOULDING

CASTING (THROWING)
see THROWING

CASTING LOTS
see LOT(S)

CASTLE
see PALACE

CATCHING
71 C 13 14   A ram caught in a thicket is
sacrificed instead of Isaac
71 D 13 31   Potiphar's wife catches Joseph
by his robe, usually while lying in bed;
Joseph escapes leaving his cloak behind
in her hands (possibly with a naked child
lying in a crib)
71 T 56   Tobias captures the fish and pulls
it on the land

CATCHING BY SURPRISE
see FINDING
see SPYING
see STRATAGEM

CATTLE
71 E 11 72 5   The plague of murrain in cattle:
all the animals of the Egyptians die

CAULDRON
see also POT
11 I 62(JEREMIAH)   Attributes of Jeremiah

CAVE
71 C 12 51   Lot, seeing the destruction of
the cities and fearing for his safety in
Zoar, flees with his daughters to a cave
in the mountains
71 C 22 41   Abraham is buried by Isaac and
Ishmael in the cave of Machpelah

CEASING
see STOPPING

CELEBRATION
71 E 11 73 13   Celebration of the first
Passover

CELL
see PRISON

CELLAR
see DUNGEON

CEREMONY
see CELEBRATION

CESSATION
see STOPPING

CHABRIS
71 U 41 1   Judith, the widow of Manasseh,
speaks with the elders Ozias, Chabris, and
Charmis

CHAIN
see CHAINING

CHAINING
see also BINDING
71 F 37 81   the blind Samson in Gaza, bound
with brass chains

CHAIR
see THRONE

CHALICE
see also CUP
71 M 53 1   An angel, holding a loaf of bread
and a jar (or chalice) wakes Elijah

CHALLENGING
see also INSULTING
71 M 4   Elijah defies the priests of Baal;
the end of the drought

CHAMBERMAID
 see TOILET (MAKING)

CHANGING
 see TRANSFORMATION

CHARACTER
 see LETTER(S)

CHARGE
 see ATTACKING

CHARIOT
 see also TRIUMPH
 71 D 16 2 Triumph of Joseph: dressed in royal attire he rides in one of Pharaoh's chariots, preceded by a herald
 71 K 29 45 When Jehoram realizes Jehu's treason, he turns his chariot round to flee, but Jehu shoots an arrow that strikes Jehoram in the back; the king falls dead in his chariot
 71 M 84 A chariot, horses of fire and a whirl-wind appear and Elijah is carried up into heaven; Elijah's cloak falls (or he hands it over to Elisha)

CHARITY
 see CLOTHING
 see DISTRIBUTING

CHARMIS
 71 U 41 1 Judith, the widow of Manasseh, speaks with the elders Ozias, Chabris, and Charmis

CHASING
 see CHASING AWAY
 see PURSUING

CHASING AWAY
 see also EXPELLING
 71 A 61 1 An angel chases Adam and Eve out of paradise with a (flaming) sword
 71 E 11 32 1 Moses drives away the shepherds who wanted to prevent Jethro's daughters from watering their father's flock

CHASTITY
 see also ORDEAL
 see also VIRGINITY
 71 D 13 Joseph in Potiphar's house; the chastity of Joseph

CHEAT
 see DECEIT

CHEERING
 see REJOICING

CHERRY
 71 E 11 27 11 Moses' trial by fire: when given the choice between two plates, one containing burning coals, the other a ruby ring (or cherries), Moses chooses the burning coals and puts them in his mouth

CHERUB(S)
 71 A 62 Adam and Eve outside Eden, whose entrance is guarded by shining cherubim

CHEST
 see ARK
 see BOX

CHIDING
 see REBUKING

CHIEFTAIN
 see OFFICER

CHILD
 see also BABY
 see also GIRL
 see also MOTHER AND CHILD
 71 A 7 The labors of Adam and Eve; infancy of Cain and Abel
 71 A 72 1 Adam engaged in agricultural activities, Eve spinning and usually their children at play
 71 C 24 Isaac's children (Esau and Jacob)
 71 C 31 5 Jacob's children
 71 D 13 31 Potiphar's wife catches Joseph by his robe, usually while lying in bed; Joseph escapes leaving his cloak behind in her hands (possibly with a naked child lying in a crib)
 71 E 11 27 1 Moses and Pharaoh's crown: Pharaoh playfully places his crown on the head of the infant Moses, who throws it to the ground and tramples on it; or Moses breaks the crown while playing
 71 W 31 41 The death of Job's children

CHILDBIRTH
 see BIRTH

CHILDLESSNESS
 see BARRENNESS

CHOICE
 see also CHOOSING
 71 E 11 27 11 Moses' trial by fire: when given the choice between two plates, one containing burning coals, the other a ruby ring (or cherries), Moses chooses the burning coals and puts them in his mouth

CHOKING
 71 F 32 5 Samson kills the lion with his bare hands

CHOOSING
 see also CHOICE
 71 E 11 27 11 Moses' trial by fire: when given the choice between two plates, one containing burning coals, the other a ruby ring (or cherries), Moses chooses the burning coals and puts them in his mouth
 71 E 12 85 Moses choosing judges
 71 H 11 David chosen as king by God

CIRCUMCISION
 71 E 11 45 1 Zipporah appeases God by circumcising one of her sons

CITHARA
 see LYRE

CITY
 see BUILDING A CITY
 see BURNING (CITY)
 see DESTRUCTION (OF CITY)

CITY-GATE
 71 C 33 27 Tamar changes from her widow's clothes and covers her face with a veil after the manner of the prostitutes; sitting at the entrance of a city on the road to Timnath she awaits Judah
 71 H 46 3 Abner, fetched by Joab's messengers, is taken aside by Joab in the gate of Hebron, and is killed by him with a sword
 71 H 85 6 David speaks to the people at the gate of the city
 71 K 31 14 Ahab's descendants are slain and their heads are piled up in two heaps at the city gate
 71 M 21 When the brook dries up, Elijah crosses over to the city of Zarephath; at the gate he meets a woman and her little son gathering wood (the woman's sticks may form a cross)

71 U 41 1   Judith and her maidservant take leave of the elders at the city gate

CLASPED HANDS
71 C 13 13 11   When Abraham has his hand raised to kill Isaac, an angel restrains Abraham's hand

CLAY
71 A 31   God fashions man from clay

CLEANSING
see PURIFICATION

CLEFT
see CAVE

CLIFF(S)
see ROCK(S)

CLIMBING
see also ASCENDING
see also LADDER
71 C 13 11 1   The servants are left behind while Abraham and Isaac (usually carrying wood) climb the mountain

CLINGING
see HANGING

CLOAK
see also ROBE
71 D 13 31   Potiphar's wife catches Joseph by his robe, usually while lying in bed; Joseph escapes leaving his cloak behind in her hands (possibly with a naked child lying in a crib)
71 D 13 4   Potiphar's wife before her husband: she accuses Joseph of trying to violate her, using the cloak as evidence
71 M 84   A chariot, horses of fire and a whirlwind appear and Elijah is carried up into heaven; Elijah's cloak falls (or he hands it over to Elisha)

CLOSING
see OPENING

CLOTH
see also VEIL
71 H 23 6   When Saul comes out of the cave, David calls him, falls down on his knees and shows him the piece of cloth
71 U 42 74 1   Holofernes' head is put on a dish, and covered with a cloth

CLOTHES
see also CLOTHING
see also TEARING ONE'S CLOTHES
71 C 21 42   Gifts of clothing, gold and jewelry are offered to Rebekah's parents
71 D 13 31   Potiphar's wife catches Joseph by his robe, usually while lying in bed; Joseph escapes leaving his cloak behind in her hands (possibly with a naked child lying in a crib)

CLOTHING
see also CLOTHES
71 A 55   Adam and Eve are clothed by God

CLOUD
see also PILLAR OF CLOUD
71 E 13 12   Moses communicating with God on Mount Sinai (the mountain may be covered by a thick cloud)
71 I 43 23 2   The Ark of the Covenant is brought into the temple; a cloud fills the house of the Lord

CLUB
71 A 82   The killing of Abel: Cain slays him with a stone, a club or a jaw-bone, alternatively with a spade or another tool as a weapon

COAL(S)
71 E 11 27 11   Moses' trial by fire: when given the choice between two plates, one containing burning coals, the other a ruby ring (or cherries), Moses chooses the burning coals and puts them in his mouth
71 O 32 2   Purification of Isaiah: an angel touches Isaiah's lips with a burning coal, taken from the altar with tongs
71 T 64 2   Tobias lies the fish's heart and liver on glowing coals; the evil spirit Asmodeus disappears

COAST
see SHORE

COAT
see also CLOAK
71 D 12 71 1   Joseph's brothers stain Joseph's coat with the kid's blood
71 D 12 8   Joseph's blood-stained coat is brought and shown to Jacob

COFFEE-HOUSE
see INN

COIN
see MONEY
see SILVER (PIECE OF)

COLLAPSING
see also FALLING
71 F 38 3   Samson breaks the pillars; the temple of Dagon collapses, killing all that are in it

COLLECTING
see GATHERING

COLUMN
see PILLAR

COMFORTING
see CONSOLING

COMING TO LIFE
see ANIMATING

COMMANDER
see OFFICER

COMMANDING
see ORDERING

COMMANDMENT(S)
see also TABLES OF THE LAW
71 A 35 4   The giving of the test commandment: God warns Adam and Eve not to eat from the tree of knowledge of good and evil
71 B 34 31   God blesses Noah and gives him his commandments

COMMUNICATING WITH GOD
71 E 13 12   Moses communicating with God on Mount Sinai (the mountain may be covered by a thick cloud)
71 H 14 44   David thanks the Lord after he has slain the giant Goliath
71 H 61 1   David communicating with God; David praying (in general)
71 W 64 (Job 38-42:6)   God speaks to Job from out of the whirlwind

COMPANION(S)
see also MAIDSERVANT
71 F 24 54   Jephthah's daughter retreats to the mountains with her companions to bewail her virginity

COMPELLING
see FORCE

COMPETITION
see CONTEST

COMPLAINING
71 C 31 45   After the wedding-night Jacob discovers that he has been deceived with Leah and complains to Laban
71 E 12 21 2   The people of Israel murmur against Moses
71 E 32 41   When the people complain again about the food, God sends poisonous snakes; many die of snake-bites - book of Numbers
71 N 11   The water of Jericho is purified: when the citizens of Jericho complain about their water, Elisha puts some salt into a jar; he then throws the salt into the water

COMPULSION
see FORCE

COMPUNCTION
see REPENTING

CONCEALING
see HIDING
see SECRECY

CONCUBINE
see HAREM

CONDEMNATION
see VERDICT

CONFIDENCE
see FAITH

CONFIDING
see SECRET

CONFINEMENT
see BIRTH

CONFRONTATION
see BEFORE

CONFUSION
71 B 42 21   The confusion of languages and the scattering of people over the earth - story of the Tower of Babel

CONQUERING
see also INVASION
see also VICTORY
71 E 52-71 E 53   The conquest of Canaan by the Israelites under Joshua's leadership

CONSECRATION
see DEDICATION

CONSENT
see PERMISSION

CONSOLING
71 H 81 3   Absalom consoles Tamar
71 W 54 1   Eliphaz, Bildad and Zophar go to Job to console him over his misfortunes (the three friends may be depicted as kings)

CONSTRUCTING
see BUILDING

CONSULTING
see ADVISING

CONTEMPLATION
see LOOKING

CONTEMPT
see INSULTING
see MOCKING

CONTEST
71 E 46 4   The contest of St. Michael and Satan for the body of Moses on Mount Nebo

CONTRACT
see MARRIAGE CONTRACT

CONTUMACY
see DISOBEDIENCE

CONVALESCENCE
see RECOVERY

CONVERSATION
see also SPEAKING
71 F 65 6   The conversation of Ruth and Boaz in the night
71 U 41 1   Judith, the widow of Manasseh, speaks with the elders Ozias, Chabris, and Charmis

CONVICT
see PRISONER(S)

COOKING
see CAULDRON

COPPER
see BRAZEN

CORD
see ROPE

CORN
see also BARLEY
see also WHEAT
71 A 81   The sacrifice of Cain and Abel: Abel offers a lamb, Cain usually a sheaf of corn
71 D 16 42 11   Joseph opens the storehouse and sells corn
71 F 34 3   Samson ties three hundred foxes two by two by their tails with a fire-brand in between; with the torches on fire he lets them go into the cornfields of the Philistines which are set aflame
71 N 15   A hundred men are fed with twenty loaves of bread: Elisha receives barley bread of the first-fruits and a sack of corn which he multiplies to feed a hundred men

CORN-SHEAF
see SHEAF

CORONATION
see CROWNING

CORPSE
see also BURIAL
see also FUNERAL
see also KILLING
see also MOURNING
see also RAISING FROM THE DEAD
71 A 82 3   Adam and Eve discover the dead body of Abel and grieve over it
71 E 46 4   The contest of St. Michael and Satan for the body of Moses on Mount Nebo
71 F 15 45   Barak comes to Jael's tent; she shows him Sisera's body

71 F 35 61   Samson drinks from the ass's jaw-
bone after having slain a thousand
Philistines
71 F 52 6   In the morning the concubine of
the Levite lies dead on the threshold
71 H 14 44   David thanks the Lord after he
has slain the giant Goliath
71 H 32 4   Saul's body
71 K 21 34 1   The body of the prophet of Judah
lies intact on the road with the donkey
and the lion beside it
71 K 31 13 2   Dogs eat Jezebel's body
71 N 71   During a funeral a band of ransacking
Moabites is seen approaching and the corpse
is thrown hastily into Elisha's tomb; when
it touches Elisha's bones the man comes
back to life
71 T 32   Old Tobit leaves the banquet and
carries the dead man into a house

CORRUPTION
see WICKEDNESS

CORTEGE
see PROCESSION

COTTAGE
71 B 35 21   The mocking of Noah: Ham finds
his father (partially) naked sleeping out
of doors (or in his tent, or in the vineyard
cottage); Ham calls his brothers

COUCH
71 Q 74 21   As Haman is kneeling at Esther's
feet or is prostrated on her couch King
Ahasuerus returns; Haman is condemned to
be hanged

COUNSEL
see ADVISING

COUPLE
see HUSBAND AND WIFE
see LOVER(S)

COURT
see also BEFORE
see also PALACE
71 H 1   David as a young man at Saul's court
71 Q   - Story of Esther

COURT OF JUSTICE
see JUDGE

COURTING
see also LOVE UNREQUITED
see also PROPOSAL
see also SEDUCING
71 X 21   Shulammite, the beloved woman - Song
of Solomon

COVENANT
see also ALLIANCE
71 B 34 2   Noah, his family and animals leave
the ark (sometimes combined with the rainbow
of the covenant)
71 B 34 3   Noah's sacrifice; various animals
are offered; possibly a lamb, a dove and
a ram (often combined with the rainbow of
the covenant)
71 B 34 31 1   God's covenant with Noah: never
again shall there be a flood; as a sign
of this covenant God puts a rainbow in the
sky
71 C 11 8   God's covenant with Abraham

COVENANT (ARK OF THE)
see ARK OF THE COVENANT

COVERING
71 A 42 4   Adam and Eve discover their
nakedness; they cover themselves with their
hands or with leaves
71 B 35 21 1   Shem and Japheth cover their
father Noah; Ham usually stands nearby
deriding him
71 E 13 12   Moses communicating with God on
Mount Sinai (the mountain may be covered
by a thick cloud)
71 U 42 74 1   Holofernes' head is put on a
dish, and covered with a cloth

COVETOUSNESS
71 K 27 41   Ahab coveting Naboth's vineyard

COW
see also CATTLE
see also OX(EN)
71 F 83 62   The Ark of the Covenant and the
box with the guilt offering, drawn by two
cows, sent back to Israel

CRADLE
71 D 13 31   Potiphar's wife catches Joseph
by his robe, usually while lying in bed;
Joseph escapes leaving his cloak behind
in her hands (possibly with a naked child
lying in a crib)

CRANE (HOISTING)
see HOISTING

CRAWLING
see PROSTRATION

CREATION
see also ORIGIN
71 A 2   The six days of creation
71 A 3   Creation of man; the Garden of Eden

CREATURE
see HUMAN BEING
see MONSTER(S)

CRIB
see CRADLE

CRIPPLE
71 C 32 22   Jacob wrestles with the angel (or
man) till daybreak; Jacob's thigh is put
out of joint

CROOK
see STAFF

CROSS
see also CROSSED...
71 M 21   When the brook dries up, Elijah
crosses over to the city of Zarephath; at
the gate he meets a woman and her little
son gathering wood (the woman's sticks may
form a cross)

CROSSED ARMS
71 D 24 21   Jacob blesses Manasseh and Ephraim
with arms crossed; Joseph may be shown
trying to uncross them or expressing (with
Asenath) his disapproval

CROSSING A RIVER
71 C 32 21   Jacob sends his family and caravan
across the river Jabbok, and stays behind

CROWD
see ARMY
see DISTRIBUTING
see REJOICING

CROWN
see also CROWNING
71 E 11 27 1   Moses and Pharaoh's crown:
Pharaoh playfully places his crown on the
head of the infant Moses, who throws it
to the ground and tramples on it; or Moses
breaks the crown while playing

CROWNING
71 Q 24   Crowning of Esther

CRUELTY
see TORTURING

CRUSHING
see TRAMPLING

CRUTCH(ES)
see CRIPPLE

CRYING (SHOUTING)
see SHOUTING

CRYING (WEEPING)
see WEEPING

CULTIVATION
see FIELDS

CUP
see also CHALICE
see also DRINK
see also DRINKING
71 D 19 1   Joseph has his silver cup placed
in Benjamin's sack
71 D 19 22   The cup is found in Benjamin's
sack

CUP-BEARER
see BUTLER

CUPIDITY
see COVETOUSNESS

CURING
see HEALING

CURSING
71 B 35 22   Noah awakes from his slumber and
curses Canaan, son of Ham

CUSHI
71 H 85 24   Cushi tells David of Absalom's
death

CUTTING OFF
see BEHEADING
see HAIR-CUTTING

CYCLONE
see WHIRLWIND

DAGGER
see STABBING

DAGON
71 F 38 3   Samson breaks the pillars; the
temple of Dagon collapses, killing all that
are in it

DALE
see VALLEY

DAMAGE
see BREAKING

DAMNED SOUL(S)
see GHOST(S)

DANCING
71 E 12 32   Miriam takes up a tambourine and
dances; all the women follow her
71 E 13 53 2   The people dance around the
golden calf - Exodus
71 D 24 53   Jephthah's daughter dances with
tambourines to meet her father on his
return from the battle; Jephthah rends his
clothes in despair
71 H 15 21   David's triumph: the women of
Israel come out to welcome David, singing,
dancing and playing tambourines and lyres;
David holding the head of Goliath
71 H 62 2   The ark is placed on a cart driven
by the sons of Abinadab; David and the
people dance and make music before the ark
71 H 62 7   David brings the ark into Jerusalem,
dancing (half-)naked before the ark and
making music, while the people rejoice

DANIEL
11 I 62(DANIEL)   Daniel (not in biblical
context)
71 P   The story of the prophet Daniel; his
visions and prophecies

DARKNESS
see also NIGHT
71 A 21   Division of light and darkness
71 C 32 22   Jacob wrestles with the angel (or
man) till daybreak; Jacob's thigh is put
out of joint
71 E 11 72 9   The plague of darkness: Moses
raises his hands towards the sky and there
is total darkness for three days

DART(S)
see ARROW(S)

DATHAN
71 E 31 7   Rebellion of Korah (Core), Dathan,
and Abiram, and their punishment

DAUGHTER
see FATHER AND DAUGHTER

DAUGHTER-IN-LAW
see FATHER-IN-LAW

DAVID
71 H   Story of David
71 H 14   Story of David and Goliath
71 X 1   Book of Psalms

DEAD (THE)
see also BURIAL
see also CORPSE
see also GHOST(S)
see also RESURRECTION
71 Z 41   Judas Maccabeus praying for the dead

DEAD BODY
see CORPSE

DEATH
see also CORPSE
see also DEAD (THE)
see also DYING PERSON
see also KILLING
see also SUICIDE
71 A 82 1   Abel's death
71 C 13 2   Sarah's death
71 C 32 6   Death of Rachel
71 D 25   Jacob's death
71 D 26 2   Joseph's death
71 E 11 72 1   The plague of water turned into
blood; as Pharaoh goes down to the Nile,
Aaron strikes the surface of the river with
with his rod; the water turns into blood
and all the fish die
71 E 11 72 5   The plague of murrain in cattle:
all the animals of the Egyptians die
71 E 32 41   When the people complain again
about the food, God sends poisonous snakes;
many die of snake-bites - book of Numbers
71 F 83 42   Eli, hearing of the capture of
the ark, falls from his seat and dies
71 H 24 53   Nabal dies
71 H 32 12   Death of Jonathan and his brothers
Abinadab and Melchi-shua
71 H 32 2   Saul's death
71 U 5(Judith 16:23: 31 E 12 2)   Judith's death
71 W 31 41   The death of Job's children

DEATH-SENTENCE
see VERDICT

DEBORAH (JUDGE)
71 F 15   The time of Deborah and Barak - the
book of Judges

DECAPITATING
see BEHEADING

DECEIT
71 C 27 4   Isaac lying in bed blesses Jacob
who, disguised in Esau's clothes, brings
food to his father; Jacob's hands and neck
are covered with goatskins
71 C 31 45   After the wedding-night Jacob
discovers that he has been deceived with
Leah and complains to Laban
71 P 41 42   Daniel exposes the elders as
deceivers

DECLARATION OF LOVE
see PROPOSAL

DECLINING
see REFUSING (GIFT, OFFER)

DECOY
71 H 16 35   Saul's soldiers discover the decoy

DECREE
see also PROCLAMATION
71 Q 82   Esther entreating Ahasuerus: she falls
at the king's feet and asks him to revoke
the decree against the Jews; the king holds
out his sceptre to her (Esther may be
holding the decree)

DEDICATION
see also PRESENTING A PERSON
71 I 43 23   The dedication of the temple of
Solomon
71 P 13 2   The dedication of the golden statue:
in the presence of King Nebuchadnezzar,
trumpets are blown and all the people
surrounding the image fall on their knees

DEFEAT
see also CHAINING
see also TRAMPLING
see also VICTORY
71 F 83 3   Second battle between the
Philistines and the Israelites at Eben-ezer,
the Israelites defeated again

DEFENDING
see PLEADING
see PROTECTION

DEFLORATION
see VIOLATING

DEITY
see GOD

DELIVERING
see LIBERATING

DELIVERY
see BIRTH

DEMANDING
see ASKING
see ORDERING

DEMOLITION
see COLLAPSING
see DESTRUCTION

DEMON(S)
see also DEVIL(S)
71 T 64 2   Tobias lies the fish's heart and
liver on glowing coals; the evil spirit
Asmodeus disappears

DENOUNCING
see BETRAYING

DEPARTING
see also EMBARKATION
see also LEAVING
see also PREPARATIONS - DEPARTURE
see also RETURNING
71 C 12 25   Abraham accompanying the departing
angels
71 C 12 83   Hagar and Ishmael (often with
bow and arrow) depart
71 D 18 1   Judah persuades the afflicted Jacob
to consent to the departure of Benjamin
71 D 19 2   Joseph's brothers set out on their
journey home
71 E 11 44   Moses departs for Egypt: he carries
his rod and is accompanied by his wife and
sons upon an ass
71 E 52 22   The Israelites leave their camp
to cross the Jordan; the priests, carrying
the ark, lead the march
71 I 33 6   The queen of Sheba sets out on the
return journey

DEPORTATION
see CAPTIVE(S)

DEPOT
see STORAGE

DERIDING
see MOCKING

DESCENDING
71 C 31 21   The dream of Jacob: while sleeping
on the ground with a stone for a pillow
Jacob sees a ladder reaching from earth
to heaven with angels going up and down;
usually with God at the top of the ladder
71 E 13 54   Moses (and Joshua) come(s) down
with stone tablets
71 E 13 74   Moses comes down with the new
tablets and is awaited by Aaron and the
assembled people, who notice that 'his face
is shining' (Moses' face is depicted with
rays of light or with horns)

DESECRATION
71 P 21   Belshazzar's great feast, during which
he and his courtiers desecrate the golden
and silver vessels that were taken from
the temple in Jerusalem

DESERT
see also WILDERNESS
71 C 11 93 1   Hagar flees into the desert
71 E 12 8   Jethro's visit to Moses: with
Zipporah and her two sons he comes to the
desert where Moses is encamped

DESIGN
71 H 92 42   David gives Solomon the plan of
the temple

DESK
see WRITING

DESPAIR
see GRIEVING
see SUICIDE
see TEARING ONE'S CLOTHES

DESTRUCTION
see also BREAKING
see also COLLAPSING
see also DESTRUCTION (OF CITY)
see also DESTRUCTION OF IDOLS
see also FLOOD
71 E 11 73 2   The plague of the first-born:
the destroying angel passes through the
land and kills every Egyptian first-born
of man and animal

DESTRUCTION (OF CITY)
see also BURNING (CITY)
71 C 12 4   The destruction of Sodom and
Gomorrah: Lot and his family flee to Zoar,
carrying their belongings; an angel may
be showing the way
71 E 52 4   The fall of Jericho
71 O 73 13   Jeremiah prophesying the
destruction of Jerusalem
71 O 78 34   Jeremiah prophesies the destruction
of Babylon
71 V 31   When Jonah arrives in the city of
Nineveh he foretells its destruction in
forty days

DESTRUCTION OF IDOLS
71 K 31 22 2   The images of Baal are destroyed
and burned

DETECTING
see FINDING

DETENTION
see PRISON

DEVIL(S)
see also DEMON(S)
see also SATAN
71 W 52   Job on the dunghill with Satan (or
devils) abusing and tormenting him; Job's
wife may be present

DEVOURING
see also SWALLOWING
71 K 31 13 2   Dogs eat Jezebel's body

DEXTERA DEI
see HAND OF GOD

DIALOGUE
see CONVERSATION

DICTATING
71 O 74 61   Jeremiah dictates his prophecies
to Baruch

DIGGING
see BURIAL
see SPADE

DIRECTING
see INSTRUCTING

DISABLED
see CRIPPLE

DISAPPEARING
71 F 31 4   Manoah's sacrifice; the angel
ascends in the flames
71 T 64 2   Tobias lies the fish's heart and
liver on glowing coals; the evil spirit
Asmodeus disappears
71 T 79 2   The angel Raphael disappears into
the sky

DISAPPROVING
see REBUKING

DISCLOSING
see REVEALING

DISCOVERING
see FINDING
see INVENTION
see RECOGNIZING

DISEASE
see SICK PERSON

DISEMBARKATION
71 B 34   The disembarkation - story of Noah

DISGUISE
71 C 27 4   Isaac lying in bed blesses Jacob
who, disguised in Esau's clothes, brings
food to his father; Jacob's hands and neck
are covered with goatskins
71 C 33 27   Tamar changes from her widow's
clothes and covers her face with a veil
after the manner of the prostitutes; sitting
at the entrance of a city on the road to
Timnath she awaits Judah
71 K 21 43   Jeroboam's wife in disguise visits
the old and blind Ahijah, but he, having
been warned by God, recognizes her; he
predicts the death of her son and Israel's
punishment for Jeroboam's sin

DISMISSING
see SENDING AWAY

DISOBEDIENCE
see also REFUSING (ORDER, REQUEST)
71 V 1   Jonah's call and disobedience

DISPLAYING
see SHOWING

DISTRIBUTING
see also DIVIDING
see also GIVING
71 H 62 8   David places the ark in a tent,
burns offerings before the Lord and
distributes bread, meat and wine to everyone

DISTRUST
    see SUSPICION

DIVIDING
    see also DISTRIBUTING
    see also SEPARATING
    71 A 21   Division of light and darkness
    71 A 22   Creation of the firmament and division
       of the waters above and below it
    71 E 54   The division of Canaan
    71 E 54 33   Joshua (assisted by Eleazar) casts
       lots and assigns to each of the remaining
       seven tribes a certain part of Canaan
    71 I 32 5   Solomon gives verdict; he commands
       a soldier to divide the living child in
       two

DIVINATION
    see PROPHESYING

DIVING
    see JUMPING

DOCUMENT
    see also DECREE
    see also WRITING
    71 T 63 2   The writing of the marriage letter
       - Tobias and Sarah

DOG
    71 K 31 13 2   Dogs eat Jezebel's body
    71 T 54   Tobias and the angel Raphael
       travelling, accompanied by Tobias' dog

DOLPHIN
    71 V 13 41   Jonah is swallowed by a great fish,
       (sea)monster, whale, dolphin, or the like

DOMINION
    see POWER

DONKEY
    see also ASS
    71 N 13 24   The Shunammite woman rides out
       with her donkey to Elisha, bows down before
       him and taking hold of his feet, entreats
       him to come with her

DOOR(S)
    see GATE(S)

DOUBT
    see UNBELIEF

DOVE
    71 B 33 22   Noah sends off a dove
    71 B 34 3   Noah's sacrifice; various animals
       are offered, possibly a lamb, a dove, and
       a ram (often combined with the rainbow of
       the covenant)

DOWNWARDS
    see DESCENDING

DOWRY
    71 C 21 42   Gifts of clothing, gold and jewelry
       are offered to Rebekah's parents

DRAGON
    see also SEA-MONSTER
    see also SERPENT
    71 E 13 53   Adoration of the golden calf (which
       may be standing on a pillar, and is
       sometimes depicted as a dragon)
    71 E 32 43   Anyone who is bitten by a snake
       is cured by looking at the brazen serpent;
       the serpent (or dragon) is usually depicted
       on a tau-shaped cross or on a pillar
    71 W 52 1   Job is smitten from head to foot
       with sores by Satan, or dragon-like monsters
       that blow poisonous smoke on Job

DRAPERY
    see VEIL

DRAUGHTSMAN
    see DRAWING

DRAWING
    see DESIGN

DRAWING (PULLING)
    see PULLING

DRAWING LOTS
    see LOT(S)

DREAD
    see FEAR

DREAM
    see also EXPLAINING
    see also VISION
    71 C 31 21   The dream of Jacob: while sleeping
       on the ground with a stone for a pillow
       Jacob sees a ladder reaching from earth
       to heaven with angels going up and down;
       usually with God at the top of the ladder
    71 C 31 21 1   Dream of Jacob, with stairway
       instead of ladder
    71 D 11 5   Joseph's dreams
    71 D 14   - Story of Joseph in prison

DRESS (COSTUME)
    see CLOTHES

DRESSING
    see CLOTHING
    see TOILET (MAKING)

DRESSING UP
    see DISGUISE

DRINK
    see also DRINKING
    see also DRUNKENNESS
    see also WATERING
    71 C 21 31 1   Rebekah offers Eliezer a drink
       from her pitcher

DRINK(ING)
    71 E 12 63   Moses strikes the rock twice in
       front of the assembled people and water
       gushes out; the people quench their thirst

DRINKING
    see also BANQUET
    see also WATERING
    see also WINE-TESTING
    71 F 21 52   Those who lap water by putting
       their hand to their mouth are separated
       from those who kneel down to drink the water
       - selection of Gideon's men
    71 F 35 61   Samson drinks from the ass's jaw-
       bone after having slain a thousand
       Philistines

DRINKING-BOUT
    see FEAST

DRIVING AWAY
    see CHASING AWAY

DROUGHT
    71 M 11   Elijah announces to King Ahab that
       God will bring a long drought in the land
       to avenge the apostasy of Israel

DROWNING
see also FLOOD
see also OVERBOARD
71 E 12 23   With his people safe on the shore,
Moses raises his hands and causes the water
to return; Pharaoh's army perishes in the
water (Red Sea)
71 E 12 23 1   Pharaoh and his army engulfed
in the Red Sea (Israelites not or barely
visible)

DRUNKENNESS
71 B 35 2   The drunkenness of Noah
71 C 12 52   Lot's daughters make their father
drunk

DRYNESS
see DROUGHT

DUNGEON
71 O 76 62 6   The princes cast Jeremiah into
a dungeon
71 O 76 62 8   Jeremiah is released from the
dungeon

DUNGHILL
71 W 5   Job on the dunghill

DYING PERSON
see also DEATH
see also WOUNDED PERSON
71 C 12 84 1   Hagar sits weeping after having
put Ishmael under a bush to die

EAR-RING
71 C 21 33   Rebekah receives ear-rings and
golden bracelets from Eliezer
71 E 13 51 1   The people bring their golden
ear-rings to Aaron

EARTH
see also CLAY
71 E 31 74 2   The ground opens and swallows
the rebels Dathan and Abiram along with
their families and possessions
71 N 16 21   Naaman urges Elisha to accept some
gifts, but Elisha refuses them; Naaman asks
two mule-loads of earth

EATING
see also DEVOURING
see also FEEDING
see also MEAL
see also SWALLOWING
71 A 42 3   Adam and Eve holding (and possibly
eating) the fruit
71 Z 35   Martyrdom of Eleazar: the old man
is forced to eat pork and voluntarily
submits to the flogging

EAVESDROPPER
see OVERHEARING

ECBATANA
71 T 5   The journey to Ecbatana - the book
of Tobit
71 T 59   The arrival at Ecbatana

ECSTASY
see also VISION

EDEN
71 A 3   Creation of man: the Garden of Eden
71 A 4-71 A 5   Temptation and Fall
71 A 6   Expulsion of Adam and Eve from paradise

EDUCATION
see TEACHING
see UPBRINGING

EGYPT
71 C 11 4   Abraham in Egypt
71 C 25 11   God appears to Isaac and warns
him not to journey into Egypt
71 D 18   Second journey of Joseph's brothers
to Egypt
71 D 21   Jacob and his family go to Egypt
71 E 11   Exodus (part I): events preceding
and preparing the exit of Israel from Egypt
71 E 11 7   The ten plagues (- Exodus)

EGYPTIANS
71 E 11 31 2-4   Moses kills the Egyptian
taskmaster

ELDER(S)
71 H 48 2   David anointed king by the elders
of Israel
71 P 41   The story of Susanna and the elders
(in which the youth Daniel intervenes on
behalf of Susanna)
71 U 41 1   Judith, the widow of Manasseh,
speaks with the elders Ozias, Chabris,
and Charmis
71 U 42 1   Judith and her maidservant take
leave of the elders at the city gate

ELEAZAR
71 E 54 33   Joshua (assisted by Eleazar) casts
lots and assigns to each of the remaining
seven tribes a certain part of Canaan

ELEAZAR (THE ELDER)
71 Z 35   Martyrdom of Eleazar: the old man
is forced to eat pork and voluntarily
submits to the flogging

ELECTION
    see CHOOSING

ELEMENTS
    71 A 2   The six days of creation

ELEVATION
    see PROMOTION

ELI
    71 F 8   Story of Samuel

ELIAS
    see ELIJAH

ELIEZER (SERVANT OF ABRAHAM)
    71 C 21   Rebekah (Rebecca) sought in marriage

ELIJAH
    11 I 62(ELIJAH)   Elijah (not in biblical
        context)
    71 M   Story of Elijah (Elias)

ELIPHAZ
    71 W 54 1   Eliphaz, Bildad and Zophar go to
        Job to console him over his misfortunes
        (the three friends may be depicted as kings)

ELISEUS
    see ELISHA

ELISHA
    71 M 8   The ascension of Elijah

ELISHA'S TOMB
    71 N 71   During a funeral a band of ransacking
        Moabites is seen approaching and the corpse
        is thrown hastily into Elisha's tomb; when
        it touches Elisha's bones the man comes
        back to life

EMBARKATION
    71 B 32 2   The embarkation of the ark

EMBRACING
    see also KISSING
    see also LOVER(S)
    71 H 17 33   David and Jonathan embracing:
        David's leave-taking from Jonathan
    71 H 82 5   Reconciliation of David and Absalom:
        Absalom kneels before David and they embrace
    71 Q 63 1   Ahasuerus leaps from his throne
        and takes Esther in his arms

EMERGING
    71 A 34 21   Eve emerges from Adam's body

EMEROD(S)
    see BOIL(S)

EMPLOYER - EMPLOYEE
    see SERVANT(S)

EN ROUTE
    see TRAVELLING

ENCOUNTERING
    see MEETING

ENDOR (WITCH OF)
    71 H 31   Saul and the witch of Endor

ENEMY
    see BATTLE

ENJOYMENT
    see REJOICING

ENOCH (CITY)
    71 A 84 2   Cain building the city of Enoch

ENOCH (SON OF JARED)
    71 B 25   Story of Enoch, son of Jared, who
        invented letters and was the first to divide
        the year into seasons and into twelve months

ENOS
    71 B 21   Story of Enos

ENQUIRING
    see ASKING

ENTERING
    see ENTRY

ENTERTAINING
    see also FEAST
    see also GUEST(S)
    71 C 12 24   Abraham entertaining the three
        angels

ENTOMBMENT
    see BURIAL

ENTRANCE
    see also DOOR(S)
    see also ENTRY
    see also GATE(S)
    see also REFUSING (ADMISSION)
    71 A 62   Adam and Eve outside Eden, whose
        entrance is guarded by shining cherubim

ENTREATING
    see ASKING

ENTRY
    see also INVASION
    see also TRIUMPH
    71 B 32 22   The animals enter the ark
    71 B 32 23   Noah and his family enter the ark
    71 H 62 7   David brings the ark into Jerusalem,
        dancing (half-)naked before the ark and
        making music, while the people rejoice

ENVOY
    see MESSENGER(S)

ENVY
    see JEALOUSY

EPHRAIM
    71 D 24 2   Joseph takes his two sons, Manasseh
        and Ephraim to see Jacob on his sick-bed
    71 D 24 21   Jacob blesses Manasseh and Ephraim
        with arms crossed; Joseph may be shown
        trying to uncross them or expressing (with
        Asenath) his disapproval

EPIDEMIC
    see PLAGUE

EPISTLE
    see LETTER (EPISTLE)

EQUESTRIAN
    see RIDING (ON HORSEBACK)

ERECTING
    see BUILDING

ERMINE CLOAK
    see CLOAK

ESAU
    71 C 24   Isaac's children (Esau and Jacob)
    71 C 27   Isaac's blessing (of Jacob and Esau)

ESCAPING
    see also FLEEING
    71 D 13 31   Potiphar's wife catches Joseph
        by his robe, usually while lying in bed;
        Joseph escapes leaving his cloak behind
        in her hands (possibly with a naked child
        lying in a crib)
    71 H 16 32   David escapes through a window;
        Michal lets him down with the help of a
        rope

ESCORTING
    see GUIDING

ESPIONAGE
    see SPY

ESTEEM
    see HONORING

ESTHER
    71 Q   The story of Esther

EVE
    11 I 62(ADAM & EVE)   Adam and Eve (not in
        biblical context)
    11 I 63(EVE)   Eve (not in biblical context)
    71 A 3   Creation of man: the Garden of Eden
    71 A 4-71 A 5   Temptation and Fall
    71 A 6   Expulsion of Adam and Eve from paradise
    71 A 7   The labors of Adam and Eve; infancy
        of Cain and Abel
    72 A 82 3   Adam and Eve discover the dead body
        of Abel and grieve over it

EVIL
    see SIN

EVIL SPIRIT
    see DEMON(S)

EVILMERODACH
    71 L 31 3   When Evilmerodach becomes king of
        Babylon, Jehoiachin is released from prison
        and permitted to dine at the king's table
        for the rest of his life

EXAMINATION
    71 P 13 5   Shadrach, Mesach and Abed-nego are
        examined; they prove to be unharmed by the
        fire, whereupon King Nebuchadnezzar decrees
        that no one may criticize them

EXECUTION
    see BEHEADING
    see KILLING

EXECUTIONER(S)
    71 P 13 3   After the furnace has been heated
        seven times more, the three Hebrews are
        bound and thrown into the fire; their
        executioners are burnt by the flames

EXHIBITION
    see SHOWING

EXHORTING
    see ADVISING
    see PERSUADING

EXILE
    see BABYLONIAN CAPTIVITY
    see BANISHING

EXODUS
    71 E 1   The book Exodus

EXPELLING
    see also BANISHING
    see also CHASING AWAY
    71 A 6   Expulsion of Adam and Eve from paradise

EXPLAINING
    see also INSTRUCTING
    71 D 14 42 1   Joseph interpreting the baker's
        dream
    71 D 14 5   Joseph interpreting the dreams of
        the butler and the baker (the two dreams
        combined)
    71 D 15 5   Joseph interpreting Pharaoh's dreams
    71 P 25   Daniel, when brought before King
        Belshazzar, interprets the writing on
        the wall

EXPOSING
    71 E 11 23   Moses is exposed in the ark on
        the banks of the Nile; Miriam, Moses'
        sister, keeps watch

EXPULSION
    see EXPELLING

EYE(S)
    see also BLINDNESS
    71 T 77   The healing of Tobit: Tobias puts
        the gall of the fish on his father's eyes

EZEKIEL
    11 I 62(EZEKIEL)   Ezekiel (not in biblical
        context)

FABRIC
    see CLOTH

FABULOUS BEING(S)
    see MONSTER(S)

FACE
    71 E 11 42 2   Moses, kneeling before the bush
       and hiding his face, listens to God
    71 E 13 74   Moses comes down with the new
       tablets and is awaited by Aaron and the
       assembled people, who notice that 'his face
       is shining' (Moses' face is depicted with
       rays of light or with horns)

FAINTING
    see SWOONING

FAITH
    71 W 54 4   Job is derided by his friends (and
       his wife) for refusing to give up his faith

FALL
    see FALLING

FALL (OF CITY)
    see DESTRUCTION (OF CITY)

FALLING
    see also COLLAPSING
    see also JUMPING
    see also PROSTRATION
    see also SWOONING
    see also THROWING (BEING THROWN)
    71 A 4-71 A 5   Temptation and Fall
    71 F 38 3   Samson breaks the pillars; the
       temple of Dagon collapses, killing all that
       are in it
    71 F 83 42   Eli, hearing of the capture of
       the ark, falls from his seat and dies

FALLING ASLEEP
    see SLEEPING

FALLING IN LOVE
    see LOVE AT FIRST SIGHT

FALSE ACCUSATION
    see ACCUSING

FAMILY
    see also PARENTS
    71 C 32 21   Jacob sends his family and caravan
       across the river Jabbok, and stays behind
    71 E 11 44   Moses departs for Egypt: he carries
       his rod and is accompanied by his wife and
       sons upon an ass
    71 E 12 8   Jethro's visit to Moses: with
       Zipporah and her two sons he comes to the
       desert where Moses in encamped
    71 H 22 21   David's family and men join him
       in the cave Adullam
    71 L 17 11   Athaliah has all the members of
       the royal family killed
    71 T 79 1   The angel makes himself known;
       Tobias and his family lie down

FAMINE
    see HUNGER

FAREWELL
    see LEAVE-TAKING

FARMER
    71 A 72   Adam (and Eve) engaged in agricultural
       activities

FASTING
    71 G 23   Saul's oath: a day of fasting
    71 H 77 2   David repentant: he lies on the
       ground praying and fasting for his child
       to recover

FATHER
    see FATHER AND CHILD

FATHER AND CHILD
    see FATHER AND DAUGHTER
    see FATHER AND SON
    see PARENTS

FATHER AND DAUGHTER
    see also INCEST
    71 C 12 5   Lot and his daughters
    71 F 24 5   The story of Jephthah's daughter
    71 W 74 1   Job and his three fair daughters

FATHER AND SON
    71 C 13 1   The sacrifice of Isaac

FATHER-IN-LAW
    71 C 33 2   Story of Judah and Tamar
    71 F 34 1   Samson goes with a kid to his wife
       and is refused entry by her father

FEAR
    see also ALARM
    71 C 12 51   Lot, seeing the destruction of
       the cities and fearing for his safety in
       Zoar, flees with his daughters to a cave
       in the mountains
    71 C 32 13   Jacob prays to God to save him
       from Esau
    71 F 21 51   To select an army for a raid
       against the Midianites Gideon sends away
       the fearful and brings the remaining
       ten thousand men to the water
    71 P 22   During Belshazzar's banquet a hand
       appears and writes on the wall (MENE, MENE,
       TEKEL and PARSIN (UPHARSIN); King Belshazzar
       is frightened
    71 T 55 1   A large fish appears while Tobias
       is washing his feet; he is frightened

FEAST
    see also BANQUET
    see also CELEBRATION
    see also MARRIAGE
    see also REJOICING
    71 B 31 1   The wickedness of mankind; the
       wicked are usually shown feasting and
       revelling
    71 D 18 5   The feast at Joseph's house: the
       amazement of his brothers at being seated
       according to their age; Benjamin is honored
       with extra food
    71 E 13 53 3   The people feasting - adoration
       of the golden calf
    71 P 21   Belshazzar's great feast, during which
       he and his courtiers desecrate the golden
       and silver vessels that were taken from
       the temple in Jerusalem
    71 Q 21   The feast of Ahasuerus (Xerxes,
       alternatively Artaxerxes); the downfall
       of Queen Vashti (Astin)
    71 Q 24 1   The wedding feast, Esther's feast
    71 T 66   The joyous feast - story of Tobias

FEEDING
    see also EATING
    see also FOOD
    see also MEAL
    see also SUCKLING
    71 M 12   Elijah fed by the raven(s): while
       the prophet is living by the brook, ravens
       bring him food
    71 N 15   A hundred men are fed with twenty
       loaves of bread: Elisha receives barley
       bread of the first-fruits and a sack of
       corn which he multiplies to feed a hundred
       men

FEET
    see FOOT (FEET)

FEMALE
see WOMAN

FEMININITY
see WOMAN

FENCE
see BOUNDARY

FESTIVITIES
see FEAST(S)

FETTERS
see BINDING
see CHAINING

FIELD(S)
71 C 21 51   Isaac, walking in the fields,
meets Rebekah
71 F 34 3   Samson ties three hundred foxes
two by two by their tails with a fire-brand
in between; with the torches on fire he
lets them go into the cornfields of the
Philistines which are set aflame
71 F 64   Ruth in the field of Boaz
71 O 93 3   Ezekiel's vision of the valley of
the dry bones

FIGHTING
see also ATTACKING
see also BATTLE
see also KILLING
see also WRESTLING
71 E 46 4   The contest of St. Michael and Satan
for the body of Moses on Mount Nebo

FIGHTING - ANIMAL
see KILLING - ANIMAL

FILIAL LOVE
see FATHER...
see MOTHER...

FILLING
71 E 12 54 2   Aaron fills a jar with manna
to be kept in the tabernacle

FINDING
see also FOUNDLING
see also INVENTION
71 A 82 3   Adam and Eve discover the dead body
of Abel and grieve over it
71 C 31 45   After the wedding-night Jacob
discovers that he has been deceived with
Leah and complains to Laban
71 D 17 71   At their camp one of Joseph's
brothers finds money in his sack
71 D 19 22   The cup is found in Benjamin's
sack
71 F 37 4   Delilah finds out Samson's secret
and warns the Philistines, who come with
the money
71 H 16 35   Saul's soldiers discover the decoy
71 U 44 2   The murder of Holofernes is
discovered (by Bagoas)

FINGER(S)
see FINGER TO THE LIPS

FINGER TO THE LIPS
71 F 37 5   Samson asleep in Delilah's lap;
she is usually shown beckoning to a
Philistine or putting a finger to her lips

FIRE
see also BURNING
see also FLAME(S)
see also PILLAR OF FIRE
see also SETTING ON FIRE
71 E 11 27 11   Moses' trial by fire: when given
the choice between two plates, one
containing burning coals, the other a ruby
ring (or cherries), Moses chooses the
burning coals and puts them in his mouth
71 E 11 72 7   The plague of hail: Moses raises
his rod towards the sky, and hail and fire
fall to the ground
71 F 21 23 3   The angel of the Lord touches
the food with his staff, fire arises from
the rock
71 M 43 21   As Elijah prays, God sends fire
which burns up not only his sacrifice but
also the altar itself; the people fall
prostrate
71 M 84   A chariot, horses of fire and a
whirlwind appear and Elijah is carried up
into heaven; Elijah's cloak falls (or he
hands it over to Elisha)
71 P 13 3   After the furnace has been heated
seven times more, the three Hebrews are
bound and thrown into the fire; their
executioners are burnt by the flames

FIRE BRAND
see BRAND

FIRE-PLACE
see FIRE

FIRMAMENT
71 A 22   Creation of the firmament and division
of the waters above and below it

FIRST-BORN
71 E 11 73 2   The plague of the first-born:
the destroying angel passes through the
land and kills every Egyptian first-born
of man and animal

FISH
71 A 25 1   Creation of birds and fish
71 E 11 72 1   The plague of water turned into
blood: as Pharaoh goes down to the Nile,
Aaron strikes the surface of the river with
his rod; the water turns into blood and
all the fish die
71 T 55 1   A large fish appears while Tobias
is washing his feet; he is frightened
71 T 64 2   Tobias lies the fish's heart and
liver on glowing coals; the evil spirit
Asmodeus disappears
71 T 77   The healing of Tobit: Tobias puts
the gall of the fish on his father's eyes
71 V 13 41   Jonah is swallowed by a great fish,
(sea)monster, whale, dolphin, or the like

FLAGELLATION
see SCOURGING

FLAME(S)
see also FIRE
see also FLAMING SWORD
71 F 31 4   Manoah's sacrifice; the angel
ascends in the flames

FLAMING SWORD
71 A 61   God expels Adam and Eve from Paradise
and has the tree of life guarded by an angel
with a flaming sword

FLASK
71 H 25 21   David takes Saul's spear and water-
flask away

FLEECE
    see also GIDEON'S FLEECE
    see also HIDE
    71 C 27 4   Isaac lying in bed blesses Jacob who, disguised in Esau's clothes, brings food to his father; Jacob's hands and neck are covered with goatskins

FLEEING
    see also ESCAPING
    see also PURSUING
    71 C 11 93 1   Hagar flees into the desert
    71 C 12 4   The destruction of Sodom and Gomorrah: Lot and his family flee to Zoar, carrying their belongings; an angel may be showing the way
    71 C 12 51   Lot, seeing the destruction of the cities and fearing for his safety in Zoar, flees with his daughters to a cave in the mountains
    71 C 31 8   Jacob's flight from Laban
    71 E 11 31 5   Moses flees to Midian
    71 E 11 42 31   Miracle of the rod changed into a serpent; Moses may be shown fleeing from the serpent
    71 H 84 9   Absalom, put to flight on a mule, remains hanging by his hair in an oak tree
    71 K 29 45   When Jehoram realizes Jehu's treason, he turns his chariot round to flee, but Jehu shoots an arrow that strikes Jehoram in the back; the king falls dead in his chariot

FLIGHT
    see FLEEING

FLIRTING
    see COURTING

FLOATING
    see also AIR (IN THE)
    71 B 33 1   The ark is floating on the waters, while life on earth is destroyed - story of Noah
    71 E 11 24   The finding of Moses: Pharaoh's daughter comes to bathe with her maidens in the river and discovers the child floating on the water

FLOCK
    see SHEEP

FLOGGING
    see SCOURGING

FLOOD
    71 B 33   The Flood and destruction of mankind - story of Noah

FLOUR
    71 N 14   The deadly pottage: Elisha purifies the poisoned pottage by throwing flour into it

FLOWERING ROD
    see ROD

FLYING
    see AIR (IN THE)

FOLLOWING
    see PURSUING

FONDLING
    see CARESSING

FOOD
    see also FEEDING
    see also MEAL
    see also PREPARATIONS - DEPARTURE
    see also PREPARATIONS - FEAST, MEAL
    71 C 21 44   The leave-taking of Rebekah; Laban gives her provisions
    71 C 24 41   Esau, returning hungry from the hunt, sells his first birthright to Jacob for a pottage of lentils
    71 C 27 4   Isaac lying in bed blesses Jacob who, disguised in Esau's clothes, brings food to his father; Jacob's hands are covered with goatskins
    71 D 18 5   The feast at Joseph's house: the amazement of his brothers at being seated according to their age; Benjamin is honored with extra food
    71 M 21 1   Elijah asks the widow of Zarephath to fetch him some food
    71 P 43 33   The prophet Habakkuk, carried by his hair by an angel, brings food to Daniel who sits unharmed between the lions

FOOT (FEET)
    see also TRAMPLING
    see also WASHING (FEET)
    71 N 13 24   The Shunammite woman rides out with her donkey to Elisha, bows down before him and taking hold of his feet, entreats him to come with her

FOOT-GEAR
    see SHOE(S)

FOOTBOY
    see SERVANT

FORCE
    71 Z 35   Martyrdom of Eleazar: the old man is forced to eat pork and voluntarily submits to the flogging

FORCING
    see FORCE

FORD
    see CROSSING A RIVER

FOREHEAD
    71 H 14 42   David slings a stone at Goliath's forehead

FORETELLING
    see PROPHESYING

FORGIVING
    see also PARDONING
    71 D 19 31   Joseph reveals his identity and in tears forgives his brothers' past misdeed

FORTY
    71 V 31   When Jonah arrives in the city of Nineveh he foretells its destruction in forty days

FOSTER-PARENT
    see FOUNDLING

FOUNDING
    see INSTITUTING

FOUNDING A CITY
    see BUILDING A CITY

FOUNDLING
    see also EXPOSING
    71 E 11 24   The finding of Moses: Pharaoh's daughter comes to bathe with her maidens in the river and discovers the child floating on the water

FOUNTAIN
    71 C 11 93 2   An angel meets Hagar at the
        fountain on the way to Shur and persuades
        her to return
    71 P 41 2   Susanna bathing, usually in or near
        a fountain and sometimes accompanied by
        two female servants

FOUR
    71 B 25   Story of Enoch, son of Jared, who
        invented letters and was the first to divide
        the year into seasons and into twelve months
    71 O 91 1   Ezekiel's vision of God sitting
        on his throne carried by four tetramorphs,
        each of them having four wings; wheels
        within wheels beside them
    71 P 13 4   To his astonishment King
        Nebuchadnezzar sees four men (one of them
        usually represented as an angel) in the
        furnace; the king commands them to come
        forth

FOX
    71 F 34 3   Samson ties three hundred foxes
        two by two by their tails with a fire-brand
        in between; with the torches on fire he
        lets them go into the cornfields of the
        Philistines which are set aflame

FRATRICIDE
    see BROTHER(S)

FRAUD
    see DECEIT

FREEING
    see LIBERATING

FRIEND(S)
    71 H 15 1   David and Jonathan, son of Saul,
        become friends

FRIGHT
    see ALARM
    see FEAR

FROG
    71 E 11 72 2   The plague of frogs: Aaron
        stretches out his hand over the water of
        Egypt: frogs come out and cover the land

FRONTIER
    see BOUNDARY

FRUIT
    71 A 4-71 A 5   Temptation and Fall
    71 E 31 52   The spies take away some of the
        fruits of Canaan and return, usually
        carrying a large bunch of grapes on a pole

FUGITIVE
    see ESCAPING

FUMES
    see SMOKE

FUNERAL
    see also BURIAL
    71 D 25 2   Joseph has his father's corpse
        brought to Canaan with great pomp
    71 N 71   During a funeral a band of ransacking
        Moabites is seen approaching and the corpse
        is thrown hastily into Elisha's tomb; when
        it touches Elisha's bones the man comes
        back to life

FURNACE
    71 P 13   The story of the three Hebrews in
        the fiery furnace

FURTIVELY
    see SECRECY

FURY
    see ANGER

FUTURE
    see DIVINATION
    see PROPHESYING

GABAEL
71 T 66 1   Tobias asks the angel to go to Gabael

GALL
71 T 77   The healing of Tobit: Tobias puts the gall of the fish on his father's eyes

GAME
71 C 27 5   Esau comes back with venison

GAMES
see CONTEST

GAOL
see PRISON

GARDEN
71 A 3   Creation of man; the Garden of Eden
71 Q 74 11   King Ahasuerus gets up in a fury and goes into the palace garden

GARMENT(S)
see CLOTHES

GARRISON
see CAMP

GATE(S)
see also CITY-GATE
71 E 13 63   Moses, standing at the gate of the camp, causes the Levites to kill the idolaters

GATHERING
see also ASSEMBLING
71 E 12 54 1   The gathering of manna (in baskets and pots)
71 M 21   When the brook dries up, Elijah crosses over to the city of Zarephath: at the gate he meets a woman and her little son gathering wood (the woman's sticks may form a cross)

GAZING
see LOOKING

GEHAZI
71 N 13 33   Gehazi fetches the Shunammite woman: when she sees her child alive she falls at Elisha's feet

GENESIS
see also ORIGIN
71 A-71 D   Genesis

GENUFLECTION
see KNEELING

GHOST(S)
see also DEAD (THE)
71 H 31 52   The ghost of Samuel appears to the witch of Endor; Saul falls prostrate to the ground

GIBEON
71 E 52 94 2   Joshua orders the sun and the moon to stand still over Gibeon and Aijalon until the Amorites who had besieged the city of Gibeon are routed

GIDEON
71 F 21   The time of Gideon (Jerubbaal) - the book of Judges

GIDEON'S FLEECE
11 I 62(GIDEON)   Attributes of Gideon
71 F 21 43   Twice Gideon asks the Lord to show him a sign with a sheep's fleece before his raid against the Midianites

GIFT
see also REFUSING (GIFT, OFFER)
71 C 11 44 1   Abraham honored with gifts by Pharaoh
71 C 21 42   Gifts of clothing, gold and jewelry are offered to Rebekah's parents
71 D 18 4   When Joseph gets home, he receives his brothers; they bow down before him and give him the presents
71 H 21 2   David receives gifts from Ahimelech
71 I 33 1   The queen of Sheba comes to Solomon with a train of camels loaded with gifts
71 T 79   Tobias and his father offer gifts to the angel

GIRDING
71 E 11 73 13 2   The Israelites eat the Passover lamb standing about a table with their loins girt, their shoes on their feet and with staves in their hands, ready to depart

GIRL
see also MAIDSERVANT
see also WOMAN
71 E 11 32   Moses at a well meets the seven daughters of Jethro, the priest of Midian
71 Q 22   Ahasuerus has the most attractive maidens of his kingdom put into his harem in order to select a new queen from among them - story of Esther

GIVING
see also DISTRIBUTING
see also GIFT
see also OFFERING
see also RECEIVING
71 F 32 73   Samson gives some of the honey he found in the lion's carcass to his parents
71 H 92 42   David gives Solomon the plan of the temple
71 M 84   A chariot, horses of fire and a whirl-wind appear and Elijah is carried up into heaven; Elijah's cloak falls (or he hands it over to Elisha)
71 R 11 4   Cyrus restores the vessels of the temple of Jerusalem that had been carried off by Nebuchadnezzar

GIVING DRINK
see DRINK

GLOWING
see COAL

GOAT
see also KID
71 C 31 61   Laban agrees to give Jacob all the black and spotted sheep and goats as wages
71 D 11 1   Joseph tending the sheep and goats with his brothers
71 T 37   Anna brings home a young goat: Tobit thinks she has stolen it

GOATSKIN
see FLEECE

GOBLET
see CUP

GOD

see also COMMUNICATING WITH GOD
see also HAND OF GOD
see also TRINITY
71 A 1-71 A 3   - Creation
71 A 31 1   The man (Adam) comes to life:
 usually God reaches out his hand or breathes
 life into his nostrils
71 A 4-71 A 5   Temptation and Fall
71 A 6   Expulsion of Adam and Eve from paradise
71 A 81 1   God (or the hand of God) appears
 and blesses Abel - sacrifice
71 B 3   Story of Noah
71 C 11 8   God's covenant with Abraham
71 C 13 13 1   When Abraham has his hand raised
 to kill Isaac, God or the hand of God
 restrains Abraham's hand
71 C 25 11   God appears to Isaac and warns
 him not to journey into Egypt
71 C 31 21   The dream of Jacob: while sleeping
 on the ground with a stone for pillow Jacob
 sees a ladder reaching from earth to heaven
 with angels going up and down; usually with
 God at the top of the ladder
71 C 32 13   Jacob prays to God to save him
 from Esau
71 E 11 42 2   Moses, kneeling before the bush
 and hiding his face, listens to God
71 E 11 45   At an inn, God (or the angel of
 God) tries to kill Moses
71 E 13 43   Moses receives the tables of the
 law from God
71 E 32 41   When the people complain again
 about the food, God sends poisonous snakes;
 many die of snake-bites - book of Numbers
71 F 82   The calling of Samuel
71 F 83 51 2   God punishes the inhabitants
 of Ashdod with emerods or boils
71 H 11   David chosen as king by God
71 H 54 63   By the command of God the angel
 stops destroying the Israelites at the
 threshing-floor of Araunah (Ornan) the
 Jebusite
71 H 62 8   David places the ark in a tent,
 burns offerings before the Lord and
 distributes bread, meat and wine to everyone
71 M 43 21   As Elijah prays, God sends fire
 which burns up not only his sacrifice but
 also the altar itself; the people fall
 prostrate
71 O 91 1   Ezekiel's vision of God sitting
 on his throne carried by four tetramorphs,
 each of them having four wings; wheels
 within wheels beside them
71 V 22 1   Jonah again receives from God the
 command to preach in Nineveh
71 V 44   When Jonah again murmurs and wishes
 to die, God rebukes him
71 W 2   The 'sons of God' (angels) with Satan
 gather before God - story of Job

GOLDEN

see also GOLDEN CALF
71 C 21 42   Gifts of clothing, gold and jewelry
 are offered to Rebekah's parents
71 E 13 51 1   The people bring their golden
 ear-rings to Aaron
71 P 21   Belshazzar's great feast, during which
 he and his courtiers desecrate the golden
 and silver vessels that were taken from
 the temple in Jerusalem
71 Z 39   A heavenly rider, in white garment
 and with weapons of gold, helps the
 Maccabees in their battle against Lysias

GOLDEN CALF

71 E 13 5   The adoration of the golden calf
 - Aaron (Exodus)
71 I 53 1   Solomon offers sacrifices to pagan
 gods (sometimes idols and/or a golden calf
 upon the altar)

GOLIATH

71 H 21 22   David receives the sword of Goliath

GOMORRAH

71 C 12 4   The destruction of Sodom and
 Gomorrah: Lot and his family flee to Zoar,
 carrying their belongings; an angel may
 showing the way

GOURD

71 V 42   The prophet Jonah withdraws from
 Nineveh; he builds a booth and while
 enjoying the shade of a plant (gourd or
 vine) which God made grow for him, he awaits
 the destiny of the city

GOWN

see ROBE

GRADING (WINE)

see WINE-TESTING

GRAIN

see CORN

GRAPE(S)

see also VINE
71 E 31 52   The spies take away some of the
 fruits of Canaan and return, usually
 carrying a large bunch of grapes on a pole

GRASPING

see GRIPPING

GRASSHOPPER(S)

71 E 11 72 8   The plague of locusts: as Moses
 raises his hands the locusts come and eat
 everything that has survived the hail

GRATITUDE

see THANKING

GRAVE

see BURIAL
see TOMB

GRAVEN IMAGE

see IDOL(S)

GREED

see COVETOUSNESS

GRIEVING

see also LAMENTING
see also MOURNING
see also REPENTING
see also TEARING ONE'S CLOTHES
see also WEEPING
71 T 53   Tobias taking leave of his parents;
 Anna mourns her son's departure

GRIPPING

71 P 43 33   The prophet Habakkuk, carried by
 his hair by an angel, brings food to Daniel
 who sits unharmed between the lions

GROTTO

see CAVE

GROUND

see EARTH
see LAND
see SAND

GROUP

see CROWD
see FAMILY

GROVE

see BUSH

GROWING
see MULTIPLYING

GROWING UP
see UPBRINGING

GRUMBLING
see COMPLAINING

GUARD
see also GUARDING
71 E 52 42   The Israelites march around
Jericho: in the procession the main body
of the soldiers comes first, next are seven
priests who blow on trumpets, followed by
the priests carrying the ark and a rear
guard

GUARDING
see also WATCHING
71 A 61   God expels Adam and Eve from paradise
and has the tree of life guarded by an angel
with a (flaming) sword
71 A 62   Adam and Eve outside Eden, whose
entrance is guarded by shining cherubim

GUESSING
see RIDDLE

GUEST(S)
see also ENTERTAINING
see also INVITING
see also RECEIVING A PERSON
see also VISITING
71 F 52 2   The Levite and his concubine in
a street in Gibeah are offered lodging by
an old man

GUIDING
see also LEADING
71 C 12 4   The destruction of Sodom and
Gomorrah: Lot and his family flee to Zoar,
carrying their belongings; an angel may
be showing the way

GUILT
see also SIN
71 F 83 62   The Ark of the Covenant and the
box with the guilt offering, drawn by two
cows, sent back to Israel

HABAKKUK
71 P 43 33   The prophet Habakkuk, carried by
his hair by an angel, brings food to Daniel
who sits unharmed between the lions

HACKING
see STABBING

HAGAR
11 I 63(HAGAR)   Hagar (not in biblical context)
71 C 11 9   Abraham and Hagar
71 C 12 8   The banishment of Hagar and Ishmael

HAIL
71 E 11 72 7   The plague of hail: Moses raises
his rod towards the sky, and hail and fire
fall to the ground

HAIR
see also HAIR-CUTTING
71 H 84 9   Absalom, put to flight on a mule,
remains hanging by his hair in an oak-tree
71 P 43 33   The prophet Habakkuk, carried by
his hair by an angel, brings food to Daniel
who sits unharmed between the lions

HAIR-CUTTING
71 F 37 6   Samson's hairlocks are shaved, or
cut off (usually with scissors) by a
Philistine
71 F 37 61   Samson's hairlocks are cut off
by Delilah

HALO (AUREOLE)
see RAY OF LIGHT

HALT
see CRIPPLE

HALTING
see STOPPING

HAM
71 B 35 21   The mocking of Noah: Ham finds
his father (partially) naked sleeping out
of doors (or in his tent, or in the vineyard
cottage); Ham calls his brothers
71 B 35 21 1   Shem and Japheth cover their
father Noah; Ham usually stands nearby
deriding him
71 B 35 22 1   Noah curses Ham (and Canaan)

HAMAN
71 Q   - Story of Esther

HAMMER
71 F 15 43   Jael takes a nail of the tent and
a hammer
71 F 15 44   Jael kills the sleeping Sisera
by hitting the nail through his temples

HAND(S)
see also HAND OF GOD
71 A 31 1   The man (Adam) comes to life:
usually God reaches out his hand or breathes
life into his nostrils
71 A 42 4   Adam and Eve discover their
nakedness; they cover themselves with their
hands or with leaves
71 C 13 13 11   When Abraham has his hand raised
to kill Isaac, an angel restrains Abraham's
hand
71 C 27 4   Isaac lying in bed blesses Jacob
who, disguised in Esau's clothes, brings
food to his father; Jacob's hands and neck
are covered with goatskins
71 F 21 52   Those who lap water by putting
their hand to their mouth are separated
from those who kneel down to drink the water
- selection of Gideon's men
71 P 22   During Belshazzar's banquet a hand
appears and writes on the wall (MENE, MENE,
TEKEL and PARSIN (UPHARSIN)); King
Belshazzar is frightened

HAND OF GOD
    71 A 81 1   God (or the hand of God) appears
    and blesses Abel - sacrifice
    71 C 13 13 1   When Abraham has his hand raised
    to kill Isaac, God or the hand of God
    restrains Abraham's hand

HANDING OVER
    see GIVING

HANDMAID
    see MAIDSERVANT

HANDS FOLDED
    see PRAYING

HANDWRITING
    see WRITING

HANGING
    see also HANGING BY THE NECK
    71 H 84 9   Absalom, put to flight on a mule,
    remains hanging by his hair in an oak-tree

HANGING BY THE NECK
    71 D 14 6   The fulfillment of the dreams:
    Pharaoh restores the butler to his former
    position, but has the baker hanged - story
    of Joseph
    71 Q 74 21   As Haman is kneeling at Esther's
    feet or is prostrated on her couch King
    Ahasuerus returns; Haman is condemned to
    be hanged

HANGMAN
    see EXECUTIONER

HARAN
    71 C 11 12   Terah takes Abraham, Sarah and
    Lot from Ur to the city of Haran
    71 C 31 3   Jacob at the well of Haran

HAREM
    71 Q 22   Ahasuerus has the most attractive
    maidens of his kingdom put into his harem
    in order to select a new queen from among
    them - story of Esther

HARLOT
    see WHORE

HARP
    11 I 62(DAVID)   Attributes of David
    11 I 62(DAVID) 32   David as musician, usually
    playing the harp
    11 I 62(DAVID) 33   David as psalmist, as author
    of the psalms, usually playing the harp
    71 H 13 6   David playing his harp before Saul
    71 H 15 3   Saul casts his spear at David when
    the latter is playing his harp before the
    king

HEAD
    see also BEHEADING
    71 F 15 44   Jael kills the sleeping Sisera
    by hitting the nail through his temples
    71 H 14 5   David with Goliath's head
    71 H 15 21   David's triumph: the women of
    Israel come out to welcome David, singing,
    dancing, and playing tambourines and lyres;
    David holding the head of Goliath
    71 H 81 23   Amnon sends Tamar away; Tamar puts
    ashes on her head, rends her garment, lays
    her hand on her head and leaves crying
    71 K 31 14   Ahab's descendants are slain and
    their heads are piled up in two heaps at
    the city gate
    71 P 41 3   The elders accusing Susanna before
    the people, laying their hands on her head
    or unveiling her
    71 U 42 73 1   Judith with Holofernes' head
    and the sword
    71 U 43 2   Judith shows Holofernes' head to
    the people

HEALING
    71 E 32 43   Anyone who is bitten by a snake
    is cured by looking at the brazen serpent;
    the serpent (or dragon) is usually depicted
    on a tau-shaped cross or on a pillar
    71 N 16 2   Naaman comes to the Jordan, dips
    himself seven times and is cured
    71 P 14 42   King Nebuchadnezzar's reason
    returns, and he praises God
    71 T 77   the healing of Tobit: Tobias puts
    the gall of the fish on his father's eyes

HEARING
    see LISTENING

HEART
    71 T 64 2   Tobias lies the fish's heart and
    liver on glowing coals; the evil spirit
    Asmodeus disappears

HEAT
    see BURNING ALIVE
    see CAULDRON

HEATHEN STATUE(S)
    see IDOL(S)

HEAVEN(S)
    see also FIRMAMENT
    see also KINGDOM
    11 I 21   The Tiburtine sibyl and Augustus:
    the sibyl reveals to the emperor a vision
    of the Madonna in heaven
    71 C 31 21   The dream of Jacob: while sleeping
    on the ground with a stone for a pillow
    Jacob sees a ladder reaching from earth
    to heaven with angels going up and down;
    usually with God at the top of the ladder
    71 M 84   A chariot, horses of fire and a whirl-
    wind appear and Elijah is carried up into
    heaven; Elijah's cloak falls (or he hands
    it over to Elisha

HEBREWS
    see also JEWS
    11 I 62(THREE HEBREWS)   Three Hebrews (not
    in biblical context)
    71 E-71 Z   From the bondage of the Israelites
    in Egypt to the revolt of the Maccabees
    71 P 13   The story of the three Hebrews in
    the fiery furnace

HEDGE
    see BUSH

HEGEMONY
    see POWER

HELIODORUS
    71 Z 31   Heliodorus in the temple, attacked
    by a man (or angel) on horseback and two
    other men (or angels)

HELMET
    see also ARMOUR
    11 I 62(GIDEON)   Attributes of Gideon

HELP
    71 B 32 11   Noah building the ark with the
    help of his sons
    71 Z 39   A heavenly rider, in white garment
    and with weapons of gold, helps the
    Maccabees in their battle against Lysias

HERALD
    71 D 16 2   Triumph of Joseph: dressed in a
    royal attire he rides in one of Pharaoh's
    chariots, preceded by a herald
    71 Q 73   Mordecai's triumph: Mordecai, mounted
    on the king's horse, is led through the
    city by Haman (Esther and Ahasuerus may
    be looking on from the palace)

HERD
see CATTLE

HERDSMAN
see CATTLE
see SHEPHERD

HIDE
see also FLEECE
11 I 62(SAMSON)   Attributes of Samson

HIDING
see also COVERING
71 C 31 94 1   Rachel hides the teraphim in
a camel's saddle and sits on it
71 E 11 42 2   Moses, kneeling before the bush
and hiding his face, listens to God

HIGH PRIEST
see also PRIEST
71 C 11 7   The meeting of Abraham and
Melchizedek, the high priest and king of
Salem, who brings bread and wine

HILARITY
see LAUGHING

HILL(S)
see also MOUNTAIN(S)
71 E 12 72   Moses goes to the top of a hill
with Aaron and Hur and raises his arms
to make the Israelites victorious

HIRING
see STRIKING

HOISTING
71 D 12 41 1   Joseph is lowered into a pit
by means of ropes or a pulley
71 D 12 51   Joseph is pulled out of the pit
71 H 16 32   David escapes through a window;
Michal lets him down with the help of a
rope

HOLDING
see EMBRACING
see GIVING

HOLE
see PIT

HOLOFERNES
71 U 4   Judith and Holofernes

HOLY CITY
see JERUSALEM

HOLY GHOST
see TRINITY

HOMAGE
see HONORING

HOME
see RETURNING

HOMICIDE
see MURDERING

HONEY
71 F 32 73   Samson gives some of the honey
he found in the lion's carcass to his
parents

HONORING
see also ADORATION
see also TRIUMPH
see also WELCOMING
71 C 11 44 1   Abraham honored with gifts by
Pharaoh
71 D 18 5   The feast at Joseph's house: the
amazement of his brothers at being seated
according to their age; Benjamin is honored
with extra food

HORN
71 E 13 74   Moses comes down with the new
tablets and is awaited by Aaron and the
assembled people, who notice that 'his face
is shining' (Moses' face is depicted with
rays of light or with horns)
71 P 52 1   The ram with two unequal horns near
a river - Daniel's visions

HORROR
see FEAR

HORSE
see also RIDING (ON HORSEBACK)
71 M 84   A chariot, horses of fire and a whirlwind appear and Elijah is carried up into
heaven; Elijah's cloak falls (or he hands
it over to Elisha)

HORSEBACK
see RIDING (ON HORSEBACK)

HOSPITALITY
see ENTERTAINING
see GUEST(S)
see RECEIVING A PERSON

HOSTAGE
see CAPTIVE(S)

HOTEL
see INN

HOUND
see DOG

HOUSE
see COTTAGE

HUMAN BEING
see also MANKIND
71 A 31   God fashions man from clay

HUMAN FIGURE
see MONSTER(S)

HUMAN LIFE
see LIFE

HUMAN SACRIFICE
71 C 13 1   The sacrifice of Isaac
71 F 24 55   Fulfilment of Jephthah's vow to
the Lord: Jephthah's daughter is sacrificed

HUMILIATION
see TRAMPLING

HUNGER
71 C 24 41   Esau, returning hungry from the
hunt, sells his first birthright to Jacob
for a pottage of lentils

HUNTER
71 C 27 5   Esau comes back with venison

HUNTING
see HUNTING ACCIDENT

HUNTING ACCIDENT
71 B 15 1   Lamech kills Cain: Cain is
accidentally shot dead by an arrow of the
blind Lamech, who is assisted in the hunt
by his son Tubalcain

HUR
71 E 12 72 1   Moses sitting on a rock, arms
held up by Aaron and Hur; the Amalekites
are defeated

HURLING
see THROWING

HURRICANE
    see WHIRLWIND

HURTING
    see WOUNDED PERSON

HUSBAND
    see HUSBAND AND WIFE

HUSBAND AND WIFE
    see also FAMILY
    see also MARRIAGE
    71 W 5   Job on the dunghill

HUSBANDMAN
    see FARMER

HUT
    see BOOTH

HYBRID
    see MONSTER(S)

IDENTITY
    see also RECOGNIZING
    71 D 19 31   Joseph reveals his identity and
       in tears forgives his brother's past misdeed

IDOL(S)
    see also DESTRUCTION OF IDOLS
    see also GOLDEN CALF
    see also IDOLATRY
    see also TERAPHIM
    71 I 53 1   Solomon offers sacrifices to pagan
       gods (sometimes idols and/or a golden calf
       upon the altar)

IDOLATRY
    see also IDOL(S)
    see also REFUSING (WORSHIP)
    71 E 13 53   Adoration of the golden calf (which
       may be standing on a pillar, and is
       sometimes depicted as a dragon)
    71 E 13 63   Moses, standing at the gate of
       the camp, causes the Levites to kill all
       the idolaters
    71 I 53   Solomon's idolatry
    71 K 21 2   Jeroboam's idolatry
    71 M 11   Elijah announces to King Ahab that
       God will bring a long drought in the land
       to avenge the apostasy of Israel
    71 P 13 2   The dedication of the golden statue:
       in the presence of King Nebuchadnezzar,
       trumpets are blown and all the people
       surrounding the image fall on their knees

ILL (SICK)
    see SICK PERSON

IMAGE
    see IDOL(S)

IMPIETY
    see UNBELIEF

IMPLORING
    see ASKING

IMPRISONMENT
    see PRISON

IMPROVEMENT
    see RECOVERY

INCEST
    71 C 12 52 1   Lot's daughters lie with their
       father in turn

INCREASING
    see MULTIPLYING

INCREDULITY
    see UNBELIEF

INCRIMINATION
    see ACCUSING

INFANCY
    see UPBRINGING
    see YOUTH

INFANT
    see BABY

INFORMATION
    see INSTRUCTING
    see REPORTING

INJURY
    see INSULTING

INJUSTICE
    see ACCUSING

INN
    71 E 11 45   At an inn, God (or the angel of
        God) tries to kill Moses

INNOCENCE
    see ACCUSING
    see ORDEAL

INQUIETUDE
    71 T 74   Old Tobit (and Anna) waiting and
        worrying about the long absence of their
        son; sometimes Anna is shown at the spinning
        wheel

INSATIABLENESS
    see HUNGER

INSPECTION
    see EXAMINATION
    see SUPERVISING

INSTITUTING
    71 A 35 2   God blesses Adam and Eve;
        institution of marriage

INSTRUCTING
    see also ORDERING
    see also TEACHING
    71 H 92   David's instructions to Solomon

INSUBORDINATION
    see DISOBEDIENCE

INSULTING
    see also MOCKING
    71 W 52   Job on the dunghill with Satan (or
        devils) abusing and tormenting him; Job's
        wife may be present
    71 W 53 11   Job scolded by his wife

INTERCEDING
    see INTERVENING
    see PLEADING

INTERFERING
    see INTERVENING

INTERPRETING
    see EXPLAINING

INTERROGATION
    see also CALLING TO ACCOUNT
    see also TRIAL
    71 F 64 2   Boaz questions his servant
        concerning Ruth
    71 P 41 41   Daniel interrogates the elders
        separately

INTERRUPTION
    see STOPPING

INTERVENING
    71 P 41   The story of Susanna and the elders
        (in which the youth Daniel intervenes on
        behalf of Susanna)

INTIMIDATION
    see THREATENING

INTOXICATION
    see DRUNKENNESS

INTRODUCING
    see PRESENTING A PERSON

INUNDATION
    see FLOOD

INVALID
    see CRIPPLE

INVASION
    71 H 25 2   David and Abishai invade Saul's
        encampment at night, while Saul and his
        soldiers are sleeping

INVENTION
    71 B 25   Story of Enoch, son of Jared, who
        invented letters and was the first to divide
        the year into seasons and into twelve months

INVENTOR
    see INVENTION

INVESTIGATION
    see INTERROGATION
    see SEARCHING

INVITING
    71 F 52 2   The Levite and his concubine in
        a street in Gibeah are offered lodging by
        an old man
    71 F 64 4   Ruth invited by Boaz to eat with
        him

INVOKING
    11 I 62(THREE HEBREWS) 21   The three Babylonian
        youths Ananias (Shedrach), Azarias (Abed-
        nego), Misael (Mesach) invoked in distress,
        and for resurrections

INVULNERABILITY
    see ORDEAL

IRREVERENCE
    see MOCKING

ISAAC
    71 C 13 1   The sacrifice of Isaac
    71 C 2   Story of Isaac

ISAIAH
    11 I 62(ISAIAH)   Isaiah (not in biblical
        context)
    71 L 24 41   King Hezekiah falls ill and is
        visited by Isaiah, who tells him to get
        ready to die; Hezekiah turns his face to
        the wall, prays and then cries

ISHMAEL
    71 C 12 8   The banishment of Hagar and Ishmael
    71 C 22 41   Abraham is buried by Isaac and
        Ishmael in the cave of Machpelah

ISRAEL (JACOB)
    see also JACOB
    71 C 32 22 1   Jacob receives a new name,
        Israel, and is blessed by the angel

ISRAEL(ITES)
    see also HEBREWS
    see also JEWS
    11 I 61 3   Kings of Israel and Judah – the
        Old Testament (not in biblical context)
    71 E-71 Z   From the bondage of the Israelites
        in Egypt to the revolt of the Maccabees

JABBOK (RIVER)
    71 C 32 21   Jacob sends his family and caravan
    across the river Jabbok, and stays behind

JABESH-GILEAD
    71 H 32 45   The inhabitants of Jabesh-gilead
    take away the bodies of Saul and his sons

JACOB
    71 C 24   Isaac's children (Esau and Jacob)
    71 C 3   Story of Jacob
    71 D 11-71 D 12   The coat of many colors:
    Joseph sold by his brothers
    71 D 17-71 D 19   Jacob sends his sons to Egypt;
    Joseph and his brothers; the missing cup
    71 D 21   Jacob and his family go to Egypt
    71 D 22   Jacob and his family in Egypt
    71 D 24   Jacob's last days
    71 D 25   Jacob's death

JACOB'S LADDER
    71 C 31 21   The dream of Jacob: while sleeping
    on the ground with a stone for a pillow
    Jacob sees a ladder reaching from earth
    to heaven with angels going up and down;
    usually with God at the top of the ladder

JAIL
    see PRISON

JAPHETH
    71 B 35 21 1   Shem and Japheth cover their
    father Noah; Ham usually stands nearby
    deriding him
    71 B 35 21 11   Shem and Japheth walking
    backwards towards Noah

JAR
    see also JUG
    see also POT
    71 E 12 54 2   Aaron fills a jar with manna
    to be kept in the tabernacle
    71 M 53   An angel wakes Elijah: a loaf of bread
    and a jar of water are usually at Elijah's
    head
    71 N 11   The water of Jericho is purified:
    when the citizens of Jericho complain about
    their water, Elisha puts some salt into
    a jar; he then throws the salt into the
    water

JAVELIN
    see SPEAR

JAW-BONE
    11 I 62(SAMSON)   Attributes of Samson
    71 A 82   The killing of Abel: Cain slays him
    with a stone, a club or a jaw-bone,
    alternatively with a spade or another tool
    as weapon

JEALOUSY
    71 A 71 22   Eve suckling Abel; Cain turns
    aside, i.e. the jealousy of Cain

JEBUS
    71 H 54 63   By the command of God the angel
    stops destroying the Israelites at the
    threshing-floor of Araunah (Ornan) the
    Jebusite

JEHU (KING)
    71 K 29 42-71 K 29 46   Jehu plots Jehoram's
    death with his fellow-officers

JEPHTHAH
    71 F 24 5   The story of Jephthah's daughter

JEREMIAH
    11 I 62(JEREMIAH)   Jeremiah (not in biblical
    context)

JERICHO
    71 E 52 4   The fall of Jericho
    71 N 11   The water of Jericho is purified:
    when the citizens of Jericho complain about
    their water, Elisha puts some salt into
    a jar; he then throws the salt into the
    water

JEROBOAM (KING)
    71 I 43 53 1   Jeroboam supervising the building
    of Millo

JERUBBAAL
    see GIDEON

JERUSALEM
    71 C 11 7   The meeting of Abraham and
    Melchizedek, the high priest and king of
    Salem, who brings bread and wine
    71 H 62   The Ark of the Covenant is brought
    to Jerusalem
    71 O 73 13   Jeremiah prophesying the
    destruction of Jerusalem
    71 O 95 1   Ezekiel prophesies against Jerusalem
    71 R 32   The rebuilding of Jerusalem's walls

JETHRO
    71 E 11 43   Moses and Jethro parting - the
    calling of Moses
    71 E 12 8   Jethro's visit to Moses: with
    Zipporah and her two sons he comes to the
    desert where Moses is encamped

JEW
    see JEWS

JEWELS
    71 C 21 42   Gifts of clothing, gold and jewelry
    are offered to Rebekah's parents
    71 E 13 81   The people bring their offerings
    for the Tabernacle: all kinds of fine
    objects, jewelry, linen, etc.

JEWS
    see also HEBREWS
    71 E-71 Z   From the bondage of the Israelites
    in Egypt to the revolt of the Maccabees
    71 L 4   The Babylonian Captivity of the Jews
    71 Q 8   The triumph of the Jews - story of
    Esther
    71 X 1 (Ps. 137:1)1:71 L 4   'By the rivers
    of Babylon...' - the Hebrews in Captivity
    lamenting by the riverside

JEZEBEL
    71 K 31 13 2   Dogs eat Jezebel's body

JOB
    71 W   The book of Job

JOB'S WIFE
    71 W 5   Job on the dunghill

JOCHEBED
    71 E 11 26   When Moses is old enough, his
    mother brings him to Pharaoh's daughter,
    who adopts him

JONAH
    71 V   The book of Jonah

JONATHAN
    71 H 15 1   David and Jonathan, son of Saul,
    become friends
    71 H 17   David and Jonathan
    71 H 32 12   Death of Jonathan and his brothers
    Abinadab and Melchi-shua

JORDAN (RIVER)
    71 E 52 2   The Israelites come to the Jordan
    71 N 16 2   Naaman comes to the Jordan, dips
    himself seven times and is cured

JOSEPH (SON OF JACOB)
   11 I 62(JOSEPH)   Joseph (not in biblical
      context)
   71 D   Story of Joseph
   71 E 12 11   Moses takes the bones of Joseph
      with him

JOURNEY
   see also DEPARTING
   see also RETURNING
   see also TRAVELLING
   71 C 21 5   The return journey and arrival
      in Canaan (Eliezer and Rebekah)
   71 D 18   Second journey of Joseph's brothers
      to Egypt
   71 D 19 2   Joseph's brothers set out on their
      journey home
   71 D 21   Jacob and his family go to Egypt
   71 E 12   Exodus (part II): journey of Israel
      to Mount Sinai
   71 F 62   Naomi's return to Bethlehem
   71 T 5   The journey to Ecbatana – the book
      of Tobit
   71 T 7   Tobias' return

JOY
   see REJOICING

JUDAH
   71 C 33 2   Story of Judah and Tamar
   71 D 18 1   Judah persuades the afflicted Jacob
      to consent to the departure of Benjamin
   71 D 19 3   The brothers before Joseph: Judah
      pleads for Benjamin and offers to be
      retained as a slave in his stead

JUDAH (KINGDOM)
   11 I 61 3   Kings of Israel and Judah - the
      Old Testament (not in biblical context)

JUDAH (TRIBE)
   71 H 41 2   David anointed king by the tribe
      of Judah

JUDAISM
   see JEWS

JUDAS MACCABEUS
   71 Z   (Books of the) Maccabees

JUDEA
   see JUDAH (KINGDOM)

JUDGE
   see also ACCUSING
   71 E 12 85   Moses choosing judges
   71 I 32   The judgement of Solomon

JUDGEMENT
   see also JUDGE
   see also VERDICT
   71 I 32   The judgement of Solomon

JUDGES
   71 F   The time of the Judges

JUDITH
   71 U   The book of Judith

JUG
   see also JAR
   see also POURING
   71 C 12 82   Abraham provides Hagar and Ishmael
      with bread and a jug of water
   71 C 21 3   The meeting at the well: Eliezer
      sees Rebekah coming with a pitcher
   71 C 21 31 1   Rebekah offers Eliezer a drink
      from her pitcher
   71 F 21 64   The attack on the Midianites:
      Gideon and his men blow their trumpets,
      break their pitchers, and hold their lamps

JUMPING
   71 Q 63 1   Ahasuerus leaps from his throne
      and takes Esther in his arms

JUSTICE
   see JUDGE

KADESH
    71 E 12 6   Moses striking water from the rock

KID
    71 D 12 71 1   Joseph's brothers stain Joseph's
      coat with the kid's blood
    71 F 34 1   Samson goes with a kid to his wife
      and is refused entry by her father

KILLING
    see also BEATING
    see also BEHEADING
    see also BURNING ALIVE
    see also DEATH
    see also DROWNING
    see also HANGING BY THE NECK
    see also HUMAN SACRIFICE
    see also KILLING - ANIMAL
    see also MASSACRE
    see also MURDERING
    see also SHOOTING
    see also STABBING
    see also STONING
    see also SUICIDE
    see also THROWING (BEING THROWN)
    see also THUNDER(BOLT)
    71 E 11 31 2-4   Moses kills the Egyptian
      taskmaster
    71 E 13 63   Moses, standing at the gate of
      the camp, causes the Levites to kill all
      the idolaters
    71 F 15 44   Jael kills the sleeping Sisera
      by hitting the nail through his temples
    71 H 46 3   Abner, fetched by Joab's messengers,
      is taken aside by Joab in the gate of
      Hebron, and is killed by him with a sword
    71 H 52 64   Benaiah kills two men, and then
      a lion, in a pit on a snowy day
    71 H 74 2   Uriah is killed in the battle
    71 K 31 14   Ahab's descendants are slain and
      their heads are piled up in two heaps at
      the city gate
    71 L 17 11   Athaliah has all the members of
      the royal family killed

KILLING - ANIMAL
    see also BITING
    see also DEVOURING
    see also SACRIFICING
    71 E 11 73 2   The plague of the first-born:
      the destroying angel passes through the
      land and kills every Egyptian first-born
      of man and animal
    71 F 32 5   Samson kills the lion with his bare
      hands
    71 H 14 31   David kills a lion and a bear (or
      tells Saul about it)
    71 H 52 64   Benaiah kills two men, and then
      a lion, in a pit on a snowy day

KINDLING
    see SETTING ON FIRE

KING
    see also BEFORE
    see also PHARAOH
    71 C 11 7   The meeting of Abraham and
      Melchizedek, the high priest and king of
      Salem, who brings bread and wine
    71 H 11   David chosen as king by God
    71 H 15 3   Saul casts his spear at David when
      the latter is playing his harp before the
      king
    71 H 41   David made king in Hebron
    71 H 42   Ish-bosheth succeeds his father Saul
      although David is already anointed king
      by the tribe of Judah
    71 H 48 2   David anointed king by the elders
      of Israel
    71 k 2-4   Story of the kingdom and kings of
      Israel

71 K 27 21 1   King Benhadad II of Syria
    besieges Samaria
71 L 1-3   Story of the kingdom and kings of
    Judah
71 l 31 3   When Evilmerodach becomes king of
    Babylon, Jehoiachin is released from prison
    and permitted to dine at the king's table
    for the rest of his life
71 M 11   Elijah announces to King Ahab that
    God will bring a long drought in the land
    to avenge the apostasy of Israel
71 P 2   Daniel and King Belshazzar
71 Q   - Story of Esther
71 W 54 1   Eliphaz, Bildad, and Zophar go to
    Job to console him over his misfortunes
    (the three friends may be depicted as kings)

KINGDOM
    71 K 2-4   Story of the kingdom and kings of
      Israel
    71 L   Story of the Southern Kingdom (Judah)
    71 O 33 4   Isaiah's prophecy of the peaceable
      kingdom: 'the wolf shall dwell with the
      lamb'

KINGSHIP
    71 H 48   Definitive acknowledgement of David's
      kingship, in Hebron

KISSING
    see also EMBRACING
    see also LOVER(S)
    71 C 31 34   Jacob kisses Rachel and is moved
      to tears
    71 E 11 46 1   Aaron meets Moses and kisses
      him

KITCHEN
    see PREPARATIONS - FEAST, MEAL

KNEELING
    see also ASKING
    see also BEFORE
    see also PRAYING
    see also PROSTRATION
    see also WORSHIPPING
    71 C 12 22   Abraham kneels before the angels
    71 E 11 42 2   Moses, kneeling before the bush
      and hiding his face, listens to God
    71 F 21 52   Those who lap water by putting
      their hand to their mouth are separated
      from those who kneel down to drink the water
      - selection of Gideon's men
    71 F 64 3   Boaz speaks to Ruth; Ruth usually
      bowing down, or kneeling before him
    71 H 23 6   When Saul comes out of the cave,
      David calls him, falls down on his knees
      and shows him the piece of cloth
    71 H 24 42   Meeting of David and Abigail, who
      kneels before him
    71 H 82 5   Reconciliation of David and Absalom;
      Absalom kneels before David and they embrace
    71 I 43 23 4   Prayer of Solomon; Solomon kneels
      before the altar
    71 P 12 51   King Nebuchadnezzar kneels before
      Daniel to show his gratitude
    71 P 13 2   The dedication of the golden statue:
      in the presence of King Nebuchadnezzar,
      trumpets are blown and all the people
      surrounding the image fall on their knees
    71 Q 64   Ahasuerus holds out his sceptre to
      Esther (Esther usually kneeling)
    71 Q 74 21   As Haman is kneeling at Esther's
      feet or is prostrated on her couch King
      Ahasuerus returns; Haman is condemned to
      be hanged

KNIFE
    71 C 13 13   Abraham picks up the knife to kill
      Isaac
    71 C 13 13 1   When Abraham has his hand raised
      to kill Isaac, God or the hand of God
      restrains Abraham's hand

KNIGHT
see SOLDIER(S)

KNOCKING
see REFUSING (ADMISSION)

KNOWLEDGE
see TREE OF KNOWLEDGE

KORAH
71 E 31 7   Rebellion of Korah (Core), Dathan
and Abiram, and their punishment

LABAN
71 C 21 35   Laban, Rebekah's brother, comes
to Eliezer at the well - Eliezer seeking
a wife for Isaac
71 C 21 44   The leave-taking of Rebekah; Laban
gives her provisions
71 C 31 4   Jacob serving Laban for Rachel and
Leah
71 C 31 6   The partnership with Laban - story
of Jacob
71 C 31 8   Jacob's flight from Laban

LABOR
71 A 7   The labors of Adam and Eve; infancy
of Cain and Abel
71 C 31 4   Jacob serving Laban for Rachel and
Leah

LACING
see SANDALS
see SHOES

LADDER
see also STAIRCASE
71 C 31 21   The dream of Jacob: while sleeping
on the ground with a stone for pillow Jacob
sees a ladder reaching from earth to heaven
with angels going up and down; usually with
God at the top of the ladder

LAMB
71 A 81   The sacrifice of Cain and Abel: Abel
offers a lamb, Cain usually a sheaf of corn
71 B 34 3   Noah's sacrifice: various animals
are offered, possibly a lamb, a dove, and
a ram (often combined with the rainbow of
the covenant)
71 E 11 73 13 2   The Israelites eat the
Passover lamb standing about a table with
their loins girt, their shoes on their feet
and with staves in their hands, ready to
depart
71 O 33 4   Isaiah's prophecy of the peaceable
kingdom: 'the wolf shall dwell with the
lamb'

LAMBSKIN
see FLEECE

LAME
see CRIPPLE

LAMENTING
see also GRIEVING
see also MOURNING
see also WEEPING
71 D 12 82   Joseph bewailed as dead by his
father; the sons and daughters are unable
to console him
71 F 24 54   Jephthah's daughter retreats to
the mountains with her companions to bewail
her virginity
71 H 81 23   Amnon sends Tamar away; Tamar puts
ashes on her head, rends her garment, lays
her hand on her head and leaves crying
71 W 54 2   When Eliphaz, Bildad and Zophar
recognize Job they weep and tear their
clothes in grief
71 X 1(Ps. 137:1)1:71 L 4   'By the rivers of
Babylon...' the Hebrews in Captivity
lamenting by the riverside

LAMP
71 F 21 64   The attack on the Midianites:
Gideon and his men blow their trumpets,
break their pitchers, and hold their lamps

LANCE
see SPEAR

LAND
see also EARTH
71 A 23   Gathering of the waters below the firmament; dry land appears and produces all kinds of plants

LANDING
see DISEMBARKATION

LANGUAGE
71 B 42 21   The confusion of languages and the scattering of people over the earth - story of the Tower of Babel

LAP
71 F 37 5   Samson asleep in Delilah's lap; she is usually shown beckoning to a Philistine or putting a finger to her lips

LAPIDATION
see STONING

LAPPING
71 F 21 52   Those who lap water by putting their hand to their mouth are separated from those who kneel down to drink the water - selection of Gideon's men

LAUGHING
see also MOCKING
71 C 12 24 3   The promise of a son is renewed; Sarah, overhearing it, laughs incredulously

LAUNDERING
see WASHING (CLOTHES)

LAW (BIBLICAL)
see COMMANDMENT(S)
see TABLES OF THE LAW

LAWSUIT
see TRIAL

LAWYER
see PLEADING

LEADER(S)
see ELDER(S)

LEADING
see also BEFORE
see also GUIDING
71 A 33 1   God brings Adam to paradise
71 A 35 1   God brings Eve to Adam
71 C 11 12   Terah takes Abraham, Sarah and Lot from Ur to the city of Haran
71 C 11 91 1   Sarah brings Hagar to Abraham, who is usually shown lying in bed
71 C 21 6   Isaac brings Rebekah into Sarah's tent
71 E 52 22   The Israelites leave their camp to cross the Jordan; the priests, carrying the ark, lead the march
71 P 41 32   Susanna is led away to be executed

LEAF
see also ROD (FLOWERING)
71 A 42 4   Adam and Eve discover their nakedness; they cover themselves with their hands or with leaves

LEAGUE
see ALLIANCE

LEAH
71 C 31 4   Jacob serving Laban for Rachel and Leah

LEAPING
see JUMPING

LEAVE-TAKING
see also DEPARTING
see also LEAVING
71 C 12 82   Abraham provides Hagar and Ishmael with bread and a jug of water
71 C 21 44   The leave-taking of Rebekah; Laban gives her provisions
71 D 18 11   Jacob's farewell to Benjamin
71 E 11 43   Moses and Jethro parting - the calling of Moses
71 H 17 33   David and Jonathan embracing; David's leave-taking from Jonathan
71 T 53   Tobias taking leave of his parents; Anna mourns her son's departure
71 U 42 1   Judith and her maidservant take leave of the elders at the city gate

LEAVING
see also DEPARTING
see also DISAPPEARING
see also LEAVE-TAKING
71 C 11 45   Abraham leaves Egypt with Sarah, Lot and his possessions

LEAVING BEHIND
71 C 13 11 1   The servants are left behind while Abraham and Isaac (usually carrying wood) climb the mountain

LEG
see THIGH

LENGTHENING
see STRETCHING

LENTIL
71 C 24 41   Esau, returning hungry from the hunt, sells his first birthright to Jacob for a pottage of lentils

LEPER
see LEPROSY

LEPROSY
71 N 16 32   Elisha rebukes Gehazi and as punishment causes him to be smitten with Naaman's leprosy

LESSON
see TEACHING

LETTER(S)
71 B 25   Story of Enoch, son of Jared, who invented letters and was the first to divide the year into seasons and into twelve months
71 P 22   During Belshazzar's banquet a hand appears and writes on the wall (MENE, MENE, TEKEL and PARSIN(UPHARSIN)); King Belshazzar is frightened

LETTER (EPISTLE)
see also DECREE
see also DOCUMENT
71 H 71 3   Bathsheba receives a letter from David
71 H 73 4   David gives Uriah a letter for Joab
71 L 24 36   Hezekiah receives a letter from Sennacherib with another threat
71 Q 83   Mordecai and Esther write letters in King Ahasuerus' name

LEVIATHAN
71 V 13 41   Jonah is swallowed by a great fish, (sea)monster, whale, dolphin, or the like

LEVITATION
see AIR (IN THE)

LEVITE(S)
71 E 13 63   Moses, standing at the gate of the camp, causes the Levites to kill all the idolaters

LEVITICUS
   71 E 2   The book Leviticus

LIBATION
   see POURING

LIBERATING
   see also RELEASING
   71 U 33 32   Achior is freed by the Israelites

LIE
   see DECEIT

LIFE
   see also ANIMATING
   see also TREE OF LIFE
   71 B 33 1   The ark is floating on the waters, while life on earth is destroyed - story of Noah

LIFTING
   see CARRYING

LIGHT
   see also LAMP
   see also RAY OF LIGHT
   71 A 21   Division of light and darkness
   71 A 62   Adam and Eve outside Eden, whose entrance is guarded by shining cherubim
   71 E 12 12 2   By night a pillar of fire gives the Israelites light
   71 E 13 74   Moses comes down with the new tablets and is awaited by Aaron and the assembled people, who notice that 'his face is shining' (Moses' face is depicted with rays of light or with horns)

LIGHTING
   see LAMP

LIGHTNING
   see THUNDER(BOLT)

LIMB(S)
   see ARM(S)

LINEN
   71 E 13 81   The people bring their offerings for the Tabernacle: all kinds of objects, jewelry, linen, etc.

LION
   71 F 32 5   Samson kills the lion with his bare hands
   71 H 14 31   David kills a lion and a bear (or tells Saul about it)
   71 H 52 64   Benaiah kills two men, and then a lion, in a pit on a snowy day

LIP(S)
   see FINGER TO THE LIPS

LISTENING
   see also BEFORE
   see also OVERHEARING
   see also SPEAKING
   71 E 11 42 2   Moses, kneeling before the bush and hiding his face, listens to God

LIVER
   71 T 64 2   Tobias lies the fish's heart and liver on glowing coals; the evil spirit Asmodeus disappears

LIVESTOCK
   see CATTLE

LIVING (THE)
   see LIFE

LOAD
   71 H 24 41   Abigail goes out with asses laden with loaves of bread and bottles of wine, to meet David

LOADING
   see PREPARATIONS - DEPARTURE

LOAF
   see also BREAD
   71 H 24 41   Abigail goes out with asses laden with loaves of bread and bottles of wine, to meet David
   71 M 53   An angel wakes Elijah; a loaf of bread and a jar of water are usually at Elijah's head
   71 N 15   A hundred men are fed with twenty loaves of bread: Elisha receives barley bread of the first-fruits and a sack of corn which he multiplies to feed a hundred men

LOAVES
   see LOAF

LOCK OF HAIR
   see HAIR
   see HAIR-CUTTING

LOCKED UP
   see PRISON(ER)

LOCUST
   see GRASSHOPPER

LODGING
   see GUEST(S)

LOINS
   71 E 11 73 13 2   The Israelites eat the Passover lamb standing about a table with their loins girt, their shoes on their feet and with staves in their hands, ready to depart

LONELINESS
   see SOLITUDE

LONGING
   see LOVE UNREQUITED

LOOK-OUT
   see WATCHING

LOOKING
   see also SPYING
   see also VISION
   see also WATCHING
   71 C 12 51   Lot, seeing the destruction of the cities and fearing for his safety in Zoar, flees with his daughters to a cave in the mountains
   71 H 62 71   David brings the ark into Jerusalem, Michal looking through a window
   71 Q 73   Mordecai's triumph: Mordecai, mounted on the king's horse, is led through the city by Haman (Esther and Ahasuerus may be looking on from the palace)

LOOTING
   see PLUNDERING

LORD (THE)
   see GOD

LORDSHIP (HEGEMONY)
   see POWER

LOST PERSON, ETC.
   see SEARCHING

LOT(S)
71 E 54 33 Joshua (assisted by Eleazar) casts lots and assigns to each of the remaining seven tribes a certain part of Canaan

LOT
71 C 11 12 Terah takes Abraham, Sarah, and Lot from Ur to the city of Haran
71 C 11 45 Abraham leaves Egypt with Sarah, Lot, and his possessions
71 C 11 6 The battle of the kings and the rescue of Lot
71 C 12 4 The destruction of Sodom and Gomorrah: Lot and his family flee to Zoar, carrying their belongings; an angel may be showing the way
71 C 12 5 Lot and his daughters

LOTTERY
see LOT(S)

LOUD SOUND
see SHOUTING

LOVE
see COURTING
see LOVE AT FIRST SIGHT
see LOVER(S)

LOVE AT FIRST SIGHT
71 C 31 34 Jacob kisses Rachel and is moved to tears
71 H 71 David, from the roof (or balcony) of his palace, sees Bathsheba bathing

LOVE UNREQUITED
see also SEDUCING
71 D 13 31 Potiphar's wife catches Joseph by his robe, usually while lying in bed; Joseph escapes leaving his cloak behind in her hands (possibly with a naked child lying in a crib)
71 P 41 22 The elders making advances towards Susanna

LOVER(S)
see also COURTING
see also LOVE UNREQUITED
71 C 25 21 1 King Abimelech, looking down from his window, sees Isaac and Rebekah making love
71 C 33 27 1 Judah's love-affair with Tamar; he gives her his signet(-ring), bracelets and staff
71 H 71 5 David and Bathsheba as lovers

LOVESICK
see LOVE UNREQUITED

LOWERING
see HOISTING

LUGGAGE
see SACK

LYING-IN
see BIRTH

LYRE
71 H 15 21 David's triumph: the women of Israel come out to welcome David, singing, dancing, and playing tambourines and lyres; David holding the head of Goliath

LYRIC (POETRY)
71 X The lyric books: Psalms and Song of Solomon

LYSIAS
71 Z 39 A heavenly rider, in white garment and with weapons of gold, helps the Maccabees in their battle against Lysias

MACHPELAH (CAVE OF)
71 C 22 41 Abraham is buried by Isaac and Ishmael in the cave of Machpelah

MAGISTRATE
see JUDGE(S)

MAIDEN
see GIRL

MAIDSERVANT
see also COMPANION(S)
71 E 11 24 The finding of Moses: Pharaoh's daughter comes to bathe with her maidens in the river and discovers the child floating on the water
71 H 71 2 Bathsheba attended by servant(s)
71 P 41 2 Susanna bathing, usually in or near a fountain and sometimes accompanied by two female servants
71 Q 63 Esther swoons on the shoulder of one of her maids
71 U 43 Judith and her maidservant on their way back to Bethuliah

MAKING MUSIC
see MUSIC MAKING

MALE
see MAN

MALTREATING
see TORTURING

MAMMALS
see ANIMAL(S)

MAN
see also HUMAN BEING
see also OLD MAN
71 C 12 2 The visit of three angels (three men) - story of Abraham

MAN OF GOD
see PROPHET

MANASSEH
71 D 24 2 Joseph takes his two sons, Manasseh and Ephraim to see Jacob on his sick-bed
71 D 24 21 Jacob blesses Manasseh and Ephraim with arms crossed; Joseph may be shown trying to uncross them or expressing (with Asenath) his disapproval

MANKIND
see also HUMAN BEING
71 B 33 1 The ark is floating on the waters, while life on earth is destroyed - story of Noah

MANNA
71 E 12 54 In the morning manna falls to the earth - Exodus
71 E 12 54 1 The gathering of manna (in baskets and pots)
71 E 12 54 2 Aaron fills a jar with manna to be kept in the tabernacle

MANOAH
71 F 31 Samson's birth and youth
71 F 31 4 Manoah's sacrifice; the angel ascends in the flames
71 F 32 Samson's journey to Timna(t)h

MANOAH'S WIFE
71 F 31 1 Annunciation of Samson's birth to the wife of Manoah by an angel

MANTLE
see CLOAK

MARCHING

71 E 52 42   The Israelites march around
Jericho: in the procession the main body
of the soldiers comes first, next are seven
priests who blow on trumpets, followed by
the priests carrying the ark and a rear
guard

MARK

see MARKING

MARKING

71 A 83 21   God puts a mark on Cain

MARRIAGE

71 A 35 2   God blesses Adam and Eve:
institution of marriage
71 C 21 7   Marriage of Isaac and Rebekah
71 C 31 44   The wedding-feast; Laban
substitutes Leah for Rachel
71 C 31 46   The marriage of Jacob and Rachel
71 D 16   Elevation and marriage of Joseph
71 E 11 34   Moses' marriage with Zipporah
71 T 63   The marriage of Tobias and Sarah

MARRIAGE...

see WEDDING...

MARRIAGE BROKER

71 C 21 4   Eliezer at Rebekah's house

MARRIAGE CONTRACT

71 T 63 2   The writing of the marriage letter
- Tobias and Sarah

MARRIAGE PROPOSAL

see PROPOSAL

MARTYR

71 Z 35   Martyrdom of Eleazar: the old man
is forced to eat pork and voluntarily
submits to the flogging

MASCULINITY

see MAN

MASSACRE

see also KILLING
71 E 11 73 2   The plague of the first-born:
the destroying angel passes through the
land and kills every Egyptian first-born
of man and animal
71 F 35 4   With an ass's jaw-bone Samson slays
a thousand Philistines
71 L 24 38   At night, an angel of the Lord
decimates the Assyrian camp: 185,000
soldiers are killed

MASTER

see SERVANT(S)

MATCH (CONTEST)

see CONTEST

MEADOW

see FIELD(S)

MEAL

see also BANQUET
see also FOOD
see also PREPARATIONS - FEAST, MEAL
71 D 18 5   The feast at Joseph's house: the
amazement of his brothers at being seated
according to their age; Benjamin is honored
with extra food
71 E 11 73 13 2   The Israelites eat the
Passover lamb standing about a table with
their loins girt, their shoes on their feet
and with staves in their hands, ready to
depart
71 F 64 4   Ruth invited by Boaz to eat with
him

71 H 78   David recovers and takes a meal
71 L 31 3   When Evilmerodach becomes king of
Babylon, Jehoiachin is released from prison
and permitted to dine at the king's table
for the rest of his life
71 M 22   Elijah fed by the widow of Zarephath

MEAL (FLOUR)

see FLOUR

MEAT

71 H 62 8   David places the ark in a tent,
burns offerings before the Lord and
distributes bread, meat and wine to everyone

MEDICINE

see HEALING

MEETING

see also BEFORE
see also EMBRACING
see also RECEIVING A PERSON
see also VISITING
71 C 11 7   The meeting of Abraham and
Melchizedek, the high priest and king of
Salem, who brings bread and wine
71 C 11 93 2   An angel meets Hagar at the
fountain on the way to Shur and persuades
her to return
71 C 21 3   The meeting at the well: Eliezer
sees Rebekah coming with a pitcher
71 C 21 35   Laban, Rebekah's brother, comes
to Eliezer at the well - Eliezer seeking
a wife for Isaac
71 C 21 51   Isaac, walking in the fields, meets
Rebekah
71 C 31 31   Jacob meets the shepherds of Haran
and their flocks of sheep lying round the
well
71 C 32 32   The meeting between Esau and Jacob
71 D 22 2   The meeting of Jacob and Joseph
in Goshen
71 E 11 32   Moses at a well meets the seven
daughters of Jethro, the priest of Midian
71 E 11 46 1   Aaron meets Moses and kisses
him
71 F 24 53   Jephthah's daughter dances with
tambourines to meet her father on his return
from the battle; Jephthah rends his clothes
in despair
71 F 64 3   Boaz speaks to Ruth; Ruth usually
bowing down, or kneeling before him
71 H 24 42   Meeting of David and Abigail, who
kneels before him
71 I 72   Meeting of Jeroboam and the prophet
Ahijah; Ahijah rends his garment in twelve
pieces, ten of which he gives to Jeroboam
71 M 21   When the brook dries up, Elijah
crosses over to the city of Zarephath; at
the gate he meets a woman and her little
son gathering wood (the woman's sticks may
form a cross)
71 T 51   The meeting of Tobias and the angel
Raphael
71 T 76   The meeting of parents and son -
Tobias' return

MELCHI-SHUA

71 H 32 12   Death of Jonathan and his brothers
Abinadab and Melchi-shua

MELCHIZEDEK

11 I 62(MELCHIZEDEK)   Melchizedek (not in
biblical context)
71 C 11 7   The meeting of Abraham and
Melchizedek, the high priest and king of
Salem, who brings bread and wine

MEN

see MAN

MENACE
see THREATENING

MENE TEKEL
71 P 22   During Belshazzar's banquet a hand
appears and writes on the wall (MENE, MENE,
TEKEL and PARSIN(UPHARSIN)); King Belshazzar
is frightened

MENORAH
see CANDLESTICK

MERIBAH
71 E 12 6   Moses striking water from the rock

MESACH
see MISAEL

MESSAGE
see LETTER (EPISTLE)
see MESSENGER

MESSENGER(S)
see also BEFORE
see also REPORTING
71 C 21 1   Eliezer taking the oath: Abraham
sends him to his relatives in Mesopotamia
to find a wife for Isaac
71 H 46 3   Abner, fetched by Joab's messengers,
is taken aside by Joab in the gate of
Hebron, and is killed by him with a sword
71 L 24 52   Hezekiah welcomes the messengers
and shows them his wealth

METAMORPHOSIS
see TRANSFORMATION

MICHAEL
71 E 46 4   The contest of St Michael and Satan
for the body of Moses on Mount Nebo

MICHAL
71 H 16 32   David escapes through a window;
Michal lets him down with the help of a
rope
71 H 62 71   David brings the ark into
Jerusalem, Michal looking through a window

MIDIAN(ITES)
71 E 11 31 5   Moses flees to Midian

MILITIA
see SOLDIER(S)

MILK
see SUCKLING

MINISTERING
see SERVANT(S)

MIRACLE
see also HEALING
see also RAISING FROM THE DEAD
71 E 11 64   Moses and Aaron before Pharaoh;
Aaron performs the miracle of the rod
changing into a snake
71 E 12 5   Miracle of the manna and the quail
- Exodus
71 E 52 23 2   While the priests with the ark
stay in the middle of the Jordan and the
waters are miraculously damned, the
Israelites cross the river
71 N 71   During a funeral a band of ransacking
Moabites is seen approaching and the corpse
is thrown hastily into Elisha's tomb; when
it touches Elisha's bones the man comes
back to life

MIRACULOUS HEALING
see HEALING

MIRIAM
71 E 11 23   Moses is exposed on the banks of
the Nile; Miriam, Moses' sister, keeps watch
71 E 12 32   Miriam takes up a tambourine and
dances; all the women follow her

MIRROR
see TOILET (MAKING)

MIRTH
see LAUGHING

MISAEL
11 I 62(THREE HEBREWS) 21   The three Babylonian
youths Ananias (Shedrach), Azarias (Abed-
nego), Misael (Mesach) invoked in distress,
and for resurrections
71 P 13   The story of the three Hebrews in
the fiery furnace

MISEMPLOYMENT
see ABUSE

MISFORTUNE
11 I 62(THREE HEBREWS) 21   The three Babylonian
youths Ananias (Shedrach), Azarias (Abed-
nego), Misael (Mesach) invoked in distress,
and for resurrections

MISHANDLING
see MALTREATING

MISLEADING
see DISGUISE

MISUSE
see ABUSE

MOAB(ITES)
71 N 71   During a funeral a band of ransacking
Moabites is seen approaching and the corpse
is thrown hastily into Elisha's tomb; when
it touches Elisha's bones the man comes
back to life

MOCKING
see also INSULTING
see also LAUGHING
71 B 35 21   The mocking of Noah: Ham finds
his father (partially) naked sleeping out
of doors (or in his tent, or in the vineyard
cottage); Ham calls his brothers
71 B 35 21 1   Shem and Japheth cover their
father Noah; Ham usually stands nearby
deriding him
71 W 54 4   Job is derided by his friends (and
his wife) for refusing to give up his faith

MONARCHY
see KINGSHIP

MONEY
see also GOLD(EN)
see also PAYING
see also SILVER (PIECE OF)
71 D 17 71   At their camp one of Joseph's
brothers finds money in his sack
71 F 37 4   Delilah finds out Samson's secret
and warns the Philistines, who come with
the money

MONEY-BOX
71 F 83 62   The Ark of the Covenant and the
box with the guilt offering, drawn by two
cows, sent back to Israel

MONSTER(S)
see also DEVIL(S)
see also DRAGON
see also SEA-MONSTER
71 W 52 1   Job is smitten from head to foot
with sores by Satan, or dragon-like monsters
that blow poisonous smoke on Job

MONSTROSITY(S)
   see MONSTER

MONTH
   71 B 25   Story of Enoch, son of Jared, who
             invented letters and was the first to divide
             the year into seasons and into twelve months

MOON
   71 A 24   Creation of sun, moon and stars
   71 E 52 94 2   Joshua orders the sun and the
             moon to stand still over Gibeon and Aijalon
             until the Amorites who had besieged the
             city of Gibeon are routed

MORDECAI
   71 Q   - Story of Esther

MORIAH
   71 C 13 11   Abraham with Isaac, an ass and
             the servants on their way to Moriah

MORTALITY
   see DEATH

MOSES
   11 I 62(MOSES)   Moses (not in biblical context)
   71 E 1-71 E 4   Story of Moses and Aaron -
             Exodus

MOTHER AND CHILD
   see also PARENTS
   71 I 32   The judgement of Solomon

MOULDING
   71 E 13 52   Aaron makes a golden calf and has
             it placed on a pedestal or altar

MOUNTAIN(S)
   see also HILL(S)
   71 B 33 2   The ark of Noah comes to rest on
             Mount Ararat
   71 C 12 51   Lot, seeing the destruction of
             the cities and fearing for his safety in
             Zoar, flees with his daughters to a cave
             in the mountains
   71 C 13 11 1   The servants are left behind
             while Abraham and Isaac (usually carrying
             wood) climb the mountain
   71 E 13   Exodus (part III): conclusion of
             the Sinaitic law and its renewal
   71 E 13 4   Moses on Mount Sinai with the tables
             of the law
   71 E 46 1   Moses from Mount Nebo views the
             promised land
   71 E 46 4   The contest of St. Michael and Satan
             for the body of Moses on Mount Nebo
   71 F 24 54   Jephthah's daughter retreats to
             the mountains with her companions to bewail
             her virginity

MOUNTING
   see ASCENDING

MOURNING
   see also FUNERAL
   see also GRIEVING
   see also LAMENTING
   see also TEARING ONE'S CLOTHES
   71 A 82 3   Adam and Eve discover the dead body
             of Abel and grieve over it
   71 C 13 2 1   Abraham mourning Sarah

MOVING
   see also TRAVELLING
   71 C 11 45   Abraham leaves Egypt with Sarah,
             Lot and his possessions
   71 C 31 84   Jacob on the way to Canaan with
             his family, his flocks, camels and all his
             possessions

MUG
   see CUP

MULE
   see also ASS
   71 H 84 9   Absalom, put to flight on a mule,
             remains hanging by his hair in an oak-tree

MULTIPLYING
   71 N 15   A hundred men are fed with twenty
             loaves of bread: Elisha receives barley
             bread of the first-fruits and a sack of
             corn which he multiplies to feed a hundred
             men

MURDERING
   see also KILLING
   71 H 81 5   Amnon is murdered at Absalom's
             banquet
   71 K 35 1   Zechariah is assassinated by Shallum

MURRAIN
   71 E 11 72 5   The plague of murrain in cattle:
             all the animals of the Egyptians die

MUSIC MAKING
   see also MUSICIAN
   see also SINGING
   11 I 62(DAVID) 32   David as musician, usually
             playing the harp
   11 I 62(DAVID) 33   David as psalmist, as author
             of the psalms, usually playing the harp
   71 E 52 42   The Israelites march around
             Jericho: in the procession the main body
             of the soldiers comes first, next are seven
             priests who blow on trumpets, followed by
             the priests carrying the ark and a rear
             guard
   71 H 13 6   David playing his harp before Saul
   71 H 15 21   David's triumph: the women of
             Israel come out to welcome David, singing,
             dancing, and playing tambourines and lyres;
             David holding the head of Goliath
   71 H 15 3   Saul casts his spear at David when
             the latter is playing his harp before the
             king
   71 H 62 2   The ark is placed on a cart driven
             by the sons of Abinadab; David and the
             people dance and make music before the ark
   71 H 62 7   David brings the ark into Jerusalem,
             dancing (half-)naked before the ark and
             making music, while the people rejoice
   71 H 88 32   Solomon anointed king by Zadok;
             all the people rejoice and blow their
             trumpets
   71 P 13 2   The dedication of the golden statue:
             in the presence of King Nebuchadnezzar,
             trumpets are blown and all the people
             surrounding the image fall on their knees
   71 W 56   Job on the dunghill visited by the
             musicians

MUSICAL INSTRUMENT(S)
   see MUSIC MAKING

MUSICIAN
   see also MUSIC MAKING
   71 W 56   Job on the dunghill visited by the
             musicians

MUSTERING
   see ASSEMBLING

MUTINY
   see REBELLION

NABAL
    71 H 24 5   The banquet in Nabal's house

NABOTH
    71 K 27 4   Naboth's vineyard (-King Ahab)

NABUCHODONOSOR
    see NEBUCHADNEZZAR

NAIL (SPIKE)
    71 F 15 43   Jael takes a nail of the tent and
        a hammer
    71 F 15 44   Jael kills the sleeping Sisera
        by hitting the nail through his temples

NAKED
    71 A 42 4   Adam and Eve discover their
        nakedness; they cover themselves with their
        hands or with leaves
    71 B 35 21   The mocking of Noah: Ham finds
        his father (partially) naked sleeping out
        of doors (or in his tent, or in the vineyard
        cottage); Ham calls his brothers
    71 H 62 7   David brings the ark into Jerusalem,
        dancing (half-)naked before the ark and
        making music, while the people rejoice
    71 V 22   After a three-day sojourn in the belly
        of the monster Jonah is cast on dry land;
        Jonah may be shown nude and bald-headed

NAME
    71 A 33 3   Adam naming the animals
    71 C 32 22 1   Jacob receives a new name,
        Israel, and is blessed by the angel

NANNY-GOAT
    see GOAT

NAOMI
    71 F 6   - The story of Ruth

NATHAN
    71 H 76   David rebuked by Nathan

NEBO (MOUNT)
    71 E 46 1   Moses from Mount Nebo views the
        promised land

NEBUCHADNEZZAR
    71 P 13   The story of the three Hebrews in
        the fiery furnace

NEMROD
    see NIMROD

NEWS
    see REPORTING

NIGHT
    see also DARKNESS
    see also WEDDING-NIGHT
    71 E 11 81   During the night Pharaoh sends
        for Moses and Aaron and begs them to depart
    71 E 12 12 2   By night a pillar of fire gives
        the Israelites light
    71 F 65 6   The conversation of Ruth and Boaz
        in the night
    71 H 25 2   David and Abishai invade Saul's
        encampment at night, while Saul and his
        soldiers are sleeping

NILE
    71 E 11 23   Moses is exposed in the ark on
        the banks of the Nile; Miriam, Moses'
        sister, keeps watch
    71 E 11 72 1   The plague of water turned into
        blood: as Pharaoh goes down to the Nile,
        Aaron strikes the surface of the river with
        his rod; the water turns into blood and
        all the fish die
    71 E 11 72 2   The plague of frogs: Aaron
        stretches out his hand over the water of
        Egypt; frogs come out and cover the land

NIMBUS (AUREOLE)
    see RAY OF LIGHT

NIMROD
    71 B 42 1   The building of the Tower of Babel;
        Nimrod may be present, supervising or
        assisting the construction

NOAH
    71 B 3   Story of Noah

NOAH'S SONS
    71 B 32 11   Noah building the ark with the
        help of his sons
    71 B 35 21   The mocking of Noah: Ham finds
        his father (partially) naked sleeping out
        of doors (or in his tent, or in the vineyard
        cottage); Ham calls his brothers

NOCTURNAL
    see NIGHT

NOSTRILS
    see ANIMATING

NUDE
    see NAKED

NUMBERS
    71 E 3   Numbers: the wandering in the
        wilderness, the Israelites leave Mount Sinai
        and reach Canaan

NURSING
    see HEALING

OAK
71 H 84 9   Absalom, put to flight on a mule, remains hanging by his hair in an oak-tree

OATH
71 C 21 1   Eliezer taking the oath: Abraham sends him to this relatives in Mesopotamia to find a wife for Isaac
71 G 23   Saul's oath: a day of fasting

OBADIAH (PROPHET)
11 I 62(OBADIAH)   Obadiah (not in biblical context)

OBJECTING
see also COMPLAINING
71 I 32 6   The true mother objects to Solomon's verdict

OFFENDING
see INSULTING

OFFERING
see also DEDICATION
see also GIVING
see also REFUSING (GIFT, OFFER)
see also SACRIFICING
71 A 42 2   Eve offers the fruit to Adam
71 C 11 7   The meeting of Abraham and Melchizedek, the high priest and king of Salem, who brings bread and wine
71 C 21 31 1   Rebekah offers Eliezer a drink from her pitcher
71 E 13 81   The people bring their offerings for the Tabernacle: all kinds of fine objects, jewelry, linen, etc.
71 H 24 42   Meeting of David and Abigail, who kneels before him
71 T 79   Tobias and his father offer gifts to the angel

OFFICER
71 K 29 42-71 K 29 46   Jehu plots Jehoram's death with his fellow-officers

OIL (BOILING)
see CAULDRON

OIL-LAMP
see LAMP

OINTMENT
see ANOINTING

OLD AGE
see OLD MAN

OLD LAW
see OLD TESTAMENT

OLD MAN
see also ELDER(S)
71 D 24   Jacob's last days
71 D 26   Later years of Joseph
71 F 52 2   The Levite and his concubine in a street in Gibeah are offered lodging by an old man
71 K 21 43   Jeroboam's wife in disguise visits the old and blind Ahijah, but he, having been warned by God, recognizes her; he predicts the death of her son and Israel's punishment for Jeroboam's sin
71 T 74   Old Tobit (and Anna) waiting and worrying about the long absence of their son; sometimes Anna is shown at the spinning-wheel

OLD TESTAMENT
11 I 6   Persons from the Old Testament (not in biblical context)
11 I 62(...)   Male persons from the Old Testament (with NAME)(not in biblical context)
11 I 63(...)   Female persons from the Old Testament (with NAME)(not in biblical context)
71   Old Testament
71 X 1(Ps....)1   The book of Psalms - scenes from the Old Testament

OMEN
see SIGN

OMER OF MANNA
71 E 12 54 21   The jar with the 'omer' of manna

OPEN
see OPENING

OPEN-AIR
see OUTDOOR

OPENING
71 B 34 1   God orders Noah to disembark and opens the ark
71 D 16 42 11   Joseph opens the storehouse and sells corn
71 E 31 74 2   The ground opens and swallows the rebels Dathan and Abiram along with their families and possessions

OPPOSITION
see OBJECTING

ORDEAL
71 P 13 3   After the furnace has been heated seven times more, the three Hebrews are bound and thrown into the fire; their executioners are burnt by the flames
71 P 13 5   Shadrach, Mesach, and Abed-nego are examined; they prove to be unharmed by the fire, whereupon King Nebuchadnezzar decrees that no one may criticize them

ORDER
see ORDERING
see PEACE

ORDERING
see also INSTRUCTING
71 B 31 21   God announces a flood and commands Noah to build an ark
71 B 34 1   God orders Noah to disembark and opens the ark
71 C 12 24 2   Abraham orders the preparation of a calf and other food
71 E 52 94 2   Joshua orders the sun and the moon to stand still over Gibeon and Aijalon until the Amorites who had beseiged the city of Gibeon are routed
71 G 36   Samuel summons Agag to be brought before him
71 H 32 21   Saul orders his armour-bearer to kill him, but he refuses
71 H 54 63   By the command of God the angel stops destroying the Israelites at the threshing-floor of Araunah (Ornan) the Jebusite
71 I 32 5   Solomon gives verdict; he commands a soldier to divide the living child in two
71 P 13 4   To his astonishment King Nebuchadnezzar sees four men (one of them usually represented as an angel) in the the furnace; the king commands them to come forth
71 V 22 1   Jonah again receives from God the command to preach in Nineveh

ORDINATION
    see DEDICATION

ORGY
    see FEAST

ORIGIN
    71 A 1   'In the beginning...' the ordering
        of chaos

ORNAMENT(S)
    see JEWELS

ORNAN
    see ARAUNAH

ORPAH
    71 F 6   - The story of Ruth

OUTDOOR
    71 B 35 21   The mocking of Noah: Ham finds
        his father (partially) naked sleeping out
        of doors (or in his tent, or in the vineyard
        cottage); Ham calls his brothers

OVEN
    see FURNACE

OVERBOARD
    71 V 13 4   The sailors reluctantly throw the
        prophet Jonah into the sea

OVERHEARING
    71 C 12 24 3   The promise of a son is renewed;
        Sarah, overhearing it, laughs incredulously

OVERSEER
    see also TASKMASTER
    71 D 16 1   Pharaoh takes off his signet-ring
        and puts it on Joseph's finger; Joseph is
        appointed overseer

OVERTAKING
    see PURSUING

OX
    see also CATTLE
    71 W 31 11   The theft of Job's oxen and asses
        by the Sabeans

OZIAS
    71 U 41 1   Judith, the widow of Manasseh,
        speaks with the elders Ozias, Chabris, and
        Charmis

PACKING
    see PREPARATIONS - DEPARTURE

PAGAN STATUE(S)
    see IDOL(S)

PAGANISM
    see IDOLATRY

PAGE (SERVANT)
    see SERVANT

PAGEANT
    see PROCESSION
    see TRIUMPH

PAIL
    see BUCKET

PAIN
    see SUFFERING
    see TORTURING
    see WOUNDED PERSON

PALACE
    see also BEFORE
    see also COURT
    71 C 11 43   Sarah attracts the attention of
        the Egyptians and is taken to Pharaoh's
        palace
    71 H 51 4   The building of David's palace
    71 H 71   David, from the roof (or balcony)
        of his palace, sees Bathsheba bathing
    71 H 71 4   Bathsheba comes to David's palace
    71 Q 73   Mordecai's triumph: Mordecai, mounted
        on the king's horse, is led through the
        city by Haman (Esther and Ahasuerus may
        be looking on from the palace)

PALM OF THE HAND
    see HAND

PALM-TREE
    71 F 15 1   Deborah (sitting under a palmtree)
        beseeches Barak to attack Sisera and his
        army

PAPER
    see DOCUMENT
    see LETTER (EPISTLE)
    see WRITING

PARADISE
    see EDEN
    see GARDEN
    see HEAVEN

PARALYSIS
    see CRIPPLE

PARDONING
    see FORGIVING

PARENTS
    see also FAMILY
    see also FATHER...
    see also MOTHER...
    71 C 21 42   Gifts of clothing, gold and jewelry
        are offered to Rebekah's parents
    71 F 32 73   Samson gives some of the honey
        he found in the lion's carcass to his
        parents

PARK
    see GARDEN

PARRICIDE
    see FATHER...

PARTING
    see DIVIDING
    see LEAVE-TAKING
    see SEPARATING

PARTNER
    71 C 31 6   The partnership with Laban - story
    of Jacob

PARTURITION
    see BIRTH

PARTY (FEAST)
    see FEAST

PASSION
    see LOVE AT FIRST SIGHT
    see LOVE UNREQUITED
    see LOVER(S)

PASSOVER
    71 E 11 73 13   Celebration of the first
    Passover
    71 E 11 73 13 2   The Israelites eat the
    Passover lamb standing about a table with
    their loins girt, their shoes on their feet
    and with staves in their hands, ready to
    depart

PATIENT
    see SICK PERSON

PATRIARCH(S)
    11 I 61 1   Patriarchs from the Old Testament
    (not in biblical context)
    11 I 62(ABRAHAM) 11   Abraham as father of all
    believers
    71 C   The patriarchs

PATRON
    see PROTECTOR

PAYING
    see also MONEY
    71 C 31 61   Laban agrees to give Jacob all
    the black and spotted sheep and goats as
    wages
    71 F 37 71   Samson is tormented by the
    Philistines, Delilah is paid

PEACE
    see also RECONCILIATION
    71 O 33 4   Isaiah's prophecy of the peaceable
    kingdom: 'the wolf shall dwell with the
    lamb'

PEASANT
    see FARMER

PEDESTAL
    71 E 13 52   Aaron makes a golden calf and has
    it placed on a pedestal or altar

PEEPING
    see SPYING

PEG
    71 F 15 43   Jael takes a nail of the tent and
    a hammer
    71 F 15 44   Jael kills the sleeping Sisera
    by hitting the nail through his temples

PELT
    see HIDE

PENANCE
    71 A 63   Adam and Eve doing penance

PENITENCE
    see PENANCE
    see REPENTING

PEOPLE (THE)
    see MANKIND

PERJURY
    see ACCUSING

PERMISSION
    71 D 18 1   Judah persuades the afflicted Jacob
    to consent to the departure of Benjamin

PERSECUTING
    see PURSUING

PERSONNEL
    see SERVANT(S)

PERSUADING
    see also PLEADING
    71 A 41 1   The serpent tries to persuade Eve
    to take some of the fruit (usually an apple)
    71 C 11 93 2   An angel meets Hagar at the
    fountain on the way to Shur and persuades
    her to return
    71 D 18 1   Judah persuades the afflicted Jacob
    to consent to the departure of Benjamin

PERVERSITY
    see WICKEDNESS

PESACH
    see PASSOVER

PEST-SORE
    see BOIL(S)

PESTILENCE
    see PLAGUE

PETITION
    see ASKING

PETRIFYING
    see STONE

PHARAOH
    71 C 11 44 1   Abraham honored with gifts by
    Pharaoh
    71 D 14 6   The fulfilment of the dreams:
    Pharaoh restores the butler to his former
    position, but has the baker hanged - story
    of Joseph
    71 D 16 1   Pharaoh takes off his signet-ring
    and puts it on Joseph's finger; Joseph is
    appointed overseer
    71 D 22 4   Jacob is presented to Pharaoh by
    Joseph
    71 E 11 27 1   Moses and Pharaoh's crown:
    Pharaoh playfully places his crown on the
    head of the infant Moses, who throws it
    to the ground and tramples on it; or Moses
    breaks the crown while playing
    71 E 11 64   Moses and Aaron before Pharaoh;
    Aaron performs the miracle of the rod
    changing into a snake
    71 E 11 7   The ten plagues (- Exodus)
    71 E 11 81   During the night Pharaoh sends
    for Moses and Aaron and begs them to depart
    71 E 12 23 1   Pharaoh and his army engulfed
    in the Red Sea (Israelites not or barely
    visible)

PHARAOH'S DAUGHTER
    71 E 11 24   The finding of Moses: Pharaoh's
    daughter comes to bathe with her maidens
    in the river and discovers the child
    floating on the water
    71 E 11 26   When Moses is old enough, his
    mother brings him to Pharaoh's daughter,
    who adopts him

PHIAL
    see FLASK

INDEX

PHILISTINES
71 F 34   Samson in conflict with the
Philistines
71 F 35 4   With an ass' jaw-bone Samson slays
a thousand Philistines
71 H 32   Battle between the Israelites and
the Philistines

PHRYGIAN BONNET
11 I 62(DANIEL)   Attributes of Daniel

PHYSICIAN
see HEALING

PIERCING
see STABBING

PIGEON
see DOVE

PILLAGING
see PLUNDERING

PILLAR
see also PILLAR OF CLOUD
see also PILLAR OF FIRE
71 E 13 53   Adoration of the golden calf (which
may be standing on a pillar, and is
sometimes depicted as a dragon)
71 E 32 43   Anyone who is bitten by a snake
is cured by looking at the brazen serpent;
the serpent (or dragon) is usually depicted
on a tau-shaped cross or on a pillar
71 F 38 3   Samson breaks the pillars; the
temple of Dagon collapses, killing all that
are in it

PILLAR OF CLOUD
71 E 12 12   The pillar of cloud and the pillar
of fire - Exodus
71 E 12 22 1   The people pass over on dry land
(Egyptians not or barely visible); the angel
of God and the pillar of cloud may be shown
at the rear

PILLAR OF FIRE
71 E 12 12   The pillar of cloud and the pillar
of fire - Exodus

PINCERS
see TONGS

PINING AWAY
see GRIEVING

PIT
see also WELL
71 D 12 41   Joseph is thrown into a pit
(usually depicted as a well or cistern)
71 D 12 51   Joseph is pulled out of the pit
71 H 52 64   Benaiah kills two men, and then
a lion, in a pit on a snowy day

PITCHER
see JUG

PLAGUE
71 E 11 7   The ten plagues (- Exodus)

PLAIN
see FIELD(S)

PLAN (DESIGN)
see DESIGN

PLANT(S)
71 A 23   Gathering of the waters below the
firmament; dry land appears and produces
all kinds of plants
71 V 42   The prophet Jonah withdraws from
Nineveh; he builds a booth and while
enjoying the shade of a plant (gourd or
vine) which God made grow for him, he awaits
the destiny of the city

PLAYING
see also MUSIC-MAKING
71 A 72 1   Adam engaged in agricultural
activities, Eve spinning and usually their
children at play
71 E 11 27 1   Moses and Pharaoh's crown:
Pharaoh playfully places his crown on the
head of the infant Moses, who throws it
to the ground and tramples on it; or Moses
breaks the crown while playing

PLAYING (MUSICAL INSTRUMENT)
see MUSIC-MAKING

PLEADING
see also PERSUADING
71 D 19 3   The brothers before Joseph: Judah
pleads for Benjamin and offers to be
retained as a slave in his stead
71 P 41 4   The youth Daniel opposes the verdict
against Susanna

PLEDGING
see PROMISING

PLOUGHING
71 A 72   Adam (and Eve) engaged in agricultural
activities

PLUNDERING
see also DESTRUCTION
71 L 32 32   The temple of Jerusalem is looted
- story of Zedekiah

POET
11 I 62(DAVID) 33   David as psalmist, as author
of the psalms, usually playing the harp

POINTING
see SHOWING

POISON
see also BITING
71 E 32 41   When the people complain again
about the food, God sends poisonous snakes;
many dies of snake-bites - book of Numbers
71 W 52 1   Job is smitten from head to foot
with sores by Satan, or dragon-like monsters
that blow poisonous smoke on Job

POLE
see CARRYING-POLE

PORK
71 Z 35   Martyrdom of Eleazar: the old man
is forced to eat pork and voluntarily
submits to the flogging

POT
see also CAULDRON
see also JAR
71 E 12 54 1   The gathering of manna (in
baskets and pots)

POTSHERD(S)
see also BREAKING
71 W 51   Job covered with sores (or boils)
takes his abode on a dunghill (pile of
ashes) and scrapes his body with a potsherd

POURING
    see also JUG
    71 F 84 12 1   Water is poured out before God
        - Samuel as judge

POWER
    71 A 35 3   Adam is given dominion over all
        created things

PRAYING
    71 C 32 13   Jacob prays to God to save him
        from Esau
    71 H 54 62   David sees the avenging angel in
        Jerusalem; he prays to God
    71 H 61 1   David communicating with God; David
        praying (in general)
    71 H 77 2   David repentant; he lies on the
        ground praying and fasting for his child
        to recover
    71 H 93   David's prayer of thanks
    71 I 31   Solomon's prayer for wisdom
    71 I 43 23 4   Prayer of Solomon; Solomon kneels
        before the altar
    71 L 24 41   King Hezekiah falls ill and is
        visited by Isaiah, who tells him to get
        ready to die; Hezekiah turns his face to
        the wall, prays and then cries
    71 M 43 21   As Elijah prays, God sends fire
        which burns up not only his sacrifice but
        also the altar itself; the people fall
        prostrate
    71 U 42 72   Judith prays before killing
        Holofernes
    71 Z 41   Judas Maccabeus praying for the dead

PRECIOUS STONE(S)
    see JEWELS

PREPARATIONS
    71 C 13 12   Preparations for the sacrifice,
        e.g. Abraham binding Isaac
    71 E 13 22   The people get ready for the coming
        legislation: they wash their clothes and
        set bounds round the mountain
    71 E 13 8   Preparation and setting up of the
        Tabernacle and its accessories - Exodus

PREPARATIONS - BATTLE, WAR
    71 C 11 65   Abraham calls all the men in his
        camp together and sets out in pursuit of
        the four kings

PREPARATIONS - DEPARTURE
    71 C 21 44   The leave-taking of Rebekah; Laban
        gives her provisions
    71 E 11 73 13 2   The Israelites eat the
        Passover lamb standing about a table with
        their loins girt, their shoes on their feet
        and with staves in their hands, ready to
        depart

PREPARATIONS - FEAST, MEAL
    71 C 12 24 2   Abraham orders the preparation
        of a calf and other food

PRESENTING A PERSON
    see also BEFORE
    71 D 22 4   Jacob is presented to Pharaoh by
        Joseph
    71 F 81 32   Samuel in the temple at Shiloh
        presented to Eli by Hannah
    71 Q 23 3   Esther is presented to King
        Ahasuerus

PRESENTING
    see INTERVENING

PRIEST
    see also HIGH PRIEST
    71 E 52 22   The Israelites leave their camp
        to cross the Jordan; the priests, carrying
        the ark, lead the march
    71 E 52 42   The Israelites march around
        Jericho: in the procession the main body
        of the soldiers comes first, next are seven
        priests who blow on trumpets, followed by
        the priests carrying the ark and a rear
        guard
    71 M 4   Elijah defies the priests of Baal;
        the end of the drought

PRISON
    71 D 13 5   Joseph is arrested and sent to
        prison
    71 D 14   - Story of Joseph in prison
    71 D 17 31   Joseph accuses his brothers of
        being spies and throws them in prison
    71 L 31 3   When Evilmerodach becomes king of
        Babylon, Jehoiachin is released from prison
        and permitted to dine at the king's table
        for the rest of his life
    71 O 76 62   Jeremiah's imprisonment

PRISONER
    see also CAPTIVE
    see also RELEASING
    71 F 37 7   Samson wakes up and finds his hair
        and strength gone; he is taken prisoner
    71 P 41 32   Susanna is led away to be executed

PROCESSION
    71 D 25 2   Joseph has his father's corpse
        brought to Canaan with great pomp

PROCLAMATION
    see also DECREE
    71 D 16 2   Triumph of Joseph: dressed in royal
        attire he rides in one of Pharaoh's
        chariots, preceded by a herald
    71 L 18 1   Joash is proclaimed king at the
        age of seven
    71 P 14 5   King Nebuchadnezzar is restored
        to the throne and in a proclamation he makes
        known what has happened to him

PROFANATION
    see DESECRATION

PROMISING
    71 C 12 24 3   The promise of a son is renewed;
        Sarah, overhearing it, laughs incredulously

PROMOTION
    71 D 16   Elevation and marriage of Joseph
    71 Q 87   Mordecai's advancement

PROPHESYING
    71 K 21 43   Jeroboam's wife in disguise visits
        the old and blind Ahijah, but he, having
        been warned by God, recognizes her; he
        predicts the death of her son and Israel's
        punishment for Jeroboam's sin
    71 L 24 41   King Hezekiah falls ill and is
        visited by Isaiah, who tells him to get
        ready to die; Hezekiah turns his face to
        the wall, prays and then cries
    71 N 61 1   Elisha tells Joash to shoot an arrow
        through the window towards Syria and
        predicts that Joash will be victorious
    71 V 31   When Jonah arrives in the city of
        Nineveh he foretells its destruction in
        forty days

PROPHET
    see also PROPHESYING
    71 I 72   Meeting of Jeroboam and the prophet
      Ahijah; Ahijah rends his garment in twelve
      pieces, ten of which he gives to Jeroboam
    71 M   Story of Elijah (Elias)
    71 N   Story of Elisha (Eliseus)
    71 O   Prophets before and during the Babylonian
      Captivity (Amos, Hosea, Isaiah, Micah,
      Zephaniah, Habakkuk, Jeremiah, Nahum,
      Ezekiel)
    71 P   The story of the prophet Daniel; his
      visions and prophecies
    71 P 43 33   The prophet Habakkuk, carried by
      his hair by an angel, brings food to Daniel
      who sits unharmed between the lions

PROPOSAL
    71 c 21   Rebekah (Rebecca) sought in marriage

PROSTRATION
    see also KNEELING
    see also PRAYING
    71 H 31 52   The ghost of Samuel appears to
      the witch of Endor; Saul falls prostrate
      to the ground
    71 H 77 2   David repentant; he lies on the
      ground praying and fasting for his child
      to recover
    71 M 43 21   As Elijah prays, God sends fire
      which burns up not only his sacrifice but
      also the altar itself; the people fall
      prostrate
    71 N 13 33   Gehazi fetches the Shunammite
      woman; when she sees her child alive she
      falls at Elisha's feet
    71 Q 74 21   As Haman is kneeling at Esther's
      feet or is prostrated on her couch King
      Ahasuerus returns; Haman is condemned to
      be hanged
    71 Q 82   Esther entreating Ahasuerus: she falls
      at the king's feet and asks him to revoke
      the decree against the Jews; the king holds
      out his sceptre to her (Esther may be
      holding the decree)
    71 T 79 1   The angel makes himself known;
      Tobias and his family lie down

PROTECTION
    71 F 65   Naomi advises Ruth to seek Boaz'
      protection

PROTECTOR
    11 I 62(THREE HEBREWS) 21   The three Babylonian
      youths Ananias (Shedrach), Azarias (Abed-
      nego), Misael (Mesach) invoked in distress,
      and for resurrections

PROTEST
    see OBJECTING

PROVING
    see ORDEAL

PROVISIONS
    see FOOD

PROVOKING
    see INSULTING

PSALMS (BOOK OF)
    71 X 1   The book of Psalms

PSALTERY
    see LYRE

PUBLIC FESTIVITIES
    see FEAST(S)

PUBLIC HOUSE
    see INN

PULLEY
    71 D 12 41 1   Joseph is lowered into a pit
      by means of ropes or a pulley

PULLING
    see also HOISTING
    see also RESCUING
    71 T 56   Tobias captures the fish and pulls
      it on the land

PUNISHMENT
    see also BEATING
    see also SCOURGING
    71 A 54   The punishment of Adam and Eve
    71 E 13 6   The punishment - adoration of the
      golden calf
    71 E 24   The blasphemer's punishment -
      Leviticus
    71 E 31 7   Rebellion of Korah (Core), Dathan
      and Abiram, and their punishment
    71 F 83 51 2   God punishes the inhabitants
      of Ashdod with emerods or boils
    71 H 92 1   David instructs Solomon to punish
      Joab
    71 H 92 2   David instructs Solomon to punish
      Shimei
    71 N 16 3   Gehazi's punishment

PUPIL(S)
    see TEACHING

PURCHASING
    see BUYING

PURIFICATION
    71 N 11   The water of Jericho is purified:
      when the citizens of Jericho complain about
      their water, Elisha puts some salt into
      a jar; he then throws the salt into the
      water
    71 N 14   The deadly pottage: Elisha purifies
      the poisoned pottage by throwing flour into
      it
    71 O 32 2   Purification of Isaiah: an angel
      touches Isaiah's lips with a burning coal,
      taken from the altar with tongs - Isaiah's
      visions
    71 Z 38   Second purification of the temple
      - Maccabees

PURSUING
    see also FLEEING
    71 C 11 65   Abraham calls all the men in his
      camp together and sets out in pursuit of
      the four kings

PUSHING
    see THROWING (BEING THROWN)

PUTTING ON SHOES
    see SANDAL(S)
    see SHOE(S)

QUEEN
    11 I 63(SHEBA)   Sheba (not in biblical context)
    71 I 33   Solomon and the queen of Sheba
    71 Q 2   Esther becomes queen
    71 Q 21   The feast of Ahasuerus (Xerxes,
        alternatively Artaxerxes); the downfall
        of Queen Vashti (Astin)

QUEST
    see SEARCHING

QUESTION
    see ASKING

QUESTIONING
    see INTERROGATION

QUIVER
    see ARROW(S)

RACHEL
    71 C 31 3-71 C 32 6   - Story of Jacob

RADIANCE
    see RAY OF LIGHT

RAG(S)
    see also TEARING ONE'S CLOTHES
    71 H 23 6   When Saul comes out of the cave,
        David calls him, falls down on his knees
        and shows him the piece of cloth

RAGE
    see ANGER

RAGUEL
    71 T 6-71 T 7   - Story of Tobias

RAIDING
    see ATTACKING

RAIN
    71 E 12 54   In the morning manna falls to the
        earth - Exodus

RAINBOW
    71 B 34 2   Noah, his family and the animals
        leave the ark (sometimes combined with the
        rainbow of the covenant)
    71 B 34 3   Noah's sacrifice; various animals
        are offered, possibly a lamb, a dove and
        a ram (often combined with the rainbow of
        the covenant)
    71 B 34 31 1   God's covenant with Noah: never
        again shall there be a flood; as a sign
        of this covenant God puts a rainbow in the
        sky

RAISED ARMS (HANDS)
    see ARM(S) RAISED

RAISING (UPBRINGING)
    see UPBRINGING

RAISING A STORM
    see STORM AT SEA

RAISING FROM THE DEAD
    see also RESURRECTION
    71 N 13 3   Raising of the Shunammite woman's
        son

RAM
    71 B 34 3   Noah's sacrifice; various animals
        are offered, possibly a lamb, a dove and
        a ram (often combined with the rainbow of
        the covenant)
    71 C 13 14   A ram caught in a thicket is
        sacrificed instead of Isaac
    71 C 13 14 1   The ram of the sacrifice -
        sacrifice of Isaac
    71 P 52 1   The ram with two unequal horns near
        a river - Daniel's visions

RAMESES
    71 E 11 8   The Israelites leave Egypt; first
        movement from Rameses to Succoth

RAPE (VIOLATION)
    see VIOLATING

RAPHAEL
    71 T 4-71 T 7   The angel Raphael - the book
        of Tobit

RAVEN
    71 M 12   Elijah fed by the raven(s): while
        the prophet is living by the brook, ravens
        bring him food

RAVISHING
    see VIOLATING

RAY OF LIGHT
see also LIGHT
71 C 31 21 2   Dream of Jacob, with beam of
light instead of ladder
71 E 13 74   Moses comes down with the new
tablets and is awaited by Aaron and the
assembled people, who notice that 'his face
is shining' (Moses' face is depicted with
rays of light or with horns)

REACHING
see also ARM(S) STRETCHED
see also TOUCHING
71 A 31 1   The man (Adam) comes to life:
usually God reaches out his hand or breathes
life into his nostrils

READINESS
see PREPARATIONS

REALM
see KINGDOM

REAPING
see GATHERING

REARING (UPBRINGING)
see UPBRINGING

REBECCA
see REBEKAH

REBEKAH
11 I 63(REBEKAH)   Rebekah (not in biblical
context)
71 C 2   - Story of Isaac

REBELLION
71 E 31 7   Rebellion of Korah (Core), Dathan
and Abiram, and their punishment

REBUKING
71 A 53   Adam and Eve reproved by God
71 D 24 21   Jacob blesses Manasseh and Ephraim
with arms crossed; Joseph may be shown
trying to uncross them or expressing (with
Asenath) his disapproval
71 G 34 2   Samuel reproving and rejecting Saul
71 H 76   David rebuked by Nathan
71 N 16 32   Elisha rebukes Gehazi and as
punishment causes him to be smitten with
Naaman's leprosy
71 V 44   When Jonah again murmurs and wishes
to die, God rebukes him

REBURIAL
see BURIAL

RECEIVING
see also GIVING
see also RECEIVING A PERSON
71 C 21 33   Rebekah receives ear-rings and
golden bracelets from Eliezer
71 E 13 43   Moses receives the tables of the
law from God
71 H 14 32   David receives Saul's armour -
story of David and Goliath

RECEIVING A PERSON
see also BEFORE
see also GUEST(S)
see also PRESENTING A PERSON
see also VISITING
71 D 18 4   When Joseph gets home, he receives
his brothers; they bow down before him and
give him the presents

RECEPTION
see RECEIVING A PERSON

RECITING
see SINGING

RECOGNIZING
see also IDENTITY
71 K 21 43   Jeroboam's wife in disguise visits
the old and blind Ahijah, but he, having
been warned by God, recognizes her; he
predicts the death of her son and Israel's
punishment for Jeroboam's sin
71 W 54 2   When Eliphaz, Bildad and Zophar
recognize Job they weep and tear their
clothes in grief

RECOMMENDATION
see PLEADING

RECONCILIATION
71 H 82 5   Reconciliation of David and Absalom;
Absalom kneels before David and they embrace

RECONNAISSANCE
see SCOUTING

RECOVERING (FINDING AGAIN)
see FINDING

RECOVERY
71 H 78   David recovers and takes a meal

RED
71 E 11 72 1   The plague of water turned into
blood: as Pharaoh goes down to the Nile,
Aaron strikes the surface of the river with
his rod; the water turns into blood and
all the fish die

REDEEMING
see BUYING

REED
71 E 11 23 1   Moses (alone) in the bulrushes

REFUSING
see FASTING
see LOVE UNREQUITED
see REFUSING (ADMISSION)
see REFUSING (GIFT, OFFER)
see REFUSING (ORDER, REQUEST)
see REFUSING (WORSHIP)
see REJECTING

REFUSING (ADMISSION)
71 F 34 1   Samson goes with a kid to his wife
and is refused entry by her father

REFUSING (GIFT, OFFER)
71 N 16 21   Naaman urges Elisha to accept some
gifts, but Elisha refuses them; Naaman asks
two mule-loads of earth

REFUSING (ORDER, REQUEST)
see also DISOBEDIENCE
see also REFUSING (WORSHIP)
71 H 32 21   Saul orders his armour-bearer to
kill him, but he refuses
71 W 54 4   Job is derided by his friends (and
his wife) for refusing to give up his faith

REFUSING (WORSHIP)
71 P 13 22   King Nebuchadnezzar calls Shadrach,
Mesach, and Abed-nego to account, but they
refuse to kneel before the golden statue

REGARDING
see LOOKING

REGRET
see REPENTING

REJECTING
    see also LOVE UNREQUITED
    see also REFUSING
    71 G 34 2   Samuel reproving and rejecting Saul

REJOICING
    see also FEAST
    see also TRIUMPH
    71 E 12 3   After crossing the Red Sea the
    Israelites rejoice and praise God
    71 G 12 5   Saul's messengers come to Jabesh-
    gilead; the people rejoice
    71 H 62 7   David brings the ark into Jerusalem,
    dancing (half-)naked before the ark and
    making music, while the people rejoice
    71 H 88 32   Solomon anointed king by Zadok;
    all the people rejoice and blow their
    trumpets

RELATIVES
    see FAMILY

RELEASING
    see also LIBERATING
    71 L 31 3   When Evilmerodach becomes king of
    Babylon, Jehoiachin is released from prison
    and permitted to dine at the king's table
    for the rest of his life
    71 O 76 62 8   Jeremiah is released from the
    dungeon

RELIGION
    see IDOLATRY

RELIGIOUS SERVICE
    see SACRIFICING

REMORSE
    see REPENTING

REMOVAL
    see MOVING

REMOVING
    71 H 32 45   The inhabitants of Jabesh-gilead
    take away the bodies of Saul and his sons

RENDING ONE'S CLOTHES
    see TEARING ONE'S CLOTHES

REPAST
    see MEAL

REPENTING
    see also GRIEVING
    71 A 51   Adam and/or Eve overcome with
    repentance
    71 H 77 2   David repentant; he lies on the
    ground praying and fasting for his child
    to recover

REPHIDIM
    71 E 12 6   Moses striking water from the rock

REPLACEMENT
    see SUBSTITUTION

REPORTING
    see also ANNOUNCING
    see also BETRAYING
    see also MESSENGER
    see also REVEALING
    71 E 31 53   The spies, except for Caleb and
    Joshua, bring startling reports which upset
    the people - reconnaissance of Canaan
    71 E 31 56   When Moses reports God's punishment
    to the people they mourn bitterly -
    reconnaissance of Canaan
    71 H 14 31   David kills a lion and a bear (or
    tells Saul about it

REPRIMANDING
    see REBUKING

REPROACHING
    see REBUKING

REPROVING
    see REBUKING

REPUDIATING
    see LOVE UNREQUITED

REQUESTING
    see ASKING

REQUITAL
    see REVENGE

RESCUING
    see also LIBERATING
    71 E 11 24 1   Moses is pulled out of the water
    by the servants

RESENTMENT
    see COMPLAINING

RESPECT
    see HONORING

RESTITUTION
    see GIVING

RESTLESSNESS
    see INQUIETUDE

RESTORATION
    see RESTORING

RESTORING
    see also GIVING
    see also HEALING
    see also RAISING FROM THE DEAD
    71 P 14 5   King Nebuchadnezzar is restored
    to the throne and in a proclamation he makes
    known what has happened to him

RESURRECTION
    see also RAISING FROM THE DEAD
    71 N 71   During a funeral a band of ransacking
    Moabites is seen approaching and the corpse
    is thrown hastily into Elisha's tomb; when
    it touches Elisha's bones the man comes
    back to life

RETALIATION
    see REVENGE

RETREATING
    see DEFEAT
    see SOLITUDE

RETURNING
    see also JOURNEY
    71 B 33 22 1   The dove returns with an olive-
    branch - story of Noah
    71 C 11 94   Hagar returns to Abraham
    71 C 27 5   Esau comes back with venison
    71 E 31 52   The spies take away some of the
    fruits of Canaan and return, usually
    carrying a large bunch of grapes on a pole
    71 F 24 53   Jephthah's daughter dances with
    tambourines to meet her father on his return
    from the battle; Jephthah rends his clothes
    in despair
    71 F 62   Naomi's return to Bethlehem
    71 F 62 2   Naomi sends away her daughters-in-
    law: Orpah returns home, Ruth stays
    71 I 33 6   The queen of Sheba sets out on the
    return journey
    71 T 7   Tobias' return
    71 U 43   Judith and her maidservant on their
    way back to Bethuliah

REVEALING
    see also BETRAYING
    see also RECOGNIZING
    71 C 12 84 11   An angel appears and reveals
       a well of water to Hagar
    71 D 19 31   Joseph reveals his identity and
       in tears forgives his brother's past misdeed
    71 P 41 42   Daniel exposes the elders as
       deceivers

REVELLING
    see FEAST(S)

REVENGE
    see also AVENGING
    71 A 83 11   Abel's blood cries out for revenge

REVERENCE
    see HONORING

REVIVING
    see ANIMATING
    see RAISING FROM THE DEAD

REVOLT
    see REBELLION

REVOLUTION
    see REBELLION

RIB(S)
    71 A 34 1   God removes a rib from the side
       of the sleeping Adam

RIDDLE
    71 I 33 2   The queen of Sheba before Solomon,
       testing him with questions

RIDICULE
    see MOCKING

RIDING
    see AIR (IN THE)
    see ASS
    see CAMEL
    see DOLPHIN
    see DONKEY
    see MULE
    see RIDING (ON HORSEBACK)

RIDING (ON HORSEBACK)
    71 Q 73   Mordecai's triumph: Mordecai, mounted
       on the king's horse, is led through the
       city by Haman (Esther and Ahasuerus may
       be looking on from the palace)
    71 Z 31   Heliodorus in the temple, attacked
       by a man (or angel) on horseback and two
       other men (or angels)
    71 Z 39   A heavenly rider, in white garment
       and with weapons of gold, helps the
       Maccabees in their battle against Lysias

RING
    see also EAR-RING(S)
    see also SIGNET-RING
    71 E 11 27 11   Moses' trial by fire: when given
       the choice between two plates, one
       containing burning coals, the other a ruby
       ring (or cherries), Moses chooses the
       burning coals and puts them in his mouth

RIOT
    see REBELLION

RISING
    see ASCENDING
    see EMERGING

RIVER
    see also CROSSING A RIVER
    see also WATERS
    71 E 11 23   Moses is exposed in the ark on
       the banks of the Nile; Miriam, Moses'
       sister, keeps watch
    71 E 11 24   The finding of Moses: Pharaoh's
       daughter comes to bathe with her maidens
       in the river and discovers the child
       floating on the water
    71 E 11 72 1   The plague of water turned into
       blood: as Pharaoh goes down to the Nile,
       Aaron strikes the surface of the river with
       his rod; the water turns into blood and
       all the fish die
    71 E 11 72 2   The plague of frogs: Aaron
       stretches out his hand over the water of
       Egypt; frogs come out and cover the land
    71 E 52 2   The Israelites come to the Jordan
    71 N 16 2   Naaman comes to the Jordan, dips
       himself seven times and is cured
    71 P 52 1   The ram with two unequal horns near
       a river - Daniel's visions
    71 X 1(Ps. 137:1)1:71 L 4   'By the rivers of
       Babylon...' - the Hebrews in Captivity
       lamenting by the riverside

RIVER-BANK
    see RIVER

ROASTING
    see BURNING ALIVE

ROBBING
    see PLUNDERING

ROBE
    see also CLOAK
    71 D 16 2   Triumph of Joseph: dressed in a
       royal attire he rides in one of Pharaoh's
       chariots, preceded by a herald
    71 Q 56   Esther puts on her royal robes

ROCK(S)
    71 E 12 63   Moses strikes the rock twice in
       front of the assembled people and water
       gushes out; the people quench their thirst
    71 E 12 72 1   Moses sitting on a rock, arms
       held up by Aaron and Hur; the Amalekites
       are defeated
    71 F 21 23 3   The angel of the Lord touches
       the food with his staff, fire arises from
       the rock

ROD
    see also ROD (FLOWERING)
    71 C 31 63   Jacob puts peeled rods in the
       animals' drinking troughs to make the beasts
       bear spotted young
    71 E 11 42 31   Miracle of the rod changed into
       a serpent; Moses may be shown fleeing from
       the serpent
    71 E 11 44   Moses departs for Egypt: he carries
       his rod and is accompanied by his wife and
       sons upon an ass
    71 E 11 64   Moses and Aaron before Pharaoh;
       Aaron performs the miracle of the rod
       changing into a snake
    71 E 11 72 1   The plague of water turned into
       blood: as Pharaoh goes down to the Nile,
       Aaron strikes the surface of the river with
       his rod; the water turns into blood and
       all the fish die
    71 E 11 72 7   The plague of hail: Moses raises
       his rod towards the sky, and hail and fire
       fall to the ground

ROD (FLOWERING)
    71 E 31 8   The flowering rod - the book of
       Numbers

ROOF
    71 H 71   David, from the roof (or balcony)
        of his palace, sees Bathsheba bathing

ROPE
    71 D 12 41 1   Joseph is lowered into a pit
        by means of ropes or a pulley
    71 F 37 32   Samson is bound by Delilah with
        new ropes
    71 H 16 32   David escapes through a window;
        Michal lets him down with the help of a
        rope

ROUND FORM
    see WHEEL

ROYAL DRESS
    see ROBE

ROYAL FAMILY
    see FAMILY

RUBY
    71 E 11 27 11   Moses' trial by fire: when given
        the choice between two plates, one
        containing burning coals, the other a ruby
        ring (or cherries), Moses chooses the
        burning coals and puts them in his mouth

RULER
    see BEFORE
    see KING

RUNNING
    see FLEEING

RUSE
    see STRATAGEM

RUSHES
    see REED(S)

RUTH
    71 F 6   The story of Ruth, the Moabitess

SABEANS
    71 W 31 11   The theft of Job's oxen and asses
        by the Sabeans

SACK
    71 D 17 71   At their camp one of Joseph's
        brothers finds money in his sack
    71 D 19 1   Joseph has his silver cup placed
        in Benjamin's sack
    71 D 19 22   The cup is found in Benjamin's
        sack
    71 N 15   A hundred men are fed with twenty
        loaves of bread: Elisha receives barley
        bread of the first-fruits and a sack of
        corn which he multiplies to feed a hundred
        men
    71 U 42 74   Judith and her maidservant put
        Holofernes' head in a sack

SACKING
    see DESTRUCTION (OF CITY)
    see PLUNDERING

SACRIFICING
    see also HUMAN SACRIFICE
    71 A 81   The sacrifice of Cain and Abel: Abel
        offers a lamb, Cain usually a sheaf of corn
    71 B 34 3   Noah's sacrifice; various animals
        are offered, possibly a lamb, a dove, and
        a ram (often combined with the rainbow of
        the covenant)
    71 C 13 14   A ram caught in a thicket is
        sacrificed instead of Isaac
    71 C 31 95   Jacob and Laban make an alliance:
        a pile of stone is erected and an animal
        is sacrificed
    71 E 13 53 1   Aaron builds an altar and offers
        a sacrifice to the golden calf
    71 E 22   Aaron offers sacrifices
    71 F 31 4   Manoah's sacrifice; the angel
        ascends in the flames
    71 F 83 62   The Ark of the Covenant and the
        box with the guilt offering, drawn by two
        cows, sent back to Israel
    71 H 61 2   David sacrificing (in general)
    71 H 62 8   David places the ark in a tent,
        burns offerings before the Lord and
        distributes bread, meat and wine to everyone
    71 I 53 1   Solomon offers sacrifices to pagan
        gods (sometimes idols and/or a golden calf
        upon the altar)

SACRILEGE
    see DESECRATION

SADDLE
    71 C 31 94 1   Rachel hides the teraphim in
        a camel's saddle and sits on it

SADNESS
    see GRIEVING

SAILOR(S)
    71 V 13   The ship is caught in a violent storm
        - Jonah and the sailors

SALE
    see SELLING

SALEM (KING OF)
    71 C 11 7   The meeting of Abraham and
        Melchizedek, the high priest and king of
        Salem, who brings bread and wine

SALT
    71 N 11   The water of Jericho is purified:
        when the citizens of Jericho complain about
        their water, Elisha puts some salt into
        a jar; he then throws the salt into the
        water

SALUTING
　　see MEETING
　　see WELCOMING

SAMSON
　　11 I 62(SAMSON)　Samson (not in biblical
　　　　context)
　　71 F 3　The time of Samson - the book of Judges

SAMSON'S WIFE
　　71 F 33　Samson's wedding and riddle

SAMUEL
　　71 F 8　Story of Samuel
　　71 G 11　Samuel and Saul
　　71 H 31 52　The ghost of Samuel appears to
　　　　the witch of Endor; Saul falls prostrate
　　　　to the ground

SANCTIFYING
　　see DEDICATION

SAND
　　see also DESERT
　　71 E 11 31 21　Moses buries the body of the
　　　　Egyptian taskmaster in the sand

SANDAL
　　71 E 11 42 1　Moses taking off his sandals

SARAH
　　71 C 1　Sarah - story of Abraham

SARAH (WIFE OF TOBIAS)
　　71 T　- The book of Tobit
　　71 T 6　Tobias and Sarah

SARCOPHAGUS
　　see TOMB

SATAN
　　71 E 46 4　The contest of St. Michael and Satan
　　　　for the body of Moses on Mount Nebo
　　71 W 2　The 'sons of God' (angels) with Satan
　　　　gather before God - story of Job
　　71 W 52　Job on the dunghill with Satan (or
　　　　devils) abusing and tormenting him; Job's
　　　　wife may be present

SAUL
　　71 G　Story of Saul
　　71 H 1　David as a young man at Saul's court
　　71 H 2　David's wanderings
　　71 H 3　Story of Saul's death

SAVING
　　see RESCUING

SCARED
　　see FEAR

SCARING AWAY
　　see CHASING AWAY

SCATTERING
　　71 B 42 21　The confusion of languages and
　　　　the scattering of people over the earth
　　　　- story of the Tower of Babel

SCEPTER
　　71 Q 64　Ahasuerus holds out his scepter to
　　　　Esther (Esther usually kneeling)
　　71 Q 82　Esther entreating Ahasuerus: she falls
　　　　at the king's feet and asks him to revoke
　　　　the decree against the Jews; the king holds
　　　　out his scepter to her (Esther may be
　　　　holding the decree)

SCISSORS
　　see HAIR-CUTTING

SCOLDING
　　see INSULTING
　　see MOCKING

SCOURGE
　　see SCOURGING

SCOURGING
　　71 Z 35　Martyrdom of Eleazar: the old man
　　　　is forced to eat pork and voluntarily
　　　　submits to the flogging

SCOUTING
　　see also SPY
　　71 E 31 5　Reconnaissance of Canaan - book
　　　　of Numbers

SCRAPING
　　71 W 51　Job covered with sores (or boils)
　　　　takes his abode on a dunghill (pile of
　　　　ashes) and scrapes his body with a potsherd

SCRIPT
　　see LETTER(S)

SCROLL
　　see also DOCUMENT
　　11 I 62(DANIEL) 31　Daniel as a prophet with
　　　　book or scroll
　　11 I 62(DAVID) 31　David as prophet, with
　　　　crown and scroll
　　11 I 62(ELIJAH)　Attributes of Elijah
　　11 I 62(EZEKIEL)　Attributes of Ezekiel
　　11 I 62(ISAIAH)　Attributes of Isaiah
　　11 I 62(JEREMIAH)　Attributes of Jeremiah
　　11 I 62(OBADIAH)　Attributes of the prophet
　　　　Obadiah
　　11 I 63(SHEBA)　Attributes of Sheba (goosefeet,
　　　　scroll, negress)

SEA
　　see also SHORE
　　see also STORM AT SEA
　　see also WATERS
　　71 E 12 1　Journey of the Israelites from
　　　　Succoth to the Red Sea
　　71 E 12 2　Passage through the Red Sea

SEA-MAMMALS
　　see SEA-MONSTER

SEA-MONSTER
　　see also LEVIATHAN
　　71 V 13 41　Jonah is swallowed by a great fish,
　　　　(sea)monster, whale, dolphin, or the like

SEA-SHORE
　　see SHORE

SEARCHING
　　71 C 31 94　Laban searches the tents and
　　　　belongings of Jacob to find the teraphim

SEASON(S)
　　71 B 25　Story of Enoch, son of Jared, who
　　　　invented letters and was the first to divide
　　　　the year into seasons and into twelve months

SEAT
　　see THRONE

SECRECY
　　71 E 11 31 21　Moses buries the body of the
　　　　Egyptian taskmaster in the sand
　　71 T 24　Tobit buries the dead in secret

SECRET
　　see SECRECY

SEDITION
  see REBELLION

SEDUCING
  see also COURTING
  see also TEMPTATION
  see also VIOLATING
  71 D 13 3   Potiphar's wife trying to seduce
    Joseph

SEEING
  see LOOKING

SEEKING
  see SEARCHING

SEER
  see PROPHESYING

SEETHING POT
  11 I 62(JEREMIAH)   Attributes of Jeremiah

SEIZING
  see GRIPPING

SELECTING
  see CHOOSING

SELLING
  see also BUYING
  71 C 24 41   Esau, returning hungry from the
    hunt, sells his first birthright to Jacob
    for a pottage of lentils
  71 D 12 52   Joseph is sold for twenty pieces
    of silver
  71 D 13 1   Joseph is sold to Potiphar
  71 D 16 42 11   Joseph opens the storehouse
    and sells corn

SENDING
  see also MESSENGER
  see also SENDING AWAY

SENDING AWAY
  see also BANISHING
  see also EXPELLING
  71 F 21 51   To select an army for a raid
    against the Midianites Gideon sends away
    the fearful and brings the remaining ten
    thousand men to the water
  71 F 62 2   Naomi sends away her daughters-in-
    law: Orpah returns home, Ruth stays
  71 H 81 23   Amnon sends Tamar away; Tamar puts
    ashes on her head, rends her garment, lays
    her hand on her head and leaves crying
  71 Q 21 31   Queen Vashti is deposed

SENTENCE
  see VERDICT

SENTRY
  see GUARD

SEPARATING
  see also DIVIDING
  see also INTERVENING
  see also LEAVE-TAKING
  71 C 11 5   Abraham and Lot separating
  71 F 21 52   Those who lap water by putting
    their hand to their mouth are separated
    from those who kneel down to drink the water
    - selection of Gideon's men

SEPULCHRE
  see TOMB

SERF(S)
  see SLAVE(S)

SERPENT
  see also DRAGON
  see also SNAKE
  71 A 4-71 A 5   Temptation and Fall
  71 E 11 42 31   Miracle of the rod changed into
    a serpent; Moses may be shown fleeing from
    the serpent
  71 E 32 4   The brazen serpent - book of Numbers

SERVANT(S)
  see also MAIDSERVANT
  see also SLAVE(S)
  71 C 13 11   Abraham with Isaac, an ass and
    the servants on their way to Moriah
  71 C 13 11 1   The servants are left behind
    while Abraham and Isaac (usually carrying
    wood) climb the mountain
  71 C 31 4   Jacob serving Laban for Rachel and
    Leah
  71 F 64 2   Boaz questions his servant
    concerning Ruth

SERVING
  see SERVANT(S)

SETH
  71 A 92   Story of Seth
  71 b 2   The descendants of Seth

SETTEE
  see COUCH

SETTING ON FIRE
  71 F 34 3   Samson ties three hundred foxes
    two by two by their tails with a fire-brand
    in between; with the torches on fire he
    lets them go into the cornfields of the
    Philistines which are set aflame

SEVEN
  71 E 11 32   Moses at a well meets the seven
    daughters of Jethro, the priest of Midian
  71 I 43 22 4   The seven-branched candlestick
    - temple of Solomon
  71 N 16 2   Naaman comes to the Jordan, dips
    himself seven times and is cured
  71 P 13 3   After the furnace has been
    heated seven times more, the three Hebrews
    are bound and thrown into the fire; their
    executioners are burnt by the flames
  71 W 54 3   Eliphaz, Bildad, and Zophar silently
    sit on the ground with Job for seven days

SEXUAL INTERCOURSE
  see INCEST
  see LOVER(S)
  see VIOLATING

SHADE(S)
  see GHOST(S)
  see SHADOW

SHADOW
  71 V 42   The prophet Jonah withdraws from
    Nineveh; he builds a booth and while
    enjoying the shade of a plant (gourd or
    vine) which God made grow for him, he awaits
    the destiny of the city

SHADRACH
  see ANANIAS (OF BABYLON)

SHALLUM
  71 K 35 1   Zechariah is assassinated by Shallum

SHAME
  see REPENTING

SHAWL
  see VEIL

SHE-WOLF
  see WOLF

SHEAF
  71 A 81   The sacrifice of Cain and Abel: Abel
    offers a lamb, Cain usually a sheaf of corn

SHEBA
  11 I 63(SHEBA)   Sheba (not in biblical context)
  71 I 33   Solomon and the queen of Sheba

SHECHEM
  71 D 12 1   Jacob sends Joseph to his brothers,
    who are taking care of their father's flock
    at Shechem

SHECHEM (SON OF HAMOR)
  71 C 32 41   The rape of Dinah by Shechem

SHEDRACH
  see ANANIAS (OF BABYLON)

SHEEP
  see also LAMB
  see also RAM
  see also SHEPHERD(S)
  71 C 31 3   Jacob at the well of Haran
  71 C 31 31   Jacob meets the shepherds of Haran
    and their flocks of sheep lying round the
    well
  71 C 31 61   Laban agrees to give Jacob all
    the black and spotted sheep and goats as
    wages
  71 C 31 61   Laban agrees to give Jacob all
    the black and spotted sheep and goats as
    wages
  71 C 31 84   Jacob on the way to Canaan with
    his family, his flocks, camels and all his
    possessions
  71 D 11 1   Joseph tending the sheep and goats
    with his brothers
  71 D 12 1   Jacob sends Joseph to his brothers,
    who are taking care of their father's flock
    at Shechem
  71 E 11 32 1   Moses drives away the shepherds
    who wanted to prevent Jethro's daughters
    from watering their father's flock
  71 E 11 32 2   Moses waters the sheep of
    Jethro's daughters

SHEM
  71 B 35 21 1   Shem and Japheth cover their
    father Noah; Ham usually stands nearby
    deriding him
  71 B 35 21 11   Shem and Japheth walking
    backwards towards Noah

SHEPHERD(S)
  see also SHEEP
  see also SHEPHERDESS
  71 C 31 31   Jacob meets the shepherds of Haran
    and their flocks of sheep lying round the
    well
  71 D 11 1   Joseph tending the sheep and goats
    with his brothers
  71 E 11 32 1   Moses drives away the shepherds
    who wanted to prevent Jethro's daughters
    from watering their father's flock

SHEPHERD'S CROOK
  see STAFF

SHEPHERDESS
  71 E 11 32   Moses at a well meets the seven
    daughters of Jethro, the priest of Midian

SHINING
  see LIGHT

SHIP
  see EMBARKATION
  see OVERBOARD

SHIPWRECK
  see STORM AT SEA

SHOE(S)
  see also SANDAL(S)
  71 E 11 73 13 2   The Israelites eat the
    Passover lamb standing about a table with
    their loins girt, their shoes on their feet
    and with staves in their hands, ready to
    depart

SHOOTING
  see also ARROW(S)
  see also KILLING
  71 B 15 1   Lamech kills Cain: Cain is
    accidentally shot dead by an arrow of the
    blind Lamech, who is assisted in the hunt
    by his son Tubalcain
  71 K 29 45   When Jehoram realizes Jehu's
    treason, he turns his chariot round to flee,
    but Jehu shoots an arrow that strikes
    Jehoram in the back; the king falls dead
    in his chariot

SHORE
  see also DISEMBARKATION
  71 V 22   After a three-day sojourn in the belly
    of the monster Jonah is cast on dry land;
    Jonah may be shown nude and bald-headed

SHOULDERS
  see CARRYING ON THE SHOULDERS

SHOUTING
  71 B 35 21   The mocking of Noah: Ham finds
    his father (partially) naked sleeping out
    of doors (or in his tent, or in the vineyard
    cottage); Ham calls his brothers

SHOVEL
  see SPADE

SHOWBREAD
  71 H 21 21   David receives the hallowed bread

SHOWING
  see also PRESENTING A PERSON
  see also REVEALING
  71 D 12 8   Joseph's blood-stained coat is
    brought and shown to Jacob
  71 F 15 45   Barak comes to Jael's tent; she
    shows him Sisera's body
  71 H 23 6   When Saul comes out of the cave,
    David calls him, falls down on his knees
    and shows him the piece of cloth
  71 U 43 2   Judith shows Holofernes' head to
    the people

SHOWING THE WAY
  see GUIDING

SHREW
  see HUSBAND AND WIFE

SHRINE
  see ARK OF THE COVENANT

SHRUB
  see BUSH

SHULAMMITE
  71 X 21   Shulammite, the beloved woman - Song
    of Solomon

SHUNAMMITE
   71 N 13   Elisha and the Shunammite woman

SHUR
   71 C 11 93 2   An angel meets Hagar at the
                fountain on the way to Shur and persuades
                her to return

SIBYL
   11 I 2(...)   Sibyls (with NAME)

SICK (THE)
      see HEALING
      see PLAGUE
      see SICK PERSON

SICK PERSON
   71 D 24 2   Joseph takes his two sons, Manasseh
                and Ephraim to see Jacob on his sick-bed
   71 L 24 41   King Hezekiah falls ill and is
                visited by Isaiah, who tells him to get
                ready to die; Hezekiah turns his face to
                the wall, prays and then cries

SICK-BED
      see SICK PERSON

SIDE
   71 A 34 1   God removes a rib from the side
                of the sleeping Adam

SIDRACH
      see ANANIAS (OF BABYLON)

SIGN
   71 F 21 43   Twice Gideon asks the Lord to
                show him a sign with a sheep's fleece before
                his raid against the Midianites

SIGNAL
      see TRUMPET

SIGNET-RING
   71 D 16 1   Pharaoh takes off his signet-ring
                and puts it on Joseph's finger; Joseph is
                appointed overseer

SILENCE
      see also FINGER TO THE LIPS
   71 W 54 3   Eliphaz, Bildad and Zophar silently
                sit on the ground with Job for seven days

SILVER
      see also SILVER (PIECE OF)
   71 D 19 1   Joseph has his silver cup placed
                in Benjamin's sack
   71 P 21   Belshazzar's great feast, during which
                he and his courtiers desecrate the golden
                and silver vessels that were taken from
                the temple in Jerusalem

SILVER (PIECE OF)
   71 C 13 21 1   Abraham weighs out four hundred
                pieces of silver
   71 D 12 52   Joseph is sold for twenty pieces
                of silver
   71 F 37 4   Delilah finds out Samson's secret
                and warns the Philistines, who come with
                the money

SIMEON
   71 D 17 52   Joseph comes back, picks out Simeon
                and has him bound

SIN
      see also WICKEDNESS
   71 E 52 5   Achan's sin (aftermath of the fall
                of Jericho)

SINAI (MOUNT)
   71 E 12   Exodus (part II): journey of Israel
                to Mount Sinai
   71 E 13   Exodus (part III): conclusion of the
                Sinaitic law and its renewal
   71 E 13 1   Recurrent themes - Mount Sinai
   71 E 13 2   Arrival of the Israelites at Mount
                Sinai
   71 E 13 4   Moses on Mount Sinai with the tables
                of the law

SINGER
      see SINGING

SINGING
      see also LAMENTING
   71 E 12 32 1   Miriam's song of praise - Exodus
   71 H 15 21   David's triumph: the women of
                Israel come out to welcome David, singing,
                dancing, and playing tambourines and lyres;
                David holding the head of Goliath
   71 W 64(Job 38:7): 24 D 0   When the morning
                stars sang together - God speaks to Job

SINGLE COMBAT
      see also CONTEST
      see also FIGHTING
      see also WRESTLING
   71 H 14 4   David fighting Goliath

SINNER(S)
      see SIN

SISERA
   71 F 15 1   Deborah (sitting under a palmtree)
                beseeches Barak to attack Sisera and his
                army
   71 F 15 4   Story of Jael and Sisera

SITTING
      see also BANQUET
      see also THRONE
   71 C 33 27   Tamar changes from her widow's
                clothes and covers her face with a veil
                after the manner of the prostitutes; sitting
                at the entrance of a city on the road to
                Timnath she awaits Judah
   71 E 12 72 1   Moses sitting on a rock, arms
                held up by Aaron and Hur; the Amalekites
                are defeated
   71 W 54 3   Eliphaz, Bildad and Zophar silently
                sit on the ground with Job for seven days

SIX
   71 A 2   The six days of creation

SKELETON
      see BONES

SKETCH
      see DESIGN

SKIN
      see HIDE

SKIN DISEASE
      see BOIL(S)
      see LEPROSY

SKY
      see also AIR (IN THE)
      see also FIRMAMENT
      see also HEAVEN
   71 T 79 2   The angel Raphael disappears into
                the sky
   71 Z 39   A heavenly rider, in white garment
                and with weapons of gold, helps the
                Maccabees in their battle against Lysias

SLANDER
      see ACCUSING

SLAPPING
    see STRIKING

SLAUGHTER
    see MASSACRE

SLAUGHTERING
    see SACRIFICING

SLAVE(S)
    see also SERVANT(S)
    71 D 12 52   Joseph is sold for twenty pieces
        of silver
    71 D 13 1   Joseph is sold to Potiphar

SLEEPING
    see also BED
    see also DREAM
    71 A 34 1   God removes a rib from the side
        of the sleeping Adam
    71 B 35 21   The mocking of Noah: Ham finds
        his father (partially) naked sleeping out
        of doors (or in his tent, or in the vineyard
        cottage); Ham calls his brothers
    71 C 31 21   The dream of Jacob: while sleeping
        on the ground with a stone for pillow Jacob
        sees a ladder reaching from earth to heaven
        with angels going up and down; usually with
        God at the top of the ladder
    71 F 15 44   Jael kills the sleeping Sisera
        by hitting the nail through his temples
    71 F 37 5   Samson asleep in Delilah's lap;
        she is usually shown beckoning to a
        Philistine or putting a finger to her lips
    71 H 25 2   David and Abishai invade Saul's
        encampment at night, while Saul and his
        soldiers are sleeping
    71 T 34   Tobit lies sleeping against a wall

SLING
    71 H 14 42   David slings a stone at Goliath's
        forehead

SMASHING
    see BREAKING

SMITING
    see VICTORY

SMOKE
    71 A 81 2   The fume of Abel's sacrifice goes
        straight to heaven, whereas the smoke of
        Cain's offering is beaten down
    71 W 52 1   Job is smitten from head to foot
        with sores by Satan, or dragon-like monsters
        that blow poisonous smoke on Job

SNAKE
    see also SERPENT
    71 E 11 64   Moses and Aaron before Pharaoh:
        Aaron performs the miracle of the rod
        changing into a snake
    71 E 32 41   When the people complain again
        about the food, God sends poisonous snakes;
        many die of snake-bites - book of Numbers

SNOW
    71 H 52 64   Benaiah kills two men, and then
        a lion, in a pit on a snowy day

SODOM
    71 C 12 4   The destruction of Sodom and
        Gomorrah: Lot and his family flee to Zoar,
        carrying their belongings; an angel may
        be showing the way

SOFA
    see COUCH

SOLDIER(S)
    see also ARMY
    see also GUARD
    see also OFFICER
    71 E 52 42   The Israelites march around
        Jericho: in the procession the main body
        of the soldiers comes first, next are seven
        priests who blow on trumpets, followed by
        priests carrying the ark and a rear guard
    71 H 25 2   David and Abishai invade Saul's
        encampment at night, while Saul and his
        soldiers are sleeping
    71 I 32 5   Solomon gives verdict; he commands
        a soldier to divide the living child in
        two

SOLICITING
    see PROPOSAL

SOLITUDE
    see also WILDERNESS
    71 F 24 54   Jephthah's daughter retreats to
        the mountains with her companions to bewail
        her virginity

SOLOMON
    71 H 92   David's instructions to Solomon
    71 I   Story of Solomon
    71 X 2   Song of Solomon, Song of Songs

SOLOMON'S TEMPLE
    71 I 43 2   Temple of Solomon

SOLVING A RIDDLE
    see RIDDLE

SON
    see also FATHER AND SON
    71 C 12 24 3   The promise of a son is renewed;
        Sarah, overhearing it, laughs incredulously
    71 F 31 2   Annunciation of the birth of a son
        to Manoah and his wife
    71 W 2   The 'sons of God' (angels) with Satan
        gather before God - story of Job

SON-IN-LAW
    see FATHER-IN-LAW

SONG
    see SINGING

SONG OF SOLOMON
    71 X 2   Song of Solomon, Song of Songs

SORCERESS
    see WITCH

SORE(S)
    see BOIL(S)

SORROW(S)
    see GRIEVING
    see SUFFERING

SOUP
    71 C 24 41   Esau, returning hungry from the
        hunt, sells his first birthright to Jacob
        for a pottage of lentils
    71 N 14   The deadly pottage: Elisha purifies
        the poisoned pottage by throwing flour into
        it

SOUTHERN KINGDOM
    71 L   Story of the Southern Kingdom (Judah)

SPADE
    71 A 82   The killing of Abel: Cain slays Abel
        with a stone, a club or a jaw-bone,
        alternatively with a spade or another tool
        as weapon

SPEAKING
see also ADVISING
see also ASKING
see also BEFORE
see also COMMUNICATING WITH GOD
see also COMPLAINING
see also CONVERSATION
see also CURSING
see also DICTATING
see also INSTRUCTING
see also LISTENING
see also ORDERING
see also PERSUADING
see also REBUKING
see also REPORTING
71 E 33 14 1   Balaam strikes his ass, whereupon the ass lies down and starts to speak

SPEAR
71 H 15 3   Saul casts his spear at David when the latter is playing his harp before the king
71 H 16 21   Saul casts his spear at David for the second time
71 H 25 21   David takes Saul's spear and water-flask away
71 H 84 92   Joab stabs Absalom with three spears

SPECTER
see GHOST(S)

SPIKE
see NAIL (SPIKE)

SPINDLE
see SPINNING

SPINNING
71 A 72 1   Adam engaged in agricultural activities, Eve spinning and usually their children at play
71 T 74   Old Tobit (and Anna) waiting and worrying about the long absence of their son; sometimes Anna is shown at the spinning-wheel

SPINNING-WHEEL
see SPINNING

SPIRIT(S)
see DEMON(S)
see GHOST(S)

SPOIL(S)
see PLUNDERING

SPOILS OF THE HUNT
71 C 27 5   Esau comes back with venison

SPOT(S)
71 C 31 61   Laban agrees to give Jacob all the black and spotted sheep and goats as wages
71 C 31 63   Jacob puts peeled rods in the animals' drinking troughs to make the beasts bear spotted young

SPRING (SOURCE)
see FOUNTAIN
see WELL

SPRINGING FROM
see EMERGING

SPROUTING
see ROD (FLOWERING)

SPURNING
see LOVE UNREQUITED

SPY
71 D 17 31   Joseph accuses his brothers of being spies and throws them in prison
71 E 31 52   The spies take away some of the fruits of Canaan and return, usually carrying a large bunch of grapes on a pole
71 E 31 53   The spies, except for Caleb and Joshua, bring startling reports which upset the people - reconnaissance of Canaan

SPYING
see also LOOKING
see also SPY
71 C 25 21 1   King Abimelech, looking down from his window, sees Isaac and Rebekah making love
71 H 71   David, from the roof (or balcony) of his palace, sees Bathsheba bathing
71 P 41 21   The elders spying upon Susanna

STABBING
see also SUICIDE
see also SWORD
71 C 13 13   Abraham picks up the knife to kill Isaac
71 H 84 92   Joab stabs Absalom with three spears

STAFF
see also SCEPTER
71 C 33 27 1   Judah's love affair with Tamar; he gives her his signet(-ring), bracelets and staff
71 E 11 73 13 2   The Israelites eat the Passover lamb standing about a table with their loins girt, their shoes on their feet and with staves in their hands, ready to depart
71 F 21 23 3   The angel of the Lord touches the food with his staff, fire arises from the rock

STAINING
71 D 12 71 1   Joseph's brothers stain Joseph's coat with the kid's blood

STAIRCASE
see also LADDER
71 C 31 21 1   Dream of Jacob, with stairway instead of ladder

STALL
see BOOTH

STANDING
71 E 11 73 13 2   The Israelites eat the Passover lamb standing about a table with their loins girt, their shoes on their feet and with staves in their hands, ready to depart

STAR(S)
71 A 24   Creation of sun, moon and stars

STARVATION
see HUNGER

STATUE(S)
see IDOL(S)

STEALING
71 H 25 21   David takes Saul's spear and water-flask away
71 W 31 11   The theft of Job's oxen and asses by the Sabeans

STEPS
see STAIRCASE

STERILITY
see BARRENNESS

STICK
see ROD
see STAFF

STIRRING THE WAVES
see STORM AT SEA

STONE(S)
see also ROCK(S)
see also STONING
71 A 82   The killing of Abel: Cain slays him
with a stone, a club or a jaw-bone,
alternatively with a spade or another tool
as weapon
71 C 31 21   The dream of Jacob: while sleeping
on the ground with a stone for a pillow
Jacob sees a ladder reaching from earth
to heaven with angels going up and
down; usually with God at the top of the
ladder
71 C 31 33   Jacob moves the stone which covers
the opening of the well and waters Rachel's
sheep
71 C 31 95   Jacob and Laban make an alliance:
a pile of stone is erected and an animal
is sacrificed
71 H 14 42   David slings a stone at Goliath's
forehead

STONING
71 E 24 2   The son of Shelomith is stoned to
death by the Israelites
71 P 41 5   The elders are stoned to death -
story of Susanna

STOPPING
see also INTERVENING
71 A 42 1   Eve takes the fruit from the serpent
(or the tree) in the presence of Adam (who
may be trying to stop her)

STORAGE
71 D 16 42 11   Joseph opens the storehouse
and sells corn

STORM
see STORM AT SEA
see WHIRLWIND

STORM AT SEA
71 V 13   The ship is caught in a violent storm
- Jonah and the sailors

STORY
see REPORTING

STRANGLING
see CHOKING

STRATAGEM
71 E 52 6   The city of Ai taken by stratagem
71 E 52 94   Joshua and his army make a surprise
attack on the Amorites who are besieging
the city of Gibeon

STREAM
see RIVER

STRENGTH
see POWER

STRETCHED ARMS (HANDS)
see ARM(S) STRETCHED

STRETCHING
71 N 13 32   Elisha stretches himself out upon
the child of the Shunammite woman

STRIFE
see STRUGGLING

STRIKING
see also BEATING
see also THUNDER(BOLT)
71 E 12 63   Moses strikes the rock twice in
front of the assembled people and water
gushes out; the people quench their thirst
71 E 33 14 1   Balaam strikes his ass, whereupon
the ass lies down and starts to speak

STRUGGLING
see also WRESTLING
71 H 4   Struggle for the hegemony between David
and Saul's descendants

SUBSTITUTION
71 C 31 44   The wedding-feast: Laban
substitutes Leah for Rachel

SUCCESSION
71 E 11 8   The Israelites leave Egypt; first
movement from Rameses to Succoth

SUCKLING
71 A 71 22   Eve suckling Abel; Cain turns
aside, i.e. the jealousy of Cain
71 A 72 2   Adam engaged in agricultural
activities, Eve suckling the children

SUFFERING
71 W 3   The first series of afflictions - the
book of Job

SUFFOCATING
see CHOKING

SUICIDE
71 H 32 22   Saul kills himself with a sword
71 H 32 23   Saul's armour-bearer kills himself

SUITOR
see COURTING
see PROPOSAL

SUMMONING
see ORDERING

SUN
71 A 24   Creation of sun, moon and stars
71 E 52 94 2   Joshua orders the sun and the
moon to stand still over Gibeon and Aijalon
until the Amorites who had besieged the
city of Gibeon are routed

SUNLIGHT
see RAY OF LIGHT

SUPERVISING
71 B 42 1   The building of the Tower of Babel;
Nimrod may be present, supervising or
assisting the construction
71 I 43 21 21   Solomon supervising the work
- temple of Solomon

SUPPLY
see FOOD

SUPPORTING
see LAP

SUSANNA
71 P 41   The story of Susanna and the elders
(in which the youth Daniel intervenes on
behalf of Susanna)

SUSPENSION
see STOPPING

SUSPICION
71 T 37   Anna brings home a young goat: Tobit
thinks she has stolen it

SWALLOWING
see also DEVOURING
71 E 31 74 2   The ground opens and swallows
the rebels Dathan and Abiram along with
their families and possessions
71 V 13 41   Jonah is swallowed by a great fish,
(sea)monster, whale, dolphin, or the like

SWARM
see GRASSHOPPER

SWEARING
see OATH
see PROMISING

SWIMMING
see DROWNING

SWOONING
71 Q 63   Esther swoons on the shoulder of one
of her maids

SWORD
see also FLAMING SWORD
see also KILLING
see also STABBING
71 A 61   God expels Adam and Eve from paradise
and has the tree of life guarded by an angel
with a flaming sword
71 E 33 14   An angel holding a sword bars the
way and causes Balaam's ass to turn aside;
the angel is invisible to Balaam
71 H 14 43   David beheads Goliath with a sword
71 H 21 22   David receives the sword of Goliath
71 H 32 22   Saul kills himself with a sword
71 H 46 3   Abner, fetched by Joab's messengers,
is taken aside by Joab in the gate of
Hebron, and is killed by him with a sword
71 H 54 6   God punishes Israel with three days
of plague; the avenging angel with his sword
drawn goes through the land; seventy
thousand men are killed
71 U 42 73   Holofernes beheaded by Judith with
his own sword; the maidservant may be
keeping watch

SYMBOL
see SIGN

T-SHAPE
see TAU-CROSS

TABERNACLE
71 E 12 54 2   Aaron fills a jar with manna
to be kept in the tabernacle
71 E 13 8   Preparation and setting up of the
Tabernacle and its accessories - Exodus

TABLE
see TABLES OF THE LAW
see WRITING

TABLES OF THE LAW
71 E 13 4   Moses on Mount Sinai with the tables
of the law
71 E 13 43 1   God writing the commandments
on the two stone tablets
71 E 13 54   Moses (and Joshua) come(s) down
with the stone tablets
71 E 13 54 1   On seeing the idolaters Moses
breaks the tables of the law
71 E 13 7   The new tables of the law - Exodus

TABLET
see TABLES OF THE LAW

TAIL(S)
71 F 34 3   Samson ties three hundred foxes
two by two by their tails with a fire-brand
in between; with the torches on fire he
lets them go into the cornfields of the
Philistines which are set aflame

TAKING OFF SHOES
see SANDAL(S)
see SHOE(S)

TALENT (MONEY)
see MONEY

TALKING
see CONVERSATION
see SPEAKING

TAMAR
71 C 33 2   Story of Judah and Tamar

TAMAR (DAVID'S DAUGHTER)
71 H 81   Tamar dishonored; story of Tamar and
Amnon

TAMBOURINE
71 E 12 32   Miriam takes up a tambourine and
dances; all the women follow her
71 F 24 53   Jephthah's daughter dances with
tambourines to meet her father on his return
from the battle; Jephthah rends his clothes
in despair
71 H 15 21   David's triumph: the women of
Israel come out to welcome David singing,
dancing, and playing tambourines and lyres;
David holding the head of Goliath

TASK
see ORDERING

TASKMASTER
see also OVERSEER
71 E 11 31 2-4   Moses kills the Egyptian
taskmaster

TASTER
see WINE-TESTING

TAU-CROSS
71 E 32 43   Anyone who is bitten by a snake
is cured by looking at the brazen serpent;
the serpent (or dragon) is usually depicted
on a tau-shaped cross or on a pillar

TAUNTING
    see INSULTING

TEACHER
    see TEACHING

TEACHING
    see also INSTRUCTING
    see also UPBRINGING
    71 A 72 3   An angel instructs Adam in
        agricultural activities
    71 E 41   Moses teaching (in general)

TEAR(S)
    see WEEPING

TEARING
    see TEARING ONE'S CLOTHES

TEARING ONE'S CLOTHES
    71 D 12 81   Jacob rending his garments on
        recognizing the robe
    71 F 24 53   Jephthah's daughter dances with
        tambourines to meet her father on his return
        from the battle; Jephthah rends his clothes
        in despair
    71 H 81 23   Amnon sends Tamar away; Tamar puts
        ashes on her head, rends her garment, lays
        her hand on her head and leaves crying
    71 I 72   Meeting of Jeroboam and the prophet
        Ahijah; Ahijah rends his garment in twelve
        pieces, ten of which he gives to Jeroboam
    71 W 54 2   When Eliphaz, Bildad and Zophar
        recognize Job they weep and tear their
        clothes in grief

TEARING TO PIECES
    see DEVOURING

TELLING
    see REPORTING

TEMPLE
    71 F 38 3   Samson breaks the pillars; the
        temple of Dagon collapses, killing all that
        are in it
    71 F 81 32   Samuel in the temple at Shiloh
        presented to Eli by Hannah
    71 F 81 4   Samuel growing up in the temple
        at Shiloh
    71 I 43 2   Temple of Solomon
    71 Z 31   Heliodorus in the temple, attacked
        by a man (or angel) on horseback and two
        other men (or angels)
    71 Z 38   Second purification of the temple
        - Maccabees

TEMPLES
    71 F 15 44   Jael kills the sleeping Sisera
        by hitting the nail through his temples

TEMPTATION
    see also SEDUCING
    71 A 4-71 A 5   Temptation and Fall

TEN
    71 E 11 7   The ten plagues (- Exodus)
    71 E 13 43 1   God writing the commandments
        on the two stone tablets

TEN THOUSAND
    71 F 21 51   To select an army for a raid
        against the Midianites Gideon sends away
        the fearful and brings the remaining ten
        thousand men to the water

TENDRIL
    see VINE

TENT
    see also BOOTH
    see also CAMP
    see also TABERNACLE
    71 B 35 21   The mocking of Noah: Ham finds
        his father (partially) naked sleeping out
        of doors (or in his tent, or in the vineyard
        cottage); Ham calls his brothers
    71 C 21 6   Isaac brings Rebekah into Sarah's
        tent
    71 C 31 94   Laban searches the tents and
        belongings of Jacob to find the teraphim
    71 H 62 8   David places the ark in a tent,
        burns offerings before the Lord and
        distributes bread, meat and wine to everyone
    71 U 42 4   Judith and her maidservant are led
        to Holofernes' tent

TERAH
    71 C 11 12   Terah takes Abraham, Sarah, and
        Lot from Ur to the city of Haran

TERAPHIM
    71 C 31 94   Laban searches the tents and
        belongings of Jacob to find the teraphim
    71 C 31 94 1   Rachel hides the teraphim in
        a camel's saddle and sits on it

TERROR
    see FEAR

TESTAMENT (OLD)
    see OLD TESTAMENT

TESTING
    see also ORDEAL
    see also WINE-TESTING
    71 A 35 4   The giving of the test commandment:
        God warns Adam and Eve not to eat from the
        tree of knowledge of good and evil

TETRAMORPH
    71 O 91 1   Ezekiel's vision of God sitting
        on his throne carried by four tetramorphs,
        each of them having four wings; wheels
        within wheels beside them

TEXT
    see DOCUMENT

TEXTILE
    see CLOTH

THANKING
    71 H 14 44   David thanks the Lord after he
        has slain the giant Goliath
    71 H 93   David's song of thanks
    71 P 12 51   King Nebuchadnezzar kneels before
        Daniel to show his gratitude
    71 W 75   Job thanking the Lord

THEFT
    see STEALING

THICKET
    see BUSH

THIEF
    see STEALING

THIGH
    71 C 32 22   Jacob wrestles with the angel (or
        man) till daybreak; Jacob's thigh is put
        out of joint

THIRST
    see DRINK(ING)

THOUSAND
71 F 35 4   With an ass's jaw-bone Samson slays
a thousand Philistines
71 F 35 61   Samson drinks from the ass's jaw-
bone after having slain a thousand
Philistines

THREATENING
71 L 24 36   Hezekiah receives a letter from
Sennacherib with another threat

THREE
71 C 12 2   The visit of the three angels (three
men) - story of Abraham
71 H 84 92   Joab stabs Absalom with three
spears
71 P 13   The story of the three Hebrews in
the fiery furnace
71 F 21 21   The angel of the Lord appears to
Gideon, who is usually shown threshing wheat

THRESHING-FLOOR
71 H 54 63   By the command of God the angel
stops destroying the Israelites at the
threshing-floor of Araunah (Ornan) the
Jebusite

THRESHOLD
71 F 52 6   In the morning the concubine of
the Levite lies dead on the threshold

THRONE
see also BEFORE
71 O 91 1   Ezekiel's vision of God sitting
on his throne carried by four tetramorphs,
each of them having four wings; wheels
within wheels beside them
71 Q 62   Esther approaching the throne

THROWING
see also LOT(S)
see also SCATTERING
see also SPEAR
see also STONING
see also THROWING (BEING THROWN)
71 E 12 41 2   Moses throws a piece of wood
into the water of Marah, which then becomes
sweet
71 N 11   The water of Jericho is purified:
when the citizens of Jericho complain about
their water, Elisha puts some salt into
a jar; he then throws the salt into the
water

THROWING (BEING THROWN)
see also EXPELLING
see also JUMPING
71 D 12 41   Joseph is thrown into a pit
(usually depicted as a well or cistern)
71 N 71   During a funeral a band of ransacking
Moabites is seen approaching and the corpse
is thrown hastily into Elisha's tomb; when
it touches Elisha's bones the man comes
back to life
71 P 13 3   After the furnace has been heated
seven times more, the three Hebrews are
bound and thrown into the fire; their
executioners are burnt by the flames
71 V 13 4   The sailors reluctantly throw the
prophet Jonah into the sea

THUNDER(BOLT)
71 G 13 4   Samuel prays for thunder and rain

TIBURTINE SIBYL
11 I 2(...)   Sibyls (with NAME)

TOBIAS
71 T   - The book of Tobit

TOBIT
71 T   - The book of Tobit

TOILET (MAKING)
71 Q 23 1   Esther makes her toilet
71 Q 56   Esther puts on her royal robes

TOKEN
see SIGN

TOMB
71 N 71   During a funeral a band of ransacking
Moabites is seen approaching and the corpse
is thrown hastily into Elisha's tomb; when
it touches Elisha's bones the man comes
back to life

TONGS
71 O 32 2   Purification of Isaiah: an angel
touches Isaiah's lips with a burning coal,
taken from the altar with tongs - Isaiah's
visions

TORCH
see BRAND
see SETTING ON FIRE

TORMENTING
see TORTURING

TORN...
see RAG(S)

TORNADO
see WHIRLWIND

TORTURING
see also MARTYR
see also ORDEAL
71 F 37 71   Samson is tortured by the
Philistines, Delilah is paid
71 W 52   Job on the dunghill with Satan (or
devils) abusing and tormenting him; Job's
wife may be present

TOUCHING
71 Q 64 1   Esther touches the tip of the
scepter
71 Q 64 2   Ahasuerus touches Esther with the
scepter

TOWEL
see CLOTH

TOWER
71 B 4   Story of the Tower of Babel

TRADE
see SELLING

TRAIN (RETINUE)
see COMPANION(S)

TRAINING
see TEACHING

TRAITOR
see BETRAYING

TRAMPLING
71 E 11 27 1   Moses and Pharaoh's crown:
Pharaoh playfully places his crown on the
head of the infant Moses, who throws it
to the ground and tramples on it; or Moses
breaks the crown while playing

TRANSFORMATION
   71 E 11 42 31   Miracle of the rod changed into
      a serpent; Moses may be shown fleeing from
      the serpent
   71 E 11 64   Moses and Aaron before Pharaoh;
      Aaron performs the miracle of the rod
      changing into a snake
   71 E 11 72 1   The plague of water turned into
      blood: as Pharaoh goes down to the Nile,
      Aaron strikes the surface of the river with
      his rod; the water turns into blood and
      all the fish die

TRANSLATION (ASCENSION)
   see ASCENSION

TRANSPORTING
   see CARRYING

TRAVELLER(S)
   see TRAVELLING

TRAVELLING
   see also ARRIVAL
   see also DEPARTING
   see also JOURNEY
   see also RETURNING
   see also WANDERING
   71 C 11 45   Abraham leaves Egypt with Sarah,
      Lot, and his possessions
   71 C 13 11   Abraham with Isaac, an ass and
      the servants on their way to Moriah
   71 C 31 84   Jacob on the way to Canaan with
      his family, his flocks, camels and all his
      possessions
   71 E 11 44   Moses departs for Egypt: he carries
      his rod and is accompanied by his wife and
      sons upon an ass
   71 E 12 22 1   The people pass over on dry land
      (Egyptians not or barely visible); the angel
      of God and the pillar of cloud may be shown
      at the rear
   71 T 54   Tobias and the angel Raphael
      travelling, accompanied by Tobias' dog

TRAVESTY
   see DISGUISE

TREACHERY
   see BETRAYING

TREADING
   see TRAMPLING

TREASON
   see BETRAYING

TREASURE(S)
   see GIFT
   see JEWELS
   see MONEY

TREASURE-CHEST
   see MONEY-BOX

TREATY
   see ALLIANCE
   see COVENANT

TREE(S)
   see TREE OF KNOWLEDGE
   see TREE OF LIFE

TREE OF KNOWLEDGE
   71 A 35 4   The giving of the test commandment:
      God warns Adam and Eve not to eat from the
      tree of knowledge of good and evil
   71 A 4-71 A 5   Temptation and Fall

TREE OF LIFE
   71 A 61   God expels Adam and Eve from paradise
      and has the tree of life guarded by an angel
      with a flaming sword

TRIAL
   see also ACCUSING
   see also JUDGE
   see also ORDEAL
   see also TESTING
   see also VERDICT
   71 E 11 27 11   Moses' trial by fire: when given
      the choice between two plates, one
      containing burning coals, the other a ruby
      ring (or cherries), Moses chooses the
      burning coals and puts them in his mouth
   71 P 41 4   The youth Daniel opposes the verdict
      against Susanna

TRIFORMIS
   see THREE

TRINITY
   71 A 2   The six days of creation

TRIUMPH
   see also ENTRY
   see also TRAMPLING
   71 D 16 2   Triumph of Joseph: dressed in a
      royal attire he rides in one of Pharaoh's
      chariots, preceded by a herald
   71 H 15 21   David's triumph: the women of
      Israel come out to welcome David, singing,
      dancing, and playing tambourines and lyres;
      David holding the head of Goliath
   71 Q 73   Mordecai's triumph: Mordecai, mounted
      on the king's horse, is led through the
      city by Haman (Esther and Ahasuerus may
      be looking on from the palace)

TRIUMPHAL CHARIOT
   see TRIUMPH

TRIUMPHAL ENTRY
   see TRIUMPH

TROOP(S)
   see ARMY

TROUGH
   71 C 31 63   Jacob puts peeled rods in the
      animal's drinking troughs to make the beasts
      bear spotted young

TRUMPET
   71 E 52 42   The Israelites march around
      Jericho: in the procession the main body
      of the soldiers comes first, next are seven
      priests who blow on trumpets, followed by
      the priests carrying the ark and a rear
      guard
   71 F 21 64   The attack on the Midianites:
      Gideon and his men blow their trumpets,
      break their pitchers, and hold their lamps
   71 H 88 32   Solomon anointed king by Zadok;
      all the people rejoice and blow their
      trumpets
   71 P 13 2   The dedication of the golden statue:
      in the presence of King Nebuchadnezzar,
      trumpets are blown and all the people
      surrounding the image fall on their knees

TRYING
   see TESTING
   see TRIAL

TUB
   see VESSEL

TWIG
    see ROD

TWIN(S)
    71 C 24 3   Birth of the twins: Jacob clutches
        Esau's heel

TYING
    see BINDING

TYPHOON
    see WHIRLWIND

ULCER
    see BOIL(S)

UNBELIEF
    71 C 12 24 3   The promise of a son is renewed;
        Sarah, overhearing it, laughs incredulously

UNCOVERING
    see UNVEILING

UNCTION
    see ANOINTING

UNILATERAL
    see LOVE UNREQUITED

UNITY
    see ALLIANCE

UNIVERSE
    71 A 1   'In the beginning...' the ordering
        of chaos

UNLOOSING
    see RELEASING

UNREQUITED LOVE
    see LOVE UNREQUITED

UNREST
    see INQUIETUDE

UNTYING
    see LIBERATING

UNTYING SHOES
    see SHOE(S)
    see SANDAL(S)

UNVEILING
    71 P 41 3   The elders accusing Susanna before
        the people, laying their hands on her head
        or unveiling her

UPBRAIDING
    see REBUKING

UPBRINGING
    see also TEACHING
    71 A 73   Education, upbringing of Cain and
        Abel
    71 F 81 41   Samuel brought up by Eli

UPWARDS
    see ASCENDING
    see HOISTING

UR
    71 C 11 12   Terah takes Abraham, Sarah and
        Lot from Ur to the city of Haran

VALET
see TOILET (MAKING)

VALLEY
see also FIELD(S)
71 O 93 3   Ezekiel's vision of the valley of
the dry bones

VANISHING
see DISAPPEARING

VANQUISHING
see VICTORY

VASHTI (QUEEN)
71 Q 21   The feast of Ahasuerus (Xerxes,
alternatively Artaxerxes); the downfall
of Queen Vashti (Astin)

VAULT
see DUNGEON

VEGETATION
see PLANT(S)

VEIL
see also UNVEILING
71 C 33 27   Tamar changes from her widow's
clothes and covers her face with a veil
after the manner of the prostitutes; sitting
at the entrance of a city on the road to
Timnath she awaits Judah

VENERATION
see ADORATION

VENGEANCE
see REVENGE

VENISON
see GAME

VERDICT
see also JUDGE
71 I 32 5   Solomon gives verdict; he commands
a soldier to divide the living child in
two
71 Q 74 21   As Haman is kneeling at Esther's
feet or is prostrated on her couch King
Ahasuerus returns; Haman is condemned to
be hanged

VERTICAL TRANSPORT
see HOISTING

VESSEL
71 P 21   Belshazzar's great feast, during which
he and his courtiers desecrate the golden
and silver vessels that were taken from
the temple in Jerusalem

VESTMENT
see ROBE

VIABILITY
see LIFE

VICE
see SIN
see WICKEDNESS

VICTOR
see also CHAINING
see also CROWNING
see also SINGLE COMBAT
see also TRAMPLING
see also TRIUMPH
see also VICTORY

VICTORY
see also VICTOR
71 E 12 72 1   Moses sitting on a rock, arms
held up by Aaron and Hur; the Amalekites
are defeated
71 N 61 1   Elisha tells Joash to shoot an arrow
through the window towards Syria and
predicts that Joash will be victorious
71 U 44   Victory of the Israelites – Judith
and Holofernes

VICTUALS
see FOOD

VIEWING
see LOOKING

VIGILANCE
see WATCHING

VINDICTIVENESS
see REVENGE

VINE
see also GRAPE(S)
see also VINEYARD
see also WINE-GROWING
71 V 42   The prophet Jonah withdraws from
Nineveh; he builds a booth and while
enjoying the shade of a plant (gourd or
vine) which God made grow for him, he awaits
the destiny of the city

VINEYARD
see also VINE
see also WINE-GROWING
71 B 35 1   Noah plants a vineyard
71 K 27 4   Naboth's vineyard (– King Ahab)

VIOLATING
see also SEDUCING
71 C 32 41   The rape of Dinah by Shechem
71 H 81 22   Tamar violated by Amnon

VIOLENCE
see FORCE
see VIOLATING

VIRGIN
see GIRL

VIRGINITY
see also CHASTITY
71 F 24 54   Jephthah's daughter retreats to
the mountains with her companions to bewail
her virginity

VISION
see also APPEARANCE
see also DREAM
71 O 91 1   Ezekiel's vision of God sitting
on his throne carried by four tetramorphs,
each of them having four wings; wheels
within wheels beside them

VISITING
see also APPEARANCE
see also BANQUET
see also BEFORE
see also GUEST(S)
see also MEETING
see also RECEIVING A PERSON
71 C 12 2   The visit of the three angels (three
men) – story of Abraham
71 D 17 3   Admitted to Joseph's presence, the
brothers bow down before him
71 D 24 2   Joseph takes his two sons, Manasseh
and Ephraim to see Jacob on his sick-bed
71 E 12 8   Jethro's visit to Moses: with
Zipporah and her two sons he comes to the
desert where Moses is encamped
71 H 71 4   Bathsheba comes to David's palace

71 K 21 43   Jeroboam's wife in disguise visits the old and blind Ahijah, but he, having been warned by God, recognizes her; he predicts the death of her son and Israel's punishment for Jeroboam's sin

71 L 24 41   King Hezekiah falls ill and is visited by Isaiah, who tells him to get ready to die; Hezekiah turns his face to the wall, prays and then cries

71 T 61   Tobias and the angel in Raguel's house

VITALITY
    see LIFE

VITICULTURE
    see WINE-GROWING

VOCAL MUSIC
    see SINGING

VOTARY
    see VOWING

VOWING
    see also PROMISING
    71 F 81 22   Hannah prays in the temple and vows to give her child to the Lord

VOYAGE
    see JOURNEY

WADING
    see CROSSING A RIVER

WAGES
    see PAYING

WAGON
    see CART
    see CHARIOT

WAILING
    see LAMENTING

WAITING
    71 C 33 27   Tamar changes from her widow's clothes with a veil after the manner of the prostitutes; sitting at the entrance of a city on the road to Timnath she awaits Judah
    71 T 74   Old Tobit (and Anna) waiting and worrying about the long absence of their son; sometimes Anna is shown at the spinning-wheel
    71 V 42   The prophet Jonah withdraws from Nineveh; he builds a booth and while enjoying the shade of a plant (gourd or vine) which God made grow for him, he awaits the destiny of the city

WAKE
    see LAMENTING

WAKING UP
    see AWAKING

WALKING
    see also MARCHING
    see also PROCESSION
    71 B 35 21 11   Shem and Japheth walking backwards towards Noah

WALL(S)
    71 L 24 41   King Hezekiah falls ill and is visited by Isaiah, who tells him to get ready to die; Hezekiah turns his face to the wall, prays and then cries
    71 P 22   During the Belshazzar's banquet a hand appears and writes on the wall (MENE, MENE, TEKEL and PARSIN (UPHARSIN)); King Belshazzar is frightened
    71 T 34   Tobit lies sleeping against a wall

WAND
    see ROD

WANDERING
    see also SEARCHING
    71 H 2   David's wanderings

WAR
    see ARMY
    see BATTLE

WAREHOUSE
    see STORAGE

WARNING
    see also INSTRUCTING
    71 A 35 4   The tree of knowledge of good and evil
    71 C 25 11   God appears to Isaac and warns him not to journey into Egypt
    71 F 37 4   Delilah finds out Samson's secret and warns the Philistines, who come with the money

WARRIOR(S)
    see SOLDIER(S)

WASHING
    see BATHING
    see WASHING (CLOTHES)
    see WASHING (FEET)

WASHING (CLOTHES)
71 E 13 22   The people get ready for the coming legislation: they wash their clothes and set bounds round the mountain

WASHING (FEET)
71 C 12 23   Abraham fetches water and washes the angel's feet

WATCHING
see also GUARDING
see also LOOKING
71 E 11 23   Moses is exposed in the ark on the banks of the Nile; Miriam, Moses' sister, keeps watch
71 U 42 73   Holofernes beheaded by Judith with his own sword; the maidservant may be keeping watch

WATER
see also CAULDRON
see also WATERING
see also WATERS
see also WELL
71 C 12 23   Abraham fetches water and washes the angels' feet
71 C 12 82   Abraham provides Hagar and Ishmael with bread and a jug of water
71 E 11 72 1   The plague of water turned into blood: as Pharaoh goes down to the Nile, Aaron strikes the surface of the river with his rod; the water turns into blood and all the fish die
71 E 12 41 2   Moses throws a piece of wood into the water of Marah, which then becomes sweet
71 E 12 63   Moses strikes the rock twice in front of the assembled people and water gushes out; the people quench their thirst
71 F 21 52   Those who lap water by putting their hand to their mouth are separated from those who kneel down to drink the water - selection of Gideon's men
71 F 35 6   Water comes from a hollow in the asses' jaw-bone
71 F 84 12 1   Water is poured out before God - Samuel as judge
71 M 53   An angel wakes Elijah; a loaf of bread and a jar of water are usually at Elijah's head
71 N 11   The water of Jericho is purified: when the citizens of Jericho complain about their water, Elisha puts some salt in a jar; he then throws the salt into the water
71 W 53 12   Job's wife pouring a bucket of water over him

WATERING
see also WELL
71 C 31 3   Jacob at the well of Haran
71 E 11 32 2   Moses waters the sheep of Jethro's daughters

WATERS
see also FLOOD
see also RIVER
see also SEA
71 A 22   Creation of the firmament and division of the waters above and below it
71 A 23   Gathering of the waters below the firmament; dry land appears and produces all kinds of plants
71 E 12 23   With his people safe on the shore, Moses raises his hands and causes the water to return; Pharaoh's army perishes in the water (Red Sea)
71 F 21 51   To select an army for a raid against the Midianites Gideon sends away the fearful and brings the remaining ten thousand men to the water

WAVE(S)
see STORM AT SEA

WAVING
see LEAVE-TAKING

WEAPON(S)
see also ARMOUR
71 Z 39   A heavenly rider, in white garment and with weapons of gold, helps the Maccabees in their battle against Lysias

WEAPON-BEARER
see ARMOUR-BEARER

WEDDING (MARRIAGE)
see MARRIAGE

WEDDING-GUEST
71 F 33 1   Samson puts forth a riddle during his wedding-festivities

WEDDING-NIGHT
71 C 31 45   After the wedding-night Jacob discovers that he has been deceived with Leah and complains to Laban

WEDDING-RING
see RING

WEEPING
see also LAMENTING
71 C 12 84 1   Hagar sits weeping after having put Ishmael under a bush to die
71 C 31 34   Jacob kisses Rachel and is moved to tears
71 D 19 31   Joseph reveals his identity and in tears forgives his brothers' past misdeed
71 L 24 41   King Hezekiah falls ill and is visited by Isaiah, who tells him to get ready to die; Hezekiah turns his face to the wall, prays and then cries

WEIGHT
see CARRYING...

WELCOMING
see also ARRIVAL
see also RECEIVING A PERSON
71 H 15 21   David's triumph: the women of Israel come out to welcome David, singing, dancing, and playing tambourines and lyres; David holding the head of Goliath
71 L 24 52   Hezekiah welcomes the messengers and shows them his wealth

WELL
see also PIT
71 C 12 84 11   An angel appears and reveals a well of water to Hagar
71 C 21 3   The meeting at the well: Eliezer sees Rebekah coming with a pitcher
71 C 21 31   Rebekah at the well (Eliezer absent)
71 C 21 35   Laban, Rebekah's brother, comes to Eliezer at the well - Eliezer seeking a wife for Isaac
71 C 31 3   Jacob at the well of Haran
71 D 12 41   Joseph is thrown into a pit (usually depicted as a well or cistern)
71 E 11 32   Moses at a well meets the seven daughters of Jethro, the priest of Midian

WHALE
71 V 13 41   Jonah is swallowed by a great fish, (sea)monster, whale, dolphin, or the like

WHEAT
see also CORN
71 F 21 21   The angel of the Lord appears to Gideon, who is usually shown threshing wheat

WHEEL
71 O 91 1   Ezekiel's vision of God sitting
on his throne carried by four tetramorphs,
each of them having four wings; wheels
within wheels beside them

WHIPPING
see SCOURGING

WHIRLWIND
71 M 84   A chariot, horses of fire and a
whirlwind appear and Elijah is carried up
into heaven; Elijah's cloak falls (or he
hands it over to Elisha)
71 W 64(Job 38-42:6)   God speaks to Job from
out of the whirlwind

WHITE
see also BLACK AND WHITE
71 Z 39   A heavenly rider, in white garment
and with weapons of gold, helps the
Maccabees in their battle against Lysias

WHORE
71 C 33 27   Tamar changes from her widow's
clothes and covers her face with a veil
after the manner of the prostitutes; sitting
at the entrance of a city on the road to
Timnath she awaits Judah

WICKEDNESS
see also SIN
71 B 31 1   The wickedness of mankind; the
wicked are usually shown feasting and
revelling

WIDOW
71 C 33 27   Tamar changes from her widow's
clothes and covers her face with a veil
after the manner of the prostitutes; sitting
at the entrance of a city on the road to
Timnath she awaits Judah
71 M 2   Elijah and the widow of Zarephath
71 U 41 1   Judith, the widow of Manasseh,
speaks with the elders Ozias, Chabris and
Charmis

WIFE
see also FAMILY
see also HUSBAND AND WIFE
71 D 13 31   Potiphar's wife catches Joseph
by his robe, usually while lying in bed;
Joseph escapes leaving his cloak behind
in her hands (possibly with a naked child
lying in a crib)
71 F 31 1   Annunciation of Samson's birth to
the wife of Manoah by an angel
71 F 33   Samson's wedding and riddle

WILDERNESS
see also DESERT
71 C 12 84   Hagar and Ishmael in the wilderness

WIND
see WHIRLWIND

WINDOW
71 C 25 21 1   King Abimelech, looking down
from his window, sees Isaac and Rebekah
making love
71 H 16 32   David escapes through a window;
Michal lets him down with the help of a
rope
71 H 62 71   David brings the ark into
Jerusalem, Michal looking through a window
71 N 61 1   Elisha tells Joash to shoot an arrow
through the window towards Syria and
predicts that Joash will be victorious

WINE
see also WINE...
71 C 11 7   The meeting of Abraham and
Melchizedek, the high priest and king of
Salem, who brings bread and wine
71 H 62 8   David places the ark in a tent,
burns offerings before the Lord and
distributes bread, meat and wine to everyone

WINE-GRADING
see WINE-TESTING

WINE-GROWING
see also VINEYARD
71 B 35   Noah as wine-grower

WINE-TESTING
71 B 35 11   Noah tests the wine

WING
71 O 91 1   Ezekiel's vision of God sitting
on his throne carried by four tetramorphs,
each of them having four wings; wheels
within wheels beside them

WINNER
see CONTEST

WINTER
see SNOW

WISDOM
71 I 3   Solomon's wisdom

WITCH
71 H 31   Saul and the witch of Endor

WITHDRAWING
see SEPARATING

WITNESSING (LOOKING)
see LOOKING

WOE
see CURSING

WOLF
71 O 33 4   Isaiah's prophecy of the peaceable
kingdom: 'the wolf shall dwell with the
lamb'

WOMAN
see also GIRL
see also WIFE
71 N 13   Elisha and the Shunammite woman

WONDER
see also MIRACLE
71 D 18 5   The feast at Joseph's house: the
amazement of his brothers at being seated
according to their age; Benjamin is honored
with extra food
71 P 13 4   To his astonishment King
Nebuchadnezzar sees four men (one of them
usually represented as an angel) in the
furnace; the king commands them to come
forth

WOOD(EN)
71 C 13 11 1   The servants are left behind
while Abraham and Isaac (usually carrying
wood) climb the mountain
71 E 12 41 2   Moses throws a piece of wood
into the water of Marah, which then becomes
sweet
71 M 21   When the brook dries up, Elijah
crosses over to the city of Zarephath; at
the gate he meets a woman and her little
son gathering wood (the woman's sticks may
form a cross)

WOODGATHERER
see GATHERING

WOOING
see COURTING

WOOL
see SPINNING

WORK
see LABOR

WORLD
see EARTH
see UNIVERSE

WORRYING
see INQUIETUDE

WORSHIPPING
see also ADORATION
see also IDOLATRY
see also PRAYING
see also REFUSING (WORSHIP)
71 E 12 3   After crossing the Red Sea the
    Israelites rejoice and praise God

WOUND
see WOUNDED PERSON

WOUNDED PERSON
see also DYING PERSON
71 H 32 13   Saul wounded by an arrow

WOUNDING
see WOUNDED PERSON

WRAPPING
see COVERING

WRATH
see ANGER

WRESTLING
see also STRUGGLING
71 C 32 22   Jacob wrestles with the angel (or
    man) till daybreak; Jacob's thigh is put
    out of joint
71 E 11 45   At an inn, God (or the angel of
    God) tries to kill Moses

WRITER
see POET

WRITING
71 E 13 43 1   God writing the commandments
    on the two stone tablets
71 O 74 61   Jeremiah dictates his prophecies
    to Baruch
71 P 22   During Belshazzar's banquet a hand
    appears and writes on the wall (MENE, MENE,
    TEKEL and PARSIN (UPHARSIN)); King
    Belshazzar is frightened
71 Q 83   Mordecai and Esther write letters
    in King Ahasuerus' name
71 T 63 2   The writing of the marriage letter
    - Tobias and Sarah

WRITING DESK
see WRITING

XERXES (AHASUERUS)
see AHASUERUS (KING)

YARN
see SPINNING

YEAR
71 B 25   Story of Enoch, son of Jared, who
    invented letters and was the first to divide
    the year into seasons and into twelve months

YOUTH
see also UPBRINGING
71 F 31 7   Samson's youth

YOUTH (ADOLESCENT)
see FATHER AND SON
see MOTHER AND SON

ZAREPHATH (WIDOW OF)
71 M 2   Elijah and the widow of Zarephath

ZECHARAIAH (KING)
71 K 35   Story of Zecharaiah, son of
    Jeroboam II, king of Israel

ZEDEKIAH (KING)
71 L 32   Story of Zedekiah, king of Judah
71 O 76   Jeremiah in the reign of Zedekiah

ZIPPORAH
71 E 11 34   Moses' marriage with Zipporah
71 E 11 45 1   Zipporah appeases God by
    circumcising one of her sons
71 E 12 8   Jethro's visit to Moses: with
    Zipporah and her two sons he comes to the
    desert where Moses is encamped

ZOAR
71 C 12 4   The destruction of Sodom and
    Gomorrah: Lot and his family flee to Zoar,
    carrying their belongings; an angel may
    be showing the way

ZOPHAR
71 W 54 1   Eliphaz, Bildad and Zophar go to
    Job to console him over his misfortunes
    (the three friends may be depicted as kings)

ICONCLASS CLASSIFICATION OF OLD TESTAMENT THEMES

LISTING OF THEMES AND PAINTINGS REPRESENTING THEM

11 C   GOD THE FATHER

ITALIAN SCHOOL

Alberti, Durante. Angels holding shield
with attribute of the Creator. Rome,
Il Gesù, Cappella della SS. Trinità,
spandrel.

Antoniazzo, Romano. David and Solomon,
and Eternal in Glory. Rome, San Pietro
in Montorio.

Castagno, Andrea del. Detail: God the Father.
Venice, S. Zaccaria, Cappella di S. Tarasio.

Ramenghi, Bartolommeo (Bagnacavallo). God
the Creator. Christie, Manson and Woods
(Sale, New York, June 12, 1981, No. 104).

SPANISH SCHOOL

Spanish School, 12th century. School of
Catalonia. Fresco decorations. Triumphal
arch, detail: the hand of the Almighty.
Tahull, Sant Climent.

11 G   ANGELS

ITALIAN SCHOOL

Alberti, Durante. Angels holding shield
with attribute of the Creator. Rome,
Il Gesù, Cappella della SS. Trinità,
spandrel.

11 G 1   SERAPHIM

ITALIAN SCHOOL

Niccolò da Foligno. Panels of Prophets:
Daniel, Abraham and a Seraph. Baltimore,
Md., Walters Art Gallery, 37.620.

SPANISH SCHOOL

Pedret Master. S. Maria de Aneu. Apsidal
decoration: Madonna and Child with the
Three Kings, Archangels and Seraphim,
etc. Barcelona, Museum of Catalan Art.

Spanish school, Wall painting. Detail: Seraphim.
Fresco decorations of apse 12th century.
Rueda, Church.

11 I 1   GROUPS OF PROPHETS

FRENCH SCHOOL

French School, Wall Painting. Frescoes.
Apse. Row of Prophets. 12th century.
Le Liget, Chapel.

GERMAN SCHOOL

Cranach, L. (the elder) ? Moses with Aaron
and two Prophets. Munich, Old Pinakothek,
16 (275)

ITALIAN SCHOOL

Allamagna, Justus d' (?). Decoration of
vaulting of gallery with Old Testament
figures. Detail: bay with Job, Hosea,
Jacob, and Micah. Genoa, S. M. du Castello,
Cloister.

Allori, Alessandro. Frescoes, 1560: Prophets,
in opposite corners. Florence, S.S.
Annunziata. Ceiling, Capella della Visitazione

Amatrice, Cola dell'. Four Prophets of
the Old Testament: Jonah, Jeremiah, Zachariah,
Elijah. c. 1516. Kansas, University
of (Lawrence), Museum of Art, 60.65.

Cresti, Domenico. Coronation of the Virgin
and Prophets. Rome, S. Maria Maggiore,
Ceiling, Baptistry.

Gaulli, Giovanni Battista. The Prophets
of Israel. c. 1676. Cleveland, Museum
of Art, 69.131.

Guercino. Prophets and Sibyls. 1626-1627?
Piacenza, Cathedral, Interior of Cupola.

Italian School, 12th century. Detail: four
Prophets. Nepi, Castel Sant'Elia, Frescoes,
south transept, fourth row.

Matteo da Viteroo and others. Prophets.
Avignon, Palace of the Popes, Audience
Hall, Vault.

Muziano, Girolamo (Brescianino). Prophets.
Rome, S. Caterina della Rota.

Pinturicchio and Assistants. Lunettes: Apostles
and Prophets.Rome, Vatican,Borgia Apartments,
Hall of Creeds.

Signorelli, Luca. Frescoes. Last Judgement
and other scenes: End of the World. Detail:
Prophets and Sibyls. Orvieto, Cathedral.

Tiepolo, G. B. Four Prophets. Venice, Scuola
del Carmine.

SPANISH SCHOOL

Gascó, Joan. Door of Cabinet: Prophets and
Sibyls.

Gascó, Perot. Prophets and Sibyls. Vich,
Museo Episcopal.

Huguet, Jaime. Panel: prophets. Junyer
- Collection (Barcelona).

Master of Losarcos. Prophets from a predalla
panel. Agapito del Valle - Collection
(Logrono)

Master of the Prelate Mur. Heads of Prophets.
Junyer - Collection (Barcelona)

Sinobas Master? Retable. Details: Prophets.
Palazuelos de Muñó, Church.

Spanish School,12th century.School of Catalonia.
Fresco decorations: Nave arches. Details:
Prophets. Tahull, Santa Maria.

Spanish School, 15th century. Prophets,
left. Barcelona, Dealer.

Spanish School, Wall Painting. New Testament
scenes destroyed by fire in 1936. Old
Testament cycle and ancestors of Christ
on arches. Two Prophets. c. 1200. Sigera,
Monastery, Chapter House.

11 I 2   SIBYLS

FLEMISH SCHOOL

Dyck, Anthony van. An Ancient Prophetess.
c. 1655/1660. Leipzig, Museum, 1593.

FRENCH SCHOOL

Subleyras, Pierre. A Sibyl. Bologna, Pinacoteca
Nationale, 728.

ITALIAN SCHOOL

Allori, Alessandro. Ceiling, Frescoes, 1560
(two sibyls in opposite corners). Florence,
SS. Annunziata, Cappella della Visitazione.

Domenichino. Sibyl. 1620-25. Rome, Museo
Capitalino.

Guercino. Cathedral. Interior of Cupola,
with Prophets and Sibyls. 1626-1627?
Piacenza, Cathedral.

Massari, Antonio. Ceiling: King David and
a Sibyl. Corneto, Cathedral.

Massari, Antonio. Ceiling: Isaiah and a
Sibyl. Corneto, Cathedral.

Massari, Antonio. Ceiling: Hosea and a Sibyl.
Corneto, Cathedral.

Peruzzi, Baldassare. Sibyls. Rome, S. Onofrio,
semi-dome and tribune.

Reni, Guido. Head of Sibyl. Mahon. Denis
- Collection (London).

Reni, Guido. Sibyl with a Scroll. Burghley
House.

Romanino, Girolamo. Scenes of the Life and
Passion of Christ. Detail: Corners: Sibyl.
Pisogne, S. Maria della Neve.

Saluiati, Francesco. Lunette: Prophet and
Sybil. Rome, Palazzo della Cancelleria,
Cappella del Pallio.

Signorelli, Luca. Frescoes. Last Judgement
and other scenes: End of the World. Detail:
Prophets and Sybils. Orvieto, Cathedral.

Sirani, Elisabetta. A Sibyl. Bologna, Pinacoteca
Nazionale.

Sirani, Elisabetta. The Sibyl. Bologna,
Pinacoteca Nazionale.

SPANISH SCHOOL

Gascó, Joan. Door of Cabinet: Prophets and
Sibyls. Detail.

OLD TESTAMENT FIGURES

11 I 2   CUMAEAN SIBYL

FLEMISH SCHOOL
Eyck, Hubert and Jan van. Altarpiece of the
Adoration of the Lamb. Exterior, center
upper panel, top right: The Cumaean Sibyl.
Ghent, St. Bavon.

ITALIAN SCHOOL
Bordone, Paris, School of. A Sibyl. Boston,
Museum of Fine Arts, 74.24.
Castagno, Andrea del. Famous Men: Frescoes
from the Villa Carducci (Villa Pandolfini,
Villa Rinuccini, Il Fornacione), Legnaia:
Pippo Spano, Farinata degli Uberti, Niccolo
Acciaiuoli, Cumaean Sibyl, Queen Esther,
Queen Tomyris, Dante, Petrarch, Boccaccio.
Frescoes. Florence, Palazzo Uffizi.
Castagno, Andrea del. Frescoes from the Villa
Pandolfini, Legnaia: Cumaean Sibyl. Florence,
S. Apollonia.
Michelangelo. Sibyls and Prophets. Detail:
Cumaean Sibyl. Rome, Vatican, Sistine Chapel.
Ceiling decorations, between lunettes.
Pitati, Bonifacio. The Cumaean Sibyl. Boston,
Museum of Fine Arts, 01.6215.

SPANISH SCHOOL
Gascó, Joan. Door of Cabinet: Prophets and
Sibyls. Detail: Cumaean Sibyl. Vich, Museo
Episcopal.
Gascó, Perot. Prophets and Sibyls. Detail:
Cumaean Sibyl. Vich, Museo Episcopal.

11 I 2   DELPHIC SIBYL

GERMAN SCHOOL
Ring, Ludger, Tom the Elder, 1496-1547. The
Delphic Sibyl. Part of a series of Sibyls
and Prophets. c.1534, Panel. Paris, Louvre,
Musée du, R.F. 2283.

ITALIAN SCHOOL
Michelangelo. Sibyls and Prophets. Detail:
Sibyl of Delphi. Rome, Vatican, Sistine
Chapel, Ceiling decorations, between lunettes.
Romanino, Girolamo. Cantoria: Sibyl Delfica.
Asolo, Duomo.

11 I 2   ERYTHRAEAN SIBYL

DUTCH SCHOOL
Heemskerck, Maerten van. The Erythraen Sibyl.
1565. Amsterdam, Rijksmuseum. A 1910.

FLEMISH SCHOOL
Eyck, Hubert and Jan van. Altarpiece of the
Adoration of the Lamb. Exterior, center
upper panel, top left: The Erythraean Sibyl.
Ghent, St. Bavon.
ITALIAN SCHOOL
Angelico, Fra. Large Crucifixion. Detail:
Erythraean Sibyl. S. Marco, Chapter House.
Cesari, Guiseppe. Prophets and Sibyls. Vault
decoration. Rome, S. Prassede, Capella
Olgiati.
Gennari, Benedetto. Erythraean Sibyl. Detroit,
Institute of Arts, 89.6.
Michelangelo. Sibyls and Prophets. Ceiling
decorations between lunettes. Detail: The
Erythraean Sibyl. Rome, Vatican, Sistine
Chapel.
Maretto da Brescia. Isaiah; Erythraean Sibyl.
Escorial, Monastery, Chapter House.
Romanino, Girolamo. Cantoria: Sibyl Eritrea.
Asolo, Duomo.

SPANISH SCHOOL
Gascó, Joan. Door of a cabinet: Prophets
and Sibyls. Detail: Erythraean Sibyl.
Vich, Museo Episcopal.
Gascó, Perot. Prophets and Sibyls. Detail:
Erythraean Sibyl. Vich, Museo Episcopal.

11 I 2   HELLESPONTIC SIBYL

ITALIAN SCHOOL
Romanino, Girolamo. Cantoria: Sibyl
Ellespontica. Asola, Duomo.

SPANISH SCHOOL
Gascó, Perot. Prophets and Sibyls. Detail:
Hellespontian Sibyl. Vich, Museo Episcopal.

11 I 2   LIBYAN SIBYL

ITALIAN SCHOOL
Michelangelo. Ceiling decorations, between
lunettes: Sibyls and Prophets. Detail:
Libyan Sibyl. Rome, Vatican, Sistine
Chapel.
Romanino, Girolamo. Cantoria: Sibyl Libica.
Asola, Duomo.

11 I 2   PERSIAN SIBYL

FLEMISH SCHOOL
Benson, Ambrose. Copy. Sibilla Persica.
London, Victoria and Albert Museum, Ionides
Bequest CAI.106.

ITALIAN SCHOOL
Italian School, 11th century. Church, nave,
left wall above pillars, fresco: Persian
Sibyl. S. Angelo in Formis.
Michelangelo. Ceiling decorations between
lunettes: Sibyls and Prophets. Detail:
Persian Sibyl. Rome, Vatican, Sistine
Chapel.
Romanino, Girolamo. Cantoria: Sibyl Persica.
Asola, Duomo.

11 I 2   PHRYGIAN SIBYL

ITALIAN SCHOOL
Sirani, Elisabeth. Sibyl. Bologna. F.A.
Ghedini Collection.

SPANISH SCHOOL
Gascó, Perot. Prophets and Sibyls. Detail:
Phrygian Sibyl. Vich, Museo Episcopal.

11 I 2   SAMIAN SIBYL

ITALIAN SCHOOL
Guercino. Samian Sibyl. Florence, Uffizi.
Guercino. Samian Sibyl (companion painting
to King David, Spencer Collection, 766).
Althorp House, Spencer Collection, 767.
Romanino, Girolamo. Cantoria: Sibyl Samia.
Asola, Duomo.

11 I 2   TIBURTINE SIBYL

ITALIAN SCHOOL
Peruzzi, Baldassare. The Sibyl predicting
the birth of Christ to Augustus. Siena,
Fonteguista.

11 I 2   TIBURTINE SIBYL AND AUGUSTUS

FLEMISH SCHOOL
Engelbrechtsz, Cornelis. The Tiburian Sibyl.
Vienna, Academy. (Inv.#568).
Provost, Jan. Vision of David and the
Tiburtine Sibyl. Leningrad, Hermitage.

ITALIAN SCHOOL
Cortona, Pietro da. The Tiburtine Sibyl.
Nancy (Meuthe-et-Moselle), Musée.

11 I 6   OLD TESTAMENT FIGURES NOT IN NARRATIVE SCENES

ITALIAN SCHOOL
Giaquinto, Corrado. Figures from the Old
Testament. Sketch for the cupola of the
Cathedral of Cesena. c. 1750. Chicago, Art
Institute, 41.830.
Vecchietta. Old Testament Scenes. Sala di
S. Pietro. Siena, Spedale di S. M. Della
Scala.

11 I 61   GROUPS OF PERSONS FROM THE OLD TESTAMENT

DUTCH SCHOOL
Bol, Ferdinand. Anna van Erckel and Erasmus
Scharlaken as Rebecca and Isaac. Late 1640s.
Dordrecht, Museum, DM /948/126.
Bray, Salomon de. Jael, Deborah and Barek.
1635. Utrecht, Rijksmuseum, on loan from
Thurkow van Huffel, Mrs. L - Collection.

ITALIAN SCHOOL
Campi, Bernardino. Old and New Testaments.
Fresco in cupola. Cremona, S. Sigismondo.
Italian School, 12th century. Prophet and
Elders in Procession. Nepi, Castel Sant'Elia.
Frescoes, south transept, second row.

11 I 61 1   PATRIARCHS

EARLY MEDIEVAL AND BYZANTINE
Byzantine school. Wall Painting. Patriarch
of the Old Testament. Fresco, 13th century.
St. Achilles, nave, central square, north
arch, east side. Arilje, Yugoslavia.

FLEMISH SCHOOL
Flemish School, 16th century. A Patriarch.
Madrid, Prado.
Provost, Jan. Altarpiece, wing: a Patriarch
of the Old Testament (?) Madrid, Prado.
ITALIAN SCHOOL
Castiglione, Giovanni Benedetto. Journey of
a Patriarch. Cleveland, Museum of Art,
69.1.

SPANISH SCHOOL
Spanish School, 13th century. Ancestors of
Christ. Fresco, c. 1200. Sigena, Monastery,
Chapter House, soffits of arches.

11 I 61 3   KINGS OF ISRAEL AND JUDAH

FRENCH SCHOOL
French School, Wall Painting. The Kings of
Judah. Fresco, copy by Louis Henri Laffillée.
Laval (Mayenne).

GERMAN SCHOOL
German school, Wall Painting. Vision of the
Prophets. Detail: A King of Judah. Fresco,
1160. Lower Rhine School. Schwarz-Rheindorf,
Lower Church.

11 I 62   SMALL PERSONS FROM THE OLD TESTAMENT

EARLY MEDIEVAL AND BYZANTINE
Byzantine school, Wall Painting, 14th-15th
century. Head of a Prophet. Fragment.
Candis, Crete, Historical Museum.
Byzantine school, Wall Painting, Mistra. Prophet.
Pantanassa Church, frescoes, dome, squinch.
Mistra.

DUTCH SCHOOL
Rosa, Salvatore. A Bearded Prophet. Sotheby
and Co., London. (Sale, April 8, 1981, No.
6).

GERMAN SCHOOL
German School, 16th century. A Prophet.
Sotheby and Co., London (Sale, New York,
Parke Bernet, No. 4778M, Jan 21, 1982,
No. 42).
Strigel, Bernhard. Heads of Prophets. Stuttgart,
Museum ?

ITALIAN SCHOOL
Carracci, Ludovico. Prophets. c. 1592. Frescoes.
Bologna, S. Bartolomeo sul Reno.
Castagno, Andrea del. Fresco of a Prophet.
Venice, S. Zaccaria, Cappella S. Farasio.
Cimabue. Prophet. S. Francesco, Upper Church:
Misc. fresco decorations, decorative band
in nave. Assisi.
Conco, Sebastiano. Prophet with an Angel.
Rome, Galleria d'Arte Antica.
Italian school, 9th century. Bust of prophet
in medallion. Fresco. Rome, S. Maria in
Cosmedin.
Italian school, 11th century. ?(Obadiah,
Habakkuk, or Nahum). S. Angelo in Formis.
Church, nave, Right wall above pillars.
Italian school, Wall painting, end of 12th
century. Prophet. Spoleto, S. Paolo.
Italian school, 13th century. Cathedral,
frescoes. Detail: Prophet. Anagni.
Italian school, 13th century. S. Francesco,
upper church. Decorations of vaults. Detail:
Prophet in fourth bay. Assisi.
Italian school, Wall painting, Bolzano S.
Giovanni (Johanneskirche), frescoes.
13th/14th c. Apse vault:
Writing of the Scriptures, c. 1230.
Italian school, 13th century. Baptistery,
ceiling decoration, religious subjects,
second zone. Detail: a saint or a prophet.
Parma.
Italian school, 13th century. Prophet in
medallion. Fresco. Rome, SS. Quatro Coronati,
Chapel of S. Silvestro, right wall.
Italian school, 18th century. Prophets and
Angels. Ceiling decorations. Naples, S.
Chiara.
Melozzo da Forli. Prophets. Designed by
Melozzo, painted by Palmezzano. Forli,
S. Biagio.
Marco da Pino ? Prophet. Rome, Villa Borghese,
Gallery.
Masucci, Agostino. Prophet. Rome, Palazzo
del Quirinale, Coffee House.
Palma, Giovane. Prophet. Boston, Morison
Collection.
Palma, Giovane. Prophet. Venice, Ateneo
Veneto.
Romanino, Girolamo. Scenes of the life and
passion of Christ: Detail: Corners: Prophet.
Pisogne, S. Maria della Neve.
Rosselli, Cosimo. A Prophet. San Miniato,
Cathedral.
Schiavone, Andrea. Prophets. Venice, S.
Giacomo dell'Orio.
Siciolante, Girolamo. Prophet. Rome, Villa
Borghese, Gallery.
Tintoretto (Jacopo Robusti). A Prophet.
Venice, Scuola di San Rocco, refectory,
walls.
Titian, School of. A prophet.
Uccello, Paolo. Heads of Prophets. Frescoes.
Florence Cathedral.

SPANISH SCHOOL

Martin de Soria. Retable, fragment: prophet.
Madrid, Prado, Collection Bosch.
Ribera, Jusepe de. The Prophets. c. 1638.
Naples, S. Martino.
Serafi, Pedro. Organ shutters: Prophets.
Barcelona, Cathedral.

Spanish school, Wall painting, Sigene. c. 1200.
Monastery, chapter house. New Testament
scenes destroyed by fire in 1936. Old
Testament cycle and ancestors of Christ
on arches. Barcelona, Museum of Catalan
Art.
Spanish school, 13th century. Fragments of
fresco decoration. Details: prophets. Toledo,
San Román.
Spanish school, 14th century. School of Navarre.
Frescoes in cloisters above tomb of Bishop
Sanchez de Asiain. Details: Medallions of
Prophets. Pamplona, Cathedral.
Támara Master. Prophets from unknown altarpiece.
Barcelona, Private Collection.

11 I 62   AARON

EARLY MEDIEVAL AND BYZANTINE
Early Medieval and Byzantine painting, 13th
century. Moses and Aaron. Sinai, Monastery
of St. Catherine, Icon 378A and B.
Byzantine school, Wall painting, 16th century.
Showing section of Last Supper. Aaron in
medallion. Mount Athos, the Laura, Church.

ITALIAN SCHOOL
Ugolino da Siena. Moses and Aaron. Detail:
Aaron. Richmond, Collection. Cook, 2.
Vasari, Giorgio and Gherardi, Cristofano.
Sacrifices and Prophets: Aaron. Fresco.
Cortona, Compagnia del Gesù.

SPANISH SCHOOL
Juanes, Juan de. Triptych: the High Priest
Aaron.
Mayno, Juan Bautista. Aaron. Wall decorations.
Toledo, San Pedro Mártir.
Ribera, Jusene de. Moses and Aaron. Florence,
Palazzo Corsini.

11 I 62   ABRAHAM

EARLY MEDIEVAL AND BYZANTINE
Coptic painting. Detail: Daniel, "Peace",
Abraham. Khargeh, Bagawat Necropolis, Tomb
Chapel, Room of Peace.

ITALIAN SCHOOL
Castagno, Andrea del. Fresco of the prophet
Abram. Venice, S. Zaccaria, Cappella S.
Farasio.
Italian school, 14th century. Series of Prophets:
Abraham and Noah. Detail: head of Noah.
Fresco, School of Rimini. Pomposa, Abbey,
Chapter Room.
Lorenzo Monaco. Abraham. New York, Metropolitan
Museum of Art, 65.14.1.
Niccolò da Foligno. Panels of Prophets: Daniel,
Abraham and a Seraph. Baltimore, Md., Walters
Art Gallery, 37.620.
Roselli, Cosimo. Patriarchs: Abraham. Florence,
Galleria Antica e Moderna.
Italian school, 14th century. Series of Prophets:
Abraham and Noah. Detail: head of Abraham.
Fresco, School of Rimini. Pomposa, Abbey,
Chapter Room.

SPANISH SCHOOL
Huguet, Jaime. Panel: Prophets. Detail: Abraham.
Barcelona, Junyer-Collection.
Spanish school, 16th century, School of Catalonia.
Prophets: Moses, Abraham, Isaiah. New York,
Hispanic Society of America.

11 I 62   ABRAHAM(II) AS FATHER OF ALL BELIEVERS

ITALIAN SCHOOL
Italian school, 16th century (North Italian)
? Series of patriarchs and prophet: Abraham.
Greenville, S.C., Bob Jones University
Collection, 1962 cat. 198.

11 I 62   ADAM

GERMAN SCHOOL
Baldung, Hans. Adam and Eve. Budapest,
Museum of Fine Arts, 715, 716.

11 I 62   ADAM AND EVE

AUSTRIAN SCHOOL
Klimt, Gustav. Adam and Eve. 1917-18. Vienna,
Osterreichische Galerie Inv. Nr. 4402.

DUTCH SCHOOL
Dongen, Kees van. Adam and Eve. 1922.
Collection Dolly A. van Dongen.

FLEMISH SCHOOL
Eyck, Hubert and Jan van. Altarpiece of
the Adoration of the Lamb. Interior. Extreme
right and left panels: Adam and Eve.
Ghent, St. Bavon.

GERMAN SCHOOL
Baldung, Hans. Adam and Eve. Lugano, Collection
Thyssen-Bornemisza, 16.

11 I 62 5   ADAM AND EVE IN LEGEND

EARLY MEDIEVAL AND BYZANTINE
Byzantine school, Wall painting, 12th-14th
century. Adam and Eve. Lagoudera, Panagia
tou Arakos, west bay, north vault, Anastasis.

11 I 62   AMOS

ITALIAN SCHOOL
Dello di Niccolo Delli. Retable with scenes
from the Lives of Christ and the Virgin.
Predella with series of prophets of the
Old Testament and other: Amos.
Italian school, 11th century. Fresco. Amos.
S. Angelo in Formis, church, nave, left
wall above pillars.
Italian school, 12th century. Frescoes,
south transept, fourth row. Detail: Prophets
Amos and Jonah. Nepi, Castel Sant 'Elia.
Italian school, 13th century. Ceiling decoration.
Religious subjects, second zone. Detail:
Amos. Parma, Baptistery.

SPANISH SCHOOL
Gascó, Joan. Door of a cabinet: Prophets
and sibyls. Detail: Amos. Vich, Museo
Episcopal.
Ribera, Jusepe de. The Prophets. Detail:
the Prophet Amos. 1638-1643. Naples,
Museo Nazionale di S. Martino.

11 I 62   ASA

AMERICAN SCHOOL
Levine, Jack. King Asa. Harvard University,
Fogg Art Museum. Collection Meta and
Paul J. Sachs.

11 I 62   BALAAM

ITALIAN SCHOOL
Italian school, 11th century. Right wall
above pillars. Balaam. S. Angelo in Formis,
church, nave.
Italian school, 13th century.Ceiling decoration.
Religious subjects, Second zone. Detail:
Balaam and Head of Balaam. Parma, Baptistery.

SPANISH SCHOOL
Luna Master. Retable, fragments: Balaam
and David. Popoff, Alexander - Collection
(Paris).
Master of Riofrío. Series of prophets: Balaam.
Greenville, S.C., Bob Jones University
Collection, 1962 cat. 191.
Serafi, Pedro. Organ shutters. Balaam.
Barcelona, Cathedral.

Villalobos Master. The Prophet Balaam. Harris
- Collection (London).

11 I 62   BARUCH

FRENCH SCHOOL
Flandrin, J.H. Baruch, the Prophet.

ITALIAN SCHOOL
Celio, Gaspare. Baruch. Rome, Il Gesù, Cappella
della Sacra Famiglia, spandrel.

SPANISH SCHOOL
Muru, Juan, and a collaborator. Retable of
High Altar. Panels by Hand B. Resurrection.
Prophets Malachi and Baruch. Ardara, Sardinia,
Parish Church.

11 I 62   DANIEL

EARLY MEDIEVAL AND BYZANTINE
Byzantine school, Wall painting. Detail: Prophet
Daniel. 10th century. Cappadocia, Goereme
Region, Elmale Kilisse, frescoes, vault.
Coptic painting. Tomb chapel: Room of Peace.
Detail: Daniel. Khargeh, Bagawat Necropolis.

DUTCH SCHOOL
Drost, Wilhelm. The Young Daniel. c. 1853-54.
Copenhagen, Art Museum, 999, Deposit, No.
6.

ITALIAN SCHOOL
Castagno, Andrea del. Fresco of the prophet
Daniel. Venice, S. Zaccaria, Cappella S.
Farasio.
Dello di Niccolo Delli. Retable with scenes
from the Lives of Christ and the Virgin.
Predella with series of prophets of the
Old Testament and others: Daniel.
Italian school, 12th century. Scenes from
the Book of Daniel: Prophet Daniel. Fresco.
Rome, S. Maria in Cosmedin, nave.
Italian school, 11th century. Left wall above
pillars. Daniel. Fresco. S. Angelo in Formis,
Church, nave.
Niccolò da Foligno. Panels of prophets: Daniel,
Abraham and an angel. Baltimore, Md. Walters
Art Gallery, 620A, D, F.
Tiepolo, G. B. Decorations: Daniel. Udine,
Palazzo Arcivescovile.

SPANISH SCHOOL
Huguet, Jaime. Panel: prophets. Detail: Daniel.
Junyer - Collection (Barcelona).
Pareja, Diego de. Panels of the life of the
Virgin and Prophets. Detail: Daniel and
Habakkuk. Arjona, Santa Maria.
Reixach, Juan (?) Retable. Panel: Daniel.
Valencia, Museo de Pinturas.

11 I 62 31   DANIEL AS PROPHET WITH BOOK AND SCROLL

EARLY MEDIEVAL AND BYZANTINE
Early Medieval and Byzantine painting. The
prophet Daniel. Athens, Byzantine Museum.
Byzantine school, Wall painting. Dome: Prophets.
Daniel, S.W. quarter. 12th-14th century.
Lagoudera, Panagia tou Arakos.

ITALIAN SCHOOL
Italian school, 13th century. Ceiling decoration,
religious subjects, second zone. Detail:
Daniel. Parma, Baptistery.
Michelangelo. Ceiling decorations, between
lunettes: Sibyls and Prophets. Detail: Daniel.
Rome, Vatican, Sistine Chapel.
Niccolò da Foligno. Panels of Prophets: Daniel,
Abraham and a Seraph. Baltimore, Md., Walters
Art Gallery, 37.620.
Romanino, Girolamo. Cantoria: Prophet Daniel.
Asolo, Duomo.
Ugolino da Siena. Daniel. Philadelphia,
Collection J.G. Johnson, 89.

11 I 62   DAVID

EARLY MEDIEVAL AND BYZANTINE
Byzantine school, Wall painting. Detail
of remains of frescoes: David and Moses.
13th century. Grottoferrata, Church.

DUTCH SCHOOL
Finson, Ludovicus. David. Stanford University,
Art Museum, 55.1.
Bray, Salomon de. David with his Sword.
1636. Malibu, J. Paul Getty Museum, 69.PA.22.
Gelder, Aert de. King David. Amsterdam,
Rijkmuseum.

FRENCH SCHOOL
French school, Wall painting. Wall decorations.
Choir, wall dividing choir and nave. The
Last Supper and Prophets. Detail of the
Prophet David. 12th century. Vic, Church.
Moreau, Gustave. King David. Chrysler,
Walter P. - Collection (New York).

GERMAN SCHOOL
German school, Wall painting. Geneaology
of Christ. Ceiling painting on wood. Detail:
King David. 12th century. Hildesheim,
S. Michael.

ITALIAN SCHOOL
Castagno, Andrea del. Fresco of prophet.
Cappella S. Farasio. Venice, S. Zaccaria.
Dello di Niccolo Delli. Retable with scenes
from the Lives of Christ and the Virgin.
Predella with series of prophets of the
Old Testament and others: David.
Domenichino. King David playing the harp.
Versailles, Palace.
Girolamo da S. Croce. King David. Kress,
S. H. - Collection (New York). 1013.
Guercino. King David. (companion painting
to Samian Sibyl). Althorp House, Spencer
Collection, 766.
Italian school, 12th-14th century. Annunciation
with medallions of Isaiah and David.
S. Vito di Normanni, S. Biagio, Crypt,
Vault.
Italian school, 13th century. Ceiling decoration.
Religious subjects, Second zone. Detail:
David. Parma, Baptistery.
Italian school, 14th century. King David.
Spinelli - Collection (Florence).
Italian school, 17th century. Boy with Sword
(David?). Kansas City, William Rockwell
Nelson Gallery of Art, 33-119.
Italian school, 13th century. David and
a Patriarch: David. Assisi, S. Francesco,
upper church.
Italian school, 14th century. Series of
Prophets: David. Fresco, School of Rimini.
Pomposa, Abbey, Chapter Room.
Massari, Antonio. Ceiling: King David and
a Sibyl. Corneto, Cathedral.
Palma, Giovane. David. Venice, S. Niccolò
da Tolentino.
Reni, Guido. The young David. Vienna,
Kunsthistorisches Museum.
Roselli, Cosimo. Patriarchs: David and Noah.
Florence, Galleria Antica e Moderna.
Salviati, Francesco. Story of David. David
talking to Soldiers. Rome, Palazzo Sachetti,
Second floor salon, East wall, far left,
upper section.

SPANISH SCHOOL
Becerril Master. David. Section of a Predella.
Madrid, Private Collection.
Becerril Master. Isaiah and David. Barcelona,
Private Collection.
Berruguete, Pedro. David. Pani, Alberto
J. - Collection (Mexico City).

Bonnat Master. Panels of the Prophets. David
    and Ezekiel. Cornellà, Marqués de -
    Collection (Barcelona).
Correa de Vivar, Juan. Retable from S. Martín
    de Valdeiglesias. Detail: David. Madrid,
    Prado.
Craz, Diego de la. Christ between David and
    Jeremiah. Bob Jones University Collection.
    (Greensville, S.C.).
Gascó, Perot. Prophets and Sibyls. Detail:
    David. Vich, Museo Episcopal.
López, Andrés, and Antonio de Vega. David.
    Madrid, Private Collection.
Luna Master. Retable, fragments: Balaam and
    David. Popoff, Alexander - Collection (Paris).
Master of Riofrió. Series of prophets: David.
    Greenville, S.C., Bob Jones University
    Collection, 1962 cat. 192.

11 I 62 31   DAVID AS A PROPHET WITH CROWN AND SCROLL

DUTCH SCHOOL
    Gelder, Aert de. King David. Amsterdam,
        Rijksmuseum, 966 B 3.

ITALIAN SCHOOL
    Antoniazzo Romano. David and Solomon, and
        Eternal in Glory. Rome, San Pietro in Montorio.
    Italian school, 11th century. Nave: Prophets:
        King David. S. Angelo in Formis, Cathedral.

SPANISH SCHOOL
    Huguet, Jaime. Panel: prophets. Detail: David.
        Junyer - Collection (Barcelona).
    Nunyes, Pedro. Panels, from the church at
        Castelldans. David. Lerida, Museo Episcopal.
    Reixach, Juan (?). Retable. Panel: David.
        Valencia, Museo de Pinturas.
    Spanish school, 16th century. School of Catalonia.
        David. New York, French and Co.
    Spanish school, 16th century. School of Catalonia.
        Prophets: Jeremiah, David, Melchizedek.
        New York, Hispanic Society of America.

11 I 62 32   DAVID AS MUSICIAN

AMERICAN SCHOOL
    Levine, Jack. King David. Mr. and Mrs. S.
        Plaut, Collection, Cambridge, Mass.

BRITISH SCHOOL
    Rossetti, D.G. The Seed of David. (Llandaff
        Cathedral Triptych), 1856, right panel.
        London, Tate Gallery, 3965.
    Rossetti, D.G. The Seed of David. (Llandaff
        Cathedral Triptych), 1858-64, right panel.
        Cardiff, National Museum of Wales.

DUTCH SCHOOL
    Dutch school, 16th century. Two panels : Donor
        and angels. David and musicians. Paris,
        Musée de Cluny.
    Honthorst, Gerard van. King David Playing
        the Harp. Utrecht, Centraal Museum.
    Lastmann, Pieter P. David Playing the Harp
        in the Temple. Brunswick, Landesmuseum.
    Rembrandt. King David with his Harp. New
        York, Schaeffer Galleries, 1939.
    Terbruggen, Hendrick. King David Playing his
        Harp, Surrounded by Angels. Versions also
        in Hartford, Kiel and Frankfurt. 1628.
        Warsaw, Nationalmuseum (Museum Narodowe).
    Terbruggen, Hendrick. King David Playing His
        Harp Surrounded by Angels. 1628. Hartford,
        Conn., Wadsworth Atheneum, 1942.29.

FLEMISH SCHOOL
    Rubens, P.P. King David. Frankfurt-on-the-Main,
        Staedel Institute.

FRENCH SCHOOL
    Vouet, Simon. King David playing the harp.
        Greenville, S.C., Bob Jones University
        Collection, 1962 cat. 99.

GERMAN SCHOOL
    Böcklin, Arnold. King David. Fresco. Basle,
        Museum, No. 1905.

ITALIAN SCHOOL
    Domenichino. King David Playing the Harp.
        Versailles, Palace.
    Giordano, Luca. Antecoro, decoration: stories
        from the life of David. Escorial, Monastery,
        Church.
    Lorenzo Monaco. King David Playing the Harp.
        c.1406. New York, Metropolitan Museum
        of Art, 65.14.4.

11 I 62 33   DAVID AS AUTHOR OF THE PSALMS

ITALIAN SCHOOL
    Cavedone, Jacopo. King David. Modena, Pinoteca
        Estense.
    Celio, Gaspare. David. Rome, Il Gesù, Cappella
        della Sacra Famiglia. Spandrel.

11 I 62 S   DAVID: LEGENDARY/HISTORICAL ADDITIONS

FLEMISH SCHOOL
    Provost, Jan. Vision of David and the Tiburtine
        Sibyl. Leningrad, Hermitage.

FRENCH SCHOOL
    Poussin, Nicolas. David, Conqueror of Goliath,
        Crowned by Victory. Madrid, Prado.

11 I 62   ELIJAH

EARLY MEDIEVAL AND BYZANTINE
    Byzantine school, Wall painting. Dome: Prophets.
        Elias (Elijah), S.E. quarter. 12th-14th
        century. Lagoudera, Panagia tou Arakos.
    Early Medieval and Byzantine painting. Prophet
        Elijah. 8th century. Sinai, Monastery
        of St. Catherine.

FRENCH SCHOOL
    Flandrin, J.H. The Prophet Elijah. c.1856-1861.
        Private Collection.

ITALIAN SCHOOL
    Dello di Niccolo Delli. Retable with scenes
        from the Lives of Christ and the Virgin.
        Predella with series of prophets of the
        Old Testament and others: Elijah.
    Finoglia, Paolo. Prophet Elijah. Naples,
        S. Martino (Capitolo dei Padri).

SPANISH SCHOOL
    Gascó, Joan. Triptych of Elijah with Sts.
        Severus and Sigismund. Vich, Private
        Collection.
    Ribera, Jusepe de. The Prophets: Elijah.
        c.1638. Naples, S. Martino.
    Ribera, Jusepe de, School of. Elijah. Probably
        Italian school. 17th century. Attributed
        to Ribera. Minneapolis, Institute of
        Art.
    Zurbaran, Francisco de. The Prophet Elijah.
        Detail: Head. Cordova, Museum.

11 I 62   ELISHA

EARLY MEDIEVAL AND BYZANTINE
    Byzantine school, Wall painting. Dome: Prophets.
        Elisaias (Elisha), S.W. quarter. 12th-14th
        century. Lagoudera, Panagia tou Arakos.

ITALIAN SCHOOL
    Dello di Niccolo Delli. Retable with scenes
        from the Lives of Christ and the Virgin.
        Predella with series of prophets of the
        Old Testament and others: Elisha.

11 I 62   EZEKIEL

EARLY MEDIEVAL AND BYZANTINE
Byzantine school, Wall painting. S. Vincenzo.
Apse. Detail: Prophet Ezekiel. Fresco. 11th
century. Galliano.
Byzantine school, Wall painting. Dome: Prophets.
Ezekiel, N.W. quarter. 12th-14th centuries.
Lagoudera, Panagia tou Arakos.

ITALIAN SCHOOL
Angelico, Fra. Large Crucifixion. Detail:
Ezekiel. Florence, S. Marco, Chapter House.
Campi, Giulio. Ezekiel. Fresco in transept.
Cremona, S. Sigismundo.
Dello di Niccolo Delli. Retable with scenes
from the Lives of Christ and the Virgin.
Predella with series of prophets of the
Old Testament and others: Ezekiel.
Italian school, 11th century. Ezekiel. Fresco.
S. Angelo in Formis, Church, Nave, right
wall above pillars.
Matteo da Viterbo and others. Prophets and
Sibyls. Vault. Detail: Ezekiel and Jeremiah
(Scala). Avignon, Palace of the Popes,
Audience Hall.
Michelangelo. Sibyls and Prophets. Detail:
Ezekiel. Rome, Vatican, Sistine Chapel.
Ceiling decorations, between lunettes.
Romanino, Girolamo. The Prophet Ezekiel.
Brescia, S. Giovanni Evangelista, Capella
del S.S. Sacramento.
Tiepolo, G.B. Decorations. Ezekiel. Udine,
Palazzo Arcivescovile, Sala Rossa.

SPANISH SCHOOL
Bonnat Master. Panels of the Prophets. David
and Ezekiel. Barcelona, Collection Marqués
de Cornellà.

11 I 62   EZRA

ITALIAN SCHOOL
Dello di Niccolo Delli. Retable with scenes
from the Lives of Christ and the Virgin.
Predella with series of prophets of Old
Testament and others: Ezra.

11 I 62   GIDEON

EARLY MEDIEVAL AND BYZANTINE
Byzantine, Wall painting. Dome: Prophets.
Gideon, S.W. quarter. 12th-14 centuries.
Lagoudera, Panagia tou Arakos.

11 I 62   HABAKKUK

EARLY MEDIEVAL AND BYZANTINE
Byzantine school, Wall painting. Dome: Prophets.
Habakkuk. N.W. quarter. Lagoudera, Panagia
tou Arakos.

FRENCH SCHOOL
Flandrin, J.H. The Prophet Habakkuk: Study
for mural in St. Germain-des-Prés, Paris.
c. 1856. Poitiers, Musée des Beaux-Arts.

ITALIAN SCHOOL
Dello di Niccolo Delli. Retable with scenes
from the Lives of Christ and the Virgin.
Predella with series of prophets of the
Old Testament and others: Habakkuk.
Italian school, 13th century. Religious subjects,
second zone. Detail: Prophet Habakkuk.
Parma, Baptistery. Ceiling decoration.
Pier Francesco Fiorentino. Abraham and six
prophets. Detail: Habakkuk. S. Gimignano,
Collegiata.
Romanino, Girolamo. The Prophet Abacuc. Brescia,
S. Giovanni Evangelista, Capella del S.
S. Sacramento.
Romanino, Girolamo. Cantoria: Prophet Abacus.
Asola, Duomo.

SPANISH SCHOOL
Gascó, Joan. Door of a cabinet: Prophets
and Sibyls. Detail: Habakkuk. Vich, Museo
Episcopal.
Pareja, Diego de. Panels of the life of the
Virgin and prophets. Detail: Daniel and
Habakkuk. Arjona, Santa Maria.
Spanish school, 13th century. Fragments
of fresco decorations. Details: Prophets.
Left, Habakkuk. Toledo, San Román.

11 I 62   HAGGAI

ITALIAN SCHOOL
Dello di Niccolo Delli. Retable with scenes
from the Lives of Christ and the Virgin.
Predella with series of prophets of the
Old Testament and others: Haggai.

SPANISH SCHOOL
Ribera, Jusepe de. The Prophets. Detail:
the Prophet Haggai in spandrel of nave
arcade. 1638-1643. Naples, Museo Nazionale
de S. Martino.

11 I 62   HILLEL

AMERICAN SCHOOL
Levine, Jack. Hillel. Spingold, Nat -
Collection (New York).

11 I 62   HOSEA

AMERICAN SCHOOL
Sargent, J.S. Frieze of the prophets. Head
of the prophet Hosea. Boston, Public
Library.

ITALIAN SCHOOL
Castagno, Andrea del. Fresco of the prophet
Hosea. Venice, S. Zaccaria, Capella S.
Farasio.
Dello di Niccolo Delli. Retable with scenes
from the Lives of Christ and the Virgin.
Predella with series of prophets of the
Old Testament and others: Hosea.
Italian school, 11th century. Prophet Hosea.
Fresco. S. Angelo in Formis, Church,
Nave, left wall above pillars.
Italian school, 13th century. Ceiling decoration.
Religious subjects, second zone. Detail:
Hosea. Parma, Baptistery.
Massari, Antonio. Ceiling: Hosea and a Sibyl.
Corneto, Cathedral.

SPANISH SCHOOL
Gascó, Joan. Door of cabinet: Prophets and
sibyls. Detail: Hosea. Vich, Museo Episcopal.
Ribera, Jusepe de. The Prophets. Detail:
the Prophet Hosea in spandrel of nave
arcade. 1638-1643. Naples, Museo Nazionale
de S. Martino.

11 I 62   ISAAC

DUTCH SCHOOL
Drost, Wilhelm. The Young Isaac. c. 1652|53.
Bader, Dr. Alfred - Collection (Milwaukee).

ITALIAN SCHOOL
Italian school, 16th century (North Italian)?
Series of patriarchs and prophet: Isaac.
Greenville, S.C., Bob Jones University
Collection, 1962 cat. 199.

11 I 62   ISAIAH

AMERICAN SCHOOL
LaFarge, John. Isaiah. Study for Mural in
Trinity Church, Boston. Coolidge, Charles
- Collection.
Sargent, J.S. Frieze of the Prophets: Isaiah.
Boston, Public Library.

EARLY MEDIEVAL AND BYZANTINE
Byzantine school, Wall painting. Dome: Prophets.
Isaiah, N.E. quarter. 12th -14th century.
Lagoudera, Panagia tou Arakos.
Coptic painting. Chapel of Flight. Detail:
Egyptians; Israelites in fiery furnace;
Prophet Isaiah; Jonah's ship. Khargeh,
Bagawat Necropolis.

DUTCH SCHOOL
Mostaert, Jan. The Prophet Isaiah. Rotterdam,
Museum Boymans, St 13.

FRENCH SCHOOL
Master of the Annunciation of Aix. The Prophet
Isaiah. Rotterdam, Museum Boymans. Inv.
Nr. 2463.

GERMAN SCHOOL
German school, 15th century. Prophet Isaiah.
Liége, Palais de Justice.
Strigel, Ivo, circle of (also attributed to
the circle of Hans Strigel the younger).
The Prophet Isaiah. Christie, Manson and
Woods (Sale, London, July 9, 1982, No. 98).

ITALIAN SCHOOL
Angelico, Fra. Large Crucifixion. Detail:
Isaiah. S. Marco, Chapter House.
Bartolommeo, Fra. Prophets: Prophet Isaiah.
Florence, Palazzo Uffizi, 1448.
Carracci, Ludovico. Prophets: Isaiah. c. 1592,
frescoes. Bologna, S. Bartolommeo sur Reno.
Castagno, Andrea del. Fresco of the Prophet
Isaiah. Venice, S. Zaccaria, Capella S.
Farasio.
Cavedone, Jacopo. The Prophet Isaiah. Bologna,
S. Benedetto.
Celio, Gaspare. Isaiah. Rome, Il Gesù, Capella
della Sacra Famiglia. Spandrel.
Italian school, 12th-14th century. Annunciation
with medallions of Isaiah and David. S.
Vito di Normanni, S. Biago, Crypt, Vault.
Italian school, 13th century. David and a
Patriarch: Patriarch. (Isaiah?). Assisi,
S. Francesco, upper church.
Italian school, 16th century (North Italian)
? Series of patriarchs and prophet: Isaiah.
Greenville, S.C., Bob Jones University
Collection, 1962 cat, 201.
Italian school, 11th century. Church, Nave,
Right wall above pillars. Isaiah. Fresco.
S. Angelo in Formis.
Massari, Antonio. Ceilings: Isaiah and a Sibyl.
Corneto, Cathedral.
Master of the Bambino Vispo. Saints and prophets.
Isaiah with angels. Boston, Museum of Fine
Arts.
Masucci, Agostino. Isaiah. Rome, Palazzo
del Quirinale, Coffe House.
Matteo da Viterbo and others. Prophets and
Sibyls: Isaiah. Avignon, Palace of the
Popes, Audience Hall.
Michelangelo. Sibyls and Prophets. Detail:
Isaiah. Rome, Vatican, Sistine Chapel.
Ceiling decorations.
Moretto da Brescia. Isaiah; Erythraen Sibyl.
Escorial, Monastery, Chapter House.
Raphael. The prophet Isaiah with two putti.
Rome, Sant' Agostino.
Romanino, Girolamo. Cantoria: Prophet Isaiah.
Asola, Duomo.
Tiepolo, G.B. Isaiah. Udine, Palazzo
Arcivescovile, Sala Rosa, Decorations.
Ugolino da Siena. The Prophet Isaiah. Dublin,
National Gallery, 1112.

SPANISH SCHOOL
Albaceta Master. Retable of various themes.
Prophet Isaiah. Albecete, S. Juan Bautista.
Artés Master. Isaiah. New York, Kende
Galleries, 1951.

Becerril Master. Isaiah and David. Barcelona,
Private Collection.
Bonnat Master. Panels of the Prophets, left.
Isaiah. Cornellà, Marqués de - Collection
(Barcelona).
Correa de Vivar, Juan. Retable from S. Martin
de Valdeiglesias. Detail: Isaiah. Madrid.
Prado.
Huguet, Jaime. Panel: prophets. Detail:
Isaiah. Yunger - Collection (Barcelona).
Master of Palanquinos (?) Isaiah. Rosenbloom,
Charles J. - Collection (Pittsburg).
Nunyes, Pedro. Panels from the church at
Caselldans. Isaiah. Lerida, Museo Episcopal.
Reixach, Juan (?). Retable. Panel: Isaiah.
Valencia, Museo de Pinturas.
Serafi, Pedro. Organ shutters. Prophet Isaiah.
Barcelona, Cathedral.
Spanish school, 16th century.School of Catalonia.
Prophets: Moses, Abraham, Isaiah. New
York, Hispanic Society of America.

11 I 62 JACOB

EARLY MEDIEVAL AND BYZANTINE
Coptic painting. Tomb Chapel: Room of Peace.
Detail: Mary, Noah, Jacob, "Prayer".
Khargeh, Bagawat Necropolis.

ITALIAN SCHOOL
Angelico, Fra. Large Crucifixion. Detail:
Jacob. S. Marco, Chapter House.
Dello di Niccolo Delli. Retable with scenes
from the Lives of Christ and the Virgin.
Predella with series of prophets of the
Old Testament and others: Jacob.
Italian school, 16th century (North Italian)
? Series of patriarchs and prophet: Jacob.
Greenville, S.C., Bob Jones University
Collection, 1962 cat. 200.
Niccolò da Foligno. Panels of prophets:
Jacob, Moses and Joseph. Baltimore, Md.,
Walters Art Gallery, 620B, C, E.
Vasari, Giorgio and Gherardi, Cristofano.
Sacrifices and prophets: Jacob. Fresco.
Cortona, Compagnia del Gesù.

SPANISH SCHOOL
Spanish school, 12th century.School of Catalonia.
Fresco decorations. Triumphal arch. Detail:
the patriarch Jacob. Tahull, Sant Climent.

11 I 62 JEREMIAH

AMERICAN SCHOOL
Allston, Washington. Study for Head of Jeremiah.
Peekskill, N.Y., St. Mary's Convent.

EARLY MEDIEVAL AND BYZANTINE
Byzantine school, Wall painting. Apse. Detail:
Archangel Michael and prophet Jeremiah
and saints. Fresco. 11th century. Galliano,
S. Vincenzo.
Byzantine school, Wall painting. Dome: Prophets.
Jeremiah; S.E. quarter. 12th-14th century.
Lagoudera, Panagia tou Arakos.

FRENCH SCHOOL
Master of the Annunciation of Aix. The Prophet
Jeremiah.

ITALIAN SCHOOL
Angelico, Fra. S. Marco, Chapter House:
Large Crucifixion. Detail: Jeremiah.
Carpaccio, Vittore. Prophets: Jeremiah.
Capodistria, Cathedral.
Castagno, Andrea del. Fresco of the prophet
Jeremiah. Cappella S. Zaccaria.
Cavedone, Jacopo. The Prophet Jeremiah.
Bologna, S. Benedetto.
Dello di Niccolo Delli. Retable with scenes
from the Lives of Christ and the Virgin.
Predella with series of prophets of the
Old Testament and others: Jeremiah.

Guercino. The Prophet Jeremiah. Greenville,
S.C., Bob Jones University Collection.
Italian school, 9th century. Bust of the prophet
Jeremiah in medallion. Fresco. Rome, S.
Maria in Cosmedin.
Italian school, 11th century. Jeremiah. Fresco.
S. Angelo in Formis, church, nave, right
wall above pillars.
Italian school, 13th century.Religious subjects,
second zone. Detail:Jeremiah.Parma,Baptistery.
Ceiling decoration.
Italian school, 14th century.Series of Prophets:
Jeremiah. Fresco, School of Rimini. Pomposa,
Abbey, Chapter Room.
Martino di Bartolommeo. Jeremiah. Harvard
University, Fogg Art Museum, 1952.94.
Master of the Bambino Vispo.Saints and prophets.
Jeremiah with angels. Boston, Museum of
Fine Arts.
Matteo da Viterbo and others. Prophets and
Sibyls. Jeremiah. Avignon, Palace of the
Popes, Audience Hall.
Michelangelo. Sibyls and Prophets. Detail:
Jeremiah. Rome, Vatican, Sistine Chapel.
Ceiling decorations, between lunettes.
Moretto da Brescia. The Prophet Jeremiah.
Milan, Museo del Castello.
Romanino, Girolamo. Cantoria: Prophet Jeremiah.
Asola, Duomo.
Salviatti, Francesco. Lunette: Prophet and
Sibyl. Rome, Palazzo della Cancelleria,
Cappella del Pallio.
Tiepolo, G.B. Jeremiah. Udine, Palazzo
Arcivescovile, Sala Rossa. Decorations.

SPANISH SCHOOL
Artés, Master. Jeremiah. Kende Galleries,
New York, 1951.
Cruz, Diego de la. Christ between David and
Jeremiah. Bob Jones University Collection,
(Greenville, S.C.).
Gascó, Perot. Prophets and Sibyls. Detail:
Jeremiah. Vich, Museo Episcopal.
Lladó Master. The Prophet Jeremiah. Barcelona,
Museo Episcopal.
Reixach, Juan, Circle of. Retable from Denia.
Fragment: Jeremiah. Valencia, Diocesan
Museum.
Spanish school, 13th century. School of Catalonia.
Painted Ciborium from Tosas. Details:spandrels.
Daniel and Jeremiah. Plandiura - Collection
(Barcelona).
Spanish school, 16th century. School of Catalonia.
Prophets: Jeremiah, David, Melchizedek.
New York, Hispanic Society of America.

11 I 62   JOB

EARLY MEDIEVAL AND BYZANTINE
Early Christian painting. "Di Orfeo", Job.
Rome, Via delle Sette Chiese, Catacomb of
Domitilla, Cubiculum IV.

DUTCH SCHOOL
Goltzius, Hendrik. Job. New York, Private
Collection.

ITALIAN SCHOOL
Angelico, Fra. Large Crucifixion. Detail:
Job. Florence, S. Marco, Chapter House.
Bartolommeo, Fra. Prophets: Job. Florence,
Palazzo Uffizi, 1448.
Dello di Niccolo Delli. Retable with scenes
from the Lives of Christ and the Virgin.
Predella with series of prophets of the
Old Testament and others: Job.

11 I 62   JOEL

GERMAN SCHOOL
Bertram (van Byrde) Master. Grabow altar.
Right side: Apostles, prophets, saints,
and magi. Detail: The Prophet Joel. Hamburg,
Kunsthalle.

ITALIAN SCHOOL
Michelangelo. Sibyls and prophets. Detail:
Joel. Rome, Vatican, Sistine Chapel.
Ceiling decorations, between lunettes.

SPANISH SCHOOL
Ribera, Jusepe de. The Prophets. Detail:
the prophet Joel, in spandrel of nave
arcade. 1638-1643. Naples, Museo Nazionale
di S. Martino.

11 I 62   JONAH

EARLY MEDIEVAL AND BYZANTINE
Early Christian painting. Jonah thrown overboard.
Detail: head of Jonah. Rome, Catacomb
of the Jordani.
Byzantine school, Wall painting. Dome: Prophets.
Jonas, N.W. quarter. 12th-14th century.
Lagoudera, Panagia tou Arakos.

ITALIAN SCHOOL
Allori, Alessandro. Jonah. Fresco (?), probably
from the Arcispedale di S. Maria Nuova.
Florence, Ognissanti, Museum.
Dello di Niccolo Delli. Retable with scenes
from the Lives of Christ and the Virgin.
Predella with series of prophets of the
Old Testament and others: Jonah.
Italian school, 12th century. Frescoes.
South transept, fourth row. Detail: Prophets
Amos and Jonah. Nepi, Castel Sant 'Elia.
Italian school, 13th century. Fresco. Detail
of two prophets in medallions: Jonah and
Micah. Rome, S.S. Quatro Coronati, Chapel
of S. Silvestro.
Michelangelo. Sibyls and prophets. Detail:
Jonah. Rome, Vatican, Sistine Chapel.
Ceiling decorations between lunettes.

SPANISH SCHOOL
Gascó, Joan. Door of a cabinet: Prophets
and sibyls. Detail: Jonah. Vich, Museo
Episcopal.
Portillo Master. Jonah. St. Helena. Madrid,
Collection Duchess of Parcent.
Solives, Francisco. Retable, fragments: Prophets
Jonah and Zachariah. Barcelona, Collection
Rómulo Bosch.

11 I 62   JOSEPH

ITALIAN SCHOOL
Niccolò da Foligno. Panels of Prophets:
Jacob, Moses and Joseph. Baltimore, Md.,
Walters Art Gallery, 37.620.

11 I 62   JOSIAH

AMERICAN SCHOOL
Levine, Jack. King Josiah. 1941. East Lansing,
Michigan, Collection Mr. and Mrs. Hugo
Munsterberg.

11 I 62   MALACHI

EARLY MEDIEVAL AND BYZANTINE
Byzantine school, Wall painting. Medallion:
Malachi. 14th century. Fresco. Veroia,
Hagios Christos. South wall. Middle zone.

ITALIAN SCHOOL
Italian school, 11th century. Prophets:
Malachia. S. Angelo in Formis, Cathedral,
Nave.
Romanino, Girolamo. The Prophet Malachi.
Brescia, S. Giovanni Evangelista, Capella
del S.S. Sacramento.

SPANISH SCHOOL
Muru, Juan and a Collaborator. Retable of
high altar. Panels by Hand B. Resurrection.
Prophets Malachi and Baruch. Ardara,
Sardinia, Parish Church.

11 I 62   MELCHIZEDEK

SPANISH SCHOOL

Juanes, Juan de. Triptych: Melchizedek.
Spanish school, 16th century, School of Catalonia.
Prophets: Jeremiah, David, Melchizedek.

11 I 62   MICAH

FLEMISH SCHOOL

Eyck, Hubert and Jan van. Altarpiece of the
Adoration of the Lamb. Exterior. Right
Upper Panel, Top: The Prophet Micah. Ghent,
St. Bavon.

ITALIAN SCHOOL

Cavedone, Jacopo. The Prophet Micah. Bologna,
S. Benedetto.
Italian school, 11th century. Micah. Fresco.
S. Angelo in Formis, Church, Nave, right
wall above pillars.
Italian school, 13th century. Fresco. Detail
of two prophets in medallions: Jonah and
Micah. Rome, SS. Quatro Coronati, Chapel
of S. Silvestro, left wall.
Romanino, Girolamo. Cantoria: Prophet Micah.
Asola, Duomo.

SPANISH SCHOOL

Huguet. Panel from lost retable of Santa Maria
de Ripoli: Melchizedek.

11 I 62   MORDECAI

ITALIAN SCHOOL

Mola, Pier Francisco, Attributed to. Mordecai.
Sarasota, Fla., Ringling Museum of Art.

11 I 62   MOSES

AUSTRIAN SCHOOL

Maulbertsch, F.A. Moses. Vienna, Barockmeuseum,
127.

BRITISH SCHOOL

English school, Wall painting. West wall:
Last Judgement. Right: Moses. Left: Carnal
man surrounded by Seven Deadly Sins. c.
1380. Trotton (Sussex), St. George.

EARLY MEDIEVAL AND BYZANTINE

Byzantine school, Wall painting. Church. Detail
of remains of frescoes: David and Moses.
13th century. Grottoferrata.
Byzantine school, Wall painting. Dome: Prophets.
Moses, N.E. quarter. 12th-14th century.
Lagoudera, Panagia tou Arakos.
Early Christian painting. Catacomb of Domitilla.
Arco delle piccole Oranti. Moses smiting
rock. Rome, Via delle Sette Chiese.
Early Medieval and Byzantine painting. Moses
and Aaron. 13th century. Sinai, Monastery
of St. Catherine.

FRENCH SCHOOL

Champaigne, Philippe de. Moses and the Tablets
of the Law. 1663. Amiens, Musée de Picardie.
Valentin de Boulogne. Moses. Vienna,
Kunthistoriches Museum, 163.

GERMAN SCHOOL

Strigel, Ivo, circle of (also attributed to
the circle of Hans Strigel the younger).
The Prophet Moses. Christie, Manson and
Woods (Sale, London, July 9, 1982, No. 98).

ITALIAN SCHOOL

Castagno, Andrea del. Fresco of Moses. Cappella
S. Farasio. Venice, S. Zaccaria.
Cesari, Giuseppe. Vault decoration. Prophets
and Sibyls. Rome, S. Prassede, Cappella
Olgiati.

Dello di Niccolo Delli. Retable with scenes
from the Lives of Christ and the Virgin.
Predella with series of prophets of the
Old Testament and others: Moses.
Girolamo, da Santa Croce. Moses. Venice,
S. Giovanni Grisostomo.
Guercino. Moses. Florence, Palazzo Pitti,
103.
Italian school, 11th century. Moses. Fresco.
S. Angelo in Formis, Church, Nave, right
wall above pillars.
Italian school, 13th century. Moses. Parma,
Baptistery. Ceiling decoration, religious
subjects, second zone.
Italian school, 14th century. Series of
Prophets: Moses. Detail. Fresco. School
of Rimini. Pomposa, Abbey, Chapter Room.
Lorenzetti, Ambrogio? Moses. London, University
of, Courtauld Institute.
Lorenzo Monaco. Moses. c. 1406. New York,
Metropolitan Museum of Art, 65.14.3.
Masucci, Agostino. Lunette: Moses. Rome,
Palazzo del Quirinale, Coffee House.
Niccolò da Foligno. Panels of Prophets:
Jacob, Moses and Joseph. Baltimore, Md.,
Walters Art Gallery; 37.620.
Romanino, Girolamo. The Prophet Moses.
Brescia, S. Giovanni Evangelista, Capella
del S. S. Sacramento.
Roselli, Cosimo. Patriarchs: Moses and Abraham.
Florence, Galleria Antica e Moderna.
Ugolino da Siena. Moses. Eszergom, Palace
of the Primate of Hungary.
Ugolino da Siena. Moses and Aaron. Detail:
Moses. Richmond, Coll. Cook, 1.
Vasari, Giorgio and Gherardi, Cristofano.
Sacrifices and prophets: Moses. Fresco.
Cortona, Compagnia del Gesù.

SPANISH SCHOOL

Frōmista Master (?) Moses. Monte Carlo,
Collection Wakefield-Mori.
Huguet, Jaime. Panel from lost retable of
Santa Maria de Ripoll: Moses. Vich, Museo
Episcopal.
Mayno, Juan Bautista. Wall decorations.
Moses. Toledo, San Pedro Mártir.
Reixach, Juan (?) Retable. Panel: Moses.
Valencia, Museo de Pinturas.
Ribera, Jusepe de. Moses and Aaron. Florence,
Palazzo Corsini.
Ribera, Jusepe de. Moses. 1638. Naples,
S. Martino.
Spanish school, 16th century. School of
Catalonia. Prophets: Moses, Abraham,
Isaiah. New York, Hispanic Society of
America.

11 I 62   NAHUM

ITALIAN SCHOOL

Dello di Niccolo Delli. Retable with scenes
from the Lives of Christ and the Virgin.
Predella with series of prophets of the
Old Testament and others: Nahum.

11 I 62   NEHEMIAH

ITALIAN SCHOOL

Vasari, Giorgio and Gherardi, Cristofano.
Sacrifices and prophets: Nehemiah. Fresco.
Cortona, Compagnia del Gesù.

11 I 62   NOAH

EARLY MEDIEVAL AND BYZANTINE

Coptic painting. Detail: Mary, Noah, Jacob,
"Prayer". Khargeh, Bagawat Necropolis,
Tomb chapel: Room of Peace.

ITALIAN SCHOOL
Italian school, 14th century. Series of Prophets:
Abraham and Noah. Fresco, School of Rimini.
Pomposa, Abbey, Chapter Room.
Rosselli, Cosimo. Patriarchs: Noah. Florence,
Galleria Antica e Moderna.

SPANISH SCHOOL
Ribera, Jusepe de. The Prophets. Detail:
the Prophet Noah. In spandrel of nave arcade.
1638-1643. Naples, Museo Nazionale di S.
Martino.

11 I 62   OBADIAH

ITALIAN SCHOOL
Dello di Niccolo Delli. Retable with scenes
from the Lives of Christ and the Virgin.
Predella with series of prophets of the
Old Testament and others: Obadiah.
Italian school, 13th century. Detail: Prophet
Obadiah. Parma, Baptistery. Ceiling decoration.
Religious subjects, second zone.

SPANISH SCHOOL
Ribera, Jusepe de. The Prophets. Detail: the
Prophet Obadiah, in spandrel of nave arcade.
1638-1643. Naples, Museo Nazionale di S.
Martino.

11 I 62   SAMSON

AMERICAN SCHOOL
Vedder, Elihu. Delilah. Pair with Samson.
1886. Williford, Graham - Collection.

BRITISH SCHOOL
Leighton, Sir Frederick. Samson. Ottawa,
National Gallery of Canada.

DUTCH SCHOOL
Gelder, Aert de. Samson. 1689. Detroit,
Institute of Arts.

FRENCH SCHOOL
Flandrin, J.H. Samson.
Valentin de Boullogne. Samson. Cleveland,
Museum of Art, 72.50.

11 I 62   SAMUEL

BRITISH SCHOOL
Reynolds, Sir Joshua. The infant Samuel kneeling
at prayer. c. 1776. London, Tate Gallery.
Reynolds, Sir Joshua. The Prophet Samuel as
a boy. Dulwich Gallery, 223.

ITALIAN SCHOOL
Dello di Niccolo Delli. Retable with scenes
from the Lives of Christ and the Virgin.
Predella with series of prophets of the
Old Testament and others: Samuel.
Vasari, Giorgio and Gherardi, Cristofano.
Sacrifices and prophets: Samuel. Fresco.
Cortona, Compagnia del Gesù.

11 I 62   SAUL

AMERICAN SCHOOL
Levine, Jack. King Saul. 1952. Collection
Dr. and Mrs. Abram Kanof.

11 I 62   SOLOMON

EARLY MEDIEVAL AND BYZANTINE
Byzantine school, Wall painting. Dome: Prophets.
Solomon, S.E. quarter. 12th-14th century.
Lagoudera, Panagia tou Arakos.
Byzantine school, Wall painting. Solomon.
14th century. Mistra, Metropolitan Church.
Frescoes, Nave, North wall.

ITALIAN SCHOOL
Antoniazzo Romano. David and Solomon, and
Eternal in glory: Eternal in glory. Rome,
San Pietro in Montorio.
Italian school, 13th century. Solomon.
Parma, Baptistery. Ceiling decoration.
Religious subjects, second zone.
Italian school, 11th century. Prophets:
King Solomon. S. Angelo in Formis, Cathedral,
Nave.
Palma Giovane. Solomon. Venice, S. Niccolò
da Tolentino.
Solimena, Francesco. Solomon. Sotheby and
Co., London (Sale, New York [5104] Nov.
3, 1983, No. 74)

SPANISH SCHOOL
Albacete Master. Retable of various themes.
Solomon. Albacete, S. Juan Bautista.
Becerril Master. Solomon. Section of a predella.
Madrid, Private Collection.
Huguet, Jaime. Panel: prophets. Detail:
Solomon. Barcelona, Coll. Junyer.
Master of Riofrió. Series of prophets: Solomon.
Greenville, S.C., Bob Jones University
Collection, 1962 cat. 193.
Reixach, Juan (?) Retable. Panel: Solomon.
Valencia, Museo de Pinturas.

11 I 62   THREE HEBREWS

BRITISH SCHOOL
Burne-Jones, Sir Edward. Three Israelites
in the Fiery Furnace; designs for stained
glass windows in St. James, Farnworth.
Port Sunlight, The Lady Lever Art Gallery.

11 I 62   UZZIAH

DUTCH SCHOOL
Rembrandt. Uzziah Stricken with Leprosy.
1635. Devonshire, Duke of - Collection
(Chatsworth).

11 I 62   ZACHARIAS

EARLY MEDIEVAL AND BYZANTINE
Byzantine school, Wall painting. Medallion:
Zachariah(?) 14th century. Fresco. Veroia,
Hagios Christos. South wall. Middle zone.

FLEMISH SCHOOL
Eyck, Hubert and Jan van. Altarpiece of
the Adoration of the Lamb. Exterior. Left
Upper Panel, Top: The Prophet Zechariah.
Ghent, St. Bavon.

ITALIAN SCHOOL
Angelico, Fra. Large Crucifixion. Detail:
Zacharias. Florence, S. Marco, Chapter
House.
Carpaccio, Vittore. Prophets: Zacharias.
Capodistria, Cathedral.
Castagno, Andrea del. Frescoes of the prophet
Zaccaria. Cappella S. Farasio. Venice,
S. Zaccario.
Cavedone, Jacopo. The Prophet Zacchariah.
Bologna, S. Benedetto.
Celio, Gaspare. Cappella della Sacra Famiglia.
Spandrel. Zachariah. Rome, Il Gesù.
Dello di Niccolo Delli. Retable with scenes
from the Lives of Christ and the Virgin.
Predella with series of the prophets of
the Old Testament and others: Zachariah.
Italian school, 14th century. Series of
Prophets: Zechariah and another figure,
partially effaced. Fresco, School of Rimini.
Pomposa, Abbey, Chapter Room.
Italian school, 11th century. Zachariah.
Fresco. S. Angelo in Formis, Church, Nave,
Right wall above pillars.

Michelangelo. Sibyls and prophets. Detail:
    Zachariah. Rome, Vatican, Sistine Chapel.
    Ceiling decorations, between lunettes.
Romanino, Girolamo. The Prophet Zaccariah.
    Brescia, S. Giovanni Evangelista, Capella
    del S.S. Sacramento.

SPANISH SCHOOL
Huguet, Jaime. Panel:prophets. Detail: Zachariah.
    Barcelona, Coll. Junyer.
Master of Riofriō. Series of prophets: Zechariah.
    Greenville, S.C. Bob Jones University
    Collection, 1962 cat. 194.
Solives, Francisco. Retable, Fragments: Prophets
    Jonah and Zachariah. Barcelona, Collection
    Rōmulo Basch.
Villalobos Master. Prophet Zechariah. New
    York, American Art Galleries.

11 I 62   ZEPHANIAH

ITALIAN SCHOOL
Italian school, 11th century. Prophet Zephaniah.
    Fresco. S. Angelo in Formis, Church, Nave,
    Left wall above pillars.

11 I 63   DELILAH

AMERICAN SCHOOL
Vedder, Elihu. Delilah. Pair with Samsom.
    Williford, Graham - Collection.

11 I 63   ESTHER

DUTCH SCHOOL
Gelder, Aert de. Esther. Dunkirk Museum.
Gelder, Aert de. Esther. Heino (Kastel het
    Nijenhuis), Hannema-se Stuers Fundatie.
Gelder, Aert de. Esther. Treul, William -
    Collection (Milwaukee).

ITALIAN SCHOOL
Castagno, Andrea del. Frescoes from Villa
    Pandolfini, Legnaia. Detail: Queen Esther.
    Florence, S. Apollonia, now in Palozzo Uffizi.
Veronese, Paolo. Esther.

11 I 63   EVE

FRENCH SCHOOL
Baudry, P.J.A. Eve.

GERMAN SCHOOL
Baldung, Hans. Adam and Eve. Budapest, Museum
    of Fine Arts, 715, 716.

ITALIAN SCHOOL
Bembo, Bonifazio. Eve. Fresco. c.1452. Cremona,
    S. Agostino, Nave.
Carlo da Camerino. Madonna and Child with
    Saints, Angels, and Eve. Cleveland, Museum
    of Art.
Lorenzetti, Ambrogio. Madonna and Child enthroned
    with saints and angels. Detail: Eve. San
    Galgano, Parish Church.

SWEDISH SCHOOL
Beskow, Bo. Eve: Study for a monumental painting.
    Stockholm, National Museum, 3392.

11 I 63   HAGAR

BRITISH SCHOOL
Geddes, Andrew. Hagar. Edinburgh, National
    Gallery, 631.

11 I 63   JAEL

DUTCH SCHOOL
Spielberg, Johannes. Jael. Berlin, Staatliche
    Museen.

11 I 63   JUDITH

AUSTRIAN SCHOOL
Klimt, Gustav. Judith I. 1901. Salzburg,
    Galerie Welz

GERMAN SCHOOL
Cranach, L. (the elder) ? Judith and Lucretia.
    Dresden, Royal Gallery, 1916A (1918)

11 I 63   REBEKAH

FRENCH SCHOOL
Lecomte- Vernet, Charles Emile Hippolyte.
    Rebecca. 1869. Hammer Galleries, New
    York.

11 I 63   RUTH

ITALIAN SCHOOL
Veronese, Paolo. Ruth and Boaz.

11 I 63   SHEBA

FRENCH SCHOOL
Bussiere, Gaston. Queen of Sheba. 1926.
    Sotheby and Co., London (Sale, Nov. 25,
    1981, No. 277).

11 I 63   SUSANNA

ITALIAN SCHOOL
Luini, Bernardo. Susanna. Milan, Coll.
    Borromeo.

11 S 16   REPRESENTATION OF CELESTIAL PARADISE
AS ABRAHAM'S BOSOM (THE BLESSED IN HIS LAP OR ARMS)

ITALIAN SCHOOL
Italian school, 12th century. Abraham with
    his children. Civate, S. Pietro, frescoes
    of narthex.

71 OLD TESTAMENT: SERIES OF SCENES AND UNIDENTIFIED
SCENES

DUTCH SCHOOL
Bramer, Leonard. Biblical subject ? Amsterdam,
Rijksmuseum.
Bramer, Leonard ? Old Testament scene. Hinton
Charterhouse,Somerset Collection - R.Robertson
Glasgow.
Bramer, Leonard. Scene of a Sacrifice. Florence,
San Marco, Museo di, n. 141.
Swaneveldt, Herman van. Old Testament Scene.
Hague, Museum Bredius, 115-1946.

FLEMISH SCHOOL
Franck, Franz, I, Studio of. Flemish Reliquary
Chest painted with scenes from the Old
Testament. c.1600. Sarasota, Fla., Ringling
Museum of Art, SN 1950.

FRENCH SCHOOL
French school, Wall painting. Scenes from
the Old Testament. 11th century. St. Savin,
(Vienne), Church.

GERMAN SCHOOL
Bertram (van Byrde) Master. Grabower Altar:
Scenes from the Old and New Testament.
1379-1383. Hamburg, Kunsthalle.
German school, 15th century. Triptych with
scenes from the Old Testament from Göttingen.
1400-1410. Hanover, Provincial Museum.

ITALIAN SCHOOL
Cresti, Domenico. Old Testament scenes and
scenes of the Church. Ceiling decorations.
Rome S.M. Maggiore, Sacristy of Cappella
Paolina.
Fontebasso, Francesco. Scene of Sacrifice.
Povo (Trento), Church.
Garafalo (Benvenuto Tisi) Scenes from the
Old and New Testaments. Ferrara, Picture
Gallery.
Novelli, Pietro (Il Monrealese). Scene from
Old Testament. Bologna, San Michele in
Bosco, Sacristy.
Peruzzi, Baldassare. Old and New Testament
subjects. Rome, S. Maria della Pace, Cappella
della Ponzetto. Arch.
Raphael. Loggie., General view of Ceiling.
1516-1519. Rome, Vatican.
Romanino, Girolamo. Old Testament scenes.
Detail, north wall. Breno, S. Antonio.

SPANISH SCHOOL
Antolinez, Antonio de (Francisco?) Unknown
biblical subject. Jerez de la Frontera,
San Miguel.
Goya. Biblical themes. 1. Moses and the brazen
serpent. 2. Moses causing water to spring
from rock. 3. Abraham and Isaac. 4.Sacrificial
scene.

71A GENESIS: SCENES IN SERIES AND UNKNOWN SCENES

FLEMISH SCHOOL
Bles, Herri met de. Garden of Eden. Amsterdam,
Rijksmuseum, 522.

GERMAN SCHOOL
Cranach, L. (the elder). Paradise. Vienna,
Imperial Gallery, 1462.
Cranach, Lucas, the elder. Adam and Eve in
Paradise. 1530. Vienna, Kunsthistorisches
Museum, 3678.

ITALIAN SCHOOL
Italian school, 12th century. Detail: Episodes
of Adam and Eve. Spoleto (near), S. Paolo.
Presbiterium. Frescoes.
Italian school, 13th century. Detail: wall
of the Grotto di San Lorenzo. Anagi, Cathedral.
Frescoes.

Italian school, 13th century. Scenes from
the Old Testament: Genesis. Assisi, S.
Francesco. Upper church.
Vecchietta. Old Testament scene. Detail;
Siena, Spedate di S. Maria della Scala,
Sala di S. Pietro.

SPANISH SCHOOL
Spanish school, 12th century. School of Cataloni.
Scenes from Genesis. Sant Sadurni d'Osomort.
Fresco decoration of apse.

URUGUAIN SCHOOL
Torres-García, Joaquin. Composition with
Adam and Eve. 1928. Buenos Aires, Coll.
Maurico and Natalia Kohen.

71 A 1 GENESIS 1:1-2 "IN THE BEGINNING;" THE
ORDERING OF CHAOS

ITALIAN SCHOOL
Ramenghi, Bartolommeo (Bagnacavallo) God,
the Creator. Christie, Manson and Woods
(Sale, New York, June 12, 1981, No. 104).
Salviati, Francesco. Scene from the Creation;
Separation of Chaos. Rome, S. Maria del
Popolo, Cappella Chigi.

71 A 2 GENESIS 1:3-25 THE SIX DAYS OF CREATION

BRITISH SCHOOL
Burne-Jones, Sir Edward. Days of Creation.
Six Panels. Harvard University, Fogg
Art Museum, 1943. 454.

ITALIAN SCHOOL
Italian school, 12th century. Wall decorations.
Old Testament subjects. Detail: Creation
of Heaven and Earth. Ferentillo, S. Pietro
e S. Paolo.
Italian school, 13th century. Creation of
the World. Assisi, S. Francesco, upper
church.
Italian school, 14th century. Thirty stories
from the Bible: Creation, top register,
1st panel. Veronese. Verona, Museo Civico,
362.
Torriti, Jacopo. Frescoes: Nave: Creation
of the World, bust of God the Father.
Assisi, S. Francesco, upper church.
Uccello, Paolo. Frescoes in cloister: Deluge
and Story of Noah; Creation of Adam and
Eve, the Fall. Florence, S. Maria Novella.

71 A 21 GENESIS 1:3-5 FIRST DAY. THE DIVISION
OF LIGHT AND DARKNESS

BRITISH SCHOOL
Burne-Jones, Sir Edward. Days of Creation.
First day: Light divided from darkness.
Harvard University, Fogg Art Museum, Winthrop
Bequest, 1943. 454.

FLEMISH SCHOOL
Flemish school, 17th century. Creation of
Light. Seville, Cathedral, Capilla de
Santiago.

FRENCH SCHOOL
Tissot, James Jacques Joseph. Illustrations
of the Hebrew Bible. No. 1: The Creation.
1896-1903. New York, Jewish Museum, 52.68.

GERMAN SCHOOL
Bertram (van Byrde) Master. Grabow altar.
Scenes from the Old and New Testament:
God separating light from darkness. Hamburg,
Kunsthalle.

ITALIAN SCHOOL
Italian school, 13th century. Creation of
the world. Detail: Light. Assisi, S.
Francesco, upper church.

Italian school, 13th century. Creation of the
world. Detail: Darkness. Assisi, S. Francesco,
upper church.
Italian school, 13th century. Creation of
Adam and division of light and darkness.
Anagni, Cathedral. Frescoes. Wall of Grotta
di S. Lorenzo.
Italian school, 13th century. Cycle of creation:
God with angels, God creating animals.
Fresco. Fossa, Santa Maria ad Cryptas.
Michelangelo. God separating light from darkness.
Rome, Vatican, Sistine chapel, ceiling
decorations.
Raphael (and assistants). Old Testament subjects:
God separating light from darkness. Rome,
Vatican, Loggie.

71 A 22 GENESIS 1:6-8 SECOND DAY. CREATION OF THE FIRMAMENT

BRITISH SCHOOL
Burne-Jones, Sir Edward. Days of Creation.
Second day: Orderign of Chaos. Harvard
University, Fogg Art Museum, Winthrop Bequest,
1943. 455.

FLEMISH SCHOOL
Flemish school, 17th century. Creation of
heaven and earth. Seville, Cathedral, Capilla
de San Antonio.

GERMAN SCHOOL
Bertram (van Byrde) Master. Grabow altar.
Scenes from the Old and New Testament: God
creating the firmament. Hamburg, Kunsthalle.

71 A 23 GENESIS 1:9-10 THIRD DAY. CREATION OF LAND AND WATER

BRITISH SCHOOL
Burne-Jones, Sir Edward. Days of creation.
Third day: Separation of the waters and
the land. Harvard University, Fogg Art
Museum, Winthrop Bequest, 1943. 456.

FLEMISH SCHOOL
Flemish school, 17th century. Creation.Separation
of the waters from the earth. Seville,
Cathedral. Capilla de San Antonio.

GERMAN SCHOOL
Bertram (van Byrde) Master. Grabow altar.
Scenes from the Old and New Testament: God
creating the earth. Hamburg, Kunsthalle.

ITALIAN SCHOOL
Bartolo di Fredi. Scenes from the Old Testament:
Creation of the world. S.Gimignano,Collegiata.
Michelangelo. Creation and Scenes from Old
Testament: Separation of land from water.
Rome, Vatican, Sistine Chapel.
Raphael (and assistants) Old Testament subjects:
Story of Creation: God separating the waters.
Rome, Vatican, Loggie.

71 A 24 GENESIS 1:14-19 FOURTH DAY. CREATION OF SUN, MOON AND STARS

BRITISH SCHOOL
Burne-Jones, Sir Edward. Days of creation.
Fourth day: Creation of sun, moon and stars.
Harvard University, Fogg Art Museum, Winthrop
Bequest, 1943. 457.

FRENCH SCHOOL
French school, Wall painting. Scenes from
the Old Testament: God creating the sun
and moon. 11th century. St. Savin, (Vienne),
church.
French school, Wall painting. St. Savin, nave.
Scenes from the Old Testament: God creating
the sun and moon. Copy. 11th century. Paris,
Musée National des Monument Français.

GERMAN SCHOOL
Bertram (van Byrde) Master. Grabow altar.
Scenes from the Old and New Testament:
God creating the larger and lesser lights.
Hamburg, Kunsthalle.
Cornelius, Peter von. Creation of the World.
c. 1836, fresco. Munich, St. Ludwig.

ITALIAN SCHOOL
Michelangelo. Central panel: Creation and
other scenes from Old Testament: Creation
of sun, moon and planets. Rome, Vatican,
Sistine chapel, ceiling decrations.
Raphael (and assistants). Old Testament
subjects: God creating the sun and moon.
Rome, Vatican, Loggie.
Salviati, Franceso. Scene from the Creation.
Creation of the sun and moon. Rome, S.
Maria del Popolo, Capella Chigi.

71 A 25 GENESIS 1:20-25 FIFTH AND SIXTH DAYS. CREATION OF ANIMALS

BRITISH SCHOOL
Burne-Jones, Sir Edward. Days Of Creation.
Fifth day: Creation of animal life. Harvard
University, Fogg Art Museum, Winthrop
Bequest, 1943. 458.

FLEMISH SCHOOL
Brueghel, Jan, the elder. The creation of
animals. Rome Palazzo Doria.
Flemish school, 17th century. Creation of
animals. Seville, Cathedral, Capilla
de Santiago.

GERMAN SCHOOL
Bertram (van Byrde) Master. Grabow altar.
Scenes from the Old and New Testament:
God creating animal life. Hamburg, Kunsthalle.

ITALIAN SCHOOL
Alberti, Durante. The Creation. Rome, Il
Gesù, Cappella della S.S. Trinità. Vault.
Albertinelli, Mariotto. The Creation and
Fall. London, University of, Courtald
Institute.
Italian school, 13th century. Creation of
the world. Detail: the animals. Assisi,
S. Francesco, upper church.
Italian school, 13th century. Cycle of creation:
God with angels, God creating animals.
Fossa, Santa Maria ad Cryptas.
Niccolò di Tommaso. The Creation of the
Animals. Fresco, Pistoia, Casa Tonini.
Raphael (and assistants). Old Testament
subjects: God creates animal life. Rome,
Vatican, Loggie.
Salviati, Francesco. Scene from the creation;
Creation of animals. Rome. S. Maria del
Popolo, Cappella Chigi.
Tintoretto. Creation of the Animals. 1550-53.
Venice, Academy.
Uccello Paolo. Creation of Man and the Animals.
Florence, S. Maria Novella, Frescoes in
the cloister.

PORTUGUESE SCHOOL
Fernandes, Vasco. The creation of the animals.
1506-1511. Lamego, Museu.

71 A 25 1 GENESIS 1:21 CREATION OF BIRDS AND FISH

ITALIAN SCHOOL
Castiglione, Giovanni Benedetto. Creation
of the Animals. Genoa, Palazzo Durazzo-
Pallavicini.
Italian school, 13th century. Creation of the
world. Detail: the fish. Assisi, S. Francesco,
upper church.

71 A 3 GENESIS 1:26 - 2 CREATION OF ADAM AND EVE

BRITISH SCHOOL
Blake, William. God Blessing the Seventh Day.
c.1805. London, Tate Gallery, 5893.
Burne-Jones, Sir Edward. Days of Creation.
Sixth day: Creation of Adam and Eve. Harvard
University, Fogg Art Museum. Winthrop Bequest,
1943. 459.

FLEMISH SCHOOL
Brueghel, Jan, the Younger. The Creation of
Adam in the Garden of Eden. Sotheby and
Co., London (Sale, New York (SAFFRON), March
13, 1985, No. 26).

FRENCH SCHOOL
French school, 11th century. Scenes from the
Old Testament: Creation of Adam and Eve.
St. Savin, Vienne, Church, Nave.

ITALIAN SCHOOL
Italian school, 12th century. Wall decorations.
Old Testament subjects. Detail: Creation
of Adam. Ferentillo, S. Pietro e S. Paolo.

71 A 31 GENESIS 2:7 GOD FASHIONS MAN FROM CLAY

FRENCH SCHOOL
Chagall, Marc. Illustrations from the *Bible*
published by Vollard. No. 18: God Creates
Man. 1930. Nice (Alpes-Maritimes), Musées
National Message Biblique Marc Chagall.

GERMAN SCHOOL
Rohlfs, Christian. Creation of Man. 1916,
München-Gladbach, Museum.

ITALIAN SCHOOL
Italian school, 13th century. Creation of
Adam and division of light and darkness.
Anagni, Cathedral, Frescoes. Detail: wall
of grotta di S. Loresnzo.
Italian school, 13th century. Cycle of creation:
God creating man and woman. Fresco. Fossa,
Santa Maria ad Cryptas.

MEXICAN SCHOOL
Figueroa, José. Earthly Paradise. Guadalajara
(Mexico), Museo del Estado de Jalisco.

71 A 31 1 GENESIS 2:7 CREATION OF ADAM. GOD BESTOWS
LIFE ON ADAM

FLEMISH SCHOOL
Brueghel, Jan, the Younger. The Life of Adam:
Creation of Adam. Koller - Gallery (Zürich).
Flemish school, 17th century. Creation of Adam.
Seville, Cathedral, Capilla de San Antonio.

GERMAN SCHOOL
Bertram (van Byrde) Master. Grabow altar.
Scenes from the Old and New Testament: God
creating Adam. Hamburg, Kunsthalle.

ITALIAN SCHOOL
Albertinelli, Mariotto. The Creation and Fall.
London, University of, Courtauld Institute.
Bartolo di Fredi. Scenes from the Old Testament:
Creation of Man. S. Gimignano, Collegiata.
Italian school, 12th century. Wall decorations.
Old Testament subjects. Detail: Creation
of Adam. Ferentillo, S. Pietro e S. Paolo.
Italian school, 13th century. Scenes from
the Old Testament: Creation of Adam. Assisi,
S. Francesco, upper church.
Master of the Apollo and Daphne Legend. Creation
of Adam and Eve. Yale University, Gallery
of Fine Arts, Jarves Collection 49.
Michelangelo. Creation of Adam. Rome, Vatican,
Sistine Chapel. Ceiling decorations.
Palma Vecchio, School of. Creation of Adam.
Philadelphia, Collection Johnson.

Puccio, Pietro di. Scenes from the Old Testament:
The Creation of Man. Pisa, Camposanto.
Salviati, Francesco. Cappella Chigi. Creation
of Adam. Rome, S. Maria del Popolo.
Siciolante, Girolamo. Wall fresco: creation
of Adam. Rome, S. Maria della Pace.
Uccello Paolo. Frescoes in the cloister:
Creation of Man and Animals. Sinopie
for fresco. Creation of Man. Florence,
S. Maria Novella.

SPANISH SCHOOL
Spanish school, Wall painting. Fresco decoration
of apse. Above: apostles. Below: scenes
from Genesis. Detail: Creation of Adam.
Osormort (Barcelona), S. Saturninus.
Spanish school, 13th century. Old Testament
cycle: Creation of Adam. Detail. Fresco,
c. 1200. Sigena, Monastery, Chapter House.

71 A 32 1 GENESIS 2:8-9 THE GARDEN OF EDEN. PARADISE

AMERICAN SCHOOL
Field, Erastus Salisbury. Garden of Eden.
c. 1865. Boston, Museum of Fine Arts,
48.1027.
Field, Erastus Salisbury. Garden of Eden.
c.1860. Shelburne, Vt., Shelburne Museum.

DUTCH SCHOOL
Savery, Roland. Paradise. 1628. Vienna,
Kunsthistorisches Museum, 1003.
Savery, Roland. Temptation in the Garden
of Eden. 1620. Buscot Park, Collection
Lord Faringdon.
Vos, Paul de. Paradise. Vienna, Kunsthistorisches
Museum, 1709.

FLEMISH SCHOOL
Bles, Herri met de. Garden of Eden. Amsterdam,
Rijksmuseum, 522.
Bosch, Jerome. Adam and Eve in Paradise.
Chicago, Art Institute.
Brueghel, Jan, the elder. Garden of Eden.
Besancon, Mus. des Beaux Arts.
Brueghel, Jan, the elder. Garden of Eden
(Fall of Man). Budapest, Museum of Fine
Arts.
Brueghel, Jan, the elder. The Garden of
Eden; in the background, the Temptation.
London, Victoria and Albert Museum, 340-1878.
Brueghel, Jan, the elder. The Garden of
Eden. Madrid, Prado.
Brueghel, Jan, the elder. Garden of Eden
(Earthly Paradise) Paris, Louvre, Musée
du, 1092.
Brueghel, Jan, the elder. Garden of Eden.
Rome, Galleria Doria.
Brueghel, Jan, the elder. Terrestrial Paradise.
Rome, Villa Borghese Gallery.
Brueghel, Jan, the elder. Garden of Eden.
Seville, Museo Provincial.
Brueghel, Jan, the Younger. The Garden of
Eden. Sotheby and Co., London (Sale [ROSE]
July 6, 1983, No. 116).
Hondt, L. de. The Garden of Eden. Weston
Park, Collection. Earl of Bradford.

71 A 33 GENESIS 2:15 - 3:42 ADAM IN THE GARDEN
OF EDEN

EARLY MEDIEVAL AND BYZANTINE
Coptic painting, Fayûm. Adam before original
sin. Fresco. 1025. From Om el-Beregete,
Fayûm. Cairo, Coptic Museum.

71 A 33 1 GENESIS 2:15 GOD BRINGS ADAM TO PARADISE

SPANISH SCHOOL
Spanish school, 12th century. School of Catalonia.
Fresco decoration of apse. Details: scenes
from Genesis. Middle: God sends Adam into
Eden. Osormort (Barcelona), S. Saturninus.

71 A 33 3 GENESIS 2:19-20 ADAM NAMING THE ANIMALS

BRITISH SCHOOL
Blake, William. Adam naming the beasts. 1810.
Art Gallery, Pollock House.

FLEMISH SCHOOL
Brueghel, Jan, the Younger. The Life of Adam:
Adam Naming the Animals. Koller - Gallery
(Zürich).

ITALIAN SCHOOL
Italian school, Wall painting. Episodes of
Adam and Eve. Adam naming the animals,
top. End of 12th century. Spoleto, Ṣ. Paolo,
Presbiterium.
Italian school, 12th century. Wall decorations.
Old Testament subjects. Detail: Adam naming
the animals. Ferentillo, S. Pietro e S.
Paolo.

71 A 34 GENESIS 2:21-25 CREATION OF EVE

BRITISH SCHOOL
Watts, G.F. Creation of Eve. Harvard University,
Fogg Art Museum, 1943.210.
Watts, George Frederic. The Creation of Eve.
Sotheby and Co., London (Belgravia, Sale,
Oct. 24, 1978).

FLEMISH SCHOOL
Bosch, Jerome. Adam and Eve in Paradise:Creation
of Eve. Chicago, Art Institute.
Brueghel, Jan, the elder. Creation of Eve.
Pommersfelden, Schloss, Gallery.
Vroylínck, Ghislain. Creation of Eve. Wing
of a triptych. Bergues, Museum, 131.

GERMAN SCHOOL
Baldung, Hans? Creation of Eve. Nüremberg,
Germanic Museum.

ITALIAN SCHOOL
Albani, Francesco, Follower of. The Creation
of Eve. Oxford, University, Ashmolean Museum,
A944.
Domenichino. Creation of Eve. Frascati, Villa
Muti.
Peruzzi, Baldassare. Cappella della Ponzetto.
Arch. Old and New Testament subjects. The
Creation of Eve, upper panel. Rome, S.
Maria della Pace.
Raphael (and assistants). Old Testament subjects:
Creation of Eve. Rome, Vatican, Loggie.
Salviati, Francesco. Creation of Eve. Two
details. Rome, S. Maria del Popolo, Cappella
Chigi.
Uccello, Paolo. Frescoes in cloister: Creation
of Eve. Florence, S. Maria Novella.
Veronese, Paolo. Creation of Eve. Chicago,
Art Institute, Coll. Mr. and Mrs. C. H.
Worcester.

**71 A 34 1 GENESIS 2:21 CREATION OF EVE. GOD REMOVES
A RIB FROM ADAM'S SIDE**

FLEMISH SCHOOL
Bles, Herri met de. Garden of Eden. Amsterdam,
Rijksmuseum, 522.

FRENCH SCHOOL
Chagall, Marc. Illustrations from the _Bible_
published by Vollard. No. 19: Creation of
Eve. Nice (Alpes-Maritimes), Musée National
Message Biblique Marc Chagall.
French school, Wall painting. Scenes from
the Old Testament: Creation of Adam and
Eve. 11th'century. St. Savin, (Vienne),
Church, Nave.

ITALIAN SCHOOL
Raphael. Standard with Crucifixion and Creation
of Eve.Citta da Castello,Pinacoteca Communale.

**71 A 34 2 GENESIS 2:22 EVE IS FASHIONED FROM
ADAM'S RIB**

GERMAN SCHOOL
Bertram (van Byrde) Master. Grabow altar.
Scenes from the Old and New Testament:
God creating Eve. Hamburg, Kunsthalle.

ITALIAN SCHOOL
Italian school, 13th century. Frescoes.
Detail: wall of the Grotta di S. Lorenzo:
Creation of Eve. Anagni, Cathedral.

**71 A 34 21 GENESIS 2:21-22 CREATION OF EVE. EVE
EMERGES FROM ADAM'S BODY**

AUSTRIAN SCHOOL
Austrian school, 18th century. The Creation
of Eve. Budapest, Museum of Fine Arts,
6108.

FLEMISH SCHOOL
Bocksberger, Hans, the Elder. Fresco decorations
for Schlosskapelle, Neuburg an der Donau.
16th century. Creation of Eve. Neuburg
an der Donau, Schloss.
Brueghel, Jan, the elder. The creation of
Eve. Budapest, Museum of Fine Arts, 625.
Brueghel, Jan, the elder. Garden of Eden.
Besancon, Mus. des Beaux Arts.
Brueghel, Jan, the elder. Paradise. Frankfort-
on-the-Main, Staedel Institute, 1097.
Gossaert, Jan (Mabuse). The metamorphosis
of Eve. Rotterdam, Museum Boymans, 2457.

GERMAN SCHOOL
Bertram (van Byrde) Master. Grabow altar.
Scenes from the Old and New Testament:
God creating Eve. Hamburg, Kunsthalle.

ITALIAN SCHOOL
Albertinelli, Mariotto. The Creation and
Fall. London, University of, Courtauld
Institute.
Bartolo di Fredi. Scenes from the Old Testament:
Creation of woman. S. Gimignano, Collegiata.
Bartolommeo, Fra. Creation of Eve. Washington,
National Gallery, 467. Keyes.
Caliari, Carletto. The Creation of Eve.
c. 1586. Florence, Palazzo Uffizi, 954.
Carpioni, Guilio. The Creation of Eve.
Christie, Manson and Woods (Sale, London
[TASMANIA-3051], Dec. 11, 1984, No. 31).
Guglielmo da Marcilla. Scenes from the Old
and New Testament: Creation of Eve. Arezzo,
Cathedral.
Italian school, 12th century. Wall decorations.
Old Testament subjects. Detail: Creation
of Eve. Ferentillo, S. Pietro e S. Paolo.
Italian school, 13th century ? Decoration.
Detail: creation of woman. Andria, S.
Croce.
Italian school, 13th century. (Cavallini,
Pietro?) Scenes from the Old Testament:
Creation of Eve. Assisi, S. Francesco,
upper church.
Italian School, 13th century. Cycle of Creation:
God creating man and woman: Creation of
Eve. Fossa, Santa Maria ad Cryptas.
Italian school, 14th century. Thirty stories
from the Bible: Creation of Eve, top register,
second panel. Veronese. Verona, Museo
Civico, 362.
Italian school, Wall painting. Episodes
of Adam and Eve, Creation of Eve, bottom.
Spoleto, S. Paolo, Presbiterium.
Master of the Apollo and Daphne Legend.
Creation of Adam and Eve. Yale University,
Gallery of Fine Arts.
Michelangelo. Creation of Eve: and four
figures on pedestals. Rome, Vatican,
Sistine chapel. Ceiling decorations.
Mingha, Andrea di Mariotto del. Creation
of Eve. Florence, Palazzo Pitti.

Nuvolone, Carlo Franceso. Creation of Eve.
Dulwich Gallery, 235.
Puccio, Pietro di. Scenes from the Old Testament.
Creation [of Eve]. Pisa, Camposanto.
Rosso, Il. Creation of Eve. Rome, S. Maria
della Pace.

SPANISH SCHOOL
Spanish school, 13th century. Old Testament
cycle: Creation of Eve. Detail. Fresco,
c. 1200. Sigena, Monastery, Chapter House.

71 A 35 GENESIS 2:25 ADAM AND EVE IN PARADISE BEFORE
THE FALL

AMERICAN SCHOOL
American school, 19th century. Adam and Eve.
c. 1830. New York, Whitney Museum of American
Art.

BRITISH SCHOOL
Martin, John. The Garden of Eden. London,
Tate Gallery, T.1007.
Wolmark, Alfred. Adam and Eve. Sotheby and
Co., London (Sale, Sept. 26, 1984. No. 208).

DUTCH SCHOOL
Poelenburgh, Cornelis. Adam and Eve in paradise.
Salm, Fürsten zu - Collection, 440.

EARLY MEDIEVAL AND BYZANTINE
Coptic painting. Chapel of Flight. Heavenly
Jerusalem in form of palace. Detail. Below:
Adam and Eve. Khargeh, Bagawat Necropolis.

FLEMISH SCHOOL
Bouttats, Frederik, the Younger. Adam and
Eve in the Garden of Eden. Sotheby and
Co., London (Sale, New York, Jan. 20, 1983,
No. 35).
Bouttats, G. The Garden of Eden. Sotheby
and Co., London (April 7, 1982, No.6).
Brueghel, Jan, the Elder. Adam and Eve in
Paradise. Ottawa, National Gallery of Canada.
Brueghel, Jan, the Elder. The Garden of Eden.
Christie, Manson and Wood (Sale, London,
June 28, 1974, No.83).
Brueghel, Jan, the Elder. The Earthly Paradise.
The Hague, Royal Gallery, 236.
Hondt, L. de. The Garden of Eden. Weston
Park, Collection. Earl of Bradford.

FRENCH SCHOOL
Duchamp, Marcel. Paradise. Painted on reverse
of the King and Queen Surrounded by Swift
Nudes. 1910. Philadelphia, Museum of Art,
'50-134-63b.
Gleyre, C. The terrestrial paradise.
Poussin, N. The Four Seasons. Spring or Adam
and Eve. 1660-64. Paris, Louvre.

GERMAN SCHOOL
Müller, Otto. Adam and Eve. Frankfort-on-the-Main,
Staedel Institute, 2020.
Rösel von Rosenhoff, Franz. The Garden of
Eden before the Fall. Copenhagen, Art Museum,
1898.
Thoma, Hans. Adam and Eve. 1886. Berlin,
Staatliche Museen, NG 1367.

ITALIAN SCHOOL
Alberti, Durante. The Creation. Rome, Il
Gesù, Cappella della S.S. Trinità. Vault.
Bassano, Jacopo. The Earthly Paradise. Rome,
Palazzo Doria Pamphili.
Solimena, Francesco. The Garden of Eden.
Sotheby and Co., London (Sale, April 16,
1980, No. 20).
Vaga, Perino del. Adam and Eve. Rome, S.
Trinità dei Monti, Cappella Pucci. Vault
of arch.

71 A 35 1 GENESIS 2:22 GOD BRINGS EVE TO ADAM

BRITISH SCHOOL
Blake, William. The Angel of the Divine Presence
Bringing Eve to Adam. c. 1803. New York,
Metropolitan Museum of Art.

71 A 35 2 GENESIS 2:25 GOD BLESSES ADAM AND EVE.
INSTITUTION OF MARRIAGE.

ITALIAN SCHOOL
Vecchietta. Old Testament scene. Detail:
Adam and Eve. Siena, Spedale di S.M.
della Scale, Sala di S. Pietro.

71 A 35 3 GENESIS 1:26 ADAM IS GIVEN DOMINION
OVER ALL CREATED THINGS

ITALIAN SCHOOL
Bartolo di Fredi. Scenes from the Old Testament:
God Gives Adam Dominion over Paradise.
S. Gimignano, Collegiata.

71 A 35 4 GENESIS 2:16-17 THE GIVING OF THE TEST
COMMANDMENT. GOD WARNS ADAM AND EVE NOT
TO EAT FROM THE TREE OF KNOWLEDGE OF GOOD
AND EVIL

FLEMISH SCHOOL
Bles, Herri met de. Garden of Eden. Amsterdam,
Rijksmuseum, 522.
Gossaert, Jan (Mabuse). Adam and Eve. Berlin,
Staatliche Museen (East Berlin).

GERMAN SCHOOL
Bertram (van Byrde) Master. Grabow altar.
Scenes from the Old and New Testament:
God warning Adam and Eve not to touch
forbidden fruit. Hamburg, Kunsthalle.
Soest, Konrad von. Adam and Eve warned not
to touch the forbidden fruit. Bielefeld,
Marienkirche.

ITALIAN SCHOOL
Bartolo di Fredi. Scenes from the Old Testament:
God forbids the picking of the fruit.
S. Gimignano, Collegiata.

SPANISH SCHOOL
Greco, El. Altarpiece with scenes of Adam
and Eve. Modena, Pinacoteca Estense.
Spanish school,12th century. School of Catalonia.
Scenes from Genesis. Top: God instructs
Adam not to eat from the tree of knowledge.
Osormort, S. Saturninus, Fresco, decoration
of apse.

71 A 41 1 GENESIS 3:1-5 THE SERPENT TRIES TO
PERSUADE EVE TO TAKE SOME OF THE FRUIT

AUSTRIAN SCHOOL
Wagenschön, Franz Xavier. Adam and Eve (a
pair). Budapest, Museum of Fine Arts,
2319, 2320.

BRITISH SCHOOL
Watts, George Frederic. The Temptation of
Eve. Paris, Louvre, Musée du, R.F. 1977-433.

EARLY MEDIEVAL AND BYZANTINE
Coptic painting. Fayûm. Eve before original
sin. Cairo, Coptic museum.

FRENCH SCHOOL
Gauguin. Eve and the serpent. 1889. Igny,
Collection G. Fayet.

71 A 41 2 GENESIS 3:5 EVE TAKES THE FRUIT

BRITISH SCHOOL
Merritt, Anna Lea. Eve. 1885. Sotheby and
Co., London (Sale, [JCB] December 14,
1983, No. 168).

Watts, G.F. Trilogy of Eve. Second picture:
Eve tempted. Compton, (Limnerslease) Watts
Picture Gallery.
Watts, G.F. Eve tempted. Aberdeen, Art Gallery.

FLEMISH SCHOOL
Memlinc, Hans. Bathsheba at her toilet. Reverse
panel: Eve. Stuttgart, Museum, 644.

GERMAN SCHOOL
Baldung, Hans. Eve, the Serpent and Death.
c. 1515. Ottawa, National Gallery of Canada.
Cranach, Lucas, the Elder. Eve. Antwerp,
Museum, 5048.

SPANISH SCHOOL
Verger, C. Eve. Valencia, Museo de Pinturas.

71 A 42   GENESIS 3:1-7   TEMPTATION AND FALL (SCENES
WITH BOTH ADAM AND EVE)

BRITISH SCHOOL
English school, 12th century, Wall painting.
The Temptation. Hardham (Sussex),St. Botolph.

DUTCH SCHOOL
Cornelisz, Cormelis. Adam and Eve(The Temptation)
Dresden, Staaliche Kunstsammlungen, 852.
Dutch school, 16th century. The Fall. c. 1540.
Vienna, Kunsthistorisches Museum, 2684.

EARLY MEDIEVAL AND BYZANTINE
Coptic painting. Adam and Eve. Khargeh, Bagawat
Necropolis, Tomb chapel: Room of Peace.
Early Medieval and Byzantine Wall Painting,
Fayûm. Om el-Beregete. Adam and Eve before
the Original Sin. 1025 A.D. Cairo, Coptic
Museum.

FLEMISH SCHOOL
Bosch, Jerome. Adam and Eve in Paradise: Creation
of Eve. Chicago, Art Institute.
Brueghel, Jan, the Younger. The Life of Adam:
The Temptation. Koller - Gallery (Zürich).
Goes, Hugo van der, Follower of. The Fall.
Ludwigshafen, Wilhelm Hack Museum.
Goes, Hugo van der, School of. Tempting of
Adam and Eve. Schloss Frens, Collection
Count Beissel van Gymnich.
Gossaert, Jan (Mabuse). Adam and Eve. New
York, Metropolitan Museum.
Kessel, Jan van I. The Garden of Eden. Christie,
Manson and Woods (Sale, New York, Jan. 19,
1982, No. 119).
Rubens, P.P. Adam and Eve. Antwerp, Rubens
House.
Rubens, P.P. Adam and Eve. (The fall of man).
Copy, with variations, of a Titian. Madrid,
Prado.

FRENCH SCHOOL
Tissot, James Jacques Joseph. Illustrations
of the Hebrew Bible. No. 2: Adam is Tempted
by Eve. 1896-1903. New York, Jewish museum,
52.69.

GERMAN SCHOOL
Baldung, Hans. Adam and Eve. c. 1520. Budapest,
Museum of Fine Arts, 715, 716 (1888).
Beckmann, Max. Adam and Eve. 1917. Dr. and
Mrs. Stephan Lackner Collection, Santa Barbara.
Cranach, Lucas, the elder. Adam and Eve.
c. 1530. Pasadena, Calif., Norton Simon
Museum.
Cranach, Lucas, the elder. Adam and Eve.
Vienna, Kunsthistorisches Museum, 861, 861A.
Cranach, Lucas, the elder. Adam and Eve. 1537.
Vienna, Kunsthistorisches Museum Inv. Nr.
1537.
Cranach, Lucas, the elder, Studio of. Adam
and Eve. c. 1520. Vienna, Kunsthistorisches
Museum, 929a, b.

NORWEGIAN SCHOOL
Munch, Edvard. Adam and Eve under the Apple
Tree. 1908. Oslo, Munch-Museet (City
Museum).

SPANISH SCHOOL
Spanish school, 13th century. Old Testament
cycle: Temptation of Eve. Fresco, c.
1200. Sigena, Monastery.

71 A 42 1   GENESIS 3:6   EVE TAKES THE FRUIT FROM
THE SERPENT (OR THE TREE) IN THE PRESENCE
OF ADAM, WHO MAY BE TRYING TO STOP HER

AMERICAN SCHOOL
Field, Erastus Salisbury. Garden of Eden.
c.1865. Boston, Museum of Fine Arts,
48.1027.
Field, Erastus Salisbury. Garden of Eden.
c. 1860. Shelburne, Vt., Shelburne Museum.

EARLY MEDIEVAL AND BYZANTINE
Early Christian Painting. Adam and Eve,
and decoration. Rome, Catacomb Maggiore.
Cubiculum II.
Early Christian Painting. Adam and Eve.
Rome, Torre Pignattara, Catacomb of Saints
Petrus and Marcellinus. Cubiculum XIII.
Vault.
Early Christian Painting. Adam and Eve.
Rome, Torre Pignattara, Catacomb of Saints
Petrus and Marcellinus. Cubiculum XIV.

FLEMISH SCHOOL
Brueghel, Jan, the Younger. Paradise Landscape
with the Fall of man. Milan, Ambrosiana,
69.
Coxie, Michiel van. Altarpiece: The Fall
and Expulsion from Paradise. Vienna,
Kunsthistorisches Museum.
Gossaert, Jan (Mabuse). Adam and Eve. Berlin,
Staatliche Museen (East Berlin).
Gossaert, Jan (Mabuse). Adam and Eve. Brussels,
Musées Royaux des Beaux-Arts, 193.
Gossaert, Jan (Mabuse). Adam and Eve. England,
Royal Collection.
Rubens, P.P. Adam and Eve (After Titian).
1628-29. Madrid, Prado.
Spranger, Bartholomew. Adam and Eve: The
Fall. c. 1595. Vienna, Kunsthistorisches
Museum.

FRENCH SCHOOL
Valaden, Suzanne. Adam and Eve. 1909. Paris,
Musée National d'Art Moderne.

GERMAN SCHOOL
Cranach, L. (the elder). Adam and Eve.
Breslau, Museum.
Cranach, Lucas, the elder. Adam and Eve.
c. 1530. Chicago, Art Institute.
Cranach, Lucas, the elder. Adam and Eve.
1528. Florence, Palazzo Uffizi, 1459.
Cranach, Lucas, the younger, Circle of.
Adam and Eve. Christie, Manson and Woods
(Sale, New York, Christie's East, [POLLY],
March 13, 1980, No. 129).
Rottenhammer, Johann. Adam and Eve in Paradise.
Stockholm, University, 271.

ITALIAN SCHOOL
Italian school, 13th century. Adam and Eve.
Anagni, Cathedral. Frescoes, Wall of the
Grotta di S. Lorenzo.
Italian school, 13th century. Decoration.
Detail: Adam and Eve. Andria, Santa Croce.
Michelangelo. First sin. Rome, Vatican,
Sistine Chapel, Ceiling decorations.
Salviati, Francesco. Adam and Eve. Rome,
Galleria Colonna.
Titian. Fall of Man. 1565-70. Madrid,
Prado.
Uccello, Paolo. Frescoes in cloister: Deluge
and Story of Adam and Eve, the Fall.
Florence, S. Maria Novella.

71 A 42 2   GENESIS 3:6   EVE OFFERS THE FRUIT TO ADAM

AMERICAN SCHOOL
Landis, John, attributed to. The Temptation.
c. 1828. Washington, D.C., National Gallery
of Art, Garbisch Collection.

AUSTRIAN SCHOOL
Bocksberger, Hans, the Elder. Fresco decorations
for Schlosskapelle. The Fall. 16th century.
Neuburg an der Donau, Schloss.

BRITISH SCHOOL
Barry, James. Adam and Eve. Dublin, National
Gallery, 762.

DUTCH SCHOOL
Cornelisz, Cornelis. Adam and Eve. Amsterdam,
Rÿksmuseum, 719.
Cornelisz, Cornelis. Adam and Eve. Hamburg,
Kunsthalle, 67.
Cornelisz, Cornelis. Adam and Eve. Haarlem,
Museum.
Scorel, Jan van. Adam and Eve. Haarlem, Frans
Hals Museum, 264.
Werff, Adriaen van der. Adam and Eve. Paris,
Louvre, Musée du, INV, 1939.

FLEMISH SCHOOL
Brueghel, Jan, the elder. Creation of Eve.
Pommersfelden, Schloss, Gallery.
Brueghel, Jan, the elder. Garden of Eden.
Budapest, Museum of Fine Arts, 621.
Brueghel, Jan, the elder. The garden of Eden.
Madrid, Prado.
Brueghel, Jan, the elder. Garden of Eden.
Rome, Galleria Doria.
Brueghel, Jan, the elder. Garden of Eden.
Seville, Museo Provincial.
Brueghel, Jan, the elder. Terrestrial Paradise.
Rome, Villa Borghese Gallery.
Floris (de Vriendt), Frans I. Adam and Eve.
1560. Florence, Palazzo Uffizi.
Gossaert, Jan (Mabuse). Adam and Eve. Berlin,
Kaiser Friedrich Museum.
Gossaert, Jan (Mabuse), Circle of. The Fall
of Man. c. 1520/30. Dulwich Gallery, 505.
Hondt, Lambert de. Adam and Eve in the Garden
of Eden. Sotheby and Co., London (Sale,
New York, March 6-7, 1975, No. 102).
Jordaens, Jacob. The Fall. Budapest, Museum
of Fine Arts, 5551 (410 a).

FRENCH SCHOOL
Dumons, J.J. Adam and Eve. Paris, Ecole des
Beaux Arts.
French School, 16th century. Adam and Eve.
Wildenstein Collection, New York.
Troy, Jean François de. Adam and Eve. 1730.
Louisville, Ky., J.B. Speed Art Museum,
77.21.

GERMAN SCHOOL
Altdorfer, Albrecht. Fall of Man. Altarpiece.
c.1525. Washington D.C., National Gallery
of Art, 1110.
Cranach, Lucas, the elder. Adam and Eve. 1528.
Detroit, Institute of Arts, 62.279.
Cranach, L. (the elder). Adam and Eve. Florence,
Uffizi, 1458.
Cranach, Lucas, the elder. Adam and Eve.
London, Univ. of, Courtauld Institute, Lee
Collection.
Cranach, L. (the elder). Adam and Eve in Paradise.
Berlin, Kaiser-Friedrich Museum, 567.
Cranach, Lucas, the elder, School of. Adam
and Eve. Antwerp, Museum.
Cranach, L. (the elder), Follower of. Adam
and Eve. Boston, Fenway Court.
Cranach, Lucas, the elder, School of. Adam
and Eve. after 1533. Eisenach, Wartburg.

Cranach, Lucas, the elder, School of. Adam
and Eve in Paradise (landscape possibly
by Flemish artist). Chicago, Art Institute.
Cranach, Lucas the Younger. Eve Tempting
Adam. Christie, Manson and Wood (Sale,
London, July 7, 1972, No. 31).
Cranach, Lucas, the younger. The fall of
man. Houston, Museum of Fine Arts, Straus
Collection, 44.546.
Dürer, Albrecht. Adam and Eve, 1507. Madrid,
Prado, 2177, 2178.
Dürer, Albrecht. Copy. Adam and Eve: Adam.
Copy of the picture in the Prado by Hans
Baldung? Florence, Pitti.
Dürer, Albrecht, School of. Rovingo, Pinacoteca
dell'Accademia dei Concordi, 299.80.
Soest, Konrad von. The Fall. Panel from
wings of altarpiece in the Marienkirche,
Bielefeld. Bielefeld, Marienkirche.
Stuck, Franz von. Adam and Eve. 1912. Galerie
Gunzenhauser (Munich).

ITALIAN SCHOOL
Albertinelli, Mariotto. The Creation and
Fall. London, University of, Courtauld
Institute.
Caliari, Carletto. Original Sin. c.1584.
Florence, Palazzo Uffizi, 960.
Castello, Valerio. Adam and Eve. Genoa,
Private Collection.
Cignani, Carlo. Adam and Eve. The Hague,
Royal Galllery.
Cignani, Carlo. The Fall. Budapest, Museum
of Fine Arts, 514 (198).
Giordano, Luca. Adam and Eve. Ottawa, National
Gallery of Canada, 93.
Italian school, 13th century. Cycle of Creation:
God creating man and woman, Temptation.
Fossa, Santa Maria ad Cryptas.
Palma Giovane. Adam and Eve. Venice, Palazzo
Vendramin Calergi.
Palma Giovane. Adam and Eve. Venice, Querini-
Stampalia.
Palma Giovane. The Fall of Man. Baltimore,
Md., Walters Art Gallery, 37.576.
Palma Vecchio. Adam and Eve. Brunswick,
Landesmuseum, 453.
Puccio, Pietro di. Scenes from the Old Testament:
Creation [The Temptation]. Pisa, Camposanto.
Raphael (and assistants). Old Testament subjects:
The fall of man. Rome, Vatican, Loggie.
Reni, Guido. The Fall of Man (The Temptation
of Adam). Dijon (Côte-d'Or), Musée Municipal.
Salviati, Francesco. The Temptation. Rome,
S. Maria del Popolo, Cappella Chigi.
Sicciolante, Girolamo. Wall fresco: the
Fall. Rome, S. Maria della Pace.
Tintoretto. Adam and Eve (The Fall). 1550-51,
Venice, Academy.
Tintoretto. Adam and Eve. Ottawa, National
Gallery of Canada, 3364.
Tintoretto. Scuola di San Rocco, upper hall,
Ceiling: Fall of man.

71 A 42 21   GENESIS 3:6   EVE SIMULTANEOUSLY OFFERS SOME OF THE FRUIT TO ADAM AND TAKES SOME MORE FROM THE SERPENT (OR THE TREE)

DUTCH SCHOOL
Dutch school, 17th century. Adam and Eve
in the Garden of Eden. Sotheby and Co.,
London (Sale, New York [5104] Nov. 3,
1983, No. 82).
Savery, Roland. Temptation in the Garden
of Eden. Buscot Park, Collection Lord
Faringdon.
Savery, Roland. The Fall. Budapest, Museum
of Fine Arts, 208 (381).

FLEMISH SCHOOL
Brueghel, Jan, the elder. Garden of Eden
(Fall of Man). Budapest, Museum of Fine
Arts.
Brueghel, Jan, the elder. Garden of Eden.
Detail: Adam and Eve. Seville, Museo Provincial.

Brueghel, Jan, the elder. Garden of Eden.
Detail:Adam and Eve.Seville, Museo Provincial.
Brueghel, Jan, the Younger. Paradise with
the Fall. Germany, Private Collection.
Rubens, P.P. and Brueghel,Jan,the elder (Brueghel
de Velours). Adam and Eve in Paradise.
The Hague, Royal Gallery, 253.

71 A 42 22 GENESIS ADAM HIMSELF TAKES THE FRUIT FROM THE TREE

FLEMISH SCHOOL
Isenbrant, Adrian. Adam and Eve. San Francisco,
Fine Arts Museum.

71 A 42 3 GENESIS 3:6 ADAM AND EVE HOLDING (AND POSSIBLY EATING) THE FRUIT

EARLY MEDIEVAL AND BYZANTINE
Early Medival and Byzantine Wall Painting,
Fayûm, Om el-Beregete. Adam and Eve before
the Original Sin. 1025 A.D. Cairo, Coptic
Museum.

DUTCH SCHOOL
Rooswyck, Engel. Adam and Eve. Milwaukee
(Wisconsin), Art Center.

FLEMISH SCHOOL
Bles, Herri met de. Adam and Eve. Bologna,
Pinacoteca.
Bertram (van Byrde) Master. Grabow altar.
Scenes from the Old and New Testament: Fall
of man. Hamburg, Kunsthalle.
Cranach, L. (the elder) ? Diptych with Adam
and Eve. Brussels, Musée de Peinture, 123a.
Cranach, Lucas, the elder. Adam and Eve. 1518.
Brunswick, Landesmuseum, 27.
Cranach, Lucas, the elder. Adam and Eve. 1531.
Dresden, Gallery, 1911.
Cranach, L. (the elder). Adam and Eve. Dresden,
Royal Gallery, 1916B (1919).
Cranach, L. (the elder). Adam and Eve. Munich,
Old Pinakothek, 720 (277).

ITALIAN SCHOOL
Celesti, Andrea, Circle of. Adam and Eve.
Sotheby and Co., London (Sale [DELPHINIUM]
July 13, 1983., No. 40).
Masaccio, Masolino and Filippino Lippi. Adam
and Eve under the tree of knowledge.Florence,
S. Maria del Carmine, Brancacci Chapel.

SPANISH SCHOOL
Spanish school, Wall painting. Fresco decoration
of apse. Above: apostles. Below: scenes
from Genesis. Detail: the sin of Adam and
Eve. Osormort, S. Saturninus.
Spanish school, School of Catalonia. Fresco
decoration of apse. Above: apostles.
Below: scenes from Genesis. Detail: the
sin of Adam and Eve. Copy in Museo de la
Ciutadella, Barcelona. Osormort,
S. Saturninus.

71 A 42 4 GENESIS 3:7 ADAM AND EVE DISCOVER THEIR NAKEDNESS. THEY COVER THEMSELVES WITH THEIR HANDS OR WITH LEAVES

EARLY MEDIEVAL AND BYZANTINE
Early Christian Painting. Detail of Adam and
Eve. Rome, Torre Pignattara, Catacomb of
Saints Petrus and Marcellinus. Cubiculum
XIII.
Early Medieval and Byzantine Wall Painting,
Fayûm. Om el-Beregete. Adam and Eve before
and after the Original Sin. 1025 A.D. Cairo,
Coptic Museum.

FLEMISH SCHOOL
Cleve, Joos van, the elder. Adam and Eve.

ITALIAN SCHOOL
Alloci, Alessandro. Frescoes, 1560: Adam
and Eve. Florence, S.S. Annunziata, Ceiling,
Cappella della Visitazione.
Domenichino. Original Sin. Rome, Galleria
Rospigliosi.

71 A 5 GENESIS 3:8-21 ADAM AND EVE IN PARADISE (AFTER THE FALL)

BRITISH SCHOOL
Watts, G.F. Trilogy of Eve. Third picture.
Eve repentant. London, Tate Gallery.

FRENCH SCHOOL
Gauguin, Paul. Adam and Eve. 1902. Ordrupgaard
Collection, Copenhagen.

ITALIAN SCHOOL
Italian school, 14th century. Thirty stories
from the Bible. Temptation of Adam and
Eve, top register, 3rd panel. Veronese.
Verona, Museo Civico.
Vecchietta. Adam and Eve. Siena, Spedale
di S.Maria della Scala, Sala di S. Pietro.

SPANISH SCHOOL
Spanish school, 12th century. Adam and Eve
instructed by the Lord. Fresco from San
Martín Sescortes. Vich, Museo Episcopal.
Spanish school, 13th century. Old Testament
cycle: Admonition of Adam and Eve. Fresco,
c.1200. Sigena, Monastery, Chapter House.

SWISS SCHOOL
Amiet, Cuno. Garden of Eden (Paradise).
1958. Private Collection.

71 A 53 GENESIS 3:8-22 ADAM AND EVE REPROVED BY GOD

FLEMISH SCHOOL
Brueghel, Jan, the Younger. Paradise Landscape
with Expulsion. Milan, Ambrosiana, 63.
Gossaert, Jan (Mabuse). Adam and Eve. Berlin,
Staatliche Museen (East Berlin).

GERMAN SCHOOL
Bertram (van Byrde) Master. Grabow altar.
Scenes from the Old and New Testament:
Discovery of sin. Hamburg, Kunsthalle.

ITALIAN SCHOOL
Bassano, Jacopo. The defense of Adam. Madrid,
Prado, 21.
Benefial, Marco. Expulsion from Paradise.
Rome, Palazzo Barberini.
Domenichino. Expulsion of Adam and Eve.
Chatsworth, Collection Duke of Devonshire.
Domenichino. Original Sin (Rebuke of Adam
and Eve). Rome, Barberini Gallery.
Furini, Francesco. Adam and Eve. Florence,
Pitti.
Furini, Francesco. Adam and Eve in garden.
Ottawa, National Gallery of Canada, 2025.
Italian school, 13th century. Scenes from
the Old Testament: Adam snd Eve and the
Serpent. Assisi, S. Francesco, upper
church.
Puccio, Pietro di. Scenes from the Old Testament:
Creation (The Fall). Pisa, Camposanto.

71 A 54 3 GENESIS 3:17-19 PUNISHMENT OF ADAM (ALONE)

BRITISH SCHOOL
Blake, William. God Judging Adam. c.1790-93.
Goyder, George, Esq. - Collection (Long
Melford, Suffolk).

<u>71 A 55 GENESIS 3:21 ADAM AND EVE ARE CLOTHED BY</u>
<u>   GOD</u>

BRITISH SCHOOL
     Blake, William. The Angel of the Divine Presence
     Clothing Adam and Eve with Coats of Skins.
     1803. Cambridge, University, Fitzwilliam
     Museum PD29-1949.

<u>71 A 6 GENESIS 3:23-24 EXPULSION FROM THE GARDEN</u>
<u>   OF EDEN</u>

BRITISH SCHOOL
     Blake, William. The Fall of Man. 1807. London,
     Victoria and Albert Museum.
     Faed, John. Expulsion from the Garden of Eden.
     Cleveland, Museum of Art, 80.258.
     Martin, John. The Expulsion of Adam and Eve
     from Paradise. Frank, Mrs. Robert - Collection.

GERMAN SCHOOL
     Rösel von Rosenhoff, Franz. The Earth after
     the Fall. 1690. Copenhagen, Art Museum,
     1899.

ITALIAN SCHOOL
     Angelico, Fra. Annunciation, with Expulsion
     from Eden in background. Madrid, Prado,
     15.
     Bassano, Francesco, the younger. Expulsion
     from Paradise (Spring). 1580-1585. Vienna,
     Kunsthistorisches Museum, 4303.
     Domenichino. Expulsion of Adam and Eve. Dublin,
     National Gallery, 1083.
     Rosso, Il. Wall decorations. Expulsion. Rome,
     S. Maria della Pace.
     Tintoretto (Jacopo Robusti). Adam and Eve
     Expulsed from Paradise. c.1550-55. Florence,
     Palazzo Uffizi, 8428.

SPANISH SCHOOL
     Spanish school, 12th century. School of Catalonia.
     Fresco decoration of Apse. Detail: Adam
     and Eve expelled from Eden. God instructing
     Adam. Copy in Museo de la Ciutadelle,Barcelona.
     Osormort, S. Saturninus.

<u>71 A 61 GENESIS 3:24 GOD EXPELS ADAM AND EVE FROM</u>
<u>   PARADISE AND HAS THE TREE OF LIFE GUARDED</u>
<u>   BY AN ANGEL WITH A FLAMING SWORD</u>

FRENCH SCHOOL
     Tissot, James Jacques Joseph. Illustrations
     of the Hebrew Bible. No. 4: Adam and Eve
     Driven from Paradise. 1896-1902. New York,
     Jewish Museum, 52.71.

ITALIAN SCHOOL
     Bartolo di Fredi. Scenes from the Old Testament.
     Expulsion. S. Gimignano, Collegiata.
     Giovanni di Paolo. Expulsion from Paradise.
     New York, Metropolitan Museum.
     Italian school, 15th century. Expulsion from
     the Garden of Eden. Lausanne, Collection
     Reber.
     Uccello, Paolo. Frescoes in the cloister:
     Adam and Eve driven from Paradise. Florence,
     S. Maria Novella.

<u>71 A 61 1 GENESIS 3:23-24 AN ANGEL CHASES ADAM</u>
<u>   AND EVE OUT OF PARADISE WITH A FLAMING SWORD</u>

DUTCH SCHOOL
     Vertangen, Daniel. Adam and Eve: The Expulsion
     from Paradise. Glasgow, Art Gallery.

FLEMISH SCHOOL
     Bles, Herri met de. Garden of Eden. Amsterdam,
     Rijksmuseum, 522.
     Brueghel, Jan, the Younger. The Life of Adam:
     The Expulsion from Eden. Koller - Gallery
     (Zürich).

Coxie, Michiel van. Altarpiece. Left wing:
     Expulsion from Paradise. Vienna,
     Kunsthistorisches Museum.
Coxie, Michiel van. Altarpiece. Left wing:
     Expulsion from Paradise. Vienna,
     Kunsthistoriches Museum.
Dyck, Anthony van. Expulsion from Paradise.
     c. 1621? Baskett and Day, London.
Flemish school, 16th century. Expulsion
     from Paradise. c.1560. Vienna,
     Kunsthistorisches Museum, 917.
Rubens, Peter Paul. The expulsion from Eden.
     Design for a painted ceiling for the Jesuit
     Church, Antwerp. Prague, Národní Galerie.

FRENCH SCHOOL
     Bauchant, Andre. Adam and Eve Expelled from
     Paradise. Lavel, Musée du Vieux-Chateau.
     Delacroix, Eugène. The Expulsion of Adam
     and Eve from Paradise. Glasgow, Art Gallery.
     Lanoüe, Félix Hippolyte. Adam and Eve Expulsed
     from the Garden of Eden. 1841. Paris,
     Ecole des Beaux-Arts (Grand Prix de Rome).

GERMAN SCHOOL
     Bertram (van Byrde) Master. Grabow altar.
     Scenes from the Old and New Testament.
     Expulsion from Eden. Hamburg, Kusthalle.
     German school, 16th century. Expulsion of
     Adam and Eve from Paradise. South German
     School, c. 1550. Philadelphia, Philadelphia
     Museum of Art, Johnson Collection, no.
     731.
     Soest, Konrad von. Eight panels from wings
     of altarpiece in the Marienkirche, Bielefeld.
     3. Adam and Eve Driven from Paradise.

ITALIAN SCHOOL
     Benvenuto di Giovanni. Expulsion from Paradise.
     Boston, Museum of Fine Arts, 56.512.
     Caliari, Carletto. Expulsion from Paradise.
     c. 1586. Florence, Palazzo Uffizi, 944.
     Cesare da Sesto. Expulsion from Paradise.
     Oxford, University, Christ Church.
     Cesari, G. Adam and Eve. Paris, Louvre.
     Cesari, Giuseppe. Expulsion. London, Apsley
     House, Collection Duke of Wellington.
     Cresti, Domenico. Expulsion of Adam and
     Eve. Rome, Palazzo Barberini.
     Guardi, Francesco. The Expulsion from Paradise.
     Paris, Finney Collection.
     Italian school, 11th century. Expulsion
     of Adam and Eve from Paradise. S. Angelo
     in Formis, Cathedral, right aisle, entrance
     wall.
     Italian school, 13th century. Scenes from
     the Old Testament: Expulsion from Paradise.
     Assisi, S. Francesco, upper church.
     Mannozzi, Giovanni. Expulsion from Paradise.
     c. 1634. Florence, Palazzo Uffizi, 5422.
     Massacio, Masolino, and Filippino Lippi.
     Expulsion from Paradise. Florence, Carmine,
     Brancacci Chapel.
     Michelangelo. First sin and Expulsion from
     Paradise. Rome, Vatican, Sistine Chapel,
     Ceiling decorations.
     Mingha, Hadrea di Mariotto del. Adam and
     Eve cast out of Eden. Florence, Palazzo
     Pitti.
     Pomarancio, Niccolò. The Expulsion from
     Paradise. Christie, Manson and Woods
     (Sale, New York, Christie's East [KAREN-5521]
     March 23, 1984, No. 48).
     Pontormo, Jacopo da. Adam and Eve expelled
     from Paradise. Florence, Palazzo Uffizi.
     Puccio, Pietro di. Scenes from the Old Testament:
     Creation (Expulsion from Eden). Pisa,
     Camposanto.
     Raphael (and assistants) Old Testament subjects:
     Adam and Eve exiled from Eden. Rome,
     Vatican, Loggie.
     Rocca, Michele. Expulsion from the Garden.
     Hartford, Wordsworth Atheneum.

Salviati, Francesco. The Expulsion. Rome,
S. Maria del Popolo, Cappella Chigi.
Siciolante, Girolamo. Wall fresco: Expulsion
of Adam and Eve from Paradise. Rome, S.
Maria della Pace.
Tintoretto. Adam and Eve: [Expulsion]. Venice,
Academy.
Vite, Antonio. Scenes from lives of Adam and
Eve. Detail: Expulsion. Pistoia, Convent
del T.

SPANISH SCHOOL
Spanish school, 12th century. Expulsion of
Adam and Eve. Fresco from San Martín Sescortes,
right. Vich, Museo Episcopal.
Spanish school, 12th century. Expulsion of
Adam and Eve. Fresco from San Martín Sescortes,
left. Vich, Museo Episcopal.
Spanish school, 13th century. Old Testament
cycle: Temptation of Eve and Expulsion from
Paradise. Fresco, c.1200. Sigena, Monastery,
Chapter House.
Spanish school, 13th century. Fragments of
fresco decoration. Details: saints; Expulsion.
Toledo, San Román.

71 A 62   GENESIS 3:24 ADAM AND EVE OUTSIDE EDEN,
          WHOSE ENTRANCE IS GUARDED BY SHINING CHERUBIM

AMERICAN SCHOOL
Cole, Thomas. Expulsion from Eden. Boston,
Museum of Fine Arts (Karolik Collection).

BRITISH SCHOOL
Strang, William. The Expulsion of Adam and
Eve. 1901. Athill, Philip and Annibel -
Collection.

MEXICAN SCHOOL
Correa, Juan. The Expulsion. Tepozotlán,
Jesuit Seminary of San Martín.

71 A 63   ADAM AND EVE DOING PENANCE

SPANISH SCHOOL
Sert, José María. Murals with scenes from
the Old and New Testaments. Panel: Adam
and Eve expelled from Paradise.Vich,Cathedral.

71 A 7   GENESIS 4:1-2 THE LABOURS OF ADAM AND EVE;
         INFANCY OF CAIN AND ABEL

DUTCH SCHOOL
Haensbergen, Johan van. Adam and Eve and Cain
and Abel. Sotheby and Co. (Sale, London,
February 22, 1984, No. 34).

FLEMISH SCHOOL
Brueghel, Jan, the Younger. The Life of Adam:
Adam and Eve Laboring. Koller - Gallery
(Zürich).
Teniers, David, the Younger. Adam and Eve
after the Expulsion, copy after Veronese.
London, University, Courtauld Institute
(Princess Gate Collection) 308.

ITALIAN SCHOOL
Bacchiacca, Francesco. Adam and Eve.Philadelphia,
Philadelphia Museum of Art, Johnson Collection.
Chimenti, Jacopo. Adam and Eve. Christie,
Manson and Woods (Sale, London, October
14, 1983, No. 229).
Master of the Register of the Bolognese Cloth
Merchant's Association of 1328. The First
Parents: Adam and Eve. Cleveland, Museum
of Art, 82.139.
Turchi, Alessandro. Adam and Eve with the
Infants Cain and Abel. Sotheby and Co.,
London (Sale, May 16, 1984, [MAGNOLIA],
no. 23).

SPANISH SCHOOL
Spanish school, 13th century. Old Testament
cycle: Adam and Eve instructed in agriculture.
Fresco, c. 1200. Sigena, Monastery, Chapter
House.

71 A 72   GENESIS 4:1-2 ADAM (AND EVE) ENGAGED
          IN AGRICULTURAL ACTIVITIES

ITALIAN SCHOOL
Caliari, Carletto. The Family of Adam. c.
1586. Florence, Palazzo Uffizi, 951.
Vaga, Perino del. Adam and Eve working.
Rome, S. Trinità dei Monti, Cappella Pucci,
Vault of arch.

71 A 72 1   GENESIS 4:1-2 [ADAM (AND EVE) ENGAGED
            IN AGRICULTURAL ACTIVITIES], WITH EVE SPINNING
            AND USUALLY THEIR CHILDREN AT PLAY

AUSTRIAN SCHOOL
Bocksberger, Hans, the Elder. Fresco decorations
for Schlosskopelle. Adam and Eve toiling.16th
century. Neuberg an der Donau, Schloss.

GERMAN SCHOOL
Bertram (van Byrde) Master. Grabow altar.
Scenes form the Old and New Testament:
Toil of Adam and Eve. Hamburg, Kunsthalle.

ITALIAN SCHOOL
Fetti, Domenico. Adam and Eve at Labour.
Paris, Louvre, Musée, 280.
Fetti, Domenico. Adam and Eve at work.
London, University, Courtauld Institute.
Peruzzi, Baldassare. Adam and Eve Laboring.
Also attributed to Perino del Vaga. Rome.
Palazzo della Cancelleria, Salone de Studio,
Vault decorations.
Raphael (and assistants). Old Testament
subjects: The labours of Adam and Eve.
Rome, Vatican, Loggie.
Uccello, Paolo. Frescoes in the cloister:
Adam and Eve laboring. Florence, S. Maria
Novella.
Vite, Antonio. Scenes from lives of Adam
and Eve. Detail: Beginning of industry.
Pistoia, Convent del T.

SPANISH SCHOOL
Cano, Alonso. Adam and Eve. Glasgow, Collection
Sir Stirling-Maxwell.
Spanish school, 13th century. Old Testament
cycle: Adam and Eve laboring. Fresco,
c. 1200. Sigena, Monastery, Chapter House.

71 A 72 2   GENESIS 4:1-2 [ADAM (AND EVE) ENGAGED
            IN AGRICULTURAL ACTIVITIES] WITH EVE SUCKLING
            THE CHILDREN

DUTCH SCHOOL
Mostaert, Jan. Eve with Four Children. c.
1520. Williamstown, Clark Art Institute,
946.

ITALIAN SCHOOL
Bacchiacca, Francesco. Adam and Eve with
their Children. Pistoia, Private Collection.
Puccio, Pietro di. Scenes from the Old Testament:
Creation [The Labor of Adam and Eve].
Pisa, Camposanto.
Veronese, Paolo. After the Expulsion from
Paradise. Vienna, Kunsthistorisches Museum.

71 A 72 3   AN ANGEL INSTRUCTS ADAM

ITALIAN SCHOOL
Italian school, 13th century. Scenes from
the creation: an angel instructs Adam?
Anagni, Cathedral. Frescoes. Detail: wall
of the Grotta di S. Lorenzo.

71 A 73   EDUCATION, UPBRINGING OF CAIN AND ABEL

ITALIAN SCHOOL
Italian school, 13th century. Detail: wall
of the Grotta di S. Lorenzo: Scenes from
the Creation; education, upbringing of Cain
and Abel. Anagni, Cathedral, Frescoes.

71 A 8   GENESIS 4:1-15   THE STORY OF CAIN AND ABEL

FRENCH SCHOOL
Cormon, Fernand. Cain.
French school, Wall painting. Scenes from
the Old Testament: the Egyptians in the
Red Sea; story of Cain and Abel. 11th century.
St. Savin (Vienne), Church.

71 A 81   GENESIS 4:3-4   THE SACRIFICE: ABEL OFFERS
A LAMB, CAIN USUALLY A SHEAF OF CORN

FLEMISH SCHOOL
Eyck, Hubert and Jan van. Altarpiece of the
Adoration of the Lamb. Interior. Extreme
Left Panel, Upper. The Sacrifice of Cain
and Abel. Ghent, St. Bavon.

FRENCH SCHOOL
French school, Wall painting. Scenes from
the Old Testament: Offering of Cain and
Abel. 11th century. St. Savin (Vienne),
Church.
French school, Wall painting. St. Savin, nave.
Scenes from the Old Testament: Offering
of Cain and Abel. Copy. 11th century. Paris,
Musée National des Monuments Français, 21432.
Vernet, Claude Joseph, attributed to. Cain
and Abel Bringing their Sacrifices. Sacramento,
Crocker Art Gallery, 1872.573.

GERMAN SCHOOL
Bertram (van Byrde) Master. Grabow altar.Scenes
from the Old and New Testament:Sacrifices
of Cain and Abel. Hamburg,Kunsthalle.

ITALIAN SCHOOL
Bartolo di Fredi. Scenes from the Old Testament:
Cain kills Abel. S. Gimignano, Collegiata.
Puccio, Pietro di. Scenes from the Old Testament:
Death of Abel and Sacrifice of Cain and
Abel. Pisa, Camposanto.

SPANISH SCHOOL
Pedret Master. Frescoes of main apse: sacrifice
of Abraham; sacrifice of Cain. Pedret, Church.
Spanish school, 12th century. School of Catalonia.
Fresco decorations, Inner triumphal arch.
Detail: Abel. Tahull, Santa Maria.

71 A 81   GENESIS 4:4   GOD (OR THE HAND OF GOD) APPEARS
AND BLESSES ABEL

ITALIAN SCHOOL
Italian school, 11th century. Cain and Abel.
Fresco. S. Angelo in Formis, Church, right
aisle, entrance wall.
Peruzzi, Baldassare. Sacrifice of Cain and
Abel. Also attributed to Perino del Vaga.
Rome, Palazzo della Cancelleria, Salone
di Studio, Vault decorations, Lunette.

SPANISH SCHOOL
Spanish school, 13th century. Old Testament
cycle. Above: Sacrifice of Cain and Abel.
Below: Slaying of Abel. Fresco, c. 1200.
Sigena, Monastery, Chapter House.

71 A 81 2   GENESIS 4:4-5   THE FUME OF ABEL'S SACRIFICE
GOES STRAIGHT TO HEAVEN, WHEREAS THE SMOKE
OF CAIN'S OFFERING IS BEATEN DOWN

BRITISH SCHOOL
Millais, Sir John E. The rejection of Cain's
sacrifice. Birmingham, England, Art Gallery,
620'06.

EARLY MEDIEVAL AND BYZANTINE
Byzantine school, Wall painting. Story of
Cain and Abel. Detail: Offering. 16th
century. Mount Athos, The Laura, Refectory.

ITALIAN SCHOOL
Albertinelli, Mariotto. Sacrifice of Cain
and Abel. Harvard University, Fogg Art
Museum, 1906.5.

71 A 82   GENESIS 4:8   THE KILLING OF ABEL: CAIN
SLAYS HIM WITH A STONE, A CLUB OR A JAW BONE,
ALTERNATIVELY WITH A SPADE OR ANOTHER
TOOL AS WEAPON

DUTCH SCHOOL
Cornelisz, Cornelis. Cain and Abel. Boston,
Museum of Fine Arts, 60.960.

EARLY MEDIEVAL AND BYZANTINE
Byzantine school, 16th century. Below: Story
of Cain and Abel. Detail of the Slaying.
Mount Athos, The Laura, Refectory.

FLEMISH SCHOOL
Eyck, Hubert and Jan van. Altarpiece of
the Adoration of the Lamb. Interior. Extreme
right panel, Upper. The Murder of Abel.
Ghent, St. Bavon.
Flemish school, 17th century. Cain and Abel.
Seville, Cathedral, Capilla de San Antonio.
Floris (de Vriendt), Frans I. Cain Slaying
Abel. Copenhagen, Art Museum, Sp. 337.
Govaerts, Abraham. Cain Slaying Abel. Salm,
Fürsten zu - Collection, 243.
Rubens, Peter Paul. Cain Slaying Abel.
London, University, Courtauld Institute
(Princess Gate Collection) 298.

FRENCH SCHOOL
French school, Wall painting. Scenes from
the Old Testament: Death of Abel and the
curse of Cain. 11th century. St. Savin,
(Vienne), Church.
Legrand, Pierre Nicolas. Cain Murders His
Brother. Bern, Art Museum, 313.

GERMAN SCHOOL
Bertram (van Byrde) Master. Grabow altar.
Scenes from the Old and New Testament:
Murder of Abel. Hamburg, Kunsthalle.
Stummel, Friedrich. Wall paintings in St.
Maria, Kevelaer. Study for Cain Killing
Abel. 1915. Kranenburg, Museum Katharinenhof.

ITALIAN SCHOOL
Asserto, Gioachino. Cain Killing Abel.
Brunswick, Landesmuseum, 490.
Bartolo di Fredi. Scenes from the Old Testament:
Cain kills Abel. S. Gimignano, Collegiata.
Giordano, Luca. Cain and Abel. Dublin,
National Gallery, 1667.
Giordano, Luca. Cain Slaying Abel. Copenhagen,
Art Museum, Sp. 63.
Italian school, 11th century. Cain kills
Abel, Cain flees. S. Angelo in Formis,
Cathedral, left aisle, entrance wall.
Italian school, 16th century (Venetian).
Cain Kills Abel. Budapest, Museum of
Fine Arts, 4239 (P.114)
Italian school, 17th century (Neapolitan).
Cain Killing Abel. Formerly attributed
to Ludovico Carracci. Edinburgh, National
Gallery, 21.
Lana, Ludovico. Cain Kills Abel. Modena,
Pinacoteca Estense.
Luti, Benedetto. Cain and Abel. Formerly
Osterley Park, Collection Earl of Jersey.
Maffei, Francesco. Cain and Abel. Venice,
Collection Conte Ludovico Foscari.
Palma Giovane (?) Cain and Abel. Longleat,
Collection Marquis of Bath.
Palma Giovane. Cain's Murder. Vienna,
Kunsthistorisches Museum, 1576.

Peruzzi, Baldassare. Cain Killing Abel. Also attributed to Perino del Vaga. Rome, Palazzo della Cancelleria, Salone di Studio, Vault decorations, Lunette.
Puccio, Pietro di. Scenes from the Old Testament: Death of Abel. Pisa, Camposanto.
Reni, Guido. Cain Slaying Abel. c.1615. Vienna, Kunsthistorisches Museum, 363.
Reni, Guido. Cain Slaying Abel. Turin, Pinacoteca, 504.
Riminaldi, Orazio. Cain and Abel. Florence, Soprintendenza alle Galleria. Inv. Gallerie, 1890, n. 5842.
Rosa, Salvatore. Cain and Abel. Rome, Doria Gallery.
Rosa, Salvator. Cain and Abel. Sotheby and Co. (Sale, February 16, 1983, No. 45).
Sirani, Elisabette. Cain Killing Abel. Turin, Pinacoteca, 504.
Spada, Lionello. Cain Killing Abel. Christie, Manson and Wood, London, (Sale, May 28, No. 90).
Spada, Lionello. Killing of Abel. Naples, Museo Nazionale, Capodimonte, 622.
Tintoretto. Death of Abel. 1550-51. Venice, Academy.
Titian. Ceiling decorations: Cain slaying Abel. Venice, S. Maria della Salute.
Trevisani, Francesco. Cain and Abel. Rome, Palazzo Barberini.

MEXICAN SCHOOL
Siqueiros, David Alfaro. Death and Burial of Cain. 1947. Private Collection.

SPANISH SCHOOL
Spanish school, 13th century. Old Testament cycle. Above: Sacrifice of Cain and Abel. Below: slaying of Abel. Fresco, c. 1200. Sigena, Monastery, Chapter House.

SWEDISH SCHOOL
Wickenburg, Per. Eve Mourning the Death of Abel. 1835. Stockholm, National Museum, 1246.

71 A 82 1 GENESIS 4:8-10 ABEL'S DEATH

AMERICAN SCHOOL
Cole, Thomas. Study of Abel. 1832. Albany, N.Y., Albany Institute of History and Art.
Grosz, George. Cain and Abel. 1935. Mrs. Lester Francis Avnet Collection, Great Neck, N.Y.

BRITISH SCHOOL
Watts, G.F. Death of Abel ("My punishment is greater than I can bear"). London, Diploma Gallery, 243.
Watts, G.F. Death of Abel. Compton (Surrey), Watts Picture Gallery, Mansell.

FLEMISH SCHOOL
Rubens, P.P. The dead Abel. Greenville, S.C., Bob Jones University, Gallery.

FRENCH SCHOOL
Falguiere, J.A.J. Cain and Abel. Carcassonne (Aude), Musée.

ITALIAN SCHOOL
Italian school, 13th century. Scenes from the Old Testament: Cain and Abel. Assisi, S. Francesco, upper church, nave.
Italian school, 17th century. Cain and Abel. Rome, Palazzo Barberini.
Italian school, 17th century (Roman). Cain and Abel. Rome, Galleria Colonna.
Lys, Giovanni. Death of Abel. Padua, Collection Fiocco.
Lys, Giovanni. Cain and Abel. New York, Coll. Walter P. Chrysler, jr.

Piazetta, Giovanni Battista. The Dead Abel. 1741? London, Sotheby and Co. (Sale, Dec. 12, No. 21, [IVY]).
Passante, Bartolomeo. Cain killing Abel. Frankfort -on- the-Main, Staedel Institute.
Reni, Guido. Abel. Bologna, Pinacoteca Nazionale, 1302.
Sacchi, Andrea. Cain and Abel. Rome, Palazzo Barberini (Formerly).

SWEDISH SCHOOL
Pilo, Carl Gustaf. Cain and Abel. Stockholm, National Museum.

71 A 82 3 ADAM AND EVE DISCOVER THE DEAD BODY OF ABEL AND GRIEVE OVER IT

AUSTRIAN SCHOOL
Rottmayr, Johann Michael, 1654-1730. The Mourning of Abel. Vienna, Österreichische Galerie, 4298.

BRITISH SCHOOL
Blake, William. The Body of Abel Found by Adam and Eve. c.1826. London, Tate Gallery, 5888.
Blake, William. The Body of Abel Found by Adam and Eve. c.1805-09. Harvard University, Fogg Art Museum, 1943.401.
Stephanoff, Francis Philip. The Death of Abel. 1810. London, Victoria and Albert Museum, F.A. 605.

DUTCH SCHOOL
Breenbergh, Bartholomeus. Death of Abel. Antwerp, Museum, 641.
Dalen, Cornelius van, after. Landscape with Adam and Eve weeping over the body of Abel. Rotterdam, Museum Boymans, Inv. 2095.

EARLY MEDIEVAL AND BYZANTINE
Byzantine school, Wall painting. Below: Story of Cain and Abel. Detail: Adam and Eve lamenting the death of Abel. 16th century. Mount Athos, the Laura, Refectory.

FLEMISH SCHOOL
Brueghel, Jan, the Younger. The Life of Adam: The Lamentation over the Death of Abel. Koller - Gallery (Zürich).
Floris, Frans, I. Adam and Eve Mourning over the Body of Abel. c.1560. Cassel, Staatliche Kunstsammlungen.

FRENCH SCHOOL
Bonnat, Léon. Adam and Eve Discovering the Dead Abel. 1860. Lille, Palais des Beaux-Arts, Musée Wicar.
Champaigne, Philippe de. Lamentation for Abel. 1656. Vienna, Kunsthistorisches Museum, 371.
Champaigne, Philippe de. Lamentation for Abel. Sketch. Vienna, Kunsthistorisches Museum, 9685.
Henner, J.J. The Death of Abel.
Henner, Jean Jacques. Adam and Eve Finding the Body of Abel. 1858. Paris, École des Beaux-Arts (Grand Prix de Rome).

ITALIAN SCHOOL
Cerquozzi, Michelangelo. Adam and Eve Finding the Body of Abel. Rome, Galleria d'Arte Antica.
Giordano, Luca. Adam and Eve Lamenting over the Body of Abel. Copenhagen, Art Museum, Sp. 64.
Italian school, 18th century (Roman). Adam and Eve Mourning Abel. 2nd half 18th century. Sotheby and Co., London (Sale, April 4, 1984, [DAFFODIL] No. 277).
Lys, Giovanni. Death of Abel. Venice, Academy, (Inc. 880, Cat. 913).
Pagani, Paolo. The Lamentation for Abel. Brunswick, Landesmuseum, 1006.

SPANISH SCHOOL
Castillo y Saavedra, Antonio del ? Death of
Abel. Zürich, Gratwohl Collection.

71 A 83   GENESIS 4:10-15   THE CURSE AND FLIGHT OF
CAIN

FRENCH SCHOOL
Coypel, N. Punishment of Cain.

GERMAN SCHOOL
Stummel, Friedrich. Wall paintings in St.
Maria, Kevelaer. Study for God Laying a
Curse on Cain. c.1897. Vinnemeier, Dr. Maria
- Collection (Velbert).

ITALIAN SCHOOL
Bartolo di Fredi. Scenes from the Old Testament:
Cain Kills Abel. S. Gimignano, Collegiata.

71 A 83 1   GENESIS 4:9-14   THE LORD CALLS ON CAIN
TO ACCOUNT FOR HIS DEED

FRENCH SCHOOL
French school, Wall painting. Scenes from the
Old Testament: Death of Abel and the curse
of Cain. 11th century. St. Savin, Vienne,
nave.

71 A 83 11   GENESIS 4:10   ABEL'S BLOOD CRIES OUT
FOR REVENGE

AMERICAN SCHOOL
Grosz, George. Cain. 1944. Estate of George
Grosz.

71 A 83 21   GENESIS 4:15   GOD PUTS A MARK ON CAIN

ITALIAN SCHOOL
Puccio, Pietro di. Scenes from the Old Testament.
Death of Abel [The Mark of Cain]. Pisa,
Camposanto.

71 A 84 2   GENESIS 4:17   CAIN BUILDING THE CITY OF
ENOCH

FRENCH SCHOOL
French school, 17th century. Cain Builds the
City of Enoch. Budapest, Museum of Fine
Arts, 9983.
La Fage, Raymond, School of. Cain building
the City of Enoch. 3rd quarter 17th century.
Budapest, Museum of Fine Arts.

71 A 92   GENESIS 4:25-58   STORY OF SETH

SPANISH SCHOOL
Oliveri, Juan. Wall decorations from San Pedro,
Olite. Seth planting tree of life on Adam's
ground. Pamplona, Museo Provincial.

71 B 15 1   GENESIS 4:23-24   LAMECH KILLS CAIN: CAIN
IS ACCIDENTALLY SHOT DEAD BY AN ARROW OF
THE BLIND LAMECH, WHO IS ASSISTED IN THE
HUNT BY HIS SON TUBALCAIN

BRITISH SCHOOL
Watts, G.F. The death of Cain. London, Diploma
Gallery, 26.

ITALIAN SCHOOL
Italian school, 15th century. Series of fresco
scenes from the Old Testament. Lamech Killing
Cain (upper left). Florence, S.M. Novella,
Cloister.

71 B 21   GENESIS 5:6-11   STORY OF ENOS

ITALIAN SCHOOL
Vasari, Giorgio and Gherardi, Cristofano.
Sacrifices and prophets: Enos. Fresco.
Cortona, Compagnia del Gesù.

71 B 25   GENESIS 5:18-24   STORY OF ENOCH, SON OF
JARED, WHO INVENTED LETTERS AND WAS THE
FIRST TO DIVIDE THE YEAR INTO SEASONS
AND INTO TWELVE MONTHS

BRITISH SCHOOL
Blake, William. Enoch Walked with God (?)
c.1780-85. Cincinnati, Museum.

FRENCH SCHOOL
French school, Wall Painting, St. Savin.
Scenes from the Old Testament: Enoch calls
upon the Lord. 11th century. St. Savin,
Vienne, Nave.

71 B 3   GENESIS 5:28-9:29   STORY OF NOAH

BRITISH SCHOOL
Epstein, Jacob. Noah and his Sons. 1931.
London, Victoria and Albert Museum, E.
422-1943.

FRENCH SCHOOL
French school, Wall painting. Scenes from
the Old Testament: Story of Noah. 11th
century. St. Savin (Vienne), Church,
Nave.

ITALIAN SCHOOL
Italian school, 12th century. Wall decorations.
Old Testament subjects. Detail: Noah and
his family in the Ark. Ferentillo, S.
Pietro e S. Paolo.

71 B 31   GENESIS 6-7:4   BEFORE THE FLOOD

BRITISH SCHOOL
Linnell, John. Noah: The Eve of the Deluge.
1848. Cleveland, Museum of Art, 72.119.
Solomon, Simeon. 'And the Sons of God saw
that the Daughters of Man that they were
Fair' 1863. Handley-Read Collection.

71 B 31 1   GENESIS 6:1-6   THE WICKEDNESS OF MANKIND;
THE WICKED ARE USUALLY SHOWN FEASTING
AND REVELLING

BRITISH SCHOOL
Scott, William Bell. The Eve of the Deluge.
1865. Christie, Manson and Woods (March
1980).
Scott, William Bell. The Eve of the Deluge.
London, Tate Gallery, 1322.

DUTCH SCHOOL
Cornelisz, Cornelis. "And God Saw that the
Wickedness of Man was Great in the Earth."
Sotheby and Co., London (Sale, June 9,
1982, No. 26).
Cornelisz, Cornelis. The Antediluvian Race.
1626. Christie, Manson and Wood, London
(Sale, December 11, 1981, No. 113).
Cornelisz, Cornelis. The corruption of men
before the Deluge. 1615. Toulouse (Haute-
Garonne), Musée des Beaux-Arts.
Mander, Karel van. Before the Deluge. Frankfort
-on- the-Main, Staedel Institute, 2088.

FLEMISH SCHOOL
Bosch, Jerome. The World Before the Flood.
Rotterdam, Museum Boymans.

<u>71 B 31 21   GENESIS 6:13-21   GOD ANNOUNCES A FLOOD
AND COMMANDS NOAH TO BUILD AN ARK</u>

FRENCH SCHOOL
   Chagall, Marc. Illustrations from the <u>Bible</u>
      published by Vollard. No. 20: Noah Receives
      the Order to Build the Ark. 1930. Nice
      (Alpes-Maritimes), Musée National Message
      Biblique Marc Chagall.
   French school, Wall painting, St. Savin. Scenes
      from the Old Testament: God speaks to Noah.
      11th century. St. Savin, (Vienne), Church,
      Nave.

GERMAN SCHOOL
   Bertram (van Byrde) Master. Grabow altar.
      Scenes from the Old and New Testament:
      Building the Ark. Hamburg, Kunsthalle.

ITALIAN SCHOOL
   Italian school, 11th century. God commands
      Noah to build the Ark. S.Angelo in Formis,
      Cathedral. Left aisle, Entrance wall.
   Italian school,12th century. Wall decorations.Old
      Testament subjects. Details:Noah receiving
      the command of the Lord. Ferentillo, S.Pietro
      e S.Paolo.
   Italian school, 13th century. Scenes from
      the Old Testament: Construction of the Ark.
      Assisi, S. Francesco, upper church.
   Uccello, Paolo. Frescoes in the cloister.
      Noah receiving the order to build the Ark.
      Florence, S. Maria Novella.

<u>71 B 32   GENESIS 7:5-9   THE BUILDING OF THE ARK,
AND THE EMBARKATION</u>

AMERICAN SCHOOL
   Peale, Charles Willson. Noah and His Ark.
      1819. Philadelphia, Pennsylvania Academy
      of Fine Arts, 1951.22.

FLEMISH SCHOOL
   Boel, Pieter. Noah's Ark. Dublin, National
      Gallery, 42.

FRENCH SCHOOL
   La Fage, Raymond, School of. Construction
      of Noah's Ark. 3rd quarter 17th century.
      Budapest, Museum of Fine Arts.

GERMAN SCHOOL
   Bertram (van Byrde) Master. Grabow altar.
      Scenes from the Old and New Testament:Building
      the ark. Hamburg, Kunsthalle.

ITALIAN SCHOOL
   Italian school, 13th century. Scenes from
      the Old Testament: Construction of the Ark.
      Assisi, S. Francesco, upper church.
   Italian school, 12th century. Wall decorations.
      Old Testament subjects. The building of
      the Ark. Ferentillo, S. Pietro e S. Paolo.
   Italian school, 15th century. Series of scenes
      from the Old Testament. Noah. Florence,
      S. M. Novella, Cloister frescoes.

SPANISH SCHOOL
   Orrente, Pedro. Noah after the Construction
      of the Ark. Orihuela, Diocesan Museum.

<u>71 B 32 1   GENESIS 7:5   NOAH BUILDING THE ARK</u>

ITALIAN SCHOOL
   Bassano, Francesco, the younger. Noah's Ark.
      Florence, Palazzo Uffizi, 6203.

<u>71 B 32 11   GENESIS 6:22   NOAH BUILDING THE ARK WITH
THE HELP OF HIS SONS</u>

FRENCH SCHOOL
   French school, 17th century. The Building
      of Noah's Ark. Budapest, Museum of Fine
      Arts, 9984.

ITALIAN SCHOOL
   Bartolo di Fredi. Scenes from the Old Testament:
      Noah building the Ark. S.Gimignano,Collegiata.
   Bassano, Jacopo. The Building of the Ark.
      Marseille (Bouches-du-Rhône), Musée Municipal.
   Bassano, Leandro. The Building of the Ark.
      Dublin, National Gallery, 954.
   Italian school, 11th century. The building
      of the Ark. Fresco. S. Angelo in Formis,
      Church, Left aisle wall.
   Italian school, 12th century. Wall decorations.
      Old Testament subjects. The building
      of the Ark. Ferentillo, S. Pietro e S.
      Paolo.
   Italian school, 13th century. Scenes from
      the Old Testament. Construction of the
      Ark. Assisi, S. Francesco. Upper Church.
   Puccio, Pietro di. Scenes from the Old Testament:
      Noah's Ark and the Deluge (Building the
      Ark). Pisa, Camposanto.
   Raphael (and assistants). Old Testament subjects:
      Noah supervising the building of the ark.
      Rome, Vatican, Loggie.

<u>71 B 32 2   GENESIS 7:1-9   THE EMBARKATION</u>

DUTCH SCHOOL
   Hondecoeter, Melchior d'. Animale with a
      View of Noah's Ark in the Background.
      Brunswick, Landesmuseum, 393.
   Hondt, L. de. Noah enters the ark. Weston
      Park, Collection Earl of Bradford.

FLEMISH SCHOOL
   Grimmer, Jacob. The Entry of the Animals
      into the Ark. Also attributed to Pieter
      Aertsen, Younger. Christie, Manson and
      Woods (Sale, New York, June 12, 1981,
      No. 238)
   Jordaens, Habs. The Entry into the Ark. Christie,
      Manson and Wood (Sale, London, April 15,
      1983, No. 68).

FRENCH SCHOOL
   Boucher, François. Noah Entering the Ark.
      Paris, Private Collection.

ITALIAN SCHOOL
   Castiglione, G.B. Noah making preparations
      to enter the ark. Schleissheim, Neues
      Schloss, Gallery.
   Castiglione, Giovanni Benedetto. Noah Loads
      the Animals in the Ark. Vienna,
      Kunsthistorisches Museum, 1633.
   Castiglione, G.B., School of. Noah Waiting
      to Enter the Ark. Christie, Manson and
      Woods (Sale, New York, July 15, 1981,
      No. 21).

<u>71 B 32 21   GENESIS 7:2-3   THE GATHERING OF THE
ANIMALS IN PAIRS</u>

FLEMISH SCHOOL
   Brueghel, Jan, the elder. The animals of
      Noah's Ark. Budapest, Museum of Fine
      Arts, 629.
   Brueghel, Jan, the elder. The animals of
      Noah's ark. Madrid, Prado.
   Brueghel, Jan, the elder. The animals of
      Noah's ark. Madrid, Private Collection.
   Brueghel, Jan, the elder. Animals gathering
      for the Ark. London, Apsley House, Collection
      Duke of Wellington.

GERMAN SCHOOL
   German school, 17th century. Noah and the
      Animals. Budapest, Museum of Fine Arts,
      56.9.

ITALIAN SCHOOL
   Castiglione, Giovanni Benedetto. Animals
      of Noah's Ark. Genoa, Private Collection.
   Castiglione, G.B. Noah' Ark. Dresden, Gallery.

71 B 32 22 GENESIS 7:8-9 THE ANIMALS ENTER THE
ARK

    AMERICAN SCHOOL
        Hicks, Edward. Noah's Ark. 1846. Philadelphia,
           Museum of Art, 50-92-7.
        Hidley, Joseph H. Noah's Ark. c. 1850.
           Williamsburg, Va., Abby Aldrich Rockefeller
           Folk Art Collection, 57.101.8.

    AUSTRIAN SCHOOL
        Austrian school, 17th century. The Entry of
           the Animals into Noah's Ark. Sotheby and
           Co., London (Sale,[PRIMROSE], Feb. 16,
           1983, No. 15).

    FLEMISH SCHOOL
        Brueghel, Jan, the Elder. The Procession into
           the Ark. Wolf, Emile E. - Collection (New
           York).

    ITALIAN SCHOOL
        Bartolo di Fredi. Scenes from the Old Testament:
           Animals entering and leaving the Ark. Detail:
           Animals entering the Ark. S. Gimignano,
           Collegiata.
        Bassano, Jacopo.The animals entering the ark.
        Bassano, Jacopo. Animals entering the Ark.
           c.1574-81. New York, Collection William
           Kennedy (1968).
        Bassano, Jacopo. Entrance of the animals into
           Noah's ark. Madrid, Prado, 22.
        Castiglione, G.B. Animals entering the Ark.
           Weston Park, Collection Earl of Bradford.
        Castiglione, G.B. Entrance of the animals
           into the ark.Genoa,Accademia di Belle Arti.
        Castiglione, Giovanni Benedetto. Noah and the
           Animals in the Ark. Vienna, Kunsthistorisches
           Museum, 1645.
        Castiglione, Giovanni Benedetto, Circle of.
           The Animals Entering the Ark. Christie,
           Manson and Woods (Sale, London,[TERNI-2813]
           Dec. 15-16, 1983, No. 216).
        Italian school, 13th century. Entry into the
           ark. Assisi, S. Francesco, upper church.
        Jacopo da Ponti, school. Entering the ark.
           Bassano, Museo Civico, inv. 325.

    SPANISH SCHOOL
        Spanish school, 13th century. Old Testament
           cycle:Noah building the Ark. Fresco,c.1200.

71 B 32 23 GENESIS 7:7-13 NOAH AND HIS FAMILY ENTER
       THE ARK

    GERMAN SCHOOL
        Olivier, Friedrich. Noah's ark. Berlin,Staatliche
           Museen.

71 B 33 GENESIS 7:10-8:17 THE FLOOD

    AMERICAN SCHOOL
        Cole, Thomas. Sotheby and Co., London (Sale,
           March 17, 1982, No.84).

    BRITISH SCHOOL
        Turner, J.M.W. Light and Colour(Goethe's Theory):
           the Morning After the Deluge: Moses Writing
           the Book of Genesis.London,Tate Gallery,532.
        Turner, J.M.W. Shade and Darkness: The Evening
           of the Deluge. London, Tate Gallery, 531.

    EARLY MEDIEVAL AND BYZANTINE
        Coptic painting. Chapel of Flight: Detail:
           Noah's Ark. Khargeh, Bagawat Necropolis.

    ITALIAN SCHOOL
        Italian school, 12th century. Wall decorations.
           Old Testament subjects. Details: Noah and
           his family in the Ark. Ferentillo, S. Pietro
           e S. Paolo.
        Peruzzi, Baldassare. Old and New Testament
           subjects. The Flood, lower middle panel.
           Rome, S. Maria della Pace, Cappella della
           Ponzetto. Arch.

        Uccello, Paolo. Frescoes in cloister: Deluge.
           Florence, S. Maria Novella.

71 B 33 1 GENESIS 7:17-24 THE ARK FLOATING ON
       THE WATERS, WHILE LIFE ON EARTH IS DESTROYED

    BRITISH SCHOOL
        Danby, Francis. Copy. The Deluge. c. 1840.
           London, Tate Gallery, 6134.
        Linnell, John, the elder. The Eve of the
           Deluge. 1848. Cleveland, Museum of Art,
           72.119.

    DUTCH SCHOOL
        Amstel, Jan van. The Deluge. Brussels,
           Musées Royaux des Beaux Arts.
         Nagel, Jan. The Deluge with the Last Survivors
           of the Human Race in the Foreground. Christie,
           Manson and Wood, London (Sale, October
           30, 1981, No. 75).
        Uytewael, Joachim Antonisz, Attributed to.
           The Flood. c. 1610-1620. Yale University,
           Gallery of Fine Arts, 1964.40.
        Uytewael, Joachim Antonisz, Circle of. The
           Flood. 1611. Christie, Manson and Woods
           (Christie's East, [POLLY], March 13, 1980,
           no. 174).

    EARLY MEDIEVAL AND BYZANTINE
        Coptic painting. Chapel of Flight. Noah's
           Ark. Khargeh, Bagawat Necropolis.

    FLEMISH SCHOOL
        Bosch, Jerome. The Ark after the Flood. Rotterdam,
           Museum Boymans.
        Teniers, David, the younger. The Flood.
           Christie, Manson and Woods (Sale, London,
           July 9, 1982, No. 100).

    FRENCH SCHOOL
        French school, Wall painting. Scenes from
           the Old Testament: Noah's Ark. 11th century.
           St. Savin, (Vienne), Church, Nave.
        Gamelin, Jacques. The Deluge. 1779. Carcassonne,
           St. Vincent.

    GERMAN SCHOOL
        Baldung, Hans. The Deluge. Bamberg, Neue
           Hofhaltung.
        Elseheimer, Adam. The Deluge. Frankfort-on-the
           Main, Staedel Institute, 1607.
        Schoenfeld, Johann Heinrich. The Deluge.
           Vienna, Kunsthistorisches Museum, 1870.

    ITALIAN SCHOOL
        Palizzi, Filippo. The Day of the Deluge.
           1864. Naples, Museo Nazionale, Capodimente,
           44.
        Puccio, Pietro di. Scenes from the Old Testament.
           The Deluge. Pisa, Camposanto.
        Turchi, Alessandro. The Deluge. Paris,
           Louvre, Musée du, 699.
        Uccello, Paolo. Frescoes in the cloister:
           the Deluge. Detail. Florence, S. Maria
           Novella.

71 B 33 11 GENESIS 7: 17-24 THE ARK FLOATING
       ON THE WATERS (DESTRUCTION OF MANKIND
       NOT VISIBLE)

    ITALIAN SCHOOL
        Castiglione, Giovanni Benedetto. Noah Loading
           the Animals into the Ark. c.1630. Florence,
           Palazzo Uffizi, 1336.
        Italian school, 11th century. The Flood:
           the Ark on the Water. Fresco. S. Angelo
           in Formis, Church, Left aisle wall.

    SWEDISH SCHOOL
        Arosenius, Ivar. Noah's Ark. 1902. Stockholm,
           National Museum, NM B 1230.

71 B 33 12 GENESIS 7:17-24 DESTRUCTION OF MANKIND
            BY THE FLOOD (THE ARK ABSENT OR BARELY VISIBLE)

AMERICAN SCHOOL
    Allston, Washington. The deluge. New York,
    Metropolitan Museum.

BRITISH SCHOOL
    Danby, Francis. The Deluge. London, Tate Gallery.
    Turner, Joseph Mallord William. The Deluge.
    Exhibited 1805? London, Tate Gallery, 493.

DUTCH SCHOOL
    Cornelisz, Cornelis. The Flood (The Deluge).
    Brunswick, Landesmuseum, No. 170.
    Mander, Karel van. The Flood. Sotheby and
    Co., London (Sale, Dec. 12, 1984, No. 41)
    IVY.
    Uytewael, Joachim Antonisz. The Flood. c.
    1585. Nuremberg, Germanic Museum.

FLEMISH SCHOOL
    Floris, Frans, I. The Flood.

FRENCH SCHOOL
    Géricault, J.L.A.T. Scene of the Deluge.
    Paris, Louvre, Musée du, R.F. 1950.40.
    Girodet-Trioson, A.L.D. The Deluge. 1806.
    Patel, Pierre Antoine, the Younger, 1648-1707.
    The Deluge. London, Sotheby and Co., London
    (Sale, Monaco, (OUDRY), Dec. 8, 1984, No.354).
    Poussin, N. The Four Seasons: Winter or the
    Deluge. 1660-64. Paris, Louvre.
    Regnault, Jean Baptiste. The Deluge. 1789?
    Paris, Louvre, Musée du, 7380.

ITALIAN SCHOOL
    Carpioni, Guilio. Flood (The Deluge). Budapest,
    Museum of Fine Arts.
    Carracci, Antonio. The Deluge. Paris, Musée
    du Louvre.
    Guglielmo da Marcilla. Scenes from the Old
    and New Testaments: The Flood. Arezzo,
    Cathedral.
    Italian school, 16th century (Lombard). The
    Deluge. Madrid, Prado.
    Italian school, 17th century. The Deluge. Florence,
    Palazzo Uffizi, 5748.
    Lelio Orsi. The Deluge. Parma, S. Paolo.
    Michelangelo. The Flood. Rome, Vatican, Sistine
    Chapel, Ceiling decorations.
    Raphael (and assistants). Old Testament subjects:
    the flood. Rome, Vatican, Loggie.
    Testa, Pietro, attributed to. The Deluge. Sotheby
    and Co., London (Sale, Monaco, (OUDRY),
    Dec. 8, 1984, No. 316)

71 B 33 2 GENESIS 8:1-14 THE ARK COMES TO REST
           ON MOUNT ARARAT

ITALIAN SCHOOL
    Uccello, Paolo. Frescoes in the cloister.
    The recession of the flood. Florence, S.
    Maria Novella.

71 B 33 22 1 GENESIS 8:11 THE DOVE RETURNS WITH
              AN OLIVE BRANCH

BRITISH SCHOOL
    Landseer, Charles. Return of the Dove to the
    Ark. Ex.1844. Forbes Magazine Collection,
    New York.
    Millais, Sir John E. The Return of the Dove
    to the Ark. 1851. Oxford University, Ashmolean
    Museum.

EARLY MEDIEVAL AND BYZANTINE
    Early Christian Painting, Rome. Noah in his
    ark. Rome, Via delle Sette Chiese, Catacomb
    of Domitillo, Cubiculum III.

Early Christian Painting, Rome. Noah in
    his ark. Rome, Catacomb of Pamphilus,
    second level.
Early Christian Painting, Rome. Noah. Rome,
    Torre Pignattara, Catacomb of Saints Petrus
    and Marcellinus, Crypt with Orpheus.
Early Christian painting, Rome. Scenes of
    Noah. Rome, Torre Pignattara, Catacomb
    of Saints Petrus and Marcellinus, Cubiculum
    XIII, Vault.
Early Christian painting, Rome. Noah in
    his ark. Rome, Torre Pignattara, Catacomb
    of Saints Petrus and Marcellinus, Cubiculum
    XXI.

SPANISH SCHOOL
    Spanish school, 13th century. Fresco fragments.
    Scenes from the New and Old Testaments.
    Detail: the Flood. Madrid, Coll. Raimundo
    Ruiz.
    Spanish school, 13th century. Old Testament
    cycle: Dove returns to the Ark. Fresco,
    c.1200. Sigena, Monastery, Chapter House.

71 B 34 GENESIS 8:1-19 THE DISEMBARKATION

FRENCH SCHOOL
    Bonnard, Pierre. After the Deluge. 1906.
    Collection Walter P. Chrysler, New York.

ITALIAN SCHOOL
    Salviati, Francesco. After the Deluge.
    Rome, Palazzo della Cancelleria, Cappella
    del Pallio, Vault.

71 B 34 1 GENESIS 8:16 GOD ORDERS NOAH TO DISEMBARK
           AND OPENS THE ARK

FRENCH SCHOOL
    French school, Wall painting. Scenes from
    the Old Testament: Noah and his family
    leaving the ark. 11th century. St. Savin,
    (Vienne), Church, Nave.
    French school, Wall painting. St. Savin,
    Nave. Scenes from the Old Testament:
    God blesses Noah and his sons. Copy. 11th
    century. Paris, Musée National des Monuments
    Français. 21430.

71 B 34 2 GENESIS 8:19 NOAH, HIS FAMILY AND THE
           ANIMALS LEAVE THE ARK (SOMETIMES COMBINED
           WITH THE RAINBOW OF THE COVENANT)

DUTCH SCHOOL
    Colonia, P. Noah Goes Forth from the Ark.
    Copenhagen, Art Museum, Sp.534.

ITALIAN SCHOOL
    Bartolo di Fredi. Scenes from the Old Testament:
    Animals Leaving the Ark. S. Gimignano,
    Collegiata.
    Castiglione, G.B. Exodus of the animals
    from the ark (?) Nantes, Museum.
    Castiglione, G.B. Exodus of the animals
    from the ark. Genoa, Palazzo Bianco.
    Raphael (and assistants). Old Testament
    subjects: Exit of animals from the ark.
    Rome, Vatican, Loggie.

71 B 34 3 GENESIS 8:20-22 NOAH'S SACRIFICE: VARIOUS
           ANIMALS ARE OFFERED, POSSIBLY A LAMB,
           A DOVE AND A RAM (OFTEN COMBINED WITH
           THE RAINBOW OF THE COVENANT)

DUTCH SCHOOL
    Moeyaert, Claes Cornelisz. The Sacrifice
    of Noah. 1628. Schickman, H. - Gallery
    (New York).
    Mulier, Pieter (Il Cavaliere Tempesta). The
    Sacrifice of Noah. Cassel, Staatliche
    Kunstsammlungen, 414.

FLEMISH SCHOOL
  Rubens, Peter Paul. The Sacrifice of Noah.
  Oxford, University, Ashmolean Museum, A
  158.

FRENCH SCHOOL
  Bourdon, Sébastien. Sacrifice of Noah.
  Bourdon, Sébastien. Sacrifice of Noah. Moscow,
    Pushkin State Museum of Fine Arts, 724.
  Chagall, Marc. Illustrations from the Bible
    published by Vollard. No.22: The Sacrifice
    of Noah. Nice (Alpes-Maritimes), Musée
    National Message Biblique Marc Chagall.
  French school, Wall painting. Scenes from
    the Old Testament: sacrifice of Noah. 11th
    century. St. Savin (Vienne), Church, Nave.
  Murat, Jean. Noah's Sacrifice. 1837. Paris,
    Ecole des Beaux-Arts (Grand Prix de Rome).
  Poussin, Nicholas, Follower of. Sacrifice of
    Noah. National Trust (Tatton Park).
  Poussin, Nicolas, Follower of. The Sacrifice
    of Noah. A pair, with the Daughters of
    Jethro.Sotheby and Co.,London(Sale(DELPHINIUM),
    July 13, 1983, No. 57.).

GERMAN SCHOOL
  Koch, Joseph Anton. Sacrifice of Noah. 1803.
    Frankfort- on-the-Main, Staedel Institute.
  Koch, Joseph Anton. Noah's Sacrifice. 1814.
    Berlin, Staatliche Museen, NG 413.
  Koch, Joseph Anton. Landscape with the Sacrifice
    of Noah. 1837-38. Sotheby and Co., London
    (Sale, New York, Nov. 25, 1981, No. 12)

ITALIAN SCHOOL
  Bassano, Jacopo. Noah after the Deluge. Madrid,
    Prado,23.
  Castiglione, Giovanni Benedetto. The Sacrifice
    of Noah. Christie, Manson and Wood (Sale,
    London, March 11, 1983, No. 11).
  Castiglione, G.B. The Sacrifice of Noah.
    Genoa, Palazzo Bianco.
  Castiglione, G.B. Sacrifice on leaving the
    ark. Nantes, Museum.
  Cavallino, Bernardino. Sacrifice of Noah.
    Washington, National Gallery of Art, 840.
    Kress Collection.
  Cortona, Pietro da. Sacrifice of Noah. Wanas,
    Collection Gustaf Wachtmeister.
  Gargiulo, Domenico (called Micco Spadaro).
    Noah's Sacrifice. Sotheby and Co., London
    (Sale, April 7, 1982, No. 81).
  Italian school, 9th century. Sacrifice of
    Noah. Fara in Sabina, Abbey of Farfa, Campanile,
    ground floor of oratory of Salvatore.
  Italian school, 11th century. Noah's Offering
    of Thanks. Fresco. S. Angelo in Formis,
    Church, left aisle wall.
  Italian school, 18th century. The Sacrifice
    of Noah. Oxford, University, Ashmoleon
    Museum, A 29.
  Michelangelo. Noah's Thank-offering. Rome,
    Vatican, Sistine Chapel, ceiling decorations.
  Palma Vechhio. Sacrifice of Noah. Companion
    piece to Drunkeness of Noah. Detroit,Institute
    of Arts, 162.
  Puccio, Pietro di. Scenes from the Old Testament:
    Noah's Ark and the Deluge (The Sacrifice
    of Noah). Pisa, Camposanto.
  Raphael (and assistants). Old Testament subjects.
    Noah's sacrifice. Rome, Vatican, Loggie.
  Uccello, Paolo. Frescoes in the cloister.
    The sacrifice of Noah. Florence, S.M. Novella,
    Cloister.

71 B 34 31 GENESIS 9:1-7 GOD BLESSES NOAH AND GIVES
            HIM HIS COMMANDMENTS

ITALIAN SCHOOL
  Lauri, Filippo. Noah Leaving the Ark. Rome,
    Galleria Colonna.
  Mullier, Peter (Il Cavaliere Tempesta) After.
    The Sacrifice of Noah. Sotheby and Co.,
    London (Sale [CHICORY] Dec. 15, 1982, No.
    15).

Spadaro, Micco, Circle of. The Sacrifice
  of Noah. Sotheby and Co., London (Sale
  [CHICORY] Dec. 15, 1982, No. 71.)

71 B 34 31 1 GENESIS 9:9-17 GOD'S COVENANT WITH
              NOAH: NEVER AGAIN SHALL THERE BE A FLOOD;
              AS A SIGN OF THIS COVENANT GOD PUTS A
              RAINBOW IN THE SKY

BRITISH SCHOOL
  Maclise, Daniel. Noah's Sacrifice. 1847.
    Leeds (Yorkshire), City Art Gallery.

FRENCH SCHOOL
  Chagall, Marc. Illustrations from the Bible
    published by Vollard. No.23: The Rainbow,
    Sign of the Covenant Between God and the
    Earth. 1930. Nice (Alpes-Maritimes),
    Musée National.
  Chagall, Marc. Illustrations from the Bible
    published by Vollard. No.24: The Rainbow,
    Sign of the Covenant Between God and the
    Earth. Nice (Alpes-Maritimes), Musée
    National Message Biblique Marc Chagall.

ITALIAN SCHOOL
  Italian school, 17th century ? (Genoese).
    God's Covenant with Noah. Greenville,
    S.C., Bob Jones University Collection,
    1962 cat. 87.

71 B 35 GENESIS 9:18-27 NOAH AS A WINE-GROWER

FRENCH SCHOOL
  French school, Wall painting. Scenes from
    the Old Testament: Noah in his vineyard.
    11th century. St. Savin (Vienne), Church,
    Nave.

ITALIAN SCHOOL
  Gozzoli, Benozzo (and assistants). Old Testament
    and other subjects: Drunkenness of Noah.
    Pisa, Camposanto.

71 B 35 61 GENESIS 9:20 NOAH TESTS THE WINE

ITALIAN SCHOOL
  Gozzoli, Benozzo, and assistants. Old Testament
    and other subjects:Drunkenness of Noah.
    Detail: testing the wine. Pisa, Camposanto.

71 B 35 21 GENESIS 9:22 THE MOCKING OF NOAH: HAM
            FINDS HIS FATHER (PARTIALLY) NAKED SLEEPING
            OUT OF DOORS (OR IN HIS TENT OR IN THE
            VINEYARD COTTAGE); HAM CALLS HIS BROTHERS

ITALIAN SCHOOL
  Brandi, Giacinte. Drunkenness of Noah.
    Rome, Galleria d'Arte Antica.

71 B 35 21 1 GENESIS 9:22-23 SHEM AND JAPHETH COVER
              THEIR FATHER; HAM USUALLY STANDS NEARBY
              DERIDING HIM

FRENCH SCHOOL
  Chagall, Marc. Illustrations from the Bible
    published by Vollard. No. 25: The Garment
    of Noah. 1930. Nice (Alpes-Maritimes),
    Musée National Message Biblique Marc Chagall.
  French school, Wall painting. Scenes from the
    Old Testament: Drunkenness of Noah. 11th
    century. St. Savin (Vienne), Church,
    Nave.

ITALIAN SCHOOL
  Bartolo di Fredi. Scenes from the Old Testament:
    Drunkenness of Noah. S. Gimignano, Collegiata.
  Bellini, Giovanni. Drunkenness of Noah.
    Besançon (Doubs), Musée.
  Cavillino, Bernardo. Noah and his sons.
    Gosford Park, Scotland, Collection Earl
    of Wemyss.

Chimenti, Jacopo. Drunkenness of Noah. c.1594.
Florence, Palazzo Uffizi, 1531.
DeBellis, Antonio. Drunkenness of Noah. Milan,
Private Collection.
Giordano, Luca. Intoxication of Noah. Escorail,
Sale Capitolari.
Gozzoli, Benozzo. Old Testament and other subjects:
Drunkenness of Noah. Pisa, Camposanto.
Luini, Bernardo. The Mocking of Noah by Ham.
Fresco transferred from S. Barnaba, Milan.
Milan, Brera, 287.
Michelangelo. Drunkenness of Noah. Rome,
Vatican, Sistine Chapel, ceiling decoration.
Moretto da Brescia. The drunkenness of Noah.
Brescia, Collection Count Mazzotti.
Sacchi, Andrea. Drunkenness of Noah. Berlin,
Staatliche Museen, 422.
Uccello, Paolo. Frescoes in cloister. Story
of Noah. Florence, S. Maria Novella.

SPANISH SCHOOL
Montero de Rojas, Juan. The Drunkenness of
Noah. Tarbes (Haute-Pyrenées).
Spanish school, 13th century. Old Testament
cycle: Drunkenness of Noah. Fresco, c.1200.
Sigena, Monastery, Chapter House.

71 B 35 21 11 GENESIS 9:23 SHEM AND JAPHETH, WALKING
BACKWARDS, COVER THEIR FATHER

FRENCH SCHOOL
Chagall, Marc. Illustrations from the Bible
published by Vollard. No.25: The Garment
of Noah. 1930. Nice (Alpes-Maritimes),
Musée National Message Biblique Marc Chagall.

ITALIAN SCHOOL
Ferrari, Andreo. Drunkenness of Noah. Parma,
Galleria Nazionale.
Palma Vecchio. Drunkenness of Noah. Companion
piece to sacrifice of Noah. Detroit, Insti-
tute of Arts, 163.
Procaccini, Cammillo. The Drunkenness of Noah.
c. 1590. Newcastle Upon Tyne (Northumberland),
University, Hatton Art Gallery.

71 B 35 22 GENESIS 9:24-25 NOAH AWAKES FROM HIS
SLUMBER AND CURSES HAM AND CANAAN, SON OF
HAM

FRENCH SCHOOL
French school, Wall painting, St. Savin. Scenes
from the Old Testament: Noah curses Canaan.
Detail. 11th century. St. Savin, (Vienne),
Church, Nave.

ITALIAN SCHOOL
Gozzoli, Benozzo. Camposanto. Old Testament
and other subjects: Curse of Ham. Pisa.

71 B 4 GENESIS 11:1-9 STORY OF THE TOWER OF BABEL

FLEMISH SCHOOL
Metsys, Cornelis, Circle of. The Tower of
Babel. Sotheby and Co., London (Sale, (LILY)
June 15, 1983, No. 107).
Vranck, Sebastian. The Tower of Babel. Cassel,
Staatliche Kunstsammlungen, 45.

GERMAN SCHOOL
Kaulbach, Wilhelm von. The Tower of Babel.
c. 1843. Berlin, Staatliche Museen, NG
8/56.

71 B 42 GENESIS 11:4-9 THE TOWER OF BABEL

FLEMISH SCHOOL
Brill, Paul. Tower of Babel. Münich, Pinakothek, Alte. Inv. no. L 1038.

71 B 42 1 GENESIS 11:1-4 THE BUILDING OF THE
TOWER; NIMROD MAY BE PRESENT, SUPERVISING
OR ASSISTING THE CONSTRUCTION

DUTCH SCHOOL
Micker, Jan Christiaensz. The Building of
the Tower of Babel. Sotheby and Co.,
(Sale, New York, [SAFFRON], March 13,
1985, No. 28).

FLEMISH SCHOOL
Brueghel, Pieter, the elder. Tower of Babel.
Vienna, Kunsthistorisches Museum.
Brueghel, Pieter, the elder. Tower of Babel.
Rotterdam, Museum Boymans (Collection
van Beunningen).
Brueghel, Pieter, the elder. Tower of Babel.
Brighton, England, Corporation Art Gallery.
Cleve, Hendrick van, III. Tower of Babel.
Hamburg, Kunsthalle.
Cleve, Hendrik van, III. The Building of
the Tower of Babel. Sotheby and Co.,
London (Sale, New York [TOMMASO] Jan.
17, 1985, No. 165).
Cleve, Hendrick van, III. The Tower of Babel.
Stockholm, University, 124.
Cleve, Hendrick van, III. The Tower of Babel.
Sarasota, Fla., Ringling Museum of Art,
SN 848.
Flemish school, 15th century. The Tower
of Babel. 1480. The Hague, Royal Gallery,
784.
Franck, Frans, II. The Building of the Tower
of Babel. Sotheby and Co., London (Sale,
New York, 4996, Jan. 20, 1983, No. 13).
Valckenborch, Lucas van. Tower of Babel.
Paris, Louvre.
Valckenborch, Martin van. The Tower of Babel.
Dresden, Staatliche Kunstsammlungen, 833.

FRENCH SCHOOL
French school, Wall painting, St. Savin.
Scenes from the Old Testament: The Tower
of Babel. 11th century. St. Savin, (Vienne),
Church, Nave.

GERMAN SCHOOL
Brentel, Friedrich. Tower of Babel. 1627.
Collection Mrs. Anne Macdonald.

ITALIAN SCHOOL
Bassano, Leandro, School of. Building of
the Tower of Babel. London, National
Gallery, 60.
Ghisolfi, Giovanni, Attributed to. The Tower
of Babel. Christie, Manson and Woods
(Sale, London, [TERNI-2813] Dec. 15-16,
1983, No. 249.
Gozzoli, Benozzo. Old Testament and other
subjects: Tower of Babel. Pisa, Camposanto.
Italian school, 11th century. The Tower
of Babel. Fresco. S. Angelo in Formis,
Church, Left aisle wall.
Italian school, 17th century. The Tower
of Babel. Christie, Manson and Woods
(Sale, New York, March 25, 1983, No.135).
Schiavone, Andrea. Tower of Babel. Longleat,
Collection Marquis of Bath.

71 B 42 11 GENESIS 11:5-6 THE TOWER OF BABEL
VISITED BY GOD

FRENCH SCHOOL
French school, Wall painting, St. Savin.
Scenes from the Old Testament: The Tower
of Babel. 11th century. St. Savin, (Vienne),
Church.

71 B 42 21 GENESIS 11:6-9 THE CONFUSION OF LANGUAGES
AND SCATTERING OF THE PEOPLE OVER THE EARTH

DUTCH SCHOOL
Goubau, Anton, follower of. The Tower of
Babel. Christie, Manson and Woods (Sale,
London, April 13, 1984, TOMATO - 2874,
No. 149).

FRENCH SCHOOL
Flandrin, J.H. Tower of Babel, confusion
of tongues. 1861.

71 C 1 GENESIS 11:26-25:10 STORY OF ABRAHAM

FLEMISH SCHOOL
Franck, Franz II. Scenes from the lives of
Abraham and Lot. Probably furniture panels.
Weston Park, Collection Earl of Bradford.

ITALIAN SCHOOL
Meloni, Marco. Madonna and Child enthroned
with saints. Predella: Story of Abraham.
Modena, Pinacoteca Estense.

71 C 11 GENESIS 11-25 STORY OF ABRAHAM (PART 1)

ITALIAN SCHOOL
Poccetti, Bernardino. Story of Abraham. 1603.
Florence, Palazzo degli Acciaiuoli.

71 C 11 12 GENESIS 11:31 TERAH TAKES ABRAHAM,
SARAH AND LOT FROM UR TO THE CITY OF HARAN

ITALIAN SCHOOL
Bartolo di Fredi. Scenes from the Old Testament:
Abraham and Lot depart from the land of
Chaldea. S. Gimignano, Collegiata.
Bassano, Francesco, the younger. The Departure
of Abraham for the Promised Land. c. 1575.
Vienna, Kunsthistorisches Museum, 4301.
Bassano, Jacopo, Copy after. Departure of
Abraham. London, National Gallery, 2148.
Castiglione, G.B. Abraham's journey. Genoa,
Galleria Brignole.

71 C 11 2 ABRAHAM COMMUNICATING WITH GOD (IN GENERAL)

FRENCH SCHOOL
French school, Wall painting, St. Savin. Scenes
from the Old Testament: God appears to
Abraham. 11th century. St. Savin, (Vienne),
Church, Nave.

71 C 11 33 1 GENESIS 12:7 ABRAHAM COMES TO THE
SACRED TREE OF MOREH AT SHECHEM, AND BUILDS
HIS FIRST ALTAR

DUTCH SCHOOL
Moeyaert, Claes Cornelisz. Abraham is Called
by God. Stockholm, University, 292.

71 C 11 4 GENESIS 12:10-20 ABRAHAM IN EGYPT

ITALIAN SCHOOL
Gozzoli, Benozzo. Old Testament and other
subjects: Abraham and Lot in Egypt. Pisa,
Camposanto.

71 C 11 45 GENESIS 13:1 ABRAHAM LEAVES EGYPT WITH
SARAH, LOT AND HIS POSSESSIONS

ITALIAN SCHOOL
Bassano, Jacopo. The Departure of Abraham.
Hampton Court Palace.

71 C 11 5 GENESIS 13 ABRAHAM AND LOT SEPARATING

FRENCH SCHOOL
French school, Wall painting, St. Savin.
Scenes from the Old Testament: Separation
of Abraham and Lot? 11th century. St.
Savin, (Vienne), Church, Nave.

ITALIAN SCHOOL
Bartolo di Fredi. Scenes from the Old Testament:
Abraham separates from Lot in the land
of Canaan. S. Gimignano, Collegiata.
Italian school, 15th century. Series of
scenes from the Old Testament: Episodes
in the life of Abraham. Florence, S.M.
Novella, Cloister frescoes.

71 C 11 6 GENESIS 14:1-17 THE BATTLE OF THE
KINGS AND THE RESCUE OF LOT

ITALIAN SCHOOL
Gozzoli, Benozzo. Old Testament and other
subjects: Abraham victorious. Pisa, Camposanto.
Italian school, 15th century. Series of
scenes from the Old Testament: Episodes
in the life of Abraham. Florence, S.M.
Novella, Cloister frescoes.

71 C 11 65 GENESIS 14:14 ABRAHAM CALLS ALL THE
MEN IN HIS CAMP TOGETHER AND SETS OUT
IN PURSUIT OF THE FOUR KINGS

FRENCH SCHOOL
French school, Wall painting, St. Savin.
Scenes from the Old Testament: Abraham
goes to battle against Chedorlaomer.
11th century. St. Savin, (Vienne), Church,
Nave.

71 C 11 7 GENESIS 14:18-20 THE MEETING OF ABRAHAM
AND MELCHIZEDEK, THE HIGH PRIEST AND
KING OF SALEM, WHO BRINGS BREAD AND WINE

AUSTRIAN SCHOOL
Baumgartner, Johann Wolfgang. Abraham and
Melchizedek. Sotheby and Co., London
(Sale, (BLUEBELL) April 4, 1984, No. 22).

BRITISH SCHOOL
Heins, J.T. Melchizedek offering bread
and wine to Abraham. Felbrigg Hall,
Coll. W. Ketton-Cremer.

DUTCH SCHOOL
Eeckout, Gerbrand van den. Abraham and
Melchizedek. 1664. Budapest, Museum
of Fine Arts, 69.44.
Eeckhout, Gerbrand van den. Abraham and
Melchizedek. c. 1670. New York, New
York, Historical Society.
Wet, Jacob Willemsz, the elder. Abraham
and Melchizedek. Dublin, National Gallery,
1315.

FLEMISH SCHOOL
Herp, Willem van. The Meeting of Abraham
and Melchizedek. Christie, Manson and
Wood, London (Sale, Dec. 17, 1981, No.99).
Rubens, Peter Paul. Abraham and Melchizedek.
Sketch for the painting in Anvers, Church
of the Jesuits. c. 1620-21. Paris, Louvre,
Musée du, M.I. 963.
Rubens, Peter Paul. Abraham and Melchizedek
Sarasota, Fla., Ringling Museum of Art,
SN 212.
Vos, Martin de, the elder. Abraham and
Melchizedek. London, Collection E. Schapiro.
Savery, Jacob I. The meeting of Abraham
and Melchizedek. 1597. Collection M.
Fernand Stuyck.

Wael, Cornelis de. Abraham and Melchizedek.
Christie, Manson and Woods (Sale, New
York, Jan. 19, 1982, No. 23).

FRENCH SCHOOL
   French school, Wall painting, St. Savin. Scenes
      from the Old Testament: Abraham and Melchi-
      zedek. 11th century. St. Savin, (Vienne),
      Church, Nave.

GERMAN SCHOOL
   Stummel, Friedrich. High Altar, Inner Wing,
      Left: The Meeting between Abraham and Melchi-
      zedek. 1887. Keeken, St. Mariae Himmel-
      fahrt.

ITALIAN SCHOOL
   Castiglione, G.B. Melchizedek and Abraham.
      Paris, Louvre.
   Italian school, 15th century. Series of scenes
      from the Old Testament: Episodes in the
      life of Abraham. Florence, S.M. Novella,
      Cloister frescoes.
   Raphael (and assistants). Old Testament subjects:
      Melchizedek offers Abraham bread and wine.
      Rome, Vatican, Loggie.
   Solimena, Francesco. Abraham and Melchizedek.
      Collection Michael Jaffe.
   Spada, Lionello. Abraham and Melchizedek.
      Bologna, Pinacoteca Nazionale, 181.
   Vasari, Giorgio and Gherardi, Cristofano.
      Sacrifices and prophets: Melchisidech.
      Fresco. Cortona, Compagnia del Gesù.
   Vasari, Giorgio, Workshop of. The Meeting
      of Abraham and Melchizedek. Baltimore,
      Md., Walters Art Gallery, 37.1176.

SPANISH SCHOOL
   Arteaga y Alfaro, Matias. Melchizedek offering
      bread and wine and blessing Abraham. Seville,
      Museo Provincial.

71 C 11 71 GENESIS 14:19 MELCHIZEDEK BLESSES ABRAHAM

   DUTCH SCHOOL
      Eeckhout, Gerbrand van den. Abraham and Melchi-
         zedek. 1648. Mäntta, Gösta Serlachiuksen
         Taidesäätiön Museo, 381.
      Meemskerck, Maerten van. Abraham and Melchi-
         zedek. Amsterdam, Art Market.

   ITALIAN SCHOOL
      Maffei, Francesco. Sacrifice of Melchizedek.
         Foscari, Conte Lodovico - Collection (Venice).
      Tintoretto (Jacopo Robusti). Scuola di San
         Rocco. Upper Hall, Ceiling: Abraham and
         Melchizedek. Venice, Scuola di San Rocco.
      Vasari, Giorgio. Abraham and Melchizedek.
         Greenville, S.C., Bob Jones University
         Collection, 1962 cat. 46.

71 C 11 8 GENESIS 15 GOD'S COVENANT WITH ABRAHAM

   DUTCH SCHOOL
      Potter, Pieter Symonsz. The Angel Speaks
         out of the Sky to Abraham. Budapest, Museum
         of Fine Arts, 58.22.

   ITALIAN SCHOOL
      Raphael (and assistants). Old Testament subjects:
         God's covenant with Abraham. Rome, Vatican,
         Loggie.

71 C 11 9 GENESIS 16 ABRAHAM AND HAGAR

   DUTCH SCHOOL
      Poelenburg, Cornelis. Sarah Suggests to Abraham
         that He Take Hagar. Paris, Louvre, Musée
         du, INV 1693.

   ITALIAN SCHOOL
      Gozzoli, Benozzo. Old Testament and other
         subjects: Abraham and Hagar. Pisa, Camposanto.

71 C 11 91 1 GENESIS 16:1-3 SARAH BRINGS HAGAR
TO ABRAHAM, WHO IS USUALLY SHOWN LYING
IN BED

DUTCH SCHOOL
   Bray, Salomon de. Sarah presenting Hagar
      to Abraham. Schapiro, E. - Collection
      (London).
   Dyk, Philip van. Sarah Presenting Hagar
      to Abraham. Paris, Louvre, Musée du,
      INV. 1265.
   Netscher, Caspar. Sarah presenting Hagar
      to Abraham. New York, H. Shickman Gallery.
   Rembrandt, imitator of. Sarah Brings Hagar
      to Abraham. Sacramento, Crocker Art Gallery,
      1872.535.
   Werff, Adriaen van der. Copy. Sarah Presenting
      Hagar to Abraham. 1699. Paris, Louvre,
      Musée du, R.F. 3709.

FLEMISH SCHOOL
   Foubus, Frans, the younger. Abraham, Sarah,
      and Hagar. Dulwich Gallery, 455.
   Stomer, Matthias. Sara, Abraham and Hagar.
      Göteborg, Museum.
   Stomer, Matthias, Follower of. Sarah presenting
      Hagar to Abraham. Christie, Manson and
      Woods (Sale, London, (TINKER-3144) May
      24, 1985, No. 167).

GERMAN SCHOOL
   Dietrich, Christian Wilhelm Ernst. Sarah
      Guides Abraham to Hagar. Brunswick,
      Landesmuseum, 619.

ITALIAN SCHOOL
   Pietro da Cortona, attributed to. Abraham
      reconciling Hagar and Sarah. Chicago,
      Art Institute, 61.335.

71 C 11 93 1 GENESIS 16:6 HAGAR FLEES INTO THE
DESERT

FLEMISH SCHOOL
   Rubens, P.P. Dismissal of Hagar. London,
      Grosvenor House, Collection Duke of West-
      minster.
   Rubens, P.P. Hagar Leaving the House of
      Abraham. c. 1615-17. Leningrad, Hermitage.

71 C 11 93 2 GENESIS 16:7-13 AN ANGEL MEETS
HAGAR AT THE FOUNTAIN ON THE WAY TO SHUR
AND PERSUADES HER TO RETURN

DUTCH SCHOOL
   Bol, Ferdinand. Hagar and the Angel at
      the Fountain on the way to Shur. Danzig,
      Museum Pormorskie MNG/50/269/M.
   Lievens, Jan. Hagar and the Angel. Rouen
      (Seine-Inférieure), Musée, 32-6-19.
   Myn, Herman van der. Hagar in the Wilderness.
      Budapest, Museum of Fine Arts, 212 (410).
   Obermüller, Erasmus Anton (Il Pistolese).
      Hagar in the Wilderness. Cologne, Wallraf-
      Richartz Museum. Dep. 343.

FRENCH SCHOOL
   Claude Lorrain. Hagar and the angel in
      landscape. London, Dr. E.S. de Beer
      Collection.
   Claude Lorrain. Hagar and the angel in
      landscape. Dunsany Castle, Lady Dunsany
      Collection.
   Claude Lorrain. Hagar and the angel in
      landscape. London, National Gallery, 61.

ITALIAN SCHOOL
   Donducci, Giovanni Andrea, Circle of. Hagar
      and the Angel. Sotheby and Co., London
      (Sale, Dec. 12, 1984, (IVY) No. 270).
   Ferrari, Andrea (Gio Andrea). Hagar and
      the Angel. Genoa, Private Collection.
   Strozzi, Bernardo. Hagar and the Angel.
      Seattle, Art Museum.

GERMAN SCHOOL
Köenig, Johann. Hagar and the Angel in the
Wilderness. Frankfort-on-the-Main, Staedel
Institute, 2089.

71 C 11 94 GENESIS 16:10-14 HAGAR RETURNS TO ABRAHAM

BRITISH SCHOOL
Lauder, James Eckford. Hagar. 1850. Edinburgh,
Royal Scottish Academy.

ITALIAN SCHOOL
Cortona, Pietro da. Hagar's Home-coming.
1637-42. Vienna, Kunsthistorisches Museum,
153.

71 C 12 2 GENESIS 18 THE VISIT OF THE THREE ANGELS
(THREE MEN)

GERMAN SCHOOL
Platzer, Johann Georg. Abraham Receives God
and the Three Angels. Budapest, Museum
of Fine Arts, 7465.

ITALIAN SCHOOL
Italian school, 17th century (Neapolitan).
Abraham and the Three Angels. Brooklyn,
N.Y., Institute of Arts and Sciences, Museum,
06.22.
Piola, Domenico. Abraham and the Angels.
Sotheby and Co., London (Sale, June 3,
1981, No. 58).

71 C 12 22 GENESIS 18:2 ABRAHAM KNEELS BEFORE
THE ANGELS

DUTCH SCHOOL
Bie, Cornelis de. Abraham and the Three Angels.
1651. U.S.A., Private Collection.
Bol, Ferdinand. Abraham Entertaining the Three
Angels. c. 1660. Amsterdam, Rijksmuseum,
A 1577, on loan to the Hague, Dienst Vers-
preide Rijkskollekties.
Heerschop, Hendrik, Attributed to. Abraham
and the Three Angels. Christie, Manson
and Woods (Sale, London (THUMP - 3441),
April 12, 1985, No. 158).
Rembrandt, School of. Abraham Entertains the
Three Angels. c. 1655. Brocart - Collection
(Moscow).

FLEMISH SCHOOL
Gassel, Lucas. Abraham visited by the angels.
New York, Collection W.C.H.M. Georgi.

FRENCH SCHOOL
Lèbre, André. Abraham and the Three Angels.
Paris, Louvre, Musée du, INV. 20006.

GERMAN SCHOOL
Loth, Johann Carl. Abraham and the Angels.
Gateshead, Shipley Art Gallery.

ITALIAN SCHOOL
Alberti, Durante. Cappella della SS. Trinità.
Lunette. Abraham adoring the three angels
in pilgrims' garb. Rome, Il Gesù.
Amigoni, Jacopo. Three Angels Appearing to
Abraham. Oxford, University, Ashmolean
Museum, A1015a.
Antonello da Saliba. Abraham and three angels.
Washington, D.C., National Gallery, 315.
Buti, Lodovico. Abraham and the Angels.
Vienna, Kunsthistorisches Musuem, 1520.
Castello, Valerio. Abraham and the Three Angels.
Christie, Manson and Woods, London (Sale,
July 10, 1981, No. 112).
Donducci, Giovanni Andrea. Three Angels Appearing
to Abraham. Modena, Pinacoteca Estense.
Gargiulo, Domenico. Decorative frescoes: Abraham
and the Angels. 1638. Naples, San Martino
(Coro dei Conversi).

Guardi, Giovanni Antonio. The angels appearing
to Abraham. Cleveland, Museum of Art,
52.237, William H. Marlatt Collection.
Italian school, 11th century. Three Angels
visit Abraham. Fresco, Church, Left aisle
wall. S. Angelo in Formis.
Italian school, 12th century. Wall decorations.
Old Testament subjects. Abraham and the
Three Angels. Ferentillo, S. Pietro e
S. Paolo.
Italian school, 13th century. Scenes from
the Old Testament: Abraham and the three
angels. Assisi, S. Francesco, upper church.
Italian school, 15th century. Series of
scenes from the Old Testament: Three angels
visit Abraham. Florence, S.M. Novella,
Cloister frescoes.
Lorenzo Monaco, Attributed to. Abraham and
the Three Angels. Illuminated Letter
B, cut from a Choral Book. London, National
Gallery, 3089.
Raphael. Old Testament subjects: The three
angels appearing to Abraham. Rome, Vatican,
Loggie.
Tiepolo, G.B. Abraham and the three angels.
Tiepolo, G.B. Decorations, Galleria: Abraham
and the three angels.
Tommaso da Vigilia. Abraham and the three
angels. Palermo, Museo Nazionale.

SPANISH SCHOOL
Gasco, Perot. Retable, panel: Abraham and
the three angels. San Esteban de Bas,
Parish Church.
Murillo. Abraham and the Three Angels. c.1670-
74. Ottawa, National Gallery of Canada.
Murillo. Works of Charity, painted for
the Hospital de la Caridad, Seville. Abraham
and the three angels. Dunrobin Castle,
Collection Duke of Sutherland.
Navarrete, Juan Fernandez. Abraham and the
Three Angels. Dublin, National Gallery,
1721.

71 C 12 23 GENESIS 18:4 ABRAHAM FETCHES WATER
AND WASHES THEIR FEET

FRENCH SCHOOL
Giacomotti, Fèlix Henri. Abraham Washing
the Feet of the Three Angels. 1854. Paris,
École des Beaux-Arts (Grand Prix du Rome).
Lefebvre, Jules Joseph. Abraham Washing
the Feet of the Angels. 1854. Paris,
École des Beaux-Arts.
Lévy, Émile. Abraham Washing the Feet of
the Three Angels. 1854. Paris, École
des Beaux-Arts (Grand Prix de Rome).
Maillot, Theodore Pierre Nicolas. Abraham
Washing the Feet of the Three Angels.
1854. Paris, École des Beaux-Arts (Grand
Prix de Rome).

ITALIAN SCHOOL
Italian school, 12th century. Wall decorations.
Old Testament subjects. Abraham and the
three angels. Ferentillo, S. Pietro e
S. Paolo.

71 C 12 24 GENESIS 18:3-5 ABRAHAM ENTERTAINING
THE THREE ANGELS

EARLY MEDIEVAL AND BYZANTINE
Byzantine school, 14th century. Icon:
"Hospitality of Abraham". Athens, Benaki
Museum.
Early Medieval and Byzantine painting.
Hospitality of Abraham. 16th century,
from Crete. Athens, Byzantine Museum.

DUTCH SCHOOL
Eeckhout, Gerbrand van den. Abraham Entertains
the Angels. Amsterdam, Rembrandt's House, 8.
Eeckhout, Gerbrandt van den. Abraham Entertaining
the Angels. Leningrad, Hermitage.
Fabritius, Bernard. Abraham Entertains the
Three Angels. 1666. Meissner, Kurt- Collection
(Zürich).
Fabritius, Bernard. Abraham Entertains the
Three Angels. 1664. Arras (Pas-de-Calais),
Musée.
Rembrandt ? Abraham entertaining the angels.
Amsterdam, Rijksmuseum.

FRENCH SCHOOL
Chagall, Marc. Illustrations from the Bible
published by Vollard. No. 26: The Three
Angels Visit Abraham. 1930. Nice (Alpes-
Maritimes), Musée National Message Biblique
Marc Chagall.

GERMAN SCHOOL
Elsheimer, Adam. Abraham entertains three
men. Frankfort-on-the-Main, Staedel Institute
13954.

ITALIAN SCHOOL
Carracci, Ludovico. Abraham and the three
angels. Bologna, Pinacoteca Nazionale.
Italian school, 15th century. Series of scenes
from the Old Testament: Three angels visit
Abraham. Florence, S.M. Novella, Cloister
frescoes.

71 C 12 24 2 GENESIS 18:7-12 ABRAHAM ORDERS THE
PREPARATION OF A CALF AND OTHER FOOD AND
FEEDS THEM

DUTCH SCHOOL
Borssum, Anthonie van. Abraham Entertaining
the Three Angels. Cassel, Staatliche Kunst-
sammlungen, 260a.
Eeckhout, Gerbrand van den (?) Abraham and
the three angels. Cassel, Gallery, 260A.
Gelder, Aert de. Abraham and the angels.
Rotterdam, Museum Boymans, 1229.
Grebber. P.F. de. Abraham receiving the angels.
Haarlem, Frans Hals Museum, No. 119.
Lairesse, Gerard de. Abraham and the Three
Angels. Paris, Louvre, Musée du, R.F.1964.8.

GERMAN SCHOOL
Zick, Januarius. Abraham before the Three
Angels. Munich, Pinakothek, Neue, 9002.

ITALIAN SCHOOL
Ferrari, Andrea. Abraham visited by three
angels. St. Louis, City Art Museum.
Preti, Mattio. Abraham entertaining the angels.
Esztergom, Palace of the Primate of Hungary.

71 C 12 24 3 GENESIS 18:12 THE PROMISE OF A SON
IS RENEWED; SARAH, OVERHEARING IT, LAUGHS
INCREDULOUSLY

FLEMISH SCHOOL
Flemish school, 17th century. Abraham and
the three angels. Seville, Cathedral,
Capilla del Cristo de Maracaibo.
Lastman, Pieter P. Abraham Entertaining the
Angels. 1616. Private Collection.
Rubens, P.P. Apparition of the angels to
Abraham. Seville, Cathedral.

FRENCH SCHOOL
French school, 16th century. Angel Announcing
to Abraham the Birth of a Son. Paris, Coll.
Durrieu.

ITALIAN SCHOOL
Guardi, Giovanni Antonio. Abraham welcoming
the three angels. Cleveland, Museum of
Art, 52.238. William H. Marlatt Collection.
Tiepolo, G.B. Decorations, Galleria: Sarah
told of her maternity. Udine, Palazzo
Arcivescoville.

SPANISH SCHOOL
Sert, José María. Murals with scenes from
the Old and New Testaments. Panel: Abraham
entertaining the three angels. Vich,
Cathedral.

71 C 12 4 GENESIS 19:15-25 THE DESTRUCTION OF
SODOM AND GOMORRAH: LOT AND HIS FAMILY
FLEE TO ZOAR, CARRYING THEIR BELONGINGS;
AN ANGEL MAY BE SHOWING THE WAY

AMERICAN SCHOOL
West, Benjamin. Lot Fleeing from Sodom.
1810. Detroit, Institute of Arts, 70.831.

AUSTRIAN SCHOOL
Bocksberger, Hans, the Elder. 16th century.
Lot saved from Sodom. Neuburg an der
Donau, Schloss. Fresco decorations for
Schlosskapelle.

DUTCH SCHOOL
Duyfhuysen, Pieter Jacobsz. Lot and his
daughters led from Sodom by an angel.
Rotterdam, Museum Boymans, Inv. 1178.

FLEMISH SCHOOL
Heil, Daniel van. Lot and his Daughters
Leaving Sodom. Christie, Manson and
Woods (Sale, London, Oct. 22, 1982, No.
58.)
Oosten, Frans van. Lot Fleeing Sodom.
Christie, Manson and Woods (Sale, New
York, June 12, 1981, No. 194.)
Patinir, Joachim. Lot and his daughters.
Oxford, University, Ashmolean Museum.
Patinir, Joachim de. Burning of Sodom and
Gomorrah. Rotterdam, Museum Boymans,
Inv. 2312.
Patinir, Joachim, attributed to. Sodom
and Gomorrah. c. 1520. Harvard University,
Dumbarton Oaks, 36.69.
Rubens, P.P. Flight of Lot from Sodom. 1625.
Paris, Louvre.
Rubens, P.P. Flight of Lot and his family
from Sodom. 1615-16. Sarasota, Fla.,
Ringling Museum of Art, 218.
Stomer, Matthias. The flight from Sodom.
Greenville, S.C., Bob Jones University
Collection, 1962 cat. 169.
Teniers, David, the younger. Lot Fleeing
Sodom. 1658? Bader, Alfred - Collection
(Milwaukee).

FRENCH SCHOOL
Corot, Jean Baptiste Camille. The Destruction
of Sodom. Study for painting in the Metro-
politan Museum of Art, New York. 1843?
Sotheby and Co., London (Sale, New York,
Feb. 29, 1984, No. 14).
Corot. Burning of Sodom. New York, Metro-
politan Museum, Havemeyer Collection.
Courtin, J.F. Lot and his daughters. Paris,
École des Beaux Arts.
Watteau, J.A. Flight of Lot (after Rubens).
Paris, Collection Jules Strauss.

GERMAN SCHOOL
Dürer, Albrecht. Madonna and Child. Reverse:
Lot and his daughters. c.1505. Washington,
D.C., National Gallery of Art, 1099.

ITALIAN SCHOOL
Fetti, Domenico. Flight from Sodom. Sandon
Hall, Collection Earl of Harrowby.
Gozzoli, Benozzo. Old Testament and other
subjects: Destruction of Sodom. Pisa, Campo-
santo.
Italian school, 15th century. Series of scenes
from the Old Testament: Lot fleeing from
Sodom. Florence, S.M. Novella, Cloister
frescoes.
Raphael (and assistants). Old Testament subjects:
Lot and family flying from Sodom. Rome,
Vatican, Loggie.
Turchi, Alessandro. Angel Leading Lot and
His Daughters. Formerly attributed to
Follower of Guercino. Dublin, National
Gallery, 1653.
Vaccaro, Andrea. Lot and his family. Escorial,
Chapter-house.
Veronese, Paolo. Burning of Sodom. Paris,
Louvre, 1157.

71 C 12 42 GENESIS 19:24 SODOM AND GOMORRAH BURNING

FLEMISH SCHOOL
Mostaert, Gillis, attributed to. Burning of
Sodom. London, Collection E. Schapiro.

71 C 12 5 GENESIS 19:30-38 LOT AND HIS DAUGHTERS

DUTCH SCHOOL
Eeckhout, Gerbrand van den. Burning of Sodom
and Gomorrah. New York, Metropolitan Museum.
Lucas van Leyden. Lot and His Daughters. Paris,
Louvre, Musée du, R.F. 1185.
Thulden, Theodor van. Lot and His Daughters.
Cassel, Staatliche Kunstsammlungen, 134.

FLEMISH SCHOOL
Bles, Henri met de. Landscape with Lot and
his daughters. Stockholm, National Museum.
Metsys, Jan. Lot and His Daughters. 1563.
Vienna, Kunsthistorisches Museum, 1015.
Mostaert, Gillis, attributed to. Burning of
Sodom. London, Collection E. Schapiro.

FRENCH SCHOOL
Greuze, Jean Baptiste. Lot and His Daughters.
Strasbourg, Private Collection.
Massé, Jean Baptiste. Lot and His Daughters.
Christie, Manson and Woods (Sale, New York,
Jan. 15, 1985, CAROL-5808, 171).
Vien, Joseph Marie. Lot and His Daughters.
Caen (Calvados), Musée Municipal.

GERMAN SCHOOL
Krodel, Wolfgang, the elder. Lot and His
Daughters. Vienna, Kunsthistorisches Museum,
899.

ITALIAN SCHOOL
Carrà, Carlo. The Daughters of Lot. 1919.
Turin, Private Collection.
Gentileschi, Orazio. Lot and His Daughters.
c. 1622-23. Berlin, Staatliche Museen.
Gentileschi, Orazio. Lot and His Daughters.
Ottawa, National Gallery of Canada.
Italian school, 17th century. Lot and his
Daughters. Christie, Manson and Woods (Sale,
New York, June 12, 1981, No. 269).
Reni, Guido. Lot and his two daughters leaving
Sodom. c.1615. London, National Gallery,193.
Veronese, Paolo. Lot and His Daughters Flee
Sodom. Vienna, Kunsthistorisches Museum,
3672.

71 C 12 51 GENESIS 19:29-30 LOT, SEEING THE
DESTRUCTION OF THE CITIES AND FEARING
FOR HIS SAFETY IN ZOAR, FLEES WITH HIS
DAUGHTERS TO A CAVE IN THE MOUNTAINS

BRITISH SCHOOL
Hamilton, William. Lot with His Wife and
Daughters Cast Out of Sodom. Sotheby
and Co., London (Sale, New York, [5104]
Nov. 3, 1983, No. 69).

ITALIAN SCHOOL
Castiglione, Francesco. Lot Fleeing Sodom.
c. 1660. Christie, Manson and Woods (Sale,
Christie's East, New York [POLLY], March
13, 1980, No. 135.).
Manetti, Rutillo di Lorenzo. The Daughters
of Lot. Florence, Collection Sergardi.
Reni, Guido. Lot and his two daughters leaving
Sodom. c.1615. London National Gallery, 193.
Veronese, Paolo, School of. Lot's Family
Fleeing Sodom. Paris, Louvre, Musée du,136.

71 C 12 52 GENESIS 19:31-32 LOT'S DAUGHTERS
MAKE THEIR FATHER DRUNK

AUSTRIAN SCHOOL
Bocksberger, Hans, the Elder. 16th century.
Lot and his Daughters. Neuburg an der
Donau, Schloss, Fresco decorations for
Schlosskapelle.
Cranach, L. (the elder) ? Copy. Lot and
his two daughters. Venice, Academy, 186.

DUTCH SCHOOL
Aersten, Pieter. Lot and his Daughters.
Salm, Fürsten zu - Collection, 765.
Engelbrechtsz, Cornelis. Lot and His Daughters.
Sotheby and Co., London (Sale, New York,
[5104] Nov. 3, 1983, No. 174).
Gelder, Aert de. Lot and His Daughter.
Brussels, Musées Royaux des Beaux-Arts.
Gelder, Aert de. Lot and His Daughters.
Moscow, Pushkin State Museum of Fine Arts.
Lucas van Leyden. Lot and his daughters.
Paris, Louvre.
Lucas van Leyden. Lot and his daughters.
Rotterdam, Museum Boymans, 2456.
Lucas van Leyden, Style of. Lot's Daughters
Make Their Father Drink Wine. London,
National Gallery, 3459.
Paudiss, Cristoph. Lot and His Daughters.
Budapest, Museum of Fine Arts, 51.2883.
Rembrandt. Drunken Lot and his daughters.
Budapest, Georg-Rath Museum.
Werff, Adriaen van der. Lot and his daughters.
London, Buckingham Palace, 98.
Zijl, Jan van. Lot and his daughters. 1630.
Rotterdam, Museum Boymans, - Van Beuningen,
Inv. 2027.

FLEMISH SCHOOL
Backer, Jacob de, workshop of. Lot and his
Daughters. c. 1580. Bern, Art Museum,
511.
Benson, Ambrose. Lot and his Daughters.
Lima, Collection of the Papal Nuncio.
Cock, Jan de. Lot and his daughters. Detroit,
Institute of Arts, 37.
Cock, Jan de. Lot and his daughters. Siena,
Palazzo Chigi-Saracini.
Franck, Franz, I, Studio of. Flemish Reliquary
Chest painted with scenes from the Old
Testament. Detail: Drawer: Lot and his
Daughters. c. 1600. Sarasota, Fla.,
Ringling Museum of Art, SN 1950.
Franck, Frans II. Lot and his daughters.
Toledo, Spain, Museo Provincial.
Metsys, Jan. Lot and his daughters.
Metsys, Jan. Lot and his Daughters. Cognac
(Charente), Musée Municipal.
Metsys, Jan. Lot and his Daughters. 1563.
Vienna, Kunsthistorisches Museum.

FRENCH SCHOOL
 Courbet, Gustave. Loth et ses filles. New
 York, Parke-Bernet Galleries, 1961.
 French school,16th century. Lot and his daughters.
 New York, Collection Wildenstein.
 Troy, J.F. de. Lot and his daughters. Lenin-
 grad, Hermitage.
 Troy, J.F. de. Lot and his daughters. Orléans,
 Musée.
 Troy, J.F. de. Lot and his daughters. Puerto
 Rico, Luis Ferré Foundation, Musée di Ponce.
 Vien, Joseph Marie. Lot and His Daughters.
 Le Havre, Musée des Beaux-Arts.

GERMAN SCHOOL
 Aldegrever, Heinrich. Lot and His Daughters.
 1555. Budapest, Museum of Fine Arts. 1477(678).
 Cranach, L. (the elder) ? Lot and his two
 daughters. Munich, Old Pinakothek, 167
 (273).
 Cranach, Lucas, the Elder. Lot and his Daughters.
 1528. Vienna, Kunsthistorisches Museum
 Inv. Nr. 9589.
 German school, 17th century. Lot and His
 Daughters. Budapest, Museum of Fine Arts,621.

ITALIAN SCHOOL
 Cavallino, Bernardo. Lot and his Daughters.
 Private Collection.
 Graziani, Ercole. Lot and his Daughters.
 Bologna, Pinacoteca Nazionale, 6.
 Guercino. Lot and His Daughters. Paris, Louvre,
 Musée du, 75.
 Guercino, School of. Lot and His Daughters.
 Sotheby and Co., London (Sale No. 4778M,
 Jan. 21, 1982, No. 13).
 Italian school, 17th century (Roman). Lot
 and His Daughters. Boston, Museum of Fine
 Arts, Res. 37.242.
 Italian school, 17th century (Neapolitan).
 Lot and his Daughters. Brooklyn, N.Y.,
 Institute of Arts and Sciences, Museum,
 06.84.
 Italian school, 17th century. Lot and his
 Daughters. Budapest, Museum of Fine Arts,541.
 Italian school, 17th century. Lot and His
 Daughters. Christie, Manson and Woods (Sale,
 New York, June 12, 1981, No. 269).
 Italian school, 17th century. Lot and his
 Daughters. Sacramento, Crocker Art Gallery,
 1872.96.
 Italian school, 17th century (Bolognese). Lot
 and his Daughters. Sotheby and Co. (Sale,
 London, February 22, 1984, No. 129).
 Lippi, Lorenzo. Lot and His Daughters. Florence,
 San Marco, Museo di, N. 55.
 Mazzoni, Sebastiano. Lot and His Daughters.
 Rovigo,Pinacoteca dell'Accademia dei Concordi,
 398.497.
 Pagani, Gasparo. Lot and His Daughters.
 Florence, Palazzo Uffizi, 3829.
 Pignoni, Simone. Lot and his Daughters. Florence,
 Palazzo Uffizi, S. Marco e Cenacoli 161.
 Pitati, Bonifacio. Lot and his Daughters.
 c. 1545. Norfolk, Va., Chrysler Museum.
 Pittoni, G.B. Lot and his Daughters. Chrysler
 Museum, Norfolk, Va.
 Rosa, Salvatore. Lot and His Daughters. Castro,
 F. Di - Collection (Rome).
 Reni, Guido. Lot and his daughters. Bologna,
 Collection Giovanni Neri.
 Spinelli, Giovanni Battista. Lot and his
 Daughters. Pisani Collection, Naples.
 Turchi, Alessandro. Lot and his Daughters.
 Dresden, Staatliche Kunstsammlungen, 1972.

71 C 12 52 1 GENESIS 19:33-36 LOT'S DAUGHTERS
 LIE WITH HIM IN TURN

FRENCH SCHOOL
 Chagall, Marc. Illustrations from the Bible
 published by Vollard. No.28: The Daughters
 of Lot. 1931. Nice (Alpes-Maritimes),
 Musée National Message Biblique Marc Chagall.

GERMAN SCHOOL
 Altdorfer, Albrecht. Lot and his Daughters.
 1537. Vienna, Kunsthistorisches, 1774.

71 C 12 8 GENESIS 21:9-21 THE BANISHMENT OF HAGAR
 AND ISHMAEL

AUSTRIAN SCHOOL
 Bocksberger, Hans, the Elder. Abraham sending
 away Hagar and Ishmael. 16th century.
 Neuburg an der Donau, Schloss, Fresco
 decorations for Schlosskapelle.

DUTCH SCHOOL
 Bartius, Willem. The Expulsion of Hagar.
 Malibu, J. Paul Getty Museum, 71.PA.70.
 Bloemaert, Abraham. The Expulsion of Hagar
 and Ishmael. 1628. Malibu, J. Paul Getty
 Museum, 69.PA.16.
 Bloemaert, Abraham. The Expulsion of Hagar.
 1635. Christie, Manson and Wood (Sale,
 July 9, 1982, No. 65).
 Bol. Ferdinand. The Expulsion of Hagar.
 c. 1650-55. Leningrad, Hermitage.
 Breenbergh, Bartholomeus. The Dismissal
 of Hagar. Leningrad, Hermitage.
 Breenbergh, Bartholomeus. Landscape with
 Departure of Hagar. Wellesley College,
 Jewett Arts Center, P 68.1.
 Cornelisz, Lucas. The Expulsion of Hagar.
 Vienna, Kunsthistorisches Museum, 6820.
 Dyk, Philip van. Abraham Rejects Hagar and
 Ishmael. Paris, Louvre, Musée du, INV.1266.
 Eeckhout, Gerbrand van den. The Expulsion
 of Hagar. 1666. Raleigh, N.C., North
 Carolina Museum of Art.
 Engelbrecht, Cornelis. Abraham casting out
 Hagar. Vienna, Kunsthistorisches Museum.
 Fabritius, Bernard. The Banishment of Hagar.
 San Francisco, M.H. De Young Memorial
 Museum.
 Fabritius, Bernard. Copy. Hagar cast out.
 Copy of picture in Turin. Stockholm,
 Museum.
 Fabritius, Bernard. Hagar cast out. Turin,
 Pinacoteca.
 Flinck, Govert. The Expulsion of Hagar.
 c. 1640/42. Berlin, Staatliche Museen,815.
 Flinck, Govert. Hagar and Ishmael. Budapest,
 Gallery, 547.
 Lastman, Pieter P. The Dismissal of Hagar.
 1612. Hamburg, Kunsthalle.
 Maes, Nicolaes. The banishing of Hagar.
 Berlin, Staatliche Museen.
 Metsu, Gabriel. The Dismissal of Hagar.
 1653? Leyden, Stedelijk Museum.
 Molyn, Pieter de. The Expulsion of Hagar.
 Budapest, Museum of Fine Arts, 1065 (521).
 Pynas, Jan. Dismissal of Hagar. Dijon (Cote
 d'Or), Musée Magnin.
 Rembrandt. Departure of the Shunammite Woman.
 Dismissal of Hagar. 1640. London, Victoria
 and Albert Museum, CAI 78.
 Steen, Jan. The dismissal of Hagar. Dresden
 Gallery.
 Victors, Jan. Abraham Dismisses Hagar and
 Ishmael. Budapest, Museum of Fine Arts,
 230(355).
 Victors, Jan. The Dismissal of Hagar. Christie,
 Manson and Woods (Sale, New York, June
 12, 1981, No. 23).
 Wet, Jacob Willemsz, the elder. The Expulsion
 of Hagar. Blaffer, Sarah Campbell - Found-
 ation (Houston, Texas).

FLEMISH SCHOOL
    Immenraet, Philips Augustijin. The Expulsion
      of Hagar. Vienna, Kusthistorisches Museum,
      1198.
    Verhagen, P.J. Abraham casting out Hagar.
      Louvain, Abbaye de Parc.

FRENCH SCHOOL
    Claude Lorrain. The Expulsion of Hagar. Munich,
      Pinakothek, Alte.
    French school, 17th century. Casting out of
      Hagar and Ishmael. Bourges, Museum.
    Le Moyne, François. Abraham and Hagar. Formerly
      attributed to Jean François de Troy. Christie,
      Manson and Woods (Sale, London, April 15,
      1983, No. 92).

ITALIAN SCHOOL
    Ferri, Ciro. The Expulsion of Hagar. Dublin,
      National Gallery, 1670.
    Giordano, Luca. Abraham Repudiating Hagar.
      Christie, Manson and Woods (Sale, London,
      July 18, 1974, No. 88).
    Guercino. Repudiation of Hagar by Abraham.
      Milan, Brera.
    Guercino, Manner of. The Dismissal of Hagar.
      Christie, Manson and Woods (Sale, New York,
      June 12, 1981, No. 161).
    Italian school, 15th century. Series of scenes
      from the Old Testament: Hagar and Ishmael
      driven away by Abraham. Florence, S.M.
      Novella, Cloister frescoes.
    Italian school, 17th century. The Banishment
      of Hagar. Prato, Cassa di Risparmi.
    Italian school, 17th century (Lombard). The
      Expulsion of Hagar and Ishmael. Sotheby
      and Co., London (Sale, May 16, 1984, MAGNOLIA,
      No. 4).
    Mola, Pier Francesco. Hagar and Ishmael (Expul-
      sion). Rome, Palazzo dei Conservatori.
    Nuvolone, Carlo Francesco. The Expulsion of
      Hagar. Brunswick, Landesmuseum, 690.
    Pellegrini, Giovanni Antonio. The Dismissal
      of Hagar. Christie, Manson and Woods (Sale,
      New York, July 15, 1981, No. 68).
    Preti, Mattia. Abraham Drives out Hagar and
      Ishmael. Milan, Fraù Collection.
    Ruschi, Francesco. The Expulsion of Hagar.
      Greenville, S.C., Bob Jones University
      Collection.
    Ruschi, Francesco. The expulsion of Hagar.
      Study for painting of same subject at Bob
      Jones University Collection, Greenville,
      S.C.
    Ruschi, Francesco. Repudiation of Hagar. Treviso,
      Museo Civico.
    Tiepolo, G.B. Repudiation of Hagar. Milan,
      Private Collection.

71 C 12 82 GENESIS 21:14 ABRAHAM PROVIDES HAGAR
      AND ISHMAEL WITH BREAD AND A JUG OF WATER

DUTCH SCHOOL
    Fabritius, Bernard. The Expulsion of Hagar.
      c. 1666. Hull (Yorkshire), Ferens Art Gallery,
      503.
    Fabritius, Bernard. The Expulsion of Hagar.
      1658. New York, Metropolitan Museum, 1976.100.23.
    Maes, Nicolaes. Abraham Dismissing Hagar and
      Ishmael. 1653. New York, Metropolitan
      Museum of Art, 1971.73.
    Pluym, Karel van der. The Dismissal of Hagar.
      Queen's University (Kingston), Agnes Ethering-
      ton Art Centre.

ITALIAN SCHOOL
    Cavarozzi, Bartolomeo. The Expulsion of Hagar.
      Louisville, Ky., J.B. Speed Art Museum,
      70.43.
    Sacchi, Andrea. Abraham, Hagar, and Ishmael.
      Holkam Hall, Collection Earl of Leicester.

71 C 12 83 GENESIS 21:14 HAGAR AND ISHMAEL (OFTEN
      WITH BOW AND ARROW) DEPART

DUTCH SCHOOL
    Eeckhout, Gerbrand van den. The Expulsion
      of Hagar. 1642. Edzard - Collection
      (Munich).

FLEMISH SCHOOL
    Franck, Franz, I, Studio of. Flemish Reliquary
      Chest painted with scenes from the Old
      Testament. Detail: Drawer: The Expulsion
      of Hagar. c.1600. Sarasota, Fla., Ringling
      Museum of Art, SN 1950.

ITALIAN SCHOOL
    Giordano, Luca. The Expulsion of Hagar.
      c. 1660. Vienna, Kunsthistorisches Museum,
      1634.
    Ricci, Sebastiano. The Repudiation of Hagar.
      Turin, Pinacoteca, 595.

SPANISH SCHOOL
    Orrente, Pedro. The Repudiation of Hagar.
      Orihuela, Diocesan Museum.

71 C 12 84 GENESIS 21:16 HAGAR AND ISHMAEL IN
      THE WILDERNESS

BRITISH SCHOOL
    Eastlake, Sir C.L. Hagar and Ishmael. London,
      Diploma Gallery, 289.

DANISH SCHOOL
    Eckersberg, Christoffer Wilhelm. Hagar and
      Ishmael in Exile. Sotheby and Co., London,
      (Sale, [DORDOGNE] Feb. 27, 1985, No. 66).

FRENCH SCHOOL
    Gros, A.J. Hagar and Ishmaël. Montargis,
      Picture Gallery.
    Millet, J.F. Hagar and Ishmael. The Hague,
      Mesdag Museum.
    Hutin, Charles François. Hagar and Ishmael
      in the Wilderness. Budapest, Museum of
      Fine Arts, 672 (818).

SPANISH SCHOOL
    Lopez, Vicente. Hagar in the desert. Copy.
      after Corregio. Valencia, Cathedral.

71 C 12 84 1 GENESIS 21:16 HAGAR SITS WEEPING
      AFTER HAVING PUT ISHMAEL UNDER A BUSH
      TO DIE

DUTCH SCHOOL
    Steen, Jan. Hagar and Ishmael. New York,
      Collection Paul Drey.

FLEMISH SCHOOL
    Rubens, Peter Paul. Hagar in the Desert.
      c. 1630. Dulwich Gallery, 131.

FRENCH SCHOOL
    Colombel, Nicolas. Hagar and Ishmaël in
      the desert. Budapest, Museum.
    Colombel, Nicolas. Hagar and Ishmael in
      the Wilderness. Budapest, Museum of Fine
      Arts, 700 (822).
    Peyron, Jean François Pierre. Hagar and
      the Angel. Paris, Private Collection.

ITALIAN SCHOOL
    Conca, Sebastiano. The Angel appearing
      to Hagar and Ishmael in the wilderness.
      Sotheby and Co., London (Sale, [DAFFODIL],
      Feb. 20, 1980, No. 25).

71 C 12 84 11   GENESIS 21:17-19   AN ANGEL APPEARS AND REVEALS A WELL OF WATER TO HAGAR

AUSTRIAN SCHOOL
   Troger, Paul. Hagar and Ishmael in the Wilderness. Budapest, Museum of Fine Arts, 2149 (745 g).

DUTCH SCHOOL
   Dujardin, Karel. Hagar and Ishmael in the Wilderness. c.1665-67. Sarasota, Fla., Ringling Museum of Art, 270.
   Lastman, Pieter P. Hagar and the Angel. Los Angeles, County Museum.
   Lastman, Pieter. Hagar and the Angel. 1614. Sotheby and Co., London (Sale, New York, [NAPLES-5348] June 6, 1985, No. 76).
   Neer, Eglon Hendrik van der. Hagar and Ishmael with an Angel. Munich, Staatsgalerie Schleissheim, 2012.

FLEMISH SCHOOL
   Franck, Franz, I, Studio of. Flemish Reliquary Chest painted with scenes from the Old Testament. Detail: Center door: Hagar and Ishmael in the Wilderness. c.1600. Sarasota, Fla., Ringling Museum of Art, SN 1950.
   Rubens, Peter Paul. Hagar in the Desert. Dulwich Gallery, 131.

FRENCH SCHOOL
   Colombel, Nicolas. Hagar in the Desert. before 1682. Budapest, Museum of Fine Arts.
   Corot, J.B.C. Hagar in the Wilderness. 1835. New York, Metropolitan Museum, 38.64.
   Dorigny, Michel. Hagar and the Angel. Sotheby and Co., London (Sale, [ROSE] July 6, 1983, No. 62).
   Hutin, Charles François. Hagar and Ishmael in the Wilderness. Budapest, Museum of Fine Arts, 672 (818).
   Natoire, Charles Joseph. Hagar in the Desert Paris, Louvre, Musée du, INV. 6845.

GERMAN SCHOOL
   Obermüller, Erasmus Anton (Il Pistolese). Hagar in the Wilderness. Cologne, Wallraf Richartz Museum, 343.
   Schirmer, J.W. God's promise to Hagar. Berlin, Staatliche Museen, 313.

ITALIAN SCHOOL
   Asserto, Gioachino. The angel appearing to Hagar and Ishmael. London, Collection Denis Mahon.
   Asserto, Gioacchino. Hagar and the Angel. Genoa, Palazzo Rosso.
   Batoni, Pompeo. Hagar in the Desert. 1773. Rome, Galleria d'Arte Antica.
   Bellucci, Antonio. Hagar on the desert with her child. Florence, Coll. Spinelli.
   Bencovich, Federigo. Hagar and Ishmail. Pommersfelden, Dr. Karl Graf van Schönborn-Wiesentheid Collection.
   Caliari, Carletto. Hagar in the Wilderness. c. 1590. Sarasota, Fla., Ringling Museum of Art, SN 84.
   Cantarini, Simone. Hagar and Ishmael. Lt. Col. A.J.E. Cranstoun Collection (Corehouse).
   Carnevali, Giovanni. Hagar in the desert. Collection Farina.
   Castiglione, Giovanni Benedetto. Hagar in the Desert. Genoa, Palazzo Durazzo-Pallavicini.
   Castiglione, Giovanni Benedetto. Hagar and the Angel. Genoa, Palazzo Rosso.
   Cignani, Carlo. Hagar and Ishmael. Boston, Museum of Fine Arts, Ath. 20.
   Cortona, Pietro da. Hagar, Ishmael and the angel in the wilderness. Sarasota, Fla., Ringling Museum of Art.
   Cozza, Francesco. Landscape with the Angel Leading Hagar to the Well. 1664. Copenhagen, Art Museum, 458.

Cozza, Francesco. Landscape with the Angel Leading Hagar to the Well. 1664. Copenhagen Art Museum, 458.
Creti, Donato. Hagar and the Angel. Bologna, Private Collection.
Dolci, Carlo. Hagar and the Angel. Christie, Manson and Woods (Sale, New York, [BETH-5258], Jan. 18, 1983, No. 69).
Domenichino. Hagar in the desert. Frascati, Villa Muti.
Fiasella, Domenico. Hagar and the Angel. Rome, Galleria d'Arte Antica.
Gargiulo, Domenico (called Micco Spadaro). Landscape with Hagar and the Angel. Private Collection.
Giaquinto, Corrado. Hagar and Ishmael. Montefortino, Pinacoteca Civica.
Gimignani, Lodovico. Hagar and Ishmael in the Desert. Sotheby and Co., London (Sale, [MARJOREM] Oct. 20, 1983, No. 76).
Giordano, Luca. Hagar. London, Apsley House, Collection Duke of Wellington.
Girolamo da Treviso, the younger. Hagar and the Angel. c.1515. Rouen (Seine-Inferieure), Musée.
Guercino. The angel appearing to Hagar and Ishmael. London, Collection Denis Mahon.
Italian school, 17th century. Hagar in the Wilderness. Stockholm, University, 266.
Lanfranco, Giovanni. Hagar in the Desert. Paris, Louvre, Musée du.
Liberi, Pietro. Hagar and the Angel. Christie, Manson and Woods (Sale, London [TIVOLI-2704] July 8, 1983, No.33).
Mola, Pier Francesco. Hagar and Ishmael. Dulwich Gallery, 32.
Mola, Pier Francesco. Hagar and Ishmael with the Angel in the Wilderness. Rome, Galleria Colonna.
Mola, Pier Francesco, Follower of. Hagar and Ishmael in the Wilderness. London, Victoria and Albert Museum, Dyce Bequest, D.6.
Novelli, Pietro (Il Monrealese). Hagar and Ishmael.
Paganini, Paolo. Dismissal of Hagar. Venice, Palazzo Salvioni.
Pellegrini, Giovanni Antonio. Hagar's Vision. Christie, Manson and Woods (Sale, New York, June 12, 1981, No. 254).
Preti, Mattia. Hagar and Ishmael. Munich, Staatsgalerie Schlessheim, 469.
Rosa, Salvatore. Wooded Landscape with the Angel Appearing to Hagar and Ishmael. Leger Galleries, London.
Rosa, Salvatore. An angel appears to Hagar and Ishmael in the Desert. London, National Gallery, 2107.
Rosa, Salvatore. Landscape with Hagar and the Angel. Toledo, Museum of Art, 61.29.
Sacchi, Andrea. Hagar in the desert. Rome, Palazzo Barberini.
Tiepolo, G.B. Hagar and Ishmael. Venice, Scuola di S. Rocco.
Tiepolo, G.B. Hagar and Ishmael.
Tiepolo, G.B. Apparition of the angel to Hagar and Ishmael in the desert. Kansas City, William Rockhill Nelson Gallery of Art.
Tiepolo, G.B. Decorations, Galleria: Hagar in the desert. Udine, Palazzo Arcivescovile.
Veronese, Paolo. Hagar and Ishmael in the Desert. Vienna, Kunsthistorisches Museum.
Vignali, Jacopo. Hagar and the Angel. 1632. Christie, Manson and Woods (Sale, June 28, 1974, No. 88).

SPANISH SCHOOL
   Collantes, Francisco. Hagar and Ishmael. Providence, Rhode Island School of Design.

71 C 13   STORY OF ABRAHAM (PART III)

   DUTCH SCHOOL
      Amstel, Jan van. The Sacrifice of Abraham.
         Paris, Louvre, Musée du, INV 1980.
      Heerschop, Hendrick. Abraham taking Isaac
         to the Sacrifice, Sarah pleading. 1669.
         Christie, Manson and Woods (Sale, London,
         October 14, 1983, No. 8).

   FLEMISH SCHOOL
      Rubens, P.P. The Sacrifice of Isaac by Abraham.
         c. 1620-21. Paris, Louvre, Musée du, M.I.962.

71 C 13 1   GENESIS 22   THE SACRIFICE OF ISAAC

   EARLY MEDIEVAL AND BYZANTINE
      Byzantine school, Wall painting, Arilje (Yugo-
         slavia). St. Achilles, Narthex, East wall,
         Middle band: Sacrifice of Isaac. Fresco.
         13th century. Arilje, Yugoslavia.
      Byzantine school, Wall painting, Ohrid (Yugo-.
         slavia). Wall decoration. Sacrifice of
         Abraham. Detail: Abraham and Donkey. Fresco.
         11th century. Ohvid, St. Sophia.
      Byzantine school, Wall painting, Ohrid (Yugo-
         slavia). S. Sophia. Choir. Sacrifice of
         Abraham. Detail. 11th century.
      Byzantine school, Wall painting, Ohrid (Yugo-
         slavia). S. Sophia. Bema, South wall. Sacri-
         fice of Abraham. Fresco. 11th century.
         Ohrid, Yugoslavia.
      Byzantine school, Wall painting, Ohrid (Yugo-
         slavia). S. Sophia. Bema, south wall. Sacri-
         fice of Abraham: Abraham preparing for the
         journey. Fresco. 11th century. Ohrid, Yugo-
         slavia.
      Coptic painting, Khargeh, Bagawat Necropolis.
         Tomb chapel: Room of Peace. Detail: "Peace";
         Abraham and Isaac.Khargeh,Bagawat Necropolis.
      Coptic painting, Khargeh, Bagawat Necropolis.
         Tomb chapel: Room of Peace. Detail: Abraham
         and Isaac; Adam. Khargeh, Bagawat Necropolis.
      Coptic painting, Khargeh, Bagawat Necropolis.
         Chapel of Flight. Detail: Abraham and Isaac.
         Khargeh, Bagawat Necropolis.
      Early Christian painting, Rome. Catacomb of
         the Jordani. Corridor. Detail: Sacrifice
         of Abraham. Rome.
      Early Christian painting, Rome. Catacombs
         of St. Calixtus. Wall decoration. Sacrifice
         of Abraham. Rome, Via Appia.

   DUTCH SCHOOL
      Claesz, Allaert. Abraham's sacrifice of Isaac.
         Paris, Louvre.
      Gherwen, Roynier van. Sacrifice of Isaac.
         Munich, Pinakothek, Alte, 354.
      Lievans, Jan. The Sacrifice of Abraham. Bruns-
         wick, Landesmuseum, 242.
      Rembrandt, School of. Abraham sacrificing
         Isaac. Dallas, Museum of Fine Arts.
      Victors, Jan. The Sacrifice of Isaac. Christie,
         Manson and Woods (Sale, New York, June 12,
         1981, No. 22).

   FLEMISH SCHOOL
      Brueghel, Pieter, the younger. The Sacrifice
         of Isaac. Montreal, Museum of Fine Art.
      Mehus, Livio. Sacrifice of Isaac. c.1670.
         Florence, Palazzo Uffizi, 527.
      Vos, Martin de, the elder. The Sacrifice of
         Isaac. Brunswick, Landesmuseum, 731.

   FRENCH SCHOOL
      Poussin, Gaspard. Landscape: Abraham and Isaac
         Approach the Place of the Sacrifice. London,
         National Gallery, 31.

   GERMAN SCHOOL
      Zick, Januarius. Abraham and Isaac. Cologne,
         Wallraf-Richartz Museum, 3811.

   ITALIAN SCHOOL
      Allori, Alessandro. Sacrifice of Abraham.
         Florence, Palazzo Uffizi.
      Andrea del Sarto. The Sacrifice of Isaac.
         1520s. Cleveland, Museum of Art, 37.577.
      Gozzoli, Benezzo. Camposanto. Old Testament.
         and other subjects: Sacrifice of Isaac.
      Italian school, 15th century. Cloister frescoes.
         Series of scenes from the Old Testament:
         Sacrifice of Isaac. Florence, S.M. Novella.
      Lys, Giovanni. The Sacrifice of Isaac. 1615-
         26. Florence, Palazzo Uffizi, 1376.

   SPANISH SCHOOL
      Pedret Master. Frescoes of Main Apse: sacri-
         fice of Abraham. Church of Pedret.

71 C 13 11   GENESIS 22:3-4   ABRAHAM WITH ISAAC,
   AN ASS AND THE SERVANTS ON THEIR WAY TO
   MORIAH

   EARLY MEDIEVAL AND BYZANTINE
      Byzantine school, Wall painting, Arilje (Yugo-
         slavia). St. Achilles, Narthex, East
         wall, Middle band: Sacrifice of Isaac.
         Fresco. 13th century. Arilje, Yugoslavia.

   DANISH SCHOOL
      Engelsted, Malthe. Abraham on his Way to
         Mount Moriah. 1892. Stockholm, National
         Museum, 1454.

   DUTCH SCHOOL
      Poelenburg, Cornelis van. The Departure
         of Abraham and Isaac. Christie, Manson
         and Woods (Sale, London [TINKER-3144]
         May 24, 1985, No. 140).
      Pynas, Jan. Abraham and Isaac Leaving for
         Mount Moriah. Schapiro, E. - Collection
         (London).

   ITALIAN SCHOOL
      Allori, Alessandro. Sacrifice of Abraham.
         Florence, Palazzo Uffizi.
      Domenichino. Sacrifice of Isaac. Holkham
         Hall,Collection Earl of Leicester. Courtauld
         Institute of Art, B60/640.
      Italian school, 11th century. Church, Left
         aisle wall. Abraham on the way to the
         sacrifice. Fresco. S. Angelo in Formis.

71 C 13 11 1   GENESIS 22:5   THE SERVANTS ARE LEFT
   BEHIND WHILE ABRAHAM AND ISAAC (USUALLY
   CARRYING WOOD) CLIMB THE MOUNTAIN

   EARLY MEDIEVAL AND BYZANTINE
      Early Christian painting, Rome. Catacomb
         of Priscilla. Cappella della Velatio.
         Sacrifice of Abraham. Rome, Via Salaria
         Nuova.

   FRENCH SCHOOL
      Chagall, Marc. Illustrations from the Bible
         published by Vollard. No. 30: Abraham
         and Isaac on Their Way to the Place of
         Sacrifice. 1931. Nice (Alpes-Maritimes),
         Musée National Message Biblique Marc Chagall.
      Puvis de Chavannes, Pierre. Abraham and
         Isaac. c. 1890. Sotheby and Co., London
         (Sale [LOHENGREN] June 15, 1982, No.115).

   ITALIAN SCHOOL
      Domenichino. The Sacrifice of Isaac. 1602.
         Fort Worth (Texas), Kimbell Art Museum.
      Domenichino. The sacrifice of Abraham. Bowood,
         Collection Marquis of Landsowne (1897
         cat. no. 164).

   SPANISH SCHOOL
      Mayno, Juan Bautista. The Sacrifice of Isaac.
         Christie, Manson and Woods (Sale, London,
         [TOLEDO-2659] May 27, 1983, No. 231).
      Murillo. Abraham and Isaac on the way to
         the Sacrifice. Aynho Park, Collection
         Cartwright.

Orrente, Pedro. Abraham and Isaac on the Way
to the Sacrifice. Madrid, Consejo de Estado.

71 C 13 12   GENESIS 22:6-9   PREPARATIONS FOR THE SACRIFICE, E.G., ABRAHAM BINDING ISAAC

BRITISH SCHOOL
Runciman, John. Abraham and Isaac. Scotland,
Private Collection.

DUTCH SCHOOL
Victors, Jan. Abraham and Isaac. Private
Collection.

GERMAN SCHOOL
Dietrich, Christian Wilhelm Ernst. The Sacrifice
of Abraham. Budapest, Museum of Fine Arts,
58.16.
Dietrich, Christian Wilhelm Ernst. The Sacrifice
of Abraham. Karlesruhe, Kunsthalle, 1737.

ITALIAN SCHOOL
Romanino, Girolamo. Cantoria: Sacrifice of
Isaac. Asola, Duomo.
Tintoretto (Jacopo Robusti). Scuola di San
Rocco.

71 C 13 13   GENESIS 22:10   ABRAHAM PICKS UP THE KNIFE TO KILL ISAAC

DUTCH SCHOOL
Gelder, Aert de. Abraham's Sacrifice of Isaac.
1696. Location unknown.
Monogramist CHK. The Sacrifice of Isaac.
Sotheby and Co., London (Sale, Monaco,
[OUDRY], Dec. 8, 1984, No. 312).
Rembrandt, School of. Abraham sacrificing
Isaac. Stockholm, National Museum, 1069.

71 C 13 13 1   GENESIS 22:11-12   WHEN ABRAHAM HAS HIS HAND RAISED TO KILL ISAAC, GOD OR THE HAND OF GOD RESTRAINS ABRAHAM'S HAND

ITALIAN SCHOOL
Allori, Alessandro. Sacrifice of Abraham. Flor-
ence, Palazzo Uffizi.
Cantarini, Simone. Sacrifice of Isaac. Venice,
Querini-Stampalia.
Italian school, 13th century. S. Francesco,
upper church. Scenes from the Old Testament.
North wall, 2nd bay, bottom. Assisi, S.Fran-
cesco.
Italian school, 13th century. S. Francesco,
upper church. Scenes from the Old Testament:
Sacrifice of Isaac. Assisi, S. Francesco.
Mantegna, Andrea. Sacrifice of Isaac. 1490.
Vienna, Kunsthistorisches Museum, Inv. 1842.

71 C 13 13 11   GENESIS 22:11-12   WHEN ABRAHAM HAS HIS HAND RAISED TO KILL ISAAC, AN ANGEL RESTRAINS ABRAHAM'S HAND

AMERICAN SCHOOL
American school, 18th century. Wall painting.
Abraham and Isaac. Portsmouth, N.H., Warner
House.

AUSTRIAN SCHOOL
Bocksberger, Hans, the Elder. Fresco decor-
ations for Schlosskapelle. 16th century.
Neuburg an der Donau, Schloss.

EARLY MEDIEVAL AND BYZANTINE
Byzantine school, Wall painting, Daphni. Sacri-
fice of Abraham. Fresco. Daphni, Convent
Church.
Byzantine school, Wall painting, Arilje (Yugo-
slavia). St. Achilles, Narthex, East wall,
Middle band: Sacrifice of Isaac. Fresco.
13th century. Arilje, Yugoslavia.
Byzantine school, Wall painting, Ohrid (Yugo-
slavia). S. Sophia. Bema, South wall. Sacri-
fice of Abraham: Sacrifice prevented. Detail.
Fresco. 11th century. Ohrid, Yugoslavia.

DUTCH SCHOOL
Bray, Salomon de. Abraham's Sacrifice. 1639.
Schapiro, E. - Collection (London).
Flinck, Govert. Abraham's Sacrifice. Late
1630's. Bader, Alfred - Collection (Mil-
waukee).
Gherwen, Reynier van. Sacrifice of Isaac.
Munich, Pinakothek, Alte, 853.
Lastman, P.P. Abraham's sacrifice. Amsterdam,
Rijksmuseum, 1425.
Lastman, Pieter. The Sacrifice of Abraham.
1616. Paris, Louvre, Musee du, R.F. 920.
Maes, Nicolas. The Sacrifice of Isaac.
Bader, Alfred - Collection (Milwaukee).
Master of Alkmaar. Abraham and Isaac.
Cologne, Wallraf-Richartz Museum, Dep.432.
Rembrandt. Abraham's sacrifice. Leningrad,
Hermitage, 727.
Rembrandt. Abraham's sacrifice. Munich,
Alte Pinakothek, 438.

FLEMISH SCHOOL
Flemish school, 17th century. Abraham's
Sacrifice of Isaac. c.1700. Budapest,
Museum of Fine Arts, 59.4.
Franck, Franz, Studio of. Flemish Reliquary
Chest painted with scenes from the Old
Testament. Detail: Drawer: Abraham and
Isaac. c.1600. Sarasota, Fla., Ringling
Museum of Art, SN 1950.
Franck, Frans II. Sacrifice of Isaac.
Amsler and Ruthardt, 7503.
Keuning, Kerstiaen de. Landscape with Abraham.
Basle, Museum, 1262.
Mehus, Livio. Sacrifice of Isaac. c.1670.
Florence, Palazzo Uffizi, 527.
Rubens, P.P. Sacrifice of Abraham. Sketch.
Paris, Louvre, Musée du.
Teniers, David the younger and Uden, Lucas
van. Abraham sacrificing Isaac. Sotheby
and Co. (Sale, February 16, 1983, No.
37).

FRENCH SCHOOL
Chagall, Marc. Illustrations from the Bible
published by Vollard. No. 31: Abraham
about to Sacrifice His Son. 1931. Nice
(Alpes-Maritimes), Musée National Message
Biblique Marc Chagall.
Valentin de Boullogne. Abraham sacrificing
Isaac. Montreal, Museum of Fine Arts,
446.

GERMAN SCHOOL
Bertram (van Byrde) Master. Grabow altar.
Scenes from the Old and New Testament:
Sacrifice of Isaac. Hamburg, Kunsthalle.
Bruyn, Barthel, the Elder, School of. The
Sacrifice of Isaac. Christie, Manson
and Wood (Sale, London, July 20, 1984,
No. 38).
Christ, Josef, Circle of. The Sacrifice
of Isaac. Sotheby and Co., London (Sale,
Dec. 12, 1984, No. 130, [IVY]).
Cranach, L. (the elder) ? Sacrifice of Abraham.
Vienna, Liechtenstein Gallery.
German school, Wall painting, Wismar. Fresco
decoration. Sacrifice of Isaac. 15th century
(and later). Wismar, Georgen-Kirche.
Veltmann, Hermann. The Sacrifice of Abraham.
1721. Salm, Fürsten zu - Collection,
810.
Zick, Januarius. Abraham and Isaac. Harvard
University, Fogg Art Museum, Winthrop
Bequest, 1943.1815.
Zick, Januarius. The Sacrifice of Isaac.
Christie, Manson and Woods (Sale, London,
[TREVI-2719] July 22, 1983, No. 212).
Zick, Januarius. Abraham's Sacrifice. Munich,
Pinakothek, Neue, 10424.
Zick, Januarius. Sacrifice of Isaac. Munich,
Pinakothek, Neue, 9001.
Zick, Januarius. Sacrifice of Isaac. Munich,
Pinakothek, Neue, 4937.

ITALIAN SCHOOL

Allori, Alessandro. Sacrifice of Abraham. Milan, Collection Alberto Saibene.

Allori, Alessandro. Sacrifice of Isaac. Florence, S. Jacopo sopr'Arno.

Allori, Cristofano.Sacrifice of Abraham.Florence, Pitti Gallery.

Andrea del Sarto. Sacrifice of Abraham. Dresden, Gallery.

Andrea del Sarto. Sacrifice of Abraham. Madrid, Prado.

Andrea del Sarto. Sacrifice of Abraham (unfinished). Cleveland, Museum of Art, Holden Collection.

Bassano, Francesco, the younger. Abraham Sacrificing Isaac (Summer). Vienna, Kunsthistorisches Museum, 4302.

Bencovich, Federigo. Sacrifice of Isaac. Zagabria, Galleria Strossmayer.

Bernardus, D. The Sacrifice of Isaac. Geneva, Musée d'Art et d'Histoire, 1855-20.

Borzone, Luciano. The Sacrifice of Isaac. Christie, Manson and Woods (Sale, London, April 15, 1983, No. 3).

Caravaggio. Sacrifice of Abraham. Florence, Palazzo Uffizi.

Carracci, Annibale. Sacrifice of Abraham. Paris, Louvre.

Carracci, Ludovico. Sacrifice of Isaac. after 1585. Rome, Vatican.

Castiglione, G.B. Sacrifice of Abraham. Rome, Palazzo Doria.

Chimienti, Jacopo. Sacrifice of Isaac. c.1594. Florence, Palazzo Uffizi, 1463.

Chimienti, Jacopo. The sacrifice of Isaac. Florence, S. Marco.

Chimienti, Jacopo. The Sacrifice of Isaac. Kansas, University of (Lawrence), Museum of Art, 59.36.

Cigoli, Il. The Sacrifice of Abraham. Florence, Pitti.

Coccapani, Sigismondo. The Sacrifice of Abraham. Sotheby and Co., London (Sale Nov. 17, 1982, No. 42).

Damini, Vincenzo. The Sacrifice of Isaac. Cassel, Staatliche Kunstsammlungen, 873a.

Domenichino. Sacrifice of Abraham. Madrid, Prado.

Ficherelli, Felice. The Sacrifice of Isaac. Dublin, National Gallery, 1070.

Fungai, Bernardino. Sacrifice of Isaac. 1485. Siena, Archivo di Stato.

Gaulli, G.B. Abraham sacrificing Isaac. Atlanta, Ga., Museum of the Atlanta Art Association.

Gentileschi, Orazio. The Sacrifice of Isaac. c. 1621. Genoa, Palazzo Cattaneo Adorno.

Guardi, Giovanni Antonio. The sacrifice of Abraham. Cleveland, Museum of Art, 52.235. William H. Marlatt Collection.

Guardi, Giovanni Antonio. The Sacrifice of Abraham. Paris, Finney Collection.

Italian school, 11th century. Church, Left aisle wall. Sacrifice of Isaac. Fresco. S. Angelo in Formis.

Italian school, 17th century. Abraham Offering Isaac. Sacramento, Crocker Art Gallery, 1872.437.

Lelio Orsi. Sacrifice of Abraham. Naples, Museum, Capodimonte, 81.

Ligozzi, Jacopo. The sacrifice of Abraham. Florence, Palazzo Uffizi.

Lys, Giovanni. The sacrifice of Isaac. Florence, Uffizi.

Lys, Giovanni. Sacrifice of Isaac. Venice, Academy, Inv. 879, Cat. 914.

Lys, Giovanni. Offering of Abraham. Hague, Museum Bredius, 180-1946.

Miradori, Luigi. Abraham's Sacrifice. Davenport, Iowa, Municipal Art Gallery.

Pagani, Paolo. Abraham's Sacrifice. Leningrad, Hermitage.

Pagani, Paolo. Sacrifice of Isaac. Venice, Palazzo Salvioni.

Palma, Giovane. Ceiling, detail: sacrifice of Isaac. Venice,Palazzo Loredan (Municipio).

Peruzzi, Baldassare. Cappella della Ponzetto. Arch. Old and New Testament subjects: the sacrifice of Abraham, upper left. Rome, S. Maria della Pace.

Piazzetta, G.B. Sacrifice of Isaac. London, National Gallery, 3163.

Piazzetta, G.B. Sacrifice of Abraham. New York, Koetser Collection.

Piazzetta, Giambattista. The Sacrifice of Isaac. Bergamo, Private Collection.

Piazzetta, Giovanni Battista. The Offering of Isaac. Dresden, Staatliche Kunstsammlungen, 569.

Pittoni, Giovanni Battista. The Sacrifice of Isaac. Louisville, Ky., J.B. Speed Art Museum, 65.19.

Preti, Mattia. The Sacrifice of Isaac. Sotheby and Co., London (Sale, April 19, 1972, no. 112).

Preti, Mattia. The sacrifice of Isaac. Bologna, Pinacoteca Nazionale, 674.

Schiavone, Giorgio, attributed to. Judith, Abraham and David. Ascott, Buchs, National Trust.

Sodoma. Sacrifice of Isaac. Pisa, Cathedral.

Tanzio, Antonio d'Enrico. Cappella dell'Angelo Custode (Cappella Nazzari): Scenes. 1629. Frescoes. Novara, S. Gaudenzio.

Tiepolo, G.B. Sacrifice of Abraham. New York, Metropolitan Museum.

Tintoretto (Jacopo Robusti). The Sacrifice of Isaac. Florence, Palazzo Uffizi, 931.

Tintoretto (Jacopo Robusti). Upper hall, ceiling: Sacrifice of Isaac. Venice, Scuola di San Rocco.

Titian. Ceiling decorations. Abraham and Isaac. S. Maria della Salute.

Vasari, Giorgio and Gherardi, Cristofano. Sacrifices and prophets: Abraham. Fresco. Cortona, Compagnia del Gesù.

Vasari, Giorgio, Workshop of. The Sacrifice of Isaac. Baltimore, Md., Walters Art Gallery, 37.1705.

Veronese, Paolo? Sacrifice of Abraham. Madrid, Private Collection.

Veronese, Paolo. Sacrifice of Isaac. Vienna, Kunsthistorisches Museum.

SPANISH SCHOOL

Goya. Biblical themes. 3.Abraham and Isaac.

Mayno, Juan Bautista. The Sacrifice of Isaac. Christie, Manson and Woods (Sale, London, [TOLEDO-2659] May 27, 1983, No. 231).

SWEDISH SCHOOL

Albertus Pictor. Ceiling painting. Detail: Sacrifice of Isaac. c.1480. Täby (Uppland), Church.

71 C 13 14 GENESIS 22:13 A RAM CAUGHT IN A THICKET IS SACRIFICED INSTEAD OF ISAAC

FLEMISH SCHOOL

Teniers, David, the younger. Abraham sacrificing the ram. Vienna, Kunsthistorisches Museum.

ITALIAN SCHOOL

Allori, Alessandro. Sacrifice of Abraham. Florence, Palazzo Uffizi.

Italian school, Wall painting, Spoleto. Sant'Ansano.Central apse. Sacrifice of Abraham. Spoleto, Sant'Ansano.

71 C 21 1 GENESIS 24:2-9 ELIEZER TAKING THE OATH.
ABRAHAM SENDS HIM TO HIS RELATIVES IN MESO-
POTAMIA TO FIND A WIFE FOR ISAAC.

FLEMISH SCHOOL
Vos, Martin, the Elder. Abraham Entrusts Eliezar
with Bridal Request. Rouen (Seine-Infèrieure),
Musée.

71 C 21 3 GENESIS 24:15-16 THE MEETING AT THE WELL:
ELIEZER SEES REBEKAH COMING WITH A PITCHER

FRENCH SCHOOL
Chagall, Marc. Illustrations from the Bible
published by Vollard. No.33: Eliezer and
Rebekah. 1931. Nice (Alpes-Maritimes),
Musée National Message Biblique Marc Chagall.

GERMAN SCHOOL
German school, 19th century. Eliezer and
Rebecca. 1826. Sotheby and Co., London
(Sale, Monaco, [TAORMINE], Dec. 9, 1984,
No. 634).
Loth, Johann Carl. Rebecca and the servant
of Abraham at the well. San Francisco,
M.H. de Young Memorial Museum.
Seekatz, Johann Konrad. Rebecca at the well.
Christie, Manson and Woods (Sale, London,
October 14, 1983, No. 164).

ITALIAN SCHOOL
Gimignani, Giacinto. Rebecca at the Well. Flor-
ence, Palazzo Pitti.
Italian school, 18th century. Eliezer and
Rebekah at the Well. London, Victoria and
Albert Museum, 554-1870.
Italian school, 19th century. Rebecca at the
well. Christie, Manson and Woods (Sale,
New York, Nov. 4, 1983, No. 68).
Torri, Flaminio. Rebecca at the Well. Turin,
Pinacoteca, 517.

71 C 21 31 REBEKAH AT THE WELL (ELIEZER ABSENT)

AMERICAN SCHOOL
Rossiter, T.P. Rebecca at the well. Washington,
D.C., Corcoran Gallery.

FRENCH SCHOOL
Boulogne, Louis, the younger, attributed to.
Rebecca and Eliezer at the Well. Christie,
Manson and Woods (Sale, New York, June 12,
1981, No. 65).
Corot, Jean Baptiste. Rebecca at the Well.
1839. Pasadena, Ca., Norton Simon Museum,
F.72.21.F
Lecomte-Vernet, Charles Emile Hippolyte. Rebecca.
1869. New York, Hammer Galleries.
Leprince, Jean Baptiste, School of. Rebecca
at the Well. Christie, Manson and Woods
(Sale, New York, July 15, 1981, No. 78,
Illus. No. 79).

GERMAN SCHOOL
Dietrich, Christian Wilhelm Ernst. Elieser
and Rebecca. Brunswick, Landesmuseum, 618.

ITALIAN SCHOOL
Italian school, 18th century (Venetian). Rebecca
at the Well. Brescia, S. Giuseppe, Museo
Diocesano.
Luti, Benedetto. Rebecca at the well. Holkam
Hall, Norfolk, Collection Earl of Leicester.
Mola, Pier Francesco. Rebecca at the Well.
Rome, Galleria Colonna.
Monti, Francesco. Rebecca at the Well. Edinburgh,
National Gallery, 2120.
Ricci, Sebastiano. Rebecca at the Well. Castel-
franco, Banca Popolaro.

71 C 21 31 1 GENESIS 24:17-18 REBEKAH OFFERS
ELIEZER A DRINK FROM HER PITCHER.

AMERICAN SCHOOL
Allston, Washington. Rebecca at the Well.
Harvard University, Fogg Art Museum, 7.1955.
Long-term loan, Boston, Museum of Fine
Arts.

BRITISH SCHOOL
Martin, John. Rebecca and Eleazar at the
well. Harvard University, Fogg Art Museum,
1965.559.

DUTCH SCHOOL
Bray, Salomon de. Eliezer and Rebecca. Douai,
(Nord), Musée, No. 2794.
Eeckhout, Gerbrand van den. Abraham's servant
with Rebecca. 1663. Leipzig, Museum.
Eeckhout, Gerbrand van den. Rebecca and
Elieser at the Well. Prague, Nároní Galerie.
Eeckhout, Gerbrand van den. Eliezer and
Rebecca. 1661. Shickman, H. - Gallery
(New York).
Moeyaert, Claes Cornelisz. Rebecca and Eliezer
ast the well. Sotheby and Co., London
(Sale, June 3, 1981, No. 39).
Troyen, Rombout van. Rebecca at the well
with Eliesar. Aix-la-Chapelle, Private
Collection.

FLEMISH SCHOOL
Franck, Franz, I, Studio of. Flemish Reliquary
Chest painted with scenes from the Old
Testament. Detail: Right door: Rebecca
at the Well. c. 1600. Sarasota, Fla.,
Ringling Museum of Art, SN 1950.
Franck, Franz, II. Rebecca at the Well.
Duault, Daniel - Gallery (Paris).
Garemyn, J.A. Rebecca at the well? Bruges?
Master of the Prodigal Son. Rebecca at the
Well. Dublin, National Gallery, 845.
Valkenborch, Lucas van. Eliezer and Rebecca.
Sotheby and Co., London (Sale, April 7,
1982, No. 159).
Verhagen, P.J. Eliezer and Rebecca. Louvain,
Abbaye de Parc.

FRENCH SCHOOL
Decamps, A.G. Rebecca at the fountain. Braun,
15721.
Poussin, Nicolas. Rebecca and Eliezer. Mont-
pellier, Musée Fabre.
Poussin, Nicolas. Rebecca and Eliezer. London,
Collection A.F. Blunt.
Poussin, Nicolas. Rebecca quenching the
thirst of Eliezer at the well. c. 1629.
London, Collection Denis Mahon.
Poussin, Nicolas, Copy after. Eliezer and
Rebecca. Mans, Le (Sarthe), Musée, 10.78.

GERMAN SCHOOL
Ramboux, Johann Anton. Rebecca and Elieser
at the Well. 1819. Berlin, Staatliche
Musée, All 726, NG 1671.

ITALIAN SCHOOL
Asserto, Gioacchino. Rebecca at the Well.
Genoa, Palazzo Durazzo-Pallavicini.
Castello, Valerio. Rebecca at the Well.
Leningrad, Hermitage.
Dandini, Pietro. Rebecca at the Well. Christie,
Manson and Woods (Sale, New York [BETH-
5258] Jan. 18, 1983, No. 70).
Lippi, Lorenzo. Rebecca at the well. Copy,
1644. Dayton, Art Institute.
Lippi, Lorenzo. Rebecca at the well.
Reni, Guido. Rebecca at the well. Florence,
Pitti.
Rosso, Il. Rebecca at the well. Pisa, Museo
Nazionale di S. Matteo.
Sagrestani, Giovanni Camillo, attributed
to. Rebecca at the Well with Abraham's
Servant. Harvard University, Fogg Art
Museum, 1973.23.

Solimena, Francesco. Rebecca and the Servant
  of Abraham. c.1700. Leningrad, Hermitage.
Solimena, Francesco. Rebecca and the Servant
  of Abraham. 1700. Venice, Academy, 847.
Strozzi, Bernardo. Rebecca with Abraham's
  Servant at the Well. Dresden, Staatliche
  Kunstsammlungen, 656.
Vannini, Ottavio. Rebecca and Eliezer. Vienna,
  Kunsthistorisches Museum, Inv. Nr. 1573.

SPANISH SCHOOL
  Murillo. Rebecca and Eliezer at the well.
    Madrid, Prado, 996.

71 C 21 33 GENESIS 24:22 REBEKAH RECEIVES EAR RINGS
            AND GOLDEN BRACELETS FROM ELIEZER

AMERICAN SCHOOL
  Trumbull, John. Abraham's Servant Meeting
    Rebekah at the Well.1773. Private Collection.

DUTCH SCHOOL
  Heerschop, Hendrick. Rebecca and the servant
    of Abraham. Amsterdam, Rijksmuseum, 1133.

FLEMISH SCHOOL
  Vos, Martin de, the elder. Rebecca and Eliezer
    at the Well. Hove, Charles van - Collection
    (Mousty).
  Vos, Martin de, the elder. Rebecca and Eliezer
    at the Well. Rouen (Seine-Infêrieure),
    Musée.

FRENCH SCHOOL
  Bourdon, Sebastien. Rebecca and Eliezer. c.1658.
    Boston, Museum of Fine Arts, 68.24.
  Colombel, Nicolas. Rebecca at the Well. Based
    on a painting by Nicolas Poussin in the
    Louvre, Paris. Sotheby and Co., London
    (Sale, June 23, 1982, No. 23).
  Coypel, A. Rebecca and Eliezer.
  Poussin, Nicolas. Rebecca and Eliezer. Paris,
    Musée du Louvre.
  Poussin, Nicolas. Rebecca and Eliezer. Copy
    of painting in the Louvre. Jerez de la
    Frontera, Private Collection.

GERMAN SCHOOL
  Seekatz, Johann Conrad. Rebecca and Eliezer.
    Sotheby and Co. (Sale, London, March 9,
    1983, No. 27).

ITALIAN SCHOOL
  Amigoni, Jacopo. Rebecca at the Well. Chrysler,
    Walter P. Jr. - Collection (New York).
  Bellucci, Antonio. Rebecca at the Well.
    Pommersfelden, Collection Dr. Karl Graf
    von Schonborn-Wiesentheid.
  Carracci, Agostino. Rebecca at the well.
    Burghley House, cat. (1954) 415.
  Chiari, Guiseppe Bartolomeo. Rebecca and
    Eliezer. Christie, Manson and Woods (Sale,
    New York, [LOUISE-5912] June 5,1985, No.116).
  Costanzi, Placido, Circle of. Rebecca and
    Eliezer. Sotheby and Co., London (Sale,
    April 8, 1981, No. 132).
  Costanzi, Placido. Rachael at the Well. c.1740.
    Florence, Palazzo Uffizi, S. Marco e Cenaculi,
    39.
  Ferri, Ciro. Rebecca at the Well. Rome, Galleria
    d'Arte Antica.
  Lauri, Filippo. Rebecca at the Well. Dublin,
    National Gallery, 989.
  Lazzarini, Gregorio. Rebecca at the well.
    Venice, Palazzo Rezzonico.
  Locatelli, Andrea. Rebecca and Eliezer. Geneva,
    Musée d'Art et d'Histoire, CR 275.
  Mura, Francesco de. Rebecca and Eleazer at
    the well. Christie, Manson and Woods (Sale,
    London, [TINKER-3144] May 24, 1985, No.159).
  Pellegrini, Giovanni Antonio. Rebecca at the
    well. Washington, D.C., National Gallery

of Art, Kress Collection.
Pellegrini, Giovanni Antonio. Rebecca at the
  well. London, National Gallery, 6332.
Piazzetta, G.B. Rebecca at the Well. Milan,
  Brera.
Tiepolo, Giovanni Domenico. Rebecca at the
  well. Companion with Christ and the Woman
  Taken in Adultery. Paris, Musée du Louvre,
  R.F. 1975-2.
Tortelli, Giuseppe. Rebecca at the Well.
  c.1705-10. Brescia, S.Giovanni Evangelista.
Veronese, Paolo. Rebecca at the Well. Glens
  Falls, N.Y., Hyde Collection.
Veronese, Paolo. Rebecca at the Well. 1580-85.
  Washington, D.C., National Gallery of
  Art, 1161.

71 C 21 35 LABAN, REBEKAH'S BROTHER, COMES TO
            ELIEZER AT THE WELL. GENESIS 24:29-31

FLEMISH SCHOOL
  Vos, Martin de, the Elder. Laban Greets
    Eliezar. Rouen (Seine-Infêrieure), Musée.

71 C 21 4 GENESIS 24:32-61 ELIEZER AT REBEKAH'S
           HOUSE

FLEMISH SCHOOL
  Vos, Martin, the Elder. Laban Introduces
    Eliezar to Rebecca's Father. Rouen (Seine-
    Infêrieure), Musée.

71 C 21 42 GENESIS 24:53 GIFTS OF CLOTHING, GOLD
            AND JEWELRY ARE OFFERED TO REBEKAH'S PARENTS

FRENCH SCHOOL
  Bourdon, Sebastien. Abraham's servants bringing
    gifts to Rebecca. Welbeck Abbey, Collection
    Duke of Portland.
  Vignon, Claude. Abraham's Servant Giving
    Gifts to the Family of Rebecca. Sotheby
    and Co., London (Sale, New York [AUINCE-
    5193] June 7, 1984, No. 54).

ITALIAN SCHOOL
  Italian school, 15th century. Cloister
    frescoes. Series of scenes from the Old
    Testament: Abraham's servants offering
    gifts to Rebecca. Florence, S.M. Novella.

71 C 21 44 THE LEAVE-TAKING OF REBEKAH; LABAN
            GIVES HER PROVISIONS

FLEMISH SCHOOL
  Vos, Martin, the Elder. Rebecca Takes Leave
    of her Parents. Rouen (Seine-Infêrieure),
    Musée.

ITALIAN SCHOOL
  Solimena, Francesco, studio of. Rebecca's
    departure from her father. Budapest,
    Museum of Fine Arts, 1044 (228 b).

71 C 21 5 GENESIS 24:61-67 THE RETURN JOURNEY AND
           ARRIVAL IN CANAAN

ITALIAN SCHOOL
  Castiglione, G.B. Rebecca and Isaac. Rome,
    Galleria Corsini.
  Giordano, Luca. The Journey of Rebecca.
    Malibu, J. Paul Getty Museum, 70.PA.31.
  Giordano, Luca. Scene from the Old Testament.
    Journey of Rebecca? Naples, San Martino.

71 C 21 51 GENESIS 24:63-65 ISAAC, WALKING IN
            THE FIELDS, MEETS REBEKAH

FRENCH SCHOOL
  Tissot, James Jacques Joseph. Illustrations
    of the Hebrew Bible. No.41: Rebecca Meets
    Isaac by the Way. 1896-1903. Gouache,
    New York, Jewish Museum, 52.108.

ITALIAN SCHOOL
    Castiglione, Giovanni Benedetto. Isaac Meeting
    Rebecca. Leningrad, Hermitage.

71 C 21 6 GENESIS 24:67 ISAAC BRINGS REBEKAH INTO
    SARAH'S TENT

DUTCH SCHOOL
    Fabritius, Bernard. Rebecca Welcomed by Abraham.
    Chicago, Art Institute 1967.594.

FLEMISH SCHOOL
    Vos, Martin de, the Elder. Rebecca Received
    by Abraham. Rouen (Seine-Inférieure), Musée.

71 C 21 7 GENESIS 24:67 MARRIAGE OF ISAAC AND
    REBEKAH

DUTCH SCHOOL
    Gelder, Aert de. The Marriage of Isaac and
    Rebecca. Brussels, Stedilijk Museum.

FRENCH SCHOOL
    Claude Lorrain. Landscape: The Marriage of
    Isaac and Rebekah (The Mill). 1648. London,
    National Gallery, 12.

ITALIAN SCHOOL
    Amigoni, Jacopo. Isaac and Rebecca. Christie,
    Manson and Woods (Sale, New York, June 12,
    1981, No. 170).
    Gozzoli, Benozzo. Old Testament and other
    subjects: Marriage of Rebecca and Isaac.
    Camposanto.

71 C 24 GENESIS 25:19-34 ISAAC'S CHILDREN

AMERICAN SCHOOL
    West, Benjamin. Esau and Jacob presented to
    Isaac. Greenville, S.C., Bob Jones University
    Collection.

71 C 24 3 GENESIS 25:24-26 BIRTH OF THE TWINS;
    JACOB CLUTCHES ESAU'S HEEL

ITALIAN SCHOOL
    Gozzoli, Benozzo. Old Testament and other
    subjects: Birth of Jacob and Esau. Detail.
    Pisa, Camposanto.

71 C 24 41 GENESIS 25:29-34 ESAU, RETURNING HUNGRY
    FROM THE HUNT, SELLS HIS BIRTHRIGHT TO JACOB
    FOR A POTTAGE OF LENTILS

BRITISH SCHOOL
    Martin, John. Esau Selling his Birthright.
    1853. Sotheby and Co., London (Sale, [LOHEN-
    GRIN] June 15, 1982, No. 14).

DUTCH SCHOOL
    Terbruggen, Hendrick. Esau selling his birth-
    right. Greenville, S.C., 1962 cat. 165.
    Terbruggen, Hendrick. Esau Selling his Birth-
    right. c.1627. Thyssen-Bornemisza Collection
    (Lugano).

FRENCH SCHOOL
    Corneille, Michel. Esau Sells his Birthright
    to Jacob. 1630. Orleans (Loiret), Musée,
    306.

GERMAN SCHOOL
    Master H.B. Portrait of a Young Woman and her
    Son as Rebecca and Jacob. 1545. Sotheby
    and Co., London (Sale, Monaco, [OUDRY] Dec.
    8, 1984, No. 308).

ITALIAN SCHOOL
    Gozzoli, Benozzo. Old Testament and other
    subjects: Birth of Jacob and Esau. Detail:
    Esau sells his birthright. Pisa, Camposanto.
    Strozzi, Bernardo. Esau and Jacob. Genoa,
    Collection Viezzoli.

SPANISH SCHOOL
    Antolinez, Francisco. Scene from the life
    of Jacob. Seville, Cathedral.
    Rubiales, Pedro de. Copy. Esau Sells his
    Birthright. Copy of fresco in chapel of
    the princes of Solmona, Church of Sant'Anna
    dei Lombardi (Monteoliceto), Naples.
    Baltimore, Md., Walters Art Gallery.
    37.1739.

71 C 25 11 GENESIS 26:2 GOD APPEARS TO ISAAC
    AND WARNS HIM NOT TO JOURNEY INTO EGYPT

ITALIAN SCHOOL
    Raphael (and assistants). Old Testament sub-
    jects: God forbids Isaac and Rebecca to
    emigrate to Egypt. Rome, Vatican, Loggie.

71 C 25 21 1 GENESIS 26:8 KING ABIMELECH, LOOKING
    DOWN FROM HIS WINDOW, SEES ISAAC AND REBEKAH
    MAKING LOVE

ITALIAN SCHOOL
    Raphael (and assistants). Old Testament sub-
    jects: Isaac and Rebecca observed by Abi-
    melech. Rome, Vatican, Loggie.

71 C 25 42 GENESIS 26:25 ISAAC BUILDS AN ALTAR

ITALIAN SCHOOL
    Vasari, Giorgio and Gherardi, Cristofano.
    Sacrifices and prophets: Isaac. Fresco.
    Cortona, Compagnia del Gesù.

71 C 27 2 ESAU HUNTING

ITALIAN SCHOOL
    Italian school, 13th century. Esau hunting.
    Stimigliano, S. Maria in Vescovo.

71 C 27 4 GENESIS 27:18-29 ISAAC LYING IN BED
    BLESSES JACOB WHO, DISGUISED IN ESAU'S
    CLOTHES, BRINGS FOOD TO HIS FATHER; JACOB'S
    HANDS AND NECK ARE COVERED WITH GOATSKINS

DUTCH SCHOOL
    Eeckhout, Gerbrand van den. Isaac Blessing
    Jacob. 1642. New York, Metropolitan
    Museum.
    Flinck, Govert. Isaac blessing Jacob. 1638.
    Amsterdam, Rijksmuseum.
    Flink, Govert. Jacob Receives Isaac's Blessing.
    c. 1637. Leeuwarden, Fries Museum.
    Herp, Willem van. Isaac Blessing Jacob.
    Private Collection, U.S.A.
    Horst, G.W. Isaac blessing Jacob. 1638.
    Dulwich Gallery, 214.
    Horst, Gerrit Willemsz. Isaac Blessing Jacob.
    c. 1633. Location Unknown.
    Horst, G.W. Jacob's Blessing. Berlin,
    Staatliche Museen.
    Victors, Jan. Isaac Blesses Jacob. 1640-50.
    Paris, Louvre, Musée du, Inv. 1285.

FLEMISH SCHOOL
    Hemessen, Jan Sanders van. Isaac Blessing
    Jacob. Budapest, Museum of Fine Arts,
    1049 (676).
    Herp, Willem van. Isaac Blessing Jacob.
    Private Collection, U.S.A.
    Jordaens, Jacob. The Blessing of Jacob.
    Christie, Manson and Woods (Sale, London,
    June 28, 1974, No. 6).
    Stomer, Matthias. Isaac Blessing Jacob. Paris,
    Louvre, Musée du, R.F. 2810.

FRENCH SCHOOL
    Jouvenet, Jean. Isaac Blessing Jacob. 1692.
    Rouen (Seine-Inférieure), Musée.

GERMAN SCHOOL
    Bertram (van Byrde) Master. Grabow altar.
    Scenes from the Old and New Testament:
    Jacob receiving the blessing. Hamburg,
    Kunsthalle.

Loth, Johann Carl. Jacob's Blessing. Modena,
Pinacoteca Estense.

ITALIAN SCHOOL
Assereto, Gioachino. Isaac Blessing Jacob.
Leningrad, Hermitage.
Bassano, Leandro. Jacob and Esau. 1612. New
York, Newhouse Galleries.
Caravaggio. The seniority of Esau. Cadiz,
Private Collection.
Cavalori, Mirabello. Blessing of Isaac. Florence,
Collection Loeser.
Girolamo da Treviso, the younger. Isaac Blessing
Jacob. c.1515. Rouen (Seine-Infèrieure),
Musée.
Italian school, 13th century. Scenes from the
Old Testament. Isaac blessing Jacob. Assisi,
S. Francesco, upper church.
Italian school, 11th century. Church, Left
aisle wall. The death of Isaac: Jacob steals
the blessing of his father.(?) Fresco.
S. Angelo in Formis.
Pitati, Bonifacio. Isaac Blessing Jacob. Also
attributed to Andrea Schiavone. Dublin,
National Gallery, 1128.
Raphael (and assistants). Old Testament subjects:
Isaac blesses Jacob. Rome, Vatican, Loggie.
Strozzi, Bernardo. Isaac blessing Jacob.
Pisa, Museo Nazionale di S. Matteo.
Strozzi, Bernardo. Isaac and Jacob. Venice,
Private Collection.
Zanchi, Antonio, Attributed to. Isaac Blessing
Jacob. Boston, Museum of Fine Arts, Res.
23.136.

SPANISH SCHOOL
Murillo. Isaac. London, Apsley House, Collection
Duke of Wellington.
Murillo. Isaac blessing Jacob.
Orrente, Pedro. The Blessing of Jacob. Madrid,
Collegio San Anton.
Orrente, Pedro. The Blessing of Jacob. Detail:
Blessing. Madrid, Colegio San Anton.
Ribera, Jusepe. The Blessing of Isaac. Madrid,
Prado.

71 C 27 5 GENESIS 27:31 ESAU COMES BACK WITH VENISON

ITALIAN SCHOOL
Italian school, 13th century. Scenes from
the Old Testament. Esau giving pottage to
Isaac. Assisi, S. Francesco, upper church.
Strozzi, Bernardo. Isaac Blessing Esau. Genoa,
Private Collection.

71 C 27 6 GENESIS 27:31-33 ESAU SEEKS HIS FATHER'S
BLESSING; ISAAC REALIZES HE HAS MISTAKENLY
BLESSED JACOB INSTEAD OF ESAU

DUTCH SCHOOL
Rembrandt. Isaac blessing Esau.

GERMAN SCHOOL
Bertram (van Byrde) Master. Grabow altar.
Scenes from the Old and New Testament: Jacob
and Esau. Hamburg, Kunsthalle.

ITALIAN SCHOOL
Giotto, Attributed to. Scenes of Old and New
Testament stories. Also attributed to the
Isaac Master and other artists of the Italian
school. 1291-95. Fresco. Assisi, San Fran-
cesco, Upper Church. Isaac Rejecting Esau.
Raphael (and assistants). Old Testament subjects:
Esau implores Jacob's blessing. Rome, Vatican,
Loggie.

SPANISH SCHOOL
March, Esteban? Esau securing Isaac's blessing.
Also attributed to Spanish school, 17th
century. Brussels, Musée de Peinture.

71 C 3 STORY OF JACOB

FRENCH SCHOOL
Chagall, Marc. The Song of Jacob. 1956-
57. Private Collection.

ITALIAN SCHOOL
Tanzio, Antonio d'Enrico (Tanzio da Varallo).
Jacob and Rachel. Turin, Pinacoteca.

71 C 31 STORY OF JACOB (PART I)

AMERICAN SCHOOL
West, Benjamin. Portrait of Mary, Wife of
Henry Thompson of Kirby Hall, as Rachel
at the Well. 1775. Norfolk, Va., Chrysler
Museum, 71.720.

FRENCH SCHOOL
Claude Lorrain. Jacob with Laban and his
daughters. Dulwich Gallery, 205.

SPANISH SCHOOL
Orrente, Pedro. The return of Jacob. Barcelona,
Collection Juan Prats Tomas.

71 C 31 21 GENESIS 28:11-16 THE DREAM OF JACOB:
WHILE SLEEPING ON THE GROUND WITH A STONE
FOR A PILLOW JACOB SEES A LADDER REACHING
FROM EARTH TO HEAVEN WITH ANGELS GOING
UP AND DOWN, USUALLY WITH GOD AT THE TOP
OF THE LADDER

EARLY MEDIEVAL AND BYZANTINE
Byzantine school, Wall painting, Prizren.
Story of Jacob: Jacob's dream. Fresco.
14th century. Bogorodica Ljeviska. Exo-
narthex, west wall. Prizren, Yugoslavia.

DUTCH SCHOOL
Bol, Ferdinand. Jacob's dream. Dresden,
Gallery, 1604.
Bol, Hans. The Vision of Jacob's Ladder.
Dresden, Staatliche Kunstsammlungen, 828.
Eeckhout, Gerbrand van den. Jacob's Dream.
1669. Dresden, Staatliche Kunstsammlungen,
1618A.
Eeckhout, Gerbrand van den. Jacob's Dream.
1672. Bader, Alfred - Collection (Mil-
waukee).
Gelder, Aert de. Jacob's dream. Dulwich
Gallery, 126.
Mieris, Frans van, the elder. Jacob's dream.
Amsterdam, Rijksmuseum, 1613.

FLEMISH SCHOOL
Franck, Franz, I, Studio of. Flemish Reliquary
Chest painted with scenes from the Old
Testament. Detail: Drawer: Jacob's Ladder.
c. 1600. Sarasota, Fla., Ringling Museum
of Art, SN 1950.
Franck Frans, II. Jacob's dream. Toledo,
Spain, Museo Provincial.

FRENCH SCHOOL
Chagall, Marc. Jacob and the Angels. 1969-
72. Private Collection.
French school, 15th century. Jacob's dream.
London, Collection George Durlacher.

GERMAN SCHOOL
Elseheimer, Adam. Jacob's Dream. Frankfort-
on-the-Main, Staedel Institute.
Willmann, Michael Leopold. Jacob's Dream.
c. 1691. Berlin, Staatliche Museen, FV2
(On loan from Leubus Monastery, Silesia.)

ITALIAN SCHOOL
Allori, Cristoforo. Jacob's Dream. Turin,
Pinacoteca, 132.
Carpioni, Giulio. Jacob's Dream of the Ladder
in the Sky. Budapest, Museum of Fine Arts, 63.7.

Carracci, Ludovico. Jacob's dream. Bologna,
Pinacoteca Nazionale.
Fetti, Domenico. Jacob's Dream. Cleveland,
Museum of Art, 40.437.
Giordano, Luca. Jacob's dream. Naples, Museo
Nazionale.
Italian school, 17th century. Dream of Jacob.
(Also attributed to Francisco Collantes).
New York, Hispanic Society of America,
Weitzner Collection.
Ligozzi, Jacopo. Jacob's dream. c.1600. Flor-
ence, S. Giovanni degli Scolopi.
Palma Giovane. Ceiling, detail: dream of Jacob.
Venice, Palazzo Loredan (Municipio).
Rosa, S| Jacob's Dream. Christie, Manson
and Woods (Sale, London, July 23, 1982,
No. 151).
Testa, Pietro. Dream of Jacob. Rome, Accademia
di S. Luca.
Vasari, Giorgio (and Workshop). Jacob's Dream.
1558. Baltimore, Md., Walters Art Gallery.
Zuccari, Federigo. Chapel, ceiling: dream
of Jacob. Rome, Il Gesù.

SPANISH SCHOOL
Goya. Jacob's dream (?) Saragossa, Collection
Gabarda.
Milá Master. Jacob's Dream. Seville, Museo
Provincial.
Murillo, Bartolomé Esteban. Jacob's Dream.
Louisville, Ky., J.B. Speed Art Museum, 74.8.
Orrente, Pedro, Attributed to. Jacob at the
Well. In the background: Jacob's Dream.
Christie, Manson and Woods (Sale, London,
[TERNI-2813] Dec. 15-16, 1983, No. 7).
Orrente, Pedro. Jacob's Dream. Barcelona,
Collection Juan Prats Tomas.
Orrente, Pedro, follower of. Jacob's Dream.
Christie, Manson and Woods (Sale, London,
Feb. 1, 1985, [TURNIP-3068] No. 19).

71 C 31 21 1 GENESIS 28:11-16 THE DREAM OF JACOB,
WITH STAIRWAY INSTEAD OF LADDER

AMERICAN SCHOOL
Allston, Washington. Jacob's Dream. 1817.
Petworth (Sussex), Petworth House, 449.

BRITISH SCHOOL
Blake, William. Jacob's Dream. c.1805, London,
British Museum, 1949-11-12-2.

EARLY MEDIEVAL AND BYZANTINE
Byzantine school, Wall Painting, Istanbul.
Mosque Kahrié. Pareclesion, Western bay,
North wall, Lunette: Jacob's Ladder. 14th
century. Istanbul.

DUTCH SCHOOL
Eeckhout, Gerbrand van den. Jacob's Dream.
1669. Dresden, Staatliche Kunstsammlungen,
1618 A.

FLEMISH SCHOOL
Desubleo, Michele. Jacob's Dream. Trafalgar
Galleries (London).

ITALIAN SCHOOL
Creti, Donato. Jacob's Dream. Rome, Galleria
d'Arte Antica.
Fetti, Domenico. Jacob's dream. Vienna, Kuns-
thistorisches Museum, 121.
Fetti, Domenico. Jacob's Dream. Detroit,
Institute of Arts, 39.669.
Fetti, Domenico. Jacob's Dream of a Ladder
to Heaven. Rome, Galleria d'Arte Antica.
Raphael (and assistants). Old Testament subjects:
Jacob's dream. Rome, Vatican, Loggie.
Tiepolo, G.B. Decorations. Jacob's dream.
Palazzo Arcivescovile, Galleria.
Tintoretto. Ceiling: Jacob's dream. Scuola
di San Rocco, upper hall.
Vasari, Giorgio (and Workshop). Jacob's Dream.
1558. Baltimore, Md., Walters Art Gallery,
37.2508.

SPANISH SCHOOL
Murillo. Jacob's dream. New York, Wildenstein
Collection.

71 C 31 21 2 GENESIS 28:11-16 THE DREAM OF JACOB,
WITH BEAM OF LIGHT INSTEAD OF LADDER

BRITISH SCHOOL
Turner, Joseph Mallord William. The Vision
of Jacob's Ladder. c.1830. London, Tate
Gallery, 5507.

DUTCH SCHOOL
Eeckhout, Gerbrand van den. Jacob's Dream.
1642. Warsaw, Nationalmuseum.
Eeckhout, Gerbrand van den. Jacob's Dream.
1672. Bader, Alfred - Collection (Mil-
waukee).
Rembrandt, School of. Jacob's Dream. c.1650.
Private Collection, U.S.A.

SPANISH SCHOOL
Ribera, Jusepe de. Jacob's Dream. 1639.
Madrid, Prado.

71 C 31 3 GENESIS 29:1-13 JACOB AT THE WELL OF
HARAN

DUTCH SCHOOL
Flinck, Govert (?) Meeting of Jacob and
Rachel?
Pynas, Jan. Jacob and Rachel at the Well.
Christie, Manson and Woods (Sale, London,
March 11, 1983, No. 78).

ITALIAN SCHOOL
Castiglione, Giovanni Benedetto. Laban and
his Flock at the Well. Los Angeles,
County Museum.
Cortona, Pietro da. Rachel at the well.
London, Collection Duke of Devonshire.
Italian school, 15th century. Series of scenes
from the Old Testament. The meeting of
Jacob and Rachel. Florence, S.M. Novella,
Cloister frescoes.
Lippi, Lorenzo. Jacob at the Well. Florence,
Palazzo Pitti, 3477.
Paciccio (Francesco Rosa). The Meeting of
Jacob and Rachael. Naples, Museo Nazionale,
Capiomonte.

SPANISH SCHOOL
Orrente, Pedro. Jacob at the Well. Christie,
Manson and Woods (Sale, London, [TOLEDO-
2659] May 27, 1983, No. 206).

71 C 31 32 GENESIS 29:10 JACOB SEES RACHEL COMING
TO THE WELL TO WATER LABAN'S SHEEP

ITALIAN SCHOOL
Bassano, Jacopo, Studio of. Jacob and Rachael.
Vienna, Kunsthistorisches Museum, 5824.

71 C 31 33 GENESIS 29:10 JACOB MOVES THE STONE
WHICH COVERED THE OPENING OF THE WELL
AND WATERS RACHEL'S SHEEP

DUTCH SCHOOL
Moeyaert, Claes Cornelisz? Jacob and Rachel
meeting at the well. Amsterdam, Rijksmuseum, 1633.

ITALIAN SCHOOL
Bassano, Francesco, the younger. Jacob at
the Well. Vienna, Kunsthistorisches Museum,
4307.
Bassano, Francesco, the younger. Jacob at
the well. Weston Park, Collection Earl
of Bradford.
Castiglione, G.B. Laban and his flock. New
York, Collection Robert Manning.
Costanzi, Placido. Rachael and Jacob. c.1740.
Florence, Palazzo Uffizi, S.Marco e Cenacoli, 25.

Giordano, Luca. Jacob and Rachael at the Well. Dresden, Gallery, 491 (1722 A 47).

Grassi, Nicola. Meeting of Jacob and Rachael. Udine, Museo Civico.

Italian school, 15th century. Series of eight panels with scenes from the Old Testament: Rachel at the Well. Venice, S. Alvise.

Italian school, 18th century. Jacob and Rachel at the Well. London, Victoria and Albert Museum, 555-1870.

Mola, Pier Francesco. Jacob Meeting Rachel. Leningrad, Hermitage.

Procaccini, G.C. Rachel. Pavia, S. Maria in Canepanova.

Raphael (and assistants). Old Testament subjects: Jacob meets Rachel at the Well. Rome, Vatican, Loggie.

Solimena, Francesco. Jacob and Rachel at the Well. Formerly attributed to Luca Giordano. Sarasota, Fla., Ringling Museum of Art, SN 158.

SPANISH SCHOOL

Antolínez, Francisco. Jacob rolling the stone from the well's mouth. Seville, Cathedral.

Antolinez, Francisco de. Jacob and Rachel at the well. Jerez de la Frontera, S. Miguel.

Murillo. Jacob and Rachel at the well. New York, Collection S. H. Kress, 484.

Murillo. Jacob and Rachel at the well. Detail. New York, Collection S. H. Kress, 484.

71 C 31 34   GENESIS 29:11   JACOB KISSES RACHEL AND
IS MOVED TO TEARS

BRITISH SCHOOL

Dyce, William. The Meeting of Jacob and Rachael. c.1853. Hamburg, Kunsthalle.

Dyce, William. The Meeting of Jacob and Rachael. c.1853. Leicester, Art Gallery.

DUTCH SCHOOL

Venant, François, Attributed to. Rachel at the Well. Christie, Manson and Woods (Sale, New York [GERTRUDE-5584], June 6, 1984, No.55).

FLEMISH SCHOOL

Goes, Hugo van der. Jacob and Rachel. Oxford, University, Christ Church.

Jordaens, Jacob. Jacob and Rachel at the Well. Sotheby and Co., London (Sale, June 9, 1982, No. 34).

Vos, Martin de, the elder. Jacob and Rachel at the Well. Sotheby and Co., London (Sale, March 24, 1976, No. 50).

GERMAN SCHOOL

Führich, Josef von. The Meeting of Jacob and Rachel. 1836. Vienna, Österreichische Gallerie.

Seekatz, Johann Konrad. Jacob and Rachel at the Well. Christie, Manson and Woods, London (Sale, July 17, 1981, No. 178).

ITALIAN SCHOOL

Palma Vecchio. Meeting of Jacob and Rachel.

SPANISH SCHOOL

Murillo, Bartolomé Esteban. Jacob and Rachel. Detroit, Institute of Arts, 30.411.

Spanish school, 17th century. Jacob and Rachel at the Well. Dulwich Gallery, 185.

71 C 31 4   GENESIS 29:14-30   JACOB SERVING LABAN
FOR RACHEL AND LEAH

DUTCH SCHOOL

Moninckx, Pieter. Jacob and Laban. Christie, Manson and Woods (Sale, New York [RACHAEL-5423] Nov. 4, 1983, No. 39).

FRENCH SCHOOL

Claude Lorraine. Landscape with Jacob, Laban and his Daughters. 1659. Pasadena, Ca., Norton Simon Museum.

ITALIAN SCHOOL

Castiglione, G.B. (?)Jacob guarding Laban's sheep. Cambridge, Cambs., Stearn & Sons.

Passante, Bartolomeo? Jacob and Laban. Paris, Collection Benito Pardo.

SPANISH SCHOOL

Antolinez, Francisco, Attributed to. Jacob with Rachael and Leah (?) Christie, Manson and Woods (Sale, London, [TOLEDO-2659] May 27, 1983, No. 206).

Ribera, Jusepe de. Jacob guarding Laban's sheep. Escorial.

Ribera, Jusepe de. Jacob with the Flock of Laban. 1638. London, National Gallery, 244.

Ribera, Jusepe de. Jacob and his sheep. Madrid, Museo Cerralbo, No. 1576.

Ribera, Jusepe de. Jacob guarding Laban's sheep. Buscot Park, Collection Lord Faringdon.

71 C 31 44   GENESIS 29:23   THE WEDDING-FEAST; LABAN
SUBSTITUTES LEAH FOR RACHEL

ITALIAN SCHOOL

Italian school, 15th century. Series of scenes from the Old Testament. The meeting of Jacob and Rachel: the wedding-feast. Florence, S.M. Novella.

SPANISH SCHOOL

Antolínez, Francisco. Jacob and Laban, with Rachel and Leah. Seville, Cathedral.

71 C 31 45   GENESIS 29:25   JACOB DISCOVERS THAT
HE HAS BEEN DECEIVED AND COMPLAINS TO
LABAN

DUTCH SCHOOL

Terbruggen, Hendrick. Tobias Seeks the Hand of Sarah. Also identified as Jacob Chastising Laban for Giving Him Leah instead of Rachel for his Wife. Cologne, Wallraf-Richartz Museum, 1026.

Terbruggen, Hendrik. Jacob and Laban. 1627. London, National Gallery, 4164.

Terbruggen, Hendrik. Jacob and Laban. c.1628. Cologne, Wallraf-Richartz Museum.

Victors, Jan. Jacob and Laban. New York, Metropolitan Museum.

FRENCH SCHOOL

Coypel, Antoine. Jacob Reproaches Laban for Having Given Him Leah Instead of Rachel. Cartoon for a tapestry. Paris, Louvre, Musée du, INV. 3503.

ITALIAN SCHOOL

Saraceni, Carlo. Jacob Reproaching Laban for Giving Him Leah in Place of Rachael. c.1607. London, National Gallery, 6446.

Raphael (and assistants). Old Testament subjects: Jacob bargains with Laban. Rome, Vatican, Loggie.

71 C 31 46   GENESIS 29:28-30   THE MARRIAGE OF JACOB
AND RACHEL

ITALIAN SCHOOL

Ferri, Ciro. The Marriage of Jacob. Corsham Court, Collection Lord Methuen. Birmingham Museum and Art Gallery.

Gozzoli, Benozzo. Old Testament and other subjects: Marriage of Jacob and Rachel. Detail. Pisa, Camposanto.

71 C 31 5   GENESIS 29:31 - 30:24   JACOB'S CHILDREN

ITALIAN SCHOOL
    Italian school, 15th century. Series of scenes
    from the Old Testament: Marriage of Jacob.
    Florence, S.M. Novella. Cloister frescoes.

SPANISH SCHOOL
    Antolínez, Francisco. Jacob and Leah. Seville,
    Cathedral.

71 C 31 63   GENESIS 30:37-38   JACOB PUTS PEELED RODS
IN THE ANIMALS' DRINKING TROUGH

SPANISH SCHOOL
    Antolinez, Francisco, Attributed to. Jacob
    setting the peeled rods before the flocks
    of Laban. Christie, Manson and Woods (Sale,
    London, [TOLEDO-2659] May 27, 1983, No.
    205).
    Murillo. Jacob setting the Peeled Rods before
    the Flocks of Laban. c.1660. Dallas, Virginia
    Meadows Museum of Art.
    Orrente, Pedro. Jacob and the Herds of Laban.
    Madrid, Colegio San Anton.

71 C 31 8   GENESIS 31:1-21   JACOB'S FLIGHT FROM LABAN

ITALIAN SCHOOL
    Italian school, 15th century. Series of scenes
    from the Old Testament: Marriage of Jacob
    (upper panel), Jacob's Flight from Laban
    (lower panel). Cloister frescoes.

71 C 31 84   GENESIS 31:17-18   JACOB ON THE WAY TO
CANAAN WITH HIS FAMILY, HIS FLOCKS, CAMELS,
AND ALL HIS POSSESSIONS

DUTCH SCHOOL
    Uytenbroeck, Moses van. Jacob's Return to Canaan.
    Private Collection.
    Victors, Jan. The Migration of Jacob. Colnaghi
    and Co., (London).

FRENCH SCHOOL
    Claude Lorrain. Landscape with the Voyage
    of Jacob. 1677. Williamstown, Clark Art
    Institute, 42.

ITALIAN SCHOOL
    Bassano, Jacopo. Jacob's Journey. Hampton
    Court Palace.
    Castiglione, Giovanni Benedetto. Voyage of
    Jacob. Genoa, Palazzo Durazzo-Pallavicini.
    Castiglione, G.B., Attributed to. The Journey
    of Jacob. Sotheby and Co., London (Sale,
    New York, March 22, 1984, No. 121).
    Lione, Andrea de. The Departure of Jacob.
    Vienna, Kunsthistorisches Museum, 6786.
    Raphael (and assistants). Old Testament subjects:
    Jacob's Flight to Canaan and Return to his
    Father. Rome, Vatican, Loggie.
    Zuccarelli, Francesco. The Journey of Jacob.
    Private Collection.

SPANISH SCHOOL
    Orrente, Pedro. The Journey of Jacob. Detail.
    Family. Murcia, Museo Provincial.
    Orrente, Pedro. The Journey of Jacob. Detail:
    Patriarch. Murcia, Museo Provincial.
    Orrente, Pedro. The Journey of Jacob. Detail:
    Men with Chest. Murcia, Museo Provincial.
    Orrente, Pedro. The Departure of Jacob. Detail:
    Rachael. Madrid, Colegio San Anton.

71 C 31 94   GENESIS 31:33-35   LABAN SEARCHES THE
TENTS AND BELONGINGS OF JACOB TO FIND THE
TERAPHIM

DUTCH SCHOOL
    Lastmann, Pieter P. Laban searching for the
    images. Bologne-sur-Mer (Pas-de-Calais),
    Musée de Beaux-Arts et d'Archéologie.

    Moeyaert, Claes Cornelisz. Laban Searching
    for his Gods. 1647. Detroit, Institute
    of Arts, 57.17.
    Steen, Jan. Laban seeks images hidden by
    Rachel. Leyden, Stedelijk Museum.

FRENCH SCHOOL
    Boucher, François. Laban Searching for his
    Gods. New York, Private Collection.
    Bourdon, Sébastien, Copy after. Laban Searching
    for his Gods. Paris, Louvre, Musée du,
    INV. 2801.
    Bourdon, Sébastien. Rachel Hiding the Idols
    of her Father. Louisville, Ky., J.B.
    Speed Art Museum, 69.22.
    La Hyre, Laurent de. Laban Seeking his Idols.
    1647. Paris, Louvre.
    Saint-Aubin, Gabriel de. Laban Searching
    for his Gods. c.1753. Cleveland, Museum
    of Art, 65.548.

GERMAN SCHOOL
    Roos, Johann Heinrich. Laban Searching for
    the Images Stolen by Rachael. Sotheby
    and Co., London (Sale, June 3, 1981, No.35).

ITALIAN SCHOOL
    Tiepolo, G.B. Laban Searches Rachael's Tent.
    Decorations. Palazzo Arcivescovile, Galleria.

SPANISH SCHOOL
    Murillo. Laban Searches for his Stolen House-
    hold Gods in Rachel's Tent. c.1660. Cleve-
    land, Museum of Art.

71 C 31 94 1   GENESIS 31:34-35   RACHEL HIDES THE
TERAPHIM IN A CAMEL'S SADDLE AND SITS
ON IT

DUTCH SCHOOL
    Bylert, Jan van. Laban and Rachel. Rotterdam,
    Museum Boymans, 1104.

FRENCH SCHOOL
    Bourdon, Sébastien. Rachael Hiding the Idols
    of her Father. Louisville, Ky., J.B.
    Speed Art Museum, 69.22.
    Le Moyne, F. Laban and Rachel.
    Saint-Aubin, Gabriel de. Laban Searching
    for His Household Gods. Paris, Louvre,
    Musée du, RF 1939.5.

71 C 31 95   GENESIS 31:44-54   JACOB AND LABAN MAKE
AN ALLIANCE: A PILE OF STONE IS ERECTED
AND AN ANIMAL IS SACRIFICED

FLEMISH SCHOOL
    Stalbemt, Adriaen van. The Reconciliation
    of Jacob and Laban. Christie, Manson
    and Woods (Sale, London, Dec. 2, 1983
    [TORINO-2790], No. 62).

ITALIAN SCHOOL
    Cortona, Pietro da. Alliance of Jacob and
    Laban. Paris, Louvre.
    Cortona, Pietro da. Scene from the story
    of Jacob version in Paris, Louvre. Holkam
    Hall, Collection Earl of Leicester.

71 C 32   STORY OF JACOB (PART II)

ITALIAN SCHOOL
    Bassano, Jacopo. Return of Jacob from Canaan.
    Venice, (Ducal Palace) Palazzo Ducale.
    Gozzoli, Benozzo. Old Testament and other
    subjects: Meeting of Jacob and Esau. Detail:
    Group of men. Pisa, Camposanto.

71 C 32 13   GENESIS 32:9-12   JACOB PRAYS TO GOD
TO SAVE HIM FROM ESAU

DUTCH SCHOOL
    Niewland, Willem van. Jacob Praying. 1644.
    Lille, Palais des Beaux-Arts.

71 C 32 2 GENESIS 32:24-32 JACOB AND THE ANGEL

DUTCH SCHOOL
   Flinck, Govert. Jacob and the Angel. 1653.
      Jerusalem, Israel Museum.

GERMAN SCHOOL
   Seekatz, Johann Konrad. Jacob Wrestling with
      the Angel. Sacramento, Crocker Art Gallery,
      1872.466.

ITALIAN SCHOOL
   Vignali, Jacopo. Jacob and the Angel. c.1637.
      Florence, Palazzo Uffizi, 5578.

71 C 32 21 GENESIS 32:22-23 JACOB SENDS HIS FAMILY
      AND CARAVAN ACROSS THE RIVER JABBOK, AND
      STAYS BEHIND

ITALIAN SCHOOL
   Andrea di Leone. Voyage of Jacob. c.1633.
      Vienna, Kunsthistorisches Museum, Inv. no.
      6786.
   Castiglione, G.B. Jacob's return. Dresden,
      Gallery.
   Castiglione, G.B. The Return of Jacob. Florence,
      Palazzo Uffizi, S. Marco e Cenacoli, 50.

71 C 32 22 GENESIS 32:24-31 JACOB WRESTLES WITH
      THE ANGEL (OR MAN) TILL DAYBREAK; JACOB'S
      THIGH IS PUT OUT OF JOINT

BRITISH SCHOOL
   Ricketts, Charles. Jacob Wrestling with the
      Angel. Oxford, University, Ashmolean Museum,
      A34.

EARLY MEDIEVAL AND BYZANTINE
   Byzantine school, Wall painting, Istanbul.
      Lunette: Jacob Wrestling with the Angel.
      14th century. Istanbul, Mosque Kahrié. Parec-
      clesion, western bay, north wall.
   Byzantine school, Wall painting, Prizren.
      Story of Jacob: Jacob's dream, Jacob wrestling
      with angel. Fresco. 14th century. Prizren,
      Yugoslavia. Bogorodica Ljeviska, Exonarthex,
      west wall.

DUTCH SCHOOL
   Breenbergh, Bartholomeus. Jacob wrestling with
      the angel. Amsterdam, Rijksmuseum, 620.
   Pynas, Jan. Jacob Struggling with an Angel.
      Sotheby and Co., London (Sale, Dec. 12,
      1984, [IVY] No. 202).
   Rembrandt. Jacob Wrestling with the Angel.
      Berlin, Staaliche Museen, 828.
   Uytenbroeck, Moses van. Jacob Wrestling with
      the Angel. Sacramento, Crocker Art Gallery.

FLEMISH SCHOOL
   Franck, Franz, I, Studio of. Flemish Reliquary
      Chest painted with scenes from the Old Testa-
      ment. Detail: Drawer: Jacob Wrestling with
      the Angel. c.1600. Sarasota, Fla., Ringling
      Museum of Art, SN 1950.

FRENCH SCHOOL
   Delacroix, Eugène. Chapelle des Saints-Anges.
      Decoration. 1861. Paris, S. Sulpice.
   Delacroix, Eugène. Jacob Wrestling with the
      Angel. Variant of fresco at St. Sulpice,
      Paris. Vienna, Kunsthistorisches Museum.
   Denis, Maurice. Jacob wrestling with the Angel.
      1893. Lausanne, Collection Paul Joséfowitz.
   Gauguin, Paul. Jacob wrestling with the angel.
      Edinburgh, National Gallery.
   Moreau, Gustave. Jacob and the angel. Harvard
      University, Fogg Art Museum, 1943.266.

GERMAN SCHOOL
   Beich, Joachim Franz. Landscape with Jacob
      and the Angel. Rome, Collection A. Caraceni.

ITALIAN SCHOOL
   Gugliemlmo da Marcilla. Scenes from the
      Old and New Testaments: Struggle of Jacob
      with the angel. Arezzo, Cathedral.
   Italian school, 17th century ? Jacob fighting
      with the angel. Rome, Palazzo Barberini.
   Lazzarini, Gregorio. Jacob Wrestling with
      the Angel. Brunswick, Landesmuseum, 1031.
   Rosa, Salvatore. Jacob wrestling with an
      angel. Chatsworth, Collection Duke of
      Devonshire.
   Tornioli, Niccolo. Jacob battling with an
      angel. Bologna, S. Paulo.

SPANISH SCHOOL
   Sert, José María. Murals with scenes from
      the Old and New Testaments. Panel: Jacob's
      struggle with the angel. Vich, Cathedral.

71 C 32 22 1 GENESIS 32:28-29 JACOB RECEIVES
      A NEW NAME, ISRAEL, AND IS BLESSED BY
      THE ANGEL

SPANISH SCHOOL
   Antolínez, Francisco. Jacob and the angel.
      Seville, Cathedral.

71 C 32 32 GENESIS 33:1-15 THE MEETING BETWEEN
      ESAU AND JACOB

BRITISH SCHOOL
   Watts, G.F. Meeting of Jacob and Esau. Compton
      (Surrey), Watts Picture Gallery (R.A.
      Ex. of Brit. Art, London, 1934, no.592).

DUTCH SCHOOL
   Cornelisz, Cornelis. The Meeting of Jacob
      and Esau. Princeton, University, Museum
      of Art.
   Delff, Jacob Willemsz I. The Reconciliation
      of Jacob and Esau. Vienna, Kunsthistorisches
      Museum, 1062.
   Dutch school, 17th century. The Meeting of
      Jacob and Esau. Christie, Manson and Woods,
      London (Sale, May 28, 1982, No. 30).
   Horst, G.W. Jacob and Esau. Stockholm, Museum,
      1046.
   Horst, Gerrit Willemsz. Jacob and his Family
      Meeting with Esau. Cassel, Staatliche
      Kunstsammlungen.
   Hogers, Jacob. Jacob and Esau. Amsterdam,
      Rijksmuseum, 1209.
   Uytenbroeck, Moses van. Jacob Wrestling with
      the Angel. Bader, Alfred - Collection
      (Milwaukee).
   Victors, Jan. Jacob and his Family Meet Esau.
      Cassel, Staatliche Kunstsammlungen, 253a.
   Werff, Adriaen van der. The Reconciliation
      of Jacob and Esau. Sarasota, Fla., Ringling
      Museum of Art, SN 373.

FLEMISH SCHOOL
   Franck, Frans, II. Jacob and the angel (?)
   Hoecke, Robert van den. The Reconciliation
      of Esau and Jacob. Vienna, Kunsthistor-
      isches Museum, 691.
   Rubens, Peter Paul. Meeting of Esau and Jacob.
      Munich, Staatsgalerie Schleissheim, 1302.
   Rubens, P.P. Reconciliation of Jacob and
      Esau. Sketch. Edinburgh, National Gallery.
   Rubens, P.P. The Reconciliation of Esau and
      Jacob. Rome, Galleria Colonna.
   Valckenborch, Martin van. Reconciliation
      of Esau and Jacob.Serge Philipson Collection.

GENESIS

GERMAN SCHOOL
Schoenfeld, Johann Heinrich. The Reconciliation
of Jacob and Esau. c.1636. Vienna, Kunsthistorisches Museum, 1143.

ITALIAN SCHOOL
Italian school, 16th century. Reconciliation
between Jacob and Esau. Rome, Palazzo Altieri.

71 C 32 41 GENESIS 34:2 THE RAPE OF DINAH BY SHECHEM

ITALIAN SCHOOL
Bugiardini, Giuliano. The Abduction of Dina.
1531. Vienna, Kunsthistorisches Museum.

71 C 32 6 GENESIS 35:16-21 DEATH OF RACHEL

ITALIAN SCHOOL
Furini, Francesco. Death of Rachael. Schleissheim, Neues Schloss, Gallery, 9884.

71 C 32 62 GENESIS 35:16-19 BIRTH OF BENJAMIN:
RACHEL DIES IN CHILDBIRTH

ITALIAN SCHOOL
Cignaroli, Gianbettino. Death of Rachel. Venice,
Academy.
Furini, Francesco. Death of Rachael. Schleiss-
heim, Neues Schloss Gallery, 9884.
Furini, Francesco. Copy. The Death of Rachel.
Paris, Louvre, Musée du, 704.

71 C 33 2 GENESIS 38 STORY OF JUDAH AND TAMAR

ITALIAN SCHOOL
Bassano, Jacopo. Judah and Tamar. Florence,
Palazzo Uffizi, 927.

71 C 33 27 GENESIS 38:14-15 TAMAR CHANGES FROM
HER WIDOW'S CLOTHES AND COVERS HER FACE
AFTER THE MANNER OF THE PROSTITUTES; SITTING
IN AN OPEN PLACE BY THE WAY OF TIMNATH SHE
AWAITS JUDAH

DUTCH SCHOOL
Gelder, Aert de. Judah and Tamar. 1667. Hoog-
steder-Naumann, Ltd. - Gallery (New York).
Gelder, Aert de. Judah and Tamar. 1681. Bader,
Alfred - Collection (Milwaukee).
Gelder, Aert de. Judah and Tamar. The Hague,
Royal Gallery, 40.
Lastman, Pieter P. Judah and Tamar. Schapiro,
E. - Collection (London).

ITALIAN SCHOOL
Lanfranco, Giovanni. Judah and Tamar. Rome,
Palazzo Barberini.

71 C 33 27 1 GENESIS 38:18 JUDAH'S LOVE-AFFAIR
WITH TAMAR; HE GIVES HER HIS SIGNET(-RING),
BRACELETS AND STAFF

DUTCH SCHOOL
Bol, Ferdinand. Judah and Tamar. 1644. Boston,
Museum of Fine Arts, 17.3268.
Eeckhout, Gerbrand van den. Judah and Tamar.
1645. Moscow, Pushkin State Museum of Fine
Arts.
Eeckhout, Gerbrand van den. The Levite and
the Prostitute in Gibea. 1645. Berlin, Staat-
liche Museen, 1771.
Gelder, Aert de. Judah and Tamar. c.1700. The
Hague, Royal Gallery, 40.
Gelder, Aert de. Judah and Tamar. Vienna,Academy.

FLEMISH SCHOOL
Coninzloo, Gillis III, van. Judah and Tamar;
a pair with Saul and the Witch of Endor.
Christie, Manson and Woods (Sale, London,
[TOLEDO-2659] May 27, 1983, No. 161).
Hemessen, Jan Sanders van. Judah and Tamar.
Hellberg - Collection (Stockholm).

FRENCH SCHOOL
Vernet, Horace. Judith and Tamar. 1840. London,

71 D STORY OF JOSEPH

ITALIAN SCHOOL
Pontormo, Jacopo da. Joseph and his kindred
in Egypt. c.1518. London, National Gallery,
1131.

71 D 1 STORY OF JOSEPH (PART I)

ITALIAN SCHOOL
Andrea del Sarto. Story of Joseph. Left:
Joseph Recounts Dream. Center: Joseph
Departs for Shechem. Right: Joseph's Brothers
Betray Him. Florence, Pitti Gallery.
Biagio d'Antonio. History of Joseph (Two
cassone panels). New York, Metropolitan
Museum, 21.100.69.
Biagio d'Antonio. History of Joseph (Two
cassone panels). 1.Jacob tells Joseph
to join his brothers. 2.Joseph walks to
his brothers. 3.Joseph pulled from well
and sold. 4.Merchants leave with Joseph.
5.Brothers show Jacob the blood-stained
coat. 6. Brothers depart for Egypt to
buy corn. Malibu, J. Paul Getty Museum.
70.PA.41.
Gozzoli, Benozzo. Old Testament and other
subjects: Innocence of Joseph.Camposanto.

71 D 11 5 GENESIS 37:5-11 JOSEPH'S DREAMS

DUTCH SCHOOL
Victors, Jan. Joseph Telling his Dreams.
Hartford, Conn., Wadsworth Atheneum, 1958.
266.

EARLY MEDIEVAL AND BYZANTINE
Byzantine school, Wall painting, Castelseprio.
Dream of Joseph. Detail. Fresco. 8th century.
Castelseprio, S. Maria foris Portas. Apse
wall, to the right of center.

ITALIAN SCHOOL
Bartolo di Fredi. Scenes from the Old Testament: Joseph's dream. S. Gimignano, Collegiata.

71 D 11 53 GENESIS 37:5-11 JOSEPH RELATING HIS
DREAMS (THE TWO DREAMS COMBINED)

DUTCH SCHOOL
Rembrandt. Joseph relating his dreams. 1637.
Amsterdam, Rijksmuseum.

FRENCH SCHOOL
Tissot, James Jacques Joseph. Illustrations
of the Hebrew Bible. No.53: Joseph Reveals
his Dream to his Brethren. 1896-1903.
New York, Jewish Museum, 52.120.

ITALIAN SCHOOL
Gozzoli, Benozzo. Old Testament and other
subjects: Innocence of Joseph. Detail:
Joseph telling Jacob of his dream. Pisa,
Camposanto.
Raphael (and assistants). Old Testament sub-
jects: Joseph telling his dreams to his
brethren. Rome, Vatican, Loggie.

71 D 12 GENESIS 37:12-35 JOSEPH SOLD INTO SLAVERY
AND TAKEN TO EGYPT

ITALIAN SCHOOL
Italian school, 13th century. Scenes from
the Old Testament: Joseph sold by his
brethren. Assisi, S. Francesco, upper

71 D 12 1   GENESIS 37:13-14 JACOB SENDS JOSEPH TO
            HIS BROTHERS WHO ARE TAKING CARE OF THEIR
            FATHER'S FLOCK AT SHECHEM

FRENCH SCHOOL
    French school, Wall painting, St. Savin. Scenes
        from the Old Testament: Jacob sends Joseph
        to join his brothers. 11th century. St.
        Savin, (Vienne). Nave.

71 D 12 41   GENESIS 37:24 JOSEPH IS THROWN INTO
             A PIT (USUALLY DEPICTED AS A WELL OR CISTERN)

DUTCH SCHOOL
    Master of the Story of Joseph. Series of six
        round panels. Panel 3: Joseph cast into
        the pit. Berlin, Staatliche Museen, 5390.
    Moeyaert, Claes Cornelisz. Joseph im brunnen.
        Dresden, Gallery.
    Pynas, Jacob. Joseph being Cast by his Brethren
        into the Pit. Dresden, Staatliche Kunstsamm-
        lungen, 1547 A.

FRENCH SCHOOL
    Collantes, Francisco. Joseph and his Brethren
        at the Well. Christie, Manson and Woods
        (Sale, London, Dec. 2, 1983 [TORINO-2790],
        No. 92).
    Richomme, Jules. Joseph and his Brothers.
        Paris, Louvre, Musée du, R.F. 3145.

ITALIAN SCHOOL
    Bartolo di Fredi. Scenes from the Old Testament:
        Joseph put into a pit by his brothers.
        S. Gimignano, Collegiata.

SPANISH SCHOOL
    Murillo. Joseph and his Brethren. London,
        Wallace Collection, P 46.

71 D 12 51   GENESIS 37:28 JOSEPH IS PULLED OUT OF
             THE PIT

AUSTRIAN SCHOOL
    Bocksberger, Hans, the elder. Joseph and his
        brothers. Fresco decorations. 16th century.
        Neuburg an der Donau, Schlosskapelle.

DUTCH SCHOOL
    Engelbrechtsz, Cornelis. Scene from the story
        of Joseph. Vienna, Gallery.
    Swanevelt, Hermann van. Joseph Being Sold
        into Slavery. Christie, Manson and Woods
        (Sale, London [TREVI-2719] July 22, 1983,
        No. 23).

71 D 12 52   GENESIS 37:28 JOSEPH IS SOLD FOR TWENTY
             PIECES OF SILVER

DUTCH SCHOOL
    Cuyp, Benjamin. Joseph Sold into Slavery.
        Christie, Manson and Woods (Sale, London
        [TINKER-3144] May 24, 1985, No. 1).
    Grebber, Pieter Fransz de, Attributed to. Joseph
        Sold by his Brethren. Sotheby and Co., London
        (Sale, Oct. 24, 1984, [DAHLIA] No. 84).
    Horst, Gerrit Willemsz. Joseph Sold for 30
        Pieces of Silver. c.1640. Hoogsteder - Gallery
        (The Hague).
    Neck, Jan van. Joseph Being Sold into Slavery.
        Milwaukee (Wisconsin), Art Center.
    Swanevelt, Herman van. Joseph being sold
        into slavery. Christie, Manson and Woods
        (Sale, London [TREVI-2719], July 22, 1983,
        No. 23).

FRENCH SCHOOL
    Bourdon, Sebastien. Selling of Joseph. Petworth
        (Sussex), Petworth House, 18.
    Chassériau, Théodore. Joseph Sold by his Brothers.
        Paris, Louvre, Musée du, R.F. 3881.
    Decamps, A.G. Joseph sold by his brothers.

GERMAN SCHOOL
    Daysinger, Johann Lorenz. Joseph Sold by
        his Brothers. Budapest, Museum of Fine
        Arts, 9831.
    Overbeck, Johann Friedrich. Selling of Joseph
        by his Brethren. 1815-17. Berlin, Staat-
        liche Museen, 581.

ITALIAN SCHOOL
    Amigoni, Jacopo. Joseph is Sold by his Brothers.
        Stockholm, University, 90.
    Biago d'Antonio. History of Joseph (two cassone
        panels). Joseph sold to merchants. Malibu,
        Ca., J. Paul Getty Museum, 70.PA.41; New
        York, Metropolitan Museum, 32.100.69.
    Carlone, Giovanni Battista (Rovio). Joseph
        sold into bondage by his brethren. Bob
        Jones University Collection, (Greenville,
        S.C.).
    Diziani, Gaspare. The Selling of Joseph.
        Sotheby and Co., London (Sale, New York
        [5104] Nov. 3, 1983, No. 177).
    Francesco di Giorgio. Story of Joseph: Joseph
        sold by his brethren. Siena, Academy.
    Guardi, Francesco. Joseph Sold by his Brothers.
        Finney - Collection (Paris).
    Guardi, Giovanni Antonio. Joseph Sold by
        his Brothers. Lutomirsky - Collection
        (Milan).
    Italian school, 17th century, (Emilian).
        The Sale of Joseph. Rovigo, Pinacoteca
        dell'Accademia dei Concordi, 272.287.
    Jacopo di Paolo. Scenes from the Old Testament.
        Joseph and his brothers. Mezzaratta (near
        Bologna), Church.
    Maffei, Francesco. Joseph sold by his brethren.
        New York, Collection Jacob M. Heimann.
    Passante, Bartolommeo. Joseph sold into slavery.
        Christie, Manson and Woods (Sale, London,
        July 9, 1982, No. 7).
    Piazzetta, G.B. Joseph and his brethren.
        New York, Metropolitan Museum.
    Raphael (and assistants).Old Testament subjects:
        Joseph sold by his brethren. Rome, Vatican,
        Loggie.
    Rosselli, Matteo. Joseph sold by his brothers.
        1620-25. Florence, Palazzo Uffizi, GDSU
        19198.

71 D 12 71 1   GENESIS 37:31 JOSEPH'S BROTHERS
               STAIN HIS COAT WITH A KID'S BLOOD

FRENCH SCHOOL
    Vernet, Horace. Joseph's Coat. 1853. London,
        Wallace Collection, P 349.

71 D 12 8   GENESIS 37:32 JOSEPH'S BLOOD-STAINED
            COAT IS BROUGHT AND SHOWN TO JACOB

BRITISH SCHOOL
    Brown, Ford Madox. The coat of many colors.
        London, Tate Gallery, 4584.
    Brown, Ford Madox. The Coat of Many Colors.
        Liverpool, Walker Art Gallery.

DUTCH SCHOOL
    Flinck, Govert. Joseph's Brothers Showing
        his Blood-stained Coat to Jacob, his Father.
        Helsinki, Ateneum.
    Rembrandt. Joseph's two brothers showing
        the bloody coat to Jacob.

FRENCH SCHOOL
    Bourdon, Sebastien, Follower of. Joseph's
        Brethren Displaying his Coat to Jacob.
        Christie, Manson and Woods (Sale, London,
        [TERNI-2813] Dec. 15-16, 1983, No. 71).
    Chagall, Marc. Illustrations from the Bible
        published by Vollard. No. 35: Jacob Mourns
        over Joseph's Coat. 1931. Nice (Alpes-
        Maritimes), Musée National Message Biblique
        Marc Chagall.

Lebouy, Auguste. Joseph's Robe Presented to
Jacob. 1841. Paris, École des Beaux-Arts
(Grand Prix de Rome).

ITALIAN SCHOOL
Carlone, Giovanni Battista (Rovio). Jacob shown
the coat of Joseph. Bob Jones University
Collection, (Greenville, S.C.).
Guercino, Copy. Reuben with his Younger Brother.
Sarasota, Fla., Ringling Museum of Art.
SN 123.

SPANISH SCHOOL
Velásquez. Joseph's Bloody Coat Brought to
Jacob. 1630. El Escorial, Monastery.

71 D 12 81   GENESIS 37:34   JACOB RENDING HIS GARMENTS
ON RECOGNIZING THE ROBE

DUTCH SCHOOL
Eeckhout, Gerbrand van den. Jacob is shown
Joseph's Coat. Derby, Earl of - Collection
(Knowsley, Lancashire).

GERMAN SCHOOL
Schadow, Wilhelm von. Frescoes from the Casa
Cartholdy, Rome. Berlin, Staatliche Museen.

71 D 12 82   GENESIS 37:35   JOSEPH BEWAILED AS DEAD
BY HIS FATHER; THE SONS AND DAUGHTERS ARE
UNABLE TO CONSOLE HIM

DUTCH SCHOOL
Flinck, Govert. Jacob Bewails over Joseph's
Bloody Coat. 1655. Helsinki, Ateneum.

ITALIAN SCHOOL
Cagnacci (Guido Canlassi). Jacob Crying. Also
attributed to Paolo Emilio Besenzi. Bologna,
Pinacoteca Nazionale, 6379.
Guercino. Jacob mourning over Joseph's coat.
Greenville, S.C., Bob Jones University Col-
lection, 1962 cat. 72.

71 D 13 1   GENESIS 37:36 - 39:1   JOSEPH IS SOLD TO
POTIPHAR

FRENCH SCHOOL
French school, Wall painting, St. Savin. Scenes
from the Old Testament: Joseph sold to Potiphar. 11th century. St.Savin,(Vienne),Nave.

ITALIAN SCHOOL
Pontormo, Jacopo da. Scenes from the story
of Joseph. Detail: Joseph sold to Potiphar.
Henfield (Sussex), Collection Lady Salmond.
On loan to the National Gallery, London.

71 D 13 3   GENESIS 39:7   POTIPHAR'S WIFE TRYING TO
SEDUCE JOSEPH

FLEMISH SCHOOL
Franck, Frans, II. Scenes from the Life of
Joseph. Christie, Manson and Woods, London,
(Sale, April 23, 1982, No. 28).

GERMAN SCHOOL
Knüpfer, Nicolaus. Joseph and Potiphar's Wife.
Schapiro, E. - Collection (London).
Schadow, Wilhelm von. Frescoes from the Casa
Cartholdy, Rome. Berlin, Staatliche Museen.
Veit, Philipp. Sketch of frescoes from the
Casa Bartholdy (Palazzo Zuccarri), Rome.
Joseph and Potiphar's Wife. 1818. Berlin,
Staatliche Museen, Nr. 47.

ITALIAN SCHOOL
Cantarini, Simone. Joseph and Potiphar's Wife.
Dresden, Staatliche Kunstsammlungen, 382.
Cignani, Carlo. The Chastity of Joseph. Copen-
hagen, Art Museum, Sp 125.
Cignani, Carlo. Joseph and Potiphar's Wife.
Sotheby and Co. (Sale, London, March 9,
1983, No. 44).

Corona, Lionardo. Joseph and Potiphar's Wife.
Brunswick, Landesmuseum, 1016.
Gandolfi, Gaetano. Joseph and Potiphar's
Wife. Sotheby and Co., London (Sale, Nov.17,
1982, No.67).
Italian school, 18th century. Joseph and
Potiphar's Wife. Budapest, Museum of Fine
Arts, 9788.
Montelatici, Francesco (Cecco Bravo). Joseph
and Potiphar's Wife. Florence, Palazzo
Uffizi, 9450.
Samacchini, Orazio. Joseph and Potiphar's
Wife. Florence, Palazzo Uffizi, 1515.

71 D 13 31   GENESIS 39:12-13   POTIPHAR'S WIFE CATCHES
JOSEPH BY HIS ROBE, USUALLY WHILE LYING
IN BED; JOSEPH ESCAPES LEAVING HIS CLOAK
BEHIND IN HER HANDS (POSSIBLY WITH A NAKED
CHILD LYING IN A CRIB)

DUTCH SCHOOL
Cleve, Cornelis van. Joseph and Potiphar's
Wife. Christie, Manson and Woods (Sale,
New York, Jan. 15, 1985, [CAROL-5808,
No. 106).
Uytewael, Joachim Antonisz. Joseph and
Potiphar's Wife. Christie, Manson and Woods,
(Sale, London, June 28, 1974, No.25).

FRENCH SCHOOL
Chagall, Marc. Illustrations from the Bible
published by Vollard. No.36: Joseph and
Potiphar's Wife. 1931. Nice (Alpes-Maritimes)
Musée National Message Biblique Marc Chagall.
Champaigne, Philippe de. Joseph and Potiphar's
Wife. c.1644-48. London, Private Collection.
Troy, Jean François de. Joseph and Potiphar's
Wife. 1744. Christie, Manson and Woods(Sale,
New York, Jan. 15, 1985 [CAROL-5808],No.81).

GERMAN SCHOOL
König, Johann. Joseph and Potiphar's Wife.
Nuremberg, Germanic Museum.

ITALIAN SCHOOL
Allori, Alessandro. Chastity of Joseph. Flor-
ence, Uffizi.
Baglioni, Giovanni. Potiphar's wife. Harvard
University, Fogg Art Museum, 1969.67.
Biliverti, Giovanni. Joseph and the wife
of Potiphar. Florence, Palazzo Uffizi.
Biliverti, Giovanni. Joseph and the Wife
of Potiphar. Copy of painting in the Uffizi,
Florence. Rome, Palazzo Barbarini.
Cignani, Carlo. Joseph and Potiphar's wife.
Dresden, Gallery.
Cignani, Carlo. The Chastity of Joseph. Copen-
hagen, Art Museum, Sp 125.
Crecolini, Giovanni Antonio. Joseph and Poti-
phar's wife. 1716. Penicuik House, Collection
Clerk.
Falciatore, Filippo. Joseph and Potiphar's
Wife. c.1750. Sacramento, Crocker Art
Gallery.
Forabosco, Girolamo. The Chastity of Joseph.
Rovigo, Pinacoteca dell'Accademia dei
Concordi, 399.64.
Francesco di Giorgio. Story of Joseph. Detail:
Joseph and Potiphar's wife. Siena, Academy.
Gentileschi, Orazio. Joseph and Potiphar's
Wife. England, Royal Collection.
Guardi, Giovanni Antonio. Joseph and Potiphar's
wife. Milan, Collection Lutomirski.
Italian school, 17th century. Joseph and
Potiphar's wife. Cassel, Staatliche Kunst-
sammlungen, 585.
Lanfranco, Giovanni. Joseph and Potiphar's
Wife. After 1614? Rome, Palazzo Mattei.
Lanfranco, Giovanni. Joseph and Potiphar's
Wife (Chastity of Joseph). Rome, Villa
Borghese Gallery.
Mazzoni, Sebastiano. Joseph and Potiphar's
wife. Private Collection.

Pagani, Gasparo. The Chastity of Joseph.
Florence, Palazzo Uffizi.
Preti, Mattia. Joseph and Potiphar's Wife.
Colnaghi and Co., London.
Raphael (and assistants).Old Testament subjects:
Joseph and Potiphar's wife. Rome, Vatican,
Loggie.
Samacchini, Orazio. Chastity of Joseph. 1570-
75. Florence, Palazzo Uffizi, 1515.
Solimena, Francesco. Joseph and Potiphar's
Wife. Brunswick, Landesmuseum.
Tintoretto (Jacopo Robusti). Joseph and Poti-
phar's Wife. 1555. Madrid, Prado, 422.
Trevisani, Francesco. Joseph and the wife of
Potiphar. Pommersfelden, Collection Dr.
Karl Grof von Schönborn-Wiesentheid.

71 D 13 4 GENESIS 39:16-18 POTIPHAR'S WIFE BEFORE
HER HUSBAND: SHE ACCUSES JOSEPH OF TRYING
TO VIOLATE HER, USING THE CLOAK AS EVIDENCE

DUTCH SCHOOL
Lucas van Leyden. Potiphar's wife with Joseph's
shirt. c.1512. Rotterdam, Museum Boymans,
Inv. 2455.
Rembrandt. Joseph accused by Potiphar's wife.
Washington, D.C., National Gallery, 79.
Rembrandt. Joseph Accused by Potiphar's Wife.
1655. Berlin, Staatliche Museen, 828H.

FLEMISH SCHOOL
Franck, Frans, II. Scenes from the Life of
Joseph. Christie, Manson and Woods, London.
(Sale, April 23, 1982, No. 28).

FRENCH SCHOOL
French school, Wall painting, St. Savin. Nave:
Scenes from the Old Testament: Joseph accused
by Potiphar's wife and cast into prison.
11th century. St. Savin, Vienne.
Hallé, N. Joseph and Potiphar's Wife. 1744.
Chicago, University of, David and Alfred
Smart Gallery.
Troy, Jean François de. Joseph accused by Poti-
phar's Wife. 1745. Christie, Manson and
Woods (Sale, New York, Jan. 15, 1985, [CAROL-
5808], No. 82).

71 D 13 5 GENESIS 39:20 JOSEPH IS ARRESTED
AND SENT TO PRISON

FLEMISH SCHOOL
Franck, Frans, II. Scenes from the Life of
Joseph. Christie, Manson and Wood, London
(Sale, April 23, 1982, No. 28).

ITALIAN SCHOOL
Granacci, Francesco. Joseph taken to prison
(formerly attributed to Pontormo). Florence,
Palazzo Uffizi.

71 D 14 42 1 GENESIS 40:6-19 JOSEPH INTERPRETING
THE DREAM

DUTCH SCHOOL
Eeckhout, Gerbrand van den. Joseph Interpreting
the Dreams of Pharoah's Butler and Baker.
1643. Bob Jones University Collection, (Greenville, S.C.).
Rembrandt, School of. Joseph and the Baker.
c.1650. Bader,Alfred - Collection (Milwaukee).

FRENCH SCHOOL
Valentin de Boullogne. Joseph, the interpreter
of dreams. Rome, Palazzo Borghese.

ITALIAN SCHOOL
Lanfranco, Giovanni. Joseph in prison. Rome,
Palazzo Mattei.
Langetti, Giovanni Battista. Joseph Interpreting
the Baker's Dream. Sotheby and Co., London
(Sale, April 7, 1982, No. 100).

71 D 14 5 GENESIS 40:6-19 JOSEPH INTERPRETING
THE DREAMS (THE TWO DREAMS COMBINED)

AMERICAN SCHOOL
West, Benjamin, Follower of. Joseph and the
Pharaoh's Butler. Sotheby and Co., London
(Sale, [DANDELION] Dec. 21, 1983, No.45).

DUTCH SCHOOL
Flinck, Govert. Joseph Interpreting the Baker's
and Butler's Dreams in Prison. c.1640.
Wijn, A.H. de - Collection (Amsterdam).
Victors, Jan. Joseph in Prison. Amsterdam,
Rijksmuseum 2552.

FRENCH SCHOOL
French school, 15th century, School of Picardy.
Dream of the chief cupbearer.Lyon,Collection
Edouard Aynard (sold 1913).
Van Loo, Carle van. Joseph Interpreting Dreams.
Christie, Manson and Woods (Sale,New York,
June 12, 1981, No. 13).

GERMAN SCHOOL
Loth, Johann Carl, Attributed to. Joseph
Interpreting the Prisoner's Dreams. Sotheby
and Co., London (Sale, New York, Nov.7,
1984, [MISSOURI] No. 59).
Schadow, Wilhelm von. Joseph's Dream. 1812.
Munich, Neue Pinakothek, 9408.
Schadow, Wilhelm von. Frescoes from the Casa
Cartholdy, Rome. Joseph's dream in prison.
Berlin, Staatliche Museen.

ITALIAN SCHOOL
Italian school, 17th century. Joseph telling
his dreams in prison. Florence, Palazzo
Uffizi, 1890, n. 6511.
Italian school, 18th century. Joseph in Prison;
the dreams of the other prisoners. Budapest,
Museum of Fine Arts, 953.
Langetti, Giovanni Battista.Joseph interpreting
dreams in prison. Budapest, Museum of
Fine Arts, 6387.
Strozzi, Bernardo. Joseph as the interpreter
of dreams. Munich, Staatsgalerie Schlessheim,
6651.
Strozzi, Bernardo. Joseph Interprets a Dream.
Genoa, Palazzo Spinola.

71 D 14 6 GENESIS 40:21-22 THE FULFILLMENT OF
THE DREAMS: PHARAOH RESTORES THE BUTLER
TO HIS FORMER POSITION, BUT HAS THE BAKER
HANGED

ITALIAN SCHOOL
Pontormo, Jacopo da. Scenes from the story
of Joseph. Detail:the Baker led to execution.
Henfield (Sussex), Collection Lady Salmond
On loan to the National Gallery, London.

71 D 15 PHARAOH'S DREAMS INTERPRETED

FRENCH SCHOOL
Chagall, Marc. Illustrations from the Bible
published by Vollard. No. 37: Joseph Inter-
prets the Dream of Pharaoh. 1931. Nice
(Alpes-Maritimes), Musée National Message
Biblique Marc Chagall.

GERMAN SCHOOL
Cornelius, Peter von. Frescoes from the Casa
Bartholdy,Rome:Joseph interpreting Pharaoh's
dream. 1815-17.Berlin,Staatliche Museen,587.

ITALIAN SCHOOL
Andrea del Sarto. Story of Joseph. Detail:
Pharaoh's Dream. Florence, Pitti Gallery.
Bastiani, Lazzaro. Joseph Interpreting Pharaoh's
Dream. Columbia, S.C., Museum of Art.

71 D 15 11   GENESIS 41:1-4   PHARAOH'S FIRST DREAM:
SEVEN FAT COWS ARE DEVOURED BY SEVEN LEAN
COWS

ITALIAN SCHOOL
Pellegrino di Mariano. The Dream of the Pharaoh.
Cologne, Wallraf-Richartz Museum, 725.

71 D 15 5   GENESIS 41:15-36   JOSEPH INTERPRETING
PHARAOH'S DREAMS

FRENCH SCHOOL
French school, Wall painting, St. Savin. Scenes
from the Old Testament: Joseph explains
Pharaoh's dream. 11th century. St. Savin,
Vienne, Nave.

GERMAN SCHOOL
Cornelius, Peter von. Sketch of Frescoes from
the Casa Bartholdy (Palazzo Zuccari). Joseph
Interpreting the Pharaoh's Dream. 1818.
Berlin, Staaliche Museen, Nr. 47.

ITALIAN SCHOOL
Bastiani, Lazzari. Joseph Interpreting Pharaoh's
Dream. Columbia, S.C., Museum of Art, K.1553.
Italian school, 17th century (Neapolitan).
Joseph Interpreting the Dreams of Pharaoh.
Sarasota, Fla., Ringling Museum of Art,
SN 145.
Peruzzi, Baldassare. Salone di Studio. Vault
decorations, lunette: Joseph interpreting
the dreams of Pharaoh. Also attributed to
Perino del Vaga.Rome,Palazzo della Cancelleria.
Raphael (and assistants). Old Testament subjects:
Joseph interpreting Pharaoh's dream. Rome,
Vatican, Loggie.

71 D 15 52   GENESIS 41:26-27   INTERPRETATION OF THE
DREAM OF THE THIN AND THE FULL EARS OF CORN

FLEMISH SCHOOL
Flemish school, 16th century. Landscape with
Joseph being Sold by his Brothers. Rome,
Galleria Colonna.

GERMAN SCHOOL
Overbeck, Johann Friedrich. Selling of Joseph
by his brethren. 1815-17. Berlin, Staatliche
Museen, 581.

71 D 16   GENESIS 41:37-57   ELEVATION AND MARRIAGE
OF JOSEPH

FRENCH SCHOOL
French school, Wall painting, St. Savin. Scenes
from the Old Testament: story of Joseph.
11th century. St. Savin, Nave.

71 D 16 1   GENESIS 41:42-44   PHARAOH TAKES OFF HIS
SIGNET-RING AND PUTS IT ON JOSEPH'S FINGER:
JOSEPH IS APPOINTED OVERSEER

FRENCH SCHOOL
French school, Wall painting, St. Savin. Scenes
from the Old Testament: Pharaoh makes Joseph
ruler of Egypt. 11th century. St. Savin,
Vienne.

ITALIAN SCHOOL
Tiepolo, G.D. Joseph receiving Pharaoh's ring.
Dulwich Gallery, 158.

71 D 16 2   GENESIS 41:43-44   TRIUMPH OF JOSEPH

FRENCH SCHOOL
French school, Wall painting, St. Savin. Scenes
from the Old Testament: Joseph in the chariot
of Pharaoh. 11th century. St. Savin, Vienne,
Nave.

ITALIAN SCHOOL
Giaquinto, Corrado. Old Testament scenes:
the Triumph of Joseph. Aranjuez, Palacio
Real. Wall decorations, Dining room.

Guardi, Giovanni Antonio. The Triumph of
Joseph. Lutomirski - Collection (Milan).

71 D 16 42 11 GENESIS 41:56   JOSEPH OPENS THE
STOREHOUSES AND SELLS CORN

DUTCH SCHOOL
Lastman, P.P. Joseph selling corn in Egypt.
1612. Dublin, National Gallery.

FLEMISH SCHOOL
Diepenbeeck, Abraham van, attributed to.
Joseph selling corn to the Egyptians.
Also attributed to Bartholomeus. Hovingham
Hall, Collection Sir William Worsley.

71 D 17 3   GENESIS 42:6   ADMITTED IN JOSEPH'S PRES-
ENCE, THE BROTHERS BOW DOWN BEFORE HIM

BRITISH SCHOOL
Blake, William. Joseph's Brethren Bowing
before Him. Cambridge, University, Fitzwilliam Museum, 456B.

71 D 17 31   GENESIS 42:9-17   JOSEPH ACCUSES THEM
OF BEING SPIES AND THROWS THEM IN PRISON

ITALIAN SCHOOL
Bacchiacca, Francesco. Story of Joseph, the
Hebrew. Rome, Borghese Gallery.

71 D 17 52   GENESIS 42:24   JOSEPH COMES BACK, PICKS
OUT SIMON AND HAS HIM BOUND

BRITISH SCHOOL
Blake, William. Joseph Ordering Simeon to
be Bound. Exhibited.1785. Cambridge, University, Fitzwilliam Museum, 456A.
Blake, William. Joseph Ordering Simeon to
be Bound. Study. c.1785. Private Collection,
Milan.

71 D 17 71   GENESIS 42:27   AT THEIR CAMP ONE OF
THEM FINDS MONEY IN HIS SACK

FRENCH SCHOOL
Bourdon, Sebastien. The Finding of Money
in Benjamin's Sack. Also attributed to
Nicolas Bertin. Another version is also
located in Dublin, National Gallery, No.
1066. Dublin, National Gallery, 1684.

71 D 17 81   GENESIS 42:38   JACOB REFUSES TO HAVE
BENJAMIN TAKEN TO EGYPT IN SPITE OF REUBEN'S
EXHORTATION

FRENCH SCHOOL
Bézard, Jean Louis. Jacob Refusing to Send
Benjamin Away. 1829. Paris, École des
Beaux-Arts (Grand Prix de Rome).
Vauchelet, Théophile Auguste. Jacob Refusing
to Send Benjamin Away. 1829. Paris, École
des Beaux-Arts (Grand Prix de Rome).

71 D 18   GENESIS 48   SECOND JOURNEY OF JOSEPH'S
BROTHERS TO EGYPT

ITALIAN SCHOOL
Ferrari, Andrea. Joseph's brethren paying
homage to him. New York,Acquavella Galleries.
Italian school, 12th century. Old Testament
subjects. Details: Joseph and his brethren?
(poor condition). Ferentillo, S.Pietro
e S.Paolo, Wall decorations.

71 D 18 1   GENESIS 43:8-9   JUDAH PERSUADES THE
AFFLICTED JACOB TO CONSENT TO THE DEPARTURE
OF BENJAMIN

FLEMISH SCHOOL
Dyck, Anthony van. Benjamin and Judah. c.1655/
60. Chicago, Art Institute, 37.463.

71 D 18 11 GENESIS 43:14 JACOB'S FAREWELL TO BENJAMIN

DUTCH SCHOOL
    Fabritius, Bernard. The Departure of Benjamin.
    The Hague, Royal Gallery, 798.

71 D 18 4 GENESIS 43:26 WHEN JOSEPH GETS HOME,
HE RECEIVES HIS BROTHERS; THEY BOW DOWN
BEFORE HIM AND GIVE HIM THE PRESENTS

DUTCH SCHOOL
    Aertsen, Pieter. Joseph and his Brethren. A
    Pair with Jacob's Journey into Egypt. Chris-
    tie, Manson and Woods (Sale, London, March
    11, 1983, No. 84a).

GERMAN SCHOOL
    Cornelius, Peter von. Frescoes from the Casa
    Bartholdy, Rome: The meeting of Joseph and
    his brethren. 1815-17. Berlin, Staatliche
    Museen, 585.

ITALIAN SCHOOL
    Bacchiacca, Francesco. History of Joseph:
    (center) Brothers present gifts to Joseph.
    London, National Gallery.

71 D 18 5 GENESIS 43:33-34 THE FEAST: THE AMAZEMENT
OF JOSEPH'S BROTHERS AT BEING SEATED ACCORDING
TO THEIR AGE; BENJAMIN IS HONORED WITH EXTRA
FOOD

ITALIAN SCHOOL
    Bronzino, Copy after. The Feast Given by Joseph
    for his Brothers. Baltimore, Md., Walters
    Art Gallery, 37.1063.

71 D 19 GENESIS 44-45 THE MISSING CUP

ITALIAN SCHOOL
    Bacchiacca, Francesco. History of Joseph. London,
    National Gallery.
    Gozzoli, Benozzo. Old Testament and other sub-
    jects: Joseph made known to his brethren.
    Detail. Pisa, Camposanto.
    Granacci, Francesco. Joseph ordering the search
    for the goblet. Florence, Magazzini della
    Sopr. alle Gallerie.

71 D 19 1 GENESIS 44:2 JOSEPH HAS HIS SILVER CUP
PLACED IN BENJAMIN'S SACK

DUTCH SCHOOL
    Gelder, Aert de. Joseph with the Golden Cup.
    Location Unknown.

ITALIAN SCHOOL
    Italian school, 13th century. Scenes from the
    Old Testament: Joseph's brothers before
    him in Egypt. Assisi, S. Francesco, upper
    church.

71 D 19 2 GENESIS 44:3 THE BROTHERS SET OUT ON
THEIR JOURNEY HOME

FLEMISH SCHOOL
    Vos, Martin de, the elder. Joseph's brethren
    preparing to depart from Egypt. Christie,
    Manson, and Woods (Sale, London, May 14,
    1965, No. 118).

ITALIAN SCHOOL
    Bacchiacca, Francesco. History of Joseph: (right)
    Brothers departing with Benjamin. London,
    National Gallery.

71 D 19 22 GENESIS 44:12 THE CUP IS FOUND IN BENJA-
MIN'S SACK

DUTCH SCHOOL
    Cornelisz, Cornelis. Pharaoh's Soldiers Finding
    the Silver Cup in Benjamin's Sack. Sotheby
    and Co., London (Sale, New York, Oarje Bernet,
    No. 4778M, Jan. 21, 1982, No. 119).

    Moyaert, Claes Cornelisz. The Finding of
    the Cup in Benjamin's Sack. Budapest,
    Museum of Fine Arts, 1048 (330 a).
    Moeyaert, Claes Cornelisz. The Finding of
    the Cup in Benjamin's Sack. 1633. Budapest,
    Museum of Fine Arts, 5259 (330 a).

FLEMISH SCHOOL
    Vranck, Sebastian, Follower of. Soldiers
    discovering the Cup in Benjamin's Sack.
    Sotheby and Co., London (Sale, New York,
    [5104], Nov. 3, 1983, No. 148).

FRENCH SCHOOL
    Bourdon, Sebastien. The Finding of Money
    in Benjamin's Sack. Also attributed to
    Nicolas Bertin. Another version of the
    painting is also in Dublin, National Gallery,
    No. 1684. Dublin, National Gallery, 1066.
    Hébert, Ernest. Joseph's Cup Found in Benjamin's
    Sack. 1839. Paris, École des Beaux-Arts
    (Grand Prix de Rome).
    Verdier, François. The Finding of Benjamin's
    Cup. Christie, Manson and Woods (Sale,
    New York, Christie's East [KAREN-5521]
    March 23, 1984, No. 45).

ITALIAN SCHOOL
    Bacchiacca, Francesco. History of Joseph.
    Brethren brought back to Joseph with cup
    discovered in Benjamin's sack.(Left).
    London, National Gallery.
    Bartolo di Fredi. Scenes from the Old Testament:
    Joseph's cup in the sack of Benjamin.
    S. Gimignano, Collegiata.

SPANISH SCHOOL
    Escalante, Juan Antonio. The Cup in Benjamin's
    Sack. 1608. La Coruna (Spain), Museo Provin-
    cial de Bellas Artes.

71 D 19 3 GENESIS 44:18-34 THE BROTHERS BEFORE
JOSEPH: JUDAH PLEADS FOR BENJAMIN AND
OFFERS TO BE RETAINED AS A SLAVE IN HIS
STEAD

DUTCH SCHOOL
    Gelder, Aert de. Judah pleads for Benjamin
    and offers to be retained as a slave in
    his stead. c.1682. Heidelberg, Palatine
    Museum.

FLEMISH SCHOOL
    Stomer, Matthias, Follower of. Joseph and
    his Brethren. Christie, Manson and Woods,
    London (Sale, April 13, 1984, [TOMATO-2874]
    No. 77).

FRENCH SCHOOL
    Tissot, James Jacques Joseph. Illustrations
    of the Hebrew Bible. No. 69: Joseph Converses
    with Judah, his Brother. 1896-1903. New
    York, Jewish Museum, 52.136.

ITALIAN SCHOOL
    Amigoni, Jacopo. Joseph Tries His Brothers.
    Stockholm, University, 91.

71 D 19 31 GENESIS 45:3-8 JOSEPH REVEALS HIS
IDENTITY AND IN TEARS FORGIVES HIS BROTHERS'
PAST MISDEED

BRITISH SCHOOL
    Blake, William. Joseph Making Himself Known
    to his Brethren. Exhibited 1785. Cambridge,
    University, Fitzwilliam, 456C.

DUTCH SCHOOL
    Eeckhout, Gerbrand van den. Joseph Reveals
    his Identity to his Brothers. c.1668-70.
    Skoklosters Slott.

FLEMISH SCHOOL
Stomer, Mattias, Follower of. Joseph and his
Brethren. Christie, Manson and Woods (Sale,
London [TREVI-2719] July 22, 1983, No.46).

FRENCH SCHOOL
Chagall, Marc. Illustrations from the Bible
published by Vollard. No. 38: Joseph Recognized by his Brothers. 1931. Nice (Alpes-
Maritimes), Musée National Message Biblique
Marc Chagall.
Gérard, François Pascal. Joseph Recognized
by his Brothers. Angers (Maine-et-Loire),
Musée Municipal.
Girodet-Trioson, A.L. de Roucy. Joseph Recog-
nized by his Brothers. 1789. Paris, École
des Beaux-Arts.
Layraud, Fortuné Joseph Séraphin. Joseph Recog-
nized by his Brothers. 1863. Paris, École
des Beaux-Arts (Grand Prix de Rome).
Tardieu, Jean Charles. Joseph Reunited with
his Brothers. 1788. Wheelock, Whitney and
Co. - Gallery (New York).

ITALIAN SCHOOL
Bacchiacca, Francesco. History of Joseph.
Brothers throw themselves on Joseph's mercy.
London, National Gallery.
Bartolo di Fredi. Scenes from the Old Testa-
ment: Joseph recognized by his brethren.
S. Gimignano, Collegiata.
Gozzoli, Benozzo. Old Testament and other sub-
jects: Joseph made known to his brethren.
Detail. Pisa, Camposanto.
Mola, Pier Francesco. Joseph making himself
known to his brethren. Fresco. 1657. Rome,
Palazzo del Quirinal.
Pontormo, Jacopo da. Scenes from the story
of Joseph. Detail: Joseph reveals himself
to his brothers. Henfield (Sussex), Col-
lection Lady Salmond. On loan to the National
Gallery, London.
Pontormo, Jacopo da. Joseph and his kindred
in Egypt. London, National Gallery.

71 D 2 STORY OF JOSEPH (PART II)

EARLY MEDIEVAL AND BYZANTINE
Byzantine school, 13th century. Story of Joseph.
Sopoćani, Yugoslavia. Monastery Church,
narthex, west wall.

71 D 21 GENESIS 46:1-27 JACOB AND HIS FAMILY GO
TO EGYPT

EARLY MEDIEVAL AND BYZANTINE
Byzantine school, Wall painting, Sopocani (Yugoslavia). The Story of Joseph: Jacob's Journey
to Egypt. Fresco. 13th century. Sopoćani,
Yugoslavia. Monastery church, narthex, west
wall.

FRENCH SCHOOL
Chagall, Marc. Illustrations from the Bible
published by Vollard. No. 39: Jacob Leaves
his Country for Egypt. 1931. Nice (Alpes-
Maritimes), Musée National Message Biblique
Marc Chagall.

71 D 21 3 GENESIS 46:5-7 JACOB WITH HIS FAMILY,
LIVESTOCK AND POSSESSIONS, SETS OUT FOR
EGYPT WITH THE WAGONS

DUTCH SCHOOL
Aertsen, Pieter. Jacob's Journey to Egypt.
A pair with Joseph and his Brethren. Christie,
Manson and Woods (Sale, London, March 11,
1983, No. 84b).

71 D 22 11 GENESIS 46:28-29 JOSEPH GOES TO GOSHEN
TO MEET HIS FATHER

DUTCH SCHOOL
Moeyaert, Nicolaes Cornelisz. Joseph Welcoming
his Father into Egypt. 1628. Hamburg,
Kunsthalle, 702.

71 D 22 2 GENESIS 46:29-30 THE MEETING OF JACOB
AND JOSEPH

DUTCH SCHOOL
Moeyaert, Claes Cornelisz. Joseph declares
himself to his father in the presence
of his brothers. Christie, Manson and
Woods (Sale, London, March 29, 1968, No.42).

ITALIAN SCHOOL
Guardi, Giovanni Antonio. Joseph meets his
father. Milan, Collection Lutomirski.
Italian school, 15th century. Series of eight
panels with scenes from the Old Testament.
1. Joseph and Jacob. Venice, S. Alvise.

71 D 22 4 GENESIS 47:7-10 JACOB IS PRESENTED
TO PHARAOH BY JOSEPH

DUTCH SCHOOL
Bol, Ferdinand. Jacob presented by Joseph
before Pharaoh. Dresden, Gallery, 1605.
Eeckhout, Gerbrand van den. Joseph Brings
Jacob before Pharaoh. 1666. Location Unknown.

GERMAN SCHOOL
Müller, Johann Jakob (called Müller von Riga?)
The Brother of Joseph before Pharaoh.
Dunkirk, Museum (?)

ITALIAN SCHOOL
Giaquinto, Corrado. Old Testament scenes.
Details: Joseph presenting his father
to Pharaoh. Aranjuez, Palacio Real. Wall
decorations, upper.
Granacci, Francesco. Joseph presenting his
brothers and his father to Pharaoh. Florence,
Palazzo Uffizi.

71 D 23 GENESIS 47:13-26 FAMINE IN EGYPT

DUTCH SCHOOL
Noord, Johannes van. Joseph Selling Grain
to the Egyptians. Bader, Alfred - Collection
(Milwaukee).

71 D 24 2 GENESIS 48:1 JOSEPH TAKES HIS TWO SONS,
MANASSEH AND EPHRAIM, TO SEE JACOB ON
HIS SICK-BED

ITALIAN SCHOOL
Pontormo, Jacopo da. Joseph and his kindred
in Egypt. c.1518. London, National Gallery,
1131.

71 D 24 21 GENESIS 48:2-20 JACOB BLESSES MANASSEH
AND EPHRAIM WITH ARMS CROSSED; JOSEPH
MAY BE SHOWN TRYING TO UNCROSS THEM OR
EXPRESSING (WITH ASENATH) HIS DISAPPROVAL

AMERICAN SCHOOL
West, Benjamin. Jacob blessing the sons of
Joseph. 1766. Oberlin College, Allan Memorial
Art Museum, 61.70.

DUTCH SCHOOL
Rembrandt. Jacob Blessing the Sons of Joseph.
1656. Cassel, Kunstsammlungen.
Victors, Jan. Jacob Blesses the Sons of Joseph.
Budapest, Museum of Fine Arts, 1344 (395).
Werff, Adriaen van der. Jacob Blessing the
Sons of Joseph. 1720-22. Oberlin College,
Allen Memorial Art Museum.

FRENCH SCHOOL
  Chagall, Marc. Illustrations from the <u>Bible</u>
     published by Vollard. No.40: The Blessing
     of Ephraim and Manassah. 1931. Nice (Alpes-
     Maritimes), Musée National Message Biblique
     Marc Chagall.

GERMAN SCHOOL
  Loth, Johann Carl. Jacob blessing the sons
     of Joseph. Vienna, Kunsthistorisches Museum,
     1551.

ITALIAN SCHOOL
  Guercino. Jacob blessing the sons of Joseph.
     London, Collection Denis Mahon.
  Pontormo, Jacopo da. Joseph and his kindred
     in Egypt. c.1518. London, National Gallery,
     1131.

SWEDISH SCHOOL
  Martin, Elias. Biblical Scene. Jacob Blessing
     the Sons of Joseph. Stockholm, National
     Museum, 3047.

71 D 25 GENESIS 49:33, 50:1-14 JACOB'S DEATH

EARLY MEDIEVAL AND BYZANTINE
  Byzantine school, Wall painting, Sopočani (Yugo-
     slavia). The Story of Joseph: Death of Jacob.
     Fresco. 13th century. Sopočani, Yugoslavia,
     Monastery church, narthex, west wall.

FRENCH SCHOOL
  Forestier, Henri-Joseph de. The Death of Jacob.
     1813. Paris, École des Beaux-Arts (Grand
     Prix de Rome).

71 D 26 2 GENESIS 50:26 DEATH OF JOSEPH

AUSTRIAN SCHOOL
  Troger, Paul. The Death of Joseph. Frankfort-
     on-the-Main, Staedel Institute, 1789.

71 E EXODUS, LEVITICUS, NUMBERS, DEUTERONOMY,
      JOSHUA, FROM THE BONDAGE OF THE ISRAELITES
      IN EGYPT TO THEIR SETTLEMENT IN CANAAN

FRENCH SCHOOL
  Poussin, Gaspard. Storm: Moses and the Angel.
     London, National Gallery, 1159.

SPANISH SCHOOL
  Viladomat, Antonio. Moses and the Israelites.
     Vich, Museo Episcopal.

71 E 11 EXODUS 1:1 - 12:30 EXODUS (PART I): EVENTS
         PRECEDING AND PREPARING THE EXIT OF ISRAEL
         FROM EGYPT

FLEMISH SCHOOL
  Franck, Frans, II. Episodes from the Life
     of Moses. Sotheby and Co., London (Sale,
     June 9, 1982, No. 124).

ITALIAN SCHOOL
  Castiglione, Giovanni Battista. The Israelites
     in the Wilderness. Sotheby and Co., London
     (Sale, Nov. 17, 1982, No. 45).

71 E 11 14 2 EXODUS 1:18-19 PHARAOH QUESTIONING
              THE MIDWIVES

DUTCH SCHOOL
  Vet, Johan de. Pharaoh Chiding Shiprah and
     Puah for Not Killing the Jewish Boys.
     1618. Schapiro, E. - Collection (London).

71 E 11 2 EXODUS 2:1-10 MOSES' BIRTH AND EDUCATION

EARLY MEDIEVAL AND BYZANTINE
  Early Medieval and Byzantine painting. Moses
     receiving the Law and scenes from the
     life of Moses. 14th century. Sinai, Monastery
     of St. Catherine, Icon 359.

ITALIAN SCHOOL
  Gargiulo, Domenico (called Micco Spadaro),
     attributed to. The Finding of Moses. Form-
     erly attributed to Bernardo Cavallino.
     London, National Gallery, 6297.
  Gozzoli, Benozzo. Old Testament and other
     subjects: Infancy and first miracle of
     of Moses. Pisa, Camposanto.
  Grassi, Niccolo. Moses in the Court of the
     Pharaoh. Sorlini - Collection (Venice).

71 E 11 23 EXODUS 2:3-4 MOSES IS EXPOSED IN THE
            ARK ON THE BANKS OF THE NILE; MIRIAM,
            MOSES' SISTER, KEEPS WATCH

FRENCH SCHOOL
  Bourdon, Sébastien. The hiding of Moses.
     Bob Jones University Collection, Greenville,
     S.C.
  Patel, P. (the elder). Landscape: Moses in
     the bulrushes. 1660. Paris, Louvre.
  Poussin, Nicolas. Moses Placed on the Banks
     of the Nile (Moses Exposed). Dresden,
     Gallery, 720.
  Poussin, NIcolas. Moses abandoned on the
     Nile. Oxford, University, Ashmolean Museum.

71 E 11 23 1 EXODUS 2:3 MOSES (ALONE) IN THE BULRUSHES

FRENCH SCHOOL
  Moreau, Gustave. Young Moses.Harvard University,
     Fogg Art Museum, 1943.262.

71 E 11 24   EXODUS 2:5   THE FINDING OF MOSES: PHARAOH'S
DAUGHTER COMES TO BATHE WITH HER MAIDENS IN
THE RIVER AND DISCOVERS THE CHILD FLOATING
ON THE WATER

AMERICAN SCHOOL
    American school, 19th century. Moses rescued
        from the bulrushes. c.1810. Collection E.W.
        Garbisch.

BRITISH SCHOOL
    Alma-Tadema, Sir Lawrence. The Finding of Moses.
        1904. Sotheby and Co., London (Sale, Nov.6,
        1973).
    Blake, William. The Finding of Moses: the Comp-
        assion of Pharaoh's Daughter. c.1805. London,
        Victoria and Albert Museum, P25-1949.

DUTCH SCHOOL
    Dutch school, 17th century. The Finding of
        Moses. Sotheby and Co., London (Sale, Oct.20,
        1982).
    Poelenburg, Cornelis van. The Finding of Moses.
        1625-35. Florence, Palazzo Uffizi, 1196.
    Poelenburg, COrnelis van. Moses Striking Water
        from the Rock. 1621-22. Florence, Palazzo
        Uffizi, 1220.
    Poelenburg, Cornelis van. The Finding of Moses.
        1621-22. Florence, Palazzo Uffizi, 1203.
    Uytenbroeck, Moses, Attributed to. The Finding
        of Moses. Amsterdam, Rijksmuseum (?).
    Wet, Jacob de, the younger. The Finding of
        Moses. Cologne, Wallraf-Richartz Museum,2331.

FLEMISH SCHOOL
    Franck, Franz, I, Studio of. Flemish Reliquary
        Chest painted with scenes from the Old
        Testament. Detail: Inside Lid: The Finding
        of Moses. c.1600. Sarasota, Fla., Ringling
        Museum of Art. SN 1950.

FRENCH SCHOOL
    Degas, H.G.E. Figures from "Finding of Moses".
        Private Collection.
    Leprince, Jean Baptiste, School of. The Finding
        of Moses. Christie, Manson and Woods (Sale,
        New York, July 15, 1981, No. 78).

ITALIAN SCHOOL
    Abbate, Nicolo Dell'. Moses Saved from the
        Waters. Paris, Louvre, Musée du, R.F. 3937.
    Cignani, Carlo. Moses Saved from the Water.
        Bologna, Private Collection.
    Crespi, Giuseppe Maria. The Daughter of the
        Pharaoh at the River. Rovigo, Pinacoteca
        dell'Accademia dei Concordi, 195.303.
    Giordano, Luca. Finding of Moses. Raleigh,N.C.,
        North Carolina Museum of Art, n. 189. Acq.
        No. 52.9.158.
    Grimaldi, Giovanfrancesco. Finding of Moses.
        Badminton, Collection Duke of Beaufort.
    Italian school, 16th century (Venetian). The
        Finding of Moses. Baltimore, Md., Walters
        Art Gallery, 533.
    Italian school, 18th century (Bolognese). The
        Finding of Moses. c.1700. Sotheby and Co.,
        London (Sale, April 4, 1984, [DAFFODIL]
        No. 145).
    Lanfranco, Giovanni. The Finding of Moses.
        Brunswick, Landesmuseum, 705.
    Raphael (and assistants). Old Testament subjects.
        Moses found by Pharaoh's daughter. Rome,
        Vatican, Loggie.
    Ricci, Sebastiano. Finding of Moses. England,
        Royal Collection.
    Rosa, Salvatore. Finding of Moses. c.1650.
        Detroit, Institute of Arts, 47.92.
    Travi, Antonio Maria. The Finding of Moses.
        Rovigo, Pinacoteca dell'Accademia dei Con-
        cordi, 192.336.
    Veronese, Paolo. Copy. Moses Brought before
        Pharaoh's Daughter. Oxford, University,
        Ashmolean Museum, A 143.

SWEDISH SCHOOL
    Josephson, Ernst. Pharaoh's Daughter finds
        Moses. Sketch. 1870. Stockholm, National
        Museum, 1909.

71 E 11 24 1   EXODUS 2:5   MOSES IS PULLED OUT OF
THE WATER BY THE SERVANTS

DANISH SCHOOL
    Abildgaard, Nikolai Abraham. Moses taken
        up from the river. 1790. Copenhagen, Art
        Museum, Spengler 862.

DUTCH SCHOOL
    Bol, Ferdinand. The Finding of Moses. c.1655-60,
        The Hague, Dient Verspreide Rijkskollekties.

FLEMISH SCHOOL
    Wildens, Jan, Follower of. The Finding of
        Moses. Sotheby and Co., London (Sale,
        New York [5104] Nov. 3, 1983, No. 149).

FRENCH SCHOOL
    La Fosse, Charles de. The Finding of Moses.
        Paris, Louvre, Musée du, INV 4527.
    La Fosse, Charles de. Moses rescued from
        the water. Paris, Louvre.
    Poussin, Nicolas. Moses saved from the Nile.
        Paris, Louvre.
    Tissot, James Jacques Joseph. Illustrations
        of the Hebrew Bible. No. 78: Pharaoh's
        Daughter has Moses Brought to Her. 1896-1903.
        New York, Jewish Museum, 52.145.

ITALIAN SCHOOL
    Grassi, Nicola, Circle of. The Finding of
        Moses. Sotheby and Co., London (Sale,
        [GOLDENROD], Oct. 12, 1983, No. 96).
    Lanfranco, Giovanni. The Finding of Moses.
        Brunswick, Landesmuseum.
    Rosa, Salvatore. Finding of Moses. Lunettes.
        c. 1644. Florence, Palazzo Pitti, Mezzanino
        della Muletta.
    Tinteretto, Domenico. The Finding of Moses.
        St. Louis, City Art Museum, 59.1928.
    Zugno, Francesco, Attributed to. The Finding
        of Moses. London, National Gallery, 3542.

71 E 11 25   EXODUS 2:6   MOSES IS EITHER PRESENTED
TO PHARAOH'S DAUGHTER OR SURROUNDED BY
WOMEN FONDLING HIM

AMERICAN SCHOOL
    Church, Frederick E. The Finding of Moses.
        c. 1860. Boston, Museum of Fine Arts,
        47.1231.
    West, Benjamin. Daughters of Pharaoh Finding
        Moses. South Bend (Indiana), University
        of Notre Dame.

DUTCH SCHOOL
    Bleker, Dirck. The Finding of Moses. Sotheby
        and Co., London (Sale, New York, March
        6-7, 1975, No. 134).
    Bor, Paulus. The Finding of Moses. Amsterdam,
        Rijksmuseum, 567.
    Bray, Jan de. Finding of Moses. 1661. Rotterdam,
        Museum Boymans.
    Breenbergh, Bartholomeus. Finding of Moses.
        Stockholm, National Museum.
    Breenbergh, Bartholomeus. Finding of the
        Infant Moses by Pharaoh's Daughter. London,
        National Gallery, 208.
    Dyck, Abraham van. The Finding of Moses.
        c.1660/70.
    Grebber, Pieter Fransz de, Circle of. The
        Finding of Moses. Sotheby and Co., London
        (Sale, New York, Nov. 7, 1984, [MISSOURI],
        No. 179).
    Rembrandt. The finding of Moses. Philadelphia,
        Collection J.G. Johnson.

FLEMISH SCHOOL
    Wolffordt, Artus. The Pharaoh's Daughter Finds
    Moses. Stockholm, University, 131.

FRENCH SCHOOL
    Bourdon, Sébastien. Finding of Moses in the
    bulrushes. London, Collection A.L. Nicholson.
    Bourdon, Sébastien. Finding of Moses. c.1650.
    Washington, D.C., National Gallery of Art,
    1617.
    Chagall, Marc. Illustrations from the Bible
    published by Vollard. No. 41: Moses Saved
    from the Water. 1931. Nice (Alpes-Maritimes),
    Musée National Message Biblique Marc Chagall.
    Claude Lorrain. Finding of Moses. Madrid, Prado.
    Colombel, Nicolas. The finding of Moses. Bob
    Jones University Collection, (Greenville,S.C.)
    Poussin, Nicolas. Moses Saved from the Waters
    (Finding of Moses). Paris, Louvre, Musée
    du, 7272.
    Poussin, Nicolas. Moses saved from the Nile.
    Dorking, Collection Mrs. Schreiber.

ITALIAN SCHOOL
    Bellucci, Antonio. Finding of Moses. Pommers-
    felden, Collection Dr. Karl Graf von Schönborn-
    Wiesenthied.
    Castello, Valerio. The Finding of Moses. London,
    Collection Denys Sutton.
    Cavallino, Bernardo. The Finding of Moses.
    Brunswick, Landesmuseum, 516.
    Cavallino, Bernardo. The finding of Moses.
    Naples, Museo Nazionale.
    Celesti, Andrea. The finding of Moses. Reggio
    Emilia, Civica Galleria Parmeggiani.
    Cignani, Carlo. Moses saved from the water.
    Bologna, Private Collection.
    Crespi, Giuseppe Maria. Moses Saved from the
    Water. Rovigo, Pinacoteca dell'Accademia
    dei Concordi, 196.309.
    Creti, Donato. The Finding of Moses. Sotheby
    and Co., London (Sale, July 7, 1982, No.305).
    Crosato, Giovanni Battista. Moses saved from
    the river. Turin, Museo Civico.
    Donducci, Giovanni Andrea. Moses Saved from
    the Waters. Modena, Pinacoteca Estense.
    Fontebasso, Francesco. The Finding of Moses.
    Sotheby and Co., London (Sale, April 7,
    1982, No. 103).
    Gennari, Benedetto, Attributed to. The Finding
    of Moses. Sotheby and Co., London (Sale,
    New York, March 24, No. 82).
    Gentileschi, Orazio. Moses Rescued by Pharaoh's
    Daughter. Madrid, Prado.
    Gentileschi, Orazio. Moses rescued by Pharaoh's
    daughter. Replica of painting in the Prado.
    Castle Howard, Collection Hon. Geoffrey
    Howard.
    Gimignani, Lodovico, Attributed to. The Discovery
    of Moses ?
    Giordano, Luca. The finding of Moses. Brighton,
    Eng. Corporation Art Gallery.
    Grassi, Nicola. The Finding of Moses. Jerusalem,
    Israel Museum, 503/125.
    Guardi, Francesco. Moses Saved from the Water.
    Milan, Collection A. Bolchini-Bonomi.
    Guardi, Giovanni Antonio. Moses Saved from
    the Waters. Conegliano, Collection P. Gera.
    Italian school, 17th century (Bolognese). The
    Finding of Moses. Formerly attributed to
    Gasparo Diziani. Christie, Manson and Woods,
    London (Sale, July 17, 1981, No. 50).
    Italian school, 17th century (Florentine).
    The Finding of Moses. Christie, Manson and
    Woods (Sale, New York, Jan. 15, 1985, [CAROL-
    5808] No. 136).
    Italian school, 18th century. The finding of
    Moses. Budapest, Museum of Fine Arts, 471.
    Molinari, Giovanni Battista. The Finding of
    Moses. Brunswick, Landesmuseum, 1089.
    Mura, Francesco de. The Finding of Moses. Sotheby
    and Co., London (Sale, New York, March 6-7,
    1975, No. 69).

    Pitati, Bonifacio. The Finding of Moses.
    Sotheby and Co., London (Sale, [ROSE]
    July 6, 1983, No. 37).
    Pitati, Bonifacio. Moses saved from the water.
    Florence, Pitti.
    Pitati, Bonifacio. Moses saved from the water.
    Milan, Brera.
    Pitati, Bonifacio. Moses saved from the water.
    Dresden, Gallery, 208.
    Pitati, Bonifacio, School of. The Finding
    of Moses. Sotheby and Co. (Sale, London,
    July 24, 1974, No. 7).
    Rosa, Salvatore. The Finding of Moses. c.1660.
    Cincinnati, Museum, 1980.255.
    Tiepolo, G.B. Finding of Moses. Edinburgh,
    National Gallery, 92.
    Tintoretto (Jacopo Robusti). Finding of Moses.
    Madrid, Prado, 396.
    Tintoretto (Jacopo Robusti). The Finding
    of Moses. New York, Metropolitan Museum
    of Art, 39.55.
    Tintoretto. The Finding of Moses. Pommers-
    felden, Schloss, Gallery.
    Tintoretto. The Finding of Moses. Repainted
    by Giuseppe Angeli. Venice, Scuola di
    San Rocco, upper hall ceiling.
    Veronese, Paolo. Moses saved from the Nile.
    c.1750. Madrid, Prado, 502.
    Veronese, Paolo. The Finding of Moses. Version
    of painting in the Prado, Madrid. Dublin,
    National Gallery, 745.
    Veronese, Paolo. Moses saved from the Nile.
    Dresden, Gallery, 229.
    Veronese, Paolo. The Finding of Moses. c.1572.
    Washington, D.C., National Gallery of
    Art.
    Veronese, Paolo, after. Finding of Moses.
    England, Private Collection(A).
    Veronese, Paolo, School of. Moses saved from
    the Nile. Dresden, Gallery.
    Zucharelli, Francesco, Attributed to. The
    Finding of Moses. Boston, Museum of Fine
    Arts, Res. 24.18.

SPANISH SCHOOL
    Mesquida, Guillermo. Finding of Moses. Palma
    de Mallorca, Collection March.

71 E 11 26   EXODUS 2:10   WHEN THE CHILD IS OLD
             ENOUGH, MOSES' MOTHER BRINGS HIM TO PHARAOH'S
             DAUGHTER, WHO ADOPTS HIM

    BRITISH SCHOOL
    Hogarth, William. Moses Brought to Pharaoh's
    Daughter. 1746. London, Foundling Hospital.

    FLEMISH SCHOOL
    Verhagen, P.J. Moses and the daughter of
    Pharaoh. Louvain, Musée Communal.

71 E 11 27 1   MOSES AND PHARAOH'S CROWN: PHARAOH
               PLAYFULLY PLACES HIS CROWN ON THE HEAD
               OF THE INFANT MOSES, WHO THROWS IT TO
               THE GROUND AND TRAMPLES ON IT; OR MOSES
               BREAKS THE CROWN WHILE PLAYING

    DUTCH SCHOOL
    Doomer, Lambert. Moses and Thermuthis. Southern
    California, University of (Los Angeles).
    Eeckhout, Gerbrand van den. Moses Treading
    on Pharaoh's Crown. 1675. London, Ronald
    Cook Gallery.
    Steen, Jan. Youthful Moses rejects Pharaoh's
    crown. Amsterdam, Collection - Dr. H.
    Wetzlar.

    FRENCH SCHOOL
    Poussin, Nicolas. Moses Trampling on Pharaoh's
    Crown. Duke of Bedford Collection, Woburn
    Abbey.
    Poussin, Nicolas. Moses spurns Pharaoh's
    Crown. Paris, Musée de Louvre.

ITALIAN SCHOOL
    Celesti, Andrea. Moses and the Pharaoh's Crown.
       Also attributed to Valerio Castello. Lvov
       (Ukraine), State Picture Gallery.
    Gozzoli, Benozzo. Old Testament subjects:
       Infancy and first miracle of Moses.
       Pisa, Camposanto.
    Tiepolo, G.B. Moses Trampling Pharaoh's Crown.
       (New York, Collection S.H. Kress, 5). Wash-
       ington, National Gallery, 117.

71 E 11 27 11 MOSES' TRIAL BY FIRE: WHEN GIVEN THE
    CHOICE BETWEEN TWO PLATES, ONE CONTAINING
    BURNING COALS, THE OTHER A RUBY RING (OR
    CHERRIES), MOSES CHOOSES THE BURNING COALS
    AND PUTS THEM IN HIS MOUTH

ITALIAN SCHOOL
    Ferrari, Andrea. The Trial by Fire of Moses'
       Childhood. Vienna, Kunsthistorisches Museum,
       1630.
    Giorgione. Trial of Moses. 1502-03. Florence,
       Palazzo Uffizi, 945.
    Gozzoli, Benozzo. Old Testament and other sub-
       jects: Infancy and first miracle of Moses.
       Detail: center. Pisa, Camposanto.
    Pitati, Bonifacio. The Trial of Moses. Oxford,
       University, Ashmolean Museum, A 730.

71 E 11 31 2 EXODUS 2:12 MOSES KILLS THE EGYPTIAN
    TASKMASTER

EARLY MEDIEVAL AND BYZANTINE
    Early medieval and Byzantine painting, Sinai.
       14th century. Scenes from the life of Moses.
       Moses killing the Egyptian. Sinai, Monastery
       of St. Catherine, Icon 359.

ITALIAN SCHOOL
    Botticelli, Sandro. Moses killing the Egyptian.
       Rome, Vatican, Sistine Chapel.

71 E 11 31 21 EXODUS 2:12 MOSES BURIES THE BODY
    OF THE EGYPTIAN TASKMASTER IN THE SAND

FRENCH SCHOOL
    Patel, P., the elder. Landscape: Moses burying
       the slain Egyptian. 1660. Paris, Musée du
       Louvre.

71 E 11 31 5 EXODUS 2:15 MOSES FLEES TO MIDIAN

ITALIAN SCHOOL
    Botticelli, Sandro. Moses flees to Midian.
       Rome, Vatican, Sistine Chapel.

71 E 11 32 EXODUS 2:16 MOSES AT A WELL MEETS THE
    SEVEN DAUGHTERS OF JETHRO, THE PRIEST OF
    MIDIAN

ITALIAN SCHOOL
    Crespi, Giuseppe Maris. Moses and the Daughters
       of Jethro. Christie, Manson and Woods (Sale,
       London, June 28, 1974, No. 95).
    Italian school, 16th century ? (Venetian).
       Moses uncovering the well for the daughters
       of Jethro. Greenville, S.C., Bob Jones Univ-
       ersity Collection.
    Ricci, Sebastiano. Moses and the daughters
       of Jethro. Budapest, Museum of Fine Arts,
       57.10.
    Sagrestani, Giovanni Camillo. Moses and the
       Daughters of Jethro. Harvard University,
       Fogg Art Museum, 1973.22.
    Tintoretto.Moses and the pool of the Midianites.
       Madrid, Prado.

71 E 11 32 1 EXODUS 2:17 MOSES DRIVES AWAY THE
    SHEPHERDS WHO WANTED TO PREVENT THE DAUGHTERS
    FROM WATERING THEIR FATHER'S FLOCK

DUTCH SCHOOL
    Limborch, Hendrik van. Moses and the Daughters
       of Jethro. Christie, Manson and Woods (Sale,
       New York [BETH-5258] Jan. 18, 1983, No.120).

FLEMISH SCHOOL
    Hondt, Philipp de. Moses and the Daughters
       of Jethro. Christie, Manson and Woods
       (Sale, London [TAORIMA-2741] Oct. 14,
       1983, No. 11).

FRENCH SCHOOL
    Bourdon, Sebastien. Moses and the Daughters
       of Jethro. Minneapolis, Institute of Arts,
       24.3.
    Colombel, Nicolas. Moses and the Daughters
       of Jethro. c.1680. Stanford University,
       Art Museum, 80.43.
    Le Brun, Charles. Moses Defends the Daughters
       of Jethro. Modena, Pinacoteca Estense.

ITALIAN SCHOOL
    Botticelli, Sandro. Moses drives away the
       shepherds. Rome, Vatican, Sistine Chapel.
    Coccapani, Sigismundo. Moses Defends the
       the Daughters of Jethro. Prato, Cassa
       di Risparmi.
    Dandini, Cesare. Moses and the Daughters
       of Jethro. Dublin, National Gallery.
    Gherardini, Alessandro. Moses and the Daughters
       of Jethro. Christie, Manson and Woods
       (Sale, London, June 28, 1974, No. 3).
    Grassi, Nicola. Moses Drives the Shepherds
       away from the Well. Jerusalem, Israel
       Museum.
    Rosso, Il. Moses and Jethro's Daughters.
       Florence, Palazzo Uffizi.

71 E 11 32 2 EXODUS 2:17 MOSES WATERS THE SHEEP

DUTCH SCHOOL
    Bol, Hans. Moses with the Daughters of Jethro
       at the Well. Dresden, Staatliche Kunst-
       sammlungen, 830.

ITALIAN SCHOOL
    Botticelli, Sandro. Moses waters the sheep.
       Rome, Vatican, Sistine Chapel.

SPANISH SCHOOL
    Orrente, Pedro. Moses and the daughters of
       Jethro. Also attributed to Bassano. Madrid,
       Collection Duke of Alba.

71 E 11 34 EXODUS 2:21 MOSES' MARRIAGE WITH ZIPPORAH

FRENCH SCHOOL
    Le Brun, Charles. Moses Marries Zipporah.
       Modena, Pinacoteca Estense.
    Le Brun, Charles, Follower of. Moses Marries
       Jethro's Daughter. Budapest, Museum of
       Fine Arts, 1808.

71 E 11 4 EXODUS 3-4 THE CALLING OF MOSES

BRITISH SCHOOL
    English school, 18th century. The Finding
       of Moses. Oxford, University, Ashmolean
       Museum, A261.

ITALIAN SCHOOL
    Moretto da Brescia. Moses and the Burning
       Bush. Brescia, Pinacoteca.
    Palma Giovane. Ceiling. Detail: Moses and
       the burning bush. Venice, Palazzo Loredan
       (Municipio).

SPANISH SCHOOL
    Collantes, Francisco. Moses and the burning
       bush. Paris, Louvre, Musée du.

71 E 11 41 1 EXODUS 3:2-3 A BURNING BUSH ATTRACTS
    HIS ATTENTION

AMERICAN SCHOOL
    Lewis, Michael. Moses and the Vision of the
       Burning Bush. Harvard University, Fogg
       Art Museum, 1979.383.

BRITISH SCHOOL
    Blake, William. Moses at the Burning Bush.
       c.1800-03. London, Victoria and Albert Museum,
       A.L. 9285.
    Lewis, Michael. Moses and the Vision of the
       Burning Bush. Harvard University, Fogg Art
       Museum, 1979.383.

71 E 11 42   EXODUS 3:2   THE BURNING BUSH

EARLY MEDIEVAL AND BYZANTINE
    Byzantine school, Wall painting, Istanbul.
       Moses and the Burning Bush. 14th century.
       Istanbul, Mosque Kahrié. Parecclesion, west-
       ern bay, north wall, eastern half of lunette.

FLEMISH SCHOOL
    Bouts, Dierick. Moses and the burning bush.
       Philadelphia, Johnson Collection, 339.

GERMAN SCHOOL
    Grund, Norbert. Moses and the Burning Bush.
       Budapest, Museum of Fine Arts, 62.15.

SPANISH SCHOOL
    Mayno, Juan Bautista. Moses. Wall decorations.
       Toledo, San Pedro Mártir.

71 EE 11 42   MARY IN THE BURNING BUSH

FRENCH SCHOOL
    Froment, N. Triptych: Moses and the burning
       bush. Aix-en-Provence, Cathedral.

71 E 11 42 1   EXODUS 3:5   MOSES TAKING OFF HIS SANDALS

EARLY MEDIEVAL AND BYZANTINE
    Byzantine school, 14th century, Istanbul. Moses
       and the Burning Bush: Moses removes his
       sandals. Istanbul, Mosque Kahrié. Parec-
       clesion, western bay, north wall, lunette.
    Early Christian Painting, Rome. Moses tying
       sandal. Rome, Via Appia, Catacomb of St.
       Callixtus, Cripta delle Pecorelle.

FLEMISH SCHOOL
    Bles, Herri met de. Moses resting in a landscape
       (the Burning Bush). Naples, Museo Nazionale,
       Capodimonte, 6.

ITALIAN SCHOOL
    Botticelli, Sandro. Moses taking off his sandals.
       Rome, Vatican, Sistine Chapel.
    Fetti, Domenico. Moses and the burning bush.
       Before 1614. Vienna, Kunsthistorisches Museum,
       118.
    Giorgione, Attributed to. Moses and the burning
       bush. London, University of, Courtauld Inst.,
       Lee Collection.
    Vignali, Jacopo. Moses and the burning bush.
       Greenville, S.C., Bob Jones University
       Collection, 1962 cat. 78.

71 E 11 42 2   EXODUS 3:4 - 4:13   MOSES, KNEELING BEFORE THE BUSH AND HIDING HIS FACE, LISTENS TO GOD

EARLY MEDIEVAL AND BYZANTINE
    Early Medieval and Byzantine painting, Sinai.
       The Burning Bush. Sinai, Monastery of St.
       Catherine, Icon 649.
    Byzantine school, 14th century, Istanbul. Moses
       and the Burning Bush: Moses Hides his Face.
       Istanbul, Mosque Kahrié. Parecclesion, north
       half of transverse arch.

FRENCH SCHOOL
    Claude Lorrain. Moses and the burning bush.
       1664. (St. Boswell's, Scotland, Collection
       Earl of Ellesmere). London, Bridgewater
       House, 41.

ITALIAN SCHOOL
    Botticelli, Sandro. Moses Listens to God.
       Rome, Vatican, Sistine Chapel.
    Domenichino. Landscape with Moses and Burning
       Bush. c.1610-12. New York, Collection Mr.
       & Mrs. Charles E. Wrightsman.
    Domenichino. Moses and the burning bush.
       Shugborough, Collection Earl of Lichfield.
    Giordano, Luca. Moses and the Burning Bush.
       Brunswick, Landesmuseum, 502.
    Raphael (and assistants).Old Testament subjects:
       God speaks to Moses from the burning bush.
       Rome, Vatican, Loggie.

71 E 11 42 31   EXODUS 4:3   MIRACLE OF THE ROD CHANGED INTO A SERPENT; MOSES MAY BE SHOWN FLEEING FROM THE SERPENT

FRENCH SCHOOL
    Chagall, Marc. Illustrations from the Bible
       published by Vollard. No. 42: Moses Throws
       His Rod. 1931. Nice (Alpes-Maritimes),
       Musée National Message Biblique Marc Chagall.
    Poussin, Nicolas. Moses and the burning bush.
       Copenhagen, Art Museum.

ITALIAN SCHOOL
    Saraceni, Carlo. Moses' Rod Turns into a
       Serpent. Rome, Palazzo del Quirinale,
       Frieze of the Sala Regia.

71 E 11 43   EXODUS 4:15   MOSES AND JETHRO PARTING

DUTCH SCHOOL
    Victors, Jan. The Departure of Moses from
       Jethro. Budapest, Museum of Fine Arts,60.3.

71 E 11 44   EXODUS 4:20   MOSES DEPARTS FOR EGYPT: HE CARRIES HIS ROD AND IS ACCOMPANIED BY HIS WIFE AND SONS UPON AN ASS

ITALIAN SCHOOL
    Botticelli, Sandro. Moses departs for Egypt.
       Rome, Vatican, Sistine Chapel.

71 E 11 45   EXODUS 4:24   AT AN INN, GOD (OR THE ANGEL OF GOD) TRIES TO KILL MOSES

ITALIAN SCHOOL
    Pinturicchio. Journey of Moses. Also attributed
       to Perugino. Rome, Vatican, Sistine Chapel.

71 E 11 45 1 EXODUS 4:25   ZIPPORAH APPEASES GOD BY CIRCUMCISING ONE OF HER SONS

ITALIAN SCHOOL
    Pinturicchio. Journey of Moses: Circumcision
       of his son. Rome, Vatican, Sistine Chapel.

71 E 11 46 1   EXODUS 4:27   AARON MEETS MOSES AND KISSES HIM

DUTCH SCHOOL
    Pynas, Jacob. Meeting of Moses and Aaron
       on Mount Sinai. Also attributed to Adam
       Elsheimer. Cassel, Staatliche Kunstsamm-
       lungen, 612.

71 E 11 5   MOSES COMMUNICATING WITH GOD (IN GENERAL)

ITALIAN SCHOOL
    Tintoretto. Moses on Mount Sinai. Scuola
       di San Rocco, upper hall, ceiling.

71 E 11 6   EXODUS 5 - 7:13   MOSES AND AARON CONFRONT PHARAOH

FRENCH SCHOOL
    Chagall, Marc. Illustrations from the Bible
       published by Vollard. No. 44: Moses and
       Aaron before Pharaoh. 1931. Nice (Alpes-
       Maritimes), Musée National Message Biblique
       Marc Chagall.

ITALIAN SCHOOL
Gozzoli, Benozzo. Old Testament and other subjects: Aaron's rod. Pisa, Camposanto.

71 E 11 64 EXODUS 7:10 MOSES AND AARON BEFORE PHARAOH:
AARON PERFORMS THE MIRACLE OF THE ROD CHANGING
INTO A SNAKE

AMERICAN SCHOOL
West, Benjamin. Moses and Aaron before Pharaoh.
Greenville, S.C., Bob Jones University
Collection.

EARLY MEDIEVAL AND BYZANTINE
Byzantine school, Wall painting, Grottaferrata.
Detail of remains of frescoes: Moses and
Aaron and the miracle of the rod. 13th
century. Grottaferrata, Church.

FRENCH SCHOOL
Poussin, Nicolas. Moses Changing Aaron's Rod
into a Serpent. Paris, Louvre, Musée du.

ITALIAN SCHOOL
Bartolo di Fredi. Scenes from the Old Testament:
Moses turns his rod into a serpent. S. Gimig-
nano, Collegiata.
Gozzoli, Benozzo. Old Testament and other subjects:
Detail: Rod turned into a serpent, right
side. Pisa, Camposanto.

71 E 11 72 1 EXODUS 7:20-21 THE PLAGUE OF WATER
TURNED INTO BLOOD: AS PHARAOH GOES DOWN
TO THE NILE, AARON STRIKES THE SURFACE OF
THE RIVER WITH HIS ROD; THE WATER TURNS
INTO BLOOD AND ALL THE FISH DIE

AMERICAN SCHOOL
Field, Erastus Salisbury. "He Turned their
Waters into Blood." c.1854-1880. Washington,
D.C., National Gallery of Art, 1935.

AUSTRIAN SCHOOL
Bocksberger, Hans, the Elder. Moses turning
water to blood. Fresco decorations. 16th
century. Neuburg an der Donau, Schloss.

DUTCH SCHOOL
Breenbergh, Bartholomeus. Moses and Aaron
Changing the Rivers of Egypt into Blood.
c.1630. Malibu, J. Paul Getty Museum,70.PB.14.

GERMAN SCHOOL
German school, 18th century. Moses Turns the
Waters into Blood. Budapest, Museum of Fine
Arts, 51.793.

71 E 11 72 2 EXODUS 7:6 THE PLAGUE OF FROGS: AARON
STRETCHES OUT HIS HAND OVER THE WATER OF
EGYPT; FROGS COME OUT AND COVER THE LAND

AUSTRIAN SCHOOL
Bocksberger, Hans, the Elder. Plague of frogs.
Fresco decorations. 16th century. Neuburg
an der Donau, Schloss.

71 E 11 72 5 EXODUS 9:6 THE PLAGUE OF MURRAIN IN
CATTLE: ALL THE ANIMALS OF THE EGYPTIANS
DIE

BRITISH SCHOOL
Turner, J.M.W. The Fifth Plague of Egypt. 1800.
Indianapolis, John Herron Art Institute.

71 E 11 72 7 EXODUS 9:18-25 THE PLAGUE OF HAIL:
MOSES RAISES HIS ROD TOWARDS THE SKY, AND
HAIL AND FIRE FALL TO THE GROUND

BRITISH SCHOOL
Martin, John. Seventh Plague of Egypt. 1823.
Boston, Museum of Fine Arts, 60.1157.
Martin, John. The Seventh Plague of Egypt.
1823. Frank, Mrs. Robert - Collection.

71 E 11 73 13 EXODUS 12:3-27 CELEBRATION OF THE
FIRST PASSOVER

FRENCH SCHOOL
Chagall, Marc. Illustrations from the Bible
published by Vollard. No. 47: The Israelites
Eat Passover Lamb. 1931. Nice (Alpes-
Maritimes), Musée National Message Biblique
Marc Chagall.

ITALIAN SCHOOL
Giolfino, Niccolo. General religious subjects:
The Pascal Lamb. Verona, S. Maria in Organo.
Stanzione, Massimo. The Sacrifice of Moses.
Naples, Museo Nazionale (Capodimonte).

71 E 11 73 13 2 EXODUS 12:11 THE ISRAELITES EAT
THE PASSOVER LAMB STANDING ABOUT A TABLE
WITH THEIR LOINS GIRT, THEIR SHOES ON
THEIR FEET AND WITH STAVES IN THEIR HANDS,
READY TO DEPART

AUSTRIAN SCHOOL
Bocksberger, Hans, the Elder. Passover. Fresco
decorations. 16th century. Neuburg an
der Donau, Schloss.

ITALIAN SCHOOL
Balducci, Giovanni. The Passover. Sotheby
and Co., London (Sale, April 4, 1984 [DAFFO-
DIL] No. 138).
Luini, Bernardo. Feast of the Israelites.
Frescoes from the Villa della Pelucca
near Monza. Milan, Brera, No. 739.
Palma Giovane. Sacrifice of the paschal lamb.
Venice, S. Giacomo dall'Orio.
Tintoretto. The Paschal Feast. Venice, Scuola
di San Rocco, upper hall, ceiling.

SPANISH SCHOOL
Escalante, Juan Antonio. Feast of the Passover.

71 E 11 73 2 EXODUS 12:29 THE PLAGUE OF THE FIRST-
BORN: THE DESTROYING ANGEL PASSES THROUGH
THE LAND AND KILLS EVERY EGYPTIAN FIRST-
BORN OF MAN AND ANIMAL

AMERICAN SCHOOL
Field, Erastus, Salisbury. Burial of the
First Born of Egypt. c.1880. Springfield,
Mass., Museum of Fine Arts.

AUSTRIAN SCHOOL
Bocksberger, Hans, the Elder. Death of the
First-Born. Fresco decorations. 16th century.
Neuburg an der Donau, Schloss.

BRITISH SCHOOL
Blake, William. Pestilence: The Death of
the First-Born. c.1805. Boston, Museum
of Fine Arts.

FRENCH SCHOOL
Chagall, Marc. Illustrations from the Bible
published by Vollard. No. 46: Moses Calls
Down Death Upon the First-Born of the
Egyptians. 1931. Nice (Alpes-Maritimes),
Musée National Message Biblique Marc Chagall.

ITALIAN SCHOOL
Italian school, 17th century (Rouen). The
Exterminating Angel. c.1640. Private Col-
lection.
Luini, Bernardo. Death of the First-Born.
Frescoes from the Villa della Pelucca
near Monza. Milan, Brera, 745.

SWEDISH SCHOOL
Hörberg, Pehr. The First-Born of the Pharaoh
is Killed by the Lord. Stockholm, University, 16.

71 E 11 8 EXODUS 12:31 - 13:16 THE ISRAELITES LEAVE
EGYPT; FIRST MOVEMENT FROM RAMESES TO SUCCOTH

BRITISH SCHOOL
Dadd, Richard. The flight out of Egypt. London,
Tate Gallery.

DUTCH SCHOOL
Ossenbeck, Jan van. Departure of the Jews from
Egypt. Budapest, Museum of Fine Arts, 53.454.

EARLY MEDIEVAL AND BYZANTINE
Coptic painting, Khargeh, Bagawat Necropolis.
Moses and the Israelites. Khargeh, Bagawat
Necropolis, Chapel of Flight.
Coptic painting, Khargeh, Bagawat Necropolis.
Pursuing Egyptians. Khargeh, Bagawat Necro-
polis, Chapel of Flight.
Coptic Painting, Khargeh, Bagawat Necropolis.
Egyptians. Khargeh, Bagawat Necropolis,
Chapel of Flight.

FRENCH SCHOOL
Chagall, Marc. Illustrations from the Bible
published by Vollard. No. 48: The Flight
from Egypt. 1931. Nice (Alpes-Maritimes),
Musée National Message Biblique Marc Chagall.

GERMAN SCHOOL
Heiss, Johann, 1640-1704. The Departure of
the Israelites from Egypt. 1677. Dresden,
Staatliche Kunstsammlungen, 2016.

ITALIAN SCHOOL
Bassano, Girolamo, Attributed to. The Departure
for Canaan. Sotheby and Co., London (Sale,
July 7, !982, No. 299).
Bassano, Jacopo. The Exodus. Sotheby and Co.,
(Sale, Monaco, [OUDRY] Dec.8, 1984, No.301).
Castiglione, Giovanni Francesco. The Exodus
of the Jews. Florence, Palazzo Uffizi, 4351.
Luini, Bernardo. The Departure of the Israelites.
Frescoes from the Villa della Pelucca near
Monza. Milan, Brera, 70.

SPANISH SCHOOL
Orrente, Pedro. Moses and the children of Israel
departing from Egypt. Madrid, Real Academia
de Bellas Artes.

71 E 11 81 EXODUS 12:30 DURING THE NIGHT PHARAOH
SENDS FOR MOSES AND AARON AND BEGS THEM
TO DEPART

FRENCH SCHOOL
Doré, P.G. Moses before the Pharaoh. Harvard
University, Fogg Art Museum, 1963.158.
French school, Wall painting, St. Savin. Scenes
from the Old Testament: Pharaoh drives the
Israelites from Egypt. 11th century. St.
Savin, Vienne, nave.

71 E 12 EXODUS (PART II): JOURNEY OF ISRAEL TO MOUNT
SINAI

ITALIAN SCHOOL
Bassano, Jacopo. The Israelites Journeying
through the Wilderness. Dresden, Staatliche
Kunstsammlungen, 253.
Castiglione, G.B. Journey through the Promised
Land. Milan, Brera.

SPANISH SCHOOL
Spanish school, 13th century. Old Testament
cycle: Israelites led out of Egypt. Fresco.
c.1200. Sigena, Monastery, Chapter House.

71 E 12 11 EXODUS 13:19 MOSES TAKES THE BONES OF
JOSEPH WITH HIM

FLEMISH SCHOOL
Franck, Frans, II. The Israelites with the
Bones of Joseph after the Crossing of the
Red Sea. Assisted by Abraham Govaerts.
Christie, Manson and Woods, London (Sale,
December 11, 1981, No. 93).

Franck, Frans, II. The Casket of Joseph.
Brunswick, Landesmuseum, 103.
Franck, Frans, II. The Casket of Joseph and
the Drowning of the Egyptians in the Red
Sea. Brunswick, Landesmuseum, 102.

71 E 12 12 1 EXODUS 13:21 DURING THE DAY A PILLAR
OF CLOUD (AND/OR THE ANGEL OF GOD) SHOWS
THE WAY TO THE PEOPLE

ITALIAN SCHOOL
Raphael (and assistants). Old Testament subjects: God speaks to Moses by the pillar
of smoke. Rome, Vatican, Loggie.

71 E 12 2 EXODUS 14 PASSAGE THROUGH THE RED SEA

AUSTRIAN SCHOOL
Austrian school, c.1700. The Israelites Prep-
aring to Cross the Red Sea. Sotheby and
Co., London (Sale, Oct. 24, 1984, [DAHLIA]
No. 143).

BRITISH SCHOOL
Martin, John. Moses Dividing the Waters of
the Red Sea. London, Victoria and Albert
Museum. P.68-1968.

DUTCH SCHOOL
Cornelisz, Cornelis. The Israelites Crossing
the Red Sea. 1594. Princeton, University,
Museum of Art.

FLEMISH SCHOOL
Jordaens, Hans, III. The Children of Israel
at the Red Sea. Stockholm, University,
52.

ITALIAN SCHOOL
Gozzoli, Benozzo. Old Testament and other
subjects: Passage of the Red Sea. Pisa,
Camposanto.
Tintoretto. Moses and the column of fire.
Scuola di San Rocco, upper hall, ceiling.

71 E 12 21 2 EXODUS 14:11-12 THE PEOPLE MURMUR
AGAINST MOSES

EARLY MEDIEVAL AND BYZANTINE
Early Christian painting, Rome. Moses and
Aaron murmured against. Rome, Catacomb
Maggiore, Arco of Zosima.

71 E 12 22 1 EXODUS 14:22 THE PEOPLE PASS OVER
ON DRY LAND (EGYPTIANS NOT OR BARELY VISIBLE);
THE ANGEL OF GOD AND THE PILLAR OF CLOUD
MOVE TO THE REAR

DUTCH SCHOOL
Cornelisz, Cornelis. The Israelites Crossing
the Red Sea. 1594. Princeton, University,
Museum of Art.

FRENCH SCHOOL
French school, Wall painting, St. Savin.
Scenes from the Old Testament: Passage
of the Red Sea. 11th century. St. Savin,
Vienne, Nave.

71 E 12 23 EXODUS 14:26-28 WITH HIS PEOPLE SAFE
ON THE SHORE, MOSES RAISES HIS HANDS AND
CAUSES THE WATER TO RETURN; PHARAOH'S
ARMY PERISHES IN THE WATER

BRITISH SCHOOL
Danby, Francis. The Delivery of Israel out
of Egypt. 1823-24. Preston (Lancashire),
Harris Museum and Art Gallery.
Martin, John. The Destruction of the Egyptians
in the Red Sea. London, Victoria and Albert
Museum, P.69-1968.

FLEMISH SCHOOL

Franck, Frans, II. The Israelites' Passage through the Red Sea. Karlsruhe, Kunsthalle, 172.

Franck, Frans, II. The Israelites with the Bones of Joseph after the Crossing of the Red Sea. Assisted by Abraham Govaerts. Christie, Manson and Wood, London (Sale, Dec. 11, 1981, No. 93).

Franck, Frans, II. The Casket of Joseph and the Drowning of the Egyptians in the Red Sea. Brunswick, Landesmuseum, 102.

Franck, Frans, II, Circle of. The Crossing of the Red Sea. Sotheby and Co., London (Sale, Feb. 16, 1983, No. 24).

Jordaens, Hans. The Egyptians Crossing the Red Sea. A Pair with The Fall of Manna. Christie, Manson and Woods (Sale, New York, June 12, 1981, No. 38a).

Jordaens, Hans, Circle of. The Crossing of the Red Sea. Christie, Manson and Woods (Sale, New York, June 12, 1981, No. 133).

Jordaens, Hans, Circle of. The Crossing of the Red Sea. Christie, Manson and Woods (Sale, New York, Nov. 4, 1983, No. 95).

Mol, Pieter van.The Israelites on Their Passage through the Red Sea. Also attributed to Hans Jordaens III. Karlsruhe, Kunsthalle, 187.

Wael, Cornelis de. The Destruction of the Egyptians in the Red Sea. Vienna, Kunsthistorisches Museum.

FRENCH SCHOOL

Chagall, Marc. Illustrations from the Bible published by Vollard. No. 49: The Israelites Cross the Red Sea. 1931. Nice (Alpes-Maritimes), Musée National Message Biblique Marc Chagall.

Flandrin, Jean Hippolyte. Commanding the Waters to Close Upon the Egyptian Host. 1858. Princeton, University, Museum of Art, 78-37.

Flandrin, J.H. Mural decoration: Moses causes the waters to overwhelm the Egyptians. Paris, St. Germain de Prés.

Poussin, Nicolas. The Passage of the Red Sea. 1635-37. Melbourne, National Gallery of Victoria.

GERMAN SCHOOL

Besserer, Johann Jacob. The Israelites and the Crossing of the Red Sea. Karlsruhe, Kunsthalle, 2438.

Cranach, L. (the elder). Passage of the Red Sea. Munich, Old Pinakothek.

ITALIAN SCHOOL

Bartolo di Fredi. Scenes from the Old Testament: Passage of the Red Sea. S.Gimignano, Collegiata.

Biagio d'Antonio. Crossing of the Red Sea. Rome, Vatican, Sistine Chapel.

Celio, Gaspare. Moses Crossing the Red Sea. Rome, Antichi Palazzo Mattei.

Diano, Giacinto. The Crossing of the Red Sea. A pair with Moses Striking the Rock.Christie, Manson, and Woods (Sale, London, April 15, 1983, No. 20b).

Donducci, G.A. Moses leading the Israelites across the Red Sea. Rome, Palazzo Spada.

Guardi, Francesco. The Passage of the Red Sea. Wendland - Collection (Paris).

Mazzolino, Ludovico. Pharaoh and his Host Overwhelmed in the Red Sea. Dublin, National Gallery, 666.

Palma Giovane. Crossing of the Red Sea. Venice, S. Giacomo dall'Orio.

Previtali, Andrea. Moses crossing the Red Sea. Venice, Academy.

Raphael. Old Testament subjects: Passage of the Red Sea. Rome, Vatican, Loggie.

Rosselli, Cosimo. Crossing of the Red Sea. Rome, Vatican, Sistine Chapel.

Titian. The Crossing of the Red Sea. Venice, Palazzo Ducale.

Vaga, Perino del. Crossing of the Red Sea. Florence, Palazzo Uffizi.

71 E 12 23 1 EXODUS 14:28 PHARAOH AND HIS ARMY ENGULFED IN THE RED SEA (ISRAELITES NOT OR BARELY VISIBLE)

FRENCH SCHOOL

French school, Wall painting, St. Savin. Scenes from the Old Testament: Passage of the Red Sea. 11th century. St. Savin, Vienne.

French school, Wall painting, St. Savin. Scenes from the Old Testament: Egyptians in the Red Sea. 11th century. St. Savin, Vienne, Nave.

ITALIAN SCHOOL

Fontebasso, Francesco. The Pharaoh Submerged in the Red Sea. Bergamo, Private Collection.

Giordano, Luca. Crossing of the Red Sea. Bergamo, Sta. Maria Maggiore.

Luini, Bernardo. Frescoes from the Villa della Pelucca near Monza. Room with Old Testament subjects. 4a.The Passage of the Red Sea. Milan, Brera, 740.

Luini, Bernardo. Frescoes from the Villa della Pelucca near Monza. Room with Old Testament subjects. 4b.The Passage of the Red Sea. Milan, Brera, 741.

SPANISH SCHOOL

Spanish school, 13th century. Old Testament cycle: the Egyptians drowned in the Red Sea. Fresco, c.1200. Sigena, Monastery, Chapter House.

71 E 12 3 EXODUS 15:1-21 AFTER CROSSING THE RED SEA THE ISRAELITES REJOICE AND PRAISE GOD

FRENCH SCHOOL

Poussin, Nicolas. Crossing of the Red Sea (The Passage of the Red Sea). 1635-37. Melbourne, National Gallery of Victoria.

Poussin, Nicolas. Israelites thanking God after crossing the Red Sea. London, Grosvenor House, Collection Duke of Westminster.

71 E 12 32 EXODUS 15:20-21 MIRIAM TAKES UP A TAMBOURINE AND DANCES; ALL THE WOMEN FOLLOW HER

FRENCH SCHOOL

Chagall, Marc. Illustrations from the Bible published by Vollard. No.50: Miriam Dancing. 1931. Nice (Alpes-Maritimes), Musée National Message Biblique Marc Chagall.

ITALIAN SCHOOL

Costa, Lorenzo, Follower of. The Story of Moses (The Dance of Miriam). London, National Gallery, 3104.

Giordano, Luca. Song of Miriam. Greenville, S.C., Bob Jones University Collection, 1962 cat. 85.

Giordano, Luca, Attributed to. The Song of Miriam. Christie, Manson and Woods (Sale, New York, June 12, 1981, No. 230).

Luini, Bernardo. Frescoes from the Villa della Pelucca near Monza. Room with Old Testament subjects. 5.The Prayer after the Passage. Milan, Brera, 742.

71 E 12 4 EXODUS 15:22-27 THE ISRAELITES AT MARAH AND ELIM

ITALIAN SCHOOL

Bassano, Jacopo. Journey of Moses and his people.

Bassano, Workshop of the. Exodus of the Israelites from Egypt. Venice, Academy, cat.n.402.

<u>71 E 12 41 2 EXODUS 15:25 MOSES THROWS A PIECE
OF WOOD INTO THE WATER, WHICH THEN BECOMES
SWEET</u>

FRENCH SCHOOL
   Poussin, Nicolas. Moses purifying the waters
   of Marah. Baltimore, Maryland, Museum of
   Art.

<u>71 E 12 5 EXODUS 16 MIRACLE OF THE MANNA AND THE
QUAILS</u>

ITALIAN SCHOOL
   Carracci, Ludovico. Gathering of Manna. 1597.
   Parma, Galleria Nazionale.
   Celesti, Andrea. Moses Feeding the Israelites
   in the Wilderness. San Cito di Cadore, Par-
   rocchiale.
   Pitati, Bonifacio, School of. Fall of Manna.
   Venice, Royal Palace.

<u>71 E 12 54 IN THE MORNING MANNA FALLS TO EARTH</u>

ITALIAN SCHOOL
   Guardi, Francesco. The Fall of Manna. Bolchini-
   Bonomi, A. - Collection (Milan).
   Palme Giovane. Fall of Manna. Venice, Gesuiti.
   Tintoretto. Fall of Manna. Scuola di San Rocco,
   upper hall, ceiling.

<u>71 E 12 54 1 EXODUS 16:16-17 THE GATHERING OF MANNA
(IN BASKETS AND POTS)</u>

FLEMISH SCHOOL
   Bouts, Dierick. Altarpiece of the Last Supper,
   detail: The Gathering of Manna. Louvain,
   St. Pierre.
   Jordaens, Hans. The Fall of Manna. A Pair with
   The Egyptians Crossing the Red Sea. Christie,
   Manson, and Woods (Sale, New York, June
   12, 1981, No. 38b).
   Master of the Manna Gathering. Gathering of
   Manna. Douai (Nord), Musée.
   Rubens, Peter Paul. Gathering of Manna. Sarasota,
   Fla., Ringling Museum of Art, SN 211.
   Vos, Martin de, the elder. Gathering of the
   manna. Pommersfelden, Schloss, Gallery.
   Vos, Martin de, the elder. The Jews gathering
   Manna. London, Collection E. Schapiro.
   Wolfvoet, Victor. The Israelites Gathering
   Manna. The Hague, Royal Gallery, 268.

FRENCH SCHOOL
   Poussin, Nicolas. The gathering of Manna. Paris,
   Louvre, Musée du.
   Tissot, James Jacques Joseph. Illustrations
   of the Hebrew Bible. No. 108: The Gathering
   of Manna. 1896-1904. New York, Jewish Museum,
   52.135.

GERMAN SCHOOL
   German school, 15th century. The Fall of Manna.
   Detroit, Institute of Arts, 61.351.

ITALIAN SCHOOL
   Allori, Alessandro. Gathering of Manna. Center:
   Madonna and child with saints, by an anonymous
   contemporary of Bicci di Lorenzo. Fresco.
   Florence, S.M. Novella, Refectory.
   Angeli, Giuseppe. Fall of the Manna. Venice,
   S. Stae.
   Bacchiacca, Francesco. The Gathering of Manna.
   Washington, D.C., National Gallery of Art,
   791, Kress Collection.
   Carracci, Ludovico. Gathering of Manna. Ferrara,
   S. Cristoforo.
   Corona, Leandro. Collection of Manna. Venice,
   S. Giovanni Elemosiario.
   Costa, Lorenzo, Follower of. The Gathering
   of Manna. London, National Gallery, 3103.
   Giolfino, Niccolo. General religious subjects.
   Gathering of the manna. Verona, S. Maria
   in Organo.
   Lazzarini, Gregorio. The Fall of Manna. Venice,
   Academy.

Luini, Bernardo. Frescoes from the Villa
   della Pelucca near Monza. Room with Old
   Testament subjects. 7.The Fall of Manna.
   Milan, Brera, 744.
Maffei, Francesco. Israelites Gathering Manna.
   Padua, S. Giustina.
Montemezzano, Francesco. Fall of manna.
   Venice, S. Francesco della Vigna.
Moretto da Brescia. Gathering Manna. Brescia,
   S. Giovanni Evangelista.
Palma Giovane. Gathering of the Manna. Venice,
   S. Giacomo dall'Orio.
Palma Giovane. The fall of manna. Venice,
   S. Bartolommeo.
Roberti, Ercole. Gathering of manna. Moses
   and Aaron. London, National Gallery, 1217.
Romanelli, Giovanni Francesco. Gathering
   of manna. Paris, Musée du Louvre.
Romanino, Girolamo. The Gathering of Manna.
   Brescia, rotondo.
Tiepolo, G.B. Israelites gathering manna.
   Sketch for picture at Verola Nuovo. Oxford
   University, Ashmolean Museum.
Tintoretto. Gathering of Manna. Venice, S.
   Giorgio Maggiore.
Vasari, Giorgio, Workshop of. The Fall of
   Manna. Baltimore, Md., Walters Art Gallery,
   37.1704.
Veronese, Paolo, School of. Fall of Manna.
   SS. Apostoli.

SPANISH SCHOOL
   Olot Master. The Gathering of Manna. Philadelphia, Coll. J.G. Johnson, 801.

<u>71 E 12 6 EXODUS 17:1-7; NUMBERS 20:2-13 WATER
FROM THE ROCK</u>

AMERICAN SCHOOL
   American school, 19th century. Wall painting.
   Moses striking the rock. Weymouth Heights,
   Mass., Senigo House.

DUTCH SCHOOL
   Jordaens, Jacob. Moses Striking Water from
   the Rock. Karlesruhe, Kunsthalle, 186.
   Jordaens, Jacob. Moses Striking Water from
   the Rock. c.1615. Ghent, Private Collection.
   Lucas van Leyden. Moses after striking the
   rock. Boston, Museum of Fine Arts, 54.1432.
   Lucas van Leyden. Moses after striking the
   rock, detail of Moses. Boston, Museum
   of Fine Arts, 54.1776.
   Steen, Jan. Moses Striking the Rock for Water.
   c.1671. Philadelphia, Philadelphia Museum
   of Art (Johnson Collection).

SPANISH SCHOOL
   Murillo. Works of Charity: Moses causing
   water to spring from rock.

<u>71 E 12 63 EXODUS 17:6 MOSES STRIKES THE ROCK
TWICE IN FRONT OF THE ASSEMBLED PEOPLE
AND WATER GUSHES OUT</u>

DUTCH SCHOOL
   Bloemaert, Abraham. Moses Striking the Rock.
   1596. New York, Metropolitan Museum of
   Art, 1972.171.
   Grebber, Pieter Fransz de. Moses causes water
   to gush from a rock. Tourcoin (Nord),
   Musée.
   Grebber, Pieter Fransz de. Moses Striking
   the Rock. Sotheby and Co., London (Sale,
   June 3, 1981, No. 38).
   Mander, Karel van, Circle of. Moses Striking
   Water from the Rock. Christie, Manson
   and Woods (Sale, New York, July 15, 1981,
   No. 12).
   Micker, Jan Christiansz. Moses Striking the
   Rock. Sotheby and Co., London (Sale, April
   4, 1984, [DAFFODIL], No. 271).
   Steen, Jan. Moses Striking the Rock. Frankfort-
   on-the-Main, Staedel Institute.

Uytewael, Joachim A. Moses Striking the Rock.
1624. Washington, D.C., National Gallery
of Art, 2610.

EARLY MEDIEVAL AND BYZANTINE

Early Christian Painting, Rome. Moses Smiting
Rock. Rome, Via Appia, Catacomb of S. Callix-
tus, Cripta delle Pecorelle.

Early Christian Painting, Rome. Moses Smiting
Rock. Catacomb of Domitilla, Arco delle
piciole Oranti.

Early Christian Painting, Rome. Moses Smiting
the Rock. Rome, Catacomb of the Jordani.

Early Christian Painting, Rome. Moses smiting
the Rock. Rome, Catacomb Maggiore, Cubiculum
II.

Early Christian Painting, Rome. Moses smiting
the rock, upper left of general view of
entrance. Rome, Torre Pignattara, Catacomb
of SS. Petrus and Marcellinus, Crypt with
Orpheus.

Early Christian Painting, Rome. Moses smiting
the rock. Rome, Torre Pignattara, Catacomb
of SS. Petrus and Marcellinus, Cubiculum
IV.

Early Christian Painting, Rome. Moses smiting
the rock. Rome, Torre Pignattara, Catacomb
of SS. Petrus and Marcellinus, Cubiculum
XIV.

Early Christian Painting, Rome. Moses smiting
the rock. Detail: Head of Moses. Rome, Torre
Pignattara, Catacomb of SS. Petrus and Marcellinus, Cubiculum XXI.

Early Christian Painting, Rome. Moses and three
youths. Rome, Via Salaria Nuova,. Catacomb
of Priscilla, Cappella Greca.

FLEMISH SCHOOL

Balen, Hendrik van. Moses Striking the Rock.
Brunswick, Landesmuseum, 82.

Elias, Mathieu. Moses striking the water from
the rock. Cambridge University, Fitzwilliam
Museum, 2829.

Flemish school, 15th century. Moses Strikes
Water from the Rock. Vienna, Kunsthistorisches
Museum, 7659.

Flemish school, 17th century. Moses Striking
the Rock. c.1625. Oxford University, Ashmolean
Museum, A 8.

Janssens, Abraham. Moses Striking the Rock.
Dublin, National Gallery, 1010.

Jordaens, Jacob. Moses striking the rock.
London, Collection Sir Joseph B. Robinson.

Jordaens, Jacob. Moses Strikes Water from the
Rock. Cassel, Staatliche Kunstsammlungen,110a.

Mostaert, Gillis, Attributed to. Moses Striking
Water from the Rock. c.1560. Vienna, Kunsthistorisches Museum, 1093.

Wouters, Frans. Moses Striking Water from the
Rock. Christie, Manson and Woods (Sale,
New York, Jan. 19, 1982, No. 69).

FRENCH SCHOOL

Blanchard, Charles Octave. Moses Striking the
Rock. 1836. Paris, École des Beaux-Arts
(Grand Prix de Rome).

Bourdon, Sebastien. Moses Striking Water from
the Rock. Christie, Manson and Woods (Sale,
New York, [BETH-5258], Jan. 18, 1983, No.68).

Chagall, Marc. Illustrations from the Bible
published by Vollard. No. 51: Moses and
the Rock of Horeb. 1931. Nice(Alpes-Maritimes)
Musée National Message Biblique Marc Chagall.

Chagall, Marc. Moses Striking Water from the
Rock. Nice (Alpes-Maritimes), Musée National
Message Biblique Marc Chagall.

Champaigne, Jean Baptiste de. Moses Striking
the Rock. Christie, Manson and Woods (Sale,
New York, Jan. 15, 1985, [CAROL-5808] no.181).

Papety, Dominique Louis Ferréol. Moses Striking
the Rock. 1836. Paris, École des Beaux-Arts
(Grand Prix de Rome).

Pierre, Jean Baptiste. Moses Striking Water
from the Rock. Dijon (Côte d'Or), Musée
Maguin.

Poussin, Nicolas. Moses striking water from
the rock. London, Bridgewater House, 62.
(Now in Sutherland Coll. on loan to Edinburgh, Nat. Gal.)

Poussin, Nicolas. Moses striking water from
the rock. Leningrad, Hermitage, 255.

GERMAN SCHOOL

German school, 18th century. Moses Strikes
Water from the Rock. Budapest, Museum
of Fine Arts, 51.792.

Tassel, Jean. Moses striking the rock. Hague,
Museum Bredius, 181-1946.

ITALIAN SCHOOL

Allegri, Pomponio. Apse vault: Moses on Sinai.
Parma, Cathedral.

Bacchiacca, Francesco. Moses striking the
Rock. Edinburgh, National Gallery.

Bambini, Nicolo. Moses Striking Water from
the Rock. Venice, S. Moisé.

Bassano, Francesco (the younger).Moses striking
the rock. Melbourne Hall, Collection Lord
Lothian.

Bassano, Jacopo, and workshop. Moses striking
Water from Rock. Vienna, Kunsthistorisches
Museum.

Bassano, Jacopo, Studio of. Moses Striking
the Rock. Paris, Louvre, Musée du, 429.

Castiglione, G.B. Moses striking the rock.
New York, Collection Walter P. Chrysler,Jr.

Coppapani, Sigismundo. Moses Striking the
Rock. Prato, Cassa di Risparmi.

Diano, Giacinto. Moses Striking the Rock.
A Pair with the Crossing of the Red Sea.
Christie, Manson and Woods (Sale, London,
April 15, 1983, No. 20a).

Donducci, G.A. Moses causes water to spring
from the rock. Rome, Palazzo Spada.

Ferrari, Gregorio de. Moses Makes the Waters
Spring Forth. Genoa, Palazzo Rosso.

Francanzano, Francesco, Circle of. Moses
Striking the Rock. Christie, Manson and
Woods (Sale, London, [THUMP-3441], April
12, 1985, No. 144).

Guardi, Giovanni Antonio. Moses Finds Water
in the Desert. Milan, Private Collection.

Lippi, Filippino. Moses Brings Forth Water
out of the Rock. Pendant to Worship of
the Egyptian Bull-God, Apis. London,National
Gallery, 4904.

Luini, Bernardo. Frescoes from the Villa
della Pelucca near Monza. Room with Old
Testament subjects. 6.Moses Striking Water
from the Rock. Fresco. Milan, Brera, 738.

Luini, Bernardo. Moses Striking the Rock.
Milan, Brera.

Moretto da Brescia. Moses. Brescia, Collection
Count Bettoni Cazzago.

Paciccio (Francesco Rosa). Moses Striking
Water from the Rock. Budapest, Museum
of Arts, 767 (319).

Paggi, Giovanni Battista. Moses striking
water from the rock. Schleissheim, Neues
Schloss, Gallery.

Preti, Mattia. Moses striking the rock. Madrid,
Prado.

Raphael (and assistants). Old Testament subjects: Moses striking water from the rock.
Rome, Vatican, Loggie.

Ricci, Sebastiano. Moses Striking Water from
the Rock. Turin, Pinacoteca, 598.

Ricci, Sebastiano. Moses Striking Water from
the Rock. Venice, Santo Stefano (Fondazione
Giorgio Cini, deposited in Venice, Academy).

Tintoretto. Moses striking the rock. Frankfort-
on-the-Main, Staedel Institute.

Tintoretto. Moses Striking the Rock. Scuola
di San Rocco, upper hall, ceiling.

SPANISH SCHOOL
  Goya. Biblical themes: 2. Moses causing water
    to spring from rock. Madrid, Collection
    Duques de Aveyro.
  Spanish school, 13th century. Old Testament:
    Moses striking the rock. Fresco, c. 1200.
    Sigena, Monastery, Chapter House.

71 E 12 72 1   EXODUS 17:12   MOSES SITTING ON A ROCK
  ON THE TOP OF A HILL, WITH HIS ARMS HELD
  UP BY AARON AND HUR; THE AMALEKITES ARE
  DEFEATED

AUSTRIAN SCHOOL
  Bocksberger, Hans, the Elder. War of Israelites
    with Amalekites. Fresco decorations. 16th
    century. Neuburg an der Donau, Schloss.

FRENCH SCHOOL
  Courtois, Jacques. Joshua Defeats the Amalekites.
    Paris, Louvre, Musée du, INV. 3437.
  Poussin, Nicolas. Victory of Joshua over the
    Amalekites. Leningrad, Hermitage.

ITALIAN SCHOOL
  Falcone, Angelo. Battle of the Hebrews and
    the Amalekites. Naples, Museo Nazionale,
    Capodimonte.

71 E 12 8   EXODUS 18   JETHRO'S VISIT TO MOSES: WITH
  ZIPPORAH AND HER TWO SONS HE COMES TO THE
  DESERT WHERE MOSES IS ENCAMPED

BRITISH SCHOOL
  Artaud, William. Moses Meeting his Wife and
    Sons. c.1791. Pittsburgh, Carnegie Institute,
    57.6.4.

71 E 12 85   EXODUS 18:25   MOSES CHOOSING JUDGES

DUTCH SCHOOL
  Bol, Ferdinand. Moses Follows Jethro's Suggestion
    and Chooses Judges. c.1655/56. Leningrad,
    Hermitage.

71 E 13 1   RECURRENT THEMES: MOUNT SINAI

ITALIAN SCHOOL
  Bartolo di Fredi. Scenes from the Old Testament:
    Moses on Mount Sinai. S. Gimignano, Col-
    legiata.
  Domenichino. Moses on the mount. Frascati,
    Villa Muti.
  Gozzoli, Benozzo. Old Testament and other
    subjects: Tables of the law. Pisa, Camposanto.
  Jacopo di Paolo. Scenes from the Old Testament:
    Moses receiving the Tables of the Law. Maz-
    zaratta (near Bologna), Church.
  Rosselli, Cosimo. Moses on Sinai. Rome, Vatican
    4, Sistine Chapel.

SPANISH SCHOOL
  Greco, El. Altarpiece including scene of View
    of Mt. Sinai. Modena, Pinacoteca Estense.

71 E 13 12   EXODUS 19:3 - 24:3   MOSES COMMUNICATING
  WITH GOD ON MOUNT SINAI

AMERICAN SCHOOL
  Cole, Thomas. Moses on the Mount. Shelburne,
    Vt., Shelburne Museum.

ITALIAN SCHOOL
  Luini, Bernardo. Frescoes from the Villa della
    Pelucca near Monza. Room with Old Testament
    subjects. 8.Moses on Mount Sinai. Fresco.
    Milan, Brera, 737.

71 E 13 22   EXODUS 19:10-15   THE PEOPLE GET READY
  FOR THE COMING LEGISLATION: THEY WASH
  THEIR CLOTHES AND SET BOUNDS ROUND THE
  MOUNTAIN

DUTCH SCHOOL
  Cornelisz, Cornelis. Children of Israel before
    Mount Sinai. Signed with monogram and
    dated 1600. London, William Hallsborough
    Gallery (1968).

71 E 13 4   EXODUS 24:9-18, 31:18   MOSES ON MOUNT
  SINAI WITH THE TABLES OF THE LAW

ITALIAN SCHOOL
  Gozzoli, Benozzo. Old Testament and other
    subjects: Tables of the Law. Pisa, Campo-
    santo.
  Reni, Guido. Moses with the Ten Commandments.
    Rome, Villa Borghese, Gallery.
  Rosselli, Cosimo. Moses destroying the tables
    of the law. Rome, Vatican, Sistine Chapel.

71 E 13 43   EXODUS 24:12-18, 31:18   MOSES RECEIVES
  THE TABLES OF THE LAW FROM GOD

AMERICAN SCHOOL
  West, Benjamin. Moses Receiving the Laws
    on Mount Sinai. Sketch for painting in
    Kings Chapel at Windsor. c.1779-81. Sotheby
    and Co., London (Sale, [CATKIN], March
    14, 1984, No. 105).

EARLY MEDIEVAL AND BYZANTINE
  Early Medieval and Byzantine painting, Sinai.
    Moses receiving the Law. 14th century.
    Sinai, Monastery of St. Catherine, Icon
    359.
  Early Medieval and Byzantine painting, Sinai.
    Moses receiving the Law. 13th century.
    Sinai, Monastery of St. Catherine, Icon
    469.

FRENCH SCHOOL
  Chagall, Marc. Illustrations from the Bible
    published by Vollard. No. 52: Moses Receives
    the Tables of the Law. 1931. Nice (Alpes-
    Maritimes), Musée National Message Biblique
    Marc Chagall.
  Chagall, Marc. Moses Receives the Tablets
    of the Law. Nice (Alpes-Maritimes), Musée
    National Message Biblique Marc Chagall.
  French school, 11th century, St. Savin. Scenes
    from the Old Testament: Moses receiving
    the tables of the law. St. Savin, Vienne,
    Nave.
  French school, Wall painting, St. Savin.
    Scenes from the Old Testament: God appearing
    to Moses upon Mount Sinai. Copy. 11th
    century. Paris, Musée National des Monuments
    Français.

ITALIAN SCHOOL
  Bassano, Francesco, the younger. Moses Receiving
    the Tablets of the Law (Autumn). Vienna,
    Kunsthistorisches Museum, 4304.
  Daniele da Volterra. Moses on Mount Sinai
    (formerly attributed to Carlo Portelli).
    Dresden, Gallery, 84.
  Guardi, Francesco. Moses Receiving the Tablets
    of the Law from Mount Sinai. Milan, Private
    Collection.
  Master of the Large Figures. Retable with
    scenes from the Old Testament and the
    life of Christ. Fragment: Moses receiving
    the Ten Commandments. San Vitores, Ermita.
  Peruzzi, Baldassare. Old and New Testament
    subjects: Moses receiving the tablets,
    upper right. Rome, S. Maria della Pace.
    Cappela della Ponzetto. Arch.
  Raphael. Old Testament subjects. Moses receives
    the tables of the law from God. Rome,
    Vatican, Loggie.

SPANISH SCHOOL
  Bayeu y Subias, Francisco. Story of Moses.
    Madrid, Art Market, 1965.
  Master of the Large Figures. Retable with scenes
    from the Old Testament and the Life of Christ.
    Fragment: Moses receiving the Ten Command-
    ments. San Vitores, Ermita.
  Spanish school, 13th century. Old Testmanet
    cycle: Moses on Mount Sinai. Fresco, c.1200.
    Sigena, Monastery, Chapter House.

71 E 13 43 1 EXODUS 32:16 GOD WRITING THE COMMAND-
              MENTS ON THE TWO STONE TABLETS

BRITISH SCHOOL
  Blake, William. God Writing upon the Tables
    of the Covenant. c.1805. Edinburgh, National
    Gallery of Scotland.

71 E 13 5 EXODUS 32:1-19 THE GOLDEN CALF

AUSTRIAN SCHOOL
  Bocksberger, Hans, the Elder. Dance of the
    Golden Calf. Fresco decorations, 16th century.
    Neuburg an der Donau, Schloss.

FRENCH SCHOOL
  Claude Lorrain. Adoration of the Golden Calf.
    1653. Karlsruhe, Kunsthalle.
  Claude Lorrain. Adoration of the Golden Calf.
    1660. Manchester (Lancashire), Art Gallery.

ITALIAN SCHOOL
  Raphael (and assistants).Old Testament subjects:
    Worship of the Golden Calf. Rome, Vatican,
    Loggie.
  Tintoretto. Worship of the golden calf. Vienna,
    Kunsthistorisches Museum.
  Tintoretto. Moses and the Worship of the Golden
    Calf. c.1545. Washington, National Gallery
    of Art, 291.

71 E 13 51 1 EXODUS 32:2-4 THE PEOPLE BRING THEIR
              GOLDEN EAR-RINGS TO AARON

ITALIAN SCHOOL
  Celesti, Andrea. The Israelites sacrificing
    to their idols. Dresden, Gallery.
  Italian school, 15th century. Series of eight
    panels with scenes from the Old Testament:
    The Golden Calf. Venice, S. Alvise.

71 E 13 52 EXODUS 32:2-5 AARON MAKES A GOLDEN CALF
            AND HAS IT PLACED ON A PEDESTAL OR ALTAR

ITALIAN SCHOOL
  Gaulli, Giovanni Battista, Attributed to. The
    Israelites and their Golden Calf. Christie,
    Manson and Woods, London, (Sale, Dec., 1981,
    No. 72).

71 E 13 53 EXODUS 32:5-6 ADORATION OF THE GOLDEN
            CALF (WHICH MAY BE STANDING ON A PILLAR,
            AND IS SOMETIMES DEPICTED AS A DRAGON)

DUTCH SCHOOL
  Moeyaert, Claes Cornelisz. The Adoration of
    the Golden Calf. 1641. Christie, Manson
    and Woods (Sale, New York, Jan. 15, 1985,
    [CAROL-5808], No. 41).
  Steen, Jan. The Worship of the Golden Calf.
    Raleigh, N.C., North Carolina Museum of
    Art.

FRENCH SCHOOL
  Chagall, Marc. Illustrations for the Bible
    published by Vollard. No.53: The Hebrews
    Worshipping the Golden Calf. 1931. Nice
    (Alpes-Maritimes), Musée National Message
    Biblique Marc Chagall.
  Poussin, Nicolas. Adoration of the Golden Calf.
    Detail: Heads of women. London, Collection
    Davis Liddell.
  Poussin, Nicolas. Adoration of the Golden Calf.
    1626. San Francisco, De Young Memorial Museum.

ITALIAN SCHOOL
  Gaulli, Giovanni Battista. The Worship of
    the Golden Calf. Sotheby and Co., London
    (Sale, Nov. 17, 1982, No. 49).
  Italian school, 15th century. Series of eight
    panels with scenes from the Old Testament.
    The Golden Calf. Venice, S. Alvise.
  Rosselli, Cosimo. Moses destroying the tables
    of the law. Rome, Vatican, Loggie.
  Tintoretto. Worship of the golden calf. Venice,
    S. Maria dell'Orto.

SPANISH SCHOOL
  Spanish school, 13th century. Old Testament
    cycle: Worship of the Golden Calf. Fresco,
    c. 1200. Sigena, Monastery, Chapter House.

71 E 13 53 1 EXODUS 32:5-6 AARON BUILDS AN ALTAR
              AND SACRIFICES TO THE GOLDEN CALF

ITALIAN SCHOOL
  Diziani, Gasparo, Circle of. Aaron Sacrificing
    to the Golden Calf. Sotheby and Co., London
    (Sale, June 3, 1981, No. 12).

71 E 13 53 2 EXODUS 32:19 THE PEOPLE DANCE AROUND
              THE GOLDEN CALF

AUSTRIAN SCHOOL
  Remp, Franz Carl. The Dance of the Golden
    Calf. Vienna, Österreichische Galerie,
    4302.

FRENCH SCHOOL
  Poussin, Nicolas. The worship of the Golden
    Calf. Salisbury, Collection Earl of Radnor.
  Poussin, Nicolas. Worship of the Golden
    Calf. 1635-37. London, National Gallery.

ITALIAN SCHOOL
  Lippi, Filippino. The Worship of the Egyptian
    Bull-God, Apis. Pendant to Moses Brings
    Forth Water out of the Rock. London,
    National Gallery, 4905.

71 E 13 53 5 EXODUS 32:19 THE PEOPLE FEASTING:
              THE GOLDEN CALF CLEARLY VISIBLE

DUTCH SCHOOL
  Lucas van Leyden. Triptych of the Worship
    of the Golden Calf. Amsterdam, Rijksmuseum.
  Mander, Karel van. The Worshipping of the
    Golden Calf. 1602. Haarlem, Frans Hals
    Museum, 204 b.
  Steen, Jan. The adoration of the golden calf.
    Raleigh, N.C., North Carolina Museum of
    Art.

FLEMISH SCHOOL
  Franck, Frans, II. The Golden Calf. Christie,
    Manson and Woods (Sale, London, July 18,
    1974, No. 82).
  Pourbus, Peter, the younger. The Golden Calf.
    Also attributed to Frans Floris (de Vriendt)
    I. Dublin, National Gallery, 189.

71 E 13 54 EXODUS 32:13-18 MOSES (AND JOSHUA)
            COMES DOWN WITH THE STONE TABLETS

ITALIAN SCHOOL
  Rosselli, Cosimo. Moses destroying the tables
    of the law. Rome, Vatican, Loggie.

71 E 13 54 1 EXODUS 32:19 ON SEEING THE IDOLATERS
              MOSES BREAKS THE TABLETS OF THE LAW

BRITISH SCHOOL
  Blake, William. Moses Indignant at the Golden
    Calf. c.1799-1800. England, Private Collection.

DUTCH SCHOOL
      Rembrandt. Moses Breaking the Tablets of the
         Law. 1659. Berlin, Staatliche Museen, 811.

FRENCH SCHOOL
      Chagall, Marc. Illustrations from the <u>Bible</u>
         published by Vollard. No. 54: Moses Breaks
         the Tables of the Law. 1931. Nice (Alpes-
         Maritimes), Musée National Message Biblique
         Marc Chagall.

ITALIAN SCHOOL
      Beccafumi, Domenico. Moses and the Tablets
         of the Law. 1538. Pisa, Cathedral, Choir.
      Carracci, Ludovico. Moses and the Golden Calf.
         Bologna, Pinacoteca Nazionale.
      Daniele da Volterra. Moses on Mount Sinai,
         (formerly attributed to Carlo Portelli).
         Dresden, Gallery, 84.
      Rosselli, Cosimo. Moses destroying the tables
         of the law. Rome, Vatican, Sistine Chapel.

71 E 13 63   EXODUS 32:26-28   MOSES, STANDING AT THE
            GATE OF THE CAMP, CAUSES THE LEVITES TO
            KILL ALL THE IDOLATERS

ITALIAN SCHOOL
      Rosselli, Cosimo. Moses destroying the tables
         of the law. Rome, Vatican, Sistine Chapel.

71 E 13 7   EXODUS 34   THE NEW TABLETS

ITALIAN SCHOOL
      Guercino. Moses with the Tablets of the Law.
         Rome, Galleria Colonna.

71 E 13 74   EXODUS 34:29-32   MOSES COMES DOWN WITH
            THE NEW TABLES AND IS AWAITED BY AARON AND
            THE ASSEMBLED PEOPLE, WHO NOTICE THAT "HIS
            FACE IS SHINING" (MOSES' FACE IS DEPICTED
            WITH RAYS OF LIGHT OR WITH HORNS)

AUSTRIAN SCHOOL
      Troger, Paul, Follower of. Moses Brings the
         Tablets of the Law from Mt. Sinai. Vienna,
         Österreichische Galerie, 5334.

DUTCH SCHOOL
      Bol, Ferdinand. Moses presents the Tablets
         of the Law to the people of Israel. c.1663/66.
         Holland, Private Collection.
      Bol, Ferdinand. Moses with the Tablets of the
         Law. Amsterdam, Royal Palace.

FLEMISH SCHOOL
      Vos, Martin de, the elder. Moses bringing the
         tables of the law to the children of Israel.
         The Hague, Royal Gallery.

ITALIAN SCHOOL
      Guglielmo da Marcilla. Scenes from the Old
         and New Testaments: Moses presenting the
         Law. Arezzo, Cathedral.
      Raphael (and assistants). Old Testament subjects:
         Moses showing tables with the law. Rome,
         Vatican, Loggie.

SPANISH SCHOOL
      Mayno, Juan Bautista. Aaron. Wall decorations.
         Toledo, San Pedro Mártir.

71 E 13 81   EXODUS 35:22-28   THE PEOPLE BRING THEIR
            OFFERINGS FOR THE TABERNACLE: ALL KINDS
            OF FINE OBJECTS, JEWELRY, LINEN, ETC.

ITALIAN SCHOOL
      Luini, Bernardo. Frescoes from the Villa della
         Pelucca near Monza. Room with Old Testament
         subjects. 9.The Offering at the Tabernacle.
         Fresco. Milan, Brera, 743.

71 E 2   LEVITICUS

FRENCH SCHOOL
      Flandrin, J.H. Mural decoration: Moses sacri-
         fices the bullock and the two rams. Paris,
         St. Germain de Prés.

71 E 22   LEVITICUS 9   AARON OFFERS SACRIFICES

AUSTRIAN SCHOOL
      Troger, Paul. The Patriarch's Sacrifice.
         Frankfort-on-the-Main, Staedel Institute,
         1641.

EARLY MEDIEVAL AND BYZANTINE
      Byzantine school, Wall painting, Istanbul.
         Aaron and his sons before the Altar. 14th
         century. Istanbul, Mosque Kahrié, par-
         ecclesion, western end, north side of
         transverse arch.

71 E 23 5   LEVITICUS 14:2-7   THE LAW OF THE LEPER'S
            CLEANSING

ITALIAN SCHOOL
      Botticelli, Sandro. Purification of the leper.
         Rome, Vatican, Sistine Chapel.

71 E 3   NUMBERS 10:11 - 34:1 NUMBERS: THE WANDERING
IN THE WILDERNESS, THE ISRAELITES LEAVE
MOUNT SINAI AND REACH CANAAN

FRENCH SCHOOL
French school, 17th century. Moses Leads the
Jews into the Promised Land. Cologne, Wallraf-
Richartz Museum, 47.

ITALIAN SCHOOL
Bassano, Francesco, the younger, Attributed
to. Israelites in the Desert. Dartmouth
College Collection (Hanover, N.H.), P 977.185.

71 E 31 5   NUMBERS 13-14   RECONNAISSANCE OF CANAAN

BRITISH SCHOOL
Martin, John. Joshua Spying out the Land of
Canaan. Sotheby and Co., London (Sale, July
19, 1979).

71 E 31 52   NUMBERS 13:23   THE SPIES TAKE AWAY SOME
OF THE FRUITS OF CANAAN AND RETURN, USUALLY
CARRYING A LARGE BUNCH OF GRAPES ON A POLE

FRENCH SCHOOL
Poussin, N. The Four Seasons: Autumn or The
Spies in the Promised Land. 1660-64. Paris,
Louvre, Musée du.

GERMAN SCHOOL
Koch, Joseph Anton. Landscape with Men Returning
from the Promised Land. 1816. Cologne,
Wallraf-Richartz Museum.

71 E 31 53   NUMBERS 13:28-33   THE SPIES, EXCEPT FOR
CALEB AND JOSHUA, BRING STARTLING REPORTS
WHICH UPSET THE PEOPLE

ITALIAN SCHOOL
Lanfranco, Giovanni. Moses and the Messengers
from Canaan. Originally executed for the
Cappella del Sacramento in S. Paolo fuori
le Mura, Rome. 1621-25. Malibu, J. Paul
Getty Museum, 69.PA.4.

71 E 31 7   NUMBERS 16   REBELLION OF KORAH (CORE),
DATHAN AND ABIRAM, AND THEIR PUNISHMENT

ITALIAN SCHOOL
Botticelli, Sandro. Punishment of Korah. Rome,
Vatican, Sistine Chapel.

71 E 31 8   NUMBERS 17   THE FLOWERING ROD

ITALIAN SCHOOL
Gozzoli, Benozzo. Old Testament and other subjects: Aaron's rod.

71 E 31 74 2   NUMBERS 16:30-33   THE GROUND OPENS
AND SWALLOWS THE REBELS ALONG WITH THEIR
FAMILIES AND POSSESSIONS

ITALIAN SCHOOL
Beccafumi, Domenico. Moses and the children
of Korah. Pisa, Cathedral, Choir.

71 E 32 4   NUMBERS 21:4-9   THE BRAZEN SERPENT

FLEMISH SCHOOL
Rubens, Peter Paul. Moses and the Brazen Serpent.
London, National Gallery, 59.
Rubens, Peter Paul. Copy. Moses and the Brazen
Serpent. Sacramento, Crocker Art Gallery,
1872.168.

FRENCH SCHOOL
Perrier, François. Worship of the Brazen Serpent.
Dijon, Musée Magnin.

GERMAN SCHOOL
Rottenhammer, Johann, Attributed to. The Brazen
Serpent. Sotheby and Co., London (Sale,
April 4, 1984 [DAFFODIL], No. 146).

ITALIAN SCHOOL
Beaumont, Claudio Francesco. The Bronze Serpent.
Turin, Pinacoteca, 83.
Gozzoli, Benozzo. Old Testament and other
subjects: the brazen serpent. Pisa, Campo-
santo.
Mazzuoli, (Bedoli, Girolamo). Moses and the
Brazen Serpent. Doors from a Tabernacle.
A Pair. Christie, Manson and Wood (Sale,
Christie East, New York, Nov. 8, 1984,
No. 79).
Michelangelo. Ceiling decorations, lunettes
in four corners with scenes from the Old
Testament: The Bronze Serpent.
Palme Giovane. The punishment of the serpents
(Moses). Venice, S. Bartolommeo.
Palma Giovane. Punishment by the serpents.
Venice, Gesuiti.
Pellegrini, Giovanni Antonio. Moses and the
Serpent of Bronze. Venice, San Moise.
Pittoni, G.B. Moses and the Brazen Serpents.
Christie, Manson and Woods (Sale, New
York, Jan. 19, 1982, No. 72).
Schiavone, Andrea. Moses in Egypt. Plague
of Serpents. Venice, S. Sebastiano, Sacristy.
Tintoretto. Brazen serpent. Scuola di San
Rocco, upper hall, ceiling.

71 E 32 41   NUMBERS 21:5-6   WHEN THE PEOPLE COMPLAIN
AGAIN ABOUT THE FOOD, GOD SENDS POISONOUS
SNAKES, MANY DIE OF SNAKE-BITES

ITALIAN SCHOOL
Tiepolo, G.B. Frieze from SS. Cosmo e Damiano:
Plague of fiery serpents.

71 E 32 43   NUMBERS 21:8-9   ANYONE WHO IS BITTEN
IS CURED BY LOOKING AT THE BRAZEN SERPENT;
THE SERPENT (OR DRAGON) IS USUALLY DEPICTED
ON A TAU-SHAPED CROSS OR ON A PILLAR

AMERICAN SCHOOL
West, Benjamin. Moses and the brazen serpent.
Greenville, S.C., Bob Jones University
Collection.

AUSTRIAN SCHOOL
Bocksberger, Hans, the Elder. Moses lifting
the serpent. 16th century. Fresco decorations. Neuburg an der Donau, Schloss.

BRITISH SCHOOL
John, Augustus. Moses and the Brazen Serpent.
1898. London, University College, Slade
School of Fine Arts.

FLEMISH SCHOOL
Dyck, Anthony van. The brazen serpent. Richmond,
Cook Collection, 246.
Dyck, Anthony van. The Brazen Serpent (Moses
and the Brazen Serpent). Madrid, Prado,
1637.
Franck, Ambrosius I. Moses and the Brazen
Serpent. Sotheby and Co., London (Sale,
Oct. 24, 1984, [DAHLIA], No. 148).
Rubens, P.P. Copy. Moses and the brazen serpent.
(Copy of Rubens' picture in National Gallery)
Seville, Private Collection.
Rubens, P.P. (?) Moses and the brazen serpent.
c. 1618-20. Madrid, Prado.
Rubens, Peter Paul. Moses and the Brazen
Serpent. London, University, Courtauld
Institute (Princess Gate Collection),15.

FRENCH SCHOOL
French school, 17th century. The Erection
of the Brazen Serpent. Budapest, Museum
of Fine Arts, 703.
Gamelin, Jacques. The bronze serpent. Car-
cassone (Aude), Cathedral.

GERMAN SCHOOL
German school, Wall painting, Soest. Mural
paintings: Brazen serpent. 13th century.
Soest, St. Maria zur Höhe.

Stummel, Friedrich. The Brazen Serpent. 1887.
Keeken, St. Mariae Himmelfahrt, High Altar,
Inner wing, right.

ITALIAN SCHOOL
Brentana, Simone. The Adoration of the Bronze
Serpent. c.1710-20. Brescia, Congrega di
Carità Apostolica.
Moretto da Brescia. The plague of serpents.
Milan, Gussalli Collection.
Palma Giovane. Punishment of the serpents (Moses)
Venice, S. Giacomo dall'Orio.
Schiavone, Andrea. Moses in Egypt. Plague of
Serpents. Venice, S. Sebastiano, Sacristy.
Vecchietta. Moses and the brazen serpent. Siena,
Spedale di S. Maria della Scala, Sala di
S. Pietro.

SPANISH SCHOOL
Goya. Biblical themes: 1. Moses and the brazen
serpent. Madrid, Collection Duques de Aveyro.

SWEDISH SCHOOL
Albertus Pictor. Moses, detail. c.1480. Täby
(Uppland), Church, Ceiling painting.

71 E 33 14   NUMBERS 22:23   AN ANGEL HOLDING A SWORD
BARS THE WAY AND CAUSES BALAAM'S ASS TO
TURN ASIDE; THE ANGEL IS INVISIBLE TO BALAAM

AUSTRIAN SCHOOL
Bocksberger, Hans, the Elder. Balaam and the
Ass. 16th century. Fresco decorations. Neuburg
an der Donau, Schloss.

DUTCH SCHOOL
Fabritius, Bernard. Balaam and his Ass. c.1672.
Unknown Location.

71 E 33 14 1   NUMBERS 22:27-28   BALAAM STRIKES HIS
ASS, WHEREUPON THE ASS LIES DOWN AND STARTS
TO SPEAK

DUTCH SCHOOL
Lastman, Pieter P. Balaam and the Ass. 1622.
Feigen, Richard - Collection (New York).
Rembrandt, attributed to. Balaam and the Ass.
c. 1625. Paris, Musée Cognac-Jay.

FLEMISH SCHOOL
Franck, Franz, I, Studio of. Flemish Reliquary
Chest painted with scenes from the Old Testament. Detail: Drawer: Balaam and the Ass.
c. 1600. Sarasota, Fla., Ringling Museum
of Art, SN 1950.

GERMAN SCHOOL
Koch, Joseph Anton. Balaam and the Angel.
Frankfort-on-the-Main, Staedel Institute.

ITALIAN SCHOOL
Vignali, Jacopo. Balaam's Ass. Prato, Cassa
di Risparmi.

71 E 4   DEUTERONOMY: THE CROWNING EVENTS OF THE
WANDERINGS; MOSES PREPARES FOR HIS DEATH

ITALIAN SCHOOL
Signorelli, Luca. History of Moses. Rome,
Vatican, Sistine Chapel.

71 E 46 11   DEUTERONOMY 34:1-4   MOSES REMOVES HIS
SANDALS AT THE SIGHT OF THE HOLY LAND

FRENCH SCHOOL
Moreau, Gustave. Moses Sheds His Sandals
in Sight of the Holy Land. 1856? Paris,
Musée Gustave Moreau.

71 E 46 4   JUDE 9   THE CONTEST OF ST. MICHAEL AND
SATAN FOR THE BODY OF MOSES

BRITISH SCHOOL
Blake, William. The Devil Rebuked; the Burial
of Moses. c.1800-03. Harvard University,
Fogg Art Museum, 1943.407.

71 E 52 2   JOSHUA 3-4   THE ISRAELITES COME TO THE
         JORDAN

   FRENCH SCHOOL
      Chagall, Marc. Illustrations from the Bible
      published by Vollard. No. 56: Joshua. 1931.
      Nice (Alpes-Maritimes), Musée National Message
      Biblique Marc Chagall.

   ITALIAN SCHOOL
      Gozzoli, Benozzo. Old Testament and other sub-
      jects: Fall of Jericho. Pisa, Camposanto.

71 E 52 22   JOSHUA 3:6   THE PEOPLE LEAVE THE CAMP;
          THE PRIESTS, CARRYING THE ARK, LEAD THE
          MARCH

   FLEMISH SCHOOL
      Jordaens, Hans, III. The Israelites Pass Over
      the Jordan with Dry Feet. Budapest, Museum
      of Fine Arts, 592 (428).

   ITALIAN SCHOOL
      Raphael (and assistants). Old Testament subjects:
      The Ark of the Covenant passing through
      Jordan. Rome, Vatican, Loggie.

71 E 52 4   JOSHUA 6   THE FALL OF JERICHO

   FRENCH SCHOOL
      Tissot, James Jacques Joseph. Illustrations
      of the Hebrew Bible. No.151: The Taking
      of Jericho. 1896-1903. New York, Jewish
      Museum.

   ITALIAN SCHOOL
      Finiguerra, Maso. Joshua Before Jericho (Flor-
      entine Picture Chronicle). London, British
      Museum.
      Italian school, 15th century. Series of eight
      panels with scenes of the Old Testament:
      The Fall of Jericho. Venice, S. Alvise.
      Raphael (and assistants). Old Testament subjects:
      Fall of the walls of Jericho. Rome, Vatican,
      Loggie.

   SPANISH SCHOOL
      March, Esteban. Joshua at the walls of Jericho.
      Barcelona, Museum of Catalan Art.

71 E 52 42   JOSHUA 6:4-16   THE ISRAELITES MARCH AROUND
          THE CITY: IN THE PROCESSION THE MAIN BODY
          OF THE SOLDIERS COMES FIRST, NEXT ARE SEVEN
          PRIESTS WHO BLOW ON TRUMPETS, FOLLOWED BY
          THE PRIESTS CARRYING THE ARK AND A REAR
          GUARD

   FRENCH SCHOOL
      Tissot, James Jacques Joseph. Illustrations
      of the Hebrew Bible. No. 150: The Seven
      Trumpets of Jericho. 1896-1903. New York,
      Jewish Museum, 52.216.

   ITALIAN SCHOOL
      Gozzoli, Benozzo. Old Testament and other sub-
      jects: Fall of Jericho. Pisa, Camposanto.

71 E 52 5   JOSHUA 7   ACHAN'S SIN

   GERMAN SCHOOL
      German school, 15th century. Triptych with
      scenes from the Old Testament from Göttingen.
      1400-10. Hanover, Provincial Museum.

71 E 52 94   JOSHUA 10:8-10   JOSHUA AND HIS ARMY MAKE
          A SURPRISE ATTACK ON THE AMORITES

   FRENCH SCHOOL
      Poussin, Nicolas. Victory of Joshua over the
      Amorites. Moscow, Pushkin State Museum of
      Fine Arts.

71 E 52 94 2   JOSHUA 10:12-13   JOSHUA ORDERS THE
           SUN AND MOON TO STAND STILL UNTIL THE
           ENEMY IS ROUTED

   BRITISH SCHOOL
      Martin, John. Joshua Commanding the Sun to
      Stand Still. Oxford, University, Ashmolean
      Museum, A448b.

   FRENCH SCHOOL
      Courtois, Jacques. Joshua Stops the Sun.
      Paris, Louvre, Musée du, INV. 3438.

   ITALIAN SCHOOL
      Raphael (and assistants). Old Testament subjects:
      Joshua makes the sun stand still. Rome,
      Vatican, Loggie.

   SPANISH SCHOOL
      March, Esteban. Joshua causing the sun to
      stand still. Valencia, Museo de Pinturas.

71 E 54 38   JOSHUA 18-19   JOSHUA (ASSISTED BY ELEA-
           ZAR) CASTS LOTS AND ASSIGNS TO EACH OF
           THE REMAINING SEVEN TRIBES A CERTAIN PART
           OF THE LAND

   ITALIAN SCHOOL
      Raphael (and assistants). Old Testament sub-
      jects: Joshua and Eleazar divide the pro-
      mised land by lot. Rome, Vatican, Loggie.
      Raphael. Old Testament subjects: Joshua and
      Eleazar divide the promised land by lot.
      Study. 1517. Windsor, Castle.

71 F 15 JUDGES 4-5 THE TIME OF DEBORAH AND BARAK

DUTCH SCHOOL
Bray, Salomon de. Jael, Deborah and Barak.
1635. Utrecht, Rijksmuseum, on loan from
Thurkow van Huffel, Mrs. L. - Collection.

71 F 15 1 JUDGES 4:5-9 DEBORAH (SITTING UNDER THE
PALM TREE) BESEECHES BARAK TO ATTACK SISERA

ITALIAN SCHOOL
Italian school, 16th century. Barak and Deborah.
Budapest, Museum of Fine Arts, 1408.
Solimena, Francesco. Deborah and Barak. Holkham
Hall, Norfolk, Collection Earl of Leicester.
Solimena, Francesco, studio of. Barak and Deborah.
Budapest, Museum of Fine Arts, 1045 (228c).
Solimena, Francesco. The Prophetess Deborah.
Turin, Pinacoteca, 616.

71 F 15 4 JUDGES 4:17-22 THE STORY OF JAEL AND
SISERA

BRITISH SCHOOL
Moore, Albert. The Mother of Sisera Looked
out at a Window. 1861. Carlisle, Museum
and Art Gallery.

71 F 15 43 JUDGES 4:21 JAEL TAKES A NAIL OF THE
TENT AND A HAMMER

ITALIAN SCHOOL
Grammatica, Antiveduto. Jael. Rome, Palazzo
Rospigliosi.

71 F 15 44 JUDGES 4:21 JAEL KILLS THE SLEEPING
SISERA BY HITTING THE NAIL THROUGH HIS TEMPLES

BRITISH SCHOOL
Northcote, James. Jael and Sisera. London,
Diploma Gallery, 184.

FLEMISH SCHOOL
Spranger, Bartholomew. Jael and Sisera. Copenhagen, Art Museum, 3089.

ITALIAN SCHOOL
Caletti, Giuseppe. Jael and Sisera. Bologna,
Pinacoteca Nazionale.

71 F 15 45 JUDGES 4:22 BARAK COMES TO JAEL WHO
SHOWS HIM SISERA'S BODY

FRENCH SCHOOL
Tissot, James Jacques Joseph. Illustrations
of the Hebrew Bible. No. 168: Jael Shows
to Barak, Sisera Lying Dead. 1896-1903.
New York, Jewish Museum, 52.234.

GERMAN SCHOOL
Zick, Januarius. Jael killing Sisera. Collection
F.K. Pächt.

71 F 21 THE TIME OF GIDEON (JERUBBAAL)

DUTCH SCHOOL
Engelbrechtsz, Cornelius, attributed to. Gideon
in Prayer. Florence, Museo Nazionale.

71 F 21 21 JUDGES 6:11 THE ANGEL OF THE LORD APPEARS
TO GIDEON, WHO IS USUALLY SHOWN THRESHING
WHEAT

DUTCH SCHOOL
Eeckhout, Gerbrand van den. The Angel Appears
to Gideon. 1647. Milan, Brera, 621.
Eeckhout, Gerbrand van den. Gideon's Offering.
1644. Stockholm, National Museum.

ITALIAN SCHOOL
Italian school, 11th century. The Calling of
Gideon, the Angel burns Gideon's Offering.
S. Angelo in Formis, Church, right aisle,
entrance wall, below.

71 F 21 23 2 JUDGES 6:21 AT THE ANGEL'S REQUEST
GIDEON PUTS THE FOOD ON A ROCK AND POURS
OUT THE BROTH

DUTCH SCHOOL
Heerschop, Hendrik. The Sacrifice of Gideon.
Christie, Manson and Woods (Sale, London,
Oct. 14, 1983, No. 33).

71 F 21 23 3 JUDGES 6:21 THE ANGEL OF THE LORD
TOUCHES THE FOOD WITH HIS STAFF; FIRE
ARISES FROM THE ROCK

DUTCH SCHOOL
Bol, Ferdinand. The Angel Appears to Gideon.
Also attributed to Eeckhout and Flinck.
1641. The Hague, Dienst Verspreide Rijks-
kollekties, NK 2484.
Eeckhout, Gerbrand van den. The Angel Touching
the Flesh and Unleavened Cakes before
Gideon. 1640. Sotheby and Co., (Sale,
London, March 9, 1983, No. 79).
Engelbrechtsz, Cornelius, attributed to.
Gideon in Prayer. Florence, Museo Nazionale.

FRENCH SCHOOL
Boucher, François (the younger). The Sacrifice
of Gideon. 1729. Paris, Louvre, Musée
du.

ITALIAN SCHOOL
Italian school, 11th century. Angel burning
Gideon's offering. S. Angelo in Formis.
Cathedral, right aisle, entrance wall.

71 F 21 43 JUDGES 16:37-40 TWICE GIDEON ASKS
THE LORD TO SHOW HIM A SIGN WITH A SHEEP'S
FLEECE

FRENCH SCHOOL
French school, 15th century, School of Avignon.
Gideon and the Fleece. London, Collection
George Durlacher.

71 F 21 51 JUDGES 7:3-5 GIDEON SENDS AWAY THE
FEARFUL AND BRINGS THE REMAINING TEN
THOUSAND MEN TO THE WATER

DUTCH SCHOOL
Dutch School, 16th century. Gideon's Men
Drinking from the Well of Harod. Christie,
Manson and Woods (Sale, New York, April
23, 1982, No. 63).

GERMAN SCHOOL
Schoenfeld, Johann Heinrich. Gideon Testing
his Troops. c.1636. Vienna, Kunsthistorisches Museum.

71 F 21 52 JUDGES 7:5-6 THOSE WHO LAP WATER BY
PUTTING THEIR HAND TO THEIR MOUTH ARE
SEPARATED FROM THOSE WHO KNEEL DOWN TO
DRINK THE WATER

DUTCH SCHOOL
Dutch school, 16th century. Gideon's Men
Drinking from the Well of Harod. Christie,
Manson and Wood, London, (Sale, April
23, 1982, No. 63).

71 F 21 64 JUDGES 7:19-20 THE ATTACK ON THE MIDIAN-
ITES: GIDEON AND HIS MEN BLOW THEIR TRUMPETS,
BREAK THEIR PITCHERS, AND HOLD THEIR LAMPS

FRENCH SCHOOL
Poussin, Nicolas. The Victory of Gideon over
the Midianites. Rome, Vatican.

71 F 24 53 JUDGES 11:34-35 JEPHTHAH'S DAUGHTER
DANCES WITH TAMBOURINES TO MEET HER FATHER
ON HIS RETURN FROM THE BATTLE; JEPHTHAH
RENDS HIS CLOTHES IN DESPAIR

AMERICAN SCHOOL
Lathrop, Betsy B. Jephthah's Return. 1812.
Williamsburg, Va., Abby Aldrich Rockefeller
Folk Art Collection, 39.401.1.

DUTCH SCHOOL
Jephta and his Daughter. c.1611. Nystad, Saskia
- Collection (The Hague).

FLEMISH SCHOOL
Flemish school, 17th century. Jephthah Met
by his Daughter. Sotheby and Co., London
(Sale, New York, Nov. 7, [MISSOURI], No.54).
Savery, Jacob I. Jephta greeted by his daughter.
1597. Collection M. Fernand Stuyck.
Witte, Pieter de. Jephta's Daughter. Munich,
Pinakothek, Alte.

FRENCH SCHOOL
Degas, H.G.E. The Daughter of Jephthah. c.1861-
64. Smith College Museum of Art, Northampton,
Mass.
LeBrun, Charles. Jephthah's daughter. Harvard
University, Fogg Art Museum, 1922.109.
Van Loo, Amédée. Jephthah's Vow. Dijon (Côte
d'Or), Musée Municipal.

ITALIAN SCHOOL
Gamberucci, Cosimo. Jephtha's Return. Sotheby
and Co., London (Sale, [GOLDEN ROD] Oct.12,
1983, No. 44).
Pellegrini, Giovanni Antonio. Jephthah returns
from battle and is greeted by his daughter.
London, Collection Denis Mahon.
Pietro di Domenico. Meeting of Jephtha and
his daughter. London, Collection Earl of
Crawford.
Romanelli, Giovanni Francesco. Jephthah sees
his daughter. Vienna, Kunsthistorisches
Museum.
Romanelli, Giovanni Francesco, Follower of.
The Return of Jephthah. Sotheby and Co.,
London (Sale, [LILY] June 15, 1983, No.
150.
Zompin, Gaetano. The Meeting of Jephthah and
his Daughter. A Pair with Solomon Sacrificing
to Ashtoreth. Sotheby and Co., London (Sale,
June 30, 1971, No. 53).

71 F 24 54 JUDGES 11:37-38 SHE ASKS TWO MONTHS
RESPITE, AND RETREATS TO THE MOUNTAINS WITH
HER COMPANIONS TO BEWAIL HER VIRGINITY

BRITISH SCHOOL
Millais, Sir John, E. Jephthah. 1867. Cardiff,
National Museum of Wales.
Ricketts, Charles. Jephthah's Daughter. Oxford,
University, Ashmolean Museum, A729.

FRENCH SCHOOL
Cabanel, Alexandre. Jephthah's Daughter. 1885.
Wheelock, Whitney and Co. - Gallery (New
York).
Tissot, James Jacques Joseph. Illustrations
of the Hebrew Bible. No. 177: The Daughter
of Jephthah and her Companions (detail).
1896-1903. New York, Jewish Museum, 52.243.

GERMAN SCHOOL
Huxoll, Anton. Jephthah's Daughter and her
Friends. 1836. Berlin, Staatliche Museen,
NG 15/66.

71 F 24 55 JUDGES 11:39 FULFILLMENT OF JEPHTHAH'S
VOW TO THE LORD: JEPHTHAH'S DAUGHTER IS
SACRIFICED

AUSTRIAN SCHOOL
Schmidt, Martin Johann. The Sacrificing of
Jephthah's Daughter. Vienna, Österreichische
Gallerie, Lg. 35.

DUTCH SCHOOL
Wet, Gerrit de. Jephthah's Daughter Being Led
to the Altar. Copenhagen, Art Museum, 471.

FRENCH SCHOOL
Bourdon, Sebastien. Jephthah's Daughter. London,
Collection A.F. Blunt.

ITALIAN SCHOOL
Mazzoni, Sebastiano. Sacrifice of Jephthah.
Pedrocco Collection (Venice).
Mazzoni, Sebastiano. Sacrifice of Jephthah.
New York, Kress Foundation.
Pittoni, G.B. The sacrifice of Jephthah.
Genoa, Palazzo Reale.
Pittoni, Giambattista. The Sacrifice of Jeph-
thah. Bergamo, Private Collection.

71 F 3 THE TIME OF SAMSON

GERMAN SCHOOL
Breu, Jörg, the Elder. The Story of Samson.
Basle, Museum, 133.

71 F 31 1 JUDGES 13:3-5 ANNUNCIATION OF SAMSON'S
BIRTH TO THE WIFE OF MANOAH BY AN ANGEL

ITALIAN SCHOOL
Saraceni, Carlo. Angel appears to the wife
of Manoah. Basle, Museum.
Tintoretto (Jacopo Robusti). The Annunciation
by the Angel to the Wife of Manoah.
1555-58. Thyssen-Bornemisza - Collection
(Lugano).
Tintoretto, Jacopo, School of.Manoah's Offering.
Gothenburg, Museum, 948.

71 F 31 2 JUDGES 13:9-18 ANNUNCIATION OF THE
BIRTH OF A SON TO MANOAH AND HIS WIFE

DUTCH SCHOOL
Lastman, Pieter P. The Angel Appearing to
Manoah and his Wife. 1617. Schapiro, E.-
Collection (London).

71 F 31 4 JUDGES 13:20 MANOAH'S SACRIFICE; THE
ANGEL ASCENDS IN THE FLAMES

AUSTRIAN SCHOOL
Brandt, Heinrich Carl. The Sacrifice of Manoah.
Christie, Manson and Woods (Sale, London,
July 23, 1982, No. 135).

DUTCH SCHOOL
Breenbergh, Bartholomeus. Landscape with
the sacrifice of Manoah. New York, Metro-
politan Museum of Art, 1983.411.
Flinck, Govert. The Angel Leaving Manoah
and his Wife. 1640. Queen's University
(Kingston), Agnes Etherington Art Centre.
Flinck, Govert. The Offering of Manoah. Buda-
pest, Museum of Fine Arts, 3829, 410a.
Hoogstraten, Samuel van. Manoah's Sacrifice.
United States, Private Collection.
Jacobez, Lambert. Manoah's Sacrifice. Schapiro,
E. - Collection (London).
Lastman, P. P. Old Testament subject. Sacri-
fice of Manoah. New York, Rosenberg and
Stiebel.
Post, Fransz Jansz. The Sacrifice of Manoah.
1647. Rotterdam, Museum Boymans, 1693.
Rembrandt. Sacrifice of Manoah. Dresden,
Gallery, 1563.

FRENCH SCHOOL
Julien, Simon. The Sacrifice of Manoah, Father
of Samson. 1760. (Prix de Rome 1760).
Mans, Le (Sarthe), Musée.

ITALIAN SCHOOL
Balestra, Antonio. Sacrifice of Manoah. Munich,
Staatsgalerie Schleissheim, 1313.

71 F 31 7 JUDGES 13:24-25 SAMSON'S YOUTH

FRENCH SCHOOL
Court, Joseph Désiré. Samson and Delilah.
1821. Paris, École des Beaux-Arts (Grand
Prix de Rome).
Court, Joseph Désiré. Samson and Delilah.
Sketch. Paris, École des Beaux-Arts (Grand
Prix de Rome).

JUDGES

71 F 32 5 JUDGES 14:5-6 SAMSON KILLS THE LION WITH
HIS BARE HANDS

BRITISH SCHOOL
Hodgekins, T.F. Samson destroying the Lion.
Dulwich Gallery, 492.

FLEMISH SCHOOL
Flemish school, 17th century. Samson and the
lion. Serge Philipson Collection.
Rubens, P.P. (?) Samson and the lion. Stockholm,
National Museum.

FRENCH SCHOOL
Bonnat, Léon. Samson Killing the Lion. Bayonne
(Vasses-Pyrénées), Musée Bonnat.

GERMAN SCHOOL
Stuck, Franz von. Samson. 1890. Private Collection.

SPANISH SCHOOL
Oliveri, Juan. Wall decorations from San Pedro,
Olite. Samson and lion. Pamplona, Museo
Provincial.

71 F 32 73 JUDGES 14:9 SAMSON GIVES SOME OF THE
HONEY TO HIS PARENTS

ITALIAN SCHOOL
Guercino. Samson brings the honey to his parents.
New York, Collection Walter P. Chrysler
Jr.
Guercino. Samson bringing the honey to his
parents. San Francisco, M. H. de Young Mem-
orial Museum (n. 65.20.2).

71 F 33 1 JUDGES 14:12-14 SAMSON PUTS FORTH A RIDDLE
DURING HIS WEDDING-FESTIVITIES

DUTCH SCHOOL
Rembrandt. Samson's wedding-feast.

71 F 34 1 JUDGES 15:1 SAMSON GOES WITH A KID TO
HIS WIFE AND IS REFUSED ENTRY BY HER FATHER

DUTCH SCHOOL
Rembrandt. Samson Threatening his Father-in-Law.
1635. Berlin, Staatliche Museen.

71 F 34 3 JUDGES 15:4-5 SAMSON TIES THREE HUNDRED
FOXES TWO BY TWO BY THEIR TAILS WITH A FIRE-
BRAND IN BETWEEN; WITH THE TORCHES ON FIRE
HE LETS THEM GO INTO THE CORNFIELDS OF THE
PHILISTINES WHICH ARE SET AFLAME

ITALIAN SCHOOL
Giordano, Luca. Samson and the foxes. Madrid,
Palacio Real.

71 F 35 4 JUDGES 15:15 WITH AN ASS'S JAW-BONE SAMSON
SLAYS A THOUSAND PHILISTINES

DUTCH SCHOOL
Bylert, Jan van, Circle of. Samson Slaying
the Philistines. Sotheby and Co., London
(Sale, New York, March 24, 1983).

FRENCH SCHOOL
Meissonier, J.L.E. Samson Battling the Philistines. Paris, Louvre.

ITALIAN SCHOOL
Assereto, Gioachino. Samson slaying the Philis-
tines. Bob Jones University Collection (Green-
ville, S.C.).
Bassano, Jacopo. Samson Slaying the Philistines.
Dresden Gallery.
Liberi, Pietro. Samson Fighting the Philistines.
Sotheby and Co., London (Sale, Dec. 12,
1984,[IVY], No. 129).
Schiavone, Andrea. Samson Killing a Philistine.
Florence, Palazzo Pitti, 152.
Tintoretto, J.R. Samson and the Philistines.
1565. Venice, Palazzo Ducale, Atrio Quadrato,
ceiling.

71 F 35 6 JUDGES 15:19 WATER COMES FROM A HOLLOW
IN THE ASS'S JAW-BONE

DUTCH SCHOOL
Bray, Salomon de. Samson. 1636. Malibu, J.
Paul Getty Museum, 69.PA.23.

71 F 35 61 JUDGES 15:19 SAMSON DRINKS FROM THE
ASS'S JAW-BONE

DUTCH SCHOOL
Bray, Salomon de. Samson Getting Water from
the Jaw-bone of an Ass. 1636. Malibu,
J. Paul Getty Museum, 69.PA.23.

ITALIAN SCHOOL
Reni, Guido. Samson. Bologna, Pinacoteca.
Tintoretto (Jacopo Robusti). Samson Drinking
from a Jaw-bone. Venice, Scuola di San
Rocco, upper hall, ceiling.

71 F 37 4 JUDGES 16:18 DELILAH FINDS OUT SAMSON'S
SECRET AND WARNS THE PHILISTINES, WHO
COME WITH THE MONEY

ITALIAN SCHOOL
Guercino. Samson and Delilah. Strasbourg
(Bas-Rhin), Musée des Beaux-Arts.
Pagani, Paolo. Samson and Delilah. Brunswick,
Landesmuseum, 707.

71 F 37 5 JUDGES 16:19 SAMSON ASLEEP IN DELILAH'S
LAP; SHE IS USUALLY SHOWN BECKONING TO
A PHILISTINE OR PUTTING A FINGER TO HER
LIPS

DUTCH SCHOOL
Lievens, Jan. Samson and Delilah. Grisaille,
Rijksmuseum, A1627.
Rembrandt. Samson and Delilah. 1628. Berlin,
Staatliche Museen, 812A.
Rembrandt. The Triumph of Delilah. Frankfort-
on-the-Main, Staedel Institute.

FLEMISH SCHOOL
Flemish school, 16th century (Antwerp). Samson
and Delilah. Sotheby and Co., London (Sale,
April 16, 1981, No. 92).
Rubens, P.P., School of. Samson and Delilah.
Dulwich Gallery, 127.

FRENCH SCHOOL
Delacroix, Eugène. Samson and Delilah. 1849-56.
Winterthur, Collection Rienhart.

ITALIAN SCHOOL
Fiasella, Domenico. Samson and Delilah. Paris,
Louvre, Musée du, 700.
Pellegrini, Giovanni Antonio. Samson and
Delilah. Duckett - Collection (Venice).
Stanzione, Massimo. Samson and Delilah.Christie,
Manson and Woods, London, (Sale, December
11, 1981, No. 108).
Turchi, Alessandro (Orbetto). Samson and
Delilah. Christie, Manson and Woods, London,
(Sale, May 28, 1982, No. 2).

71 F 37 6 JUDGES 16:19 SAMSON'S HAIRLOCKS ARE
SHAVED, OR CUT OFF (USUALLY WITH SCISSORS)
BY A PHILISTINE

DUTCH SCHOOL
Natur, Antony. Samson and Delilah. 1658.
Private Collection, U.S.A.
Soutman, Pieter Claesz. Samson and Delilah.
1642. York (Yorkshire), City Art Gallery,15.
Steen, Jan. Samson and Delilah. The Hague,
Bachstitz Gallery, Dealer.

FLEMISH SCHOOL
Dyck, Anthony van. Samson and Delilah. c.1620.
Dulwich Gallery, 127.
Rubens, Peter Paul. Samson and Delilah. London,
National Gallery, 6481.
Rubens, P.P. Samson and Delilah. Sketch.
1609. Cincinnati, Museum, 1972.459.

Vos, Cornelis de. Samson and Delilah. Salm,
Fürsten zu - Collection, 662.

ITALIAN SCHOOL
Morone, Francesco. Samson and Delilah. Milan,
Museo Poldi-Pezzoli.
Schiavone, Andrea. Samson and Delilah. Rome,
Galleria d'Arte Antica.
Tintoretto (Jacopo Robusti). Samson and Delilah.
Sarasota, Fla., Ringling Museum of Art,
SN 75.
Tintoretto, School of. Samson and Delilah.
Turchi, Alessandro. Samson and Delilah. Paris,
Louvre.
Turchi, Alessandro. Samson and Delilah. Sotheby
and Co., London (Sale, [DAFFODIL] Feb. 20,
1980, No. 104).

SPANISH SCHOOL
Spanish school, 17th century (?) (or Flemish?).
Samson and Delilah.

71 F 37 61 JUDGES 16:19 SAMSON'S HAIRLOCKS ARE
SHAVED, OR CUT OFF (USUALLY WITH SCISSORS)
BY DELILAH

DUTCH SCHOOL
Honthorst, Gerard van. Samson and Delilah.
1616-1620. Cleveland, Museum of Art, 68.23.

GERMAN SCHOOL
Cranach, Lucas, the elder. Samson and Delilah.
1529. Augsburg, Maximilian Museum.
Cranach, Lucas, the elder, School of. Samson
and Delilah. C.1537. Dresden, Gallery, 1929.

ITALIAN SCHOOL
Cignani, Carlo. Samson and Delilah. Bologna,
Pinacoteca Nazionale, 512.
Gentileschi, Artemisia. Delilah Cutting Samson's
Hair. Naples, Museo Nazionale, Capodimonte.
Giordano, Luca. Samson and Delilah. London,
Apsley House, Collection Duke of Wellington.
Mannozzi, Giovanni. Samson and Delilah. c.1634.
Fresco. Florence, Palazzo Uffizi, 5424.
Mantegna, Andrea. Samson and Delilah. London,
National Gallery, 1145.
Rocca, Michele. Samson and Delilah. Budapest,
Museum of Fine Arts, 2312 (826).
Segala, Giovanni. Delilah. Verona, Private
Collection.
Strozzi, Bernardo. Delilah. Bologna, Pinacoteca
Nazionale, 654.

71 F 37 7 JUDGES 16:20-21 SAMSON WAKES UP AND FINDS
HIS HAIR AND STRENGTH GONE; HE IS TAKEN
PRISONER

BRITISH SCHOOL
Rigaud, J.F. Samson and Delilah. London, Diploma
Gallery, 207.

FLEMISH SCHOOL
Dyck, Anthony van. Samson and Delilah. Vienna,
Kunsthistorisches Museum, 1043.
Rubens, Peter Paul. The Capture of Samson.
Munich, Staatsgalerie Schleissheim, 348.
Rubens, P.P., School of. Samson Taken Prisoner.
Innsbruck, Tiroler Landesmuseum Ferdinandeum.
Rubens, P.P. Samson and Delilah. Chicago, Art
Institute.
Wolffordt, Artus. Samson Captured by the Philis-
tines. Hoogsteder-Naumann, Ltd. - Gallery
(New York).

ITALIAN SCHOOL
Guercino. Samson Seized by the Philistines.
1619. Wrightsman, Mr. and Mrs. Chase B.--
Collection (New York), on loan to Metropolitan
Museum of Art.
Pagani, Paolo. The Capture of Samson. Brunswick,
Landesmuseum, 708.
Pagani, Paolo. Samson. Bologna,Private Collection.
Preti, Mattia. The Capture of Samson. Geneva,
Musée d'Art et d'Histoire, 1893-4.

SPANISH SCHOOL
Garcia de Miranda, Juan. Samson betrayed
by Delilah, copy after Rubens, signed.
Brooklyn, Collection Mrs. Benjamin F.
Stephens, Jr.

71 F 37 71 JUDGES 16:21 HE IS TORMENTED BY THE
PHILISTINES; DELILAH IS PAID

DUTCH SCHOOL
Steen, Jan. Samson in the hands of the Philis-
tines. Cologne, Wallraf-Richartz Museum.
Steen, Jan. Samson tricked by the Philistines.
Antwerp, Museum, 338.

71 F 37 8 JUDGES 16:21 THE BLINDING OF SAMSON

DUTCH SCHOOL
Rembrandt. The Blinding of Samson by the
Philistines. 1636. Frankfort-on-the-Main,
Staedel Institute.
Rembrandt. Blinding of Samson. Cassel, Gallery.

GERMAN SCHOOL
Zick, Januarius. The Blinding of Samson.
Augsburg, Museum.
Zick, Johann. The Blinding of Samson. Cologne,
Wallraf-Richartz Museum, 2387.

ITALIAN SCHOOL
Giani, Felice. Samson and Delilah. Parma,
Picture Gallery.

71 F 37 81 JUDGES 16:21 THE BLIND SAMSON IN GAZA,
BOUND WITH BRASS CHAINS

ITALIAN SCHOOL
Carracci, Annibale. Samson Imprisoned. c.1590-
95. Rome, Villa Borghese, Gallery.

71 F 38 3 JUDGES 16:29-30 SAMSON BREAKS THE PILLARS;
THE TEMPLE COLLAPSES, KILLING ALL WHO
ARE IN IT

BRITISH SCHOOL
Hodgkins, T.F. Samson destroying the Philistines. Dulwich Gallery, 493.

GERMAN SCHOOL
Platzer, Johann Georg. Samson's Revenge.
Vienna, Österreichische Galerie, 2410.
Schoenfeld, Johann Heinrich. Samson's Revenge.
c.1633/34. Vienna, Kunsthistorisches Museum,
2666.

ITALIAN SCHOOL
Molinari, Antonio. Samson pulls down pillars.
Polcenigo, Maria Scolari - Collection.
Tintoretto. Samson's Revenge on the Philis-
tines. 1545-48. Vienna, Kunsthistorisches
Museum, 3828.

71 F 52 2 JUDGES 19:10-30 THE LEVITE AND HIS
CONCUBINE IN A STREET IN GIBEAH ARE OFFERED
LODGING BY AN OLD MAN

DUTCH SCHOOL
Eeckhout, Gerbrandt van der. The Levite at
Gibeah. Wolf, Emile E. - Collection (New
York).
Eeckhout, Gerbrand van den. The Levite and
His Concubine in Gibea. Moscow, Pushkin
State Museum of Fine Arts.
Eeckhout, Gerbrand van den. The Lèvite and
His Concubine in Gibea. Wolf, Emile E.
- Collection (New York).
Eeckhout, Gerbrandt van der. The Old Laborer
of Gibea Offers Shelter to the Levite
and His Concubine. Budapest, Museum of
Fine Arts, 9822.
Victors, Jan. Levite and His Concubine at
Gibeah. Dublin, National Gallery, 879.

152

<u>71 F 52 6 JUDGES 19:27-28 IN THE MORNING SHE LIES</u>
<u>DEAD ON THE THRESHOLD</u>

FRENCH SCHOOL
    Couder, Auguste. The Levite at Mount Ephraim.
    Henner, J.J. The Levite of Ephraim and his
       Dead Wife. c.1898. Toronto, Joseph M. Tanen-
      baum - Collection.

<u>71 F 6 RUTH THE STORY OF RUTH, THE MOABITESS</u>

BRITISH SCHOOL
    Rooke, Thomas Matthews. The Story of Ruth.
      1876-77. London, Tate Gallery.

<u>71 F 62 RUTH 1:6-22 NAOMI'S RETURN TO BETHLEHEM</u>

DUTCH SCHOOL
    Eeckhout, Gerbrand van den. Ruth Vows Faithful-
      ness to Naomi. Schwartz - Collection (Stock-
      holm).
    Scoral, Jan van, Follower of. Ruth and Naomi
      go to the land of Boaz. c.1530-40. Vienna,
      Kunsthistorisches Museum, 6409.

<u>71 F 62 2 RUTH 1:8-18 NAOMI SENDS AWAY HER DAUGHTERS-</u>
<u>IN-LAW: ORPAH RETURNS HOME, RUTH STAYS</u>

BRITISH SCHOOL
    Blake, William. Ruth. Southampton, Art Gallery,
      G/1368.
    Russell, John. Ruth and Naomi. London, Diploma
      Gallery, 292.

DUTCH SCHOOL
    Lastman, Pieter P. Ruth Vows Her Faithfulness
      to Naomi. 1614. Hanover, Niedersächsiche
      Landesgalerie.

<u>71 F 64 RUTH 2:3-17 RUTH IN THE FIELD OF BOAZ</u>

DUTCH SCHOOL
    Eeckhout, Gerbrand van den. Ruth and Boas.
      1651. Bremen, Kunsthalle.
    Eeckhout, Gerbrand van den. Ruth and Boas.
      1656. Deun, Bert van - Collection (Beerse).
    Eeckhout, Gerbrand van den. Ruth and Boas.
      1655. Rotterdam, Museum Boymans, 1192.

FRENCH SCHOOL
    Puvis de Chavannes, Pierre. Summer:Ruth and
      Boas. 1854. Sotheby and Co., London (Sale,
      June 18, 1985).

GERMAN SCHOOL
    Peters, Johann Anton de. Ruth, Naomi and
      Boas. Cologne, Wallraf-Richartz Museum,
      1065.

ITALIAN SCHOOL
    Bassano, Jacopo. Ruth and Boaz. Hampton Court.
    Veronese, Paolo ?. Ruth and Boaz.

<u>71 F 64 2 RUTH 2:4-6 BOAZ QUESTIONS HIS SERVANTS</u>
<u>CONCERNING RUTH</u>

FRENCH SCHOOL
    Gleyre, C. Ruth and Boaz.

<u>71 F 64 3 RUTH 2:7-13 BOAZ SPEAKS TO RUTH; RUTH</u>
<u>USUALLY BOWING DOWN, OR KNEELING BEFORE</u>
<u>HIM</u>

BRITISH SCHOOL
    English school, 19th century. Ruth and Boaz.
      Downton Castle, Collection W.M.P. Kincaid-
      Lennox.

DUTCH SCHOOL
    Eeckhout, Gerbrand van den. Boas and Ruth.
      1656. Private Collection, U.S.A.
    Eeckhout, Gerbrand van den. Ruth and Boaz.
      1651. Bremen, Kunsthalle, 37.
    Eeckhout, Gerbrand van den. Ruth and Boaz.
      1661. Katz - Collection (Dieren).
    Eeckhout, Gerbrand van den. Ruth and Boas.
      1672. Norfolk, Va., Chrysler Museum.
    Eeckhout, Gerbrand van den. Ruth and Boas.
      1666. Rosenthal, P. - Art Dealer (Berlin).
    Fabritius, Bernard. Ruth and Boas. 1660.
      Leningrad, Hermitage.
    Gelder, Aert de. Ruth and Boaz. 1641 ?.
      Destroyed.
    Grebber, Pieter Fransz de. Boaz and Ruth.
      Copenhagen, Art Museum, Sp 356.

Noord, Johannes van. Ruth and Boas. Butôt,
F.C. - Collection.
Victors, Jan. Boaz and Ruth. Copenhagen, Art
Museum, Sp. 463.

FLEMISH SCHOOL
Franck, Franz, I, Studio of. Flemish Reliquary
Chest painted with scenes from the Old Testament. Detail: drawer: Ruth and Boaz (?).
c.1600. Sarasota, Fla., Ringling Museum
of Art, SN 1950.

FRENCH SCHOOL
Poussin, Nicolas. The Four Seasons: Summer
or Ruth and Boaz. 1660-64. Paris, Louvre.

GERMAN SCHOOL
Hopfgarten, August Ferdinand. Ruth and Boas.
1827/29. Berlin, Staatliche Museen, 184,II,14.
Koch, Joseph Anton. Ruth and Boaz. 1815-20.
Sotheby and Co., London (Sale, June 23,
1980).

ITALIAN SCHOOL
Ricci, Marco. Landscape with Boaz and Ruth.
Sarasota, Fla., Ringling Museum of Art,
SN 180.

71 F 64 4 RUTH 2:14 RUTH INVITED BY BOAZ TO EAT
WITH HIM

DUTCH SCHOOL
Victors, Jan. Ruth and Boaz. 1653. Feigen,
Richard - Gallery (Chicago).

71 F 65 RUTH 2:18 - 3:18 BOAZ COMMANDS HIS SERVANTS
TO LET RUTH GLEAN EVEN AMONG THE SHEAVES

DUTCH SCHOOL
Drost, Wilhelm. Ruth and Naomi. Oxford, University, Ashmolean Museum, A 390.

71 F 65 1 RUTH 2:18-22 RUTH BRINGS THE BARLEY HOME
TO NAOMI AND TELLS HER WHAT HAS OCCURRED
IN THE FIELDS OF BOAZ

AMERICAN SCHOOL
American school, 19th century. Ruth and Naomi.
c. 1820. Louisville, Ky., J.B. Speed Art
Museum, 74 32.1.

GERMAN SCHOOL
Peters, Johann Anton de. Ruth, Naomi and Boaz.
Cologne, Wallraf-Richartz Museum, 1065.

71 F 65 6 RUTH 3:9-15 THE CONVERSATION OF RUTH
AND BOAZ IN THE NIGHT

DUTCH SCHOOL
Gelder, Aert de. Ruth and Boaz. Vienna, Academy.

71 F 8 I SAMUEL STORY OF SAMUEL

ITALIAN SCHOOL
Italian school, 13th century. Detail: fresco
in vault of crypt: Christ surrounded by
scenes from the Old Testament. Anagni,
Cathedral.

71 F 81 I SAMUEL 1 - 2:21 BIRTH AND CHILDHOOD
OF SAMUEL

BRITISH SCHOOL
Reynolds, Sir Joshua. The infant Samuel kneeling
at prayer. c.1776. London, Tate Gallery,162.
Reynolds, Sir Joshua. The prophet Samuel
as a boy. Dulwich Gallery, 223.

DUTCH SCHOOL
Rembrandt. Hannah and Samuel. Edinburgh,
National Gallery.
Rembrandt ? Prophetess Anna teaching her
son Samuel to read. Leningrad, Hermitage.

71 F 81 25 I SAMUEL 1:18-19 ELKANAH RETURNING
TO RAMAH WITH HANNAH AND PENINNAH; HANNAH
RELIEVED OF HER DEPRESSION

DUTCH SCHOOL
Victors, Jan. Elkanah and his Wife, Hannah,
before Eli. Dublin, National Gallery,879.

71 F 81 32 I SAMUEL 1:24-28 SAMUEL IN THE TEMPLE
AT SHILOH PRESENTED TO ELI BY HANNAH

DUTCH SCHOOL
Doomer, Lambert. Hannah Bringing Samuel to
Eli. 1668. Orleans (Loiret), Musée.
Eeckhout, Gerbrand van den. Hannah Bringing
to Eli. Paris, Louvre, Musée du, 1267.
Eeckhout, Gerbrand van den. The Infant Samuel
Brought by Hannah to Eli. Oxford, University,
Ashmolean Museum, A 734.
Fabritius, Bernard. Jacob and Benjamin. Also
identified as Eli and Samuel. Also attributed
to Wilhelm Drost. c. 1650. Chicago, Art
Institute, 37.465.
Wet, Jacob Willemsz, the Elder, Circle of.
Samuel before Eli. Christie, Manson and
Woods (Sale, New York, [LOUISE-5912],
June 5, 1985, No. 15).

71 F 81 41 I SAMUEL 2:18-21 SAMUEL BROUGHT UP
BY ELI

DUTCH SCHOOL
Dou, Gerard. Eli Instructing Samuel. Amsterdam,
Rijksmuseum.
Lievensz, Jan. Prince Charles Ludwig of the
Palatinate and his Governor as Alexander
and Aristotle. (Eli Instructing Samuel).
c.1628. Malibu, J. Paul Getty Museum.

71 F 83 51 2 I SAMUEL 5:6 GOD PUNISHES THE INHAB-
ITANTS OF ASHDOD WITH EMERODS OR BOILS

FRENCH SCHOOL
Poussin, Nicolas. The Plague of Ashdod. Paris,
Musée du Louvre.
Poussin, Nicolas. The Plague at Ashdod (The
Philistines Struck by the Plague). 1630-31.
Paris, Louvre, 710.
Poussin, Nicolas. The Philistines struck
by the plague. (The plague at Ashdod).
London, National Gallery, 165.
Poussin, Nicolas. The Philistines struck
by the plague. Variant. Lisbon, Academy.

71 F 83 62 I SAMUEL 6:10-12 THE ARK AND THE BOX
WITH THE GUILT OFFERING, DRAWN BY TWO COWS,
SENT BACK TO ISRAEL

FRENCH SCHOOL
Bourdon, Sébastien. Return of the ark from
captivity. London, National Gallery, 64.

71 F 83 3 I SAMUEL 4:10 SECOND BATTLE BETWEEN THE
PHILISTINES AND THE ISRAELITES AT EBEN-EZER;
THE ISRAELITES DEFEATED AGAIN

ITALIAN SCHOOL
Italian school, 13th century. Detail: ark of
the covenant. Anagni, Cathedral, frescoes.

71 F 83 31 I SAMUEL 4:11 THE ARK IS CAPTURED BY
THE PHILISTINES

ITALIAN SCHOOL
Italian school, 13th century. Detail: ark of
the covenant. Anagni, Cathedral, frescoes.

71 F 83 42 I SAMUEL 4:18 ELI, HEARING OF THE CAPTURE
OF THE ARK, FALLS FROM HIS SEAT AND DIES

ITALIAN SCHOOL
Italian school, 13th century. Detail: ark of
the covenant. Anagni, Cathedral, frecoes.

71 F 84 12 1 I SAMUEL 7:6 WATER IS POURED OUT BEFORE
GOD

ITALIAN SCHOOL
Italian school, Wall painting, Anagni. Story
of Samuel. 13th century. Anagni, Cathedral.

71 G 11 31 I SAMUEL 10:1 THE ANOINTMENT OF SAUL
BY SAMUEL, WITH PEOPLE LOOKING ON

ITALIAN SCHOOL
Tintoretto (Jacopo Robusti). Samuel and Saul.
Venice, Scuola di San Rocco, upper hall,
ceiling.

71 G 12 5 I SAMUEL 11:9 SAUL'S MESSENGERS COME
TO JABESH-GILEAD; THE PEOPLE REJOICE

GERMAN SCHOOL
Monogramist, A.H. Lot and his Daughters. Brunswick, Landesmuseum, 30.

ITALIAN SCHOOL
Beltrano, Agostino. The Angels Driving Lot
and his Family Out of Sodom. Sotheby and
Co., London (Sale, New York, March 6-7,
1975, No. 4).

71 F 23 I SAMUEL 14:24 SAUL'S OATH: A DAY OF FASTING

GERMAN SCHOOL
German school, 15th century. Triptych with
scenes from the Old Testament from Göttingen,
upper left panel. 1400-1410. Hanover, Provincial Museum.

71 G 34 2 I SAMUEL 15:13-23 SAMUEL REPROVING AND
REJECTING SAUL

AMERICAN SCHOOL
Copley, J.S. Saul reproved by Samuel. Boston,
Museum of Fine Arts, 25.99.

71 G 36 I SAMUEL 15:32 SAMUEL SUMMONS AGAG TO BE
BROUGHT BEFORE HIM

DUTCH SCHOOL
Witt, Emanuel de. Samuel destroys Agag, King
of the Amalekites. Dunkirk, Museum, 362.

71 H STORY OF DAVID

FLEMISH SCHOOL
Memling, Hans. King David and a boy. Chicago,
Collection Max Epstein.

GERMAN SCHOOL
Beham, H.S. Design for table top (?). Executed
for Cardinal Albert, Archbishop of Mainz:
Scenes of Story of David. Paris, Louvre,
2701.
German school, 15th century. Scenes from
the life of King David. c.1500. Madrid,
Collection Baugá.

ITALIAN SCHOOL
Fetti, Domenico. David. Brunswick, Landesmuseum, 798.

71 H 1 DAVID AT SAUL'S COURT

ITALIAN SCHOOL
Caro, Lorenzo de. Saul Baptizing David.Christie,
Manson and Woods (Sale, New York, June
12, 1981, No. 209).

71 H 11 I SAMUEL 16:1-13 DAVID CHOSEN AS KING
BY GOD

ITALIAN SCHOOL
Sellaio, Jacopo del (?). Triumph of David.
Cassone panel.

71 H 11 5 I SAMUEL 16:13 SAMUEL ANOINTING DAVID

FRENCH SCHOOL
Biennourry, Victor François Éloi. Samuel
Anointing David. 1842. Paris, École des
Beaux-Arts (Grand Prix de Rome).
Claude Lorraine. David Annointed King by
Samuel. A Pair with the Disembarkment
of Cleopatra at Tarsus. Paris, Louvre,
Musée du, 4717.

ITALIAN SCHOOL
Chiari, Giuseppe Bartolomeo. Saul Baptising
David. Christie, Manson and Woods (Sale,
New York, CHristie's East [KAREN-5521]
March 23, 1984, No. 124).
Raphael (and assistants). Old Testament sub-
jects: Samuel anoints David king of Israel.
Rome, Vatican, Loggie.
Salviati, Francesco. Story of David. Rome,
Palazzo Sacchetti, second floor salon,
west wall, upper border, center section.
Veronese, Paolo. Annointment of David. 1555-60.
Vienna, Kunsthistorisches Museum.

SPANISH SCHOOL
Spanish school, 13th century. Old Testament:
Samuel Anointing David. Fresco, c.1200.
Sigena, Monastery, Chapter house.

71 H 13 I SAMUEL 16:14-23 DAVID AS HARPIST AT
SAUL'S COURT

ITALIAN SCHOOL
Italian school, 18th century. King David
Playing the Harp. Budapest, Museum of
Fine Arts, 58.41.

<u>71 H 13 5 I SAMUEL 16:23 DAVID IS APPOINTED WEAPON-
BEARER TO SAUL</u>

ITALIAN SCHOOL
    Cavallino, Bernardo. David Playing Before Saul.
       c.1645. Vienna, Kunsthistorisches Museum.

<u>71 H 13 6 I SAMUEL 16:23 DAVID PLAYING HIS HARP
BEFORE SAUL</u>

AMERICAN SCHOOL
    Allston, Washington. David playing before Saul.
       Charleston, S.C., Gibbes Memorial Art Gallery,
       36.7.3.

DUTCH SCHOOL
    Gelder, Aert de. David Playing the Harp to Saul.
       1682. Bremen, Kunsthalle.
    Rembrandt. David before Saul. Frankfort-on-the-
       Main, Staedel Institute, 498.
    Rembrandt. David Playing the Harp Before Saul.
       1657. The Hague, Royal Gallery.

FLEMISH SCHOOL
    Quellin, Erasmus. David Plays the Harp to the
       Sick Saul. Budapest, Museum of Fine Arts,
       4276 (P.96).

FRENCH SCHOOL
    Tissot, James Jacques Joseph. Illustrations
       of the Hebrew Bible. No.144: David Plays
       the Harp Before Saul. 1896-1903. New York,
       Jewish Museum, 52.290.

GERMAN SCHOOL
    Schick, Gottlieb. David Playing for Saul. 1803.
       Stuttgart, Museum Inv.N.703.

ITALIAN SCHOOL
    Cavallino, Bernardo. David Playing before Saul.
       c.1645. Vienna, Kunsthistorisches Museum,
       509B.
    Spinelli, Giovanni Battista. David Playing Saul's
       Harp. Florence, Palazzo Uffizi, 1890, n.9467.

SWEDISH SCHOOL
    Josephson, Ernest. David and Saul. 1878. Stock-
       holm, National Museum, 1805.
    Kronberg, Julius. David and Saul. 1885. Stock-
       holm, National Museum, 1381.

<u>71 H 14 I SAMUEL 17 STORY OF DAVID AND GOLIATH</u>

GERMAN SCHOOL
    German school, 15th century. Scenes from the
       life of King David. c.1500. Madrid, Collection
       Baugá.

<u>71 H 14 31 I SAMUEL 17:34-36 DAVID KILLING A LION
AND A BEAR</u>

AMERICAN SCHOOL
    Bougereau, Elizabeth Jane Gardner. The Shepherd
       David. Sotheby and Co., London (Sale, New
       York, Oct. 19, 1984, No. 122).

BRITISH SCHOOL
    Linnell, John. David and the Lion. 1850. Sotheby
       and Co., London (Sale, June 16, 1982, No.209).

ITALIAN SCHOOL
    Cappella, Francesco. David Killing the Lion.
       Bergamo, S. Alessandro della Croce.
    Giordano, Luca. Scenes from the Old Testament:
       David Kills a Lion and a Bear. Madrid, Palacio
       Real.

<u>71 H 14 32 I SAMUEL 17:38-39 DAVID RECEIVES SAUL'S
ARMOR</u>

DUTCH SCHOOL
    Verdael, Adriaen. David Receives Saul's Armor.
       A Pair with A Messenger Brings Saul's Crown
       and Bracelet to David. Sotheby and Co., London
       (Sale, [SNOWDROP] Feb. 13, 1985, No. 150).

ITALIAN SCHOOL
    Giordano, Luca. Scenes from the Old Testament:
       David armed by Saul for the Battle with
       Goliath. Madrid, Palacio Real.

<u>71 H 14 4 I SAMUEL 17:40-51 DAVID FIGHTING GOLIATH</u>

BRITISH SCHOOL
    Rossetti, D.G. The Seed of David. 1858-64.
       (Llandaff Cathedral Triptych). Cardiff,
       National Museum of Wales.
    Rossetti, D.G. The Seed of David. (Llandaff
       Cathedral Triptych). 1856. London, Tate
       Gallery, 3965.

FLEMISH SCHOOL
    Rubens, Peter Paul. David Slaying Goliath.
       c.1630. Pasadena, Ca., Norton Simon Museum.

FRENCH SCHOOL
    Degas, H.G.E. David and Goliath. Cambridge,
       University, Fitzwilliam Museum.
    French school, 17th century. David and Goliath.
       Budapest, Museum of Fine Arts, 954.

ITALIAN SCHOOL
    Bernini, G.L. David. Rome, Collection Eleanora
       Incisa Rocchetti.
    Borgianni, Orazio. David and Goliath. Madrid,
       Real Academia de Belles Artes.
    Burrini, Antonio. David with the Head of
       Goliath. Bologna, S. Salvatore.
    Caravaggio. David with the head of Goliath.
       Rome, Villa Borghese.
    Caravaggio. David with the head of Goliath.
       Rome, Villa Borghese, Gallery.
    Caravaggio. David with the head of Goliath.
       Vienna, Kunsthistorisches Museum, 485.
    Caravaggio. David. New York, Ehrich Galleries.
    Caravaggio. David and Goliath. Turin,Collection
       Duca d'Aosta.
    Caravaggio. David and Goliath. Madrid, Prado.
    Caravaggio, School of. David and Goliath.
       Madrid, Prado.
    Caravaggio, School of. David and Goliath.
       Warwick (Warwickshire) Castle.
    Cassone Master. Triumph of David. Florence,
       Villa Reale de Castello.
    Castagno, Andrea del. The Youthful David.
       c.1450. Washington, D.C., National Gallery
       of Art, 604.
    Dolci, Carlo. David with the head of Goliath.
       Milan, Brera, 757.
    Dolci, Carlo. David with the head of Goliath.
       Colnagi and Co., London.
    Domenichino. David with the head of Goliath.
       Haddo House, Collection David Gordon.
    Dossi, Dosso. David and Goliath. Rome, Villa
       Borghese, Gallery.
    Dossi, Dosso. David with the head of Goliath.
       Copy of the one in the Borghese. Stuttgart,
       Museum, 137.
    Dossi, Dosso. David with the head of Goliath.
       New York, Schaeffer Galleries.
    Fetti, Domenico. David. Genoa, Collection
       Viezzoli.
    Fetti, Domenico. David with the head of Goliath.
       Venice, Academy.
    Gentileschi, Orazio. David. Also attributed
       to Caravaggio. Berlin, Staatliche Museen.
    Gentileschi, Orazio. David with the head
       of Goliath. c.1610. Rome, Palazzo Spada.
    Giorgione, School of. David with the head
       of Goliath. Vienna, Kunsthistorisches
       Museum, 21.
    Guercino. David with the head of Goliath.
       London, Thomas Agnew and Sons.
    Lippi, Lorenzo. Triumph of David. Florence,
       Loeser Collection.
    Lippi, Lorenzo. Triumph of David. Florence,
       Galleria Antica e Moderna.
    Mantegna, Andrea. David with Head of Goliath.
       c.1490. Vienna, Kunsthistorisches Museum,
       Inv. 1965.

Pasinelli, Lorenzo. David with the head of Goliath. Bologna, Cremonini Tamburi Collection.

Pesellino, Francesco. Two cassone panels with the life of David. Lockinge House, Collection A. Thomas Loyd.

Pinturicchio and Assistants. Hall of Saints, vault: Story of Isis and Osiris. Detail: David with Head of Goliath. Rome, Vatican, Borgia apartments.

Poccetti, Bernardino. David. Florence, Palazzo Pitti, Sala di Bona.

Pollaiuolo, Antonio. David with the head of Goliath. Berlin, Staatliche Museen, 73 A.

Reni, Guido. David conquering Goliath. Paris, Louvre.

Reni, Guido. David. Rome, Palazzo Barberini.

Reni, Guido. David with head of Goliath. Sarasota, Fla., Ringling Museum of Art.

Reni, Guido. David with the Head of Goliath. Florence, Palazzo Uffizi, 1890, n. 3830.

Riminaldi, Orazio. David with the head of Goliath. Turin, Pinacoteca.

Schiavone, Giorgio, Attributed to. Judith, Abraham and David. Ascott, Buchs, National Trust.

Sellaio, Jacopo del. David. Philadelphia, Collection J.G. Johnson, 51.

Soada, Lionello. David with the head of Goliath. Corsham COurt, Collection Lord Methuen.

Strozzi, Bernardo. David. (Venice, Collection Brass) Vierhouten, Collection D.G. van Beuningen.

Strozzi, Bernardo. David with the head of Goliath. New York, Metropolitan Museum.

Strozzi, Bernardo. David with the head of Goliath. New York, Collection Dr. Paul Drey.

Turchi, Alessandro. David with the head of Goliath. Dresden, Gallery.

71 H 14 42 I SAMUEL 17:49 DAVID SLINGS A STONE AT GOLIATH'S FOREHEAD

ITALIAN SCHOOL
Giordano, Luca. David and Goliath. Madrid, Palacio Real.

71 H 14 43 I SAMUEL 17:51 DAVID BEHEADS GOLIATH WITH A SWORD

FLEMISH SCHOOL
Rubens, P.P. Ceiling decorations for the Church of the Jesuits at Antwerp. Sketch: David and Goliath. Paris, Collection Pierre Dubaut.

Rubens, P.P. David Slaying Goliath. (Study for Jesuit Church). London, University, Courtauld Institute (Princess Gate Collection), 25.

FRENCH SCHOOL
Tissot, James Jacques Joseph. Illustrations of the Hebrew Bible. No. 149: David Cuts off the Head of Goliath. 1896-1903. New York, Jewish Museum, 52.295.

ITALIAN SCHOOL
Allori, Cristofano. David and Goliath. Study. Florence, Palazzo Uffizi, 586.

Borgianni, Orazio. David and Goliath. Madrid, Real Academia de Belles Artes.

Daniele da Volterra. David and Goliath. Paris, Louvre. (Reverse).

Daniele da Volterra. David and Goliath. Obverse. Paris, Louvre.

Gentileschi, Orazio. David and Goliath. Dublin, National Gallery, 980.

Italian school, 17th century. David and Goliath. c.1600. Venice, Collection Asta (dealer).

Italian school, 17th century (Genoese). David's Triumph. Vienna, Kunsthistorisches Museum, 2640.

Michelangelo. Ceiling decorations, lunettes in four corners with scenes from Old Testament: David and Goliath.

Peruzzi, Baldassare. David Beheading Goliath, lower left. Rome, S. Maria della Pace, Cappella della Ponzetto, arch.

Salviati, Francesco. Story of David. Rome, Palazzo Sacchetti. Second floor salon, North wall, upper section, medallion at top.

Scarsella, Ippolito. David and Goliath. Rovigo, Pinacoteca dell'Accademia dei Concordi, 150.197.

71 H 14 43 1 I SAMUEL 17:51 DAVID BEHEADS GOLIATH WITH A SWORD, THE PHILISTINES FLEE, PURSUED BY THE ISRAELITES

FLEMISH SCHOOL
Meulener, Pieter. David and Goliath. Sotheby and Co., London (Sale, New York, [SAFFRON-5298], March 13, 1985, No. 56).

ITALIAN SCHOOL
Furini, Francesco. David Conquers Goliath. Prato, Cassa di Risparmi.

Raphael (and assistants). Old Testament subjects: David Killing Goliath. Rome, Vatican, Loggie.

71 H 14 44 DAVID THANKS THE LORD

ITALIAN SCHOOL
Titian. David and Goliath. S.Maria della Salute, Ceiling decorations.

71 H 14 5 I SAMUEL 17:51-58 DAVID WITH GOLIATH'S HEAD

DUTCH SCHOOL
Backer, Jacob Adriaensz. David with Goliath's Head. Copenhagen, Art Museum, Sp 220.

Rembrandt, School of. David. c.1640. Schapiro, E. - Collection (London).

Stomer, Matthias, Circle of. David. Christie, Manson and Woods (Sale, New York, June 12, 1981, No. 9).

FLEMISH SCHOOL
Bouts, Albert. David with the Head of Goliath. Sarasota, Fla., Ringling Museum of Art, SN 197.

Stomer, Matthias, Circle of. David. Christie, Manson and Woods (Sale, New York, June 12, 1981, No. 9).

FRENCH SCHOOL
Tournier, Nicolas. David and the Head of Goliath. Rome, Galleria d'Arte Antica.

Valentin de Boullogne. David and Goliath. Formerly, Rome, Palazzo Barberini.

Valentin de Boullogne, copy. David with the Head of Goliath. Cologne, Wallraf-Richartz Museum, 1456.

GERMAN SCHOOL
Sing, Johann Caspar. David and the Head of Goliath. Sotheby and Co., London (Sale, May 16, 1984, [MAGNOLIA], No. 10).

ITALIAN SCHOOL
Allori, Cristofano. David with the Head of Goliath. Dresden, Staatliche Kunstsammlungen, 523.

Cagnacci (Guido Canlassi). David with the Head of Goliath. Columbia, S.C., Museum of Art.

Cagnacci (Guido Canlassi). David with the Head of Goliath. Sotheby and Co., London (Sale, Monaco [OUDRY], Dec. 8, 1984, No. 318).

Caravaggio, Copy. David with the Head of Goliath. Copy of painting in Galleria Borghese, Rome, Nr.455. Cassel, Staatliche Kunstsammlungen, 910.

Cima, G.B. David and Jonathan. London, National Gallery, 2505.

Dolci, Carlo. David with the Head of Goliath. 1670. Milan, Brera, 757.

Domenichino. David with the Head of Goliath. Budapest, Museum of Fine Arts, 499 (200).

Fetti, Domenico. David with the Head of Goliath. Dresden, Staatliche Kunstsammlungen, 415.

Forabosco, Girolamo. David with the Head of Goliath. Vienna, Liechtenstein Gallery.

Gennari, Benedetto. David. Florence, Palazzo Pitti, 143.

Gentileschi, Orazio. David. Also attributed to Caravaggio. c.1610. Berlin, Staatliche Museen, 1723.

Gentileschi, Orazio. David with the Head of Goliath. c.1610. Rome, Palazzo Spada.

Guardi, Francesco. David with the Head of Goliath. New York, French and Co. Gallery.

Italian school, 17th century. David with the Head of Goliath. Budapest, Museum of Fine Arts, 1008.

Italian school, 17th century. David with the Head of Goliath. Also attributed to Onorio Marinari. 1630-40. Florence, Palazzo Uffizi, 1555.

Piazzetta, Giovanni Battista. David with the Head of Goliath. Dresden, Staatliche Kunstsammlungen, 570.

Piazzetta, Giovanni Battista. David with the Head of Goliath. Sotheby and Co., London (Sale, May 16, 1984, [MAGNOLIA], No. 100).

Reni, Guido. David with the Head of Goliath. c.1618-20. Sotheby and Co., London (Sale, April 3, 1985).

Riminaldi, Orazio. David with the Head of Goliath. Turin, Pinacoteca.

Sellaio, Jacopo del. David. Philadelphia, Philadelphia Museum of Art, Johnson Collection, 51.

Strozzi, Bernardo. David with the Head of Goliath. Christie, Manson and Woods (Sale, London, July 19, 1974, No. 218).

Strozzi, Bernardo. David with the Head of Goliath. New York, Metropolitan Museum of Art, 27.93.

Strozzi, Bernardo. David with the Head of Goliath. c.1620-30. Cincinnati, Art Museum, 38.10501.

Strozzi, Bernardo. David with the Head of Goliath. Leningrad, Hermitage.

Strozzi, Bernardo. David with the Head of Goliath. Budapest, Museum of Fine Arts, 53.480.

Tanzio, Antonio d'Enrico. David with the Head of Goliath. Varallo Sesia, Pinacoteca.

Tanzio, Antonio d'Enrico (Tanzio da Varallo). David with the Head of Goliath. Varallo, Pinacoteca.

SPANISH SCHOOL

March, Miguel. David with the Head of Goliath. Valencia, Museo de Pinturas.

Spanish school, 17th century. David with the Head of Goliath. Valencia, Museo de Pinturas.

71 H 14 51 I SAMUEL 17:57 DAVID BRINGS GOLIATH'S HEAD TO SAUL

DUTCH SCHOOL

Rembrandt. David Presenting the Head of Goliath to Saul. 1626. Basle, Museum.

71 H 15 1 I SAMUEL 18:1-3 DAVID AND JONATHAN, SON OF SAUL, BECOME FRIENDS

DUTCH SCHOOL

Bol, Ferdinand. David and Jonathan. Sotheby and Co., London (Sale, [BLUEBELL], April 4, 1984, No. 58).

71 H 15 21 I SAMUEL 18:6-7 DAVID'S TRIUMPH: THE WOMEN OF ISRAEL COME OUT TO WELCOME DAVID, SINGING, DANCING AND PLAYING TAMBOURINES AND LYRES; DAVID HOLDING THE HEAD OF GOLIATH

DUTCH SCHOOL

Noord, Johannes van. The Triumph of David. London, Art Market.

Steen, Jan. David's triumph. Copenhagen, Picture Gallery.

FLEMISH SCHOOL

Cossiers, Jan. The Triumph of David. Christie, Manson and Woods (Sale, New York, June 12, 1981, No. 158).

Flemish school, 17th century (Antwerp). The Triumph of David. Budapest, Museum of Fine Arts, 9837.

Franck, Franz I, school of. David with the head of Goliath (pair to Marriage feast at Cana). England, Private Collection(A)

Rubens, P.P. Triumph of David. c.1638. Fort Worth, Texas, Kimbell Art Museum, AP 66.3.

FRENCH SCHOOL

Poussin, Nicolas. The Triumph of David. London, Dulwich College Art Gallery.

Tournier, Nicolas. David and the Head of Goliath. Rome, Galleria d'Arte Antica.

GERMAN SCHOOL

Schoenfeld, Johann Heinrich. The Triumph of David. Karlsruhe, Kunsthalle, 2473.

Strigel, Bernhard. David returning the head of Goliath. Munich, Old Pinakothek, H.G., 1063.

ITALIAN SCHOOL

Brandi, Giacinto. David with the Head of Goliath. Rome, Galleria d'Arte Antica.

Diziani, Gasparo. The Triumph of David. Christie, Manson and Woods (Sale, London, June 28, 1974, No. 54).

Gargiulo, Domenico (called Micco Spadaro). The Israelites Celebrating David's Return. Sarasota, Fla., Ringling Museum of Art, SN 155.

Gargiulo, Domenico (called Micco Spadaro). David's Triumph. Vienna, Kunsthistorisches Museum, 1593.

Guercino. The Triumph of David. Dublin, National Gallery, 1323.

Lazzarini, Gregorio. The Triumph of David. Borca di Cadore, S. Simon.

Lippi, Lorenzo. Triumph of David. Florence, Palazzo Pitti, 3476.

Manetti, Rutilio di Lorenzo. Triumph of David. Lucca, Palazzo Provinciale, Pinacoteca.

Rosselli, Matteo. Triumph of David. Florence, Pitti.

Rosselli, Matteo. Triumph of David. Paris, Louvre, Musée du.

Rosselli, Matteo. The Triumph of David. Also attributed to Jacopo Vignali. Greenville, S.C., Bob Jones University Collection, 1962, Cat. 64.

Spinelli, Giovan Battista. David Dances with the Handmaidens. Florence, Palazzo Uffizi, 1890 n.1468.

Vaccaro, Andrea. The Triumph of David. Geneva, Musée d'Art et d'Histoire, 1839-9.

Vaccaro, Andrea. Triumph of David. Naples, Museo Nazionale, Capodimente, 1736.

71 H 15 3 1 SAMUEL 18:11 SAUL CASTS HIS SPEAR AT
    DAVID

ITALIAN SCHOOL
    Salviati, Francesco. Story of David: Saul
    Attempting to Kill David. Rome, Palazzo
    Sacchetti, Second floor salon, west wall,
    far left side.

71 H 16 21 I SAMUEL 19:9-10 SAUL CASTS HIS SPEAR
    AT DAVID AGAIN

GERMAN SCHOOL
    German school, 15th century. Scenes from the
    life of King David. c.1500. Madrid, Col-
    lection Baugá.

ITALIAN SCHOOL
    Salviati, Francesco. Story of David: Saul
    attempting to kill David. Rome, Palazzo
    Sacchetti. Second floor salon, west wall,
    far left side.

71 H 16 35 I SAMUEL 19:16 SAUL'S SOLDIERS DISCOVER
    THE DECOY

ITALIAN SCHOOL
    Salviati, Francesco. Story of David: Messengers
    of Saul attempt to kill David. Rome, Palazzo
    Sacchetti. Second floor salon, south wall,
    left side, upper section.

71 H 17 I SAMUEL 20 DAVID AND JONATHAN

ITALIAN SCHOOL
    Cima, G.B. David and Jonathan. London, National
    Gallery, 2505.

71 H 17 33 I SAMUEL 20:41-42 DAVID AND JONATHAN
    EMBRACING; DAVID'S LEAVE-TAKING FROM JONATHAN

DUTCH SCHOOL
    Rembrandt. The reconciliation of David and
    Absalom. Also called David's Farewell to
    Jonathan. 1642. Leningrad, Hermitage.

71 H 21 2 I SAMUEL 21:6-9 DAVID RECEIVES GIFTS FROM
    ABIMELECH

ITALIAN SCHOOL
    Palma Giovane. David and Abimelech. Venice,
    Gesuiti, sacristy ceiling.
    Pellegrini, Giovanni Antonio. David Receives
    Bread from Abimelech. c.1724. Brescia,Chiesa
    di Sant'Agata.

SPANISH SCHOOL
    Escalante, Juan Antonio. David and the high
    priest.

71 H 21 21 I SAMUEL 21:6 DAVID RECEIVES THE HALLOWED
    BREAD

SPANISH SCHOOL
    Arteaga y Alfaro, Matias. Ahimelech offering
    David the show-bread. Seville, Museo Prov-
    incial.

71 H 21 22 I SAMUEL 21:9 DAVID RECEIVES GOLIATH'S
    SWORD

DUTCH SCHOOL
    Gelder, Aert de. Ahimelech gives Goliath's
    Sword to David. Malibu, J.Paul Getty Museum,
    78 PA 219.

71 H 22 21 I SAMUEL 22:1-2 DAVID'S FAMILY AND MEN
    JOIN HIM IN THE CAVE ADULLAM

FRENCH SCHOOL
    Claude Lorrain. Landscape: David at the cave
    of Adullam("The Chigi Claude", or Sinon
    brought prisoner to Priam. London, National
    Gallery, 6.

Claude Lorrain, Copy after. David at the
    Cave of Adullam. New York, Metropolitan
    Museum, 21.184.

71 H 23 6 I SAMUEL 24:8-11 WHEN SAUL COMES OUT
    OF THE CAVE, DAVID CALLS HIM, FALLS DOWN
    ON HIS KNEES AND SHOWS HIM THE PIECE OF
    CLOTH

GERMAN SCHOOL
    German school, 15th century. Scenes from
    the life of King David. c.1500. Madrid,
    Collection Baugá.

71 H 24 I SAMUEL 25 DAVID AND ABIGAIL

FLEMISH SCHOOL
    Flocquet, Lucas. Meeting of David and Abigail.
    1617. Northwick Park, Collection E.G.
    Spencer-Churchill (formerly).
    Goes, Hugo van der, copy after. The story
    of David and Abigail. Barcelona, Collection
    Col. Raap.
    Goes, Hugo van der, copy after. The story
    of David and Abigail. Brussels, Musées
    Royaux des Beaux Arts.

71 H 24 4 I SAMUEL 14-17 ABIGAIL, NABAL'S WIFE,
    IS TOLD ABOUT NABAL'S REFUSAL AND DAVID'S
    ADVANCE

DUTCH SCHOOL
    Jacobsz, Lambert. Abigail and Nabal. London,
    University, Courtauld Institute (Princess
    Gate Collection), 177.

FLEMISH SCHOOL
    Vos, Martin de, the Elder. David and Abigail.
    Vienna, Kunsthistorisches Museum, 1096.

71 H 24 42 I SAMUEL 25:20-35 MEETING OF DAVID
    AND ABIGAIL, WHO KNEELS BEFORE HIM

DUTCH SCHOOL
    Cornelisz van Oostsanen, Jacob. David and
    Abigail. Copenhagen, Art Museum, Sp.734.
    Engelbrechtsz, Cornelis. David and Abigail.
    Florence, Museo Nazionale.
    Uytewael, J.A. David and Abigail. Gateshead,
    Shipley Art Gallery.
    Uytewael, Joachim Antonisz. The Encounter
    Between David and Abigail. 1597. Amsterdam,
    Rijksmuseum.

FLEMISH SCHOOL
    Flemish school, 17th century. Meeting of
    David and Abigail with the Septizonium
    of Septimius Serverus in the landscape.
    Rome, Galleria Colonna.
    Franck, Franz, I, Studio of. Flemish Reliquary
    Chest painted with scenes from the Old
    Testament. Detail: Left Door: David and
    Abigail. c.1600. Sarasota, Fla., Ringling
    Museum of Art, SN 1950.
    Franck, Frans II. David and Abigail. 1630.
    Private Collection, U.S.A.
    Goes, Hugo van der, copy after. The story
    of David and Abigail. Detail. Barcelona,
    Col. Raap Collection.
    Jordaens, Hans, III. David and Abigail.Christie,
    Manson and Woods (Sale, London [TREVI-2729]
    July 22, 1983, No. 186).
    Rubens, Peter Paul (and assistants). Meeting
    of David and Abigail. 1625-30. Detroit,
    Institute of the Arts, 89.63.
    Rubens, P.P. Meeting of David and Abigail.
    In Rubens' style or a copy after his Detroit
    painting. Wanas, Collection Gustaf Wacht-
    meister.
    Tulden, Theodoor van. David and Abigail.
    Bergues, Museum.
    Vos, Martin, the Elder. David and Abigail.
    Rouen (Seine-Inférieure), Musée.
    Vos, Maerten de. David and Abigail. Vienna,
    Kunsthistorisches Museum, 1096.

FRENCH SCHOOL
    Le Brun, Charles, School of. David and Abigail.
    Christie, Manson and Woods (Sale, Christie's
    East, New York, Nov. 8, 1984, No. 79).

ITALIAN SCHOOL
    Cavallino, Bernardo. Abigail and David.Brunswick,
    Landesmuseum, 517.
    Guardi, Francesco. David and Abigail. Milan,
    Private Collection.
    Reni, Guido. Meeting of David and Abigail.Walter
    P. Chrysler Jr. Collection, New York.
    Reni, Guido. David and Abigail. Budapest, Museum
    of Fine Arts, 490.

71 H 24 5 I SAMUEL 25:36-38 THE BANQUET IN NABAL'S
    HOUSE

GERMAN SCHOOL
    Rottenhammer, Johann, Attributed to. The Meeting
    of David and Abigail.The Hague,Royal Gallery,
    281.

ITALIAN SCHOOL
    Tiepolo, G.B. Abigail and Nabal. Venice, Museo
    Civico.
    Tiepolo, G.B. Abigail and Nabal. Paris, Musée
    Cognac-Jay.

71 H 25 2 I SAMUEL 26:7 DAVID AND ABISHAI INVADE
    SAUL'S ENCAMPMENT AT NIGHT, WHILE SAUL AND
    HIS SOLDIERS ARE SLEEPING

FLEMISH SCHOOL
    Seghers, Gerard. David and Abishai with the
    Sleeping Saul and Abner. Gergel, Max - Col-
    lection (Columbia, S.C.).

71 H 25 21 I SAMUEL 26:11 DAVID TAKES SAUL'S SPEAR
    AND WATER-FLASK AWAY

DUTCH SCHOOL
    Flinck, Govert. David with Saul's Spear and
    Cask. c.1636/37. Schapiro, E. - Collection
    (London).

GERMAN SCHOOL
    German school, 15th century. Scenes from the
    life of King David. c.1500. Madrid, Col-
    lection Baugá.

ITALIAN SCHOOL
    Salviati, Francesco. David sparing the life
    of Saul. Rome, Palazzo Scchetti.Second floor
    salon, south wall, upper section.

71 H 31 52 I SAMUEL 28:14 THE GHOST OF SAMUEL
    APPEARS TO THE WITCH AT ENDOR; SAUL FALLS
    PROSTRATE TO THE GROUND

DUTCH SCHOOL
    Bol, Ferdinand. The Ghost of Samuel Appearing
    to King Saul and the Witch of Endor. Also
    attributed to Willem de Poorter Leonard
    Bramer and the School of Rembrandt. Bader,
    Alfred - Collection (Milwaukee).

ITALIAN SCHOOL
    Cavallino, Bernardo.The Shade of Samuel Invoked
    by Saul. c.1650-56. Malibu, J.Paul Getty
    Museum, 83.PC.365.
    Rosa, Salvatore. Apparition of the Shade of
    Samuel to Saul (Saul and the Witch of Endor)
    1668. Paris, Louvre, Musée du.
    Salviati, Francesco. Saul before the ghost of
    Samuel. Rome, Palazzo Sacchetti. Second floor
    salon, west wall, far right side.

71 H 31 I SAMUEL 28:3-25 SAUL AND THE WITCH OF ENDOR

DUTCH SCHOOL
    Cornelisz van Oostsanen, Jacob. Saul visiting
    the witch of Endor. Signed and dated, 1526.
    Amsterdam, Rijksmuseum, 722.

    Coninxloo, Gillis III, van. Saul and the
    Witch of Endor; a pair with Judah and
    Tamar. Christie, Manson and Woods (Sale,
    London, [TOLEDO-2659] May 27, 1983, No.161).

AMERICAN SCHOOL
    Allston, Washington. Saul and the Witch of
    Endor. c.1820. Amherst College, Mead Art
    Museum.
    Allston, Washington. Saul and the Witch of
    Endor. Study for a Foot. c.1820. Miami,
    University of, Joe and Emily Lowe Art
    Gallery.
    Mount, William Sidney. Saul and the Witch
    of Endor. 1828. Wasington, D.C., Smithsonian
    Institution, National Collection of Fine
    Arts.
    West, Benjamin. Saul and the Witch of Endor.
    Hartford, Wadsworth Atheneum, 1948.186.

BRITISH SCHOOL
    Blake, William. The Witch of Endor Raising
    the Spirit of Samuel. 1783. New York,
    Public Library.
    Blake, William. The Ghost of Samuel Appearing
    to Saul. c.1800. Washington, D.C., National
    Gallery of Art, Rosenwald Collection,
    B 11061.

71 H 32 I SAMUEL 31 BATTLE BETWEEN THE ISRAELITES
    AND THE PHILISTINES

FLEMISH SCHOOL
    Brueghel, Pieter, the Elder. Suicide of Saul
    (The Battle of Gilbon). Vienna, Kunsthistor-
    isches Museum.

71 H 32 12 I SAMUEL 31:2 DEATH OF JONATHAN AND
    HIS BROTHERS ABINADAB AND MELCHI-SHUA

ITALIAN SCHOOL
    Salviati, Francesco. Story of David: Death
    of Saul and Jonathan. Rome, Palazzo Sac-
    chetti. Second floor salon, west wall,
    center.

71 H 32 13 I SAMUEL 31:3 SAUL WOUNDED BY AN ARROW

ITALIAN SCHOOL
    Salviati, Francesco. Story of David: Death
    of Saul and Jonathan. Rome, Palazzo Sac-
    chetti. Second floor salon, west wall,
    center.

71 H 32 2 I SAMUEL 31:3-5 SAUL'S DEATH

FLEMISH SCHOOL
    Brueghel, Pieter, the Elder. Suicide of Saul
    (The Battle of Gilboa). Vienna, Kunsthistor-
    isches Museum.
    Rubens, A.F. (or Broers, J.). Death of Saul.
    Melbourne Hall, Collection Lord Lothian.

ITALIAN SCHOOL
    Salviati, Francesco. Story of David: Death
    of Saul and Jonathan. Rome, Palazzo Sac-
    chetti. Second floor salon, west wall,
    center.

71 H 32 4 I SAMUEL 31:8-13 SAUL'S BODY

ITALIAN SCHOOL
    Salviati, Francesco. Story of David: Death
    of Saul and Jonathan. Rome, Palazzo Sac-
    chetti. Second floor salon, west wall,
    center.

71 H 32 45 I SAMUEL 31:11-13 THE INHABITANTS
    OF JABESH-GILEAD TAKE AWAY THE BODIES

BRITISH SCHOOL
    Varley, John. The Burial of Saul. London,
    Victoria and Albert Museum, 1517-1882.

71 H 41 2 II SAMUEL 2:4 DAVID ANOINTED KING BY THE
    TRIBE OF JUDAH

FRENCH SCHOOL
    Claude Lorrain. David anointed king of Israel.

71 H 46 3 II SAMUEL 3:27 ABNER, FETCHED BY JOAB'S
    MESSENGERS, IS TAKEN ASIDE BY JOAB IN THE
    GATE OF HEBRON, AND IS KILLED BY HIM WITH
    A SWORD

ITALIAN SCHOOL
    Michelangelo. Joab kills Abner. Rome, Vatican,
    Sistine Chapel.

71 H 48 2 II SAMUEL 5:3 DAVID ANOINTED BY THE ELDERS
    OF ISRAEL

GERMAN SCHOOL
    German school, 15th century. Scenes from the
    life of King David. c.1500. Madrid, Collection
    Baugá.

SWEDISH SCHOOL
    Hörberg, Per. David is Anointed King over Israel.
    Stockholm, National Museum, 968.

71 H 51 4 I CHRONICLES 14:1; II SAMUEL 5:11 THE
    BUILDING OF DAVID'S PALACE

ITALIAN SCHOOL
    Pesellino, Francesco. Building of King David's
    house. Harvard University, Fogg Art Museum.

71 H 52 THE WARS OF DAVID

ITALIAN SCHOOL
    Raphael (and assistants). Old Testament subjects:
    Truimphant return of David from battle.
    Rome, Vatican, Loggie.
    Salviati, Francesco. Story of David: David talk-
    ing to soldiers. Rome, Palazzo Sacchetti.
    Second floor salon, east wall, far left,
    upper section.

71 H 52 64 I CHRONICLES 11:22 BENAIAH KILLS TWO
    MEN AND THEN A LION IN A PIT ON A SNOWY DAY

BRITISH SCHOOL
    Etty, William. Benaiah Slaying Two Lion-like
    Men of Moab. Edinburgh, National Gallery,188.

71 H 54 62 I CHRONICLES 21:16 DAVID SEES THE AVENGING
    ANGEL IN JERUSALEM; HE PRAYS TO GOD

FRENCH SCHOOL
    Ménageot, F.G. David Offering His Life to God
    to Save his People. 1779. Douai (Nord),
    St. Pierre.

71 H 54 63 I CHRONICLES 21:15 BY THE COMMANDMENT
    OF GOD THE ANGEL STOPS DESTROYING THE ISRAEL-
    ITES AT THE THRESHING-FLOOR OF ARAUNAH
    (ORNAN) THE JEBUSITE

DUTCH SCHOOL
    Eeckhout, Gerbrand van den. Angel appearing
    to Araunah. Signed, 1647. Milan, Brera,621.

71 H 61 1 DAVID COMMUNICATING WITH GOD; DAVID PRAYING
    (IN GENERAL)

GERMAN SCHOOL
    Wertinger, Hans. David in Prayer. Prague,Narodni
    Galerie.

ITALIAN SCHOOL
    Tintoretto. Scenes from the Old Testament: The
    Promise to David. c.1545. Vienna, Kunsthis-
    torisches Museum, 3832.

71 H 61 2 DAVID SACRIFICING (IN GENERAL)

ITALIAN SCHOOL
    Giordano, Luca. Stories from the life of David.
    Escorial, Monastery, Church, antecoro.

71 H 62 II SAMUEL 6 THE ARK OF THE COVENANT IS
    BROUGHT TO JERUSALEM

ITALIAN SCHOOL
    Diziani, Gaspare. David and the Israelites
    transporting the Ark of the Covenant.
    Sotheby and Co., London (Sale,[BLUEBELL],
    April 4, 1984, No. 105).

SPANISH SCHOOL
    Arteaga y Alfaro, Matias. Old Testament sub-
    ject. Seville, Cathedral, Archicofradia
    Sacramental del Sagrario.

71 H 62 2 II SAMUEL 6:14-15 THE ARK IS PLACED
    ON A CART DRIVEN BY THE SONS OF ABINADAB;
    DAVID AND THE PEOPLE DANCE AND MAKE MUSIC
    BEFORE THE ARK

AUSTRIAN SCHOOL
    Remp, Franz Carl. David Dancing and Singing
    before the Ark of the Covenant. Vienna,
    Österreichische Galerie, 4303.

DUTCH SCHOOL
    Bray, Jan de. David playing before the Ark.
    Signed Bray/1670. Variant in Brunswick
    dated 1674. Gosford Park, Scotland, Col-
    lection Earl of Wemyss.

ITALIAN SCHOOL
    Giordano, Luca. The Moving of the Ark by
    David. Vienna, Kunsthistorisches Museum,
    6208.
    Giordano, Luca. Scenes from the Old Testament:
    David and the Ark of the Covenant. Madrid,
    Palacio Real.
    Pesellino, Francesco. David and the Ark of
    the Lord. Kansas City, William Rockhill
    Nelson Gallery of Art, 32-82.
    Procaccini, Camillo, Circle of. King David
    Dancing before the Ark. A Pair with Feeding
    the Five Thousand. Sotheby and Co., London
    (Sale, [PRIMROSE], Feb. 16, 1983, No.12).
    Salviati, Francesco. Story of David: David
    dancing before the ark. Rome, Palazzo
    Sacchetti. Second floor salon, south wall,
    center.
    Tintoretto. Scenes from the Old Testament:
    The Moving of the Sacred Ark. c.1545.
    Vienna, Kunsthistorisches Museum, 3831.

71 H 62 7 II SAMUEL 6:5 DAVID BRINGS THE ARK
    INTO JERUSALEM, DANCING (HALF-) NAKED
    BEFORE THE ARK AND MAKING MUSIC, WHILE
    THE PEOPLE REJOICE

DUTCH SCHOOL
    Bray, Jan de. David Playing the Harp. 1674.
    Brunswick, Landesmuseum, 286.

ITALIAN SCHOOL
    Conca, Sebastiano. Ceiling decoration: trans-
    porting the Ark of the Holy Covenant.
    Naples, S. Chiara.
    Giordano, Luca. David before the Ark. Kansas,
    University of (Lawrence), Museum of Art,
    50.67.
    Salviati, Francesco. Story of David: David
    dancing before the Ark. Rome, Palazzo
    Sacchetti. Second floor salon, south wall,
    center.

71 H 62 8 II SAMUEL 6:17 DAVID PLACES THE ARK
    IN A TENT, BURNS OFFERINGS BEFORE THE
    LORD AND DISTRIBUTES BREAD, MEAT AND WINE
    TO EVERYONE

DUTCH SCHOOL
    Sibilla, Gijsbert. David's Thanksgiving.
    Klenk, Hans - Collection (Zurich).
    Tengnagel, Jan. King David Worshipping in
    the Tabernacle upon the Arrival of the
    Ark in Jerusalem. Christie, Manson and
    Woods (Sale, London, July 23, 1982, No.6).

GERMAN SCHOOL
Zick, Januarius. David before the Ark of the Covenant. Munich, Pinakothek, Neue, 9818.

ITALIAN SCHOOL
Pittoni, Giovanni Battista. David before the Ark. 1725-27. Florence, Palazzo Uffizi, 3940.
Pittoni, Giovanni Battista. King David in Adoration of the Ark. Sotheby and Co., London (Sale, New York, [NAPLES-5348] June 6,1985, no. 88).

71 H 71 II SAMUEL 11:2 DAVID, FROM THE ROOF (OR BALCONY) OF HIS PALACE, SEES BATHSHEBA BATHING

DUTCH SCHOOL
Lisse, Dirk van der. Bathsheba Bathing. Sotheby and Co., London (Sale, New York, March 24, 1983, No. 54).
Rembrandt. Susanna at the Bath (Bathsheba). 1637(?). The Hague, Royal Gallery.
Scorel, Jan van. Bathsheba. Amsterdam, Rijksmuseum, 2191.

FLEMISH SCHOOL
Bles, Herri met de. The story of David and Bathsheba. Boston, Fenway Court.
Dyck, Anthony van. Bathsheba. Madrid, Collection Duke of Alba.
Gassel, Lucas. Courtly Grounds with Scenes from the Story of David and Bathsheba. Hartford, Conn., Wadsworth Atheneum, 1956.618.
Huysman, Jacob. Bathsheba. 1696. London, Collection Miss Y. Ffrench.
Toeput, Lodewijk. David and Bathsheba. A Pair with Diana and Callisto. Sotheby and Co., London (Sale, April 8, 1981, No. 52).

FRENCH SCHOOL
Bourdichon, Jean, Workshop of. Bathsheba Bathing, From the Book of Hours (Prayer Book of Henri de Valois, p. 213). Early 16th century, School of Tours. Cracow, Czartoryski Museum, Ms. Czart. 3020.
Jerome, J.L. Copy. Bathsheba. 1889.

GERMAN SCHOOL
Cranach, Lucas, the elder. David and Bathsheba. 1526. Berlin, Staatliche Museen, 567B.
Douven, Bartholomeus Frans. Bathsheba. 1726. Cassel, Staatliche Kunstsammlungen, 324.
König, Johann. The Toilet of Bathsheba. Oxford, University, Ashmolean Museum, A 718.
Krodel, Wolfgang. David and Bathsheba. Vienna, Kunsthistorisches Museum, 899.

ITALIAN SCHOOL
Bellucci, Antonio. Bathsheba at the Bath. Venice, Private Collection.
Bordone, Paris. David and Bathsheba. Baltimore, Md., Walters Art Gallery, 37.2371.
Brusasorci, Domenico. Bathsheba. Florence, Palazzo Uffizi.
Castello, Valerio. The Bath of Bathsheba. Genoa, Private Collection.
Franciabigio. Bathsheba. Dresden, Gallery.
Gennari, Benedetto. Bathsheba at her Bath. Baltimore, Md., Walters Art Gallery, 37.765.
Gentileschi, Artemisia. Bathsheba at the Bath. Florence, Soprintendenza alle Gallerie, Inv. Oggetti d'arte, n. 1803.
Gentileschi, Artemisia. David and Bathsheba. c.1640-45. Columbus, Ohio, Gallery of Fine Arts.
Liberi, Pietro, circle of. David Observing Bathsheba. Sotheby and Co., London (Sale, New York, Jan. 20, 1983, No. 54).
Maratti, Carlo. Toilette of Bathsheba. Vienna, Liechtenstein Gallery.
Pellegrini, Giovanni Antonio. Bathsheba.

Pittoni, Giovanni Battista. Bathsheba in the Bath. Pordenone, Private Collection.
Raphael (and assistants). Old Testament subjects: David sees Bathsheba. Rome, Vatican, Loggie.
Ricci, Sebastiano. Bathsheba at her Bath. Budapest, Museum of Fine Arts, 57.9.
Ricci, Sebastiano. Bathsheba at her Bath. Venice, Private Collection.
Rocca, Michele. Bathsheba at her Bath. Cassel, Staatliche Kunstsammlungen, 561.
Salviati, Francesco. Story of David: Bath of Bathsheba. Rome, Palazzo Sacchetti. Second floor salon, north wall, center.
Trevisani, Francesco. Bathsheba in her bath. Pommersfelden, Collection Dr. Karl Grof von Schönborn-Wiesentheid.

SWISS SCHOOL
Deutsch, N.M., the elder. Bathsheba watched by David. 1517. Basle, Museum, 419.

71 H 71 2 II SAMUEL 11:2 BATHSHEBA ATTENDED BY MAIDSERVANT(S)

BRITISH SCHOOL
Blake, William. Bathsheba at the Bath. c.1790-1800. London, Tate Gallery, 3007.

DUTCH SCHOOL
Cornelisz, Cornelis. Bathsheba in bath. 1594. Amsterdam, Rijksmuseum, 719 A 3.
Cornelisz, Cornelis. Bathsheba in Bath. Pommersfelden, Schloss, Gallery.
Loo, Jacob van. Bathsheba in her Bath. Paris, Louvre, Musée du, M.N.R. 498.
Rembrandt. Bathsheba. 1654. Paris, Louvre, LP.
Rembrandt. Toilet of Bathsheba. New York, Metropolitan Museum.
Rembrandt. The Toilet of Bathsheba. c. 1632. Ottawa, National Gallery of Canada.
Swart, Jan van Groningen. Bathsheba in the Bath. Cologne, Wallraf-Richartz Museum, 664.

FLEMISH SCHOOL
Memlinc, Hans. Bathsheba at her toilet. Stuttgart, Museum, 644.
Rubens, P.P. Bathsheba at the fountain. Dresden, Gallery.

FRENCH SCHOOL
Cézanne, Paul. Bathsheba. Paris, Collection Pellerin.
Van Loo, Jean-Baptiste, Manner of. Bathsheba at the Bath. Sacramento, Crocker Art Gallery, 1872.153.

GERMAN SCHOOL
Aachen, Hans von. Bathsheba at the Bath. Vienna, Kunsthistorisches Museum, Inv.Nr. 1094.
Füger, Friedrich Heinrich. Bathsheba in the Bath. Budapest, Museum of Fine Arts, 438(751).

ITALIAN SCHOOL
Bordone, Paris. Bathsheba. 1545. Cologne, Wallraf-Richartz Museum.
Bordone, Paris. Bathsheba. 1552. Hamburg, Kunsthalle.
Conca, Sebastiano. David and Bathsheba. Sotheby and Co., London (Sale, April 16, 1980, No.5a).
Franceschini, Marcantonio. Bathsheba at the Bath. Genoa, Palazzo Durazzo-Pallavicini.
Furini, Francesco. Bathsheba. Sotheby and Co., London (Sale, June 9, 1982, No. 45).
Matteis, Paolo de. Bathsheba. Treviso, Private Collection.

71 H 71 3 II SAMUEL 11:4 BATHSHEBA RECEIVES A LETTER
          FROM DAVID

DUTCH SCHOOL
    Koninck, Salomon. Bathsheba. Copenhagen, Picture
    Gallery.

FLEMISH SCHOOL
    Heere, Lucas de. Bathsheba at the Bath. Salm,
    Fürsten zu - Collection, 268.
    Metsys, Jan. David and Bathsheba. Paris, Louvre,
    2030b.

GERMAN SCHOOL
    Huber, Conrad. Bathsheba Receiving the Letter
    from David. Sotheby and Co., London (Sale,
    Sept. 23, 1981, No. 129).
    Rottenhammer, Johann, Follower of. Bathsheba.
    Christie, Manson and Woods (Sale, London,
    Dec. 2, 1983 [TORINO-2790], No. 72).

ITALIAN SCHOOL
    Carraci, Ludovico, Style of. Bathsheba at the
    Bath. Christie, Manson and Wood (Sale, Chris-
    tie's East, New York, March 25, 1983, No.98).
    Mei, Bernardino. David and Bathsheba. Siena,
    Palazzo Chigi-Saracini.
    Pittoni, Giovanni Battista. Bathsheba in the
    Bath. Pordenone, Private Collection.

71 H 71 31 II SAMUEL 11:4 BATHSHEBA (ALONE) WITH
           DAVID'S LETTER

DUTCH SCHOOL
    Drost, Wilhelm. Bathsheba. 1654. Paris, Louvre,
    Musée du, 2359A.
    Flinck, Govert. Bathsheba with David's Letter.
    1659. Leningrad, Hermitage.

71 H 71 4 II SAMUEL 11:4 BATHSHEBA COMES TO DAVID'S
          PALACE

ITALIAN SCHOOL
    Salviati, Francesco. Story of David: Bathsheba
    goes to David. Rome, Palazzo Sacchetti.Second
    floor salon, north wall, right side.
    Tintoretto. David and Bathsheba. 1545-48.Vienna,
    Kunsthistorisches Museum, 3833.

71 H 71 5 II SAMUEL 11:4 DAVID AND BATHSHEBA AS
          LOVERS

FRENCH SCHOOL
    Chagall, Marc. Bathsheba. 1962-63. Private Col-
    lection.

ITALIAN SCHOOL
    Salviati, Francesco. Story of David. Rome, Pal-
    azzo Sacchetti. Second floor salon, north
    wall, detail of upper section, right.

71 H 73 4 II SAMUEL 11:14-15 DAVID GIVES URIAH A
          LETTER FOR JOAB

DUTCH SCHOOL
    Lastman, Pieter P. David and Uriah. 1619. The
    Hague, Dienst voor's Rijks Verspreide Kunst-
    voorverpen on loan to Groningen, Groninger
    Museum.
    Lastman, Pieter P. King David Handling the
    Letter to Uriah. 1611. Detroit, Institute
    of Arts, 60.63.

FLEMISH SCHOOL
    Gassel, Lucas. King David Giving Uriah His
    Letter to Joab. Christie, Manson and Wood,
    (Sale, Nov. 28, 1975).

71 H 74 2 II SAMUEL 11:17 URIAH IS KILLED IN BATTLE

ITALIAN SCHOOL
    Michelangelo. Ceiling decorations: detail: Med-
    allion between pedestals on right: Death
    of Uriah, the Hittite. Rome, Sistine Chapel.

Salviati, Francesco. Story of David: Killing
of Uriah. Rome, Palazzo Sacchetti. Second
floor salon, north wall, left side.

71 H 76 II SAMUEL 12:1-15 DAVID IS REBUKED BY
         NATHAN

DUTCH SCHOOL
    Gelder, Aert de. Nathan Rebukes David. 1683.
    Location Unknown.

GERMAN SCHOOL
    Zick, Johann. King David Admonished by the
    Prophet Nathan. Budapest, Museum of Fine
    Arts, 6510.

ITALIAN SCHOOL
    Italian school, 15th century. David Reproved
    by Nathan. 1430-50. Oxford, University,
    Ashmolean Museum, A 334.

71 H 77 2 II SAMUEL 12:16-17 DAVID REPENTANT;
          HE LIES ON THE GROUND PRAYING AND FASTING
          FOR HIS CHILD TO RECOVER

ITALIAN SCHOOL
    Guercino. King David penitent. Greenville,
    S.C., Bob Jones University Collection.
    Michelangelo. Ceiling decoration: Detail:
    medallion between pedestals: David and
    Nathan. Rome, Vatican, Sistine Chapel.
    Pesellino, Francesco. Penitence of King David.
    Le Mans, Musée.

71 H 78 II SAMUEL 12:20 DAVID RECOVERS AND TAKES
         A MEAL

DUTCH SCHOOL
    Eeckhout, Gerbrand van den. David Recovers
    from Mourning Bathsheba's Child. 1668.
    Vienna, Liechtenstein Gallery, 645.

71 H 8 II SAMUEL 13-20; I KINGS 1 REBELLIONS
        AGAINST DAVID

DUTCH SCHOOL
    Eeckhout, Gerbrand van den. King David's
    dream. 1668. Vienna, Liechtenstein Gallery.
    No. 645.

71 H 81 22 II SAMUEL 13:11-14 TAMAR VIOLATED
           BY AMNON

DUTCH SCHOOL
    Steen, Jan. Tamar and Amnon. Cologne, Wallraf-
    Richartz Museum.

FLEMISH SCHOOL
    Santvoort, Philippus van. Rape of Tamar by
    Amnon. London, National Gallery, 3404.

ITALIAN SCHOOL
    Molinari, Antonio. Amnon and Tamar. Atlanta,
    High Museum of Art.

71 H 81 23 II SAMUEL 13:18-19 AMNON SENDS TAMAR
           AWAY; TAMAR PUTS ASHES ON HER HEAD, RENDS
           HER GARMENT, LAYS HER HAND ON HER HEAD
           AND LEAVES CRYING

ITALIAN SCHOOL
    Guercino. Amon Dismisses his Sister Tamar.
    Modena, Pinacoteca Estense.

71 H 81 3 II SAMUEL 13:20 ABSALOM CONSOLES TAMAR

ITALIAN SCHOOL
    Guercino. Absalom and Tamar. National Trust,
    (Tatton Park).

Cavallino, Bernardo. The Feast of Absalom.
Rohoncz, Schloss - Collection (Hungary).
Palma, Giovane, Circle of. The Death of Amnon
in Absalom's Tent. Sotheby and Co., London
(Sale, [CHICORY] Dec. 15, 1982, No. 95).
Preti, Mattia. The Feast of Absalom. Naples,
Museo Nazionale.
Preti, Mattia. The Feast of Absalom. c.1656-61.
Ottawa, National Gallery of Canada.
Traversi, Gaspare. Feast of Absalom. Rome, San
Paolo Fuori le Mura.

SPANISH SCHOOL
Arteaga y Alfaro, Matias. Old Testament subject.
Seville, Cathedral, Archicofradia Sacra-
mental del Sagrario.

71 H 82 5 II SAMUEL 14:33 RECONCILIATION OF DAVID
AND ABSALOM; ABSALOM KNEELS BEFORE DAVID
AND THEY EMBRACE

BRITISH SCHOOL
Blake, William. David Pardoning Absalom.
c.1800-03. Bedford (Bedfordshire), Cecil
Higgins Art Gallery.

DUTCH SCHOOL
Rembrandt. The Reconciliation of David and Absalom. 1642. Leningrad, Hermitage.

71 H 84 9 II SAMUEL 18:9 ABSALOM, PUT TO FLIGHT
ON A MULE, REMAINS HANGING BY HIS HAIR IN
AN OAK-TREE

FLEMISH SCHOOL
Flemish school, 17th century. The Death of
Absalom. Vienna, Kunsthistorisches Museum,
1788.

GERMAN SCHOOL
Weisgerber, Albert. Absalom. Hamburg, Kunsthalle.

71 H 84 92 II SAMUEL 18:14 JOAB STABS ABSALOM WITH
THREE SPEARS

ITALIAN SCHOOL
Giordano, Luca. Death of Absalom. Aranjuez,
Palacio Real.
Italian school, 17th century. Death of Absalom.
Paris, Louvre.
Michelangelo. Medallions: Death of Absalom.
Rome, Vatican, Sistine Chapel.
Pesellino, Francesco. Death of Absalom. Le
Mans, Musée.
Salviati, Francesco. Story of David: Death of
Absalom. Rome, Palazzo Sacchetti. Second
floor salon, east wall, center.
Viola, Giovanni Battista. Landscape with Ab-
salom pierced by the lance of Joab. Paris,
Louvre, Musée du, 189.

71 H 85 24 II SAMUEL 19:32 CUSHI TELLS DAVID OF
ABSALOM'S DEATH

FLEMISH SCHOOL
Franck, Frans, II, Manner of. Incidents from
the Life of King David. Sotheby and Co.,
London (Sale, Oct. 24, 1984, [DAHLIA] no.
118).

ITALIAN SCHOOL
Salviati, Francesco. Story of David: David
learns of the death of Absalom. Rome, Palazzo Sacchetti. Second floor salon, east
wall, right side.

71 H 85 6 II SAMUEL 19:8 DAVID SPEAKS TO THE
PEOPLE AT THE GATE OF THE CITY

ITALIAN SCHOOL
Salviati, Francesco. Story of David: David
talking to soldiers. Rome, Palazzo Sacchetti. Second floor salon, east wall,
far left, upper section.

71 H 88 22 II SAMUEL 1:16-21 BATHSHEBA KNEELS
BEFORE DAVID AND ASKS HIM TO PROCLAIM
SOLOMON KING

DUTCH SCHOOL
Eeckhout, Gerbrand van den. David Promises
Bathsheba that Solomon will Succeed Him.
1646. Prague, Národní Galerie.
Flinck, Govert. Bathsheba Kneels before
David Asking Him to Proclaim Solomon
King. c.1651. Dublin, National Gallery, 64.
Gelder, Aert de. Bathsheba Pleads with David
to Proclaim Solomon King. Haab-Escher, E.
- Collection (Zurich).

ITALIAN SCHOOL
Strozzi, Bernardo. Bathsheba asking David
to Proclaim Solomon King. Dresden, Staatliche Kunstsammlungen, 655.

71 H 88 32 I KINGS 1:39 SOLOMON ANOINTED KING BY ZADOK; ALL THE PEOPLE REJOICE AND BLOW THEIR TRUMPETS

FLEMISH SCHOOL
Vos, Cornelis de. The Anointing of Solomon. Paris, Louvre, Musée du, INV. 953.

ITALIAN SCHOOL
Giordano, Luca. Scenes from the Old Testament: Solomon Anointed King. Madrid, Palacio Real.
Raphael (and assistants). Old Testament subjects: Solomon anointed king. Rome, Vatican, Loggie.

71 H 9 I KINGS 2; I CHRONICLES 28-29 DAVID'S LAST DAYS

ITALIAN SCHOOL
Strozzi, Bernardo. David and Solomon. Corsham Court, Collection Lord Methuen.

71 H 92 I KINGS 2:1-9 DAVID'S INSTRUCTIONS TO SOLOMON

DUTCH SCHOOL
Horst, G.W. David's dying charge to Solomon. Dublin, National Gallery, 47.
Victors, Jan. The Dying David Admonishes Solomon. 1642 or 1644. Copenhagen, Art Museum, Sp. 464.

FLEMISH SCHOOL
Cossiers, Jan. David's dying advice to Solomon. Bob Jones University Collection, (Greenville, S.C.).
Cossiers, Jan. David's Dying Advice to Solomon. Christie, Manson and Woods (Sale, New York, June 12, 1981, No. 159).

71 H 92 42 I CHRONICLES 28:11-19 DAVID GIVES SOLOMON THE PLAN OF THE TEMPLE

ITALIAN SCHOOL
Giordano, Luca. David Shows to Solomon the Plan of the Temple. c.1700. Florence, Palazzo Uffizi, 9469.

71 H 93 I CHRONICLES 29:10-19 DAVID'S PRAYER OF THANKS

ITALIAN SCHOOL
Beccafumi, Domenico. David with a Psalter. Study. 1525-29. Florence, Palazzo Uffizi, GDSU, 19109.

71 I I KINGS 1:10 – 11:43 STORY OF SOLOMON

71 I 13 I KINGS 2:19 BATHSHEBA COMES BEFORE SOLOMON

DUTCH SCHOOL
Bol, Ferdinand. Bathsheba's Appeal. Also attributed to Govert Flinck. Dublin, National Gallery, 64.

71 I 31 I KINGS 3:4-15 SOLOMON'S PRAYER FOR WISDOM

DUTCH SCHOOL
Flinck, Govert. Solomon's prayer for wisdom. Bob Jones University Collection, (Greenville, S.C.).
Flinck, Govert. Solomon's prayer for wisdom. 1658. Amsterdam, Royal Palace.

71 I 32 I KINGS 3:16-28 THE JUDGEMENT OF SOLOMON

BRITISH SCHOOL
Blake, William. The Judgement of Solomon. c.1799-1800. Cambridge, University, Fitzwilliam Museum, PD28-1949.
Dyce, William. The Judgement of Solomon. 1864. Edinburgh, National Gallery, 521.

DUTCH SCHOOL
Werff, Adriaen van der. The judgement of Solomon. 1697. Florence, Palazzo Uffizi, 1313.

FLEMISH SCHOOL
Claeissins, Pieter I, 1500-1576. The Judgement of Solomon. Sotheby and Co., London (Sale, Monaco, [TAORMINE] dec. 9, 1984, No. 506).
Herp, Willem van. The Judgement of Solomon. Christie, Manson and Woods (Sale, New York, June 12, 1981, No.117).

FRENCH SCHOOL
Boulogne, Louis, the younger. The Judgement of Solomon. 1710. Moscow, Pushkin State Museum of Fine Arts, 1221.

ITALIAN SCHOOL
Italian school, 15th century. Judgement of Solomon. (Obverse). By Ferrarese master. New York, Gimbel Brothers, 1926.
Pitati, Bonifacio. Judgement of Solomon. Venice, Academy.
Pitati, Bonifacio. The Judgement of Solomon. Oxford, University, Ashmolean Museum, A914.
Raphael (and assistants) Old Testament subjects: Judgement of Solomon. Rome, Vatican, Loggie.
Sebastiano del Piombo. The Judgement of Solomon. 1511. National Trust (Kingston Lacy).
Solimena, Francesco. Solomon and the Queen of Sheba. Chaucer Fine Arts - Gallery (London).
Tiepolo, G.B. Judgement of Solomon. Palazzo Arcivescovile, Sala Rossa, decorations.

71 I 32 4 I KINGS 3:16 BOTH MOTHERS COME BEFORE SOLOMON

GERMAN SCHOOL
Holbein, Hans, the younger. Judgement of Solomon. Basle, Museum.

ITALIAN SCHOOL
Italian school, 17th century. The Judgement of Solomon. Brooklyn, N.Y., Institute of Arts and Sciences, Museum, 06.23.

71 I 32 5 I KINGS 3:25 SOLOMON GIVES VERDICT; HE COMMANDS A SOLDIER TO DIVIDE THE LIVING CHILD IN TWO

DUTCH SCHOOL
Hoet, Gerard. The Judgement of Solomon. Sotheby and Co., London (Sale, April 21, 1982, No. 23).

FLEMISH SCHOOL
Crayer, Gaspar de. Judgement of Solomon. Ghent, Museum.
Rillaer, Jan van. Judgement of Solomon. 1528. Berlin, Staatliche Museen.

FRENCH SCHOOL
Tassel, Jean. Judgement of Solomon. Sarasota, Fla., Ringling Museum of Art.
Valentin de Boullogne. Judgement of Solomon. Paris, Louvre.

ITALIAN SCHOOL
Campi, Giulio. Judgement of Solomon. Budapest, Museum of Fine Arts, 1083.
Dossi, Dosso, Follower of. The Judgement of Solomon. Sotheby and Co., London (Sale, [DAFFODIL] Feb. 20, 1980, No. 92).
Guardi, Francesco. The Judgement of Solomon. Finney - Collection (Paris).
Preti, Mattia. Judgement of Solomon. Naples, Palazzo Serra di Cassano.

**71 I 32 6   I KINGS 3:26: THE TRUE MOTHER OBJECTS
TO SOLOMON'S VERDICT**

AUSTRIAN SCHOOL
Schmidt, Martin Johann. The Judgement of Solomon. Budapest, Museum of Fine Arts, 6676.

BRITISH SCHOOL
Dyce, William. Judgement of Solomon. Edinburgh,
National Gallery of Scotland, 521.

DUTCH SCHOOL
Bramer, Leonard. Judgement of Solomon. New York,
Metropolitan Museum of Art.

FLEMISH SCHOOL
Jordaens, Jacob (or Crayer, Gaspar de). Judgement of Solomon. Madrid, Prado, 1.543.
Rubens, P.P. Judgement of Solomon. Madrid,Prado,
1543.
Rubens, Peter Paul. Wisdom of Solomon. Copenhagen, Art Museum, Inv. 1690 (Sp.185).

FRENCH SCHOOL
Poussin, Nicolas. The judgement of Solomon.
Troy, Jean François de. The Judgement of Sol-
omon. Lyons (Rhône), Musée Municipal.

GERMAN SCHOOL
Knüpfer, Nicolaus. The Judgement of Solomon.
Bourges, Museum, D-957-2-1.

ITALIAN SCHOOL
Balducci, Matteo. Judgement of Solomon. Paris,
Louvre, 1571.
Carlone, Giovanni Andrea. Judgement of Solomon.
Fresco. Genoa, Palazzo Spinola.
Francesco da Urbino. Judgement of Solomon.
Escorial, Monastery.
Giorgione. Judgement of Solomon. Florence, Pal-
azzo Uffizi.
Martinelli, Giovanni. The Judgement of Solomon.
Christie, Manson and Woods (Sale, New York,
June 12, 1981, No. 163).
Tintoretto (Jacopo Robusti). The Judgement of
Solomon. 1565. Venice, Palazzo Ducale, Atrio
Quadrato, ceiling.

**71 I 33   I KINGS 10:1-13; 2 CHRONICLES 9:1-9 SOLOMON
AND THE QUEEN OF SHEBA**

BRITISH SCHOOL
Ruskin, John. Solomon and the Queen cf Sheba.
Detail: Negro. Copy of painting by Veronese.
Harvard University, Fogg Art Museum, 1907.2.

DUTCH SCHOOL
Bramer, Leonard. The Queen of Sheba's Visit
to King Solomon. Bader, Alfred - Collection
(Milwaukee).
Dutch school, 16th century. Solomon and the
Queen of Sheba. Brunswick, Landesmuseum,
1289.
Koninck, Philips. The Queen of Sheba before
Solomon. Sotheby and Co. (Sale, London, March
26, 1969, No. 120).
Scorel, Jan van. Solomon and the Queen of Sheba.
Amsterdam, Rijksmuseum, 2190.

FLEMISH SCHOOL
Delen, Dirck van. Solomon and the Queen of
Sheba. 1632? Christie, Manson and Woods
(Sale, London [TIVOLI-2704] July 8, 1983,
No. 90).
Flemish school, 15th century. Solomon receivng
the Queen of Sheba. Florence,Museo Nazionale.
Flemish school, 17th century. Solomon before
the Queen of Sheba. Sotheby and Co., (Sale,
London, February 22, 1984, No. 12).
Geldorp, Gortzius. Solomon and the Queen of
Sheba. 1602. Cologne,Wallraf-Richartz Museum,
2937.

Master of the Groote Adoration. Solomon and
the Queen of Sheba. 1510-20. Chicago,
Art Institute, 36.127.
Master of the Legend of St. Barbara. Wings
of an altarpiece. Detail: Solomon and
the Queen of Sheba. New York, Metropolitan
Museum.
Quellin, Erasmus. Copy. The Queen of Sheba
Bringing Gifts to King Solomon. Cassel,
Staatliche Kunstsammlungen, 133.
Rubens, P.P. The Queen of Sheba visiting
Solomon. Salamanca, Seminario Conciliar.
Rubens, Peter Paul. Solomon Receiving the
Queen of Sheba. London, University, Court-
auld Institute (Princess Gate Collection),
26.
Rubens, P.P. Ceiling decorations for the
Church of the Jesuits at Antwerp. Sketch:
Solomon Receiving the Queen of Sheba.
Richmond, Cook Collection, 333.

FRENCH SCHOOL
French school, 17th century. Solomon and
the Queen of Sheba. Sotheby and Co., London
(Sale, New York, March 6-7, 1975, No.
176.).

GERMAN SCHOOL
German school, 16th century. The Queen of
Sheba before Solomon. Sometimes attributed
to Melchior Feselen. South German school,
c.1545. Philadelphia, Philadelphia Museum
of Art, Johnson Collection, no. 734.
Platzer, Johann Georg. The Queen of Sheba
at the Court of Solomon. Sotheby and Co.,
(Sale, London, March 26, 1968, No.100).

ITALIAN SCHOOL
Apollonio di Giovanni. Solomon and the Queen
of Sheba. Yale University, Gallery of
Fine Arts, 36.
Bassano, Leandro. Visit of the Queen of Sheba
to Solomon. Dublin, National Gallery,
97.
Cassone Master. Meeting of Solomon and Queen
of Sheba, right panel. London, Collection
Lord Crawford.
Conca, Sebastiano. Ceiling decoration: the
Queen of Sheba. Naples, S. Chiara.
Cortona, Pietro da. Solomon and Sheba. Rome,
Palazzo Mattei.
Cossa, Francesco, School of. Meeting of Solomon
and the Queen of Sheba. Boston, Museum
of Fine Arts.
Fontana, Lavinia. The Visit of the Queen
of Sheba. Dublin, National Gallery.
Gherardini, Alessandro. Solomon receiving
the Queen of Sheba. Schleissheim, Neues
Schloss, Gallery.
Gozzoli, Benozzo. Old Testament and other
subjects: The Queen of Sheba, and Solomon.
Detail. Pisa, Camposanto.
Italian school, 15th century. Series of eight
panels with scenes from the Old Testament:
Solomon and the Queen of Sheba. Venice,
S. Alvise.
Italian school, 15th century, School of Ferrara.
Solomon and the Queen of Sheba. Houston,
Museum of Fine Arts.
Italian school, 15th century. Solomon and
the Queen of Sheba. Late 15th century.
Siennese School, formerly attributed to
Sano di Pietro. New York, Metropolitan
Museum, 14.44.
Italian school, 15th century (Ferrarese).
Marriage Salver: Solomon and the Queen
of Sheba. Boston, Museum of Fine Arts,
17.198.
Italian school, 18th century. Solomon and
the Queen of Sheba. Salver. Houston, Museum
of Fine Arts, 44-574.

Peruzzi, Baldassare. Lunette: Solomon Receiving the Queen of Sheba. Also attributed to Perino del Vaga. Rome, Palazzo della Cancelleria. Salone di Studio, vault decorations.

Pitati, Bonifacio, School of. Queen of Sheba. Venice, Palazzo Reale.

Pittoni, G.B. Solomon and the Queen of Sheba. Liverpool, Walker Art Gallery.

Raphael (and assistants). Old Testament subjects: Solomon and the Queen of Sheba. Rome,Vatican, Loggie.

Tintoretto (Jacopo Robusti). Scenes from the 1545. Vienna, Kunsthistorisches Museum, 3828-3833.

Tintoretto. Scenes from the Old Testament: Solomon and the Queen of Sheba. c.1545. Vienna, Kunsthistorisches Museum, 3830.

Tintoretto. The visit of the Queen of Sheba to Solomon. Greenville, S.C., Bob Jones University Collection, 1962 cat. 53.

Tintoretto. Visit of the Queen of Sheba to Solomon. Madrid, Prado.

Tintoretto, Jacopo, School of. Queen of Sheba before Solomon. New York,Schaeffer Galleries.

Tintoretto (Jacopo Robusti). Solomon and the Queen of Sheba. 1565. Venice, Palazzo Ducale. Atrio Quadrato, ceiling.

Veneziano, Domenico. The Meeting of Solomon and the Queen of Sheba. Houston, Museum of Fine Arts, Straus Collection, 44.574.

Veronese, Paolo. The Queen of Sheba Offering Gifts to Solomon.

Vicentino, Andrea. The Queen of Sheba. Florence, Palazzo Uffizi, 536.

71 I 33 1 I KINGS 10:2 THE QUEEN OF SHEBA COMES TO SOLOMON WITH A TRAIN OF CAMELS LOADED WITH GIFTS

DUTCH SCHOOL
Valckenborch, Gillis. The Entry of the Queen of Sheba into Jerusalem. Cologna, Wallraf-Richartz Museum, 2190.

FRENCH SCHOOL
Gleyre, Charles. The Queen of Sheba. c.1838-39. Lausanne, Musée Municipal.

GERMAN SCHOOL
Schoenfeld, Johann Heinrich. The Queen of Sheba before Solomon. Sotheby and Co., London(Sale, [BLUEBELL] April 4, 1984, No. 24).

ITALIAN SCHOOL
Apollonio di Giovanni. Procession of the Queen of Sheba. Boston, Museum of Fine Arts,23.252.

Apollonio di Giovanni. Procession of the Queen of Sheba. Washington, D.C., National Gallery of Art, 233.

Cassone Master. Progress of the Queen of Sheba, left panel. London, Collection Lord Crawford.

Dandini, Pietro. Solomon and the Queen of Sheba. A Pair with Rebecca at the Well. Christie, Manson and Woods (Sale, New York, [BETH-5258] Jan. 18, 1983, No. 70).

Gozzoli, Benozzo. Copy. Old Testament and other subjects: Queen of Sheba and Solomon. Copy of detail of fresco. Pisa, Camposanto.

Italian school, 15th century. Solomon and the Queen of Sheba. Late 15th century. New York, Metropolitan Museum.

71 I 33 2 THE QUEEN OF SHEBA BEFORE SOLOMON, TESTING HIM WITH QUESTIONS

BRITISH SCHOOL
Grant, Duncan. The Queen of Sheba. 1912. London, Tate Gallery, 3169.

FLEMISH SCHOOL
Beer, Jan de. King Solomon and the Queen of Sheba. Stockholm, University, 299.

Heere, Lucas de. The Queen of Sheba Visiting Solomon. Ghent, St. Bavon.

ITALIAN SCHOOL
Bassano, Leandre. The Queen of Sheba on the steps of King Solomon's throne. New York, Collection Ethan Hillman.

Campi, Giulio. The queen of Sheba before Solomon. Fresco. Cremona, S. Sigismondo, transept.

Carducci, Bartolommeo. Solomon and the Queen of Sheba. Escorial, Library.

Salviati, Francesco. Story of David. General view of west and north walls, second floor salon. Rome, Palazzo Sacchetti.

71 I 33 6 I KINGS 10:13 THE QUEEN OF SHEBA SETS OUT ON THE RETURN JOURNEY

FRENCH SCHOOL
Claude Lorrain. Seaport: The Embarkation of the Queen of Sheba. 1648. London, National Gallery, 14.

71 I 43 21 2 I KINGS 6:1-10 CONSTRUCTION OF THE TEMPLE OF SOLOMON

ITALIAN SCHOOL
Bonito, Giuseppe. Building the temple of Solomon (?). Naples, St. Clara.

Giordano, Luca. Construction of the Temple. c.1700. Florence, Palazzo Uffizi, 9471.

Giordano, Luca. Solomon Presides over the Construction of the Temple. c.1700. Florence, Palazzo Uffizi, 9472.

Raphael (and assistants).Old Testament subjects: Solomon builds the temple. Rome, Vatican, Loggie.

71 I 43 22 4 I KINGS 7:49 THE SEVEN-BRANCHED CANDLESTICK

EARLY MEDIEVAL AND BYZANTINE
Byzantine school, 14th century, Wall painting, Istanbul. Bearing of the Sacred Vessels. Istanbul, Mosque Kahrié. Parecclesion, south half of transverse arch.

71 I 43 22 5 I KINGS 7:50-51 OTHER DECORATIONS OF THE TEMPLE

EARLY MEDIEVAL AND BYZANTINE
Byzantine school, 14th century, Wall painting, Istanbul. Bearing of the Sacred Vessels. Istanbul, Mosque Kahrié. Parecclesion, south half of transverse arch.

FLEMISH SCHOOL
Franck, Frans, II. Solomon and the Treasures of the Temple. 1633. Paris, Louvre, Musée du, INV.1297.

71 I 43 23 I KINGS THE DEDICATION OF THE TEMPLE

EARLY MEDIEVAL AND BYZANTINE
Byzantine school, 14th century, Wall painting, Istanbul. Bearing of the Ark of the Covenant. Istanbul, Mosque Kahrié. Parecclesion, eastern bay, south wall, lunette.

Byzantine school, 14th century, Wall painting, Istanbul. The Installation of the Ark in the Holy of Holies. Istanbul, Mosque Kahrié. Parècclesion, western bay, south wall, lunette.

FRENCH SCHOOL
Restout, Jean, the Younger. The Dedication of the Temple by Solomon. 1732. Paris, Louvre, Musée du, M.I.54.

Tissot, J.J.J. Illustrations of the Hebrew Bible. No. 195: Solomon Dedicates the Temple at Jerusalem. 1896-1903. New York, Jewish Museum, 52.341.

ITALIAN SCHOOL
   Diano, Giacinto. The Dedication of the Temple
      at Jerusalem. Dublin, National Gallery, 357.
   Bonito, Giuseppe. The Idolatry of the Temple
      of Solomon. Sketch for a destroyed fresco
      painting in St. Clara, Naples. 1752-53.
      Naples, Museo Nazionale, Capodimonte, 211.

71 I 43 23 2 I KINGS 8:4-11 THE ARK OF THE COVENANT
   IS BROUGHT INTO THE TEMPLE; A CLOUD FILLS
   THE HOUSE OF THE LORD

EARLY MEDIEVAL AND BYZANTINE
   Byzantine school, Wall painting, Istanbul. The
      Installation of the Ark in the Holy of Holies.
      14th century. Istanbul, Mosque Kahrié. Parec-
      clesion, western bay, south wall, lunette.

ITALIAN SCHOOL
   Italian school, 13th century. Detail: Ark of
      the Covenant. Anagni, Cathedral, frescoes.

71 I 43 23 4 I KINGS 5:22-53 PRAYER OF SOLOMON;
   SOLOMON KNEELS BEFORE THE ALTAR

DUTCH SCHOOL
   Eeckhout, Gerbrand van den. Solomon Praying
      in the Temple. Bader, Alfred - Collection
      (Milwaukee).

ITALIAN SCHOOL
   Bonito, Giuseppe. The Dedication of the Temple
      of Solomon. Sketch for a destroyed fresco
      painting in St. Clara, Naples. 1752-52.
      Naples, Museo Nazionale, Capodimonte, 211.
   Bonito, Giuseppe. Solomon in his temple. Naples,
      St. Clara.
   Giordano, Luca. Dedication of the Temple of
      Solomon. c.1700. Florence, Palazzo Uffizi,
      9473.

71 I 5 I KINGS 11:4-8 SOLOMON'S WOMEN AND IDOLATRY

DUTCH SCHOOL
   Hoet, Gerard. The Idolatry of King Solomon.
      Sotheby and Co., London (Sale, Feb. 13, 1985,
      [SNOWDROP], No. 63).

GERMAN SCHOOL
   Cranach, Lucas, the elder, Follower of. Solomon,
      influenced by his wives, worshipping idols.
      1534? Kleinberger Gallery (New York).

ITALIAN SCHOOL
   Batoni, Pompeo. Solomon Worshipping False Gods.
      1766. Christie, Manson and Woods (Sale,
      London [TASMANIA-3051], Dec.11, 1984,No.75).
   Cortona, Pietro da. Idolatry of Solomon. Rome,
      Palazzo Mattei.
   Giaquinto, Corrado. Solomon's Sacrifice. Col-
      lection Eric E. Young.
   Nuvolone, Carlo Francesco. Solomon's Idolatry.
      Sarasota, Fla., Ringling Museum of Art, SN
      140.

71 I 53 I KINGS 11:4-8 SOLOMON'S IDOLATRY

DUTCH SCHOOL
   Franck, Frans, II. Solomon worshipping false
      idols. Christie, Manson and Woods (Sale,
      London, July 23, 1982, No. 9).
   Lucas van Leyden. Copy. The Idolatry of Solomon.
      Budapest, Museum of Fine Arts, 4323 (p.68).

FLEMISH SCHOOL
   Delen, Dirk van. King Solomon Worshipping Idols.
      1627. Christie, Manson and Woods (Sale, New
      York, Jan. 15, 1985, [CAROL-5808], No.28).
   Franck, Franz II. Solomon worshipping false
      gods. Malahide, Collection Lord Talbot de
      Malahide.
   Franck, Frans, II. Solomon Worshipping False
      Idols. Christie, Manson and Woods (Sale,
      London, July 23, 1982, No. 9).

   Franck, Frans, II. King Solomon Worshipping
      Idols. Missouri, University of, Museum
      of Art and Archaeology, 66.9.
   Franck, Frans, II. The Idolatry of Solomon.
      1622. Malibu, J. Paul Getty Museum, 71.PB.42.
   Franck, Frans II, Follower of. The Idolatry
      of King Solomon. Sotheby and Co., London
      (Sale, April 4, 1984 [DAFFODIL], No. 147).
   Vos, Martin de, the elder, School of. Solomon's
      Idolatry. Lewinski, Baron von - Collection
      (Steinekirch).

GERMAN SCHOOL
   Knüpfer, Nicolaus. Solomon Sacrificing to
      the Idols. Brunswick, Landesmuseum, 193.

ITALIAN SCHOOL
   Ricci, Sebastiano. Solomon Worshipping the
      Idols. Turin, Pinacoteca.

71 I 53 1 I KINGS 11:8 SOLOMON OFFERS SACRIFICES
   TO PAGAN GODS (SOMETIMES IDOLS AND/OR
   A GOLDEN CALF UPON THE ALTAR)

DUTCH SCHOOL
   Bramer, Leonard. Solomon sacrificing to the
      idols. Lille, Palais des Beaux Arts, Musée
      de Peinture (287).
   Eeckhout, Gerbrand van den. Solomon's Sacrifice.
      Petrograd, Hermitage.
   Eeckhout, Gerbrand van den. Solomon sacrificing
      to false gods. Brunswick, Gallery.
   Koninck, Salamon. The idolatry of King Solomon.
      Signed and dated 1644. Amsterdam, Rijks-
      museum, 1375 A 1.
   Paulyn, Horatius. Idolatry of KIng Solomon.
      North Carolina, University of, Art Center,
      Cat.no.9, 56.1.1.
   Poorter, Willem de. Salomon sacrificing to
      idols. Amsterdam, Rijksmuseum, 1898.
   Poorter, Willem de. The Idolatry of Solomon.
      Sotheby and Co., London (Sale, July 7,
      1982, No. 223).

FLEMISH SCHOOL
   Franck, Frans, II. Solomon Worshipping False
      Idols. Christie, Manson and Woods (Sale,
      Amsterdam, [SALLY] Dec. 7, 1982, No. 120).

FRENCH SCHOOL
   Bourdon, Sébastien. Solomon sacrificing to
      idols. Paris, Louvre.

71 I 72 I KINGS 11:29-31 MEETING OF JEROBOAM
   AND THE PROPHET AHIJAH; AHIJAH RENDS HIS
   GARMENT IN TWELVE PIECES, TEN OF WHICH
   HE GIVES TO JEROBOAM

FRENCH SCHOOL
   Fragonard, Jean Honoré. Jereboam Sacrificing
      to Idols. 1752. Paris, École des Beaux
      Arts.

71 K 21 23 1 I KINGS 13:1-3 "A MAN OF GOD" FROM
   JUDAH COMES TO BETHEL AND PROPHESIES TO
   JEROBOAM THE DESTRUCTION OF THE ALTAR

DUTCH SCHOOL
   Poorter, Willem de. Jeroboam's Idol Worship
      Rebuked. Bob Jones University Collection
      (Greensville, S.C.).

71 K 21 34 1 I KINGS 13:25 THE PROPHET OF JUDAH'S
   BODY LIES INTACT ON THE ROAD WITH THE
   DONKEY AND THE LION BESIDE IT

DUTCH SCHOOL
   Noord, Johannes van. The Disobedient Prophet.
      1653. Reedtz-Thott, Baron - Collection
      (Gavno).

FLEMISH SCHOOL
   Lamen, C.J., van der. Disobedient prophet
      slain by the lion. Greenville, S.C., Bob
      Jones University Collection.

71 K 21 43   I KINGS 14:3-16   JEROBOAM'S WIFE IN DIS-
GUISE VISITS THE OLD AND BLIND AHIJAH, BUT
HE, HAVING BEEN WARNED BY GOD, RECOGNIZES
HER; HE PREDICTS THE DEATH OF HER SON AND
ISRAEL'S PUNISHMENT FOR JEROBOAM'S SIN

DUTCH SCHOOL
Mieris, Frans van, the elder. The prophet Ahi-
jah and the wife of Jeroboam. Lille, Musée
Municipal.

71 K 29 45   II KINGS 9:23-25   WHEN JEHORAM REALIZES
JEHER'S TREASON, HE TURNS HIS CHARIOT ROUND
TO FLEE, BUT JEHER SHOOTS AN ARROW THAT
STRIKES JEHORAM IN THE BACK; THE KING FALLS
DEAD IN HIS CHARIOT

ITALIAN SCHOOL
Michelangelo. Death of Joram. Rome, Vatican,
Sistine Chapel.

71 K 31 13 2   II KINGS 9:35-37   DOGS EAT JEZEBEL'S
BODY

ITALIAN SCHOOL
Giordano, Luca. The Death of Jezebel. Private
Collection.

71 K 31 41   II KINGS 10:6-8   AHAB'S DESCENDANTS ARE
SLAIN AND THEIR HEADS ARE PILED UP IN TWO
HEAPS AT THE CITY GATE

ITALIAN SCHOOL
Michelangelo. Sons of Ahab. Rome, Vatican,
Sistine Chapel.

71 K 31 22 2   II KINGS 10:26-27   THE IMAGES OF BAAL
ARE DESTROYED AND BURNED

ITALIAN SCHOOL
Michelangelo. Hebrews destroy statue of Baal.
Sistine chapel, ceiling decorations.

71 K 35 1   II KINGS 15:10   ZECHARIAH IS ASSASSINATED
BY SHALLUM

ITALIAN SCHOOL
Fumiani, Giovanni Antonio. The Stoning of Zechariah. c.1699-1700. Florence, Palazzo Uffizi,
5491.

71 1 17 11   II KINGS 11:1; II CHRONICLES 22:10
ATHALIA HAS ALL THE MEMBERS OF THE ROYAL
FAMILY KILLED

FRENCH SCHOOL
Sigalon, X. Athaliah and the massacre of the
princes of the house of David.

71 L 18 1   II KINGS 11:4-12; II CHRONICLES 23:1-11
JOASH IS PROCLAIMED KING AT THE AGE OF SEVEN

BRITISH SCHOOL
Bird, Edward. Proclaiming Joash King. London,
Diploma Gallery, 203.

71 L 24 38   II KINGS 19:35; ISAIAH 37:36   THAT NIGHT,
AN ANGEL OF THE LORD DECIMATES THE ASSYRIAN
CAMP: 185,000 SOLDIERS ARE KILLED

EARLY MEDIEVAL AND BYZANTINE
Byzantine school, Wall painting, Istanbul.
The Angel Smiting the Assyrians before Jeru-
salem. 14th century. Istanbul, Mosque Kahrié.
Parecclesion, western end, south side of
transverse arch.
Byzantine school, Wall painting, Istanbul.
Detail: Scroll of Isaiah and the Gate of
Jerusalem. 14th century. Istanbul, Mosque
Kahrié. Parecclesion, western end, south
side of transverse arch.

ITALIAN SCHOOL
Spolverini, Ilario. The destruction of the
army of Sennacherib. Greenville, S.C.,
Bob Jones University Collection.
Tanzio, Antonio d'Enrico. Battle of Senná-
cherib. Bozzeto. 1627. Navara, Museo.
Tanzio, Antonio d'Enrico (Tanzio da Varallo).
The Battle of Sennacherib. Novara, S.
Gaudenzio.

71 L 24 41   II KINGS 20:1; ISAIAH 38:1-3   THE KING
FALLS ILL AND IS VISITED BY ISAIAH, WHO
TELLS HIM TO GET READY TO DIE; HEZEKIAH
TURNS HIS FACE TO THE WALL, PRAYS AND
THEN CRIES

EARLY MEDIEVAL AND BYZANTINE
Byzantine school, Wall painting, Rome. Hezekiah and Isaiah. 7th-10th century. Rome,
S.M. Antiqua. Nave, Choir screen, mural
decorations.

71 L 24 52   II KINGS 20:13; ISAIAH 39:2   HEZEKIAH
WELCOMES THE MESSENGERS AND SHOWS THEM
HIS WEALTH

SPANISH SCHOOL
Lopez, Vicente. Hezekiah displays his treasures. 1789. Valencia, Museo de Pinturas.

71 L 27 13   II KINGS 22:8-14   SAPHAN READS THE
BOOK ALOUD TO THE KING WHO TEARS HIS
CLOTHES IN DISMAY

DUTCH SCHOOL
Bramer, Leonard. The Discovery of Deuteronomy. Private Collection, U.S.A.

71 L 31 3   II KINGS 24:5; JEREMIAH 52:31   WHEN
EVILMERODACH BECOMES KING OF BABYLON,
JEHOIACHIN IS RELEASED FROM PRISON AND
PERMITTED TO DINE AT THE KING'S TABLE
FOR THE REST OF HIS LIFE

FRENCH SCHOOL
Boucher, Francois. Evilmerodach Frees Jeho-
iachin from Prison. 1723. Columbia, S.C.,
Museum of Art.

71 L 32 32   II KINGS 25:13-21; II CHRONICLES 36:
18-19   THE TEMPLE IS LOOTED DURING THE
FALL OF JERUSALEM

ITALIAN SCHOOL
Guardi, Francesco. The Capture and Destruc-
tion of the Temple of Jerusalem. Bergamo,
Private Collection.

71 L 4   JEREMIAH, EZEKIEL, DANIEL, ESTHER

FRENCH SCHOOL
Delacroix, Eugène. The Captivity in Babylon.
New York, Collection Adolph Lewisohn.

71 M   I KINGS 17 – II KINGS 2   STORY OF ELIJAH
(ELIAS)

RUSSIAN SCHOOL
Russian school, 16th century. The Prophet
and the Fiery Chariot with Scenes from
his Life. Second half of 16th century.
Kostroma (?). Moscow, Tretyakov Museum,
Inv. No. 12072.

71 M 11   I KINGS 17:1   ELIJAH ANNOUNCES TO KING
AHAB THAT GOD WILL BRING A LONG DROUGHT
IN THE LAND TO AVENGE THE APOSTASY OF
OF ISRAEL

SPANISH SCHOOL
Miranda, Pedro Rodriguez de. Elijah before
King Ahab. Madrid, S. José.

71 M 12   I KINGS 17:4-6   ELIJAH FED BY THE RAVEN(S):
<u>WHILE THE PROPHET IS LIVING BY THE BROOK,</u>
<u>RAVENS BRING HIM FOOD</u>

AMERICAN SCHOOL
    Allston, Washington. Elijah fed by the ravens.
    Boston, Museum of Fine Arts, 70.1.

DUTCH SCHOOL
    Bloemaert, Abraham. Elijah Fed by Ravens. Lenin-
    grad, Hermitage.
    Camphuysen, Rafel. Elijah fed by the ravens.
    Bob Jones University Collection, Greenville,
    S.C.
    Dutch school, 17th century. Elijah Being Fed
    by the Ravens. c.1645. Private Collection,
    U.S.A.
    Savery, Roland. Elijah fed by the Ravens. Am-
    sterdam, Rijksmuseum, 2137.

EARLY MEDIEVAL AND BYZANTINE
    Byzantine school, Wall painting, Gracanica
    (Yugoslavia). Detail: Elijah in the Cave.
    c. 1320. Gracanica (Grachanitza), Yugoslavia,
    Monastery Church, frescoes, south chapel.
    Byzantine school, 15th century. Elijah fed by
    the Raven. From Salonica. Athens, Byzantine
    Museum.

FLEMISH SCHOOL
    Coninxloo, Gillis III van. Elijah in a landscape
    fed by ravens. Brussels, Musée de Peinture.
    Flemish school, 17th century. Elijah and the
    Raven. Serge Philipson Collection.
    Teniers, David, the elder. Elijah Being Fed
    by the Ravens. Private Collection, U.S.A.

GERMAN SCHOOL
    Olivier, Ferdinand. Elijah in the Wilderness.
    Munich, New State Gallery.

ITALIAN SCHOOL
    Guercino. Elijah fed by the raven. Collection
    Denis Mahon.
    Lanfranco, Giovanni. Elijah Being Fed by the
    Raven. Marseille (Bouches-du-Rhone), Musée
    Municipal.
    Savoldo, Giovanni Girolamo. Elijah fed by the
    raven. Washington, D.C., National Gallery
    of Art (on loan from Samuel H. Kress, K.340).

71 M 2   I KINGS 17:7-24   ELIJAH AND THE WIDOW OF
<u>ZAREPHATH</u>

DUTCH SCHOOL
    Dyck, Abraham van. The Widow of Zarephath and
    her Son. Bader, Alfred - Collection (Mil-
    waukee).

FLEMISH SCHOOL
    Mirou, Antoine. The Prophet Elijah with the
    Widow of Zarephath. Stockholm, University,
    306.

ITALIAN SCHOOL
    Mola, Pier Francesco. The Prophet Elijah and
    the Widow of Zarephath. Sarasota, Fla.,
    Ringling Museum of Art, SN 138.
    Strozzi, Bernardo. Prophet Elijah and the widow
    of Zarephath. Sarasota, Fla., Ringling Museum
    of Art, 50.2.
    Strozzi, Bernardo. The Prophet Elijah and the
    Widow. Sacramento, Crocker Art Gallery,
    1872.452.

71 M 21   I KINGS 17:7-10   WHEN THE BROOK DRIES
<u>UP, ELIJAH CROSSES OVER TO THE CITY OF</u>
<u>ZAREPHATH; AT THE GATE HE MEETS A WOMAN</u>
<u>AND HER LITTLE SON GATHERING WOOD (THE</u>
<u>WOMAN'S STICKS MAY FORM A CROSS)</u>

DUTCH SCHOOL
    Fabritius, Bernard. Elijah and the Widow
    of Zarephath. c.1660. Location Unknown.
    Houbraken, Arnold. The Widow of Zarephath
    Collecting Weeds. Sotheby and Co., London
    (Sale, New York, March 22, 1984, No. 5).
    Rembrandt, School of. Elijah and the Widow
    of Zarephath. c.1655. Heino (Kastel Het
    Nijenhuis), Hannemade Stuers Fundatie.
    Victors, Jan. Elijah and the Widow of Zare-
    phath. Christie's, (July 9, 1982, No. 63.)

71 M 21 1   I KINGS 17:11   ELIJAH ASKS THE WIDOW
<u>OF ZAREPHATH TO FETCH HIM SOME FOOD</u>

ITALIAN SCHOOL
    Mola, Pier Francesco. The Prophet Elijah
    and the Widow of Zarephath. Sarasota,
    Fla., Ringling Museum of Art, SN 138.
    Strozzi, Bernardo. Prophet Elijah and the
    widow of Zarephath. 1640s. Vienna, Kunsthis-
    torisches Museum.

71 M 21 22   I KINGS 17:15   ELIJAH FED BY THE WIDOW

FLEMISH SCHOOL
    Dyck, Anthony van. The Widow of Zarephath
    and her Son. c.1655-60. Bader, Alfred
    - Collection (Milwaukee).
    Dyck, Anthony van. Elijah and the Widow of
    Zarephath. c.1655. Copenhagen, Art Museum,
    3578.

71 M 22   I KINGS 17:15   ELIJAH FED BY THE WIDOW
<u>OF ZAREPHATH</u>

DUTCH SCHOOL
    Fabritius, Bernard. Elijah Fed by the Widow
    at Zarephath. Copenhagen, Art Museum, 3578.

71 M 43 21   I KINGS 18:36-39   AS ELIJAH PRAYS,
<u>GOD SENDS FIRE WHICH BURNS UP NOT ONLY</u>
<u>HIS SACRIFICE BUT ALSO THE ALTAR ITSELF;</u>
<u>THE PEOPLE FALL PROSTRATE</u>

BRITISH SCHOOL
    Moore, Albert. Elijah's Sacrifice. 1863.
    Bury (Lancashire), Corporation Art Gallery.

DUTCH SCHOOL
    Breenbergh, Bartholmeus. Elijah's Sacrifice.
    1645. Copenhagen, Art Museum, Sp 500.

ITALIAN SCHOOL
    Fetti, Domenico. Elijah and the worshippers
    of Baal. Hampton Court.
    Gargiulo, Domenico (called Micco Spadaro).
    Elijah's Sacrifice on Mount Carmel. Colnagi
    and Co., London.

71 M 52   I KINGS 19:4   ELIJAH FLEES INTO THE WILDERNESS
<u>(DESERT)</u>

ITALIAN SCHOOL
    Grassi, Nicola. Elijah in the desert. Christie,
    Manson and Woods (Sale, London, October
    22, 1982, No. 28).

71 M 53   I KINGS 19:5-6   AN ANGEL WAKES ELIJAH;
<u>A LOAF OF BREAD AND A JAR OF WATER ARE</u>
<u>USUALLY AT ELIJAH'S HEAD</u>

AUSTRIAN SCHOOL
    Reysschoot, Pieter Norbert. Elijah Sleeping
    Under a Tree.

DUTCH SCHOOL
Bisschop, Cornelis. Elijah and the Angel of God. Moore, Harry - Collection (Kenilworth, Il.).
Flinck, Govert. Elijah and the Angel. c.1640. Kiev, Museum for Western and Oriental Art.
Willeboirts, Thomas. The Prophet Elijah with the Angel. Vienna, Kunsthistorisches Museum, 1723.

FLEMISH SCHOOL
Arthois, Jacques d'. A Wooded Landscape with the Feeding of Elijah. Sotheby and Co., London (Sale,New York,March 6-7,1975,No.177)
Deyster, Lodewyk de.Elijah and the angel.Bruges, Cathedral.
Patinir, Joachim. Elijah and the angel. St. Louis, City Art Museum, 6:46.

GERMAN SCHOOL
Geyer, Johann. The Prophet Elijah in the Desert. c.1845. Bern, Art Museum, 209.

ITALIAN SCHOOL
Cairo, Francesco del. The Dream of Elijah.Milan, S. Antonio Abate.
Donducci, Giovanni Andrea. An Angel Appears to Elijah. Modena, Pinacoteca Estense.
Fetti, Domenico ?. Elijah in the desert. Possibly by Francesco Maffei. Berlin, Staatliche Museen, 380 B.
Luini, Bernardo. Elijah and the Angel. Frescoes from the Monastery of Vetere (Santa Maria della Purificazione). Milan, Brera.
Magnasco, Alessandro. Angel appearing to Elijah (?). Lucerne, Collection Hoyt.
Morazzoni, Il. The Dream of Elijah. Bozzeto. c.1616-18. Varese, S. Vittore.
Moreto da Brescia. Elijah and the angel.Brescia, S. Giovanni Evangelista.
Moreto da Brescia. Elijah sleeping. Brescia, Rotondo.
Palma Giovane. Elijah and the angel. Venice, S. Giacomo dall'Orio.
Palma Giovane. Elijah receiving bread from the angel sacristry. Venice, Gesuiti.
Pelligrini, Giovanni Antonio. Elijah Visited by an Angel. c.1724. Brescia, Sant'Agata.
Tintoretto. Elijah in the desert. Scuola di San Rocco, upper hall, ceiling.

RUSSIAN SCHOOL
Russian school, 16th century. Prophet Elijah in a fiery chariot. Icon. Sewickley, Pa., George R. Hann Collection.

SPANISH SCHOOL
Arteaga y Alfaro, Matias. Elijah in the wilderness. Seville, Cathedral, el Sagrario.
Escalante, Juan Antonio. An Angel Awakens the Prophet Elijah in the Wilderness. Berlin, Staatliche Museen, 380 B.
Murillo (?). Elijah fed by an angel. Paris, Collection Jean Hahn.

<u>71 M 84</u>   II KINGS 2:11-13 A CHARIOT, HORSES OF FIRE AND A WHIRLWIND APPEAR AND ELIJAH IS CARRIED UP INTO HEAVEN; ELIJAH'S CLOAK FALLS (OR HE HANDS IT OVER TO ELISHA)

BRITISH SCHOOL
Blake, William. Elijah in the Chariot of Fire. c.1790-93. Goyder, George, Esq. - Collection (Long Melford, Suffolk).

EARLY MEDIEVAL AND BYZANTINE
Byzantine school, Wall painting, Galliano.Elijah taken up by the chariot of fire. Fresco. 11th century. Galliano, S. Vincenzo. Nave, north wall.
Early Christain painting, Rome.Chariot of Elijah. Rome, Torre Pignattara, Catacomb of SS Petrus and Marcellinus. Arcosolium, vault, Crypt of the Trichniarch.

FLEMISH SCHOOL
Rubens, P.P. Study: Elijah. Ceiling decorations for the Church of the Jesuits at Antwerp. New York, Private Collection.

ITALIAN SCHOOL
Michelangelo. Elijah in the Chariot. Rome, Vatican, Sistine Chapel.
Piazetta, Giovanni Battista. Elijah Taken Up in a Chariot of Fire. c.1745. Washington, D.C., National Gallery of Art, 1149.
Tintoretto. Elijah Ascending in a chariot. Scuola di San Rocco, upper hall, ceiling.

RUSSIAN SCHOOL
Russian school, 16th century. Prophet Elijah in a Fiery Chariot. Icon.
Russian school, 16th century. The Prophet Elijah and the Fiery Chariot. Moscow, Tretyakov Museum, Inv. No. 12072.

SWEDISH SCHOOL
Albertus Pictor. Detail: Elijah taken up by the chariot of fire. C.1480. Härkeberga (Uppland), Church, ceiling painting.

<u>71 N 11</u>   II KINGS 2:19-22 THE WATER OF JERICHO IS PURIFIED: WHEN THE CITIZENS OF JERICHO COMPLAIN ABOUT THEIR WATER, ELISHA PUTS SOME SALT INTO A JAR; HE THEN THROWS THE SALT INTO THE WATER

ITALIAN SCHOOL
Gimignani, Lodovico. Elisha Pouring Salt into the waters of Jericho. 1664. Rome, S. Lorenzo in Lucina (4th Chapel, right wall).

<u>71 N 13</u>   II KINGS 4:8-37, 8:1-6 ELISHA AND THE SHUNAMMITE WOMAN

DUTCH SCHOOL
Fabritius, Bernard. Elisha in the House of the Shunammite Woman. Blaffer, Sarah Campbell - Foundation (Houston, Texas).

FLEMISH SCHOOL
Nieulandt, Adriaen van. The Prophet Elisha and the Shunammite Woman. Copenhagen, Art Museum, Trj. 257.

ITALIAN SCHOOL
Mola, Pier Francesco. The Prophet Elisha and the Rich Woman of Shunem. Sarasota, Fla., Ringling Museum of Art, SN 139.

<u>71 N 13 24</u>   II KINGS 4:27 THE WOMAN RIDES OUT WITH HER DONKEY TO ELISHA, BOWS DOWN BEFORE HIM AND TAKING HOLD OF HIS FEET, ENTREATS HIM TO COME WITH HER

DUTCH SCHOOL
Eeckhout, Gerbrand van den. Elisha and the Shunammite. Budapest, Museum of Fine Arts, 5610 (394 a).
Rembrandt. Departure of the Shunammite Woman. 1640. London, Victoria and Albert Museum.

<u>71 N 13 3</u>   II KINGS 4:33-36 RAISING OF THE SHUNAM-MITE WOMAN'S SON

AMERICAN SCHOOL
Peale, Charles Willson. Elisha Restoring to Life the Shunammite's Son. Copy of painting by Benjamin West. 1767. Private Collection.
Trumbull, John. Elisha Restoring the Shunamite's Son. 1777. Hartford, Conn., Wadsworth Atheneum.

FLEMISH SCHOOL
Eeckhout, Gerbrand van den. Elisha and the
Shunamite. Budapest, Museum of Fine Arts,
5610 (394a).

GERMAN SCHOOL
Zick, Januarius. The Prophet Elisha Heals the
Son of the Shunammite. Budapest, Museum of
Fine Arts, 6671.

71 N 13 32   II KINGS 4:32-37   ELISHA STRETCHES HIMSELF
OUT ON THE CHILD

BRITISH SCHOOL
Leighton, Sir Frederick. Elisha Healing the
Shunammite Woman's Son. London, Leighton
House.

71 N 13 33   II KINGS 4:36-37   GEHAZI FETCHES THE MOTHER;
WHEN SHE SEES HER CHILD ALIVE SHE FALLS AT
ELISHA'S FEET

DUTCH SCHOOL
Eeckhout, Gerbrand van den. Elisha and the Shunam-
mite Woman. 1649. Warsaw, Nationalmuseum,
46560.
Victors, Jan. The Son of the Shunammite Woman
Revived by Elisha. Private Collection, U.S.A.

71 N 14   II KINGS 4:40-41   THE DEADLY POTTAGE: ELISHA
PURIFIES THE POISONED POTTAGE BY THROWING
FLOUR INTO IT

ITALIAN SCHOOL
Vasari, Giorgio. The prophet Elisha. Florence,
Palazzo Uffizi.

71 N 15   II KINGS 4:42-44   A HUNDRED MEN ARE FED WITH
TWENTY LOAVES OF BREAD: ELISHA RECEIVES BARLEY
BREAD OF THE FIRST-FRUITS AND A STACK OF
CORN WHICH HE MULTIPLIES TO FEED A HUNDRED
MEN

ITALIAN SCHOOL
Tintoretto (Jacopo Robusti). Elijah Feeding
the People. Venice, Scuola di San Rocco.
Upper hall, ceiling.

71 N 16 2   II KINGS 5:14   NAAMAN COMES TO THE JORDAN,
DIPS HIMSELF SEVEN TIMES AND IS CURED

DUTCH SCHOOL
Dyck, Abraham van. Elisha Refuses Naaman's
Gifts. Germany, Private Collection.
Engelbrechtsz, Cornelis. The Prophet Elija.
Altarpiece. c.1520. Vienna, Kunsthistorisches
Museum.
Velde, Esaias van de. Naaman Washing in the
Jordan. Christie, Manson and Woods (Sale,
London, July 19, No. 128).

71 N 16 21   II KINGS 5:15-17   NAAMAN URGES ELISHA
TO ACCEPT SOME GIFTS, BUT ELISHA REFUSES
THEM; NAAMAN ASKS TWO MULE-LOADS OF EARTH

DUTCH SCHOOL
Bol, Ferdinand. Elisha Refuses Naaman's Gifts.
1661. Amsterdam, Historisch Museum.
Dutch School, 17th century. Elisha Refusing
Naaman's Gifts. Bob Jones University Col-
lection (Greenville, S.C.).
Dyck, Abraham van. Elisha Refuses Naaman's Gifts.
Germany, Private Collection.
Grebber, P.F. de. Prophet Elisha refusing the
gifts of Naaman. Haarlem, Frans Hals Museum,
no. 118.
Jacobsz, Lambert. Elisha rejects Naaman's gifts.
Porkay, M. – Collection (Munich).

71 N 16 32   II KINGS 5:27   ELISHA REBUKES GEHAZI
AND AS PUNISHMENT CAUSES HIM TO BE SMITTEN
WITH NAAMAN'S LEPROSY

DUTCH SCHOOL
Jacobsz, Lambert. Elijah and Gehazi. Meissner,
Kurt – Collection (Zürich).

71 N 61 1   II KINGS 13:17   ELISHA TELLS JOASH TO
SHOOT AN ARROW THROUGH THE WINDOW TOWARDS
SYRIA AND PREDICTS THAT JOASH WILL BE
VICTORIOUS

BRITISH SCHOOL
Dyce, William. Joash Shooting the Arrow of
Deliverance. 1844. Hamburg, Kunsthalle.

71 N 71   II KINGS 13:20-21   DURING A FUNERAL A
BAND OF RANSACKING MOABITES IS SEEN APPROACH-
ING AND THE CORPSE IS THROWN HASTILY INTO
ELISHA'S TOMB; WHEN IT TOUCHES ELISHA'S
BONES THE MAN COMES BACK TO LIFE

AMERICAN SCHOOL
Allston, Washington. The dead man restored
to life by the bones of Elisha. Philadelphia,
Pennsylvania Academy of Fine Arts, 25.

71 O 32 2   ISAIAH 6:5-13   PURIFICATION OF ISAIAH:
          AN ANGEL TOUCHES ISAIAH'S LIPS WITH A BURNING
          COAL, TAKEN FROM THE ALTAR WITH TONGS

AMERICAN SCHOOL
     West, Benjamin. The Inspiration of the Prophet
          Isaiah. 1782. Kansas, University of (Law-
          rence), Museum of Art, 53.71.
     West, Benjamin. Isaiah's lips anointed with
          fire. Greenville, S.C., Bob Jones University
          Collection.

71 O 33 4   ISAIAH 11:6-9   ISAIAH'S PROPHECY OF THE
          PEACEABLE KINGDOM: 'THE WOLF SHALL DWELL
          WITH THE LAMB'

AMERICAN SCHOOL
     Hicks, Edward. Peaceable Kingdom.
     Hicks, Edward. The Peaceable Kingdom. c.1840-
          45. Brooklyn, N.Y., Institute of Arts and
          Sciences, Museum, 40.340.
     Hicks, Edward. Peaceable Kingdom. Denver, Art
          Museum, A-625, 1954.236.

71 O 33 7   II KINGS 19:35   OTHER PROPHECIES OF ISAIAH:
          KILLING OF THE ASSYRIANS

EARLY MEDIEVAL AND BYZANTINE
     Byzantine school, Wall painting, Istanbul. Isaiah
          prophesying; the Angel smiting the Assyrians
          before Jerusalem. 14th century. Istanbul,
          Mosque Kahrié. Parecclesion, western end,
          south side of transverse arch.
     Byzantine school, Wall painting, Istanbul.
          Detail: Isaiah prophesying. 14th century.
          Istanbul, Mosque Kahrié. Parecclesion, western
          end, south side of transverse arch.
     Byzantine school, Wall painting, Istanbul.
          Detail: Scroll of Isaiah and the Gate of
          Jerusalem. 14th century. Istanbul, Mosque
          Kahrié. Parecclesion, western end, south
          side of transverse arch.

71 O 73 13   JEREMIAH 4:27 - 5:18   JEREMIAH PROPHESYING
          THE DESTRUCTION OF JERUSALEM

DUTCH SCHOOL
     Rembrandt. Jeremiah Lamenting the Destruction
          of Jerusalem. 1630. Amsterdam, Rijksmuseum.

71 O 74 61   JEREMIAH 36:4   JEREMIAH DICTATES HIS
          PROPHESIES TO BARUCH

AMERICAN SCHOOL
     Allston, Washington. The Prophet Jeremiah
          Dictating to his Scribe Baruch. 1820.
          Yale University, Gallery of Fine Arts.

71 O 76 62 8   JEREMIAH 40:4-6   JEREMIAH IS RELEASED
          FROM THE DUNGEON

ITALIAN SCHOOL
     Rosa, Salvator. Jeremiah. Chantilly, Museé
          Condé, 84.

71 O 91 1 EZEKIEL 1:4-28 EZEKIEL'S VISION OF GOD
          SITTING ON HIS THRONE CARRIED BY FOUR TETRA-
          MORPHS, EACH OF THEM HAVING FOUR WINGS; WHEELS
          BESIDE THEM

    BRITISH SCHOOL
        Blake, William. Ezekiel's vision: the whirlwind.
            Boston, Museum of Fine Arts.

    ITALIAN SCHOOL
        Raphael. Vision of Ezekiel. Florence, Palazzo
            Pitti.
        Raphael, School of. Vision of Ezekiel. Tapestry
            cartoon. Boughton House, Collection Duke
            of Buccleuch.

71 O 93 3 EZEKIEL 37:1-10 THE VISION OF THE VALLEY
          OF THE DRY BONES

    ITALIAN SCHOOL
        Tintoretto. Ezekiel's vision. Venice, Scuola
            di San Rocco. Upper hall, ceiling.

    SPANISH SCHOOL
        Collantes, Francisco. Vision of Ezekiel.

    SWISS SCHOOL
        Memberger, Philipp, d. 1584. The Vision of the
            Prophet Ezekiel in the Valley of Dry Bones.
            Karlsruhe, Kunsthalle, 1167.

71 O 95 1 (ETC.) EZEKIEL 9:1 - 10:7 EZEKIEL'S PRO-
          PHESIES AGAINST JERUSALEM

    AMERICAN SCHOOL
        Sargent, J.S. Children of Israel oppressed by
            pagan neighbors. Boston, Public Library.
            Decorations, north end, lunette.

71 P DANIEL THE STORY OF THE PROPHET DANIEL; HIS VISIONS AND PROPHECIES

SPANISH SCHOOL
   Huguet, Jaime (?). Fragments:Vision of Daniel.
   Tamarite de Litera, Monasterio del Patro-
   cinio.

71 P 12 51 DANIEL 2:46 KING NEBUCHADNEZZAR KNEELS BEFORE DANIEL TO SHOW HIS GRATITUDE

ITALIAN SCHOOL
   D'Andrea. Daniel interprets dream of Nebuchadnezzar. Venice, Academy.

71 P 13 DANIEL 3 THE STORY OF THE THREE HEBREWS IN THE FIERY FURNACE

BRITISH SCHOOL
   Burne-Jones, Sir Edward. Three Israelites in
   the Fiery Furnace; designs for stained glass
   windows in St. James, Farnworth. Detail:
   Ananias. Port Sunlight, The Lady Lever Art
   Gallery.
   Jones, George. The Burning Fiery Furnace: Study.
   c.1832. London, Tate Gallery, 1958.
   Solomon, Simeon. Shadrach, Meschach, and Abed-
   nego Preserved from the Burning Fiery Furn-
   ace. 1863. Private Collection.
   Turner, J.M.W. Shadrach, Meshach and Abednego
   Coming from the Fiery Furnace. 1832. London,
   Tate Gallery, 517.

EARLY MEDIEVAL AND BYZANTINE
   Byzantine school; Wall painting, Sveti Naum
   (Yugoslavia). Three youths in the fiery furn-
   ace. 16th century. Sveti Naum, Yugoslavia,
   Church, narthex, capital.
   Coptic painting, Khargeh, Bagawat Necropolis.
   Israelites in fiery furnace. Khargeh, Bagawat
   Necropolis. Chapel of Flight.

ITALIAN SCHOOL
   Italian school, 15th century. Series of eight
   panels with scenes from the Old Testament:
   1. The Fiery Furnace. Venice, S. Alvise.
   Tintoretto (Jacopo Robusti). Three Children
   in the Fiery Furnace. Venice, Scuola di
   San Rocco. Upper hall, ceiling.

71 P 13 2 DANIEL 3:7 THE DEDICATION OF THE IMAGE: IN THE PRESENCE OF THE KING, TRUMPETS ARE BLOWN AND ALL THE PEOPLE SURROUNDING THE IMAGE FALL ON THEIR KNEES

ITALIAN SCHOOL
   Italian school, 12th century. Scenes from the
   Book of Daniel: The golden statue of Nebu-
   chadnezzar worshiped by the mob. Fresco.
   Rome, S. Maria in Cosmedin. Nave.
   Italian school, 16th century. Adoration of the
   statue of Nebuchadnezzar. Venetian? Boston,
   Fenway Court.

71 P 13 22 DANIEL 3:13-18 KING NEBUCHADNEZZAR CALLS THE THREE MEN TO ACCOUNT, BUT THEY REFUSE TO KNEEL BEFORE THE IMAGE

EARLY MEDIEVAL AND BYZANTINE
   Early Christian painting, Rome. Nebuchadnezzar
   and three youths. Rome, Catacomb of SS Marcus
   and Marcellianus.

ITALIAN SCHOOL
   Italian school, 12th century. Scenes from the
   Book of Daniel: Nebuchadnezzar inveighs
   against the young men who refuse to worship
   his statue. Fresco. Rome, S. Maria in Cosmedin, nave.

71 P 13 3 DANIEL 3:14-22 AFTER THE FURNACE HAS BEEN HEATED THREE TIMES MORE, THE THREE MEN ARE BOUND AND THROWN INTO THE FIRE, THEIR EXECUTIONERS ARE BURNT BY THE FLAMES

BRITISH SCHOOL
   Burne-Jones, Sir Edward. Three Israelites
   in the Fiery Furnace; designs for stained
   glass windows in St. James, Farnworth.
   Ananias. Port Sunlight, The Lady Lever Art
   Gallery.

EARLY MEDIEVAL AND BYZANTINE
   Early Christian painting, Rome. Moses and
   three youths. Rome, Cappella Greca, Catacomb of Priscilla.

GERMAN SCHOOL
   German school, 15th century. Wings of altar-
   piece: Meshack, Shadrack, and Abednego.
   Augsburg, 15th century. Merion, Pa.,
   Barnes Foundation, 788.

ITALIAN SCHOOL
   Italian school, 12th century. Scenes from
   the Book of Daniel: The fiery furnace.
   Fresco. Rome, S. Maria in Cosmedin, nave.
   Rosselli, Matteo. The Three Brothers in the
   Fiery Furnace. Florence, Palazzo Pitti,
   3560.

71 P 13 4 DANIEL 3:24-26 TO HIS ASTONISHMENT KING NEBUCHADNEZZAR SEES FOUR MEN (ONE OF THEM USUALLY REPRESENTED AS AN ANGEL) IN THE FURNACE; THE KING COMMANDS THEM TO COME FORTH

DUTCH SCHOOL
   Micker, Jan Christiansz. The Burning Fiery
   Furnace. Sotheby and Co., London (Sale,
   Oct. 7, 1981, No. 23).

EARLY MEDIEVAL AND BYZANTINE
   Early Christian painting, Rome. Three youths
   in the furnace. Fresco. Rome, Via Salaria
   Nuova. Catacombs of Priscilla.
   Early Medieval and Byzantine painting. Three
   Hebrews in the Fiery Furnace, Saved by
   an Angel. 7th century. Sinai, Monastery
   of St. Catherine, Icon 419.

ITALIAN SCHOOL
   Bassano, Jacopo. The three brothers: Shadrach,
   Mishach, and Abednego in the furnace.
   Bassano, Museo Civico.

71 P 13 5 DANIEL 3:27-29 SHADRACH, MESACH, AND ABED-NEGO ARE EXAMINED; THEY PROVE TO BE UNHARMED, WHEREUPON KING NEBUCHADNEZZAR DECREES THAT NO ONE MAY CRITICIZE THEM

ITALIAN SCHOOL
   Italian school, 12th century. Scenes from
   the Book of Daniel: Nebuchadnezzar's dream
   of the four world-empires; Nebuchadnezzar
   extoling Shadrach, Meshach and Abednego.
   Fresco. Rome, S. Maria in Cosmedin, nave.

71 P 14 5 DANIEL 4 KING NEBUCHADNEZZAR IS RESTORED TO THE THRONE AND IN A PROCLAMATION HE MAKES KNOWN WHAT HAS HAPPENED TO HIM

DUTCH SCHOOL
   Pynas, Jacob. Nebuchadnezzar's Crown Restored.
   1616. Munich, Pinakothek, Alte.

71 P 2 DANIEL 5 DANIEL AND KING BELSHAZZAR

ITALIAN SCHOOL
   Balducci, Matteo. Judgement of Daniel. Paris,
   Louvre, 1572.

71 P 21 DANIEL 5:1-3 BELSHAZZAR'S GREAT FEAST,
DURING WHICH HE AND HIS COURTIERS DESECRATE
THE GOLDEN AND SILVER VESSELS THAT WERE
TAKEN FROM THE TEMPLE IN JERUSALEM

BRITISH SCHOOL
Martin, John. Belshazzar's Feast. 1820. Wright,
Rugh, F. - Collection.

DUTCH SCHOOL
Gelder, Aert de. The Feast of Belshazzar. 1682-
85. Malibu, J. Paul Getty Museum.

FLEMISH SCHOOL
Flemish school, 16th century. Feast of Belshaz-
zar. Madrid, Collection Countess Andes.
Flemish school, 17th century. The Feast of
Belshazzar. 1st quarter 17th century. Hart-
ford, Conn., Wadsworth Atheneum, 1961.652.
Franck, Frans, II. The Banquet of Belshazzar.
Stockholm, University, 285.
Franck, Frans, II, Studio of. The Feast of
Balthazar. Paris, Louvre, Musée du, M.N.R.
582.
Valckenborch, Frederik van. Belshazzar's Feast.
Vienna, Kunsthistorisches Museum, 2333.
Valckenborch, Frederik van. Balthazar's Feast.
Clermont-Ferrand, Musée Bergoin.
Valckenborch, Frederik van, Follower of. Bal-
shazzar's Feast. Christie, Manson and Woods
(Sale, London, [TINKER-3144] May 24, 1985,
No. 145).

ITALIAN SCHOOL
Bigari, Vittorio. Feast of Belshazzar. Bologna,
(Academy) Pinacoteca.
Tintoretto. Belshazzar's Feast. 1545-48. Vienna,
Kunsthistorisches Museum, 3829.

71 P 22 DANIEL 5:5-6 DURING THE BANQUET A HAND
APPEARS AND WRITES ON THE WALL (MENE, MENE,
TEKEL AND PARSIN [UPHARSIN]); KING BELSHAZZAR
IS FRIGHTENED

BRITISH SCHOOL
Runciman, Alexander. Belshazzar's Feast. Penicuik House, Collection Clerk.

DUTCH SCHOOL
Dutch school, 17th century. Belshazzar's Feast.
1650. Copenhagen, Art Museum.
Grebber, Pieter Fransz de. King Belshazzar's
Feast. 1625. Cassel, Staatliche Kunstsamm-
lungen.
Rembrandt. Belshazzar's Feast. 1635/37. London,
National Gallery, 6350.

FLEMISH SCHOOL
Valckenborch, Frederik van. Belshazzar's Feast.
Vienna, Kunsthistorisches Museum, 2333.

FRENCH SCHOOL
Collin de Vermont, Hyacinthe. Belchazzar's
Feast. c.1737. Dijon (Côte d'Or), Musée
Maguin.

GERMAN SCHOOL
German school, 18th century. The Feast of Bal-
shazzar. Sotheby and Co., London (Sale, New
York, March 24, 1983).

ITALIAN SCHOOL
Preti, Mattia. Feast of Belshazzar. Naples,
Museo Nazionale, Capodimente, 263.

SPANISH SCHOOL
Ribera, Jusepe de. Vision of Belshazzar. 1635.
Milan, Arcivescovado.

71 P 25 DANIEL 5:13-28 DANIEL, WHEN BROUGHT BEFORE
THE KING, INTERPRETS THE WRITING

AMERICAN SCHOOL
Allston, Washington. Belshazzar's Feast.
1817-43. Detroit, Institute of Arts,
55.515.
Allston, Washington. Belshazzar's Feast.
Sketch, Recto. (Boston, Museum of Fine
Arts) Harvard University, Fogg Art Museum,
122.1942.
Allston, Washington. Study for Belshazzar's
Feast. 1817. Boston, Museum of Fine Arts,
70.1.

ITALIAN SCHOOL
Fedini, Giovanni. Study of Francesco I de
Medici. Daniel at the Feast of Baldassare.
Florence, Palazzo Vecchio.

71 P 34 11 DANIEL 6:16-22 DANIEL SITTING UNHARMED
IN THE LION'S DEN, SURROUNDED BY LIONS

AMERICAN SCHOOL
Tanner, Henry Ossawa. Daniel in the Lion's
Den. c.1916. Los Angeles, County Museum.

BRITISH SCHOOL
Ward, James. Daniel in the Lion's Den. Sketch.
1841 or 1852. London, Tate Gallery, 4985.

EARLY MEDIEVAL AND BYZANTINE
Early Christian painting, Rome. Daniel in
the Lion's Den. Rome, Catacomb of the
Jordani.
Early Christian painting, Rome. Daniel in
the Lion's Den. Rome, Torre Pignattara.
Catacomb of SS Petrus and Marcellinus,
Cripta Heliodora, center.

FLEMISH SCHOOL
Rubens, P.P. Daniel in the Lion's Den. Wash-
ington, D.C., National Gallery of Art.
Rubens, Peter Paul. Daniel in the Lion's
Den. 1663. Vienna, Kunsthistorisches Museum,
1695.

FRENCH SCHOOL
Tissot, James Jacques Joseph. Illustrations
of the Hebrew Bible. No. 276: Daniel in
the Lion's Den. 1896-1903. New York, Jewish
Museum, 52.422.

ITALIAN SCHOOL
Agostino del Quirinale. Daniel in the Lion's
Den. Rome, Palazzo del Quirinale, Coffee
House.
Cima, Giovanni Battista. Daniel in the Lion's
Den. Milan, Ambrosiana, 90.
Cortona, Pietro da. Daniel in the lion's
den. Venice, Academy.
Domenichino. Detail: Daniel and the Lions.
Villa Muti.
Grassi, Nicola. Daniel in the Lion's Den.
Ampezzo, Parrocchiale.
Guarana, Jacopo. Daniel in the lion's den.
Udine, Museo Civico.
Rosa, Salvatore. Daniel in the lion's den.
Chantilly, Musée Condé, 63.
Tintoretto (Jacopo Robusti). Daniel in the
Lion's Den. Venice, Scuola di San Rocco.
Upper hall, ceiling.

71 P 41   DANIEL 13   THE STORY OF SUSANNAH AND THE
          ELDERS (IN WHICH THE YOUTH DANIEL INTERVENES
          ON BEHALF OF SUSANNAH)

FRENCH SCHOOL
     French school, 14th century. Story of Susanna.
        Reims, Musée (?).

ITALIAN SCHOOL
     Franchi, Rossello di Jacopo. The Story of Susan-
        nah. Probably Cassone. Sotheby and Co.,
        London (Sale, New York, Jan. 17, 1985 [TOM-
        MASO], No. 42).
     Lotto, Lorenzo. Susannah and the Elders. 1517.
        Florence, Palazzo Uffizi, 9491.
     Marco del Buono. Episodes from the Story of
        Susannah: the Elders as Judges; Susannah
        Unbolting the Door of her Private Garden.
        Mid-15th century. Baltimore, Md., Walters
        Art Gallery, 37.2503.
     Master of the Apollo and Daphne Legend. Susanna
        and the Elders. Chicago, Art Institute.
     Ricci, Sebastiano. Susanna before Daniel. 1724.
        Turin, Pinacoteca.
     Sellaio, Jacopo del. Susannah and the Elders.
        First panel: the Crime. c.1475-1500. Chicago,
        Institute, 33.1029. 22.1030.
     Tintoretto (Jacopo Robusti). Susannah. Private
        Collection.

71 P 41 2   DANIEL 13   SUSANNAH BATHING, USUALLY IN
          OR NEAR A FOUNTAIN AND SOMETIMES ACCOMPANIED
          BY TWO FEMALE SERVANTS

GERMAN SCHOOL
     Altdorfer, Albrecht. Susanna Bathing. 1526.
        Munich, Pinakothek, Alte.

ITALIAN SCHOOL
     Chimenti, Jacopo. Susanna at her Bath. c.1600.
        Vienna, Kunsthistorisches Museum.
     Tintoretto (Jacopo Robusti). Susannah and the
        Elders. 1550. Paris, Louvre, Musée du.

71 P 41 21   DANIEL 13   THE ELDERS SPYING UPON HER

DUTCH SCHOOL
     Flinck, Govert. Susannah in the Bath. c.1640.
        Berlin, Staatliche Museen (East Berlin).
     Rembrandt. Susanna at the Bath. 1637 (?). The
        Hague, Royal Gallery.
     Rembrandt, School of. Susanna at the bath. Copy
        of Rembrandt's painting at the Hague.
        Arnhem, Collection Van Hengel.
     Rembrandt. Copy after. Susannah in the Bath.
        Paris, Louvre, Musée du, M.I. 958.
     Werff, Adriaen van der. Susanna in the Bath.
        Budapest, Museum of Fine Arts 396 (586).

EARLY MEDIEVAL AND BYZANTINE
     Early Christian painting, Rome. Susanna and
        the Elders. Rome, Catacomb Maggiore, Cubi-
        culum V.
     Early Christian Painting, Rome. Susanna and
        the Elders. Rome, Torre Pignattara. Catacomb
        of SS Petrus and Marcellinus, Cubiculum XIII,
        lunette.

FLEMISH SCHOOL
     Dyk, Philip van. Susannah and the Elders. 1721.
        Christie, Manson and Woods (Sale, New York,
        [GERTRUDE-5584] June 6, 1984, No. 71).
     Metsys, Jan. Susanna and the elders. 1565.
        Brussels, Museum, 297.
     Metsys, Jan. Susannah and the Elders. 1564.
        Pasedena, Ca., Norton Simon Museum.
     Rubens, P.P. Susanna and the elders. Munich,
        Alte Pinakothek, 317.
     Rubens, P.P. Copy. Susannah and the Elders.
        Copy of painting in the Pinakothek, Alte,
        Munich. New York, Metropolitan Museum,91.26.4.

FRENCH SCHOOL
     Chassériau, T. The chaste Susanna.
     French school, 17th century. Susannah. Weston
        Park, Collection Earl of Bradford.
     Henner, J.J. Chaste Susanna, or Susanna at
        the Bath. 1864. Paris, Louvre.
     Santerre, J.B. Susanna at the Bath.

GERMAN SCHOOL
     Altdorfer, Albrecht. Susanna bathing. Munich,
        Alte Pinakothek.
     Corinth, Louis. Susanna in the Bath. 1890.
        Essen, Folkwang Museum, 349.
     Stuck, Franz von. Susannah in the Bath. 1913.
        Private Collection.

ITALIAN SCHOOL
     Bassano, Leandro. Susanne and the Elders.
        Venice, Collection Italico Brass.
     Francesco di Giorgio. Susannah and the elders.
        Siena, Academy.
     Guercino. Susanna and the elders. Schleiss-
        heim, Neues Schloss, Gallery.
     Guercino. Susanna and the elders. Madrid,
        Prado, 201.
     Guercino, Copy after. Bearded Man Holding
        a Lamp. Derived from foreground Elder
        in Susannah and the Elders, Madrid, Prado.
        London, National Gallery, 5537.
     Guercino. Susanna and the Elders. Parma,
        Galleria Nazionale, 1077.
     Liberi, Pietro. Susanna in the Bath. Cassel,
        Staatliche Kunstsammlungen, 525.
     Luini, Bernardo. Susanna. Milan, Collection
        Borromeo.
     Pagani, Gasparo. Susanna at the bath. Florence,
        Palazzo Uffizi.
     Palma Giovane. Susannah in the Bath. Paris,
        Louvre, Musée du, M.I. 877.
     Samacchini, Orazio. Susannah at the Bath.
        Also attributed to Gregorio Pagini. Florence,
        Palazzo Uffizi, 1511.
     Samacchini, Orazio. Susanna at her Bath.
        1570-75. Florence, Palazzo Uffizi, 1511.
     Schiavone, Andrea. Susannah and the elders.
        London, Collection of Sir George Leon.
     Tintoretto. Susannah and the elders. Munich,
        Pinakothek.
     Tintoretto (J.R.) Susannah and the Elders.
        1555. Nemes, Marczeil von - Collection
        (Monaco).
     Tintoretto, Domenico. Susannah and the Elders.
        1550. Paris, Louvre, Musée du, 568.
     Tintoretto (J.R.) Susannah and the Elders.
        1560. Vienna, Kunsthistorisches Museum.
     Tintoretto, School of. Susanna at the Bath.
        c.1575. Washington, D.C., National Gallery
        of Art, 342.
     Veronese, Paolo, School of. Susannah and
        the Elders. Dresden, Gallery.

SPANISH SCHOOL
     Goya. Susanna. New York, Collection S.H.
        Kress, 365.

71 P 41 22   DANIEL 15-21   THE ELDERS MAKING ADVANCES

BRITISH SCHOOL
     English School. Susanna and the elders. Dulwich
        Gallery, 408.

DANISH SCHOOL
     Tuxen, Laurits Regner. Susannah Bathing.
        1882. Copenhagen, Ny-Carlsberg Glyptotek,
        I.N. 948.

DUTCH SCHOOL
     Cornelisz, Cornelis. Susanna and the Elders.
        1585/87. Nuremberg, Germanic Museum.
     Dutch school, 17th century. Susannah and
        the Elders. c.1620-30. Bader, Alfred -
        Collection (Milwaukee).

Floris (de Vriendt), Frans I. Susannah and the
Elders. 1562-63. Florence, Palazzo Uffizi,
S. Marco e Cenacoli, 24.
Goltzius, Hendrik. Susanna and the Elders.
Douai (Nord), Musée, 2800.
Honthorst, Gerard van. Susanna and the elders.
Rome, Villa Borghese.
Houbraken, Arnold. Susannah and the Elders.
Sotheby and Co., London (Sale, Dec.16, 1981,
No. 72).
Loo, Jacob van. Susannah and the Elders. Glasgow,
Art Gallery, 623.
Neck, Jan van. Susannah in the Bath. Copenhagen,
Art Museum, Sp.476.
Noord, Johannes van. Susannah in her Bath.
Munich, Art Market.
Noord, Johannes van. Susannah and the Elders.
c.1660. The Hague, Dienst Verspreide Rijk-
collecties, on loan to Utrecht, Centraal
Museum.
Rembrandt. Susanna and the Elders. 1647. Berlin,
Staatliche Museen, 826E.

FLEMISH SCHOOL
Balen, Hendrik van. Susannah and the Elders.
Perhaps by Jan van Balen. Sotheby and Co.,
London (Sale, April 15, 1981, No. 57).
Diepenbeeck, Abraham van. Susanna and the Elders.
Mexico City, Mus., de San Carlos.
Dyck, Anthony van. Susanna and the Elders. 1622-
23. Munich, Alte Pinakothek.
Jordaens, Jacob. Susanna and the elders.Brussels,
Musées Royaux des Beaux Arts.
Jordaens, Jacob. Susanna at her Bath. 1657.
Berlin, Jagdschloss Grunewald.
Jordaens, Jacob. Susanna and the Elders. 1653.
Copenhagen, Art Museum, Sp. 235.
Metsys, Jan, School of. Susanna and the elders.
Bergues, Museum, 76.
Rubens, Peter Paul. Susannah and the Elders.
1614.
Rubens, P.P. Susanna and the Elders. Madrid,
Acad. S. Fernando.
Rubens, P.P. Susanna and the Elders. Munich,
Alte Pinakothek.
Rubens, P.P. Susannah and the Elders. Rome,
Borghese Gallery.
Rubens, P.P. Susanna at the bath. Stockholm,
National Museum, 596.
Rubens, P.P. Susanna in the Bath. Turin, Pina-
coteca.
Teniers, David, the Younger. Susannah and the
Elders. London, University, Courtauld Insti-
tute, (Princess Gate Collection) 311.
Vos, Martin de, the elder. Susannah and the
Elders. Location Unknown.

FRENCH SCHOOL
La Fosse, Charles de. Susannah and the Elders.
c.1715. Moscow, Pushkin State Museum of Fine
Arts, 1138.
Troy, J.F. de. Susannah at the bath. Leningrad,
Hermitage.
Troy, Jean François de. Susannah and the Elders.
Poitiers (Vienne), Musée des Beaux Arts.
Troy, J.F. de. Susanna and the elders. Puerto
Rico, Luis Ferré Foundation, Musée di Ponce.
Troy, J.F. de. Susannah at the bath. Rouen,
Musée.
Van Loo, Jacques. Susanna and the Elders. Glas-
gow Art Gallery.
Vien, Joseph Marie. Susanna and the Elders.
Nantes, Museum.
Vouet, S. The chaste Susanna.

GERMAN SCHOOL
Corinth, Louis. Susanna in the Bath. 1909.
Berlin, Private Collection.
Douven, Bartholomeus Frans. Susanna. 1722.
Cassel, Staatliche Kunstsammlungen, 323.
Elsheimer, Adam. Susanna and the elders. Dulwich
Gallery, 22.

König, Johann. Susanna Surprised by Elders.
Augsburg, Museum (?).
König, Johann. Susannah and the Two Old Men.
Nuremburg, Germanic Museum.
Loth, Johann Carl. Susannah and the Elders.
Malibu, J. Paul Getty Museum, 69.PA.2.
Refinger, Ludwig (attributed to) Story of
Susanna. Munich, Old Pinakothek.
Rottenhammer, Johann. Susannah and the Elders.
1605. Bologna, Private Collection.
Rottmayr, Johann Michael. Susannah and the
Elders. Vienna, Österreichische Galerie,
3798.
Schäufelein, H.L. Susanna and the elders.
Stuttgart, Museum.
Stuck, Franz von. Susanna in the Bath. Munich,
Private Collection.

ITALIAN SCHOOL
Allori, Cristofano. Susanna. Schleissheim,
Neues Schloss, Gallery.
Allori, Cristofano. Susanna. Study. Florence,
Palazzo Uffizi, 7605.
Altomonte, Martino. Susanna and the Elders.
Vienna, Österreichische Galerie, 4243.
Amigoni, Jacopo. Chaste Susannah. Trieste,
Museo Civico.
Bassano, Jacopo. Susannah and the Elders.
Bassano, Museo Civico.
Bassano, Jacopo. Susanna and the Elders.
1585. Nimes, Musée de Peinture et Sculpture.
Bassano, Leandro. Susanna and the Elders.
Longleat, Collection Marquis of Bath.
Bassano, Leandro. Susanna and the Elders.
Ottawa, National Gallery of Canada.
Bortoloni, Mattia. Susannah. Venice, Museo
Civico Correr, 5696.
Burrini, Antonio. Susanna and the Elders.
Paris, Galerie Pardo.
Burrini, Antonio. Susannah and the Elders.
Bologna, Pinacoteca Nazionale.
Cagnacci (Guido Canlassi). Susanna and the
Elders. Leningrad, Hermitage.
Cantarini, Simone. Susannah and the Elders.
Bologna, Pinacoteca Nazionale.
Carneo, Antonio. Susannah and the Elders.
Christie, Manson and Woods (Sale, London,
Dec.17, 1982, No.66).
Carracci, Agostino, attributed to. Susanna
and the elders. Bologna, Private Collection.
Carracci, Agostino. Susannah and the elders.
Sarasota, Fla., Ringling Museum of Art,
SN 111.
Carracci, Ludovico. Susannah and the two
elders in the garden of Joachim. 1616.
London, National Gallery, 28.
Carracci, Ludovico. Susannah and the elders.
New York, Ehrich Galleries.
Castello, Valerio. Susannah and the Elders.
Genoa, Private Collection.
Chiari, Giuseppe Bartolomeo. Susannah and
the Elders. Baltimore, Md., Walters Art
Gallery, 31.1880.
Chimienti, Jacopo, Studio of. Susannah and
and the Elders. Dublin, National Gallery,
1671.
Conca, Sebastiano. Susannah and the Elders.
Sotheby and Co., London (Sale, April 16,
1980, No. 5b).
Domenichino. Susanna and the elders. Munich,
Pinakothek, Alte, 466.
Fabris, Pietro, attributed to. Susanna and
the Elders. 1770. Sotheby and Co., London
(Sale, April 4, 1984 [DAFFODIL] No. 178).
Gentile da Fabriano, Follower of. Susannah
and the Elders. Sotheby and Co., London
(Sale, [PRIMROSE] Feb. 16, 1983, No. 10).
Gentileschi, Artemisia. Susanna and the elders.
Pommersfelden, Schloss, Gallery.
Giordano, Luca. Copy. Susannah and the Elders.
Sarasota, Fla., Ringling Museum of Art,
SN 162.

Graziani, Ercole. Susanna and the Elders.
Bologna, Pinacoteca Nazionale, 3872.
Guercino. The Chastity of Susannah. Florence,
Palazzo Pitti, 234.
Guercino. Susanna and the Elders. Parma, Gal-
leria Nazionale, 1077.
Guidobono, Bartolommeo. Susannah and the Elders.
Paris, Louvre, Musée du, R.F. 2331.
Italian school, 18th century. Susanna and the
Elders. Madrid, Collection Antonio Anselmo
Torre.
Lanfranco, Giovanni. Susanna and the Elders.
Rome, Palazzo Doria-Pamphili.
Lazzarini, Gregorio. Susannah in the Bath.
Brunswick, Landesmuseum, 1030.
Mannozzi, Giovanni. Susannah and the Elders.
c.1634, Fresco. Florence, Palazzo Uffizi,
5418.
Master of the Apollo and Daphne Legend. Susanna
and the elders: the crime. Chicago, Art
Institute.
Mola, Pier Francesco, Circle of. Susanna and
the Elders. Sotheby and Co., London (Sale,
April 4, 1984, [DAFFODIL], No. 187).
Paciccio (Francesco Rosa). Susannah and the
Elders. Naples, Museo Nazionale, Capodimonte.
Palma Giovane. Susannah and the Elders. Siena,
Palazzo Chigi-Saracini.
Procaccini, Camillo, attributed to. Susanna
and the Elders. c. 1610. Harvard University,
Fogg Art Museum, 1973.56.
Procaccini, Guilio Cesare. Susannah and the
Elders. c.1620?. Oxford, University, Christ
Church.
Reni, Guido. Copy. Susannah and the two elders.
London, National Gallery, 196.
Ricci, Sebastiano. Susanna and the Elders. 1713.
Chatsworth, Trustees of the Chatsworth Set-
tlement.
Saraceni, Carlo. Susannah and the Elders. c.1610.
Detroit, Institute of Arts, 41.89.
Tintoretto. Susanna and the elders.
Veronese, Paolo. Susanna and the two elders.
Veronese, Paolo. Susanna and the two Elders.
Paris, Louvre, Musée du.
Veronese, Paolo. Susanna and the Elders. Brockles-
by Park, Collection Earl of Yarborough.
Veronese, Paolo. Susanna and two elders. Genoa,
Collection Marchese Ambrogio Doria.
Veronese, Paolo. Susannah and the Elders. Vienna,
Kunsthistorisches Museum, 3676.
Veronese, Paolo, School of. Susanna and the
elders.

SPANISH SCHOOL
Spanish school, 18th century. Susanna and the
elders. Cordova, Private Collection.

71 P 41 3 DANIEL 28-42 THE ELDERS ACCUSING SUSANNA
BEFORE THE PEOPLE, LAYING THEIR HANDS ON
HER HEAD OR UNVEILING HER

AUSTRIAN SCHOOL
Maulbertsch, F.A. Susanna and the Elders. 1750.
Vienna, Osterreichische Galerie.

DUTCH SCHOOL
Rosendael, Nicolas. Susannah before the Judges.
1673. Cologne, Wallraf-Richartz Museum, 1449.

EARLY MEDIEVAL AND BYZANTINE
Early Christian Painting, Rome. Susanna and
the Elders. Rome, Via Salaria Nuova. Catacomb of Priscilla, Cappella Greca.

FRENCH SCHOOL
Coypel, Antoine. Susannah Accused of Adultery.
Madrid, Prado, 2247.
French School, 14th century. Story of Susannah.
Reims, Musée (?).

GERMAN SCHOOL
German school, 16th century. (Upper German).
Story of Susanna. Vienna, Gallery, 1420.

ITALIAN SCHOOL
Lotto, Lorenzo. Susanna and the elders.
Florence, Collection Bonacossi.
Master of the Apollo and Daphne Legend. Susanna
and the Elders: Condemnation of Susanna.
Baltimore, Md., Walters Art Gallery, 37.480.
Master of the Apollo and Daphne Legend. Susan-
nah and the elders: the crime. Chicago,
Art Institute.

71 P 41 32 DANIEL 45 SUSANNAH IS LED AWAY TO
BE EXECUTED

AUSTRIAN SCHOOL
Maulbertsch, Franz Anton. Susanna before
the Judges. c.1750/52. Vienna, Österreichische Galerie, 3224.

ITALIAN SCHOOL
Master of the Apollo and Daphne Legend. Susannah
and the Elders: Susanna Led to Execution.
Baltimore, Md., Walters Art Gallery, 37.485.
Master of the Apollo and Daphne Legend. Susannah
and the Elders: the judgement. Chicago,
Art Institute.

71 P 41 4 DANIEL 45-46 THE YOUTH DANIEL OPPOSES
THE VERDICT

DUTCH SCHOOL
Lucas van Leyden. Daniel as judge. Bremen,
Kunsthalle, 62.

FRENCH SCHOOL
French school, 14th century. Story of Susanna.
Reims, Musée (?).

ITALIAN SCHOOL
Master of the Apollo and Daphne Legend. Susannah
and the Elders: Susannah Led to Execution.
Baltimore, Md., Walters Art Gallery, 37.485.

71 P 41 41 DANIEL 51-59 DANIEL INTERROGATES THE
ELDERS SEPARATELY

ITALIAN SCHOOL
Costa, Lorenzo. The Story of Susannah: The
Elders as Judges. Baltimore, Md., Walters
Art Gallery, 37.476.

71 P 41 42 DANIEL 51-60 DANIEL EXPOSES THE ELDERS
AS DECEIVERS

DUTCH SCHOOL
Eeckhout, Gerbrand van den. Daniel Proving
the Innocence of Susannah. Hartford, Conn.,
Wadsworth Athenaeum.

FLEMISH SCHOOL
Delen, Dirk van. Susanna and the elders.
Rotterdam, Museum Boymans, Inv.1159.

FRENCH SCHOOL
Ménageot, F.G. The Chaste Susannah Delivered
by Daniel. 1779. Douai (Nord), St. Pierre.
Valentin de Boulogne. The Judgement of Daniel.
Paris, Louvre, Musée du, 8245.
Valentin de Boullogne. Susanna Declared Inno-
cent. Paris, Musée du Louvre, 8245.

GERMAN SCHOOL
German school, 15th century. Triptych with
scenes from the Old Testament from Göttingen,
lower middle panel. 1400-10. Hanover,
Provincial Museum.
Willmann, Michael Leopold. Susannah at the
Bath. Nuremberg, Germanic Museum.

ITALIAN SCHOOL
   Master of the Apollo and Daphne Legend. Susannah
      and the Elders: Trial and Stoning of the
      Elders. Baltimore, Md., Walters Art Gallery,
      37.490.
   Master of the Apollo and Daphne Legend. Susanna
      and the elders: the judgement. Chicago, Art
      Institute.
   Ricci, Sebastiano. Susannah before Daniel. 1724.
      Turin, Pinacoteca, 581.

71 P 41 5 DANIEL 62 THE ELDERS ARE STONED TO DEATH

FRENCH SCHOOL
   French school, 14th century. Story of Susanna.
      Reims, Musée (?).

ITALIAN SCHOOL
   Master of the Apollo and Daphne Legend. Susannah
      and the Elders: Trial and Stoning of the
      Elders. Baltimore, Md., Walters Art Gallery,
      37.490.
   Master of the Apollo and Daphne Legend. Susanna
      and the Elders: the Judgement. Chicago, Art
      Institute.

71 P 43 33 APOCRYPHA DANIEL 36 THE PROPHET HABAKKUK,
   CARRIED BY HIS HAIR BY AN ANGEL, BRINGS FOOD
   TO DANIEL WHO SITS UNHARMED BETWEEN THE LIONS

FRENCH SCHOOL
   Flandrin, J.H. The Prophet Habakkuk: Study for
      mural in St. Germain-des-Prés, Paris. c.1856.
      Poitiers, Musée des Beaux-Arts.

GERMAN SCHOOL
   German school, 18th century. The Prophet Habak-
      kuk and an Angel. South German School. Buda-
      pest, Museum of Fine Arts, 63.16.

ITALIAN SCHOOL
   Veronese, Paolo, Studio of. The Prophet Habak-
      kuk, Carried by an Angel, Bringing Food to
      Daniel in the Lion's Den. Sotheby and Co.,
      London (Sale, April 7, 1982, No. 39).

71 P 52 1 DANIEL 8:3 THE RAM WITH TWO UNEQUAL HORNS
   NEAR A RIVER

DUTCH SCHOOL
   Rembrandt, School of. Daniel's Vision of the
      Ram and the He-Goat. Berlin, Staatliche
      Museen, 828 F.

71 Q ESTHER THE STORY OF ESTHER

DUTCH SCHOOL
   Gelder, Aert de. Esther. Private Collection,
      U.S.A.
   Gelder, Aert de. Esther. Hannema, D. - Collec-
      tion (Heino).

FLEMISH SCHOOL
   Bles, Herri met de. Esther and Ahasuerus.
      Bologna, Pinacoteca.
   Ehrenberg, Wilhelm van. Scene from the life
      of Esther. Weston Park, Collection Earl
      of Bradford.
   Franck, Frans, II. Ahasuerus and Haman. Bergues,
      Museum, 54.

ITALIAN SCHOOL
   Andrea di Giusto Manzini. Esther in the Temple.
      Philadelphia, Philadelphia Museum of Art.
   Beccafumi. Story of Esther. London, National
      Gallery, 1430.
   Cavallino, Bernardo. Esther and Ahasuerus.
      Florence, Uffizi.
   Graziani, Ercole. Esther and Ahasuerus. Bologna,
      Pinacoteca Nazionale, 2.
   Lippi, Filippino. Three Scenes in the History
      of Esther: Mordecai Lamenting; Esther
      Fainting in the Presence of Ahasuerus;
      Haman imploring in Vain for Grace. Paris,
      Louvre, Musée du, R.F. 1972-15.
   Michelangelo. Lunettes in four corners with
      scenes from Old Testament: Triumph of
      Esther (Punishment of Haman).Sistine chapel,
      ceiling decorations.
   Schiavone, Andreas, Attributed to. King Ahasue-
      rus. Scotland, Private Collection.

71 Q 21 ESTHER 1:5-8 THE FEAST OF AHASUERUS (XERXES,
   ALTERNATIVELY ARTAXERXES)

DUTCH SCHOOL
   Gelder, Aert de. Ahasuerus' Feast. Malibu,
      J. Paul Getty Museum.

ITALIAN SCHOOL
   Bonone, Carlo. Dinner of Ahasuerus. Ravenna,
      Cathedral.

71 Q 22 ESTHER 2:2-5 AHASUREUS HAS THE MOST ATTRACTIVE
   MAIDENS OF HIS KINGDOM PUT INTO HIS HAREM
   IN ORDER TO SELECT A NEW QUEEN FROM AMONG
   THEM

ITALIAN SCHOOL
   Lippi, Filippino. The Story of Esther. c.1475.
      Ottawa, National Gallery of Canada, 1953.

71 Q 23 1 ESTHER 2:15-16 ESTHER MAKES HER TOILET

DUTCH SCHOOL
   Gelder, Aert de. Esther Robes Herself for
      the Feast. 1684. Munich, Pinakothek, Alte,
      841.
   Gelder, Aert de. Esther Robes Herself for
      the Feast. Wengraf, Herner - Collection
      (London).

FRENCH SCHOOL
   Barrias, Félix Joseph. Esther before Ahasuerus.
      1894. Sotheby and Co., London (Sale [DORDOGNE]
      Feb.27, 1985, No. 194).
   Chassériau, Théodore. Esther preparing to
      appear before Ahazuerus. 1842. (Paris,
      Collection Baron Arthur Chassériau, Formerly)
      Paris, Louvre, Musée du, R.F. 3900.
   Troy, J.F. de. Toilet of Esther.

71 Q 23 2 ESTHER 2:16 ESTHER ON HER WAY TO THE
   KING

DUTCH SCHOOL
   Doomer, Lambert. Esther. 1666. Private Collec-
      tion, U.S.A.
   Meegeren, Hans van. Esther and Ahasuerus.
      Tournai, Musée des Beaux-Arts (on loan).

ITALIAN SCHOOL
Apollonio di Giovanni. The Story of Esther.
1460-70. New York, Metropolitan, 18.117.2.
Lippi, Filippino (?). Esther.
Lippi, Filippino. Story of Esther: Esther by
the town wall. (Vienna, Liechtenstein Gallery)
Ottawa, National Gallery, 1953.

71 Q 23 3   ESTHER 2:16   ESTHER IS PRESENTED TO THE KING

ITALIAN SCHOOL
Cavallino, Bernardo. Esther and Ahasuerus.
Vienna, Harrach Gallery.
Lippi, Filippino. Story of Esther. Detail:
Esther before Ahasuerus. Chantilly, Musée
Condé.
Tintoretto (Jacopo Robusti). Esther before Aha-
suerus. Seilern, Antoine, Count - Collection
(London).
Veronese, Paolo. Story of Esther. Detail: Meet-
ing of Esther and Ahasuerus. S. Sebastiano,
ceiling decorations.

71 Q 24   ESTHER 2:17   CROWNING OF ESTHER

ITALIAN SCHOOL
Apollonio di Giovanni. The Story of Esther.
1460-70. New York, Metropolitan Museum, 18.
117.2. Right center: Ahasuerus places ring
on Esther's finger.
Veronese, Paolo. Story of Esther. Detail: Coronation of Esther. Venice, S. Sebastiano,
ceiling decoration.

71 Q 24 1   ESTHER 2:18   THE WEDDING FEAST, ESTHER'S FEAST (USUALLY ESTHER IS NOT PRESENT)

ITALIAN SCHOOL
Apollonio di Giovanni. The Story of Esther.
Far right: Esther seated next to Ahasuerus.
1460-70. New York, Metropolitan Museum, 18.
117.2.

71 Q 5   ESTHER 4   MORDECAI ASKS ESTHER'S HELP

ITALIAN SCHOOL
Mantegna, Andrea. Tarquin and the Cumaean sibyl
(also thought to be Esther and Mordecai).
Cincinnati, Museum.

71 Q 56   ESTHER 5:1, 15:1-2   ESTHER PUTS ON HER ROYAL ROBES

DUTCH SCHOOL
Gelder, Aert de. Esther's Toilet. Potsdam, Sans
Souci, GK I.5255.
Poorter, Willem de. The Robing of Esther. Dublin,
National Gallery, 380.

71 Q 6   ESTHER 5:1-4   ESTHER BEFORE AHASUERUS

DUTCH SCHOOL
Dyck, Abraham van. Esther before Ahasueras.
c. 1655. Baltimore, Walters Art Gallery,
37.2013.

FLEMISH SCHOOL
Jordaens, Hans. Esther before Ahasuarus. Signed.
Serge Philipson Collection.

FRENCH SCHOOL
Vignon, Claude. Esther before Ahazuerus. Paris,
Musée du Louvre.

71 Q 62   ESTHER 5:2   ESTHER APPROACHING THE THRONE

DUTCH SCHOOL
Gelder, Aert de. Esther before Ahasuerus. Bader,
Alfred - Collection (Milwaukee).

ITALIAN SCHOOL
Cavallino, Bernardo. Esther and Ahasuerus.
c. 1645-60. Florence, Palazzo Uffizi.

Tintoretto, Jacopo. Esther before Ahasuerus.
London University, Courtauld Institute
(Princess Gate Collection), 76.

71 Q 63   ESTHER 15:7   ESTHER SWOONS ON THE SHOULDER OF ONE OF HER MAIDS

DUTCH SCHOOL
Mieris, Frans van, the elder. Esther before
Ahasuerus. Milan, Brera.

FRENCH SCHOOL
Berthélemy, Jean Simon. Esther's Faint. 1768.
Cambrai, Musée Municipal, N.C. 41.
Poussin, Nicolas. Esther Before Ahasuerus.
Leningrad, Hermitage.
Tissot, James Jacques Joseph. Illustrations
of the Hebrew Bible. No. 237: Esther
before Ahasuerus. 1896-1903. New York,
Jewish Museum, 52.383.
Troy, J.F. de. Esther swooning.

ITALIAN SCHOOL
Angeli, Giuseppe., The Swooning of Esther.
Padua, Private Collection.
Coli, Giovanni. Esther before Ahasuerus.
Also attributed to Filippe Gherardi.
Christie, Manson and Woods (Sale, London,
Dec. 2, 1983 [TORINO-2790], No. 112).
Gentileschi, Artemsia. Esther and Ahasuerus.
New York, Metropolitan Museum.
Mantegna, Andrea. Esther and Mordecai. c.1480.
Cincinnati, Art Museum, 1927.406.
Mariotti, Giovanni Battista. Esther and Aha-
suerus. Dorta - Collection (Udine).
Menescardi, Giustino. Esther Before Ahasuerus.
Christie, Manson, and Woods (Sale, [SUSAN-
5213] November 5, 1982. Nr. 121).
Pasinelli, Lorenzo. The swooning of Esther.
Bologna, Collection Prince Hercolani.
Tintoretto (?). Esther and Ahasuerus.
Tintoretto. Esther and Ahasuerus. Bowood,
Collection Marquis of Lansdowne (Formerly).
Tintoretto. Esther before Ahasuerus. London,
Collection Lord Crawford.
Tintoretto (Jacopo Robusti). Ducal Palace,
Atrio Quadrato, ceiling: Esther before
Ahasuarus. 1565. Venice, Palazzo Ducale.
Veronese, Paolo. The Swooning of Esther.
Paris, Louvre, Musée du.
Veronese, Paolo. Esther and Ahasuerus. Vienna,
Kunsthistorisches Museum, 3677.
Veronese, Paolo, School of. Scene from the
life of Esther. Paris, Louvre.

SPANISH SCHOOL
Viló, José. Esther before Ahasuerus. Valencia,
Museo de Pinturas.

71 Q 63 1   ESTHER 15:8   AHASUERUS LEAPS FROM HIS THRONE AND TAKES ESTHER IN HIS ARMS

FRENCH SCHOOL
Coypel, A. Esther before Ahasuerus. Paris,
Louvre.

71 Q 64   ESTHER 15:11   AHASUERUS HOLDS OUT HIS SCEPTER TO HER (ESTHER USUALLY KNEELING)

DUTCH SCHOOL
Neer, Eglon Hendrik van der. Esther before
Ahasuerus. 1696. Florence, Palazzo Uffizi,
1186.
Steen, Jan. Esther Before Ahasuerus. Leningrad,
Hermitage.

FLEMISH SCHOOL
Rubens, Peter Paul. Esther before Ahasuerus.
Sketch panel. London, Universtiy, Courtauld
Institute (Princess Gate Collection),27.
Rubens, P.P. Ceiling decorations for Church
of the Jesuits at Antwerp. Sketch: Meeting
of Esther and Ahasuerus. Richmond, Cook
Collection, 334.

Stradanus, Johannes. The Coronation of Esther. Florence, Palazzo Vecchio, Sala D'Ester.

GERMAN SCHOOL

Burgkmair, Hans. Esther before Ahasuerus. 1528. Munich, Pinakothek, Alte.

ITALIAN SCHOOL

Palma, Antonio. Esther before Ahasuerus. Sarasota, Fla., Ringling Museum of Art, SN 85.
Ricci, Sebastiano. Esther before Ahasuerus. London, National Gallery, 2101.
Sellaio, Jacopo del. Esther before Ahasuerus. Budapest, Museum of Fine Arts, 2537 (56).
Tintoretto. Esther before Ahasuerus. Sketch. Madrid, Prado.

71 Q 64 1   ESTHER 15:11   ESTHER TOUCHES THE TIP OF THE SCEPTER

GERMAN SCHOOL

Burgkmair, Hans. Esther before Ahasuerus. Munich, Old Pinakothek, 689.

ITALIAN SCHOOL

Castello, Valerio. Esther and Ahasuerus. Genoa, Palazzo Negrone.
Pagani, Gregorio. Esther and Ahasuerus. 1600. Vienna, Kunsthistorisches Museum, Inv. Nr. 3841.
Ricci, Sebastiano. Esther Before Ahasuerus. London, National Gallery, 2101.

71 Q 64 2   ESTHER 15:12   AHASUERUS TOUCHES ESTHER WITH THE SCEPTER

DUTCH SCHOOL

Steen, Jan. Esther before Ahasuerus. Leningrad, Hermitage, 878.

FLEMISH SCHOOL

Bles, Herri met de. Esther and Ahasuerus: Ahasuerus touches Esther with the scepter, middle panel. Bologna, Pinacoteca.
Rubens, Peter Paul. Esther and Ahasuerus. Sketch for a painting in the Church of the Jesuits, Antwerp. Vienna, Academy, 652.

ITALIAN SCHOOL

Signorelli, Luca. Predella with scenes of St. Jerome and Esther: Esther before Ahasuerus. London, National Gallery, 3946.

71 Q 73   ESTHER 6:11   MORDECAI'S TRIUMPH: MORDECAI, MOUNTED ON THE KING'S HORSE, IS LED THROUGH THE CITY BY HAMAN (ESTHER AND AHASUERUS MAY BE LOOKING ON FROM THE PALACE)

DUTCH SCHOOL

Eeckhout, Gerbrand van den. Mordecai's Triumph. 1664. Bobrinsky, Graf - Collection (London).

ITALIAN SCHOOL

Lippi, Filippino. Story of Esther: Mordecai led by Haman. Ottawa, National Gallery, 1953.
Veronese, Paolo. Story of Esther. Detail: Triumph of Mordecai. S. Sebastiano, ceiling decoration.

71 Q 74   ESTHER 7:1-9   ESTHER'S BANQUET

DUTCH SCHOOL

Gelder, Aert de. Esther's Banquet. Amiens, Musée de Picardie.
Poorter, Willem de. Esther and Ahasuerus. Sotheby and Co., London (Sale, [DAFFODIL] Feb. 20, 1980, No. 8).
Steen, Jan. Esther, Ahasuerus, and Haman. Cleveland Museum of Art.

FLEMISH SCHOOL

Bles, Herri met de. Esther and Ahasuerus: Esther's Banquet, right panel. Bologna, Pinacoteca.

71 Q 74 1   ESTHER 7:1-6   ESTHER ACCUSES HAMAN

BRITISH SCHOOL

Normand, Ernest. Esther Denouncing Haman. Sunderland (Tyne and Wear), Museum.

DUTCH SCHOOL

Eeckhout, Gerbrand van den. Esther, Haman and Ahasuerus (also attributed to Govert Flinck). Cologne, Wallraf Richartz Museum, 670.
Grebber, P.F. de. Ahasuerus, Esther and Haman. Stockholm, National Museum, 448.
Lievens, Jans. The Feast of Esther. 1625/26. Raleigh, N.C., North Carolina Museum of Art.
Rembrandt. Esther's feast for Ahasuerus and Haman. Amsterdam, Collection P. de Boer.
Steen, Jan. The Wrath of Ahasuerus. Christie, Manson and Woods (Sale, London, July 7, 1972, No. 95).
Victors, Jan. Esther and Haman with Ahasuerus. Cologne, Wallraf-Richartz Museum, 1016.

ITALIAN SCHOOL

Paolini, Pietro. Queen Esther. Denver, Art Museum, 1933.28.

71 Q 74 11   ESTHER 7:7   THE KING GETS UP IN A FURY AND GOES INTO THE PALACE GARDEN

DUTCH SCHOOL

Steen, Jan. The Wrath of Ahasuerus. Birmingham University, Barber Institute of Fine Arts.
Steen, Jan. Esther, Ahasuerus, and Haman. c.1668. Cleveland, Museum of Art.

71 Q 74 2   ESTHER 8:7   HAMAN BEGS ESTHER FOR HIS LIFE

DUTCH SCHOOL

Rembrandt. Haman begging for mercy before Esther. Leningrad, Hermitage.

71 Q 74 21   ESTHER 7:7-8   AS HAMAN IS KNEELING AT HER FEET OR IS PROSTRATED ON HER COUCH THE KING RETURNS; HAMAN IS CONDEMNED TO BE HANGED

BRITISH SCHOOL

Armitage, Edward. The festival of Esther. London, Diploma Gallery, 33.

DUTCH SCHOOL

Gelder, Aert de. King Ahasuerus Condemning Haman. c.1685. Melbourne, National Gallery of Victoria.
Poorter, Willem de. The Fear of Hamen before Esther and Ahasuerus. Sotheby and Co., London (Sale, Oct. 20, 1982, No. 58).
Victors, Jan. Esther and Haman. 1642. Brunswick, Landes-Museum, 253.

71 Q 82   ESTHER 8:5   ESTHER ENTREATING AHASUERUS: SHE FALLS AT THE KING'S FEET AND ASKS HIM TO REVOKE THE DECREE AGAINST THE JEWS; THE KING HOLDS OUT HIS SCEPTER TO HER (ESTHER MAY BE HOLDING THE DECREE)

DUTCH SCHOOL

Poorter, Willem de. Esther before Ahasuerus. Dresden, Gallery, 1392.

FLEMISH SCHOOL

Master of the Story of Joseph. Series of six round panels. Panel 4: Esther entreating Ahasuerus for her people? Berlin, Kaiser Friedrich Museum, 539D.

FRENCH SCHOOL
 French school, 14th century. Paintings on cloth.
  Story of Esther. Reims, Musée (?).
 Le Brun, Charles. Esther before Ahasuerus.
  Quimper, Musée.

ITALIAN SCHOOL
 Fiasella, Domenico. Esther and Ahasuerus. Fresco
  cycle. Genoa, Palazzo Lomellini.
 Fontebasso, Francesco. Esther and Ahasuerus.
  Povo, Church.
 Italian school, 17th century. Esther and Aha-
  suerus. c.1600. Budapest, Museum of Fine
  Arts, 9640.
 Palma, Antonio. Esther before Ahasuerus. Sara-
  sota, Fla., Ringling Museum of Art, SN 85.

SPANISH SCHOOL
 Spanish school, 17th century. Esther Kneeling
  before Ahasuerus. Copenhagen, Art Museum.

71 Q 83 ESTHER 8:9-13, 9:29 MORDECAI AND ESTHER
    WRITE LETTERS IN THE KING'S NAME

DUTCH SCHOOL
 Gelder, Aert de. The Document (Esther and Mord-
  ecai). c.1685. Dresden, Staatliche Kunst-
  sammlungen, 1792 A.
 Gelder, Aert de. Esther and Mordecai. Budapest,
  Museum.
 Gelder, Aert de. Esther and Mordecai. Provi-
  dence, Rhode Island School of Design.

ITALIAN SCHOOL
 Mantegna, Andrea. Esther and Mordecai. c.1480.
  Cincinnati, Art Museum, 1927.406.

71 Q 87 ESTHER 10:3 MORDECAI'S ADVANCEMENT

DUTCH SCHOOL
 Gelder, Arent. King Ahasuerus Honors Mordecai.
  Copenhagen, Art Museum, 1526.

71 R 11 4 EZRA 1:7-11 CYRUS RESTORES THE VESSELS
    OF THE TEMPLE OF JERUSALEM THAT HAD BEEN
    CARRIED OFF BY NEBUCHADNEZZAR

DUTCH SCHOOL
 Keyser, Thomas de. King Cyrus Returns the
  Vessels from the Temple of the Lord to
  the Jews. 1660. Paris, Institut Neerlan-
  dais.

71 S 52 2 JOEL 3:18 "THE MOUNTAINS SHALL DRIP SWEET
           WINE, AND THE HILLS SHALL FLOW WITH MILK"

FLEMISH SCHOOL
    Mostaert, Gillis. The Last Days of the World,
        According to Joel. Dayton (Ohio), Art Insti-
        tute, 61.91.

71 T   THE BOOK OF TOBIT

GERMAN SCHOOL
    German school, 15th century. Triptych with
        scenes from the Old Testament from Gött-
        ingen, upper right panel. 1400-10. Hanover,
        Provincial Museum.

ITALIAN SCHOOL
    Francesco di Giorgio. Story of Tobit.
    Francesco di Giorgio. Cassone: Story of
        Tobias. Kansas City, William Rickhill
        Nelson Gallery of Art, 41-9.
    Italian school, 15th century. Scenes from
        the story of Tobias. Florentine, c.1400.
        Florence, Museo Stibbert, 8.
    Italian school, 15th century. Scenes from
        the life of Tobias. Detail. Florence,
        Loggia Orfanotrofio del Bigallo.
    Tassi, Agostino. The Old Tobias with Friends.
        Rome, Palazzo Doria Pamphili.
    Volterrano. Tobias and the Angel. Fresco.
        Christie, Manson and Woods (Sale, New
        York, June 12, 1981, No. 196).

71 T 24 TOBIT 2:7 TOBIT BURIES THE DEAD IN SECRET

DUTCH SCHOOL
    Sweertz, Michael. Tobit Burying the Dead.
        Hartford, Conn., Wadsworth Atheneum, 1941.
        595.

FRENCH SCHOOL
    Bourdon, Sebastien. Tobias Burying the Israel-
        ites. Vienna, Academy.

ITALIAN SCHOOL
    Castiglione, Giovanni Benedetto. Tobit Burying
        the Dead in Defiance of the Orders of
        Sennacherib. Christie, Manson and Woods
        London (Sale, December 11, 1981, No. 105).
    Italian school, 15th century. Scenes from
        the story of Tobias. Cassone panel, first
        in series of five. Florentine, c.1400.
        Florence, Museo Stibbert, 8.
    Italian school, 16th century (Venetian).
        Tobit Buries a Jew in Niniveh. c.1550.
        Vienna, Kunsthistorisches Museum, 6641.

71 T 3 TOBIT 2-3:6 TOBIT'S BLINDNESS

DUTCH SCHOOL
    Cuyp, Benjamin. Blind Tobias. Rotterdam,
        Museum, Boymans, 1144.

71 T 31 1 TOBIT 2:3 ON HIS RETURN TOBIAS TELLS
           TOBIT OF A DEAD MAN IN THE STREET

ITALIAN SCHOOL
    Italian school, 15th century. Scenes from
        the life of Tobias. Detail. Florence,
        Loggia Orfanotrofio del Bigallo.

71 T 32 TOBIT 2:4 OLD TOBIT LEAVES THE BANQUET
         AND CARRIES THE DEAD MAN INTO A HOUSE

ITALIAN SCHOOL
    Italian school, 15th century. Scenes from
        the life of Tobias. Detail. Florence,
        Loggia Orfanotrofio del Bigallo.

71 T 34 TOBIT 2:4 TOBIT LIES SLEEPING AGAINST
         A WALL

DUTCH SCHOOL
    Weenix, Jan Baptist, the elder. Tobias sleeping
        under the vineyard. Rotterdam, Museum
        Boymans-Van Beuningen, inv. 1204.

71 T 37 TOBIT 2:13 ANNA BRINGS HOME A YOUNG GOAT: TOBIT THINKS SHE HAS STOLEN IT

DUTCH SCHOOL
Fabritius, Carel. Tobias and his Wife. Innsbruck, Ferdinandeum, 600.
Rembrandt. Tobit Accusing Anna of Stealing the Kid. 1626. Amsterdam, Rijksmuseum, C 1448.
Rembrandt. Wife of Tobit with Goat. 1645. Berlin, Staatliche Museen, 805.
Rembrandt, Follower of. Tobit and Hannah with the Kid. Bouwfonds, N.V. - Collection (Hoevelaken).

71 T 51 TOBIT 5:4 THE MEETING OF TOBIAS AND THE ANGEL RAPHAEL

DUTCH SCHOOL
Bloemaert, Abraham, Follower of. Tobias and the Fish. Sotheby and Co., London (Sale, Dec. 16, 1981, No. 124).

ITALIAN SCHOOL
Domenichino. Landscape with Tobias and the Angel. Sotheby and Co., (Sale, London, March 26, 1969, No. 63).

71 T 52 TOBIT 5:9-16 TOBIAS AND THE ANGEL WITH TOBIT (AND ANNA)

ITALIAN SCHOOL
Puccinelli, Angelo. Tobit blessing his son. Washington, D.C., National Gallery of Art, 180.
Rosa, Salvatore. Angel leaving Tobias. Chantilly, Musée Condé, 85.
Rosselli, Matteo. Tobias and the Angel. Boston, Museum of Fine Arts, 78.7.

71 T 53 TOBIT 5:17 TOBIAS TAKING LEAVE OF HIS PARENTS; ANNA MOURNS HER SON'S DEPARTURE

FRENCH SCHOOL
Le Sueur, Eustache, Studio of. Tobias Departs from his Parents. Budapest, Museum of Fine Arts 701 (837).
Tournier, Nicolas. Tobias Taking Leave of his Parents. Formerly attributed to Bartolomeo Manfredi as Dismissal of Hagar. Sarasota, Fla., Ringling Museum of Art, 110.

ITALIAN SCHOOL
Cavallino, Bernardo. Departure of Tobias. Rome, Galeria d'Arte Antica.
Francesco di Giorgio. Story of Tobit.
Guardi, Giovanni Antonio. The story of Tobit. The departure of Tobias. Venice, Chiesa Angelo Raffaele, Cantoria.
Traversi, Gaspare. The sending away of Tobias by his father. Rome, San Paolo Fuori le Mura.

71 T 54 TOBIT 5:16 TOBIAS AND THE ANGEL TRAVELLING, ACCOMPANIED BY TOBIAS' DOG

DUTCH SCHOOL
Bloemaert, Abraham. Shepherd Boy Pointing at Tobias and the Angel. Minneapolis, Institute of Arts, 61.30.
Bloemaert, Abraham. Landscape with Tobias and the Angel. 1612. Leningrad, Hermitage.
Dyck, Abraham van. The Departure of Tobias and the Angel. c.1655/60.
Dyck, Abraham van. Tobias and the Angel at the Tigris. Berlin, Staatliche Museen (Dahlem), 828N.
Gelton, Toussaint. Tobias and the Angel. Copenhagen, Art Museum, Sp. 362.
Hondecoeter, Gillis Claesz de. A Mountainous River Landscape with Tobias and the Angel. Christie, Manson and Woods (Sale, New York, Jan. 15, 1985 [CAROL-5808], No. 209).

Keirincx, Alexander. A Wooded Landscape with Tobias and the Angel. Sotheby and Co., London (Sale, April 8, 1981, No. 132).
Savery, Jacob, I. Rocky Landscape with Tobias and the Angel. 1592. Vienna, Kunsthistorisches Museum, 952.

FLEMISH SCHOOL
Alsloot, Denis van. Landscape with Tobias and the Angel. 1610. Antwerp, Museum, 865.
Brueghel, Jan, the elder. Landscape with the Young Tobias. 1598. Vienna, Liechtenstein Gallery, 477.
Mirou, Antoine, Attributed to. Landscape with Tobias and the Angel. Gray (Haute-Saône), Musée Baron Martin, 323.
Verhaecht, Tobias. Landscape with Tobias and the Angel. Karlesruhe, Kunsthalle, 2466.

FRENCH SCHOOL
Cazin, Jean Charles. Tobias and the Angel, No. 104. 1878. Chicago, Art Institute, 94.1036.
François, Claude (Frère Luc). The Archangel Raphael Guiding Tobias. c.1670. Quebec, Musée du Quebec.

GERMAN SCHOOL
König, Johann. Landscape with Tobias and the Angel. Christie, Manson and Woods (Sale, Nov. 5, 1982 [SUSAN] No. 169).

ITALIAN SCHOOL
Guercino. Tobit and the archangel. Rome, Palazzo Colonna.
Luini, Bernardo, School of. Tobias and the Angel. Fresco. Milan, Brera.
Maffei, Francesco. Tobias and the Angel. Venice, SS. Apostoli.
Pollaiuolo, Piero. Tobias and the Archangel Raphael. Turin, Pinacoteca, 117.
Titian, attributed to. Tobias and the Angel. Venice, Academy.

71 T 55 1 TOBIT 6:2 A LARGE FISH APPEARS; TOBIAS IS FRIGHTENED

DUTCH SCHOOL
Fabritius, Bernard. Landscape with Tobias and the Angel. Glasgow, Art Gallery.
Glauber, Johannes. Tobias and the Fish. Figures by Lairesse. Hovingham Hall, Collection Sir William Worsley.
Neer, E.H. van der. Tobit and the angel. Amsterdam, Rijksmuseum, 1722.

ITALIAN SCHOOL
Biliverti, Giovanni. Tobias and the angel. Southampton (Hampshire), Art Gallery.
Italian school, 16th century (Venetian). Tobias and the Angel. c.1550. Vienna, Kunsthistorisches Museum, 6641.
Savoldo, Giovanni Girolamo. Tobias and the Angel. Rome, Villa Borghese.
Zelotti, Battista. The Archangel Raphael and Tobias. Madrid, Collection Perez Asencio.

MEXICAN SCHOOL
Mexican school, 17th century. Tobias and the Archangel Raphael. Davenport, Iowa, Municipal Art Gallery, 25.263F.

71 T 56 TOBIT 6:3 TOBIAS CAPTURES THE FISH AND PULLS IT ON LAND

BRITISH SCHOOL
Turner, Joseph Mallord William. Tivoli: Tobias and the Angel. c.1835. London, Tate Gallery of Art, 2067.

DUTCH SCHOOL
Fabritius, Bernard. Tobias Pulls the Fish onto
Land. 1660. Nimes, Musée de Peinture et
Sculpture.
Lastman, Pieter P. Landscape with Tobias and
Angel. Budapest, Museum of Fine Arts.
Lastman, Pieter P. Landscape with Tobias and
Angel. Version of painting in Budapest.
1615. Leeuwarden, Gemeentilijk Museum Het
Princessehop.

FRENCH SCHOOL
Delacroix, Eugéne. Tobias and the Angel. 1863.
Sotheby and Co., London (Sale, [LOHENGRIN]
June 15, 1982, No. 12).

ITALIAN SCHOOL
Domenichino. Tobias and the Angel. London,
National Gallery, 48.
Fetti, Domenico. Tobias and the Angel. Dresden,
Gallery, 416.
Francesco di Giorgio. Story of Tobit.
Guardi, Giovanni Antonio. Tobias and the Angel.
(companion piece to the Abraham series).
Cleveland, Museum of Art, 52.236, Mr. and
Mrs. William H. Marlatt Collection.
Guardi, Giovanni Antonio. The Story of Tobit:
Tobit fishes with help of the angel. Venice,
Chiesa Angelo Raffaele, Cantoria.
Lippi, Lorenzo. Tobias and the Angel Catching
Fish. Pendant for the University's Moses
and the burning bush. Greenville, S.C.,
Bob Jones University Collection.
Mura, Francesco de. Raphael and Tobias. Oxford,
University, Ashmolean Museum, A 1090.
Ricci, Marco. Landscape with Tobias and the
Angel. Sarasota, Fla., Ringling Museum of
Art SN 179.
Rosa, Salvatore. Tobias and the Fish (Tobias
and the Angel). Paris, Louvre, Musée du,
583.
Rosa, Salvatore. Landscape with Tobias and
the Angel. London, National Gallery, 6298.
Rosa, Salvatore. Landscape with Tobias and the
angel (copy after painting in the Wadsworth
Atheneum, Hartford). Harvard University,
Fogg Art Museum, 1937.181.
Rosa, Salvatore. Tobias and the Angel. Berlin,
Private Collection.
Rosa, Salvatore, Style of. Tobias and the
Angel. London, National Gallery, 811.
Tavella, Carlo Antonio. Landscape with Tobias
and the Angel. Geneva, Musée d'Art et
d'Histoire, 1833-1.
Varotari, Alessandro (Il Padovanino). Tobias
and the Angel. Princeton, University, Museum
of Art, 78-14.
Zuccari, Federigo. Tobias and the archangel
Raphael. Rome, Il Gèsu, chapel, ceiling.

71 T 57   TOBIT 6:4   THE ANGEL TELLS HIM TO CUT THE
FISH TO PIECES

DUTCH SCHOOL
Dujardin, Karel. Tobias and the angel. Budapest,
Museum of Fine Arts.
Eeckhout, Gerbrand van den. Tobias and the
Angel. Brunswick Landesmuseum, 259.
Gelton, Toussaint. Young Tobias and the Angel.
Copenhagen, Art Museum, Sp. 363.
Rembrandt, School of. Tobias and the Angel.
Berlin, Staatliche Museen, 828N.

FLEMISH SCHOOL
Alsloot, Denis van. Landscape with Tobias and
the Angel. 1610. Antwerp, Museum, 865.
Crayer, Gaspar de. Tobias and the Angel. Bruns-
wick, Landesmuseum, 80.
Crayer, Gaspar de. Tobias and the Angel.
Detail: Dog. Madrid, Private Collection.

FRENCH SCHOOL
Delacroix, Eugène. Tobias and the Angel.
1863. Winterthur, Collection Dr. Oskar
Reinhart.

GERMAN SCHOOL
Elsheimer, Adam, Follower of. Tobias and
the Angel. Sotheby and Co., London (Sale,
Dec. 16, 1981, No. 90).
Elsheimer, Adam, School of. Tobias and the
Angel. Ludlow, Oakley Park, Collection
Earl of Plymouth.

ITALIAN SCHOOL
Caracciolo, G.B. Tobias and the Angel. Col-
nagi & Co. (London).
Domenichino, Attributed to. Landscape with
Tobias and the Angel. Oxford, University,
Ashmolean Museum, A970.
Guardi, Giovanni Antonio. The story of Tobit:
Tobit fishes with help of the angel, detail,
right. Venice, Chiesa Angelo Raffaele.
Lippi, Lorenzo. Tobias gutting the fish.
Sotheby and Co., London (Sale, November
17, 1982, No. 43).
Rosa, Salvatore, follower of. Tobias and
the angel. Sotheby and Co., (Sale, London,
Feb. 22, 1984, No. 130).
Rosa, Salvatore. Landscape with Tobias and
the angel. Hartford, Wadsworth Museum.

71 T 58   TOBIT 6:5   THEY CONTINUE THEIR JOURNEY,
USUALLY TOBIAS CARRYING THE FISH

AMERICAN SCHOOL
Berman, Eugene. Tobias and the Angel. New
York, Levy Galleries.

BRITISH SCHOOL
Bourgeois, P.F. Tobit and the angel. Dulwich
Gallery, 344.
De Morgan, Evelyn Pickering. Tobias and the
Angel. 1875. Sotheby and Co., London (Bel-
gravia, Sale, Oct. 24, 1978).

DUTCH SCHOOL
Jansz, Govert. Tobias and the Angel. Detroit,
Institute of Arts, 41.39.
Lievens, Jan. Landscape with Tobias and the
Angel. London, National Gallery, 72.
Poelenburg, Cornelis. Tobit and the Angel.
Osterley Park, Collection Earl of Jersey,
Cat. no. 142.
Swaneveldt, Herman van. Landscape with Tobias
and the Angel. Brighton, Eng. Corporation
Art Gallery.
Dutch School, 17th century. Tobias and the
Angel. Private Collection, U.S.A.

FLEMISH SCHOOL
Franck, Franz, I, Studio of. Flemish Reliquary
Chest painted with scenes from the Old
Testament. Detail: drawer: Tobias and
the Angel. c.1600. Sarasota, Fla., Ringling
Museum of Art, SN 1950.
Keuning, Kerstiaen de. Tobias and the Angel.
Leningrad, Hermitage.
Rubens, P.P. Landscape (Tobias and the Angel
in the left foreground). New York, Knoedler,
1951.
Sustris, Lambert. Tobias and the angel. Vienna,
Kunsthistorisches Museum.

FRENCH SCHOOL
Sérusier, Paul. Tobias and the Angel. 1895.
Kirkman, James - Collection (London).

GERMAN SCHOOL
Elsheimer, Adam, copy after. Tobias and the
angel. Copenhagen, Art Museum.
Elsheimer, Adam. Tobias and the Archangel
Raphael. London, National Gallery, 1424.
Elsheimer, Adam. Copy. Tobias and the Angel.
Copenhagen, Art Museum, Sp. 745.

König, Johann. Landscape with Tobias and angel. Karlsruhe, Kunsthalle, 1410.

Rehbenitz, Theodor Markus. Tobias and the Angel. c. 1824. Berlin, Staatliche Museen, NG1441.

ITALIAN SCHOOL

Alunno di Benozzo. Archangel Raphael and Tobias. Pisa, Museo Civico.

Andrea del Sarto, School of. Archangel Raphael and Tobias. Florence, Pitti.

Bacchiacca, Francesco. Tobias and the Angel. A.S. Drey, dealer. Formerly Collection Dr. James Simon, Berlin (?).

Belbello da Pavia, Attributed to. Tobias and the Angel. Early 15th century. Genoa, Palazzo Bianco.

Biagio d'Antonio. Tobias and the angel. New York, Collection S.H. Kress, 1139.

Botticini, Francesco. Tobias and the three angels. 1467/71. Florence, Palazzo Uffizi.

Caravaggio, School of. Tobias and the angel. Corsham Court, Collection Lord Methuen.

Evangelista da Pian di Meleto. Tobias and the Angel (Formerly attributed to Giovanni Santi). Urbino, Palazzo Ducale.

Ghirlandaio, Ridolfo, School of. Archangel Raphael and Tobias (given to Beccafumi, Zampieri, and others). Rome, Galleria Doria.

Granacci, Francesco. Tobias and the angel. New York, Metropolitan Museum, 22.60.50.

Italian school, 15th century. Altarpiece of Tobias and the Archangel Raphael. Florentine, close to A. Baldovinetti. Florence, S. Maria Novella.

Italian school, 15th century, (Florentine). Tobias and the Angel, with God the Father in the Pediment above, the Donor and his Family in Adoration below. 2nd quarter of 15th century. Sotheby and Co., London (Sale, New York, Jan. 17, 1985 [TOMMASO], No. 41).

Italian school, 15th century. Tobias and the Angel. S. Giovanni Valdarno, S. Maria delle Grazie.

Italian school, 16th century. Tobias and the Angel. Budapest, Museum of Fine Arts, 5416.

Lippi, Filippino. Tobias and the Angel. c.1480. Washington, D.C., National Gallery of Art, 340.

Master of Pratovécchio. Tobias and three archangels. Formerly attributed to Giovanni Boccatis. Berlin, Staatliche Museen.

Melone, Altobello. Tobias and the Angel. Oxford, University, Ashmolean Museum, A 290.

Morandini, Francesco. Tobit and the angel. Prato, Galleria Communale.

Motta, Raffaello. Tobias and the Archangel Raphael. Rome, Villa Borghese, Gallery, 298.

Neri di Bicci. Tobias and archangel Raphael. New Jersey, Platt Collection.

Neri di Bicci. Tobias and the angel. Florence, Collection Pazzagli.

Pollaiuolo, Piero. Tobias and the archangel Raphael. Turin, Pinacoteca.

Rosa, Salvatore. Landscape with Tobias and the Angel. London, National Gallery, 6298.

Rosa, Salvatore, Circle of. A Wooded Landscape with Tobias and the Angel. London, Sotheby and Co, (Sale, [CATKIN] April 8, 1981, No. 158).

Tassi, Agostino. Tobias and the Angel. Harvard University, Fogg Art Museum, 1979.5.

Tassi, Agostino. The Young Tobias with the Angel. Rome, Palazzo Doria Pamphili.

Titian. Tobias and the angel.

Torbido, Francesco. Tobias and the angel. Verona, Museo Civico.

Toschi, Paolo. Tobias and the angel. Rome, Villa Borghese, Gallery.

Tosini, Michele. Tobias and the angel. New York, Collection S.H. Kress, 1236.

Udine, Giovanni da. The Archangel Gabriel with Tobias. Rovigo, Pinacoteca dell'Accademia dei Concordi, 91.93.

Verrocchio, Andrea, Follower of. Tobias and the Angel. Formerly attributed to Perugino. London, National Gallery, 781.

Viola, Giovanni Battista. Tobias and the Angel. Formerly attributed to Agostino Tassi. Harvard University, Fogg Art Museum.

Zago, Sante. Tobias and the archangel Raphael. Venice, S. Caterina.

SPANISH SCHOOL

Castillo y Saavedra, Antonio del. Tobias and the angel. Detail. Cordova, Museum.

Gascó, Perot. Retable, panel: Tobias and the angel. San Esteban de Bas, Parish Church.

Martínez Master. Tobias and the Archangel Raphael. Valencia, Collection Miguel Martí.

Murillo. Tobias and the Angel. Aynho Park, Collection Cartwright.

71 T 58 1 TOBIT 6:5 TOBIAS AND RAPHAEL WITH OTHER SAINTS AND ANGELS

ITALIAN SCHOOL

Andrea del Sarto. Tobias and the Archangel Raphael with St. Leonard and a donor. Vienna, Kunsthistorisches Museum.

Botticelli, Sandro. Tobias and an Archangel. Florence, Academy.

Caroto, F. Two archangels and Tobias. Verona, Museo Civico.

Lippi, Filippino. Tobias and the three archangels. Turin, Pinacoteca, 113.

Neri di Bicci. Tobias and the Angel. Esztergom, Palace of the Primate of Hungary.

Neri di Bicci. Tobias and the three archangels. Detroit, Institute of Arts, 158.

Pacchiarotto, G. Tobias with angel Raphael and St. Cosmo or Damian. Siena, Gallery, 421.

Palma Giovane. Tobias and the angel. Christie, Manson and Woods (Sale, New York, June 12, 1981, No. 118).

Savery, Jacob, the Elder. Rocky Landscape with Tobias and the Angel. 1592. Vienna, Kunsthistorisches Museum, 952.

71 T 59 TOBIT 7 THE ARRIVAL AT ECBATANA

ITALIAN SCHOOL

Guardi, Francesco. Tobias and the Angel. Finney - Collection (Paris).

Zuccarelli, Francesco. Tobias and the Angel. Louisville, Ky., J.B. Speed Art Museum, 70.31.

71 T 61 TOBIT 7:1 TOBIAS AND THE ANGEL IN RAGUEL'S HOUSE

ITALIAN SCHOOL

Italian school, 15th century. Series of eight panels with scenes from the Old Testament. 1. Tobias and the Angel. Venice, S. Alvise.

71 T 63 TOBIT 9:6 THE MARRIAGE OF TOBIAS AND SARAH

DUTCH SCHOOL

Gelder, Aert de. The Blessing of Tobias and Sarah. The Hague, Dienst Verspriede Rijkskollekties.

Terbruggen, Hendrick. Tobias Seeks the Hand of Sarah. Also identified as Jacob Chastising Laban for Giving Him Leah instead of Rachael for his Wife. Cologne, Wallraf-Richartz Museum, 1026.

ITALIAN SCHOOL

Biliverti, Giovanni. Marriage of Sarah and Tobias. Mexico City, Palace of Fine Arts.

Italian school, 15th century. Scenes from story of Tobias: second in series of five cassone panels. Florentine, c.1400. Florence, Museo Stibbert, 8.

71 T 63 2 TOBIT 7:14 THE WRITING OF THE MARRIAGE
          LETTER

   DUTCH SCHOOL
      Gelder, Aert de. The Marriage Contract of Sara
         and Tobit. Brighton, Eng., Corporation Art
         Gallery.
      Steen, Jan. The Marriage of Tobias. Brunswick,
         Landesmuseum, 313.

   ITALIAN SCHOOL
      Italian school, 15th century. Scenes from the
         life of Tobias. Detail. Florence, Loggia
         Orfanotrofio del Bigallo.

71 T 64 2   TOBIT 8:2-3 TOBIAS LAYS THE FISH'S HEART
          AND LIVER ON THE GLOWING COALS; THE EVIL
          SPIRIT ASMODEUS DISAPPEARS

   DUTCH SCHOOL
      Lastman, P.P. The Wedding Night of Tobias and
         Sarah. Boston, Museum of Fine Arts, 62.895.
      Steen, Jan. The Angel Raphael and the Devil
         Asmodeiüs. The Hague, Museum Bredius, 112-
         1946.

71 T 64 21 TOBIT 8:3 THE ANGEL BINDING ASMODEUS

   DUTCH SCHOOL
      Lastman, P.P. The Wedding Night of Tobias and
         Sarah. Boston, Museum of Fine Arts, 62.895.

71 T 66 1 TOBIT 9:1-4 TOBIAS ASKS THE ANGEL TO GO
          TO GABAEL

   ITALIAN SCHOOL
      Italian school, 15th century. Scenes from the
         life of Tobias. Detail. Florence, Loggia
         Orfanotrofio del Bigallo.

71 T 66 12 TOBIT 9:5-6 RAPHAEL RETURNS WITH THE
          MONEY

   ITALIAN SCHOOL
      Italian school, 15th century. Scenes from the
         life of Tobias. Detail. Florence. Loggia
         Orfanotrofio del Bigallo.

71 T 7   TOBIT 10-13 TOBIAS' RETURN

   ITALIAN SCHOOL
      Bassano, Jacopo. The Return of Young Tobias.
         Dresden, Staatliche Kunstsammlungen, 254.
      Francesco di Giorgio. Story of Tobit.
      Italian school, 15th century. Scenes from the
         life of Tobias. Detail. Frescoes. Florence,
         Loggia del Bigallo.
      Luini, Bernardo. Healing of Tobias. Milan, Amb-
         rosiana, Sala G.

   SPANISH SCHOOL
      Orrente, Pedro. Journey of Tobias and Sara.
         Detail: Sara and Camels. Murcia, Museo Pro-
         vincial.
      Orrente, Pedro. Journey of Tobias and Sara.
         Detail: Tobias and the Angel Raphael. Murcia,
         Museo Provincial.

71 T 73 TOBIT 11:1-4 TOBIAS ON THE WAY BACK

   ITALIAN SCHOOL
      Castiglione, G.B. Copy. Tobit Burying the Dead.
         Paris, Louvre, Musée du, R.F. 1941.2.
      Italian school, 15th century. Scenes from the
         life of Tobias. Detail. Florence, Loggia
         Orfanotrofio del Bigallo.
      Maratti, Carlo. Tobias and the Angel. New York,
         Durlacher Brothers.

71 T 74 TOBIT 10 OLD TOBIT (AND ANNA) WAITING
          AND WORRYING ABOUT THE LONG ABSENCE OF
          THEIR SON; SOMETIMES ANNA IS SHOWN AT
          THE SPINNING-WHEEL

   AUSTRIAN SCHOOL
      Troger, Paul. Tobias and Anna. Vienna, Öster-
         reichische Galerie, 3159.

   DUTCH SCHOOL
      Brouwer, Cornelis. The Blind Tobit and Hannah.
         Kronig, J.O. - Collection (The Hague).
      Dou, Gerard. Hannah and the Blind Tobit.
         Boer, P. de - Collection (Amsterdam).
      Rembrandt. Tobit and his Wife in an Interior.
         Rotterdam, Collection W. van der Vorm.
      Rembrandt. The blind Tobit and his wife.
         Old Copy. Philadephia, Collection J.G.
         Johnson, 482.
      Rembrandt. Anna and the Blind Tobit. Also
         attributed to Gerrit Dou. London, National
         Gallery, 4189.
      Rembrandt. Tobit and his wife. Detail: Tobit.
         1650. Rotterdam, Collection W. van der
         Vorm.
      Rembrandt. Tobit and his wife. Detail: Wife.
         1650. Rotterdam, Collection W. van der
         Vorm.

71 T 76 TOBIT 10:9-10 THE MEETING OF PARENTS
          AND SON

   FLEMISH SCHOOL
      Master of the Prodigal Son. The Return of
         Tobias. Sotheby and Co., London (Sale,
         New York, [SAFFRON - 5298], March 13,
         1985, No. 97).

   FRENCH SCHOOL
      Bouguereau, W.A. Return of Tobias (restored?).
         Dijon, Musée Municipal.
      Clement, Félix August. The Return of Tobias.
         Paris, École des Beaux-Arts (Grand Prix
         de Rome).
      Delaunay, Jules Élie. The Return of Tobias.
         Paris, École des Beaux-Arts (grand Prix
         de Rome).

   ITALIAN SCHOOL
      Italian school, 15th century. Scenes from
         the story of Tobias: third in series of
         five cassone panels. Florentine, c.1400.
         Florence, Museo Stibbert, 8.

   SPANISH SCHOOL
      Sert, José María. Murals with scenes from
         the Old Testament and New Testament. Panel:
         Arrival of Tobias. Vich, Cathedral.

71 T 77 TOBIT 10:11-15 THE HEALING OF TOBIT:
          TOBIAS PUTS THE GALL OF THE FISH ON HIS
          FATHER'S EYES

   AUSTRIAN SCHOOL
      Sigrist, Franz, the Elder. The Young Tobias
         Heals his Father. Vienna, Osterreichische
         Galerie, 6309.

   DUTCH SCHOOL
      Horst, Gerrit Willemsz. Tobias Healing his
         Father. The Hague, Dienst Verspreide Rijks-
         kollekties.
      Lesire, Paulus. Tobias Healing his Father.
         Bader, Alfred - Collection (Milwaukee).
      Rembrandt. Tobias Healing his Father's Blind-
         ness. 1636. Stuttgart, Museum.
      Venne, Pseudo van de. Tobias Healing his
         Father. Private Collection, U.S.A.
      Venne, Pseudo van de. Tobias Healing his
         Father. Vienna, Art Market.
      Verelst, Pieter. Tobias Restoring his Father's
         Sight. Sotheby and Co., London (Sale,
         New York, [SAFFRON-5298], March 13, 1985,
         No. 105).

FLEMISH SCHOOL
    Floris, Franz, I. Young Tobit Healing the
      Blindness of his Father. Sotheby and Co.,
      London (Sale, Dec. 12, 1984, [IVY] No.111).
    Hemessen, Jan Sanders van. Tobit's Sight
      Restored. 1555. Paris, Louvre, Musée du,
      1335.
    Metsys, Jan. Tobit's Sight Restored. 1564. Ant-
      werp, Museum, 252.
    Vos, Martin, the elder. The Healing of Tobit.
      Ankacrona, M.T. - Collection (Boserup).

FRENCH SCHOOL
    Boulogne, Bon. Tobit Cures his Father. Lille,
      Musée des Beaux-Arts, 973-6-1 (P.1876).

GERMAN SCHOOL
    Sorgh, Hendrick. Tobias Restoring Tobit's Sight.
      Christie, Manson and Woods (Sale, London,
      Dec. 2, 1983 [TORINO-2790] No. 107).
    Vinne, Jan van der, I. Tobias Restoring Tobit's
      Sight. Christie, Manson and Woods (Sale,
      London, Dec. 2, 1983 [TORINO-2790], No. 55).

ITALIAN SCHOOL
    Caravaggio, Follower of (Dutch). The Healing
      of Tobit. Vienna, Kunsthistorisches Museum,
      145.
    Caravaggio, Follower of. The Healing of Tobias.
      c.1615-20. Berlin, Staatliche Museen, 1/72.
    Carracci, Annibale, attributed to. Tobias Heals
      his Father's Blindness. c.1590-95. Cassel,
      Gallery, 568.
    Cavallino, Bernardo. Tobias Heals his Father's
      Eye. Cassel, Staatliche Kunstsammlungen,
      477.
    Fetti, Domenico. Tobias Healing his Father.
      Leningrad, Hermitage.
    Guardi, Giovanni Antonio. The story of Tobit:
      Tobias returns to his father. Venice, Chiesa
      Angelo Raffaele.
    Italian school, 15th century. Scenes from the
      story of Tobias: fourth in series of five
      cassone panels. Florentine, c.1400. Florence,
      Museo Stibbert, 8.
    Italian school, 16th century. Tobit restoring
      the old man's vision. Catania, Museo dei
      Benedettini.
    Pagani, Gasparo. The healing of Tobit. 1604.
      Florence, Palazzo Uffizi, 1539.
    Strozzi, Bernardo. Tobit healed by angels.
      Venice, S. Zaccaria.
    Strozzi, Bernardo, Copy. The Healing of Tobit.
      Cologne, Wallraf-Richartz Museum, 1886.
    Strozzi, Bernardo. Tobit Healed by Angels.
      Variant of Painting in S. Zaccaria, Venice.
      New York, Metropolitan Museum of Art.
    Traversi, Gaspare. Tobias healing his father.
      Rome, San Paolo Fuori le Mura.

71 T 78 TOBIT 11 ARRIVAL OF SARAH

DUTCH SCHOOL
    Janssens, Pieter. The Blind Tobit Greeting his
      Returning Son Tobias and his Bride Sarah.
      Christie, Manson and Woods (Sale, Amsterdam,
      [SALLY] Dec. 7, 1982, No. 126).

71 T 79 TOBIT 12:5 TOBIAS AND HIS FATHER OFFER GIFTS TO THE ANGEL

DUTCH SCHOOL
    Lastman, Pieter P. Old Tobit and his Son Kneeling
      Before the Angel. 1618. Copenhagen, Art
      Museum, 3922.

ITALIAN SCHOOL
    Biliverti, Giovanni. The Angel Refusing the
      Gifts of Tobias. Florence, Palazzo Pitti.

71 T 79 1 TOBIT 12:16 THE ANGEL MAKES HIMSELF KNOWN; TOBIAS AND HIS FAMILY LIE DOWN

ITALIAN SCHOOL
    Biliverti, Giovanni. The Angel Departing from
      the Family of Tobias. Leningrad, Hermitage.

SPANISH SCHOOL
    Murillo. Tobias and the angel.

71 T 79 2 TOBIT 12:21 THE ANGEL RAPHAEL DISAPPEARS INTO THE SKY

DUTCH SCHOOL
    Rembrandt. The Angel (Raphael) Leaving the
      Family of Tobias. 1637. Paris, Louvre,
      Musée du.
    Victors, Jan. The Angel Leaving Tobit and
      his Family. 1649. Malibu, J. Paul Getty
      Museum.

FRENCH SCHOOL
    Boucher, François. Tobias and the Angel.
      Schäfer, George - Collection (Schweinfurt)
      73272865.
    Delacroix, Eugene. Angel Raphael leaves Tobias.
      Copy after Rembrandt. Lille, Palais des
      Beaux-Arts, Musée de Peinture (491).
    Doré, Paul Gustave. Tobias and the Angel.
      1865. Colmar, Musée d'Unterlinden.

ITALIAN SCHOOL
    Guardi, Giovanni Antonio. The story of Tobit:
      The Angel Raphael Leaves. Venice, Chiesa
      Angelo Raffaele, Cantoria.
    Italian school, 18th century. The Angel with
      the Family of Tobias. Budapest, Museum
      of Fine Arts, 9826.

71 T 79 3 TOBIT 11:21 BANQUET AT HOUSE OF TOBIT FOLLOWING TOBIAS' RETURN

ITALIAN SCHOOL
    Italian school, 15th century. Scene from
      the life of Tobias. Detail. Florence,
      Loggia Orfanotrofio del Bigallo.

71 T 9 OTHER SCENES FROM THE BOOK OF TOBIT

ITALIAN SCHOOL
    Maffei, Francesco. Tobias and the angel.
      Venice, SS. Apostoli.
    Tiarini, Alessandro. The Father of Tobias
      with the Angel. Bologna, Pinacoteca Nazionale.

71 U JUDITH STORY OF JUDITH

ITALIAN SCHOOL
    Daniele da Volterra. Story of Judith and Holo-
        fernes. Rome, Palazzo Massimo alle Colonne,
        façade.

71 U 33 32 JUDITH 6:14 ACHIOR IS FREED BY THE
    ISRAELITES

ITALIAN SCHOOL
    Veronese, Paolo. Scenes from the story of Judith.
        1. The Flight of Achior from the Camp of
        Holofernes. c.1565-70. Oxford, University,
        Ashmolean Museum, 450.

71 U 4 JUDITH 11-13 JUDITH AND HOLOFERNES

ITALIAN SCHOOL
    Sellaio, Jacopo del. The Story of Judith and
        Holofernes. Dayton (Ohio), Art Institute,
        64.10.

71 U 41 1 JUDITH 8:9-36 JUDITH, THE WIDOW OF MAN-
    ASSEH, SPEAKS WITH THE ELDERS OZIAS, CHABRIS
    AND CHARMIS

ITALIAN SCHOOL
    Veronese, Paolo. Scenes from the Story of Judith.
        2. Judith Receiving the Elders of Bethulia.
        c.1565-70. Oxford, University, Ashmolean
        Museum, 451.

71 U 42 1 JUDITH 10:6-10 JUDITH AND HER MAID SERVANT
    TAKE LEAVE OF THE ELDERS AT THE CITY GATE

ITALIAN SCHOOL
    Veronese, Paolo. Scenes from the Story of Judith.
        3. Judith Leaving Bethulia. c.1565-70. Oxford,
        University, Ashmolean Museum, 452.

71 U 42 4 JUDITH 10:20-22 JUDITH AND HER MAID-SERVANT
    ARE LED TO HOLOFERNES' TENT

ITALIAN SCHOOL
    Gionima, Antonio. Judith Presented to Holofernes.
        Also attributed to Ercole Graziani. Minnea-
        polis, Institute of Arts, 62.45.
    Marchesi, Giuseppe (Il Sansone). Judith in the
        Tent of Holofernes. Bologna, Pinacoteca Naz-
        ionale.
    Pasinelli, Lorenzo. Judith in front of Holofernes.
        Bologna, Collection Count G. de Basdari.
    Veronese, Paolo. The Story of Judith: Judith
        Received by Holofernes. c.1565-70. Oxford,
        University, Ashmolean Museum, 453.

71 U 42 61 JUDITH 12:16-20 MEAL WITH HOLOFERNES
    AND COHORTS

FLEMISH SCHOOL
    Franck, Franz, II. Judith Feasting with Holo-
        fernes. Christie, Manson and Woods (Sale,
        London [TAORIMA-2741] Oct. 14, 1983, No.
        37).

ITALIAN SCHOOL
    Veronese, Paolo. The Story of Judith. Judith
        Feasted by Holofernes. c.1565-70. Oxford,
        University, Ashmolean Museum, 454.

71 U 42 71 JUDITH 13:2 HOLOFERNES DRINKS TOO MUCH,
    AND FALLS ASLEEP ON THE BED

FRENCH SCHOOL
    Vernet, Horace. Judith and Holofernes.

71 U 42 72 JUDITH 13:7 JUDITH PRAYS BEFORE KILLING
    HOLOFERNES

BRITISH SCHOOL
    Etty, William. Judith and Holofernes. Edinburgh,
        National Gallery, 186.

ITALIAN SCHOOL
    Piazetta, G.B. Judith and Holofernes. Milan,
        Private Collection.

71 U 42 73 JUDITH 13:8 HOLOFERNES BEHEADED BY
    JUDITH WITH HIS OWN SWORD; THE MAID-SERVANT
    MAY BE KEEPING WATCH

BRITISH SCHOOL
    Etty, William. Judith's Maid Waiting Outside
        the Tent of Holofernes. Edinburgh, National
        Gallery, 185.
    Etty, William. Studies for Judith and Holo-
        fernes. Edinburgh, Royal Scottish Academy.

DUTCH SCHOOL
    Bray, Jan de. Judith and Holofernes. 1659.
        Amsterdam, Rijksmuseum, 614 A1.
    Honthorst, Gerard van. Judith beheading
        Holofernes. Baltimore, Md., Walters Art
        Gallery, 653.
    Rembrandt, School of. Judith and Holofernes.
        Sacramento, Crocker Art Gallery, 1872.139.

FLEMISH SCHOOL
    Rubens, P.P. Judith with the head of Holofernes.
        Brunswick, (Gallery) Landesmuseum.

FRENCH SCHOOL
    Regnault, A.G.H. Judith and Holofernes. Mar-
        seilles, Musée Municipal.
    Valentin de Boullogne. Judith, Holofernes,
        and servant. Valetta, Malta, Museum.

GERMAN SCHOOL
    Elseheimer, Adam. Judith. London, Apsley
        House, COllection Duke of Wellington.
    Feselen, Melchior. Judith and the Head of
        Holofernes. Dublin, National Gallery,1176.
    Stuck, Franz von. Judith and Holofernes.
        1927. Private Collection.

ITALIAN SCHOOL
    Caravaggio. Judith and Holofernes. Rome,
        Galleria d'Arte Antica.
    Cavallino, Bernardo. Judith with the Head
        of Holofernes. Stockholm, National Museum,80.
    Damini, Vincenzo. Judith with the Head of
        Holofernes. Sarasota, Fla., Ringling Museum
        of Art, SN 178.
    Gentileschi, Artemsia (?). Death of Holofernes.
        Florence, Palazzi Uffizi.
    Gentileschi, Artemsia. Judith. Naples, Museo
        Nazionale, Capodimonte, 378.
    Gentileschi, Artemsia. Judith with the head
        of Holofernes. Detroit, Institute of Arts,
        52.253.
    Gentileschi, Artemsia, attributed to. Judith
        and Holofernes. Upsala, University.
    Italian school, 15th century. Judith and
        Holofernes (said to be in the manner of
        Bartolommeo della Gatta). Pisa, Museo
        Civico.
    Ligozzi, Jacopo. Judith cutting off the
        head of Holofernes. Florence, Palazzo
        Pitti.
    Lys, Giovanni. Judith with the head of Holo-
        fernes. Venice, Palazzo Rezzonico.
    Lys, Giovanni. Judith with the head of Holo-
        fernes. Budapest, Museum of Fine Arts,
        4913 (620 d).
    Lys, Giovanni. Judith with the Head of Holo-
        fernes. Vienna, Kunsthistorisches Museum,
        2324.
    Lys, Giovanni. Judith in the tent of Holo-
        fernes. London, National Gallery, 4597.
    Maratti, Carlo. Judith. Bückeburg, Schloss.
    Peruzzi, Baldassare. Old and New Testament
        subjects: Judith beheading Holofernes,
        lower right. Rome, S. Maria della Pace,
        Cappella della Ponzetto, arch.
    Piazzetta, G.B. Judith and Holofernes. Rome,
        Collection - Baron Lazzaroni.

Preti, Mattia. Judith. Naples, Museo Nazionale,
Capodimonte, 255.
Tintoretto (Jacopo Robusti). Judith and Holo-
fernes. 1555. Madrid, Prado, 389.
Tintoretto. Judith and Holofernes. Madrid, Prado.
Tintoretto. Death of Holofernes. Madrid, Prado.
Vasari, Giorgio. Judith and Holofernes. c.1554.
Colnaghi and Co. (London).
Veronese, Paolo. Judith. Genoa, Palazzo Rosso.
Veronese, Paul. Judith and Holofernes. Caen,
Museo Municipal.
Veronese, Paolo. The Story of Judith: Judith
about to Kill Holofernes. c.1565-70. Oxford,
University, Ashmolean Museum, 455.

SPANISH SCHOOL
Goya. Judith and Holofernes. Madrid, Prado.

SWEDISH SCHOOL
Pauli, Georg. Judith and Holofernes. 1930.
Stockholm, National Museum, 2862.

71 U 42 73 1 JUDITH 13:9 JUDITH WITH HOLOFERNES'
HEAD AND THE SWORD

AUSTRIAN SCHOOL
Klimt, Gustav. Judith I (Judith with the Head
of Holofernes). 1901. Salzburg, Galerie Welz.
Klimt, Gustav. Judith I (Judith with the Head
of Holofernes). 1901. Vienna, Österreichische
Galerie.

DUTCH SCHOOL
Cornelisz, Cornelis, Attributed to. Judith with
the Head of Holofernes. Sotheby and Co.,
London (Sale, New York, March 6-7, 1975,
No. 89).

FLEMISH SCHOOL
Hemessen, Jan Sanders van. Judith. c.1560.
Chicago, Art Institute, 56.1109.
Master of the Mansi Magdalen. Judith and the
the Infant Hercules. London, National Gallery,
4891.
Metsys, Jan. Judith with the Head of Holofernes.
1543. Boston, Museum of Fine Arts, 12.1048.
Metsys, Jan. Judith. Paris, Louvre.

FRENCH SCHOOL
Valentin de Boullogne. Judith. Toulouse, Musée
des Beaux-Arts.
Vernet, Horace. Judith. Boston, Museum of Fine
Arts.
Vouet, Simon. Judith with the Head of Holofernes.
Vienna, Kunsthistorisches Museum, 581A.
Vouet, Simon. Judith. Munich, New State Gallery,
2279.

GERMAN SCHOOL
Baldung, Hans. Judith with the Head of Holofernes.
1525. Nuremburg, Germanic Museum.
Busch, Ludwig Wilhelm. Judith. Brunswick, Landes-
museum, 1100.
Cranach, Lucas, the elder. Judith with the Head
of Holofernes. 1530. Vienna, Kunsthistorisches
Museum, 1458.
Cranach, L. (the elder) ?. Judith. Schwerin,
Gallery.
Cranach, Lucas (the elder). Copy. Judith with
the Head of Holofernes. Syracuse, N.Y.,
Collection Congdon.
Cranach, Lucas, the elder. Judith with the
Head of Holofernes. Cassel, Gallery.
Cranach, Lucas, the elder. Judith with the Head
of Holofernes. New York, Metropolitan Museum,
11.15.
Cranach, Lucas, the elder. Judith with the head
of Holofernes. c.1520. Stuttgart, Museum.
Cranach, Lucas, the elder. Judith with the head
of Holofernes. c.1530. New York, Collection
Wilfrid Greif.
Cranach, Lucas the elder. Judith with the Head
of Holofernes. 1526-37. Minneapolis, Collection
J.R. Vanderlip.

Cranach, Lucas, the elder. Judith with head
of Holofernes. Dublin, National Gallery.
Cranach, Lucas, the elder. Judith with the
Head of Holofernes. Kinnaird Castle, Col-
lection of Earl of Southesk.
Cranach, Lucas, the Younger. (also attributed
to Jan Metsys). Judith with the Head of
Holofernes. Grenoble (Isère), Musée Muni-
cipal.
Ostendorfer, Michael. Judith with the Head
of Holofernes. Budapest, Museum of Fine
Arts, 129(723).
Ostendorfer, Michael. Judith woth the Head
of Holofernes. Cologne, Wallraf-Richartz
Museum, 395.
Riedel, August Heinrich. Judith. 1840. Munich,
Neue Pinakothek, WAF 826.

ITALIAN SCHOOL
Allori, Cristofano. Judith with the head
of Holofernes. Florence, Pitti, 96.
Allori, Cristofano. Replica. Judith with
the head of Holofernes. Replica of picture
in the Pitti. Florence, Corsini.
Allori, Cristofano. Replica. Judith with
the head of Holofernes. Replica of picture
in the Pitti. Florence, Uffizi.
Allori, Cristofano. Copy. Judith with the
Head of Holofernes. Geneva, Musee d'Art
et d'Histoire, 1908-92.
Allori, Christofano. Replica. Judith with
the head of Holofernes. Replica of picture
in the Pitti. Brookline, Mass., Collection
Dr. George C. Shattuck.
Allori, Cristofano, Copy. Judith with the
head of Holofernes. Dulwich Gallery, 267.
Baglioni, Giovanni. Judith and Holofernes.
Rome, Villa Borghese, Gallery.
Beccafumi, Domenico. Judith with the Head
of Holofernes. Also attributed to Giomo
del Sodoma. London, Wallace Collection,
P 525.
Cariani (Giovanni de' Busi). Judith. 1516-17.
Milan, Private Collection.
Catena, Vincenzo. Judith with head of Holofernes.
Dossi, Dosso. Judith. Modena, Pinacoteca
Estense.
Furini, Francesco. Judith with the Head of
Holofernes. Stockholm, University, 286.
Gambara, Lattanzio. Judith with the Head
of Holofernes. Sotheby and Co., London
(Sale, Nov. 17, 1982, No. 40).
Giorgione. Judith. Leningrad, Hermitage.
Girolamo da Carpi. Judith. Dresden, Gallery.
Italian school, 17th century (Naples). Judith
with the Head of Holofernes. Boston,
Museum of Fine Arts, 94.181.
Lys, Giovanni. Judith with the Head of Holo-
fernes. Faenza, Pinacoteca Comunale.
Maratti, Carlo. Judith. Bückeburg, Schloss.
Marinari, Onorio. Judith with the Head of
Holofernes. Budapest, Museum of Fine Arts,
480 (273).
Martinelli, Giovanni. Judith. 1650. Chicago,
Art Institute, 39.2240.
Matteo di Giovanni ? Judith. Washington,
National Gallery, 389.
Palma Vecchio. Judith. Florence, Uffizi.
Pinturicchio. Old Testament scenes. Rome,
Palazzina di Giuliano della Rovere, vault.
Preti, Mattia. Judith with the head of Holo-
fernes. Cologne, Wallraf-Richartz Museum,
1435.
Reni, Guido. Judith. Rome, Museo Capitalino.
Sebastiano del Piombo. Judith with the head
of Holofernes. Berlin, Staatliche
Museen.
Schiavone, Giorgio, Attributed to. Judith.
Possibly by Bonifazio Veronese. Ascott,
Bucks., National Trust.
Sirani, Elizabetta. Judith with the head
of Holofernes. Baltimore, Md., Walters
Art Gallery, 37.253.

Sodoma. Judith. Siena, Academy.
Stanzioni, Massimo. Judith. Christie, Manson
and Woods (Sale, New York, June 12, 1981,
No. 69).
Strozzi, Bernardo. Judith.
Titian ? Judith with the Head of Holofernes.
London, University of, Courtauld Institute,
Lee Collection.
Vaccaro, Andrea. Judith with the Head of Holo-
fernes. Malibu, J. Paul Getty Museum, 69.PA.17.
Varotari, Alessandro (Il Padovanino). Judith.
Dresden, Royal Gallery.
Varotari, Alessandro (Il Padovanino). Judith
with the Head of Holofernes. Vienna, Kuns-
thistorisches Museum, 80.
Veronese, Paolo, School of. Judith with head
of Holofernes.
Zoboli, Jacopo. Judith with the Head of Holo-
fernes. Modena, Pinacoteca Estense.

71 U 42 74 JUDITH 13:10 JUDITH AND HER MAID-SERVANT PUT THE HEAD IN A SACK

AUSTRIAN SCHOOL
Austrian school, 18th century. Judith with the
Head of Holofernes. Budapest, Museum of Fine
Arts, 2139.

BRITISH SCHOOL
Etty, William. Judith Coming Out of the Tent.
Edinburgh, National Gallery, 187.
Wright, Joseph, of Derby. Judith with Head of
Holofernes.

DUTCH SCHOOL
Dijk, Philip van. Judith. The Hague, Royal Gal-
lery, 27.
Neer, Eglon Hendrik van der. Judith. London,
National Gallery, 2535.

FLEMISH SCHOOL
Jordaens, Jacob. Judith and Holofernes. Phila-
delphia, Philadelphia Museum of Art, 36-26-1.
Metsys, Jan. Judith and Holofernes. Rome, Gal-
leria Nazionale.
Seghers, Gerard. Judith and Holofernes. Rome,
Galleria d'Arte Antica.
Rubens, P.P. Judith with the head of Holofernes.
Brunswick, Landesmuseum, 87.
Seghers, Gerard. Judith and the Maid. Rome,
Galleria d'Arte Antica.
Sellaio, Jacopo del. Judith with the Head of
Holofernes. 1530-40. Bern, Art Museum, 185.
Sustria, Lambert. Judith. Lille, Musée.

FRENCH SCHOOL
French school, 14th century. Judith and Holo-
fernes. Reims, Musée. (?)
Vouet, Simon. Judith with the Head of Holofernes.
Vienna, Kunsthistorisches Museum, 5795.
Vouet, Simon. Judith with the Head of Holofernes.
1623-25. Kansas City, William Rockhill Nelson
Gallery of Art, 62-44.

GERMAN SCHOOL
Aachen, Hans Von. Judith. Shickman, H. - Gallery
(New York).
Cranach, Lucas, the elder, school of. Judith
with the Head of Holofernes and a Servant.
Vienna, Kunsthistorisches Museum, 1457.
Feselen, Melchior. Judith in the camp of Holo-
fernes. c. 1538. Lucerne, Collection Böhler
and Steinmeyer.
German school, 18th century (South German).
Judith with the Head of Holofernes. Early
18th century. Sotheby and Co., London (Sale,
Feb. 13, 1985 [SNOWDROP], No. 36).

ITALIAN SCHOOL
Allori, Cristofano. Judith with the Head of
Holofernes. Detail. Florence, Palazzo Pitti.
Allori. Christofano. Replica. Judith with the
Head of Holofernes. Replica of painting in
the Palazzo Pitti, Florence. Vienna, Liech-
tenstein Gallery, 225.

Amigoni, Jacopo. Judith with the Head of
Holofernes and attendant. Venice, Ca'
Rezzonico.
Cagnacci (Guido Canlassi). Judith with the
Head of Holofernes. Bologna, Pinacoteca
Nazionale.
Cairo, Francesco del. Judith with the Head
of Holofernes. Rome, Private Collection.
Cairo, Francesco del. Judith with the Head
of Holofernes. Sarasota, Fla., Ringling
Museum of Art, SN798.
Campi, Giulio (?). Judith. Rome, Villa Borghese.
Cariani (Giovanni de' Busi). Judith. 1516-17.
Neeld, Sir Audley - Collection (Grittleton
House, Wilts).
Cavallino, Bernardo. Judith and Holofernes.
Naples, Museo Nazionale, Capodimonte,283.
Cavallino, Bernardo. Judith with the head
of Holophernes. London, Collection Christ-
opher Norris.
Cavallino, Bernardo. Judith with the head
of Holofernes. Collection Brinsley Ford.
Dossi, Dosso, School of. Judith with the
Head of Holofernes. Modena, Pinacoteca
Estense.
Gentileschi, Artemisia. Judith and the Serving
Maid. Version of painting in Detroit.
1630. Naples, Museo Nazionale (Capodimonte),
375.
Gentileschi, Orazio. Judith and Maidservant
with Head of Holofernes. 1620. Hartford,
Wadsworth Atheneum, 1949.52.
Gentileschi, Orazio. Copy. Judith and Maid-
servant with the Head of Holofernes. Copy
of painting in Hartford. c. 1611-12. Rome,
Vatican (Pinacoteca).
Giaquinto, Corrado. Judith and Holofernes.
Prato, Cassa di Risparmi.
Guercino. Copy. Judith and the Head of Holofernes. Cassel, Staatliche Kunstsammlungen,
579.
Guercino, Copy. Judith with the Head of Holo-
phernes. Sarasota, Fla., Ringling Museum
of Art, SN 125.
Italian school, 17th century. Judith and
Holofernes. Princeton, University, Museum
of Art, 77-70.
Italian school, 17th century. Judith Holding
the Head of Holofernes. London, Victoria
and Albert Museum, 519-1870.
Italian school, 17th cneuty (Venetian). Judith
with the Head of Holofernes. Sotheby and
Co., London (Sale, New York, Jan. 17,
1985 [TOMMASO], No. 136).
Mantegna, Andrea. Judith with the head of
Holofernes. Dublin, National Gallery.
Mantegna, Andrea. Judith and Holofernes.
c.1495. Washington, D.C., National Gallery
of Art, 638.
Mantegna, Andrea. Judith with the Head of
Holofernes. Montreal, Museum of Fine Arts.
Mantegna, Andrea, School of. Judith. Paris,
Galerie Czartoryski.
Maratti, Carlo. Judith with the Head of Holo-
fernes. Holkham Hall, Norfolk, Collection
Earl of Leicester.
Marchesi, Giuseppe (Il Sansone). Judith with
the Head of Holofernes. Bologna, Pinacoteca
Nazionale.
Molinari, Antonio. Judith. Zecchine - Collection
(Milan).
Muttoni, Pietro (called della Vecchia). Judith
with the Head of Holofernes. Minneapolis,
Institute of Arts, 66.49.
Palma Giovane. Judith. Venice, Querini-Stamp-
alia.
Palma Giovane. Judith Holding the Head of
Holofernes. Paris, Louvre, Musée du, 8549.
Renieri, Niccolo. Judith with the Head of
Holofernes. Brunswick, Landesmuseum, 1105.
Saracini, Carlo. Judith. Modena, Pinacoteca
Estense.
Saraceni, Carlo. Judith with the Head of
Holofernes. c.1615-20. Dayton (Ohio),
Art Institute, 64.16.

Saraceni, Carlo. Judith with the Head of Holofernes. Christie, Manson and Woods (Sale,
New York, [GERTRUDE-5584] June 6, 1984, No.
179).
Saraceni, Carlo. Judith with the Head of Holofernes. Vienna, Kunsthistorisches Museum,
41.
Saraceni, Carlo. Judith with the Head of Holofernes. Vienna, Kunsthistorisches Museum.
Sirani, Elizabeth. Judith with the Head of Holo-
fernes. Christie, Manson and Woods (Sale,
New York [GERTRUDE-5584] June 6, 1984, No.
177).
Sirani, Elizabetta. Judith with the Head of
Holofernes. Baltimore, Md., Walters Art Gallery.
Spada, Lionello. Judith. Parma, Galleria Nazion-
ale.
Strozzi, Bernardo. Judith with the Head of Holo-
fernes. Oxford, University, Christ Church.
Titian. Judith with the head of Holofernes.
c.1570. Detroit, Institute of Arts.
Veronese, Paolo. Judith and Holofernes. Genoa,
Palazzo Rosso.
Veronese, Paolo. Judith and Holofernes. 1570s.
Vienna, Kunsthistorisches Museum.

71 U 42 74 1   JUDITH AND HER MAID-SERVANT PUT THE
HEAD ON A DISK AND COVER IT WITH A CLOTH

GERMAN SCHOOL
Pencz, Georg. Judith with the Head of Holofernes. 1541. New York, Weitzner Collection.

ITALIAN SCHOOL
Caravaggio, School of. Judith. Madrid, Collection Bernaldo de Qiuros.
Galizia, Fede. Judith with the Head of Holofernes. 1596. Sarasota, Fla., Ringling Museum
of Art.
Gentileschi, Artemisia. Judith with the head
of Holofernes. Florence, Pitti.
Gentileschi, Orazio. Judith and maidservant
with head of Holofernes. Hartford, Wads-
worth Atheneum, 1949.52.
Grammatica, Antiveduto. Judith with the head
of Holofernes. Stockholm, National Museum.
Lys, Giovanni. Judith with head of Holofernes
on a platter. Faenza, Pinacoteca Comunale.
Michelangelo. Lunettes in four corners with
scenes from Old Testament, etc.: Judith with
Head of Holofernes. Rome, Vatican, Sistine
Chapel, ceiling decorations.
Strozzi, Bernardo. Judith and the head of Holo-
fernes. Berlin, Staatliche Museen, 1727.
Traversi, Gaspare. Judith with the head of Holo-
fernes. Genoa, Private Collection.

71 U 42 74 2   JUDITH AND MAID-SERVANT WITH SWORD

DUTCH SCHOOL
Uytewael, Joachim A. Judith with the Head of
Holofernes. c.1595-1600. Princeton, Univer-
sity, Museum of Art, 75-11.

ITALIAN SCHOOL
Ficherelli, Felice. Judith. Chicago, Art Insti-
tute.
Italian school, 16th century (Ferrarese). Judith.
Modena, Pinacoteca Estense.
Scorel, Jan van. Judith with the Head of Holo-
fernes. Ottawa, National Gallery of Canada,
3695.

71 U 43   JUDITH 13:10   JUDITH AND HER MAID-SERVANT
ON THEIR WAY BACK TO BETHULIAH

ITALIAN SCHOOL
Botticelli, Sandro. Return of Judith. 1467-68.
Florence, Palazzo Uffizi, 484.
Botticelli, Sandro. Judith with the head of
Holofernes. c.1468-69. Cincinnati, Museum,
1954.463.
Garofalo (Benvenuto Tisi) ? Judith with the
Head of Holofernes. Knole (Kent), Collection
Lord Sackville.

Ghirlandaio, Domenico. Judith. 1489. Berlin,
Staatliche Museen, 21.
Palmezzano, Marco. Judith Holding the Head
of Holofernes. Geneva, Musée d'Art et
d'Histoire, CR 120.
Spade, Lionello. Judith. Bologna, Pinacoteca
Nazionale, 69.
Torri, Flaminio. Judith with the head of
Holofernes. Greenville, S.C., Bob Jones
University Collection, 1962 cat.77.

71 U 43 2   JUDITH 13:15-20   JUDITH SHOWS HOLOFERNES'
HEAD TO THE PEOPLE

AUSTRIAN SCHOOL
Schmidt, Martin Johann. Judith with the Head
of Holofernes. Vienna, Österreichische
Galerie, Lg. 36.

DUTCH SCHOOL
Bloemaert, Abraham. Judith Showing the Head
of Holofernes to the People. 1593. Vienna,
Kunsthistorisches Museum, 6514.
Bloemaert, Abraham. Judith with the Head
of Holofernes. Frankfort-on-the-Main,
Staedel Institute, 1583.
Venne, Adriaen Pietersz van de. The Triumph
of Judith. 1643. Sotheby and Co., London
(Sale, April 4, 1984 [DAFFODIL] No. 206).

GERMAN SCHOOL
Zick, Johann. Judith with the head of Holo-
fernes and detail of inscription. New
York, Collection Victor Spark, S2866.

ITALIAN SCHOOL
Benevuti, Pietro. Judith Shows to the People
the Head of Holofernes. 1798. Naples,
Museo Nazionale, Capodimonte, 6587.
Caro, Lorenzo de. The Triumph of Judith.
c.1758. Pradelli, Francesco Molinari -
Collection (Bologna).
Fontebasso, Francesco. The Triumph of Judith.
Venice, Private Collection.
Giordano, Luca. Triumph of Judith. Fresco,
1704. Naples, S. Martino, Cappella del
Tesoro.
Giordano, Luca. Study for Triumph of Judith
in Cappella del Tesoro, S. Martino, Naples.
Barnard Castle, Bowes Museum.
Solimena, Francesco. Judith Shows the Head
of Holofernes to the People. c.1730. Vienna,
Kunsthistorisches Museum, 6915 (529A).

71 U 44   JUDITH 15:3-7   VICTORY OF THE ISRAELITES

ITALIAN SCHOOL
Giordano, Luca. Triumph of Judith. 1704,
fresco. Naples, S. Martino, Cappella del
Tesoro.
Giordano, Luca. Study for Triumph of Judith
in Cappella del Tesora, S. Martino, Naples.
Barnard Castle, Bowes Museum.
Giordano, Luca. Judith with the Head of Holo-
fernes. St. Louis, City Art Museum.

71 U 44 2   JUDITH 13:13-18   THE MURDER OF HOLOFERNES
IS DISCOVERED (BY BAGOAS)

ITALIAN SCHOOL
Botticelli, Sandro. Discovery of Dead Holofernes.
1467-68. Florence, Uffizi.

71 U 45 JUDITH 15:13-16   THE WOMEN OF BETHULIAH
CELEBRATING THE TRIUMPH OF JUDITH

ITALIAN SCHOOL
Reni, Guido. The Women of Bethulia Celebrating
the Triumph of Judith over Holophernes.
Baltimore, Md., Walters Art Gallery, 37.574.

71 V   JONAH   THE BOOK OF JONAH

AUSTRIAN SCHOOL
> Bocksberger, Hans, the Elder. Fresco decora-
> tions for Schlosskapelle, Neuburg an der
> Donau. 16th century. Neuburg an der Donau,
> Schloss. Jonah and the Whale.

EARLY MEDIEVAL AND BYZANTINE
> Early Christian Painting, Rome. Jonah scenes.
> Rome, Torre Pignattara. Catacomb of SS Petrus
> and Marcellinus, Cubiculum XXI, Vault.

FLEMISH SCHOOL
> Brueghel, Pieter, the elder. Seascape with
> story of Jonah (unfinished). Vienna, (Gal-
> lery) Kunsthistorisches Museum.

71 V 1   JONAH 1   JONAH'S CALL AND DISOBEDIENCE

EARLY MEDIEVAL AND BYZANTINE
> Coptic painting, Khargeh, Bagawat Necropolis.
> Detail: Jonah's Ship. Khargeh, Bagawat Necro-
> polis, Chapel of Flight.
> Early Christian Painting, Rome. Catacomb of
> of the Jordani, corridorm with scenes of
> Jonah. Rome, Catacomb of the Jordani.

**71 V 13 4   JONAH 1:15   THE SAILORS RELUCTANTLY THROW
THE PROPHET INTO THE SEA**

AMERICAN SCHOOL
> Ryder, Albert Pinkham. Jonah. Washington, D.C.,
> Smithsonian Institution, National Collection
> of Fine Arts.

FLEMISH SCHOOL
> Brill, Paul. Jonah and the Whale. Brussels,
> Musées Royaux des Beaux-Arts.
> Vos, Martin de, the elder. Jonah Falls into
> the Sea. Reverse of Jesus Discloses Himself
> to His Disciples on the Tiberian Sea. Berlin,
> Staatliche Museum, Inv. No. 709.

EARLY MEDIEVAL AND BYZANTINE SCHOOL
> Early Christian painting, Rome. Catacombs of
> St. Calixtus. Jonah and the whale. Rome,
> Via Appia.
> Early Christian Painting, Rome. Detail: Jonah
> thrown overboard. Rome, Catacomb of the
> Jordani, corridor.

SWEDISH SCHOOL
> Albertus Pictor. Ceiling painting. Detail: Jonah
> and the Whale. c.1480. Härkeberga (Uppland),
> Church.

**71 V 13 41   JONAH   JONAH IS SWALLOWED BY A GREAT FISH
(SEA) MONSTER, WHALE, DOLPHIN, OR THE LIKE**

EARLY MEDIEVAL AND BYZANTINE
> Early Christian painting, Rome. Catacombs of
> of St. Calixtus, wall decorations: Jonah
> and the Whale. Rome, Via Appia, 110.

FLEMISH SCHOOL
> Franck, Franz, I Studio of. Flemish Reliquary
> Chest painted with scenes from the Old Testa-
> ment. Detail: Drawer: Jonah and the Whale.
> c.1600. Sarasota, Fla., Ringling Museum of
> Art, SN 1950.
> Patenier, Joachim. Seascape with Jonah and the
> Whale. Sotheby and Co. (Sale, London, March
> 26, 1969, No. 72).

ITALIAN SCHOOL
> Girolamo da Santa Croce. Jonah. Venice, S. Gio-
> vanni Grisostomo.
> Salviati, Francesco. Jonah and the Whale. Rome,
> Palazzo della Cancelleria, Cappella del
> Pallio.

**71 V 22   JONAH 2:10   AFTER A THREE-DAY SOJOURN
IN THE BELLY OF THE MONSTER, JONAH IS
CAST OM DRY LAND; JONAH MAY BE SHOWN
NUDE AND BALD-HEADED**

FLEMISH SCHOOL
> Brueghel, Jan, the elder. Jonah Leaving the
> Whale. Munich, Pinakothek, Alte.
> Flemish school, 17th century. Four Paintings:
> 2)Jonah and the Whale. Serge Philipson
> Collection.
> Teniers, David, the younger. Jonah and the
> Whale. Sotheby and Co., London (Sale,
> [DAFFODIL] Feb. 20, 1980, No. 64).

FRENCH SCHOOL
> Flandrin, J.H. Mural paintings: Jonah expelled
> by the sea monster. 1839-63. Paris, St.
> Germain-des-Prés.

GERMAN SCHOOL
> Lorichs, Melchior. Jonah and the Whale. 1555.
> London, British Museum, 1884-3-8-35.

ITALIAN SCHOOL
> Tintoretto (Jacopo Robusti). Upper Hall,
> Ceiling: Jonah and the Whale. Venice,
> Scuola di San Rocco.

**71 V 22 1   JONAH 3:2   JONAH AGAIN RECEIVES FROM
GOD THE COMMAND TO PREACH IN NINEVEH**

ITALIAN SCHOOL
> Neri, Pietro Matire. Jonah and the Angel.
> Sotheby and Co., London (Sale, Dec. 12,
> 1984, [IVY] No. 112).

**71 V 31   JONAH 3:4   WHEN JONAH ARRIVES IN THE CITY
HE FORETELLS ITS DESTRUCTION IN FORTY
DAYS**

ITALIAN SCHOOL
> Rosa, Salvatore. Jonah preaching to the people
> of Nineveh. Copenhagen, Art Museum, Sp.57.

**71 V 42   JONAH 4:5   THE PROPHET WITHDRAWS FROM
NINEVEH; HE BUILDS A BOOTH AND WHILE
ENJOYING THE SHADE OF A PLANT (GOURD OR
VINE) WHICH GOD MADE GROW FOR HIM, JONAH
AWAITS THE DESTINY OF THE CITY**

DUTCH SCHOOL
> Dutch school, 16th century. Jonah Lamenting
> over Nineveh (attributed to Maertan van
> Heemskerck). Haarlem, Frans Hals Museum.

EARLY MEDIEVAL AND BYZANTINE
> Early Christian Painting, Rome. Jonah and
> the Whale. Detail: Jonah Reclining. Rome,
> Via Appia, Catacomb of St. Calixtus.
> Early Christian Painting, Rome. Jonah reclining,
> and decoration. Rome, Catacomb Maggiore,
> Cubiculum II.

**71 V 44   JONAH 4:8-11   WHEN JONAH AGAIN MURMURS
AND WISHES TO DIE, GOD REBUKES HIM**

DUTCH SCHOOL
> Heemskerck, Maerten van. Jonah under the
> gourd vine at Nineveh. Greenville, S.C.,
> Bob Jones University Collection, 1962
> cat. 150.

71 W   JOB   THE BOOK OF JOB

FLEMISH SCHOOL
    Antwerp, School of, 16th century. Altar with
      scenes from the life of Job. Schoonbroek,
      St. Job.
    Master of the Legend of St. Catherine. Atar-
      piece of Job. Four panels: Scenes from the
      life of Job. Cologne, Wallraf-Richartz Museum.

ITALIAN SCHOOL
    Gaddi, Taddeo. Story of Job. Detail. Pisa, Cam-
      posanto.

SPANISH SCHOOL
    Velasquez ? Job. Chicago, Art Institute.

71 W 1   JOB 1:1-5   JOB'S WEALTH AND PIETY

ITALIAN SCHOOL
    Bartolo di Fredi. Scenes from the Old Testament:
      Job's Wealth and Piety? S. Gimignano, Col-
      legiata.

71 W 3   JOB 1:13-22   FIRST SERIES OF AFFLICTIONS

FLEMISH SCHOOL
    Master of the Legend of St. Catherine. Altar-
      piece of Job. Four panels: Job's plague.
      Cologne, Wallraf-Richartz Museum.

71 W 31 11   JOB 1:14-15   THE THEFT OF JOB'S OXEN
AND ASSES

FLEMISH SCHOOL
    Orley, Bernard van. Altarpiece of the Trials
      of Job. Brussels, Musées Royaux des Beaux-
      Arts, 235.

ITALIAN SCHOOL
    Bartolo di Fredi. Scenes from the Old Testa-
      ment: Job's army and cattle destroyed.

71 W 31 41   JOB 1:19   THE DEATH OF JOB'S CHILDREN

FLEMISH SCHOOL
    Orley, Bernard van. Altarpiece of the Trials
      of Job. Brussels, Musées Royaux des Beaux-
      Arts, 235.

ITALIAN SCHOOL
    Bartolo di Fredi. Scenes from the Old Testament:
      Destruction of Job's children. S. Gimignano,
      Collegiata.
    Garbieri, Carlo. The Fall of the House of Job.
      Bologna, S. Maria della Pieta.

71 W 51   JOB 2:7-8   JOB COVERED WITH SORES (OR BOILS)
TAKES HIS ABODE ON A DUNG-HILL (PILE OF
ASHES) AND SCRAPES HIS BODY WITH A POTSHERD

EARLY MEDIEVAL AND BYZANTINE
    Early Christian Painting, Rome. Job. Rome, Torre
      Pignattara. Catacomb of SS Petrus and Mar-
      cellinus. Cubiculum XXI.

SPANISH SCHOOL
    Ribera, Jusepe de. Job. Parma, Picture Gallery.
    Velasquez ? Job. Chicago, Art Institute, Charles
      Deering Collection.

71 W 52   JOB 2:8   JOB ON THE DUNG-HILL WITH SATAN
(OR DEVILS) ABUSING OR TORMENTING HIM; JOB'S
WIFE MAY BE PRESENT

DUTCH SCHOOL
    Lievens, Jan. Job. 1631. Ottawa, National Gallery
      of Canada.
    Saftleven, Cornelis. The Trials of Job. 1631.
      Karlesruhe, Kunsthalle.

FLEMISH SCHOOL
    Rubens, Peter Paul. Copy. Job Tormented by Demons.
      Modena, Pinacoteca Estense.

71 W 52 1   JOB 2:8   JOB IS SMITTEN FROM HEAD TO
FOOT WITH SORES BY SATAN, OR DRAGON-LIKE
MONSTERS THAT BLOW POISONOUS SMOKE ON
JOB

BRITISH SCHOOL
    Blake, William. Satan smiting Job. London,
      Tate Gallery, 3340.

ITALIAN SCHOOL
    Pagani, Paolo. Job. Rome, Private Collection.

71 W 53   JOB 2:4   JOB ON THE DUNG-HILL VISITED
BY HIS WIFE

FLEMISH SCHOOL
    Flemish school, 17th century. Four paintings:
      1) Job and the messenger. Serge Philipson
      Collection.

FRENCH SCHOOL
    LaTour, Georges de. Job and his Wife. Epinal
      (Vosges), Musée, 152.
    La Tour, Georges de. Job and his Wife. Detail:
      Head of Job's Wife. Epinal (Vosges), Musée,
      152.

71 W 53 11   JOB 2:9   JOB SCOLDED BY HIS WIFE

FLEMISH SCHOOL
    Franck, Franz, I, Studio of. Flemish Reliquary
      Chest painted with scenes from the Old
      Testament. Detail: Drawer: Job on the
      Dung Heap. c.1600. Sarasota, Fla., Ringling
      Museum of Art, SN 1950.

ITALIAN SCHOOL
    Brusasorci, Domenico. Job on the Dung Heap.
      Rovigo, Pinacoteca dell'Accademia dei
      Concordi, 129.18.

71 W 53 12   JOB 2:9   JOB'S WIFE POURING A BUCKET
OF WATER OVER HIM

GERMAN SCHOOL
    Dürer, Albrecht. Jabach Altarpiece, left
      wing: Job mocked by his wife. c.1500.
      Frankfort-on-the-Main, Staedel Institute,
      890.

71 W 54 1   JOB 2:11   ELIPHAZ, BILDAD AND ZOPHAR
GO TO JOB TO CONSOLE HIM OVER HIS MIS-
FORTUNES (THE THREE FRIENDS MAY BE DEPICTED
AS KINGS)

FLEMISH SCHOOL
    Orley, Bernard van. Altarpiece of the Trials
      of Job. Right wing. Interior: Job and
      his friends.

FRENCH SCHOOL
    Valentin de Boullogne, Circle of. Job. Christie,
      Manson and Woods (Sale, New York, [LOUISE-
      5912], June 5, 1985, No. 17).

ITALIAN SCHOOL
    Assereto, Gioachino. The Mocking of Job.
      Budapest, Museum of Fine Arts, 783 (290).
    Giordano, Luca. Job and his friends. Escorial,
      Monastery.
    Italian school, 15th century. Series of eight
      panels with scenes from the Old Testament:
      Job. Venice, S. Alvise.
    Preti, Mattia. Job Visited by his Friends.
      Brussels, Musées Royaux des Beaux-Arts.

71 W 54 2   JOB 2:12   WHEN THE THREE FRIENDS RECOGNIZE
JOB THEY WEEP AND TEAR THEIR CLOTHES IN
GRIEF

FRENCH SCHOOL
    Decamps, A.G. Job and his Friends. c.1853.
      Minneapolis, Institute of Arts.

71 W 54 3 JOB 2:11-13 THE THREE FRIENDS SILENTLY
SIT ON THE GROUND WITH JOB FOR SEVEN DAYS

GERMAN SCHOOL
Wächter, Eberhard. Job and his Friends. Stuttgart,
Staatsgalerie.

71 W 54 4 JOB IS DERIDED BY HIS FRIENDS (AND HIS
WIFE) FOR REFUSING TO GIVE UP HIS FAITH

DUTCH SCHOOL
Cornelisz, Cornelis. Job. London,Agnew Collection.

ITALIAN SCHOOL
Garbieri, Carlo. Job's chastisement. Bologna,
S. Maria della Pieta.
Rosa, Salvatore. Job. C. 1663. Florence, Palazzo
Uffizi, 3083.

71 W 56 JOB ON THE DUNG-HILL VISITED BY MUSICIANS

DUTCH SCHOOL
Lucas van Leyden. Job ? London, University of,
Courtauld Institute, Lee Collection.

71 W 64 (ETC.) JOB 38:42 - 6 GOD SPEAKS TO JOB FROM
OUT OF THE WHIRLWIND

BRITISH SCHOOL
Blake, William. Job Confessing His Presumption
to God Who Answers from the Whirlwind. c.1800-
03. Edinburgh, National Gallery.
Blake, William. When Morning Stars Sang Together.

71 W 7 JOB 42:10-17 JOB'S PROSPERITY RESTORED; THE
LAST PART OF HIS LIFE

BRITISH SCHOOL
Blake, William. Job and his Daughters. c.1799-
1800. Washington, D.C., National Gallery
of Art, Rosenwald Collection, 763.

FRENCH SCHOOL
Tissot, James Jacques Joseph. Illustrations
of the Hebrew Bible. No. 246: Job Joins his
Family in Happiness. 1896-1903. New York,
Jewish Museum, 52.392.

71 W 75 JOB 42:1-6 JOB THANKING THE LORD

ITALIAN SCHOOL
Bartolo di Fredi. Scenes from the Old Testament:
Job Gives Thanks to God. S. Gimignano, Colleg-
iata.

71 X 1(PS. 137)1: 71 L 4: 25 H 21 7 "BY THE RIVERS
OF BABYLON..." THE HEBREWS IN CAPTIVITY
LAMENTING BY THE RIVERSIDE

AMERICAN SCHOOL
American school, 19th century. By the waters
of Babylon. Weymouth Heights, Mass., Senigo
House.

BRITISH SCHOOL
Blake, William. By the Waters of Babylon.
1806. Harvard University, Fogg Art Museum,
1943.404.

SONG OF SOLOMON

71 X 2 (ETC.) SONG OF SOLOMON

BRITISH SCHOOL
Webbe, William J. The Rose of Sharon. 1868.
Sotheby and Co., London (Belgravia, Sale,
Nov. 20, 1973).

71 X 21 SHULAMMITE, THE BELOVED WOMAN

BRITISH SCHOOL
Moore, Albert. The Shulamite. Liverpool,
Walker Art Gallery.
Rossetti, D.G. The Beloved or The Bride.
1865-66. London, Tate Gallery, 3053.

FRENCH SCHOOL
Cabanel, Alexandre. The Shulamite. New York,
Metropolitan Museum.

APOCRYPHA - MACCABEES

71 Z 31 2 MACCABEES 3:7-35 HELIODORUS IN THE
TEMPLE, ATTACKED BY A MAN (OR ANGEL) ON
HORSEBACK AND TWO OTHER MEN (OR ANGELS)

FLEMISH SCHOOL
Flemish school, 16th century (Antwerp). The
Martyrdom of the Machabees. Sotheby and
Co., London (Sale [HAREBELL] June 3, 1981,
No. 74).

FRENCH SCHOOL
Delacroix, Eugène. Heliodorus driven from
the temple. Paris, St. Sulpice, Chapelle
des Saints Anges, decoration.
Delacroix, Eugène. Heliodorus driven from
the temple. Study for painting at St.
Sulpice. 1850. Oslo, National Gallery.
Delacroix, Eugène. Heliodorus chased from
the temple. Variant of fresco in St. Sulpice,
Paris.

ITALIAN SCHOOL
Cavallino, Bernardo. Heliodorus Driven from
the Temple. Moscow, Pushkin State Museum
of Fine Arts.
Solimena, Francesco. Heliodorus in the Temple
of Jerusalem. Turin, Pinacoteca, 621.

SPANISH SCHOOL
Sert, José María. Murals with scenes from
the Old and New Testaments. Panel: Heliodorus driven from the temple. Vich, Cathedral.

71 Z 35   2 MACCABEES 6:18-31   MARTYRDOM OF ELEAZAR:
THE OLD MAN IS FORCED TO EAT PORK AND VOLUNT-
ARILY SUBMITS TO THE FLOGGING

FRENCH SCHOOL
Gros, A.J. Eleazar and Antiochus. Saint-Lo
(Manche), Musée.

71 Z 38   2 MACCABEES 10:1-8   SECOND PURIFICATION OF
THE TEMPLE

FRENCH SCHOOL
Subleyras, Pierre. Judas Maccabee Destroying
the Pagan Altar. Düsseldorf, Kunstmuseum.

71 Z 39   2 MACCABEES 11:6-12   A HEAVENLY RIDER, IN
WHITE GARMENT AND WITH WEAPONS OF GOLD, HELPS
THE MACCABEES IN THEIR BATTLE AGAINST LYSIAS

SPANISH SCHOOL
Sert, José María. Murals with scenes from the
Old and New Testaments. Panel: Victory of
the Macabees. Vich, Cathedral.

TYPOLOGY   OLD AND NEW TESTAMENT

72 A (ETC.)   TYPOLOGICAL JUXTAPOSITIONS --   THIS NOTA-
TION IS TO BE FOLLOWED BY: 1) A NOTATION
FROM DIVISION 73 (NEW TESTAMENT), AND 2)
A NOTATION FROM DIVISION 71 (OLD TESTAMENT),
E.G.: GIDEON'S FLEECE TYPOLOGICALLY USED
IN RELATION WITH THE ANNUNCIATION 72 A: 73
A 52: 71 F 21 43

FLEMISH SCHOOL
Noort, Adam van (?) Left wing of triptych: Moses
and the brazen serpent. Courtrai, St. Martin.
72 A: 73 D 64: 71 E 32 64.
Noort, Adam van (?). Right wing of triptych:
Jonah and the Whale. Courtrai, St. Martin.
72 A: 73 D 76: 71 V
Noort, Adam van (?). Right wing of a triptych:
Jonah and the Whale. Detail. Courtrai, St.
Martin.   72 A: 73 D 64: 71 V.

GERMAN SCHOOL
Holbein, Hans, the Younger. The Old and the
New Law. Edinburgh, National Gallery, 2407.
72 A: 11 L 12: 11 L 54 13 4.

ITALIAN SCHOOL
Botticelli, Sandro. Christ tempted by Satan
(Purification of the Leper). Rome, Vatican,
Sistine Chapel. 72A: 73 C 2: 71 E 23 5.
Italian school, 12th -14th century. Annunciation.
S. Vito di Normaine, Crypt of St. Biago,
Vault. 72 A: 73 A 5.
Pitati, Bonifacio. The Holy Family with Tobias
and the Angel. Milan, Ambrosiana, 205.   72
A: 73 B 82 1: 71 T 58.
Raphael. Standard with Crucifixion and Creation
of Eve. Città di Castello, Pinacoteca Commun-
ale.   72 A: 73 D 64 6: 71 A 34 1.

SPANISH SCHOOL
Cruz, Diego de la. Christ between David and
Jeremiah. Bob Jones University Collection,
(Greenville, S.C.O.   72 A: 11 D 33.

72 C: (ETC.)

FRENCH SCHOOL
French School, 15th century. School of Amiens.
Diptych: Coronation of King David and of
a King of France. Paris, Musée de Cluny,725.
72 C: 44 B 16 2: 71 H 48 2.

72 C: 44 B 42 11: 71 O 33 4

AMERICAN SCHOOL
Hicks, Edward. The peaceable kingdom. Wor-
cester, Mass., Art Museum.
Hicks, Edward. Peaceable Kingdom. 1826. Phila-
delphia, Philadelphia Museum of Art,
56-59-1.
Hicks, Edward. Peaceable Kingdom. c. 1830.
New York, Whitney Museum of Modern Art.
Hicks, Edward. Peaceable Kingdom. Philadelphia,
Pennsylvania Academy of Fine Arts.
Hicks, Edward. The Peaceable Kingdom. 1830-40.
Williamsburg, Va., Abby Aldrich Rockefeller
Art Collection.
Hicks, Edward. Peaceable Kingdom and Penn's
Treaty. 1845. Yale University, Gallery
of Fine Arts, 1965.46.3.
Hicks, Edward. Peaceable Kingdom. 1844. Williams-
burg, Va., Abby Aldrich Rockefeller Art
Collection.
Hicks, Edward. Peaceable Kingdom. 1849. Galerie
St. Etienne, New York.

72 C: 44 B 42 12: 71 O 33 4

AMERICAN SCHOOL
Hicks, Edward. The peaceable kingdom. New
York, Collection Duveen.
Hicks, Edward. Peaceable Kingdom (Kingdom
of Conflict) c. 1839. Swarthmore College,
Friends Historical Library.
Hicks, Edward. The peaceable kingdom. Yale
University, Gallery of Fine Arts, 1965.
46.2.